Classifying the Universe

CLASSIFYING THE UNIVERSE

The Ancient Indian *Varṇa* System and the Origins of Caste

BRIAN K. SMITH

New York Oxford
OXFORD UNIVERSITY PRESS
1994

Oxford University Press

Oxford New York Toronto
Delhi Bombay Calcutta Madras Karachi
Kuala Lumpur Singapore Hong Kong Tokyo
Nairobi Dar es Salaam Cape Town
Melbourne Auckland Madrid
and associate companies in
Berlin Ibadan

Published by Oxford University Press, Inc.
200 Madison Avenue, New York, New York 10016

Library of Congress Cataloging-in-Publication Data
Smith, Brian K., 1953–
Classifying the universe : the ancient Indian varṇa system
and the origins of caste
Brian K. Smith
p. cm. Includes bibliographical references and index
ISBN 0–19–506054–7 ISBN 0–19–508498–5 pbk.
1. Caste—India—History. I. Title.
DS422.C3S64 1994 305.5'122'0954—dc20 93–9363

2 4 6 8 9 7 5 3 1
Printed in the United States of America
on acid-free paper

To Katy,
who defies classification

Preface

Although this work on ancient Indian classification schemes must stand on its own, it might also be regarded and employed as a companion volume to my first book, *Reflections on Resemblance, Ritual, and Religion* (Oxford, 1989). In that earlier volume, I argued that Vedic ritual ideology and practice were governed by what I called "hierarchical resemblance." By this term I meant to encapsulate the ancient Indian notion that the universe was composed of mutually resembling and interconnected, but also hierarchically distinguished and ranked, components. The constituents of the universe—sometimes categorized as belonging to the realms of ritual (*adhiyajña*), microcosmos or self (*adhyātman*), and macrocosmos or world (*adhidevatā*, literally "belonging to the divine")—were joined together within a ritual that was regarded as primarily a *constructive*, or as I would now also put it, a *classificatory* activity.

The *bandhus* or connections I focused on in *Reflections* were those that linked higher to lower, prototypes to counterparts, forms to counterforms, and in some cases the "ideal" to the "real." I noted, however, that Vedic connections were really of two types: in addition to the "vertical" *bandhus* that brought together a prototype (e.g., the creator god Prajāpati) and its counterpart (e.g., the sacrificer and, indeed, the sacrificial ritual itself), Vedic ritual epistemology also encompassed what I termed "horizontal" linkages. *Reflections* dealt almost exclusively with the former. Here I am predominantly concerned with the latter.

While vertically oriented linkages fasten the universe from top to bottom, horizontal connections fuse it on all sides. They conjoin resembling components (e.g., the earth, the god of fire or Agni, and the Brahmin social class) of different hierarchically (i.e., vertically) organized registers (e.g., cosmology, theology, and sociology). The vertically connected prototypes and counterparts were thought to participate in the same essence although in different degrees; members of various orders of things and beings, located at the same rank within their respective realms, were horizontally connected—and were regarded as cosmic kin in the same degree. Vertical *bandhus* were drawn between higher and lower classes within the same category (e.g., Brahmins and the servant class called Shūdras);

horizontal ones linked elements of the same class within different categories (e.g. Brahmins and the season of spring).

Horizontal connections and vertical connections were interdependent: elements from different classes could be horizontally connected because they were located in the same hierarchical place within their respective vertically oriented classes. And both kinds of connections were made possible by the system we investigate in this book, that of *varṇa* or "class." Whereas *Reflections* sought to establish the longitudes of the Vedic map of universal resemblances, this book is an attempt to fill in the latitudes.

Both books are also about, *inter alia*, what I believe is one of the foremost questions in Indian studies: What is Hinduism? In *Reflections* I pursued the possibility that a working definition might center around the Veda and its function as the legitimating source of authority for all subsequent "orthodox" traditions. Here I examine another of the definitional criteria often put forward for "Hinduism," the peculiar social system of the Indic subcontinent generally known as "caste" but which has its basis in an ancient classification scheme called *varṇa* ("class"). Although neither of the two books will "solve" the definitional problem, my hope is that both will contribute (in rather different ways) to the scholarly activity of reflecting upon the supposed object of study, in this case, "Hinduism."

Over the course of the past several years, portions of this book were delivered as papers or appeared in article form. Parts of Chapters 2 and 7 were published in "Eaters, Food, and Social Hierarchy in Ancient India: A Dietary Guide to a Revolution of Values," *Journal of the American Academy of Religion* 58, 2 (Summer 1990): 201–29. Sections of Chapter 3 were brought together as a paper, "Classification and Interpretation: Repetition and Reductionism in Religion and the Human Sciences," delivered to the Institute for the Advanced Study of Religion at the University of Chicago's Divinity School, January 6, 1988 and were also presented in a lecture entitled "*Varṇa*: Supernatural, Natural, and Social Classes in Vedic Cosmogonies," presented to the Columbia University Seminar in Oriental Thought and Religion, October 6, 1989. Some of this material eventually was published as "Classifying the Universe: Ancient Indian Cosmogonies and the *Varṇa* System," *Contributions to Indian Sociology* (n.s.) 23, 2 (1989): 241–60.

Materials from Chapter 8 were incorporated into a paper, "Outcast Animals and Beastly Men: The Classification of Animals and Humans in Ancient India," delivered on November 6, 1988, at the seventeenth Annual Conference on South Asia, University of Wisconsin, Madison. A revised version was published as "Classifying Animals and Humans in Ancient India," *Man* (n.s.) 26 (September 1991): 323–41, copyright © 1991 by the Royal Anthropological Institute of Great Britain and Ireland. Portions of Chapter 9 were delivered as a paper entitled "Classifying the Veda: 'Revelation' and Social Class in Ancient India," at the 1988 Annual Meeting of the American Academy of Religion, Chicago, November 20, 1988. Some of the material in that chapter was published as "Canonical Authority and Social Classification: Veda and *varṇa* in Ancient Indian Texts," *History of Religions* 32, 2 (November, 1992): 103–25, copyright © 1992 by The University of Chicago, all rights reserved; and as "The Veda and the Authority of Class," in Laurie Patton (ed.), *Authority, Anxiety and Canon: Essays in Vedic Interpretation* (Albany, N.Y.: SUNY Press, 1993).

Overviews of the whole work were presented under the title of "*Varṇa* and the Origins of Caste" at UCLA, April 29, 1992 (sponsored by the Interdisciplinary Center for the Study of Religion), and at the University of California, Santa Barbara, May 28, 1992 (sponsored by the Department of Religious Studies). My thanks to all those who endured and responded to these oral summaries of my research.

I have worked on this book, on and off, long enough to accumulate debts to many people and institutions. I take the opportunity to thank some of them here. For financial assistance, I am very grateful to the National Endowment to the Humanities, the American Institute of Indian Studies, Barnard College, and the University of California, Riverside. Institutions that provided academic support of various sorts include the University of Chicago's Institute for the Advanced Study of Religion; the University of Chicago's Regenstein Library; the Bhandarkar Oriental Research Institution; and the libraries at the University of California, Riverside and Berkeley.

Colleagues and friends who helped along the way include Beatrice Briggs, Wendy Doniger, Arthur Droge, Daniel Gold, William Harman, Bruce Lincoln, McKim Marriott, David Shulman, Frederick Smith, and David Tracy. I am especially grateful to Barbara Holdrege, whose careful and intelligent reading of the manuscript made this a better book than it otherwise would have been. I am also most appreciative to Hameed and Nazura Sattar for their infinite graciousness while I was in Poona, and to Madhav Bhandare of the American Institute of Indian Studies for his helpfulness and friendship. My work was much aided and abetted by Arshia Sattar and Richard Wilner, who acted at different times as my research assistants. Finally, I thank my wife, Katherine E. Fleming, whose assistance in all things and constant encouragement kept me afloat, and to whom I dedicate this book.

Riverside, California B. K. S.
March 1993

Contents

Abbreviations

AitĀ	Aitareya Āranyaka
AitB	Aitareya Brāhmaṇa
AitU	Aitareya Upaniṣad
ĀpDhS	Āpastamba Dharma Sūtra
ĀpGS	Āpastamba Gṛhya Sūtra
ĀpŚS	Āpastamba Śrauta Sūtra
ĀśvGS	Āśvalāyana Gṛhya Sūtra
ĀśvŚS	Āśvalāyana Śrauta Sūtra
AV	Atharva Veda Saṃhitā (Śaunaka recension)
AVP	Atharva Veda Saṃhitā (Paippalāda recension)
BĀU	Bṛhadāraṇyaka Upaniṣad
BDhS	Baudhāyana Dharma Sūtra
BGS	Baudhāyana Gṛhya Sūtra
BGPariS	Baudhāyana Gṛhya Paribhāṣā Sūtra
BGŚeṣaS	Baudhāyana Gṛhya Śeṣa Sūtra
BPitṛS	Baudhāyana Pitṛmedha Sūtra
BŚS	Baudhāyana Śrauta Sūtra
BhGS	Bhāradvāja Gṛhya Sūtra
BhŚS	Bhāradvāja Śrauta Sūtra
ChU	Chandogya Upaniṣad
GautDhS	Gautama Dharma Sūtra
GB	Gopatha Brāhmaṇa
GGS	Gobhila Gṛhya Sūtra
HGS	Hiraṇyakeśin Gṛhya Sūtra
HŚS	Hiraṇyakesin Śrauta Sūtra
JB	Jaiminīya Brāhmaṇa

JGS	Jaiminīya Gṛhya Sūtra
JMS	Jaimini Mīmāṃsā Sūtras
JŚS	Jaiminīya Śrauta Sūtra
JUB	Jaiminīya Upaniṣad Brāhmaṇa
KauśS	Kauśika Sūtra
KauṣU	Kauṣītaki Upaniṣad
KB	Kauṣītaki Brāhmaṇa
KGS	Kāṭhaka Gṛhya Sūtra
KhGS	Khādira Gṛhya Sūtra
KS	Kāṭhaka Saṃhitā
KŚS	Kātyāyana Śrauta Sūtra
KU	Kaṭha Upaniṣad
KūrmaP	Kūrma Purāṇa
LŚS	Lātyāyana Śrauta Sūtra
MaitU	Maitrāyaṇī Upaniṣad
Manu	Manu Smṛti
MārkP	Mārkaṇḍeya Purāṇa
MatsyaP	Matsya Purāṇa
Mbh	Mahābhārata
MGS	Mānava Gṛhya Sūtra
MS	Maitrāyaṇī Saṃhitā
MŚS	Mānava Śrauta Sūtra
PB	Pañcaviṃśa Brāhmaṇa
PGS	Pāraskāra Gṛhya Sūtra
PraśnaU	Praśna Upaniṣad
ṚV	Ṛg Veda Saṃhitā
ṢaḍB	Ṣaḍviṃśa Brāhmaṇa
ŚānĀ	Śankhāyana Āraṇyaka
ŚB	Śatapatha Brāhmaṇa (Mādhyaṇdina recension)
ŚBK	Śatapatha Brāhmana (Kāṇva recension)
ŚGS	Śānkhāyana Gṛhya Sūtra
ŚŚS	Śānkhāyana Śrauta Sūtra
TĀ	Taittirīya Āraṇyaka
TB	Taittirīya Brāhmaṇa
TS	Taittirīya Saṃhitā
TU	Taittirīya Upaniṣad
VādhŚS	Vādhūla Śrauta Sūtra
VaikhSmS	Vaikhānasa Smārta Sūtra
VaikhŚS	Vaikhānasa Śrauta Sūtra

VaitŚS	Vaitāna Śrauta Sūtra
VāsDhS	Vāsiṣṭha Dharma Sūtra
VGS	Vārāha Gṛhya Sūtra
VishnuP	Viṣṇu Purāṇa
VishnuSm	Viṣṇu Smṛti
VS	Vājasaneya Saṃhitā
VŚS	Vārāha Śrauta Sūtra
YājSm	Yājñavalkya Smṛti

Classifying the Universe

This has given me the greatest trouble and still does: to realize that what things *are called* is incomparably more important than what they are. The reputation, name, and appearance, the usual measure and weight of a thing, what it counts for—originally almost always wrong and arbitrary, thrown over things like a dress and altogether foreign to their nature and even to their skin—all this grows from generation unto generation, merely because people believe in it, until it gradually grows to be part of the thing and turns into its very body. What at first was appearance becomes in the end, almost invariably, the essence and is effective as such.

— Friedrich Nietzsche, *The Gay Science*, II.58

To give a thing a name, a label, a handle; to rescue it from anonymity, to pluck it out of the Place of Namelessness, in short to identify it—well, that's a way of bringing the said thing into being.

— Salman Rushdie, *Haroun and the Sea of Stories*

In the animal kingdom, the rule is, eat or be eaten; in the human kingdom, define or be defined.

— Thomas Szasz, *The Second Sin*

1

Classifying the Universe

Classification and Society

This is a book about the way ancient Indians classified, and thereby claimed to know, the universe and their own place in it. It also concerns the various sources of authority which the ancient Indian classifiers tapped to legitimate their epistemological claims. The system I will explore was articulated in the texts called the Vedas (mostly composed between the middle of the second millennium B.C.E. and the middle of the first millennium B.C.E.) and centers around the concept of *varṇa*.

Varṇa means "color" in the sense of "characteristic" or "attribute." I translate the word throughout this work as "category" or "class."[1] Among the things and beings so categorized into *varṇa*s was ancient Indian society, which was theoretically (and perhaps also in actuality) divided into three or four classes: Brahmin priests, Kshatriya rulers and warriors, and Vaishya commoners or peasants; sometimes also included in the social hierarchy were the Shūdras, the servant class. This book thus concerns the ways in which a social hierarchy was integrated into—and therefore ratified and legitimated by—a categorical system with universal scope and persuasive power.

Classification is the basis for all of what we call thought, reason, or logic. "All thinking is sorting, classifying," as E. H. Gombrich, among others, has observed.[2] To make sense of things is to bring order to them, to organize and structure them by dividing them into classes or categories. Conversely, without general classes or categories the world of particulars would remain utterly chaotic and therefore unknown and unknowable. Classification is not only central to human thought; it is its very condition of possibility. To know about something is to know how to categorize it, to know where it belongs in relation to other things, to know what it is like and what it is not like. It may be assumed that the capacity and necessity to classify are innate to human beings, and therefore a universal trait of the species. The examination of categories can thus reveal a great deal about the nature of the human mind, as the relatively new field of cognitive science has shown.[3] One major figure in that discipline has given notice that "categorization is not a matter to be taken lightly."

> There is nothing more basic than categorization to our thought, perception, action, and speech. Every time we see something as a *kind* of thing, for example, a tree, we are categorizing. Whenever we reason about *kinds* of things—chairs, nations, illnesses, emotions, any kind of thing at all—we are employing categories. Whenever we intentionally perform any kind of action, say something as mundane as writing with a pencil, hammering with a hammer, or ironing clothes, we are using categories. . . . Without the ability to categorize, we could not function at all, either in the physical world or in our social and intellectual lives. An understanding of how we categorize is central to any understanding of how we think and how we function, and therefore central to an understanding of what makes us human.[4]

Classification may be at the heart of what makes us all human, but the differences in the forms categorical systems take, differences in the principles for as well as the content of classificatory schemes, also are indicative of the differences in the ways peoples from different times and places think. It is now almost a truism (at least in postmodern Western societies) that perceptions of reality are socially constructed; all systems of classification must therefore be the specific products of their particular cultural and historical matrix.[5]

But it is important to remember that there are people behind such abstractions as "cultures." Different ways of classifying things and beings are more than just "cultural products." They were invented and passed down by particular human beings living in particular communities under particular social conditions. If classification is fundamental to thought, those who control the form classification takes—its principles and contents—have a rather obvious advantage: knowledge is power, as the saying goes, and knowledge is a product of categorization.

I assume in this work that a classification system like that of *varṇa* is ultimately the invention of a specific group of people whose power and privilege were in part based on their very ability to "seize the enunciative function" (as Michel Foucault might say) and expatiate on how the universe is organized. But more than this, since human beings are themselves inevitably implicated in their own classificatory schemes,[6] those who generated the categorical system also placed themselves in an advantageous position within it. I assume, in other words, a social and political dimension to a classificatory system which is presented as pure knowledge.

Earlier in this century, Émile Durkheim argued that the classes that constitute different people's categorical systems could be traced to the social frameworks out of which they emerged. Durkheim disputed earlier assumptions, put forward by thinkers like Emmanuel Kant, that certain categories (such as those concerning the divisions we make in space and time) are "hard-wired" into the human brain. For Durkheim, thinking (i.e., classifying) is not a biological given but one of the gifts of social life; all forms of categorization were modeled on and presupposed social classes. Classification of other realms was made possible by a prior classification of society:

> Society was not simply a model which classificatory thought followed; it was its own divisions which served as divisions for the system of classification. The first logical categories were social categories; the first classes of things were classes of men, into which these things were integrated. It was because men were grouped, and thought of themselves in the form of groups, that in their ideas they grouped other things, and in the beginning the two modes of grouping were merged to the point of being indistinct.[7]

Logical classes are founded on social classes. Thus, because social structures differ between cultures, so too will the categories or what Durkheim called the "collective representations" they generate.

Certain features of Durkheim's argumentation have subsequently been found to be faulty. Critics often point out, for example, that Durkheim begs the question of origins: if the first classes were social classes, how did humans learn to categorize in the first place (and thereby recognize the social classes as classes)?[8] Nevertheless, stripped of its problematic etiological dimension, Durkheim's insistence on the social roots of classificatory systems still has considerable currency and interpretive utility. Even among scholars who reject the notion that the mind owes its every operational function to society, many accept the equally important idea that society, as Barry Schwartz puts it, appropriates and exploits the cognitive information the human mind generates. A particular social order lies behind every classificatory system:

> I have tried to show how this "uninvited guest"—the mind—is exploited by society in its own interests and for the sake of its own ends. I have argued that the categories of objects formed by its neural apparatus have no intrinsic cultural significance; that these objects are "socialized" only when they have been transformed into semiotic systems, which, in turn, bend them to the imperatives and needs of social order. It is in and through semiotic codes that we come to much of our knowledge of social structure. Semiosis, then, is the middle term between cognitive discrimination and classification. Behind the latter are the constants of societal organization itself.[9]

It seems to me fairly obvious that, at the very least, social concerns lie behind the classificatory scheme of *varṇa*, and probably did from its inception in Indo-European antiquity. The *varṇa* system does appear to have ancient roots; it is fundamentally a version of a classificatory strategy brought to India by the Indo-European invaders during the second millennium B.C.E. Georges Dumézil has labeled this system an "idéologie tripartie"[10] and has argued that the Indo-European forebears of civilizations ranging from the Celtic to the Greek to the

Indic shared a mode of thinking or method of classifying—inclusive of but not restricted to social classification—characterized by the division into three categories or principles he calls "fonctions" or "activités fondamentales": (1) that which is concerned with religion, the "sacred," and the relations between humans and gods, on the one hand; and with sovereignty and kingship, on the other;[11] (2) that which centers on physical force, the military, and defense; and (3) the function concerned with what Dumézil calls "fecundity, to be certain, human, animal, and vegetable, but at the same time nourishment and wealth, and health, and peace—with the delights and advantages of peace—and often pleasure, beauty, and also the important idea of a '*grand nombre*,' applied not only to goods (abundance), but also to men who comprise the social body."[12]

At least one of Dumézil's opponents insists that tripartition in the Veda cannot be understood in terms of a tripartite social structure, echoing the much-voiced (and wrongheaded) contention that religious discourse cannot be "reduced" to its social bases. In a book entitled *Triads in the Veda*,[13] Jan Gonda claims that the ubiquitous triadic classificatory structures found in the Veda were produced from nothing other than a deeply ingrained fondness for threes. It was not, in Gonda's view, a tripartite social structure (Brahmins, Kshatriyas, and commoners) that lay at the foundation of tripartite classifications. Rather, "it was the very triadic mode of thought that was the fundamental principle."[14] Gonda notes that the texts themselves do not say that the basic triad is the social triad, and therefore neither should we:

> What is however worth noticing is . . . the three classes of the Aryan society are only seldom mentioned as a group. And, what is no less interesting, their triad is, as far as I am able to see, neither paradigmatic nor made the basis of an argument. That means that as compared with the above macrocosmic, microcosmic and ritual triads the 'social triad' does not play a fundamental role in the speculations and classificatory system of the ritualists. The conclusion seems therefore to be obvious that any attempt at viewing the phenomena and at explaining the meaning and origin of the triadic line of thought on the basis of sociological arguments should, as far as Vedic antiquity is concerned, be judged with due caution and considerable reserve. . . . In the Veda the number three, as such, as a 'holy,' 'typical,' 'favourite' number was of a more fundamental significance and in any case much greater frequency than the tripartite social division. . . . And, what is more important, the cosmic triad, and not the social tripartition, was regarded as exemplary and made a basic principle of classification and "weltanschauliche" speculations.[15]

It is thus not only because tripartition was an ingrained "mode of thought" that it should not be reduced to social tripartition; it is also because three was a "holy" number reducible not to society but only to "the cosmic triad" of Vedic myth. Gonda, in sum, argues that reproducing what the texts themselves "regarded as exemplary and made a basic principle of classification" provides a sufficient analysis and interpretation of the data.

Dumézil, in his prodigious *oeuvre* on Indo-European thought, has consistently pointed to the wide application of the tripartite ideology, ranging from social structure to the categorization of illnesses and medicines. In his earlier work, Dumézil was inclined to a straightforward explanation of the basis for this ideology: "The tripartite social organization of the Indo-Europeans instigated the principle of the classification, the type of ideology," which has furnished "the philosophical thought of the Indo-Europeans with . . . a means of exploring material and moral reality, . . . a means of putting order into the capital of ideas accepted by society."[16] In later publications, however, Dumézil softened his reductionism, saying that

> a decisive advancement was accomplished the day that I realized, around 1950, that the "tripartite ideology" is not inevitably accompanied, in the life of a society, by the *actual* tripartite division of that society, as in the Indian model;[17] that it can, on the contrary, where one ascertains it, be nothing (no longer be, perhaps never have been) but an ideal, and at the same time, a mode of analyzing, of interpreting the forces which ensure the course of the world and the life of man.[18]

While renouncing the "hard" reductionism of his past—and not without provoking criticism for beating such a retreat[19]—even Dumézil's later position stands in sharp contrast to assumptions like Gonda's. Gonda argues that both the theory and possible concrete manifestation of a tripartite social order are epiphenomena of a more basic "cosmic" or religious triad; Dumézil sees tripartite representations as projections either from an original social structure (leading to the interpretive position I have called "hard reductionism"), or from the *ideal* for such a social structure, whether or not that ideal was actually realized (entailing the hermeneutic of "soft reductionism").[20]

The reductionist stance (in both its hard and soft versions) argues that tripartition in, for example, ancient Indian texts derives from an actual or idealized social situation in which the (or the idea of the) three (and later four) classes of Indian society are primary, and only secondarily are re-presented in other realms. From this point of view, the Brahmin priests (who composed these texts, and not without an eye to their own advantage) and the Kshatriya rulers and warriors (who also materially benefited from these classificatory schemes) displaced their superior social statuses, or aspirations for them, onto the natural, supernatural, religious, and ritual worlds—*and did so surreptitiously*. As we will see in Chapter 3, several of the cosmogonies or myths of the origins of the universe that lay out the *varṇa* scheme do not even mention the social hierarchy in their taxonomies.

The end result of classification schemes organized around the concept of *varṇa* was that certain humans could present what was an arbitrary social status or status claim as natural and sacred; that is, social hierarchy was presented as inexorably part of the immutable and divinely given order of things. In a philosophy like that of the Veda no less than that of ancient Indo-Europeans in general, where "every strand within the whole fabric of thought was thus reinforced by every other strand," it was difficult indeed for those whose interests were not best served by such a mode of thought (i.e., the vast majority of commoners) to think their way out of it: "Sociohistoric contingencies and natural 'laws' were treated within the same mythico-ritual discourse, and were endowed with the same status of utter facticity and eternal truth. To challenge any part of the system was to challenge all, and a challenge to any part could be refuted with overpowering arguments."[21]

Hinduism and *Varṇa*

It is, then, one of the chief aims of this work to demonstrate that although *varṇa* had a much wider application in the ancient Indian texts than is ordinarily realized (it was a totalistic classificatory system), social interests informed and impinged upon this enterprise at every turn. The *varṇa* system managed to organize under one basic structure such seemingly diverse realms as the world of the gods, the divisions of space and time, spheres of what we would call the "natural world" (i.e., flora and fauna), and the realm of revelation or "scripture." *Varṇa*, in other words, was a classificatory system which attempted to encompass within it all of the major sectors of the visible and invisible universe. But included within the reach of the *varṇa* system, and lying at its conceptual base, was the classification of society. Indeed, the class that the term "*varṇa*" has usually been exclusively understood to denote is social class; ancient Indian society was theoretically divided into three or four *varṇa*s. Although I argue throughout that *varṇa* had a much wider scope that merely the social, it is far from unimportant that society (in addition to the supernatural and natural realms) was also "discovered" to be divisible into three (or sometimes four) classes.

Varṇa, in addition to being a universalistic order of things in the Veda, provides the historical roots and theoretical backbone for the later caste system, a social institution that many regard as distinctively, perhaps uniquely, South Asian.[22] Furthermore, caste is sometimes identified as one of the only, if not *the* only, definitional features of the many-sided religion we call "Hinduism." Another purpose of this book is to determine why the Indic social system has achieved such a status in Indian studies and also, it would seem, within some parts of the indigenous tradition itself.

In an earlier work, I explored the notion that "Hinduism," a category created by outsiders largely in order to organize and unify a bewildering variety of otherwise independent South Asian religious traditions, might be best defined (provisionally, tentatively, experimentally) as "the religion of those humans who create, perpetuate, and transform traditions with legitimizing reference to the authority of the Veda."[23] In defining "Hinduism" in this way, I did *not* wish to indicate that the Veda primarily functions to provide Hindus with doctrinal truth or a guide to actual practice. The Veda is, in this respect at least, mostly irrelevant to Hindu life; the traditions we call Hindu largely ignore the doctrines and practices enshrined between "the covers" of their (until recently orally preserved) canon. The authority of the Veda is nominal or "symbolic." It is because the Veda has been constituted by the variety of traditions we call Hindu as the prototype for all subsequent authoritative (and orthodox, under this definition) declarations of absolute truth that it has attained its canonical status. Concomitantly, the Vedic fire sacrifice (*yajña*) in like manner forms the prototype for subsequent orthodox Hindu religious praxis. Veda and *yajña*, or so I argued, were *canonical categories* which made it possible for later Hindu texts, truth claims, and practices to present themselves as counterparts—and thus borrow all the authority of the ultimately and absolutely authoritative prototype.[24]

The history of post-Vedic orthodoxy, from this perspective at least, perpetuates an epistemological strategy first laid out in the Veda itself: to forge connections or *bandhus* between the counterpart and the prototype, the actual and the ideal, the immanent and the transcendent. The Vedic quest is neatly summed up in the form of a cosmic query at ṚV 10.130.3: "What was the prototype, what was the counterpart, and what was the connection between them?"[25] Later Hindu arguments that their texts were "equivalent" to the Veda and their practices "the same as" (or "procuring the same fruit as") the Vedic sacrifice appear to be reapplications of an ancient and typically Vedic strategy of conjoining and homologizing different elements within a universe governed by a principle of "hierarchical resemblance." Canonical authority for subsequent truth claims, dogmas, beliefs, doctrines, practices, and especially the scriptures in which they are codified, is obtained by claiming connection to the prototype of all canonical authority, the Veda. It is this process of "eternally returning" to the Veda that defines Hindu orthodoxy.[26]

In the course of developing such a thesis, however, I gave short shrift to the other criterion many have suggested for defining Hinduism: the distinctive social structure and ideological concomitants of caste. Indian castes are grounded in a social theory positing four principal hierarchically ordered classes (*varṇas*). Each class has its own distinctive set of duties and functions. Brahmins are charged with religious and priestly tasks, Kshatriyas with defense and political rule, Vaishyas with agriculture and trade, and Shūdras with servitude. As we shall see in Chapter 10, the thousands of castes (*jātis*) of the historical and contemporary caste system are theoretically reducible to one or another of the four classes and the system as a whole is clearly ideologically dependent on the earlier *varṇa* system. What's more, Indian texts often explain the existence of the *jātis* as the result of interbreeding among the original four *varṇas*. For these reasons, among others, the *varṇa* system can with some justification be identified as the origin of the caste system.

Some have claimed it is this idealized social scheme of *varṇa* and the institutions and ideologies underlying or derived from it that truly constitute Hinduism as such. Thus, whereas certain definitions center on the canonical status of the Veda within Hinduism, definitions of a second sort construe the religion in terms of its distinctive social theory—classifying the religion of Hinduism turns on Hinduism's classificatory scheme for the social order. Hinduism, under this definitional criterion, is "as much a social system as a religion. . . . Its social framework has from very early times been the caste system, and this has . . . become . . . increasingly identified with Hinduism as such."[27] Caste, according to another scholar, is "the very soul of this somewhat indeterminate fluid collection of customs and beliefs which is called Hinduism."[28]

The privileged position within the caste system of the Brahmin or priestly class, which is invariably placed at the top of the pecking order, is often regarded as the centerpiece of such definitions of Hinduism. It is "the spiritual prerogative of the Brahman caste which is the cornerstone on which the whole Hindu social edifice was built."[29] Implied also here is the definitional status of two traditional entailments of the caste system, and guarantors of the superior place of the Brahmin within the system: (1) the notion that one's particular duty (*dharma* or *svadharma*) is calibrated to the class (*varṇa*) into which one was born and the stage of life (*āśrama*) one is presently passing through; and (2) the belief in *karma* and the cycle of rebirth (*saṃsāra*) whereby one's social position in this life is ethically determined by moral actions in past lives.[30]

While I am inclined now, as I was when writing *Reflections*, to reject the assertion that the caste system, *varṇāśrama dharma*, or traditional Brahmin social and religious hegemony provide adequate definitional criteria for "Hinduism,"[31] this book is dedicated in part to uncovering the historical roots and ideological props that make such an assertion possible. We shall see in Chapter 9 that the two types of definitions of Hinduism mentioned here need not be regarded as mutually exclusive. For the authority of caste is in some ways dependent on the authority of the Veda in which caste (at least *in nuce*, in the form of the *varṇa* system) is first propagated. In any event, "Hinduism" defined by caste hierarchy and Brahmin supremacy is an idea which seems to have gripped many both within and outside of the tradition, and in the following pages we will discover some of the reasons why such an idea holds such persuasive power.

Although other scholars may continue to find this criterion the best one for defining Hinduism, my hope is that they will do so having become a bit more cognizant of the fact that the Brahmin authors of the ancient Veda made a much stronger case than they for Brahmin superiority within an immutable social, and indeed cosmic, order. One might also wish to ponder whether the views and interests of the Brahmin class—fascinating and intellectually sophisticated as they may be and persuasive as they undoubtedly were in Indian social and religious history—should be simply reiterated and reinforced by Indologists and scholars of religion.[32]

Vertical and Horizontal Connections in the Veda

The *varṇa* system was first formulated within the ancient Indian culture and religion we call "Vedism" (to distinguish it from, among other things, later Indian formations one characterizes as "Hindu"). Vedism is known to us entirely from its texts, and therefore one must be careful about what claims one makes. This book centers on the idealized depiction of reality that is presented in the Veda by the Brahmins who wrote it. This is no reason to dismiss the Veda or other works of the Brahmin literati in India. The Brahmins, as Francis X. Clooney points out, "were never the majority" but nevertheless "were always among the foremost and most influential representatives of the Hindu effort to relate the 'givens' of their social order to their wider beliefs and general worldview: they try to make sense of four castes . . . precisely in terms of other things that make sense to them: the rules voiced in a 'beginningless, unchanging' scripture constitutive of society and nature as we know them."[33]

My study is about representations and their persuasiveness, and not about historical, social, economic, and political realities per se. The Veda paints a picture of how things ought to be; it is an ideological tractate rather than a descriptive narrative. But, as Bruce Lincoln reminds us, "an ideology—any ideology—is not just an ideal against which social reality is measured or an end toward the fulfillment of which groups and individuals aspire." It also serves to persuade members of a given society "of the rightness of their lot in life, whatever that may be, and of the total social order."[34] Furthermore, as Franco and Chand point out, "like all ideologies, *varṇa* ideology survives only within the matrix of material affirmations and sanctions."[35]

The Veda, a collective term for a rather large corpus of ancient Sanskrit works, was preserved only orally (and perhaps not without emendations and additions along the way) until relatively recent times. It was transmitted from teacher to pupil largely within the Brahmin class of Indian society who had staked a special claim to knowledge of it. Indeed, the social privileges the Brahmin class enjoyed, and still do to some extent, were justified in part by this special relationship they maintained with the sacred Veda.[36] Such privileges, as we shall have abundant opportunity to witness in the following pages, were also authorized by the teachings of the very Veda the Brahmins have preserved. This is not surprising given the fact that it was members of the Brahmin class who were not only the historical perpetuators but also the authors of these authoritative texts.

The composers of the Veda, and most especially of those sections within the Veda called the *Brāhmaṇa*s, were preoccupied with the connections and interrelations which they believed organized reality. Supposedly resembling, and therefore potentially homologous, things, entities, and phenomena were linked by these connections or *bandhus*. Human beings in possession of this esoteric analogical knowledge could therefore claim to understand and manipulate the natural, supernatural, and social realms from within the confines of their ritual world. While no attempt at an exhaustive explication of all the guiding principles assumed and exploited by Vedic ritualists need be undertaken here,[37] their philosophy of universal resemblance can be generally described in terms of connections organized along two axes.

First, resemblances were postulated along a vertical axis. This type of homology often, but not always, connected an immanent form and its transcendent correlative: "Deux plans, mais un être," as Paul Mus observes.[38] More precisely, vertically oriented homologies operated between the hierarchically ordered elements of the same type of things or beings. The components of a particular type, however, could be located on different cosmological levels of reality, inhabitants of different "worlds" or *loka*s, the god Indra's thunderbolt and the wooden sword used in the ritual, for example. Vertical connections thus could link the visible and manifest counterpart to its invisible and transcendent prototype.

But vertical connections need not reach out only to the unseen. The prototype could be considered, from a more limited perspective, as simply the "most excellent" manifest member of the class, the paradigmatic but immanent component of a category whose other (equally manifest and immanent) components were defined in relation to it. This kind of hierarchical and vertically oriented connection, restricted to the visible components of a given category, is frequently encountered in Vedic texts on substitutions within the ritual. The prototype, in such cases, is the substance ordinarily prescribed (it being the case that the prescribed substance is also regarded as the best representative of the class). The substitutes are listed in order of their relative resemblance to the original; that is, the counterparts are ranked according to their relative degree of realization of the prototype.[39] On the social plane, the Brahmin usually functions as such a prototype, the potentially perfect realization of the human being in relation to whom members of other classes are only approximations.

The second axis along which Vedic homologies and connections were located can be pictured as horizontally oriented. Horizontal connections link resembling components of two different hierarchically (i.e., vertically) organized orders. Members of the different categories of things and beings, located at the same rank within their respective orders, were in this way also conjoined. The Brahmin, for example, was not only vertically connected to the other, if lesser, classes of human society, but also was horizontally linked to Agni among the gods, the goat among the animals, the spring among the seasons, and the *gāyatrī* among the meters. Vertically connected prototypes and counterparts were thought to participate in the same essence although in different degrees; horizontally connected members of various orders of things and beings were regarded as cosmic kin in the same degree. Vertically oriented linkages lash the universe from top to bottom; horizontal connections gird it.

Moreover, the two types of connections were obviously interdependent. Elements from different species could be horizontally connected because they were stationed at the same hierarchical levels within their respective vertically oriented orders. When put into play (and this was done within the bounds of the omnipotent ritual) such connections traverse and thus interrelate the different orders of things in such a way as to result, ultimately, in a constructed unity of parts, that is, the cosmos itself.[40]

Taken together, then, the *bandhus* of ancient Indian ritualistic philosophy theoretically can account for and hook together everything in the universe. Such high ambitions can indeed be witnessed within Vedic texts, culminating perhaps in the Upanishads with the apotheosis of "knowledge" or "wisdom" (*jñāna*) and its ultimate product, the equation of the microcosm (*ātman*) and macrocosm (*brahman*). In order to proceed with this quest to know and manage everything in the cosmos, the potentially unlimited connections needed to be organized in a manageable way, systematized into coherent classifications, and guided by principles that could justify linkages between apparently widely disparate things and beings.

This organizational framework was provided by the *varṇa* system. *Varṇa* furnished the Vedic ritualists with the only organizational concept capable of generating and negotiating connections of both the vertical and horizontal type; as such, *varṇa* might be regarded as the "root metaphor" or "master narrative" of Vedic thought. *Varṇa* provided a set of main routes along which vertical and horizontal connections could be channeled. Otherwise put, the *varṇa*s functioned as supercategories which cut across the boundaries of the species or discrete classes and thus ordered all the realms of the visible and invisible cosmos. There are, as we shall see, Brahmin parts of the human anatomy, deities, cosmological worlds, cardinal directions, times of the day and year, animals, food, plants, trees, Vedas, and meters and hymns, in addition to the Brahmin social class—and there are also Kshatriya and Vaishya counterparts for each.

Varṇa thus describes the classificatory scheme in which components were vertically or hierarchically ordered and interconnected as well as horizontally categorized, linking together components from different species. It was through *varṇa* that the parts of the cosmos could be tied together—up, down, and sideways —and it was through *varṇa* that humans were both organized into social groups and also conjoined to resembling things and beings in the natural and supernatural worlds.

Problems of Consistency

I attempt to demonstrate in this book that the *varṇa*s did indeed function as supercategories in the Vedic quest to "classify the universe." To carry out this self-appointed task, I re-present and systematize a categorical system; in other words, I reconstruct out of textual fragments taken from throughout the massive corpus of Vedic texts a system of classification according to *varṇa*. The work thus strives, among other things, to serve as a map for the symbolic system assumed and utilized within Vedic ritual and philosophy. It might be regarded as something of a handbook for deciphering Vedic codes, for understanding why the ritualists connected things and beings in the way they did, and for uncovering the logic guiding the manipulation of what we would call "symbols" within the Vedic sacrifice.

Some readers familiar with past scholarship on the Veda will be surprised that I represent Vedic thought as so orderly. For whatever else the Veda is, or so we have been told over the past century and a half, it is not systematic. Rather, it is comprised of poetic flights of fancy, mystical esotericism, and/or priestly conceits (take your pick), and it is distinguished by its proclivity toward drawing equivalences or identities (the *bandhus* mentioned earlier) that are variously described as inconsistent, fanciful, and absurd.[41]

I intend here to dispute such depictions of the categorizations one finds in the Veda. My book is long, and it is encumbered by tedious detail and a vast number of textual citations. This is necessary because my thesis runs so counter to the received opinion. I beg the indulgence of the reader in advance; but I justify the detail this work puts forward in making its case by the fact that the case has not been made before. If the reader who struggles through comes away with a sense that there is, after all, a consistency and logic to the Vedic connections others have dismissed, I will have succeeded in overturning a basic truism of Indology.

I do not wish, however, to avoid or ignore the real and potential problems my thesis faces. Let us consider at the outset three possible objections to the argument that *varṇa* provided the authors of the Veda with an overarching and systematic method for drawing consistent "equivalences" and connections between things and beings, for classifying the universe.

One such potential problem we shall encounter involves the number of classes things and beings are divided into. I referred earlier to the fact that the *varṇa* system is a reflex of a larger Indo-European pattern of tripartition. Whether or not Dumézil's thesis holds in other sectors of the Indo-European world I am not qualified to say. In ancient Indian texts, however, the tripartite ideology Dumézil described is pervasive. The *varṇa* system usually presupposes that three is the number of totality: "As much as the *brahman*, the *kṣatra* and the *viś* are"—here we have the neuter metaphysical powers that underlie the three principal classes of Vedic society—"that is this all (*idam sarvam*)," says a *Brāhmaṇa* (ŚB 4.2.2.14; cf. ŚB 14.2.2.30). When it comes to the divisions of society, the three social classes of Brahmins, Kshatriyas, and Vaishyas (who in the Veda are often generally referred to as the *viś*, the commoners, peasantry, or the masses in general) are the only ones that usually are of interest to the Vedic authors. They are set off from all others in that they are regarded as the sole members of the Āryan community; they are the only groups allowed to learn the Veda; and, most important, they are the only groups allowed within the confines of the all-important sacrifice or *yajña*.

As we shall see in abundant detail in the following chapters, this tripartite pattern is reproduced in the classification of many realms. There are, among other triads, three categories of gods, three worlds in Vedic cosmology (earth, atmosphere, and sky), three principal parts of the day (morning, midday, and afternoon), three principal Vedas (Ṛg, Yajur, and Sāma) and three principal meters in which the sacred scripture was composed (*gāyatrī*, *triṣṭubh*, and *jagatī*). Or, as one Vedic texts puts it, "There are three meters, there are three breaths—exhalation, inhalation, and circulation—and there are three worlds here. They say, 'Among the gods [everything] is three[fold]' " (JB 1.156).

Moreover, these triads are explicitly assimilated to the three social classes. Each social class corresponds to one or another of the gods, worlds, times of day, Vedas, meters, and so on. The tripartite social structure, in other words, is easily overlaid upon or correlated to other tripartite structures. The system of correspondences also follows a fairly obvious logic, a code, as it were, which is the essence of the *varṇa* classification scheme. The matching of social classes to worlds and day parts is guided by the invariable traits, characteristics, and functions of the Brahmins, Kshatriyas, and Vaishyas which are "rediscovered" in one or another of the components of such "natural" triads. I return to this point later.

But other kinds of classification schemes besides the tripartite one are also encountered, and such alternative structures might be viewed as a counterargument to the contention that the *varṇa* pattern is the dominant taxonomical mode in the Veda. In some cases, a neat correlation of the dominant social triad and triads in other realms is impossible. The four cardinal directions (east, south, west, and north) present one instance of this sort of classificatory problem. If the *varṇa* structure is fundamentally triadic and is, as I claim, the principal classificatory mold of ancient Indian texts, what is to be made of quadripartite structures found also in those texts?

Sometimes the answer to this query is fairly straightforward: the social dimension of the system has expanded to accommodate a fourth class, the Shūdras. The Veda thus sometimes makes mention of not just three but four social classes,[42] and later Hindu texts regularly assume that society includes the Shūdra or servant class as the fourth *varṇa*.[43] The enlargement of the tripartite classification system into a quadripartite one may very well have been stimulated by an analogous (or causative) historical expansion of Vedic society to include within it the non-Āryan indigenous inhabitants of South Asia. These natives the Indo-European invaders originally called *dāsas* or *dasyus*, "slaves."[44] Over time, as the invaders themselves became natives and as some of the original inhabitants were assimilated to some degree within Āryan society, the latter came to be known as "Shūdras" and took over the bottom rung in the social order—the place which was formerly occupied by the "third function" in Dumézil's reconstruction, i.e. the Vaishyas or *viś*.

Furthermore, it is perhaps telling that the traits we will observe to be characteristic of the Vaishya class—a close association with fecundity, nourishment, multiplicity, as well as subservience and weakness relative to the ruling class composed of Brahmins and Kshatriyas—we find also attributed to the Shūdras in the Veda. Sharing many of the same features, the two classes of Vaishyas and Shūdras seem to have been the result of a bifurcation of the lower strata of Vedic society. The components of the third category are divided and redistributed between the two lower classes of a now quadripartite hierarchical whole. The north, for example, the "extra" direction from the perspective of the tripartite classification mode, is thus sometimes assigned to the Shūdra, the fourth social class, but is often characterized in terms that could just as well fit the Vaishyas.

This historical and sociological shift from a tripartite to a quadripartite social structure—a shift that is only occasionally registered in the texts of our period—thus seems to be reflected in some of the four-part categorizations we shall encounter in the course of this work. This is not the only method for dealing with an "extra" fourth, however; our problem is not so easily solved in every instance. The reduplication of the third chain, the Vaishya set of associations, into a "lower" fourth or Shūdra category is only one way the systematizers formulated the quadripartite structure. Elsewhere the fourth category becomes a generalized summary of the previous three, "something which on the one hand is added to a threefold totality and on the other hand includes the three preceding items."[45] The fourth category can thus contain entities which signify the encompassing summation of the first three, or as a "transcendent fourth" which rises above the lower three. "The fourth," as Jan Gonda correctly observes, "can be interpreted in various ways and its relation with the three can vary with the context."[46]

To complicate matters even further, in yet other instances what appears to be a "standard" or even "original" tripartite mode of classification stretches out into a five-part or even six-part structure (as we shall see in Chapter 3). Stimulated by the classificatory need to correlate various sets of pentads and sextets and the *varṇa* categories, the Vedic systematizers again took recourse to the strategies of reduplication of those categories, summarizing and "transcending" the prior categories in subsequent ones, or adding to the bottom of the structure as well as to the top. I shall contend that the *varṇa* classificatory scheme is in these cases not discarded or ignored; it is, however, adjusted to meet new and more complex categorical contingencies.

A second possible stumbling block to the argument put forward here that *varṇa* is the dominant mode of classifying all realms of things and beings is the fact that there are other principles of classification besides that of *varṇa* for organizing certain realms. I return to this problem again at the beginning of Chapter 8 in relation to alternative kinds of divisions in the animal kingdom. For now, let it simply be said that it is not the purpose of this book to take into account *all* the ways the Vedic ritualists classified things and beings. My topic is limited to *varṇa*. Nevertheless, since I am arguing that *varṇa* is *the* master template for classifying the universe in Vedic texts, I might also note here that when alternatives and competitors are encountered we often seem to observe the Vedic systematizers at work harmonizing and interrelating other classification modalities to that of *varṇa*. Animals may be classified as domesticated or wild, edible or nonedible, sacrificable or nonsacrificable, but all such dichotomies ultimately are put into the service of the *varṇa* scheme. Furthermore, there exists no such alternative classification program or set of principles that has anything like the pervasive scope of *varṇa*. Other schemes exist, although they usually are specific to one or another realm and not generalized, and they will be mentioned in their proper contexts—but only when they recur with some frequency will it be necessary to burden the discussion with how they overlap and interact with the *varṇas*.

A third difficulty, and perhaps the most serious and puzzling, should also be confronted at the outset. I will be concerned to demonstrate that the connections (*bandhus*) that the *varṇa* system makes possible between things and beings (which, although of different orders or realms, share the same "class") are systematically formulated and observe a high degree of regularity. This does not mean, however, that here, any more than in other traditions that attempted to organize a universe, there were not variations, anomalies, exceptions, diverging views, and differing perspectives. I take some pains throughout this book to at least point to—if not always adequately account for—such discrepancies in what is, after all, my own reconstruction of this taxonomy. Some introductory words as to why there should be inconsistencies and alternatives in categorizing by *varṇa*, and just what kinds of inconsistencies and alternatives we will be encountering, may be in order.

In some cases, undoubtedly, different classificatory choices might be traced to different chronologically and geographically based traditions in ancient India—had we any sure method of determining such things, but alas we do not.[47] In other instances, it seems likely that individual authors left their idiosyncratic marks by creatively manipulating standardized patterns; there is no reason to think that certain Vedic ritualists were prevented from making such innovative departures from the norm. But since the particular authors of the Veda are, like those of most other sacred texts, almost always unnamed and unknown, this explanation also can only be posited and not proved. Still, it is probable that localized and individualistic classificatory choices may have subsequently been brought together by the final redactors of the Veda, keeping diversity while constructing a textual unity in an attempt to lend a synthetic and pan-Indian authority to the texts. It would be surprising if there *were not* divergencies in a set of texts composed at various places by different authors over a span hundreds, perhaps thousands, of years.

The alternatives, inconsistencies, and contradictions in categorizing by *varṇa* are of two main types. The first is when several entities within a given realm receive the same *varṇa* assignment according to various texts. For example, we will see that goats, cows, and black antelopes are all, in one passage or another, classified as "Brahmin" animals. The other type of discrepancy is the converse of the first. One individual entity sometimes receives different *varṇa* classifications in different textual passages: for example, the cow is in some texts said to be the animal of the Brahmin, but elsewhere it is regarded as a Vaishya animal.

It is precisely examples like this that Indologists cite when dismissing Vedic connections or correlations (*bandhus*) as haphazardly formulated, random, arbitrary, contradictory, and ultimately absurd. And surely not all such instances can be explained away by assuming different eras of composition, different geographical traditions, or different individual predilections among the various authors of the Veda: there are too many found too close together in too many texts. Perhaps another explanation might be put forward that accounts for categorical alternatives and apparent contradictions—and without abandoning (1) the premise that the *varṇa* scheme was pervasive and predominant, and (2) the assumption that the connections the scheme made possible between entities of different social, natural, and supernatural realms followed a discernible and ruled logic.

What I put forward in this book is the supposition that the three (and sometimes four) primary classes of the *varṇa* system, and a certain number of the definitional criteria for these classes, are fixed and invariable. What is placed within the classes, however, what is classified by means of the three or four *varṇa*s, is indeed subject to some variability. The categorization of a particular entity—the cow, let us say—can proceed according to different assumptions in different circumstances. Different features of the animal are at different times isolated and brought to the fore, thus calling up different *varṇa* attributions. The cow is sometimes thought of as the very embodiment of the sacrifice, its products (milk, clarified butter, dung, etc.) being so essential to the performance of the ritual. The animal will, under this view, be assimilated to the Brahmin, who is invariably identified with the ritual he controls and manipulates: the Brahmin "is" the sacrifice. Alternatively, the cow might be more generally conceived as material wealth, or productive of food, in which case the association with the Vaishya class is called forth. Furthermore, such differing *varṇa* indicators can occur in one and the same passage, thus precluding any necessity to suppose variant traditions: "They [the gods] said, 'What we gods have created in the cow is auspicious indeed, for truly she is the sacrifice and without the cow no sacrifice is performed. She is also food, for the cow, indeed, is all food' " (ŚB 2.2.4.13).

Nor is the cow the *only* animal that may be classified as "Brahmin" or as "Vaishya," as the case may be. The goat is also an animal intimately associated with the ritual (being the victim most often used in the animal sacrifice) and is thus often regarded as a Brahmin animal, like the cow. Or the well-known reproductive capacities of the goat may be highlighted, in which case the animal is designated "Vaishya."

In any case the animal—or any other entity subjected to this form of categorization—is classified according to predetermined and unchanging *varṇa* assumptions, for example, that the Brahmin is intimately connected to the sacrifice, and that the Vaishya is characterized by wealth, fecundity, and material productivity. It is the fixed class structure, its theoretical underpinnings, and the operative classificatory principles in Vedic texts that I wish to highlight in this work. In underscoring the consistencies, I do not mean to ignore or render insignificant the instances of the varying categorizations of particular things and beings. What is more impressive, I think, and what should not be dismissed simply because there are variations, are the considerable number of regularities in categorization one finds in Vedic texts. We shall see by the end of this work, I hope, how overwhelming the number of these recurrences within the *varṇa* system are in comparison to the relatively few divergences.

Varṇa and Its Scope

The outlines of the general system of classification by *varṇa* always remain recognizable regardless of the occasional variants at the level of application. Furthermore, a totalistic homological system such as this one—in which there is considerable confusion (from the outsider's point of view) between ordinarily separated things and beings; in which there is a confounding of the natural, the supernatural, the religious and ritual, and the social—is in all probability more than just the consequence of differing traditions and classificatory methodologies haphazardly colliding and re-forming in ancient Indian texts. It more likely was the result of an intentional strategy on the part of the composers who supplemented and revised one another's work in order to account for—and to control, in one way or another—more and more under the umbrella of the *varṇa* scheme.

Although *varṇa* is a taxonomical system with universal scope, designed and deployed in order to classify the cosmos as a whole, the brunt of scholarship on the *varṇa*s has thus far been borne almost exclusively by the social realm—and the focus of that scholarship has almost exclusively been on later literature and not on the Vedic texts that deal with social classification.[48] Because of this exclusive focus on its social application, scholars have failed to recognize and represent the *varṇa* system *in situ* and in all its fullness, and have therefore also failed to appreciate the reasons for its enduring ideological persuasiveness.

Here I am be concerned to track the *varṇa* scheme in all its applications. As a holistic system of impressive scope and explanatory power, and one with an unimpeachable Vedic pedigree, it is not all that surprising that the *varṇa* system (and the later caste system which found theoretical underpinnings in the *varṇa*s) has had such a long reign in Indian social and religious history. In subsequent chapters of this book, I trace the system's reach and the various sources of authority to which the Brahmin architects of social hierarchy and authors of the Veda appealed in order to undergird their system.

After surveying the social application of *varṇa* in the next chapter, I turn attention in Chapter 3 to the fact that the *varṇa* system was not simply postulated as one among many possible methods for social organization. Its exclusive authority was guaranteed by the fact that it was supposedly aboriginal. Because *varṇa* was the pattern in which the universe was cast in the beginning of time, a society structured in this way can be portrayed as simply perpetuating the form into which everything was made in the time of pristine perfection. Chapter 3, then, reviews the principal cosmogonic myths in which the *varṇa* system is coterminous with the origins of the cosmos and functions as the organizational template for the universe in all its manifestations.

Chapter 4 examines the way this classificatory scheme operates in the divine realm. Social class was projected onto the "world of the gods" and, conversely, drew on the authority of the divine to buttress and legitimate this human construct in its social applications. If the gods themselves were organized into *varṇa*s, the texts seem to say, how could such a method of classifying humans be disputed? Furthermore, if space and time could be shown to be guided by the categories of *varṇa*, another extremely powerful source of authority could also be marshaled to buttress a social hierarchy thus conceived. The categorization of space (Chapter 5) and time (Chapter 6) according to *varṇa* injects the *varṇa* system into the metaphysical coordinates of reality and the structures of perception. That which we call nature—the order of things in the realm of flora and fauna—is also categorized according to *varṇa*, and implicitly and yet powerfully functions as testimony to the indisputable authority of the scheme in all its applications, as we shall see in Chapters 7 ("Classifying Flora") and 8 ("Classifying Fauna"). Finally, the authority of the religious canon, the "eternal" Veda, is recruited into the service of placing the *varṇa* system beyond the reach of contestation or criticism. The Vedic texts in which the *varṇa* system is transmitted lend their authority to the scheme in part by being themselves subject to its tripartite format, as we shall observe in Chapter 9.

I do not, by casting my net this widely, minimize the importance of the social dimension of *varṇa*. It is only by revealing *varṇa* as a categorical system with enormous and wideranging epistemological capabilities that we can truly appreciate its social implications. One already begins to understand how such a social system could survive fundamentally unchanged over several millennia; indeed, caste as a social institution still persists in much of India to this day. Its formulators and beneficiaries had wrapped it within the most powerful sources of authority human beings have designed for their truth claims. Among other things, then, this work is about what kinds of authoritative sources people have at their disposal to transform the subjective and all-too-human into the objective and transcendent.

NOTES

1. See K. N. Sharma, "On the Word 'varṇa,' " *Contributions to Indian Sociology* n.s., 9, 2 (1975): 293–97, for an etymological survey of the Sanskrit connotations of the term.

2. E. H. Gombrich, *Art and Illusion: A Study in the Psychology of Pictorial Representation*, 2d ed., rev. (Princeton: Princeton University Press, 1960), p. 301.

3. See, e.g., George Lakoff, *Women, Fire, and Dangerous Things: What Categories Reveal about the Mind* (Chicago: University of Chicago Press, 1987); E. Rosch and B. B. Lloyd, eds., *Cognition and Categorization* (Hillsdale, N.J.: Lawrence Erlbaum Associates, 1978); Stevan Harnad, ed., *Categorical Perception: The Groundwork of Cognition* (Cambridge: Cambridge University Press, 1987).

4. Lakoff, *Women, Fire, and Dangerous Things*, pp. 5–6.

5. For an interesting overview of constructivist epistemology in contemporary culture, I recommend Walter Truett Anderson's *Reality Isn't What It Used to Be: Theatrical Politics, Ready-to-Wear Religion, Global Myths, Primitive Chic, and Other Wonders of the Postmodern World* (San Francisco: Harper & Row, 1990).

6. "One must recognize that insofar as knowers cannot and do not stand apart from the known, being objects as well as subjects of knowledge, they themselves also come to be categorized within their own taxonomic systems. Taxonomy is thus not only a means for organizing information, but is also—as it comes to organize the organizers—an apparatus for the classification and manipulation of society." Bruce Lincoln, "The Tyranny of Taxonomy," Center for Humanistic Studies, University of Minnesota, Occasional Papers no. 1 (1985), p. 1.

7. Émile Durkheim and Marcel Mauss, *Primitive Classification*, trans. by Rodney Needham (Chicago: University of Chicago Press, 1963), pp. 82–83. Cf. Durkheim's statement that "cosmic space was primitively constructed on the model of social space, that is, on the territory occupied by society and as society conceives it; time expresses the rhythm of collective life; the notion of class was at first no more than another aspect of the notion of a human group; collective force and its power over men's minds served as prototypes for the notion of force and causality, etc." Cited in Steven Lukes, *Émile Durkheim: His Life and Work: A Historical and Critical Study* (Harmondsworth, Middlesex, England: Penguin Books, 1973), p. 442.

8. See, e.g., Rodney Needham, from his preface to Durkheim and Mauss, *Primitive Classification*, p. xxvii: "The notion of space has first to exist before social groups can be perceived to exhibit in their disposition any spatial relations which may then be applied to the universe; the categories of quantity have to exist in order that an individual mind shall ever recognize the one, the many, and the totality of the divisions of his society; the notion of class necessarily precedes the apprehension that social groups, in concordance with which natural phenomena are classed, are themselves classified. In other words, the social 'model' must itself be perceived to possess the characteristics which make it useful in classifying other things, but this cannot be done without the very categories which Durkheim and Mauss derive from the model." For other logical difficulties with the classical Durkheimian position, see Lukes, *Émile Durkheim*, pp. 436ff., where the author enumerates six different claims made in Durkheim's sociology of knowledge "which he did not constantly and clearly distinguish one from another. In so far as he did distinguish them, he none the less assumed, mistakenly, that they were logically related, and that arguments and evidence in favour of one therefore lent support to others."

9. Barry Schwartz, *Vertical Classification: A Study in Structuralism and the Sociology of Knowledge* (Chicago: University of Chicago Press, 1981), p. 184.

10. Georges Dumézil, "La Préhistoire indo-iranienne des castes," *Journal asiatique* 216 (1930): 109–30; and idem, *L'Idéologie tripartie des Indo-Européens* (Brusels: Collection Latomus, 1958). Dumézil's work was reviewed from a number of perspectives in the *Journal of Asian Studies* 34, 1 (Nov. 1974): 127–67. See also F. B. J. Kuiper, "Some Observations on Dumézil's Theory," *Numen* 8 (1961) 34–45; Pierre Smith and Dan Sperber, "Mythologiques de Georges Dumézil," *Annales: économies, sociétés, civilisations* 26 (May–Aug. 1971): 559–86; Huguette Fugier, "Quarante ans de récherchés sur l'idéologie indo-européens: La methode de M. Georges Dumézil," *Revue d'histoire et de philosophie religieuses* 45 (1965): 358–74; and F. Scott Littleton, *The New Comparative Mythology: An Anthropological Assessment of the Theories of Georges Dumézil* (Berkeley: University of California Press, 1973). For the Indo-European origins of the ancient Indian *varṇa* system, also consult Émile Benveniste, *Le Vocabulaire des institutions Indo-Européens, Vol. 1: Économie, parenté, société* (Paris: Éditions de minuit, 1969); and idem, "Traditions indo-iraniennes sur les classes sociales," *Journal asiatique* 230 (1938): 529-49.

11. In the Indian context, Dumézil's "first function" has been bifurcated and rulership lumped with the "second function," as we shall see in the next chapter.

12. Dumézil, *L'Idéologie tripartie des Indo-Européens*, p. 19: "fécondité certes, humaine, animale, et végétale, mais en même temps nourriture et richesse, et santé, et paix—avec les jouissances et les avantages de la paix—et souvent volupté, beauté, et aussi l'importante idée du 'grand nombre,' appliquée non seulement aux biens (abondance), mais aussi aux hommes qui composent le corps social."

13. Jan Gonda, *Triads in the Veda* (Amsterdam: North-Holland, 1976). See also Gonda's articles entitled "Some Observations on Dumézil's View of Indo-European Mythology," *Mnemosyne* 4 (1960): 1–14; and "Dumézil's Tripartite Ideology: Some Critical Observations," *Journal of Asian Studies* 34, 1 (Nov. 1974): 139–49.

14. Gonda, *Triads in the Veda*, p. 177. Cf. Gonda's reiteration elsewhere: "Is it not worth investigating, in connection with Dumézil's theory, the problem of how far the 'symbolism' of the very number three, and not the social structure, has been the basic principle?" "Dumézil's Tripartite Ideology," p. 141.

15. Gonda, *Triads in the Veda*, pp. 125, 196.

16. Georges Dumézil, *Naissance d'Archanges*, vol. 3 of *Jupiter, Mars, Quirinus*, 4 vols. (Paris: Gallimard, 1941–45), p. 54.

17. Note the assumption here that, regardless of the situations elsewhere in Indo-European antiquity, in India, at least, there was certainly a "real" tripartite social structure in place. Cf. *L'Idéologie tripartie des Indo-Européens*, p. 7, where Dumézil speaks of the *varṇa* theory in the Veda as "n'a été que le durcissement d'une doctrine et sans doute d'une pratique sociale préexistantes."

18. Georges Dumézil, *Mythe et épopée*, 3 vols. (Paris: Gallimard, 1968–73), I:15. For a sympathetic treatment of Dumézil's more recent position, see Alf Hiltebeitel, "Dumézil and Indian Studies," *Journal of Asian Studies* 34, 1 (Nov. 1974): 129–37.

19. See, e.g., Cristiano Grottanelli, "Temi Duméziliani fuori dal mondo indoeuropeo," *Opus 2* (1983): 378: "To admit that a trifunctional ideology could have preceded, or— worse yet—determined an articulation of society following the three functions would strike me as absurd." This quotation, cited by Bruce Lincoln *Myths, Cosmos, and Society: Indo-European Themes of Creation and Destruction* [Cambridge, Mass.: Harvard Univerity Press, 1986] p. 228, fn. 57) is accompanied by Lincoln's own critique: "Since

at least 1958, Dumézil has consistently used the term *ideology* to describe the object of his Indo-European researches. He uses this term in an idiosyncratic, depoliticized fashion, however, denoting—if I read him rightly—the fundamental tripartite structural pattern that, as he sees it, informed not only the organization of IE society but virtually all realms of life and thought. I use *ideology* in a more conventionally Marxist sense, to denote the body of ideas, claimed to be objective or even eternal truths, that are propagated by members of certain classes and serve to legitimate a state of affairs beneficial to their own class interests." For a review of the issues, see Daniel Dubuisson, "Structure sociales et structure idéologique: l'apport de Georges Dumézil," in *Georges Dumézil*, ed. by J. Bonnet (Paris: Centre Georges Pompidou, 1981), pp. 147–58; and now also Bruce Lincoln, *Death, War, and Sacrifice: Studies in Ideology and Practice* (Chicago: University of Chicago Press, 1991), esp. pp. 1–19, 231–43, and 259–68.

20. Note that "soft reductionism," as the term is used here, still assumes that structural correspondences between symbolic classification schemes and social theory (and possibly social organization as well) have definite social purposes and must be assumed to represent and further the interests of the classifiers. Yet another interpretive option, and one which I do not pursue here, is loosely described as "deconstructionist," whereby there is an "abandonment of all reference to a *center*, to a *subject*, to a privileged reference, to an origin, or to an absolute *archia*. . . . The absence of a center is here the absence of a subject and the absence of an author"—thus Jacques Derrida, "Structure, Sign, and Play in the Discourse of the Human Sciences," in *Writing and Difference*, trans. with an introduction and additional notes by Alan Bass (Chicago: University of Chicago Press, 1978), pp. 286, 287. I find this position to be irresponsible in its attempt to "deconstruct" particular authors and to ignore the interests authors propagate through discourse and texts of all sorts. For similar objections, see Edward Said, *Orientalism* (New York: Pantheon Books, 1978), pp. 15, 23–24.

21. Lincoln, *Myth, Cosmos, and Society*, p. 171.

22. For the importance of caste in Western discourse about India, consult also Ronald Inden's chapter entitled "India in Asia: The Caste Society" in his *Imagining India* (Oxford: Basil Blackwell, 1990), pp. 49–84. Inden argues that caste, in Indology, has become "a substantialized agent, the unitary, unchanging subject of India's history" (p. 74). For a similar critique of the Indological and anthropological fetishizing of caste, see Arjun Appadhurai, "Is Homo Hierarchicus?" *American Ethnologist* 13, 4 (Nov. 1986): 745–61.

23. Brian K. Smith, *Reflections on Resemblance, Ritual, and Religion* (New York: Oxford University Press, 1989), pp. 13–14. See also my "Exorcising the Transcendent: Strategies for Defining Hinduism and Religion," *History of Religions* 27, 1 (August, 1987): 32–55.

24. See Smith, *Reflections*, Chapters 1 and 8.

25. All Sanskrit texts in this work are cited by abbreviation. A list of texts and their abbreviations is found at the beginning of this book and full publication information appears in the bibliography. All translations, unless otherwise noted, are my own.

26. It is possible, however, that such a strategy describes the relations *all* religious traditions have with their constitutive and authoritative canon and canonical categories. In other words, this kind of relationship between prototype and counterparts may not be uniquely Vedic and Hindu but generalizable to those traditions we call "religious," and very possibly to other kinds of traditions as well (e.g., constitutional law).

27. R. C. Zaehner, *Hinduism* (New York: Oxford University Press, 1966), p. 8. Similar definitions are surveyed in my *Reflections*, pp. 9–13.

28. Émile Senart, *Caste in India: The Facts and the System*, trans. by Sir E. Denison Ross (London: Methuen, 1930), p. 13, cited in Inden, *Imagining India*, p. 57.

29. Zaehner, *Hinduism*, p. 5.

30. See the observation made by F. Franco and Sarvar V. Sherry Chand in their "Ideology as Social Practice: The Functioning of *Varṇa*," *Economic and Political Weekly* 24, 47 (Nov. 25, 1989), p. 2606: "In terms of the types of ideology discussed above, *varṇa* ideology reveals two dimensions: an existential-inclusive dimension, since it incorporates various religious concepts like those of *karma* and *saṃsāra*, and a religious ritual offering expiation. It provides individuals with answers to the ultimate questions of life and death; it legitimises, with inexorable logic, the positional-historical dimension, by seeing it as part of a cosmic pattern and making it dependent on the individual subject's own 'past lives'. The positional-historical dimension of *varṇa* ideology forms individuals to occupy determined positions in a patterned social hierarchy."

31. "Hinduism" cannot, it seems to me, be reduced to its theory of social structure since it does entail more than just a social theory (although it is, as I argue in this book, the product of social forces). Second, there are traditions that do not appear to be "Hindu" (e.g., Islam, Christianity, Sikhism, Buddhism, and Jainism) that also participate in the caste system in India. Third, some apparently "Hindu" traditions reject caste and Brahmin authority. While it is possible to exclude such traditions from the rubric of "Hinduism," I would prefer not to. See Smith, *Reflections*, pp. 11–12. I would now add that this criterion for defining "Hinduism" is insufficient because its authority is not independent; the authority for the caste system is derived, ultimately, from the authority of the Veda.

32. The pernicious "trickle-down" effects of such a scholarly stance may be observed in an article by Thomas Beaudry, "Social Paradigm: For the Synthesis of Material Difference and Spiritual Oneness," *Clarion Call* 2, 3 (Summer 1989): 32–35, 59–63. Beaudry finds "spiritual India's" *varṇāśrama* system both "natural" and superior to those issuing forth from modern capitalist and communist systems.

33. Francis X. Clooney, "Finding One's Place in the Text: A Look at the Theological Treatment of Caste in Traditional India," *Journal of Religious Ethics* 17, 1 (Spring 1989), p. 6.

34. Lincoln, *Myth, Cosmos, and Society*, p. 164.

35. Franco and Chand, "Ideology as Social Practice," p. 2608.

36. See *Reflections*, pp. 12–13, and below, pp. 32–33.

37. I have attempted in my *Reflections* to survey the underlying principles of the Vedic theory of resemblance. In that work I try to demonstrate something of the range of the theory's application in the realms of cosmogony, anthropogony, epistemology, sociology, etc. For a recent study of the ritual terminology of resemblance and interconnection in the somewhat later *Mīmāṃsā* tradition, see Francis X. Clooney, S.J., *Thinking Ritually: Rediscovering the Pūrva Mīmāṃsā of Jaimini* (Vienna: Institut fur Indologie, 1990), esp. pp. 95–125.

38. Paul Mus, *Barabadur: Esquisse d'une histoire du Bouddhism fondée sur la critique archéologique des textes* (Paris and Hanoi: Paul Geuthner, 1935), p. 121.

39. For the Vedic theory of ritual substitution, consult Chapter 5 of my *Reflections*; S. C. Chakrabarti, *The Paribhāṣās in the Śrautasūtras* (Calcutta: Sanskrit Pustak Bhandar, 1980); Frederick Marcus Smith, *The Vedic Sacrifice in Transition: A Translation and Study of the Trikāṇḍamāṇḍana of Bhāskara Miśra*, Bhandarkar Oriental Series, no. 22 (Poona: Bhandarkar Oriental Research Institute, 1987); and Brian K. Smith and Wendy Doniger, "Sacrifice and Substitution: Ritual Mystification and Mythical Demystification," *Numen* 36, 2 (1989): 189–224.

40. The attempt to achieve such a totalistic "constructed unity of parts" might well serve as a shorthand summary of the purpose of the Vedic ritual as the Vedic ritualists,

at least, conceived of it. Consult Jean-Marie Verpoorten, "Unité et distinction dans les spéculations rituelles védique," *Archiv für Begriffsgeschichte* 21 (1977): 59–85.

41. For such Indological characterizations of Vedic thought, consult *Reflections*, pp. 32–34; and Herman Tull, *The Vedic Origins of Karma: Cosmos as Man in Ancient Indian Myth and Ritual* (Albany, NY: SUNY Press, 1989), pp. 7–11.

42. Four social *varṇas* are already mentioned in what is usually regarded as the earliest stratum of Vedic literature, the *Saṃhitās* (e.g., ṚV 10.90.12; TS 2.5.10.1, 7.1.1.4–6, 5.7.6.3–4; VS 30.5).

43. Manu 10.4, for example, regards society as comprised of the three "twice-born" classes and the Shūdras: "The Brahmin, the Kshatriya, and the Vaishya are the three twice-born classes, but the fourth, the Shūdra, has only one birth, and there is no fifth [*varṇa*]." Translations from this text cited in the present work closely follow, and often simply duplicate, the translation of Wendy Doniger with Brian K. Smith, *The Laws of Manu* (London: Penguin Books, 1991).

44. Or so goes the generally accepted historical interpretation, for which see, e.g., Louis Dumont, *Homo Hierarchicus: The Caste System and Its Implications*, rev. ed., trans. by Mark Sainsbury, Louis Dumont, and Basia Gulati (Chicago: University of Chicago Press, 1980), p. 68; Dumézil, *L'Idéology tripartie des Indo-Européens*, p. 7; and A. M. Hocart, *Caste: A Comparative Study* (London: Methuen, 1950), pp. 27ff. A different story of the origins of the Shūdra class (they were once Kshatriyas who subsequently fell from their status) has been put forward by B. R. Ambedkar in *Who Were the Shūdras? How they came to be the Fourth Varṇa in the Indo-Aryan Society* (Bombay: Thackers, 1946); and a kind of mediating position has been taken by R. S. Sharma in his *Śūdras in Ancient India*, 2d ed. (Delhi: Motilal Banarsidass, 1980). Wash Edward Hale, *Asura- in Early Vedic Religion* (Delhi: Motilal Banarsidass, 1986), connects the aboriginal peoples also to the Vedic *asuras* or "anti-gods" in the process of arguing that the Shūdras are the descendants of the *dasyus*. For the *dāsas/dasyus* as a *varṇa* in contrast to the "Āryan *varṇa*," see ṚV 3.34.9 ("Having killed the *dasyus*, he [Indra] aided the Āryan *varṇa*"), and cf. ṚV 1.51.8, 1.117.21, 1.103.3, 2.11.19, 2.12.4, 6.18.3; 7.5.6, 10.49.3, etc. For the Shūdra as the "demonic" *varṇa* (*asurya varṇa*) vs. the Brahmins as the "godly" (*daivya*) class, TB 1.2.6.6–7.

45. H. W. Bodewitz, "The Waters in Vedic Cosmic Classification," *Indologica Taurinensia* 10 (1982), p. 47. See also, by the same author, "The Fourth Priest (the *brahman*) in Vedic Ritual," in *Selected Studies on Ritual in the Indian Religions: Essays to D. J. Hoens*, ed. by Ria Kloppenborg (Leiden: E. J. Brill, 1983), pp. 33–68.

46. Gonda, *Triads in the Veda*, p. 119. The expansion of Vedic categorical systems from three to four is an ancient instance of a recurring phenomenon in Indian intellectual history. In later Hindu texts, to the three *puruṣārthas* or "goals of man" (pleasure, power, and principle—*kāma*, *artha*, and *dharma*) is added liberation (*mokṣa*) as a "transcendent fourth." The three *āśramas* or stages of life—student, householder, and forest-dweller—are similarly expanded to included the life of the renunciate (*samnyāsa*). Another example of the expansion of a triad into a quartet, but one more comparable to the addition of the Shūdra class at the bottom of the social hierarchy, is the supplementation of the Atharva Veda to the "triple wisdom" of the original three Vedas. For the phenomenon in general, consult Troy Organ, "Three into Four in Hinduism," *Ohio Journal of Religious Studies* 1 (1973): 7–13.

47. For attempts to trace the original localities of the various Vedic schools, see Louis Renou's *Les Écoles védiques et la formation de Veda* (Paris: Imprimerie nationale, 1947); and more recently, Michael Witzel, "On the Localisation of Vedic Texts and Schools," in *India and the Ancient World*, ed. by G. Pollet, (Louvain: Departement Orientalistiek,

1987), pp. 173–213. I have found no consistent pattern in the classificatory variants as one moves among the various recensions and schools of the Veda.

48. I do not know what to make of statements that seem to deny the importance to the social realm of *varṇa* in the Veda. I have already quoted Gonda's statement that "the three classes of the Aryan society are only seldom mentioned as a group." See also Arthur Berriedale Keith, *The Religion and Philosophy of the Veda and Upanishads*, 2 vols. (Cambridge: Harvard University Press, 1925; reprint Delhi: Motilal Banarsidass, 1976), II:480–81: "The duties and privileges of the castes are often mentioned incidentally, occasionally in more completeness, but there is no effort to develop a theoretic version of the matter." The present work might be conceived as a long refutation of such contentions.

2

Classifying Society

The Social *Varṇas* in the Veda

The *varṇa* system was first and foremost a scheme for dividing society into separate, if functionally interdependent, classes, and only secondarily a means for similarly classifying other realms by projecting social truisms into them. When applied to these other domains, to the "natural" and supernatural worlds, for example, the system follows a consistent logic: the invariable traits, characteristics, powers, skills, and functions that defined the Brahmin priests, Kshatriya warriors and rulers, and the commoner social class were recast as templates for the divisions within these other rcalms. Moreover, relationships (ideal, if not actual) between the social classes—usually hierarchically governed—were also reproduced in other realms subject to the *varṇa* scheme.

Social classes, in their essences and relations, were the prototype for the classification of other realms. Because of the priority of the social dimension to the *varṇa* system as a whole, it is therefore appropriate that we begin with the Vedic texts that concern themselves directly and explicitly with ancient India's version of sociology.

The *varṇa* system is, it will be remembered, the Indian variant of what Dumézil has identified as a generally Indo-European "tripartite ideology," the social manifestation of which divides society into three "functions": religion and rule, defense, and productivity. In ancient India, however, this "ideology" was modified in two ways.

First, rulership dropped from Dumézil's "first function" and was repositioned into the "second function." In India, Brahmins are ideally occupied exclusively with religion and the priesthood while the Kshatriyas monopolized kingship as well as the military. It may very well be too much to say, as Louis Dumont among others has, that "the king has lost his religious prerogatives" as a result of this "absolute" split between "status and power, and consequently spiritual authority and temporal authority."[1] In the Veda, at least, such dichotomies are probably misapplied—the Kshatriya's royal and military power are infused with "spirituality," and the Brahmin's "sprituality" is represented as one kind, indeed the best kind, of coercive power. It is nevertheless true that in Vedic texts Dumézil's "first function" has been bifurcated and rulership lumped with the military.

Second, the tripartite scheme of the Indo-Europeans (at least as it is portrayed by Dumézil) was sometimes expanded into a quadripartite one in ancient India, apparently in response to the expansion of Vedic society to include within it the non-Āryan indigenous inhabitants of South Asia. The Indo-European "third function" eventually subdivides into the Vaishyas (agriculturalists, traders, merchants) and the Shūdras, who are charged with serving the rest of the social body. In the texts that we draw upon here, it seems as though we are witnessing this social and more generally classificatory transition while it still is in process. The "third function" is sometimes fully embodied in the Vaishyas; sometimes that "function" is bifurcated into both the Vaishya class and the Shūdra servants; and sometimes the configuration of these traits is concentrated into the more generalized category of the *viś* ("commoners" or "peasantry," the *lumpen* masses) that may very well include both Vaishyas and those that would become "Shūdras."

Other scholars searching for the roots of the Indian theory of the social classes concentrate less on putative Indo-European origins and more on indigenous evidence found in texts called the Dharma Sūtras and Śāstras. These texts, although composed relatively late in ancient Indian history (beginning ca. third century B.C.E.), are often constituted as the *locus classicus* of the Indian formulation of *varṇa*.

The Dharma Sūtras and Śāstras had as their chief aim the expansion of the ritualistic universe of the Vedas to every corner of everyday life, to bring within their purview all aspects of what was called *dharma*, "duty" or "law." While the Vedas and the ritual texts appended to them (e.g., the Śrauta and Gṛhya Sūtras) attempted to provide comprehensive rulings for the minutiae of the ritual domain, the Dharma Sūtras and Śāstras had as their purpose to enlarge such rules and regulations so that virtually all aspects of human life would be enveloped within the reign of *dharma*. "The controlled world of the sacrifice is expanded to encompass life as it is lived and as a whole; ritual rules (*vidhis*) are blown up and out into *dharma*."[2]

In the course of such a hegemonic project, the Dharma Sūtras and Śāstras focused on the four social classes, each with its own set of distinctive traits (innate, but also to be realized through behavior) and specific duties. In the literature on *dharma*, as in the cosmogonic texts from the Veda we examine in Chapter 3, the social classes and the *dharma* assigned to each were created in the beginning of time from the body parts of the creator god. The most famous of the paradigmatic Vedic texts for such a notion is ṚV 10.90.11–12: "When they divided the Cosmic Man, into how many parts did they apportion him? What do they call his mouth, his two arms and thighs and feet? His mouth became the Brahmin; his arms were made into the Kshatriya; his thighs the Vaishya; and from his feet the Shūdras were born." Such a cosmogony becomes the starting point for the enunciation of the duties or *dharmas* the creator allocated to each of the social classes:

> But to protect this whole creation, the lustrous one made separate innate activities for those born of his mouth, arms, thighs, and feet. For Brahmins, he ordained teaching and learning [the Veda], sacrificing for themselves and sacrificing for others, giving and receiving. Protecting his subjects, giving [to the Brahmins], having sacrifices performed [by the Brahmins], studying [the Veda], and remaining unaddicted to the sensory objects are, in summary, for a Kshatriya. Protecting his livestock, giving, having sacrifices performed, studying, trading, lending money, and farming the land are for a Vaishya. The Lord assigned only one activity to a Shūdra: serving these [other] classes without resentment.[3]

This kind of conception of the "separate innate activities" of the social classes was prefigured in the Veda; indeed, the full context for this social theory cannot, I maintain, be properly understood without recourse to the earlier literature—and the Vedic texts dealing with *varṇa* are far more extensive than the Ṛgvedic hymn of origins quoted above. The theoretical enunciation of the caste system found in the Dharma Sūtras and Śāstras is nothing but a continuation and reworking of the earlier social theory inscribed in the Veda. What's more, this later Hindu social doctrine, revolving around the concept of *dharma*, depends on the legitimation provided to it by its Vedic, and therefore canonical, origins.

Although it has sometimes been argued that originally the social classes we encounter in the most ancient texts of India were fluid groups, without the restrictive boundaries provided by heredity and with ritually induced role reversals,[4] evidence for this is sparse indeed and inconclusive at best. It is far more demonstrable that the three or four social classes are in the Veda, no less than in later enunciations, regarded as separate and hereditary, each class having definite functions that are best not filled by members of other classes.

As we shall see in this chapter, the Veda defines these distinctive functions in terms not unlike the later *dharma* texts: the Brahmins are to maintain sole control over the workings of the sacrifice (and all that it entails); the Kshatriyas are rulers and warriors in whose hands coercive physical force is consolidated; and the commoners are charged with material productivity, increase, and prosperity. And also as in the Dharma Sūtras and Śāstras, the social system articulated in the Veda was hierarchically organized. The classes of society not only had different definitive qualities but also different rights and privileges and, in general, different values placed upon them by the Brahmin systematizers.

As many scholars have pointed out, the tripartite or quadripartite social hierarchy is really formed out of a series of binary oppositions which creates divisions of several sorts between the three or four classes. First, Brahmins are in various ways separated from and placed above everyone else. As we shall see repeatedly in the following chapters, the Brahmin element is invariably found in the top spot in any taxonomy; in the classification of society, the Brahmins are also and always given the highest position. Next, Brahmins and Kshatriyas united are together regarded as the ruling classes, with all others becoming the ruled in relation to them. Third, Brahmins, Kshatriyas, and Vaishyas, as "twice-born" or "initiated" full members of Āryan society are sometimes distinguished from the lowly Shūdra servants, especially when it comes to the Vedic sacrifice, from which the latter are excluded.

This relational organization of the social classes may be understood in terms of overlapping and more or less comprehensive domains of "mastery" or "lordship."[5] The Brahmin, as the hierarchically superior social entity, is the "lord" of the sacrifice, which is, in the Veda, the realm in which the cosmos as a whole is controlled. Thus the Brahmin encircles within his domain what the texts call "this all" (*idam sarvam*) and is himself "this all" (e.g., JB 1.86). From an ontological point of view, the Brahmin is the most complete manifestation of the human being and encompasses within his lordship all the domains of the other social classes. The Kshatriya, as ruler, is master over the "earth," that is, society and all its parts, save for the Brahmins who exempt themselves from the Kshatriya's overlordship and demand protection from him.[6] The Kshatriya's lordship, then, is primarily over the *viś* or subjects of the body politic and also over "immovable wealth," that is, the land or kingdom. The Vaishyas control the more limited domain of "movable wealth" of various sorts, most particularly agricultural produce and livestock,[7] while the lowly Shūdras (when they are differentiated from the other components of the *viś*) are assigned mastery over nothing other than their own households and bodies.[8]

The social classes, then, are each assigned a particular set of affinities correlated to the series of overlapping, hierarchically ordered domains over which each *varṇa* exerts mastery. Each domain, and each social class, is encompassed within the realm of the higher, and each domain is assigned to a particular social class because of the inherent traits that class reputedly possesses. Thus Brahmins are given lordship over the sacrifice because the Brahmin class has innate qualities and powers (intellectual ability, a spiritual predisposition, etc.) that are supposed to "naturally" incline them toward mastery of that realm—and the same is true with the other social classes and their domains.

One of the most frequently encountered idioms in which the texts discuss these differing intrinsic qualities is that of metaphysics. Certain metaphysical powers were thought both to course through the universe and to find particular expression in social entities. Brahmins, Kshatriyas, and commoners are who they are in part because of the abstract and neuter powers that enliven and animate each class. These powers I call the "elemental qualities" of the *varṇa* system; they are the *brahman*, the *kṣatra*, and the *viś*. The ascribed properties distinguishing each of the social classes are in this way projected and reproduced in the realm of metaphysics, while social functions and skills are represented as ontological verities.

In the Vedic ritual called the Puruṣamedha or "human sacrifice," victims from each of the three social classes are dedicated to their respective elemental quality, matching the mutually resembling social form and metaphysical power. A fourth social class, the Shūdra, is assimilated with "austerity" or *tapas* :

> For the *brahman*, he seizes a Brahmin, for the Brahmin is the *brahman* : he thus makes the *brahman* flourish with the *brahman*. For the *kṣatra*, he seizes a Kshatriya (*rājanya*),[9] for the Kshatriya is the *kṣatra*; he thus makes the *kṣatra* flourish with the *kṣatra*. For the Maruts [a group of deities, he seizes] a Vaishya, for the Maruts are the power of the *viś*. He thus makes the *viś* flourish with *viś*. For austerity (*tapas*), a Shūdra, for the Shūdra is austerity. He thus makes austerity flourish with austerity. According to their particular form he thus makes these divinities flourish with sacrificial victims. Thus supplied, they make him [the sacrificer] flourish with all his objects of desire. (ŚB 13.6.2.10; cf. TB 3.4.1)

These universal forces, here described as "divinities," that share the same "form" (*rūpa*) as the social classes are the Vedic forerunners of the three "strands" or *guṇas* undergirding the universe in Hindu metaphysics: *sattva* or "purity" corresponds to the Vedic *brahman*, *rajas* or "activity" is the descendant of the *kṣatra*, and *tamas* or "inertia" is the later transformation of the power of the *viś*.[10] In the Veda, the elemental qualities obviously found their principal expression (and also their source) in the social classes.[11] But because they were also supposed to manifest themselves in other entities located within other realms, these elemental qualities are the most important markers of *varṇa* in various taxonomies we shall encounter in this and the following chapters.

In addition to the forces of the *brahman*, *kṣatra*, and *viś*, other abstract metaphysical powers posited in Vedic texts may also be understood as simultaneously symbols and descriptions of the definitional essences of the social classes. These secondary metaphysical forces I therefore call "essential powers."[12] Thus both the Brahmin social class and the elemental quality of the *brahman* are very often correlated to such essential powers as *brahmavarcasa* ("the splendor of the *brahman* power," also connoting the "glow" obtained from knowledge of the Veda),[13] and *tejas* ("fiery luminousity or energy").[14] Other correlates to the Brahmin *varṇa* include qualities that, although not precisely of the same sort of neuter forces I have labeled "essential powers," are comparable and describe the inherent qualities and functions of this class. Because of the connection to the orally recited Veda, the (feminine) quality of "speech" (*vāc*) is directly connected to the elemental Brahmin power, the *brahman*,[15] as is the (masculine) sphere of Brahmin influence, the sacrifice (*yajña*).[16] The Brahmins are frequently said to be "foremost" (or "connected to the mouth," *mukhya*) and thus taking "precedence" over all others.[17] The hierarchical position of this class can also be gauged by the fact that the *brahman* is also equated with *ṛta*, "cosmic-moral order,"[18] and with *satya*, "truth" or "reality."[19]

The Kshatriya rulers and warriors, and the elemental quality of *kṣatra* which they in particular manifest, are consistently associated with three closely associated essential powers—*vīrya* ("virility"),[20] *ojas* ("power," "force," or "might"),[21] and *indriya* ("the command of the body")[22]—as well as with others connected to physical or military power such as *bala* ("physical strength"),[23] *sahas* ("force" or "might"),[24] and *vayas* ("youthful vigor").[25] The Kshatriya is, naturally enough, also characterized by various forms of the word *rāj* or "rule" (e.g., AitB 7.23, 8.24; AV 3.5.2) and by the "realm" (*rāṣṭra*) which is his domain (e.g., TS 2.6.5.6;

TB 3.9.14.1–2). His dominating essence is also captured by connections to the "eating of food" (*annādya*),[26] for all the subjects of his realm become "food" for the Kshatriya ruler.[27] Other essential powers frequently found directly juxtaposed to the Kshatriya or the *kṣatra* include "fame" or "glory" (*yaśas*),[28] "distinction" (*vyāvṛt*, TS 6.6.11.4), and "renown" (*kīrti*, AitB 7.23).[29]

The Vaishya and the elemental quality of the *viś* are, as the social and metaphysical signifiers of prosperity and fecundity, regularly connected to the appropriate essential powers: *puṣṭi* ("material prosperity"),[30] *ūrj* ("nourishment"),[31] "livestock" or "animals" (*paśus*),[32] and "food" (*anna*) or "nourishment" (*annādya*).[33] Another set of such equally apt characterizations include "progeny" or "offspring" (*prajā*, ŚB 2.1.3.8), "sexual coupling" (*mithuna*),[34] "productivity" or "procreation" (*prajanana*, JB 1.68–69), and "generative power" or "vigor" (*vāja*).[35] Very often the Vaishya is connected to the multiplicity (*bahuna*) or abundance (*bhūman*) he both represents and is charged with producing.[36] The Shūdra, when he appears in the texts, is depicted here (as in the Dharma Sūtras and Śāstras) solely in terms of service and dependency on others.[37]

These secondary metaphysical forces, these "essential powers," are thoroughly implicated in the *varṇa* system and very often function as ciphers for both the "elemental qualities" and social classes themselves. Indeed, the linkage between certain essential powers and the *varṇas* is often quite explicit.[38] At TĀ 6.1.3 the three *varṇas* are correlated with *tejas* (= the Brahmin), *ojas* (= the Kshatriya), and *śrī* and *puṣṭi* (= the Vaishya); VādhŚS 1.1.1.4 gives a different set of essential powers for the three social classes (*brahmavarcasa*, *indriya*, *puṣṭi*), as do other texts[39]—but in every case there is a regularity and clear logic in the connections posited between the *varṇas* and the powers connected to them.

Like the elemental qualities, the essential powers are not limited to the social realm in their applications or "manifestations" but are also attached to various entities in different supernatural, natural, and ritual contexts. I regard these essential powers as secondary indicators of *varṇa*: when a thing or being is identified with *brahmavarcasa*, or with *vīrya*, or with *puṣṭi*, one can be almost certain that connections, implicit though they may be, to Brahmins, Kshatriyas, and Vaishyas respectively are entailed.

The three (and sometimes four) primary classes of the *varṇa* system are fixed and invariable. The class of things and beings that partakes in "Brahmin-ness" (*brahmatva*) is characterized by priority and predominance, intimate connections to the Veda and the sacrifice, the elemental quality of the *brahman*, or by secondary essential powers like *brahmavarcasa* and *tejas*. Conversely, one never encounters an entity that is, in the same passage, classified both as "Brahmin" and as subservient, "food" for others, or infused with the essential power of *puṣṭi*—for these are invariably the criteria constituting the class that includes within it the social class of Vaishyas.

Let us now turn to those texts explicitly articulating the social dimension of the *varṇa* system, both in terms of essence (the traits and functions of each class) and relations (the ways each class is located in the hierarchy vis-à-vis the others). I begin, as is appropriate with texts written by and almost entirely in the interest of the Brahmin class, with the "first" class.

The Brahmins

The Brahmins stand apart from, and above, the others in the social hierarchy for four principal reasons according to the Brahmin authors of Vedic texts: (1) they were created prior to others and therefore take precedence; (2) they are the most complete and perfect instance of the human being; (3) they are learned in the Veda; and (4) they had a monopoly on the priesthood and control of the powerful sacrifice.

The Brahmin class is said to have been the first group "emitted" by the creator god, as we shall see again in Chapter 3. The priority the Brahmins claim in creation stories establishes the precedence of that class in social affairs; they are "first" among humans in both a temporal and hierarchical sense and are thus the "lords of the classes."[40] Both the *brahman* power and the Brahmin social class are regarded as the "mouth," "head" or "foremost" (*mukha*) component of "this all,"[41] for the *brahman* is the "first born."[42] The elemental quality which the Brahmin class embodies is also "first" in another sense: it is the creator of everything else. "The *brahman* generated the gods; the *brahman* generated this whole world," and therefore "The *brahman* is the best of all beings" (TB 2.8.8.9–10). The exalted claims for the *brahman* power (which can in Vedic texts also signify a generalized and omnipresent universal force that underlies all creation) that can follow from this cosmogonic presupposition are often quite unrestrained, and can be tapped for the Brahmin ritualist who possesses the proper knowledge:

> This *brahman* power is the most excellent (*jyeṣṭha*); there is nothing more excellent than this. He who knows this, being himself the most excellent, becomes the highest (*śreṣṭha*) among his own people. This *brahman* has nothing before it and nothing after it. And for the one who knows this *brahman* to have nothing before it and nothing after it there is no one higher among his compatriots. And his descendants will be higher still. (ŚB 10.3.5.10–11)

Closely related to the claim of precedence and predominance is the notion that the Brahmins are the ontologically complete and most perfect representatives of the human species; all others are inferior approximations of the Brahmin standard. It can therefore be asserted that other classes are contained within and produced from the Brahmin, "for all beings pass into (*apiyanti*) the Brahmin, and from the Brahmin are again produced (*punar visṛjyante*)" (ŚB 11.5.3.12).[43] The man of the Brahmin class, it is succinctly put elsewhere, is "everything" or "all" (*sarva*);[44] it is therefore not surprising to learn that the *brahman* "is the *kṣatra*, the *viś*, and the Shūdra" (BĀU 1.4.15).

The third reason given for Brahmin superiority is that they are learned, versed in the supposedly sacrosanct and transcendentally originated knowledge called, even in the Veda, "the Veda" (i.e., The Truth) or the "triple wisdom" (*trayī-vidyā*, the Veda being divided into three main parts—the Ṛg, Yajur, and Sāma Vedas). The *brahman* power is the very essence of the three Vedas ("*brahman*" can, in certain contexts, even mean "Veda"), and also of closely related concepts like "truth" (*satya*) and "speech" (*vāc*), as we observed earlier. Knowledge of the

Veda is thus, for a Brahmin, in a certain sense nothing but self-knowledge;[45] that is why this class is characterized by the essential power of *brahmavarcasa*, the "splendor of the *brahman* power (which is also the Veda)."

The "priority" of the Brahmin and the intimate link this class has to the Veda are combined in the following creation myth, which plays also on the double meaning of "*brahman*" as both the essential quality underlying the Brahmin class and the essence of the Veda:

> This Man (*puruṣa*) Prajāpati wished, "May I be more [than one], may I be reproduced." He exerted himself; he practiced austerity. When he had exerted himself and practiced austerity, he emitted the *brahman* power first, which is the triple wisdom. It became a firm foundation (*pratiṣṭhā*) for him. Therefore they say, "The *brahman* is the firm foundation of everything here." Therefore, when one has studied [the Veda = the *brahman*] one is firmly founded on a firm foundation, for this, the *brahman*, is his firm foundation. . . . Therefore they say, "The *brahman* is the first born of this all." For even before that Man the *brahman* was emitted—it was emitted as his mouth. Therefore they say that one who has studied the Veda is like Agni (*agnikalpa*), for the *brahman* power is Agni's mouth. (ŚB 6.1.1.8,10)

The creator's first creation is the *brahman* which is the Veda, the "firm foundation" on which all else subsequently will rest. Study of the Veda for the Brahmin thus returns him to his foundational source. Finally, we learn in this passage that the *brahman* power is prior even to the creator god himself; it is the *brahman* that becomes the Creator's mouth, the mouth of Agni (the sacrificial fire), and, as we observed earlier of the Brahmin human.

The Brahmin's knowledge of the Veda, this "self-knowledge" of the *brahman* qua "triple wisdom," is cultivated and displayed in daily recitation (*svādhyāya*).[46] In one text such daily recitation is said to be the origin of Brahminical duties, and also their privileges:

> The growing intelligence (*prajñā*) [that comes from Veda study] causes four duties (*dharmas*) relating to the Brahmin to come to fruition: the character of a Brahmin (*brahmaṇya*), a befitting deportment (*pratirūpacarya*), fame (*yaśas*), and the development of the whole world (*lokapakti*). The developing world utilizes the Brahmin with four [attendant] duties: respect (*arcaya*), liberality (*dāna*), security against oppression (*ajyeyatāya*), and security against capital punishment (*avadhyatāya*). (ŚB 11.5.7.1)

Note here that through the powers conferred on the Brahmin by virtue of Veda study, he may demand certain perquisites from "the world" he is so instrumental in "developing" (or "cooking").[47] People should respect the Brahmin, give him gifts, and not politically oppress him or subject him to the ultimate punishment to which others are liable. Vedic learning thus underwrites some of the social status and privileges the Brahmins here (and elsewhere) claim.

The fourth justification for the superiority of the Brahmin is not unrelated to the third: it centers on the fact that it was the Brahmin class that monopolized the sacerdotal occupation in ancient India. Brahmins were the priests of the Vedic fire sacrifice, the "technicians of the sacred." One of the reasons for claiming exclusive control over the operations of the sacrifice was that the *brahman* metaphysical power has one of its most concentrated expressions in the ritual: "He who takes refuge in the sacrifice takes refuge in the *brahman*, for the sacrifice is the *brahman*" (AitB 7.22; cf., e.g., ŚB 3.1.4.15, 5.3.2.4).

The connection to the sacrifice also justifies the claim that the Brahmin social class are "gods on earth." It is not only that the Brahmins "carry the sacrifice to the gods" (ŚB 1.3.4.9; cf. AitB 3.45) which grants them this divine status. The *brahman* power, it is claimed, has the same origin as that of the gods; it was born out of the "womb of the gods" (the *devayoni*) (AitB 3.19), which is another term for the sacrifice. Therefore, we read elsewhere, the Brahmin class is called the "divine *varṇa*" (*daivya varṇa*, TB 1.2.6.6).

As priests, the Brahmins are the only ones—apart from the gods themselves—allowed to consume the sacrificial oblations; certain rites in the Vedic sacrifice entail the officiants eating portions of the sacrificial food as a kind of "oblation" to these "gods on earth." For the mouth of a Brahmin is equated with the sacrificial fire (e.g., PB 16.6.14) or, as we have seen, the Brahmin is the "mouth of Agni," the fire.[48] They are for this reason also put on a par with the gods, and separated from other humans:

> Prajāpati emitted the sacrifice, and after the sacrifice the *brahman* power and the *kṣatra* power were emitted. After them were emitted those creatures who eat sacrificial oblations and those who don't. The Brahmins are those creatures who eat sacrificial oblations; the Kshatriyas, Vaishyas, and Shūdras are those who don't. (AitB 7.19)

The possession of Vedic knowledge and sacrificial techniques can, in ancient India, be regarded as more or less the same thing. Brahmin learning buttresses the Brahmin monopoly over the sacrifice. "The Brahmins who have studied and teach the Veda,"[49] one reads, "are who make the sacrifice prosper. They spread it and they bring it forth. These [Brahmins] he [the sacrificer] thus propitiates."[50] Vedic knowledge and sacrificial know-how, taken together, justify the assertion that members of this class are "human gods" (*mānuṣyadevas*):

> There are two kinds of gods, for the gods are gods, and those Brahmins who have studied and teach the Veda are human gods. The sacrifice of these [sacrificers] is divided into two. Oblations into the fire are [sacrifices] to the gods, and sacrificial fees [are sacrifices] to the human gods, the Brahmins who have studied and teach the Veda. With oblations into the fire one pleases the gods, with sacrificial fees on pleases the human gods, the Brahmins who have studied and teach the Veda. Both these gods, when gratified, place him in a condition of well-being.[51]

The Brahmins derived economic as well as status advantages from their exclusive claim to the priesthood and divinity. In the sacrifice, food offerings to the gods were required of sacrificers regardless of class; but so were "offerings" of various kinds of wealth (cows, garments, gold, as well as food) given to the Brahmin "gods" or officiants as *dakṣiṇās* or sacrificial fees.

The sacrifice, whose importance to the ideology of the Veda cannot be overestimated, was thus regarded as the exclusive domain of the gods, on the one hand, and of the Brahmin class on the other—and the latter group identified itself with the former. So closely associated was the sacrifice with the Brahmins that members of other classes who sponsored such activities, and thus acted as the sacrificer or *yajamāna*, had to first be ritually reborn into the Brahmin *varṇa*.

When a sacrificer of any class became consecrated for the soma sacrifice (and thus became a *dīkṣita*), "he passes from the world of men to the world of the gods" (ŚB 1.1.1.4). Having thus entered the "world of the gods," the sacrificer, regardless of social class, was to be addressed as "Brahmin" because a "birth out of the sacrifice" was equated with a birth out of the womb of a Brahmin mother. "Now he is truly born who is born of the *brahman*, of the sacrifice. Therefore he should address even a Kshatriya or a Vaishya as 'Brahmin', since he who is born of the sacrifice is born of the *brahman*."[52]

Upon being consecrated, the Kshatriya sacrificer in particular loses his distinctive qualities and takes on those of the Brahmin and his domain of the sacrifice. His former and Kshatriya powers are then supposed to declare, "He is becoming other than we; he is becoming the *brahman*; he is joining the *brahman*."[53] During the course of the consecration rite, the Kshatriya "attains Brahminhood (*brāhmaṇatām abhyupaiti*) in that he puts on the black antelope skin, in that he carries out the vow of a *dīkṣita*, in that [other] Brahmins [i.e., the priests] come around him" (AitB 7.23). It is thus said that the Kshatriya assumes the form of the *brahman* in the ritual in an "invisible" or "mysterious" (*parokṣa*) way (AitB 7.31). But when the sacrifice is over, the *dīkṣita*s of classes other than the Brahmin cease to be Brahmins and return to their extraritual social class. "I take refuge with the *kṣatra* power, may the *kṣatra* protect me against the *brahman*. . . . I become a Kshatriya . . . I offer being he who I am . . . I who am I am I" (AitB 7.22–24).

Reconstituting a Kshatriya or a Vaishya as a "Brahmin" for the purposes of the sacrifice may have also been a way to sidestep certain prohibitions one finds in other texts. For it is sometimes said that no one but Brahmins can participate in the soma sacrifice, no one but they can drink of the "immortal" juices.[54] Even in lesser rituals which do not employ the soma within them the Brahmins reserve rights to themselves as those who "offer and drink the soma." In the New and Full Moon sacrifice, for example, there is an oblation to Agni (the god of fire), broken in four for each of the cardinal directions: "This is the oblation for the Brahmins who offer the soma and drink the soma. He who is not a Brahmin is excluded from sharing it. There is nothing here for one who is not a Brahmin."[55]

Brahmins are in these ways (and many others we survey in following chapters) separated from all other social classes and claim the highest social status. In one rite, the bulk of the verses recited are correlated to the *brahman*, and thus the priest "bestows on the *brahman* might (*ojas*) and virility (*vīrya*), and makes the *kṣatra* and the *viś* follow after it" (PB 2.8.2). They are superior to others in that they were created first and because they encompass within their being all other social classes and their potentialities. Their learning and, most important, their control over the sacrificial domain were meant to justify their claim that their "lordship" extends over all. These and other status claims and rationales were designed by the Brahmin authors of the Veda to ensure that there would be no mistake as to which of the social classes took precedence in the social order. The highest position in the class hierarchy they took for themselves.

Brahmins and Kshatriyas

At the second level of analysis, it will be recalled, the Brahmins and the Kshatriya rulers and warriors are opposed to the masses. Conjoined, the Brahmins and Kshatriyas are regarded as the two "virile" social entities (*vīrya*, ŚB 1.2.1.7, 3.5.2.11, 3.6.1.17) and may be viewed as the ruling class in relation to others. This, then, is the second binary opposition in the Vedic social order: Brahmins and Kshatriyas as rulers vs. all others as the ruled.

Each of the two classes had their own discrete set of powers and privileges; Brahmins and Kshatriyas had separate spheres of interest, domains over which they exercised mastery—and these were supposed to be complementary. While the Brahmins monopolized the sacrifice and Vedic learning (and were characterized by related essential powers such as *brahmavarcasa* and *tejas*), they also assumed that military might and political rule were the sole preserves of the Kshatriya. It is their respective "weapons" of ritual and war, mythologically traced back to the god Indra's thunderbolt or *vajra*, that both defines the individual functions of the Brahmins and Kshatriyas and undergirds the power they jointly assume over the masses. When the warrior god Indra hurled his thunderbolt at his enemy, the serpent demon Vṛtra, it broke into four pieces:

> Thus the Brahmins make use of two [of these pieces] in the sacrifice, and Kshatriyas [make use of] two in battle. The Brahmins [perform the ritual] with the sacrificial sword (*sphya*) and the stake to which the sacrificial victim is bound; and the Kshatriyas [fight] with the chariot and the bow and arrow. (ŚB 1.2.4.2)

The specialties of the two classes are also portrayed in one rite where two singers and lute players, one a Brahmin and the other a Kshatriya, extol the different virtues of the king, who is here acting as the sacrificer:

> "Such and such sacrifices he offered, such and such he gave away!" [These are the topics about which] the Brahmin sings. For to the Brahmin belongs the fulfillment of wishes (*iṣṭapūrta*). It is the fulfillment of wishes he [the priest] thus bestows on him [the sacrificer]. "Such and such a battle he fought, such and such a war he won!" [These are the topics about which] the Kshatriya sings. For the battle is the Kshatriya's virility. It is virility he thus bestows upon him. (ŚB 13.1.5.6; cf. 13.4.3.5ff.; TB 3.9.14.1–2)

The Kshatriyas thus possess distinctive potentialities revolving around the elemental quality that defines them, the *kṣatra*, and their sphere of influence, the world of politics and power (with the attendent essential powers that world requires and entails). The tools of physical and military coercion, the weapons of war and violence, are clustered in the hands of the warrior class. The ideal Kshatriya is described as "an archer, a hero, and a great charioteer"[56] and as "one who kills his enemies and contests with rivals" (ŚB 2.1.2.17). Strong in arms and legs and fitted with armor, he is to go around performing "manly" or "heroic" (*vīrya*) deeds (TB 3.8.23.3).

The Brahmins, on the other hand, possess the "weapons" of the *brahman* and the sacrifice, and as we read in the following it is these "weapons" that define and distinguish the Brahmin class from the Kshatriya warriors:

> Prajāpati [the lord of creation] emitted the sacrifice, and after the sacrifice the *brahman* power and the *kṣatra* power were emitted. . . . The sacrifice departed from them. The *brahman* power and the *kṣatra* power followed after it, each with their own weapons. The weapons of the *brahman* power are the weapons of the sacrifice; those of the *kṣatra* are the horse chariot, armor, and bow and arrow. The sacrifice escaped, recoiling, from the *kṣatra*'s weapons, and the *kṣatra* did not catch it. The *brahman* followed it, caught it, and restrained it, standing from above. Caught, restrained from above, and recognizing its own weapons, [the sacrifice] returned to the *brahman*. Therefore, even now the sacrifice finds support in the *brahman* power and in the Brahmins. (AitB 7.19)

Here again we observe the Brahmins separating themselves from all others on the basis of their sacrificial privileges: first, they are the class that has the exclusive right to partake of the oblations in the ritual (as we have seen, there are rites where the officiants eat portions of the sacrificial food, just as the gods supposedly eat the oblations offered into the fire); and second, while the Kshatriyas may have the weapons of war it is only the Brahmins who possess the "weapons" (i.e., the sacrificial implements) that tame the powerful sacrifice.

Brahmins and Kshatriyas should keep to their own spheres of influence—the former's is the sacrifice, the latter's the military and kingship. When they do so, the powers of each "guard" or "protect" the other, and the two form a phalanx of complementary powers:

> He who takes refuge in the sacrifice takes refuge in the *brahman*, for the sacrifice is the *brahman*. Moreover, the one who is consecrated [i.e., the king] is born again out of the sacrifice. He who has thus taken refuge in the *brahman* the *kṣatra* does not oppress. "May the *brahman* protect me from the *kṣatra*," he says, so that the *brahman* may protect him from the *kṣatra*. . . . He who takes refuge in the kingdom (*rāṣṭra*) takes refuge in the *kṣatra*, for the kingdom is the *kṣatra*. He who has thus taken refuge in the *kṣatra* the *brahman* does not oppress. "May the *kṣatra* protect me from the *brahman*," he says, so that the *kṣatra* may protect him from the *brahman*. (AitB 7.22)

Ritual power, wielded by the Brahmins, is more or less equated to—when it is not presented as superior to—military power; the powers of the sacrifice[57] are often juxtaposed or even assimilated with those of the martial arts or kingship. But in fact the possession of powers of such very different sorts would have rather different practical results in the real world, or so one would think. A well-aimed arrow from the bow of a warrior careering about on his chariot would instantly render ineffectual the priest ritually engaged in drawing lines in the earth with his toy wooden sword, "fulfilling his wishes" as one previously cited text so revealingly puts it. Otherwise stated, it would seem fairly obvious that actualized physical and military force could easily and whenever it wished overpower ritual technicians. And perhaps it did in the reality that was ancient India.

Even as that world was portrayed by the Brahmins, there are indications that the Kshatriyas had certain undeniable powers over even the Brahmins themselves, as well as over the other classes. In one rite, if the sacrificer is a Kshatriya, certain verses are to be repeated three times, for "there are three other sorts of men besides the Kshatriya—the Brahmin, Vaishya, and Shūdra. He thus makes them subordinate (*anuka*) to him" (TS 2.5.10.1). Elsewhere it is said that both the Brahmins and the Vaishyas "approach the Kshatriya respectfully" and "are subject to him" (JB 1.285).

The Brahmin is sometimes presented as less glorious (less possessed of the Kshatriya trait of *yaśas*) than the ruler (ŚB 5.4.2.7; TB 3.9.14.2) or as one who merely follows his ruler around (ŚB 1.2.3.2). Elsewhere the Kshatriya is characterized as "harsh" (*krūra*) (TS 6.2.5.2), whereas the Brahmin is a "friend" (*mitra*, cf. KS 7.11; MS 1.5.14). A remarkable Vedic text posits that a Kshatriya sacrificer who mistakenly consumes soma, a symbol (and "the king") of the Brahmin class, is doomed to have Brahmin-like progeny:

> Among your offspring will be born one who is a sort of a Brahmin (*brāhmaṇakalpa*), an acceptor of gifts, a drinker [of soma], a seeker of a livelihood, one to be pushed around at will. When misfortune comes to a Kshatriya, one who is Brahmin-like is liable to be born among his offspring; the second or third [generation] from him enters into the state of Brahminhood—he is wont to live as one connected to the *brahman* power. (AitB 7.29)

Several passages transmit dire warnings as to the consequences of a Kshatriya appropriating to himself the property (usually signified by livestock) of the Brahmin,[58] possibly because the latter really was quite vulnerable on this score. Similarly, the Kshatriya king is warned against double-crossing his Brahmin priest (as perhaps kings all too often did) lest he lose both his kingdom and his life (AitB 8.23). In one text, a Kshatriya deity is said to have felt the pangs of guilt for even contemplating the oppression of a divine representative of the Brahmin class (ŚB 4.1.2.4).

The Brahmins and Kshatriyas are thus sometimes portrayed in the Veda as competitors, or even enemies. At ŚB 13.1.5.2–3, the *brahman* is said not to be fond of (*na ramata*) the *kṣatra* and vice versa. The all-too-real advantages of the Kshatriyas and the fears provoked by them are occasionally confronted head-on by the Brahmin literati. In one myth, the gods (who, as we have seen, are supposedly close kin to the Brahmins) "were afraid of the Kshatriya when he was born." But gods, and those who speak for them, have their ways of ensuring that the human warriors and rulers will ultimately subject themselves to the authority of the priests. Mythologically, at least, the Kshatriya's power is allowed expression only through the medium of Brahmin interests:

> When the Kshatriya was born, the gods became fearful. Being still within [the womb] they fettered him with a rope. The Kshatriya therefore is born fettered. If the Kshatriya were to be born unfettered, he would continually kill his enemies. If one [viz., an officiating priest] desires regarding a Kshatriya, "May he be born unfettered; may he continually kill his enemies," then one should offer for him the boiled offering dedicated to Indra and Bṛhaspati. For the Kshatriya has the nature of Indra, and Bṛhaspati is the *brahman* power. By means of the *brahman* power he thus liberates him from the rope that fetters him. (TS 2.4.13.1)

While it may very well have been that the Kshatriyas in actuality determined the conditions under which life was really led, as warriors and rulers so often do, the Brahmin authors of the Veda generally project a rather different image—possibly a mere hope—about the relative power of their own class vis-à-vis the Kshatriyas. Writers and intellectuals in our day like to say that the pen is mightier than the sword; the Brahminical version of this optimistic wish was expressed in terms of the awesome force of *their* sword, the little wooden *sphya* they wielded in the sacrifice. In the description of one rite within a ritual designed to consecrate a king we read the following:

> Then a Brahmin, either the *adhvaryu* priest or his [the king's] personal priest (*purohita*), hands him the wooden sword [saying], "You are Indra's thunderbolt. With that, you become subject to me." The thunderbolt is the wooden sword. The Brahmin, by means of the "thunderbolt," makes the king weaker (*abalīya*) than himself, for the king who is weaker than the Brahmin becomes stronger (*balīya*) than his enemies. Thus he makes him stronger than his enemies. (ŚB 5.4.4.15)

The text continues by following the journey of the wooden sword as it passes from the king's hand to, consecutively, the king's brother, the *sūta* or governor, the village headman (*grāmaṇī*), and the tribesman, and each is made "weaker" in relation to the preceding one. "They do so," the passage concludes, "lest there should be categorical confusion (*pāpavasyasa*) and so that [the kingdom or society] may be in the proper order (*yathāpūrva*)" (ŚB 5.4.4.16–19; cf. 13.4.4.1).

Only by placing himself under the supposedly superior power of the Brahmin can the Kshatriya in turn become superior to his rivals (external and internal to the kingdom). Many other texts shift the scene to the sacrificial grounds where the Brahmins manipulate their rites so as to claim dominance over the Kshatriyas.[59] The placement of certain mantras or offerings to the deified representatives of the two classes are in such an order as to make the Brahmins "come first" and the Kshatriyas "follow after," since the former is declared "prior" to the latter (both in the sense of being created first and being therefore "predominant" or "first," "preeminent").[60] Another rite is designed to ensure that the Kshatriya will be generous in his sacrifices and gift-giving and place his faith in the effectiveness of the Brahmins and their sacrifices and be characterized by "friendliness toward Brahmins" (JB 1.244).

This (Brahminical) ideal was especially to be realized in the relationship between the Kshatriya king and his Brahmin priest, the *purohita*—a word that means, literally, "one who is put ahead."[61] The Brahmin *purohita* is said to be half of the very self of the Kshatriya he serves;[62] it is also declared that one who is not either a Kshatriya or a *purohita* is "incomplete," whereas he who is one or the other is "everything" (ŚB 6.6.3.13–14). The office of the *purohita* is "the food of the *brahman*" (PB 12.8.6, 13.9.27, 14.9.38), presumably because of its economic advantages and the protection the royal patron gives to the Brahmin. On the other hand, the king who has a *purohita* in his retinue can say, "I destroy enemies and lead forth my own subjects with the help of the *brahman*" (ŚB 6.6.3.15).

It is in this relationship that the two *varṇa*s are conjoined in what is supposed to be a mutually advantageous consortium. The *kṣatra* and the *brahman* should be "united" (AitB 3.11); elsewhere it is said that the *brahman* and *kṣatra* should be "allied" and, again, "closely united" (ŚB 2.5.4.8), or that they should "speak with one voice."[63] The powers of the *brahman* and *kṣatra* are (ideally, at least) as complementary as inhalation and exhalation, food and drink.[64]

When such a union occurs it can then be said that "on the *brahman* is the *kṣatra* established, on the *kṣatra* the *brahman*."[65] Then "by means of the *brahman* he quickens the *kṣatra*, and by the *kṣatra* the *brahman*. Therefore a Brahmin [priest] who has a Kshatriya [patron] is superior to another Brahmin; and therefore a Kshatriya [king] who has a Brahmin [*purohita*] is superior to another Kshatriya" (TS 5.1.10.3; cf. ŚB 5.4.4.15ff., cited above; ŚB 6.3.1.28, 6.4.4.12–13).

In frequently cited paradigmatic text (ŚB 4.1.4.1ff.),[66] the *purohita*–king relationship is given divine pedigree in the form of the union between the divine priest Mitra and the Kshatriya royal god Varuṇa. The two are represented as the divine representatives of the powers of *brahman* and *kṣatra*, and also as two complementary principles: the Brahmin entity is intelligence or inspiration (*kratu*); the Kshatriya embodies the capacity for action or skillfulness (*dakṣa*). The Brahmin priest, as Coomaraswamy puts it, "at once inspirits and inspires the King."[67] The text portrays the two powers as originally separate. But whereas "Mitra, the *brahman*, could stand without Varuṇa, the *kṣatra*," things were otherwise for Varuṇa: "Whatever action Varuṇa did uninspired by Mitra, the *brahman*, did not succeed." Only when the two deities, powers, and principles were united, and the Brahmin was made "foremost" (*puras*) in the relationship, could the divine king effectively rule: "Whatever action, inspired by Mitra, the *brahman*, Varuṇa subsequently did succeeded."[68]

While both Brahmin and Kshatriya benefit from the union—the Brahmin authors of the Veda insist, for their part, that the king acts as the protector (*gopa*) of the Brahmins (AitB 8.17)—it is the advantages to the ruler of this relationship that are most often highlighted. It is said that the gods do not eat the sacrificial food offerings of the king who is without a *purohita*: "Therefore a king when about to sacrifice should put a Brahmin foremost [i.e., employ a *purohita*, thinking], 'May the gods eat my food' " (AitB 8.24). Similarly, according to another text, the *kṣatra* obtains the "sap of food" because of this association with the *brahman* power (TB 2.6.2.2). When the Kshatriya is properly subservient to the Brahmin, it is written elsewhere, the kingdom prospers and is filled with heroes (AitB 8.9). One who has a Brahmin *purohita* who will "protect the kingdom" obtains the following benefits: his "kingdom does not come to an early end, life does not leave him before his time, he lives to a ripe old age, he lives life to its fullest, and he does not die again" (AitB 8.25). The *purohita* is, in sum, the king's "safe abode" (*āyatana*).[69]

Furthermore, despite the occasional statement that might lead the unsuspecting reader to believe that the union between Brahmin and Kshatriya encapsulated in the *purohita*–king relationship was one between two equals, many other texts disabuse one quickly of any such thought. BĀU 1.4.11, for example, proclaims generously that "there is nothing higher than the *kṣatra* power. Therefore at the Rājasūya ritual the Brahmin sits below the Kshatriya. Thus he bestows glory (*yaśas*) upon the *kṣatra*."[70] Immediately following, however, we read: "This same *brahman* is the womb of the *kṣatra*. Therefore, even if the king attains "supremacy he still clings to the *brahman* as his own womb. Whoever injures him [the Brahmin or the *purohita*] moves against his own womb. When one harms his betters, he becomes worse."[71]

Again we witness the Brahmins proclaiming themselves as prior to and the source of their royal and military "inferiors." Brahmins, as the very womb and origin of others, are to be safeguarded from injury, the rationale for which is cleverly formulated: if you hurt me, the Brahmin, you are really hurting yourself, your "own womb." "The *brahman* generated the gods," we read in another text; indeed, "the *brahman* generated the whole world. It is out of the *brahman* that the power of the *kṣatra* has been fashioned."[72]

Because the Brahmins are in this way portrayed as the source, the "womb," of the Kshatriyas, they can also claim to ontologically encompass within themselves the powers of the latter. We observed earlier that the Brahmin and his elemental quality, the *brahman*, are the all-enveloping entities of the universe as a whole. Here we note that, specifically, the *brahman* encompasses the *kṣatra*, Brahmin encompasses the Kshatriya, the priest encompasses his king. The *kṣatra* is not only generated out of, and therefore secondary to, the *brahman*; the *brahman* is, we learn, the true essence of the *kṣatra*: "The *brahman* power is called the real (*sat*) *kṣatra*" (AV 10.2.23). Thus the *purohita* perfects "both his *brahman* and *kṣatra* powers" when he takes on his office (ŚB 6.6.3.14)—because he innately possesses both to begin with.

While the priests may therefore admit that they are "unsuited for kingship," the ritual by which the Kshatriya is elevated to that office is declared "lower" (*avara*) than another ritual identified with the Brahmins which is "higher" (*para*).[73] The Brahmins do not, at least according to the texts they wrote, submit to the rule of Kshatriyas; the Brahmins have a different "king," "King Soma," the divine ruler of the sacrifice.[74] Brahmin writers go so far as to appropriate to themselves one of the principal functions of the king: "punishment" or the administration of justice (*daṇḍa*). In the royal consecration ritual or Rājasūya, the nine-versed hymn of praise (consistently identified with the Brahmin class) is withheld from the recitations, for

> if they were to perform the sprinkling rite (*abhiṣeka*) using the nine-versed [hymn of praise] they would give over the *brahman* power to the *kṣatra*. In that they leave out the nine-versed [hymn of praise], they extricate the *brahman* from the *kṣatra*. Therefore the Brahmins exert countercontrol (*pratidaṇḍa*) over their patrons [i.e., the Kshatriyas], for they do not perform the sprinkling rite using the nine-versed [hymn of praise].[75]

Despite such machinations on the part of the Brahmin class, in general the Brahmins and Kshatriyas can be regarded as united into a ruling class vis-à-vis the populace at large. Priests and warriors are said to be "better" than or "superior" to (*śreyan*) other sorts of people,[76] and in the ritual the Brahmin officiants and Kshatriya patrons would sometimes join hands to ensure that, together, they would rule over the *viś*:

> The first [verse of the chant] is the safe abode (*āyatana*) of the *brahman*, the middle one belongs to the *kṣatra*, and the last is the *viś*. In that the first two [verses] occur each fifteen times, and the last [the verse] fourteen times, he thereby puts might (*ojas*) and virility (*vīrya*) into the *brahman* and the *kṣatra* and he makes the *viś* subservient (*upaga*) to them. (PB 3.9.2)

But although the Brahmins and Kshatriyas together might be proclaimed as superior to the commoners, the Brahmins did not hesitate to declare their own class as higher (*suyan*) than the Kshatriyas (AitB 7.15; cf. AV 5.17.9). The Brahmins, as the ontologically complete form of the human being, present themselves in the Veda as ultimately self-sufficient, and the Kshatriyas as dependent on priests. Thus it is said that Brahmins can live without rulers, but rulers cannot adequately carry out their tasks without the aid of Brahmins: "It is perfectly in order for a Brahmin to be without a Kshatriya, but were he to obtain a king that would be advantageous. It is, however, quite improper for a Kshatriya to be without a Brahmin. . . . Therefore a Brahmin is indeed to be approached by a Kshatriya who intends to take any action, for his success depends on the act having been impelled by a Brahmin" (ŚB 4.1.4.6). In another rite, sacrificial machinations are performed in such a way that "he places the *kṣatra* behind the *brahman*. Therefore the Brahmin is foremost (*mukhya*), and he who know this also becomes foremost" (TS 2.6.2.5).

The Ruling Class and the Masses

If Vedic knowledge and sacrificial skills are the principal traits of the Brahmins, and physical and military power those of the Kshatriya, it is multiplicity, fecundity, productivity, and most especially subservience to the higher classes which are the characteristics most often associated with the Vaishyas in Vedic texts.

The *viś* exist so that the ruling classes might utilize them; they are there to be thoroughly and guiltlessly exploited. The Brahmins and the Kshatriyas, it is unabashedly admitted, live their privileged lives on the backs of the commoners: the two higher classes "are established upon the people."[77]

The two upper classes are ritually constituted as superior to the lower classes. The Brahmin and Kshatriya, by means of the ritual correlates of the goat and the horse, are led before the ass who "is" the Vaishya and Shūdra: "And since the ass does not go first . . . therefore the Brahmin and Kshatriya never follow behind the Vaishya and Shūdra. Therefore this is the way they go, so that there is no categorical confusion (*apāpavasyasa*)." Furthermore, the *brahman* and the *kṣatra* should "surround on both sides" the Vaishya and Shūdra classes, and the reason for this is so that the two higher social powers will establish and maintain their control: "And he in this way surrounds on both sides those two *varṇa*s with the Brahmin and the Kshatriya, and makes them stay in their place (*anapakramiṇa*)" (ŚB 6.4.4.13; cf. ŚB 6.3.1.28).

Whereas the Brahmin's all-encompassing mastery (concentrated in the microcosm that is the sacrifice) makes him "lord of all," it is the Kshatriya king who is specifically the "lord of the people" (AV 3.4.1). It is out of the Brahmin that a Kshatriya is produced, but the Kshatriya is also generated out of the *viś*—that is, his ruling power and material well-being are derived from his subjects (ŚB 12.7.3.8–12,15). The Kshatriya is thus said to be the offspring of the *viś* (ŚB 5.3.4.11); it is "through the people that the power of the *kṣatra* becomes strong (*balavat*)" (ŚB 4.3.3.6,9; cf. AitB 8.24); and it is "by means of his *viś* that the Kshatriya wins what he desires to win."[78]

The ruler should thus be "surrounded" and "guarded" on all sides by his people,[79] for the *viś* are his "protection" (*kṣema*, AV 3.3.5) or are "stability" in general (KB 16.4). The relationship is sometimes portrayed as advantageous to the commoners, for "wherever the *kṣatra* conquers, there the *viś* is entitled a share" (ŚB 2.4.3.6). But it is also pointed out that the ruler also has a "share in the people" so "whatever there is among the people, in that the ruler also has a share" (ŚB 9.1.1.18).

One of the most frequently mentioned properties of the peasantry is their sheer numbers, their "multiplicity," and this is contrasted to the singular nature of the ruler: the Kshatriya "being one, rules over many," that is, many commoners (ŚB 5.1.5.14; cf. PB 20.12.4–5). In one rite, a cake is made as an offering to a single deity and another oblation is designated for a group of divinities; the first is equated to the Kshatriya and the second to the *viś*:

> That [cake], being one, has only a single deity. He concentrates the *kṣatra* in one [person] and concentrates excellence (*śriyā*) in one [person]. The other, the boiled offering, has many deities. The boiled offering is an abundance (*bhūman*) of rice-grains, and those Ādityas are an abundance of gods. He thus bestows abundance on the people (ŚB 6.6.1.8).

In another rite, the single fire altar is equated with the ruler and the multiple hearths with the commoners; thus the *kṣatra* power and "distinction" (*śriyā*) are given to a single Kshatriya, whereas because the other hearths are "numerous" (*bahava*), abundance is ritually transferred to the people (ŚB 9.4.3.2).

Still another rite has the same purpose—to attach power and excellence to a single Kshatriya[80] and multiplicity to his Vaishya subjects—and goes on to add that the Kshatriya is "distinct" (*nirukta*) while the Vaishya is "indistinct" (*anirukta*):[81]

> This is a single [oblation]. He concentrates the *kṣatra* in one [person] and concentrates excellence (*śriyā*) in one [person]. The other [oblations] are numerous; he thus bestows abundance on the *viś*. The first [is offered in] a distinct [voice], for the Kshatriya is distinct, as it were. The others are indistinct, for indistinct, as it were, are the *viś*. (ŚB 9.3.1.14-15)

Jan Gonda commented that on the basis of this passage "it may be inferred that in the eyes of the author the 'second' and the 'third estate' were dissimilar in that the latter, as opposed to the former, could not be defined, or said to be 'bounded,' 'limited,' or 'clearly organized.' "[82] The social class known as the *viś* were indeed "indistinct,"[83] both in the sense of lacking distinction and also in the sense of being a multitudinous and variegated class, a kind of catch-all category for all who were neither Brahmins nor Kshatriyas in Vedic society.[84]

This motley group had to be kept in line. The *viś* are to be "restrained" (TB 3.3.6.10), "brought into order" (AitB 1.9), and made "steady and faithful" to their ruler.[85] Above all, hierarchical distinctions are to be established and maintained between the king and his people, and this is often done ritually by having the element representing the Kshatriya come before that symbolizing the commoners. Thus, for example, the multiple hearths "are the *viś*, and the built-up fire-altar is the *kṣatra*. He thus constructs both the *kṣatra* and the *viś*. The former [fire altar which is the *kṣatra*] he constructs first, then these [hearths which are the *viś*]. Thus he constructs the *viś* after having first constructed the *kṣatra*."[86]

Another method for ritually constituting the proper order between the Kshatriyas and the commoners was to endow activities that entail things and beings that are higher or lower with social meanings. One stands to offer an oblation connected to the Kshatriya and sits when offering that related to the Vaishya: "He thus makes the *viś* compliant (*anukara*) and obedient (*anuvartman*) to the Kshatriya" (ŚB 9.3.1.15–16). One type of altar is built up into five layers of brick, while another is wider but of a single layer: "He builds that one up. He thus builds the *kṣatra* up, and he builds the others across. He thus makes the *viś* devoted to and below the *kṣatra*" (ŚB 9.4.3.3). A single ladle representing the Kshatriya is placed on top of the many spoons that symbolize the people: "He thereby makes the *kṣatra* higher than the commoners. Therefore the subjects here [on earth] serve, from a lower position, the Kshatriya seated above them" (ŚB 1.3.4.15). A northern or "higher" (*uttara*) portion of the sacrificial ground which is connected to the Kshatriyas is constructed in order to make "the *kṣatra* higher (*uttara*) than the people, and therefore the subjects here serve, from a lower position the Kshatriya who is placed above them" (ŚB 2.5.2.6). Or, again, the "seasonal" bricks representing the power of the Kshatriyas are strategically placed among and on top of other bricks associated with the *viś*:

> The seasonal [bricks], indeed, are the *kṣatra*. With the [different] layers he thus builds up the *kṣatra* above [the *viś*]. . . . He should not thereafter place over them any other brick with a sacrificial formula, for then he would place the *viś* over the *kṣatra*. (ŚB 8.7.1.12)

Many rites performed by the Brahmins for Kshatriya patrons were designed to produce the same result: to establish the superiority of the ruler over his people, and to invoke the obedience and subservience of the *viś*. The latter was also insured by unifying the otherwise fractious masses. If a king properly takes on a Brahmin *purohita*, his subjects (the *viś*) will be united (*samjanate*) under him, with a common visage (*sammukha*) and a "unified mind" (*ekamanas*).[87] Another text agrees with this strategy for rule through unification of the subjects. Representing the soma plant as the *kṣatra* and the pressing stones for extracting the juice of the soma as the *viś*, the author recommends that the soma plant be put over the stones: "He thereby raises the *kṣatra* over the *viś*. And as to why they [the pressing stones] are lying with their heads (*mukhas*) together [toward each other, i.e., broad sides turned toward each other]. He thereby makes the *viś* one-headed (*ekamukha*) and uncontentious towards the *kṣatra*" (ŚB 3.9.3.3). In another ritual, the priest symbolically "intertwines" (*vyatiṣajati*) the people and the Kshatriya ruler (TB 2.7.18.5).

While some texts thus emphasize the necessity to unify the people in order to conjoin them to the rule of the Kshatriya, others recommend a different tack. The Kshatriya should keep the people in their fragmented state in order to control them most effectively—divided they fall in the face of his ruling power. Certain bricks, identified with the peasantry, are stacked on the fire altar one by one, each with a different mantra: "He thereby makes the *viś* less virile than the *kṣatra*, divided by language and differing in thought (or will, *cetas*)" (ŚB 8.7.2.3).

Many other ritual actions also have as their stated purpose to bestow upon the Kshatriya more power than that of his subjects. "He thus places the *kṣatra* in an imposing position by means of virility, he makes the *kṣatra* more virile than the peasantry, and the peasantry less virile than the *kṣatra*" (ŚB 9.4.3.4; cf. 8.7.2.3; JB 1.80). Other rites were also designed to infuse the Kshatriya with strength while they drained it from the people. At ŚB 2.5.2.36 we learn that the male ram belongs to a deity representing the Kshatriyas, and the female ewe is connected with Vaishya divinities. Furthermore, "the male represents virility; hence they thereby put virility into the *kṣatra*. The female, on the other hand, is without virility. . . . Hence they thereby cause the peasantry to be without virility."

No matter how it was to be effected, the main desideratum, as we have seen, was to maintain the hierarchical distinction between Kshatriya rulers and Vaishya subjects. There should never be a "categorical confusion" between the inferior and superior (*pāpavasyasa*) and one must take care not to "make the peasantry equal (*pratiprati*) and resistant (*pratyudyāmin*) to the *kṣatra*" (ŚB 10.4.3.22; cf. ŚB 4.3.3.10; AitB 6.21). In one rite, cups of milk represent the *kṣatra* and cups of liquor stand for the *viś*. If the two types of liquid are not symbolically conjoined (by alternating them), "he would cut off the *viś* from the *kṣatra*, and the *kṣatra* from the *viś*; he would cause confusion between the inferior and the superior and the sacrifice would fail" (ŚB 12.7.3.15). Elsewhere, one is cautioned not to make an error in the sacrifice for fear that the *viś* would "step over" or "ascend to the heights of" (*abhyārohaya*) the *kṣatra*; insofar as the rite is performed correctly, "the *kṣatra* is not stepped over (*anabhyārūḍha*) [by the *viś*]" (ŚB 2.4.3.7). One must always be careful lest one make "the *viś* resistant to the *kṣatra*" instead of making them, as is proper, "compliant and obedient to the *kṣatra*" (ŚB 2.5.2.34).

Eaters and Food

While the peasantry is thus depicted as the particular subjects of the Kshatriya overlord, it should not be forgotten that the Brahmins—or so claim these texts written by the Brahmin class—are at the top of the social heap. The hierarchy is straightforward: "He makes the *kṣatra* dependent on (*anuniyukta*) the *brahman* . . . and the *viś* dependent on the *kṣatra*" (AitB 2.33). This ideal rank order, which we have seen above is often enough articulated outright, was sometimes encoded within the discourse of "food" and "eaters," which in ancient India was a means of speaking about the whole order of the "natural" world.[88]

We shall return to this theme in Chapter 7. For now, let it be said that this rather basic and literal description of the world endlessly divided into food and eaters of food was also applied in a seemingly more figurative way to the interrelations between the classes in the social world: the higher orders "live on" the lower, "for the eater is superior to his food. He who knows this lords over his peers" (AitĀ 2.3.1). But it may be just a prejudice to regard as symbolic the image of the lower classes as "food" for their superiors. Perhaps we are not dealing with metaphor but rather with an accurate, if unadorned, depiction of relations within Vedic society—at least as that society was depicted in the Veda.

A natural world categorized into dominating feeders and dominated food was reprojected as the paradigm for the order of the social world. The eater is superior to his food, in society as well as in nature; the social world, no less than the natural, is one of rulers and ruled, of consumers and consumed, of exploiters and exploited, of the strong and the weak. No text puts the case of continuity between nature and culture more starkly than Manu 5.29: "Immobile beings are the food of those which are mobile, those without teeth are the food of those with teeth, those without hands are the food of those with hands, and the cowards are the food of the brave."

Society's classes, like nature's, are divided into eaters and food, and supposedly immutable hierarchical distinctions are drawn between the *varṇa*s on this basis. The creator god Prajāpati is manifest on earth in the form of a series of hierarchically ordered mouths: "The Brahmin is one of your mouths. With that mouth you eat Kshatriyas. With that mouth make me an eater of food. The king is one of your mouths. With that mouth you eat the Vaishyas. With that mouth make me an eater of food" (KU 2.9; cf. ŚānĀ 4.9). The encompassment of the lower by the higher in society is here articulated in alimentary (and elementary) terms: you are more than the one you eat, and less than the one by whom you are eaten.

The Brahmins, at the top of the pecking order, claim to be "eaters of Kshatriyas" (and everybody else), but, as we have seen, the Veda also makes it clear that Brahmins are not to be "eaten." In the consecration ceremony for a Kshatriya ruler, the officiating priest "makes all this food for him [the king]; only the Brahmin he excepts. Therefore the Brahmin is not food, for he has Soma as his king."[89] Elsewhere we read that one who regards the Brahmin as food consumes poison (AV 5.18.4). The Kshatriya king was limited to the "eating" of the Vaisyas, for members of that class essentially are defined by their status as food for all others.

The commoners are sometimes equated with the animals in general, or more particularly with the domesticated animals they are charged with tending.[90] As "animals," the masses are the natural food[91] and prey of the higher two classes, as well as the class held responsible for producing food, both animal and vegetable. In texts to which we return in the next chapter, the Brahmin is said to be "emitted" from the mouth of the creator god, the Kshatriya from his chest and arms, and the Vaishya is generated out of Prajapati's penis, thereby ensuring that this "food" will be ever replenishing: "Therefore the Vaishya, although devoured [by the others] does not decrease, for he was emitted from the penis. Therefore he has abundant animals. . . . Therefore he is the food of the Brahmin and the Kshatriya, for he was emitted below [them]" (PB 6.1.10). Or again, the Vaishyas were created out of the stomach of the creator, and "therefore they are to be eaten, for they were created from the receptacle of food" (TS 7.1.1.5). The hierarchically inferior Vaishya exists, or so it is said, solely in order to be "eaten up" by the two ruling classes.[92]

Brahmins and Kshatriyas are thus both "eaters" of the ordinary folk. But the *viś* or "masses" are regarded as the special delicacy of the Kshatriyas who are directly above them in society's version of nature's food chain and who, it will be recalled, are often associated with the essential power called the "eating of food" (*annādya*). "The Kshatriya is the eater, and the commoners are food," it is said in many passages. "Where there is abundant food for the eater, that kingdom is prosperous and grows."[93] Thus several different rites manipulate symbols of the Kshatriya and commoner classes so that the priest "thereby places the *kṣatra*, as the eater, among the *viś*" (ŚB 8.7.1.2, 8.7.2.2, 9.4.3.5, etc.). In one the *kṣatra* is equated with a deer, while the *viś* are grain. "He thus makes the people to be food for the *kṣatra*, which is why the wielder of the *kṣatra* power feeds on the people" (ŚB 13.2.9.8).

The ŚB spells out some of the consequences of designating one numerically small class as the "eater" of another and much larger class. The text first constitutes the sacrificial *juhū* ladle as the analogue of "the eater," and the *upabhṛt* ladle as the symbol of "that which is eaten." It then goes on to extract certain social meanings from particular ritual acts:

> When he draws butter [with the spoon] four times [and places it] into the

> *juhū*, he makes the eater more limited and less numerous; and when he draws butter eight times [and places it] into the *upabhṛt*, he makes that which is to be eaten more unlimited, more numerous. For there is prosperity (*samṛddha*) wherever the eater is less numerous and that which is to be eaten is more numerous. When he draws butter only four times [and places it] into the *juhū*, he nevertheless draws up a greater quantity of butter; and when he draws butter eight times [and places it] into the *upabhṛt* he takes less butter. . . . While thus making the eater more limited and less numerous, he still puts virility and physical strength into him. . . . And while making that which is to be eaten more unlimited more numerous, he makes it impotent and weaker. Therefore a ruler who has come to dwell among unlimited commoners exploits them while just sitting in his own palace, and takes whatever he likes. . . . Now if he were to offer [the oblation] with the *upabhṛt*, the subjects would become separated from him, and there would not be either eater or what is to be eaten. When, on the other hand, he mixes [the butter] together and offers it with the *juhū*, then the commoners pay tribute to the Kshatriya. Thus, when he draws butter [and places it] into the *upabhṛt*, the Vaishya, being in the power of the Kshatriya, becomes one who possesses many animals. And when he mixes [the butter] together and offers it into the fire with the *juhū*, the Kshatriya says whenever he wants to, "Hey Vaishya, bring me whatever you have laid away!"[94]

The "food" or Vaishya class is here desired to be "more unlimited, more numerous" in relation to the "eater" or Kshatriya simply so that there will be more for the latter to "eat."[95] But the Vaishyas are also to be "weaker" than Kshatriyas to ensure that they will be infinitely exploitable. They are not to escape the ruler's power and "separate" from him, for then "there would not be either eater or what is to be eaten"—the Kshatriya would lose his "food" (meaning, among other things, the tribute the Vaishya brings him), and hierarchical distinctions would collapse. When, however, proper hierarchy is maintained the Vaishyas become wealthy in livestock and the Kshatriya's "wealth" ("Hey Vaishya, bring me whatever you have laid away!") remains secure.[96] This is, one might say, taxonomy in the interest of taxation.[97] It is no wonder that the Vaishya class is said to shrink from the Kshatriyas (JB 1.286).

Classifying Society

We observed earlier that the three social *varṇas* are depicted in terms of certain traits and qualities unique to each, and by certain relations with the others that further define their roles. The Brahmin class is essentially defined by its supposed priority (as the class created first by the creator god), by knowledge of the Veda, and by the monopoly this class holds on the operation of the sacrifice. These traits justify the social position of the class vis-à-vis others: they are predominant because they are prior, and they claim to stand outside of the power relations that govern social life for others because of their superior knowledge and sole possession of the ultimate "weapons," sacrificial techniques.

The Kshatriya, in his turn, is characterized by physical and martial strength. Such supposedly ontological qualities also determine his relations with others:

the Kshatriya is charged with the protection of the higher Brahmin class and with rule over (and unrestricted exploitation of) the lower Vaishya class.

The *viś*, the vaguely conceived "masses," are also somewhat more vaguely defined. They are depicted in terms of their vast numbers and their productivity—both in the sense of human reproduction and the production of wealth and material goods. The peasantry guarded the herds and nurtured the crops; their own numbers as well as the productivity they were expected to deliver were both included in the qualities of "multiplicity," "increase," and so forth, so intimately associated with this class. The Vaishyas were to be subservient and weak in comparison to their rulers, infinitely exploitable and infinitely regenerative—and this was presented as a natural state of affairs in the social realm. In relation to others they are "food" (being it and making it) and are to be kept obedient and hierarchically inferior to the two ruling classes.[98] The Vaishya is thus succinctly and brutally described in one text as a "tributary to another, to be eaten by another, and one who may be dispossessed at will" (AitB 7.29).[99]

Classifying society was thus seemingly a matter of assigning certain definitive traits to each class, representing those traits as manifestations of metaphysical forces, and establishing by means of ritual machinations the hierarchical relations that were to order the social body. Had it been left at that, the Vedic texts would have provided a rather detailed and interesting foreshadowing of the later conceptions of the *dharmas* assigned to each of the social *varṇas*. Furthermore, because such statements of social organization were to be found in the canonical Veda, subsequent social theory could tap the authority those texts came to assume in Hindu thought.

But the Veda went much further both in terms of the project of classifying the social world and in terms of supplying a set of authoritative legitimations for its particular class structure. Explicit articulations of the social aspect of the *varṇa* system are but the proverbial tip of the iceberg. The *varṇa* system projected itself into cosmological, supernatural, natural, and ritual contexts; the structure of society was mirrored in the structure of reality in all its dimensions. Such a universal application in and of itself would lend to the social structure an authority far more pervasive, and far more persuasive, than anything the direct discourse we have surveyed in this chapter could muster.

This cosmic pattern of *varṇa*, always encrusted with social connotations, was not only pervasive; it was aboriginal. The universe as a whole, including but not limited to the social realm, was created in the shape of the *varṇa* scheme, as we shall see in the next chapter.

NOTES

1. Louis Dumont, *Homo Hierarchicus: The Caste System and Its Implications*, rev. ed., trans. by Mark Sainsbury, Louis Dumont, and Basia Gulati (Chicago: University of Chicago Press, 1980), pp. 71–72. See also Dumont's "The Conception of Kingship in Ancient India," *Contributions to Indian Sociology* 6 (1962): 48–77; and Ananda K. Coomaraswamy, *Spiritual Authority and Temporal Power in the Indian Theory of Govern-*

ment (New Haven, Conn.: American Oriental Society, 1942). For an alternative view that emphasizes the Indian king's ritual and religious functions, see A. M. Hocart, *Caste: A Comparative Study* (reprint London: Methuen, 1950) and idem, *Kings and Councillors* (reprint Chicago: University of Chicago Press, 1970); and more recently, Gloria Goodwin Raheja, *The Poison in the Gift: Ritual, Prestation, and the Dominant Caste in a North Indian Village* (Chicago: University of Chicago Press, 1988). For opposition from another quarter, claiming that Dumont has simply repeated the "Brahmin optic" on the caste system and ignored the sociopolitical implications of caste hierarchy by separating it from power, consult F. Franco and Sarvar V. Sherry Chand, "Ideology as Social Practice: The Functioning of *Varṇa*," *Economic and Political Weekly* 24, 47 (Nov. 25, 1989), pp. 2601, 2607–8.

2. Wendy Doniger with Brian K. Smith, trans., *The Laws of Manu* (London: Penguin Books, 1991), pp. xxxv–xxxvi.

3. Manu 1.87–91. For the duties assigned to each of the four *varṇa*s in the Dharma Sūtras and Śāstras, see also the texts accumulated and analyzed by P. V. Kane in his *History of Dharmaśāstra: Ancient and Mediaeval, Religious and Civil Law*, 2d ed., vol. II, no. 1 (Poona: Bhandarkar Oriental Research Institute, 1974), pp. 50–179.

4. This argument has been put forward by Jan Heesterman, who posits a "preclassical" period in which "originally brahmins and ksatriyas were not closed, separate groups" but rather participated in "reversal of roles." See "Brahmin, Ritual, and Renouncer," reprinted as Chapter 2 of *The Inner Conflict of Tradition: Essays in Indian Ritual, Kingship, and Society* (Chicago: University of Chicago Press, 1985), esp. pp. 29–30.

5. I refer to Ronald Inden's "Lordship and Caste in Hindu Discourse," in *Indian Religion*, ed. by R. Burghart and A. Cantlie (London: Curzon Press, 1985), pp. 159–179.

6. See below, pp. 39–41. While the Kshatriya, and especially the Kshatriya king, can be given all kinds of grandiose titles in the texts, those same texts assume, as we see later that the ruler and warrior are inferior vis-à-vis the supposedly all-encompassing Brahmin. Ananda Coomaraswamy is quite right to point out that "in any Hierarchy, the individual is necessarily related in one way to what is above him, and in another to his own domain." *Spiritual Authority and Temporal Power*, p. 50.

7. And are therefore "encompassed" within the lordship of the Kshatriya: "The mastery of the Kshatriya was more complete than that of the Vaishya (and Shūdra). The Kshatriya had mastery over not only movable wealth—cash, grain, and the like, but also over immovable wealth, namely the land, which was thought to be the ultimate source of movable wealth. Similarly, he had mastery over not only domestic animals, but also over people as well. He was not simply master of a productive household, he was lord of a fraction or share of a kingdom." Inden, "Lordship and Caste," pp. 171–72.

8. "The hierarchic relationship of the Vaishya with the Shūdra is clear. The Shūdra was master of his body, his own labour, his own household, if he had one, but he was not the master of wealth beyond what he required for subsistence. The Vaishya was not only master in all these domains, he was master of wealth, of things produced and traded, and of animals domesticated, expert at causing them to increase." Ibid., p. 170.

9. Here and throughout this work I translate this older name for the ruling and warrior social class, *rājanya*, as "Kshatriya" for the sake of consistency.

10. For the explicit correlation of the three *guṇa*s with three social *varṇa*s (Brahmin = *sattva*, Kshatriya = *rajas*, and the Shūdra [who is, it will be recalled, often incorporated within the Vedic conception of the *viś*] = *tamas*), see Manu 12.43–48 and Mbh 14.39.11. This contra Gonda, who declaims that "the origin of the doctrine of the three *guṇa*s has nothing to do with Dumézil's three functions." Jan Gonda, *Triads in the Veda* (Amsterdam: North-Holland, 1976), p. 210.

11. For the identification of the elemental qualities and the social classes, see also, e.g., VS 30.5; ŚB 5.1.1.11, 5.1.5.2ff., 5.3.4.27–28, 13.1.5.3, 13.1.9.1–2, 13.4.4.1; and TB 3.8.5.1. Jan Gonda's study *Notes on Brahman* (Utrecht: J. L. Beyers, 1950) remains the only work that wholly concentrates on any of these three neuter powers and their relation to their respective social classes.

12. For studies of these neuter powers in Vedism, see J. Manessy, *Les substantifs an –as– dans la Ṛk–Saṃhitā* (Dakar, 1961); Jan Gonda, *Ancient Indian ojas, Latin *augos and the Indo-European Nouns –es/–os* (Utrecht: Oosthoek's Uitgevers Mij., 1952); and idem, *Some Observations on the Relations between "Gods" and "Powers" in the Veda à propos of the Phrase śunuh sahasā* (The Hague: Mouton, 1957). Gonda defines them as "Daseinsmächte" or "power-substances," which constitute "a sort of 'entity', 'substance', or 'potency', supposed to be present in beings, objects, or phenomena, and by virtue of which these are powerful, effective or influential" (*Some Observations*, p. 14).

13. For the Brahmin or the *brahman* as possessing *brahmavarcasa*, VS 22.22; ŚB 1.9.3.16, 2.1.3.6, 2.3.2.13, 4.2.2.16, 13.1.5.2–3, 13.1.9.1, 13.2.6.9, 13.3.7.8; AitB 1.28; TB 1.1.2.6, 3.8.13.1, 3.8.18.5, 3.9.19.3; TS 6.2.5.2–3, 7.5.18.1; AV 15.10.8; MS 3.12.6; PB 19.17.6; BŚS 9.1-2; VādhŚS 1.1.1.4. The Brahmin class is also connected to similar powers such as *tviṣ* ("brilliance" or "luster") and *varcas* ("splendor") at TS 5.3.4.4, 4.3.9.2; ŚB 8.4.2.10, 8.5.1.11, etc.

14. For the equation of the Brahmin and *tejas*, TS 6.2.5.3; TB 2.6.1.3, 3.7.6.6, 3.12.9.1–2; ŚB 2.5.4.8, 13.2.6.9; AitB 1.28; 7.24; TĀ 6.1.3. According to Mbh 13.104.63, the *brahman* is a manifestation of *tejas*. For *tejas* in Indian literature, see J. P. Vogel, *Het Sanskrit woord tejas (= gloed, vuur) in de beteekenis van magische kracht* (Amsterdam: Mededelingen der Koninktijke Nederlandse Akademie van Wetenschappen, 1930); and Gonda, *Some Observations*, pp. 58–63. At least one text (PB 8.10.2) regards *tejas* and *brahmavarcasa* as interchangeable.

15. E.g., TS 7.3.14.1; KS 37.2; ŚB 2.1.4.10, 5.3.3.5, 8.4.2.3; JB 1.82, 1.102, 1.115, 1.140; JUB 2.9.6; AitĀ 1.1.1, 1.3.8; BĀU 4.1.2; and below, p. 32. Vāc deified as a goddess makes a person a Brahmin according to ṚV 10.125.5 (cf. 1.164.35). For the connection between the Vedas and speech, ŚB 10.1.1.8, 10.2.4.6; JUB 4.25.2; and for the *brahman* and the Vedas, see, e.g., ŚB 2.6.4.5 and below, Chapter 9, p. 288.

16. "The sacrifice is the *brahman*" or is established on or born from the *brahman* according to MS 1.22.10, 3.6.4, 4.8.2; KS 2.2, 23.2; AitB 4.11, 7.19, 7.22; ŚB 3.1.4.9,15, 3.2.2.7,9, 5.3.2.4, 14.2.1.15; PB 13.3.2; TS 5.3.4.1. For the related notion that the Vedas are equatable to the *brahman*, see, e.g., KauṣU 1.7; and for the correlation of speech (*vāc*) and sacrifice, consult G. U. Thite, *Sacrifice in the Brāhmaṇa-Texts* (Poona: University of Poona, 1975), pp. 288–290. Other Brahmin traits related to their sacrificial domain include "the drinking of soma" (*somapa*) and the "sacrificial quality" (*medha*), which is particularly strong in the priestly class.

17. "Therefore they are foremost (*mukhya*), for they were emitted from the mouth," TS 7.1.1.4–6; cf. 5.3.4.1–6; ŚB 8.1.1.4, 8.4.2.3, 13.8.4.1; TB 1.1.2.6–7. The Brahmins, as the "prior" class, are connected to the power of "generation" at JB 1.68–69.

18. E.g., ŚB 4.1.4.10; cf. 5.3.2.4.

19. BĀU 5.4; cf. ŚB 5.3.3.8, 10.6.3.1.

20. TS 7.1.1.4–6; AitB 1.28, 7.23, 8.2, 8.3, 8.4; ŚB 2.5.4.8, 2.5.2.36, 9.4.2.16; PB 14.1.5, 14.5.19, 14.7.10; JB 1.68–69; GB 2.6.7; and cf. ṚV 5.27.6, 6.8.6 (*suvīrya*).

21. ṚV 10.160.5, 10.180.3; AV 10.3.12, 11.8.20; AitB 1.28, 8.3, 8.4, 8.24; PB 14.1.5, 14.5.19, 14.7.10; TB 3.7.6.6; TĀ 6.1.3; TS 4.3.9.1, 5.3.4.2–3,6; 5.7.4.3; ŚB 8.4.2.4; BGS 2.5.20. AitB 8.2 says that *ojas* is a "form" (*rūpa*) of the *kṣatra* and the Kshatriya "is" *ojas*, the *kṣatra* and *vīrya*. According to PB 6.10.11 a Kshatriya takes possession of the

viś through employing a mantra having in it the word "*ojas*." *Ojas* and *vīrya* are similar concepts and sometimes found together, e.g., PB 22.3.3, 22.10.2. For an overview of *ojas*, consult also Gonda, *Ancient Indian ojas*, passim; and for the meaning of *ojas* in Āyurveda ("vital force"), see Jean Filliozat, *The Classical Doctrine of Indian Medicine: Its Origins and Greek Parallels*, trans. by Dev Raj Chanana (Delhi: Munshiram Manoharlal, 1964), esp. pp. 27–28, 166–68.

22. For *indriya* and the Kshatriya, AV 15.10.7,10–11; AitB 1.28, 7.23, 8.2, 8.3, 8.4; PB 14.1.5, 14.5.19, 14.7.10; TB 1.1.2.7, 2.6.1.3, 2.8.5.7; ŚB 2.5.4.8; VādhŚS 1.1.1.4. Jan Gonda, *The Dual Deities in the Religion of the Veda* (Amsterdam: North-Holland, 1974), defines this term as "a complete command of all bodily and psychical faculties" (p. 248, n. 97).

23. For *bala* as a Kshatriya power, AV 11.8.20; TS 5.7.4.3; AitB 3.41. *Bala* and *ojas* are conceptually and semantically very close. See ŚB 3.3.4.15; AitB 1.23, 2.16; GB 2.2.13; and Gonda, *Ancient Indian ojas*, p. 9.

24. E.g., AitB 3.41; TB 2.8.5.7. See also Gonda, *Some Observations*, esp. pp. 14–23. Gonda's definition of this concept is "victorious or conquering power, Ueberlegenheit, irresistibility, preponderating power, overwhelming force, that particular strength, power or ability by which its bearer can vanquish his enemies . . . *sahas* is a power-substance ('Daseinsmächt') of a more or less independent or autonomous character, which is often in the possession of gods and other powerful beings or objects; it is a potency, of which they, and even men, may dispose, enabling them to be irresistible, to conquer, to gain supremacy, to resist and sustain" (pp. 15, 18).

25. For *vayas* and the Kshatriya, TB 2.6.17.7 and ŚB 8.2.3.11 ("*vayas* is the *kṣatra*").

26. For the Kshatriya as the "eater of food," see TS 4.4.8.1; AV 15.8.1–3, 12.5.5–11; AitB 8.12; ŚB 1.3.2.12ff., 8.7.1.2, 9.4.3.5, 8.7.2.2; PB 20.12.4–5, and below, pp. 46–48. At AitB 8.7 the *kṣatra* power is juxtaposed with the "eating of food," the "sap of food" (cf. AitB 8.8), the "sap of the plants and waters," and other comparable essences.

27. All the wealth of the kingdom also ultimately belongs to the ruler. This is the reason why the Kshatriya may be connected to the (more usually Vaishya) powers of *śrīyā* or *śrī*, "wealth," e.g., AV 6.54.1; ŚB 2.1.3.5–8; TB 3.9.14.1–2.

28. AitB 7.23; JB 1.243, 1.272; ŚB 2.1.3.5–8, 14.4.2.23ff.; TB 2.6.19.1–2; BĀU 1.4.11. For the somewhat unusual notion that it is the Brahmin who is so endowed with *yaśas* or "fame," see ŚB 11.5.7.1; and ŚB 4.2.4.9 ("Brahmins . . . take unto themselves (*ātmandadhate*) that *yaśas* [which is soma] when they drink [the soma juice]. He who drinks knowing this becomes famous"). The reason for this particular homology may very well be that "Soma" is also regarded as a "king." For the Vaishya's connection to "fame," TB 3.8.7.2; and below, Chapter 3, p. 64.

29. The Kshatriya also is sometimes related to the control of livestock (GB 2.6.7; cf. AitB 6.15; and esp. JB 1.350, where the Kshatriya is the giver of cattle while the Vaishya is the possessor of livestock). Several texts may be cited in which a whole list of essential powers are attributed to the Kshatriya, e.g., AV 12.5.5–11 (where in addition to *kṣatra* are listed the warrior-ruler capabilities of *ojas*, *sahas*, *bala*, *vīrya*, *indriya*, *śrī*, *rāṣṭra*, *annādya*, among others); AitB 7.23 (*indriya*, *vīrya*, *āyus* ("long life," cf. AitB 7.23), *rājya*, *yaśas*, and *kīrti*), cf. TS 4.4.8.1. See also the texts at TB 2.6.5.3–6 and AitB 8.12, where the various parts of the king's body are correlated to such powers.

30. E.g., TS 6.2.5.3; TB 2.7.2.1–2, 3.7.6.6; AitĀ 1.1.1; VādhŚS 1.1.1.4. At JB 1.243 the *viś* is equated to *puṣṭi* and *rayi* ("wealth"). See also TĀ 6.1.3, where the *viś* is equated with *śrī* or "wealth" and also, rather anomalously, with the Kshatriya essential power of *bala* or physical power.

31. Texts which assimilate the Vaishya or *viś* and *ūrj* (and, in this case, also food) include TB 2.7.2.2.

32. ŚB 2.1.3.5–8; TB 1.1.2.7–8; AitB 1.28; BŚS 9.1–2; BhŚS 11.3.10–4.14; ĀpŚS 15.1.1–3.16; HŚS 24.1.19–22; VaikhŚS 13.5–6; JB 1.350. According to ŚB 3.1.4.9, animals are *puṣṭi*, while MS 2.5.1 connects animals to *ūrj*.

33. TS 3.5.7.1–3; ŚB 2.1.3.8, 3.9.1.16, 4.2.1.12, 5.1.3.3, 6.7.3.7, 8.7.3.21; TB 2.7.2.2; PB 6.6.2ff.; and TS 7.1.1.4–6 (the Vaishya was created in order to be eaten). TB 1.7.5.2 draws, *inter alia*, equivalences between the *viś*, the waters, *ojas*, and food. For the Vaishya's somewhat rare connection to the ordinarily Kshatriya essential power of *ojas*, see also TB 2.6.19.2.

34. Which is connected to *puṣṭi* at TS 2.1.9.3. A coupling is in order to achieve *puṣṭi* and "generation" (*prajāti*) according to MS 1.6.4 and 1.6.8. *Mithuna* is elsewhere connected with offspring (*prajā*) and domestic animals (e.g. MS 1.9.6, 2.3.7; TS 6.5.11.3; KS 12.5).

35. PB 13.9.13 declares that "strength (*vāja*) is food. . . . For when there is food, cow, horse and man are strong."

36. TS 7.1.1.4–6; ŚB 3.9.1.17, 5.3.1.6, 5.5.1.10, 6.6.1.8, 9.4.3.2. See also Georges Dumézil, *Les Dieux des Indo-Européens* (Paris: Presses Universitaires de France, 1952), p. 7, for this quality ("*le nombre*") of the "third function."

37. See JB 1.69 and TS 7.1.1.4–6. The Shūdra, like the Vaishya, may also be connected to *puṣṭi* or material prosperity (BĀU 1.4.11–15; ŚB 14.4.2.23ff.) and with the deity *Pūṣan*, who is the apotheosis of this essential power, for which see below, Chapter 4, pp. 98–100. For the Shūdra (together with the woman, the dog, and the black bird) as the embodiment of "disorder" (*anṛta*), ŚB 14.1.1.31.

38. Elsewhere, the *varṇa* correlations are easily inferred, e.g., PB 9.10.7 (*tejas, indriya* and *vīrya*, and food, offspring, and animals); PB 13.4.7,18 (*brahmavarcasa, ojas, paśus*); ŚB 13.2.6.1–7 (*tejas, indriya*, and *paśus* and *śrī*); ŚB 11.4.4.1 (*tejas, yaśas*, and *śrī*); TS 7.1.8.2 (*tejas*, indriya, *annādya*); GB 2.6.7 (*brahman, vīrya*, and *paśus*). For an examination of the ways these essential powers serve as markers for the "three functions" of Dumézilian theory, see Alf Hiltebeitel, *The Ritual of Battle: Krishna in the Mahābhārata* (Ithaca, N.Y.: Cornell University Press, 1976), esp. pp. 215–22.

39. E.g., LŚS 10.13.13–15 (*brahmavarcasa, kṣatra*, and *paśus*); TB 1.1.2.6–8 (*brahmavarcasa, indriya, paśus*); TB 3.7.6.6 (*tejas, ojas*, and *puṣṭi*); AitB 1.28 (*brahmavarcasa* and *tejas* for the Brahmin; *ojas, indriya*, and *vīrya* for the Kshatriya; and for the Vaishya, *paśus*).

40. Cf. ŚB 8.4.1.3 where *Brahman*, here regarded as a deity, is declared to be the "highest among the gods"; and below, ŚB 10.3.5.10–11. Note, however, the text at JB 1.244, where it is stated that "the Brahmin obtains his position by birth, but makes this [position] more or less important by his course of life (or conduct, *caraṇa*)."

41. ŚB 3.9.1.14; cf. AV 19.22.21, where the *brahman* is said to be the chief among the powers.

42. VS 13.13; ŚB 7.4.1.14, 14.1.3.3.

43. In Vedic texts also the *brahman* qua deity is sometimes found in the role of creator, e.g., ŚB 11.2.3.1ff., and that role is more often assigned to this power/deity in the Upanishads.

44. ŚB 13.6.2.19; JB 1.86; cf. ŚB 10.2.4.6.

45. That is why when a king instructs a Brahmin it is regarded as a breach of protocol, if not of natural law itself. See ŚB 1.6.2.5; ŚānĀ 6.19; BĀU 2.1.15; 6.2.8; ChU 5.3.7; KauṣU 4.19.

46. Consult Charles Malamoud, *Le Svādhyāya: Recitation personelle du Veda* (Paris: Institut de Civilisation Indienne, 1977).

47. See Charles Malamoud, "Cruire le monde," *Puruṣartha* 1 (1975): 91–135; reprinted in the author's *Cruire le monde: Rite et pensée dans l'Inde ancienne* (Paris: Éditions la Découverte, 1989), pp. 35–70.

48. Thus the Brahmins are also connected with Agni, the god of fire, as we shall see in the next chapter. Elsewhere we learn that the Brahmin officiants at the sacrifice are called "the place of sacrifice to the gods" (*devayajana*), ŚB 3.1.1.5.

49. For other occurrences of the phrase, see ŚB 1.3.3.8, 3.1.1.5, etc.

50. ŚB 1.8.1.28. Cf. ŚB 1.5.1.12, where the Brahmins who are versed in the Veda are said to be the "guardians" (*pravitaras*) of the sacrifice who, again, spread and produce the sacrifice and therefore are to be propitiated.

51. ŚB 2.2.2.6; cf. ŚB 2.4.3.14, 4.3.4.4. Other texts that refer to the Brahmins as "gods" include AV 6.12.2, 12.2.6, 12.4.10, 19.9.12, 19.35.2; ŚB 3.3.4.20; and ChU 2.20.2.

52. ŚB 3.2.1.39–40; cf. ŚB 13.4.1.3; AitB 7.25. For the rite according to the Śrauta Sūtras, see ĀpŚS 10.11.5–15.16; VaikhŚS 12.10–12; KŚS 7.4.10–13.

53. For the Kshatriya addressed in the ritual as "Brahmin," see also TS 3.5.2.1; ŚB 4.6.6.5; BĀU 1.4.11. Cf. AitB 7.19, where the *kṣatra* power has to set aside its "weapons" and take up those of the *brahman* power when participating in the sacrifice. "Thus the *kṣatra*, having laid aside its own weapons, with the weapons of the *brahman* went to the sacrifice. Therefore now also the Kshatriya, as sacrificer, having laid aside his own weapons, with the weapons of the *brahman*, with the form of the *brahman*, becoming the *brahman*, goes to the sacrifice."

54. For the prohibition against a Kshatriya drinking the soma juice, AitB 7.29, 7.30, 8.20. At AitB 7.28, we learn that Indra, the Kshatriya deity, was deprived of Soma drinking because of the sin of Brahminicide, and thus "even today the Kshatriya is deprived of soma drinking." See also AitB 7.31 for a Kshatriya substitute that is said to be soma in a "invisible" way.

55. TB 3.7.5.9–10. Cf. ŚB 2.3.1.39 for another instance in which only Brahmins are to drink the remainder of the Agnihotra milk since it has been put on the fire (and therefore is connected to the Brahmin deity Agni?). PB 18.10.8 also excludes the Kshatriyas from the order of the Brahmins.

56. TS 7.5.18.1; TB 3.8.13.1; cf. VS 22.22 and ŚB 13.1.9.1–2; MS 3.12.6; JUB 1.1.4.2. See also ŚB 13.3.7.9 where the Kshatriya is supposed to be a good marksman (*ativyādhi*); and AitB 7.19 and ŚB 1.2.4.2, where the weapons of the Kshatriya (chariot, armor, bow and arrow, etc.) are listed.

57. Or of speech, which were also supposedly as effective as, even more effective than, the military might of the Kshatriyas. See, e.g., Manu 11.33: "He should not hesitate to deploy the revealed canonical texts of the Atharva Veda. Speech is the weapon of the Brahmin, with it a twice-born man can slay his enemies."

58. E.g., AV 12.5.5–11 and 5.18.1–4 (where stealing Brahmin's cow is said to take away the Kshatriya's *kṣatra*).

59. In addition to the examples cited below, consider the intriguing text at AitB 2.33, where instructions are given to the Brahmin priests for secretly depriving the unwitting Kshatriya sacrificer of his power and rule by means of manipulation of certain recitations. A similar passage at AitB 3.19 additionally provides the method for inciting a rebellion among the commoners against their ruler should the priests wish to do so.

60. E.g., PB 2.16.4, 11.1.2, 15.6.3; AitB 8.1, 8.4. At PB 2.8.2 and 11.11.8 such methods are used to make both the Kshatriyas and the commoners subject to the Brahmin class.

61. See Jan Gonda, "Purohita," in *Studia Indologica: Festschrift für Willibald Kirfel*, ed. by O. Spies (Bonn: Universität Bonns, 1955), pp. 107–24. For the relationship between the Indian king and the *purohita*, consult also Gonda, *Ancient Indian Kingship from the Religious Point of View* (Leiden: E. J. Brill, 1966), pp. 62–70.

62. AitB 7.26. Thus the Brahmin must be careful as to the particular Kshatriya with whom he takes employ, and vice versa: "A Brahmin should not desire to become the *purohita* of just any Kshatriya, for thereby that which is well made (*sukṛtam*) and that which is poorly made (*duṣkṛtam*) unite. Nor should a Kshatriya make just any Brahmin his *purohita*, for thereby that which is well made and that which is poorly made unite" (ŚB 4.1.4.5). For the Brahmin *purohita* as taking on the traits of the Kshatriya he serves, see, e.g. AitB 8.24. The ambivalence inherent in the relationship for the Brahmin is explored by Jan Heesterman in "Brahmin, Ritual, and Renouncer," pp. 36–38.

63. JUB 2.2.8. For other references that refer to the cooperation between the first two classes, see ŚB 1.2.3.2 and 5.4.4.5.

64. AitB 8.9; cf. ŚB 14.2.2.27. See also the pairs listed at AitB 8.27, including sky (= *purohita*) and earth (= the king) which are interpreted as male and female. Coomaraswamy remarks that "it is clear that the relationship of the Sacredotium to the Regnum, or that of Man to Woman, or that of any Director to any Executive, can be more briefly expressed as that of Sky to Earth." *Spiritual Authority and Temporal Power*, p. 49.

65. AitB 8.2. See also Manu 9.322, where it is declared that "Kshatriyas do not prosper without Brahmins, and Brahmins do not prosper without Kshatriyas; Brahmins and Kshatriyas closely united thrive here on earth and in the world beyond."

66. See especially Ananda K. Coomaraswamy, *Spiritual Authority and Temporal Power*, which is a long meditation on the significances the author finds in the passage.

67. Ibid., p. 12.

68. Cf. the claim that the *brahman* and the *kṣatra* are, together, the two "masters" of all action, and thus "whatever is done uninspired by these two is really not done at all. 'He has done nothing at all,' they say scornfully" (AitB 2.38).

69. AitB 4.27. For the concept of *āyatana* in Vedic texts, see Jan Gonda *The Meaning of the Sanskrit Term Āyatana* (Adyar: Adyar Library and Research Centre, 1969).

70. Cf. TS 1.6.16, 3.5.2.1; ŚB 4.6.6.5, 5.4.4.9–13. For the Kshatriya as "superior" (*uttara*) to his fellows, see AV 6.54.1.

71. Verse 14 of the passage declares *dharma*, the enunciation of which is also the sole prerogative of the Brahmin, as the "*kṣatra* of Kshatriya," that is, the true essence of the ruling warrior. "Thus," the text concludes, "a weak man controls a strong man by *dharma*, just as if by a king."

72. TB 2.8.8.9. Cf. AV 15.10.3; ŚB 10.4.1.9, 12.7.3.12; and Manu 9.320–21: "Kshatriyas were born from Brahmins. Fire arose from the waters, Kshatriyas from Brahmins, and iron from stone; their all-pervading brilliant energy is quenched in their own wombs."

73. ŚB 5.1.1.12. Cf. KŚS 14.1.2ff., 15.1.1–2; ĀśvŚS 9.9.19; LŚS 8.11.1ff.

74. ŚB 5.3.3.12, 5.4.2.3; AitB 7.29ff.; KU 2.9.

75. PB 18.10.8. The power of punishment and "restraint" that the Brahmins claim over the Kshatriyas even in the Veda is also justified at Manu 9.320: "If the Kshatriyas become overbearing toward the Brahmins in any way, the priests themselves should subdue them, for the Kshatriyas were born from the Brahmins." Cf. Manu 11.31–32: "A Brahmin who knows the law need not report anything to the king. By means of his own virility, he may chastise those men who have wronged him. Between his own virility and the virility of the king, his own virility is stronger; therefore a twice-born [Brahmin] may suppress his enemies by means of his own virility alone."

76. ŚB 2.4.1.10. See also KS 29.10; TS 2.5.10.1; AitB 2.33.1ff.; PB 2.8.2, 15.6.3; ŚB 6.4.4.13, 11.2.7.16; KB 16.4; etc.

77. ŚB 11.2.7.16; cf. TB 2.4.2.8 and 2.6.5.6.

78. ŚB 5.4.3.8. See also texts like BŚS 9.1–2; BhŚS 11.3.10–4.14; ĀpŚS 15.1.1–3.16; HŚS 24.1.19–22; and VaikhŚS 13.5–6, where the Kshatriya sacrificer modifies the mantras in a particular ritual to effect the desired result "by means of the *viś*."

79. ŚB 3.6.1.24, 3.9.1.18; PB 6.10.11, 18.10.9.

80. Cf. ŚB 8.7.2.3 and esp. AV 4.22.1: "Increase, o Indra, the Kshatriya for me; make this man sole chief (*ekavṛṣa*) of the *viś*."

81. For these concepts in Vedic ritualism in general, see Louis Renou and Lillian Silburn, "Nirukta and Anirukta in Vedic," in *Sarūpa-Bhāratī or the Homage of Indology: The Dr. Lakshman Sarup Memorial Volume*, ed. by J. N. Agrawal and B. D. Shastri (Hoshiarpur: Vishveshvaranand Institute Publications, 1954), pp. 68–79.

82. Gonda, *Triads in the Veda*, p. 140.

83. See also ŚB 9.4.3.10, where an oblation connected to this class is to be offered silently, "for indistinct is the *viś*."

84. See also ŚB 4.2.1.12, where the *viś* are equated with "the creatures" in general, as well as with food; and ŚB 8.7.3.21, where the *viś* are identified with the sacrifice, "for all beings are ranged (*viṣṭa*) under the sacrifice."

85. ŚB 5.3.4.15. In addition to texts cited below, see also the other ritual actions designed to obtain the same end described at ŚB 4.3.3.10, 12.7.3.12, and 13.2.2.15.

86. ŚB 9.4.3.1; cf. ŚB 9.3.1.13. Even when ritual necessities demand that a Vaishya analogue be placed "before" a Kshatriya one, a hierarchical significance can still be drawn: "And as to why it [the animal victim dedicated to Indra] comes after that [victim intended] for the Viśva Devas—Indra is the *kṣatra* and the Viśva Devas are the *viś*; he thus places the food [= the Viśva Devas = the *viś*] before him [= Indra = the Kshatriya]" (ŚB 3.9.1.16).

87. AitB 8.25; cf. AitB 1.9, 8.27; AV 7.94.1; ŚB 4.2.4.23; TS 6.1.5.3.

88. I discuss this subject at length in an article entitled "Eaters, Food, and Social Hierarchy in Ancient India: A Dietary Guide to a Revolution of Values," *Journal of the American Academy of Religion* 58, 2 (Summer, 1990): 201-29.

89. ŚB 5.3.3.12. Cf. ŚB 5.4.2.3; AitB 7.29ff.; and KauṣU 2.9.

90. Both connotations adhere to the word "*paśu*." See, e.g., ŚB 4.4.1.15–18; PB 19.16.6; AitB 1.28.

91. For Vaishyas as food, see above, n. 33. This class is also homologically assigned the time of year that is most closely associated with the fertility of the crops, the rainy season, "for the rainy season is the *viś*, and the *viś* are food" (ŚB 2.1.3.8). For Vaishyas as animals, and therefore also "food," consult ŚB 2.1.4.11ff., 4.4.1.15ff.; and AitĀ 5.3.2.

92. The Shūdras, who are created from the feet of the creator, are also food. "Therefore the Shūdra has abundant animals," that is, this *varṇa* too is "food" for others, "but is unable to sacrifice, for he has no deity emitted along with him. Therefore he does not rise above simply the washing of feet, for from the feet he was emitted" (PB 6.1.11).

93. ŚB 6.1.2.25. Cf. ŚB 3.9.1.16 and the remarkable text at PB 18.5.6 where the *viś* are said to drain out of the expelled king like the fecal matter of a man sick with diarrhea. According to AV 15.18.1–3, the Kshatriya (*rājanya*) came into being when the creator god became impassioned (*raj*) and immediately went for the Vaishyas, who were his food.

94. ŚB 1.3.2.12–15. For similar meanings extracted out of the same ritual act, consult also ŚB 1.5.2.1–2, 1.5.3.17–20, 1.8.2.17, and 1.8.3.5–6. Most of these comparable texts, interestingly enough, regard the *upabhṛt* ladle (= food) not as the Vaishyas but as the enemy or rival.

95. Thus at ŚB 13.2.6.8 the royal sacrificer performs a rite intended to supply his subjects with abundant food and make his *viś* "eaters"—if there is "food" for the subjects, there will be "food" for the king.

96. Cf. ŚB 11.2.6.14 where the sacrificer's offerings to gods are likened to the tribute brought to the king by the *viś*.

97. I owe the observation and the phrase to Norvin Hein.

98. When the Shūdras are specifically mentioned, they are inevitably described in terms of their relative baseness and condition of servitude.

99. The passage goes on to depict the Shūdra in even less flattering terms as "a servant of another, to be dismissed at will, and to be murdered at will."

3

The Origins of Class

In the Beginning

The origins of most things are shrouded in the haze of prehistory, unknowable and mysterious. The beginning of many stories cannot be discerned, at least by ordinary means. Origins occur off the historical record. Myths, however, recount what history cannot. Indeed, myths in general often enough arise precisely in those areas where other and more verifiable modes of explanation and rationality fail. Claude Lévi-Strauss wrote that "the purpose of myth is to provide a logical model capable of overcoming a contradiction" and then added parenthetically, "an impossible achievement if, as it happens, the contradiction is real."[1] People tell myths when logic is stymied, when rational methods fail to solve the conundrums of life. One of these occasions occurs when dealing with origins; a myth will be told when other means of recovering the past are either unavailable or impossible. Myths claim to remember what history has forgotten.

The control of a group's collective memory, the power to declare what happened in the past, is also, of course, a significant means of controlling the here and now. The ability to account for the past entails the power to put it into the service of the present—and into the service of those who pronounce on what has happened in the past. To paraphrase Santayana's maxim, those who cannot remember the past are doomed to repeat other people's versions of it.

If there is always power inherent in control over memory, how much more leverage is there in control over the "memory" of how things began? Herein lies some of the persuasive significance of myth. For many myths—*all* myths, according to Mircea Eliade—are about beginnings. A myth "is always an account of a 'creation'; it relates how something was produced, began to *be*."[2] And such myths of origins are obviously, if tautologically, "true." For the things these tales explain—death, sin, men and women, flora and fauna, or the cosmos in its entirety—unquestionably exist: "The cosmogonic myth is 'true' because the existence of the World is there to prove it."[3] Mythical knowledge is in this sense self-evident, and it is also efficacious. Knowing how things began is also to have power over them: "For knowing the origin of an object, an animal, a plant, and so on is equivalent to acquiring a magical power over them by which they can be controlled, multiplied, or reproduced at will."[4]

Cosmogonic myths carry considerable weight. They account for what could not otherwise be known; they relate how things were "in the beginning" and thus why they are the way they are now; and they reveal the inner essence of things and beings through telling the tale of their nativity. Furthermore, myths of origins are oftentimes also stories of the first deeds of the divine, the creation of things and beings by the gods or God. Because these things and beings are products of divine command, because their beginning derives from the very hand of God, the time of origins is also the time of perfection. Departures from the pristine conditions of the original creation can be discounted and refuted as degenerations, the manifest evidence of some kind of "fall." Cosmogonic myths comment on the present: they legitimize the present state of affairs and ensure that any challenges to the status quo be cast as deviations from the norm; or they can decry the degeneracy of the times by positing a past, and lost, ideal situation.

Vedic classification according to *varṇa*, like all other religiously oriented taxonomies, is rooted and legitimated in cosmogony. The *varṇa*s or classes that comprise Indian society, as well as realms in the natural, supernatural, and ritual worlds, were supposedly created in the beginning, often by the procreative act of the creator god. Taxonomy by *varṇa* is thus represented as aboriginal, as hard-wired into the essence of reality, as the "way things are" because they were created that way. In Vedic cosmogonic myths, the *varṇa* scheme is not just a map providing a useful interpretation of the world; *varṇa* claims to be the territory itself.

Portraying the *varṇa* system as coeval with creation was one of the primary means by which the Brahmin authors of the Veda represented their worldview as authoritative. This particular organizational modality was original and therefore "natural." Furthermore, the system was supposed to be universal. If space and time, the congregation of the gods and goddesses, the natural world, scripture and ritual, and the human body itself—if all these realms bear witness to classification according to *varṇa*, how could an organization of society along these lines be regarded as anything other than the way things should be?

In this chapter we review a set of texts in which the individual components of the cosmos are said to have been created in groups or clusters, that is, in classes or *varṇa*s. Because certain things and beings share common origins, they are, as we might be tempted to say, "symbols" of each other. The texts we analyze in this chapter present us with the ideological underpinnings for the theory of *bandhus* or connections that so pervade Vedic philosophy and ritual, a system of homologies rooted in common origins.

We also see here that the specific connections stated in the course of recounting the origins of things tend to remain remarkably fixed; certain homologies between things and beings are repeated in text after text. To gain an overview of the system as a whole and its peculiar contours, we are not overconcerned here to explicate the technical or exotic terms and concepts our cosmogonic texts trade in. It is rather the systemic consistencies, repetitions, and reiterations that I want to call attention to by means of these texts and the taxonomies they generate. Contra the received wisdom of Indology, I wish to demonstrate here that many specific *bandhus* of Vedic thought recur with great frequency in text after text. And these homologies are guided by and organized into the metacategories of the *varṇa*s.

Further, these myths of origins provide us with some indication of the scope of the *varṇa* system, its epistemological power to render the universe explicable through classifying it. We shall see that the system is both efficient and flexible. It operates well as a tripartite organizational structure, coordinating a variety of triads into a categorical nexus. But the *varṇa* scheme can also expand into a quadripartite, pentadic, or six-part classificatory whole to accommodate more and more within its fold.

In these myths of origins, the classes that make up the natural, supernatural, and ritual worlds are hierarchically ordered. In each text we will encounter, without exception, the category of things and beings that can be shown to connect to the Brahmin social class is said to have been created first. This is not, we must assume, coincidental; the authors purposefully insinuated their own class interests into the cosmogonies they invented and disseminated. They did not always clearly tip their hand, however. More often than not, the myths do not explicitly deal with the social classes at all, and when they do the social *varṇa*s are buried among the many other applications of the classificatory scheme.

The *varṇa* scheme is, as I indicated in Chapter 1, much more than a means for classifying society; its real influence cannot be fully appreciated unless all the realms in which it is applied are taken into account. In this chapter I set before the reader something of the breadth of the *varṇa* system. The point is not to confuse but to impress the reader with the grandeur, persuasiveness, consistency, and elasticity of the system. In the course of the survey, however, we should not lose sight of the fact that classification according to *varṇa*, regardless of its pretensions to universality, had as its first and foremost ramification the representation of the social hierarchy as inherent in the original order of things.

Tripartite Schemes for Classifying the Universe

The cosmogonic myths I analyze here range from relatively simple and straightforward accounts that classify the universe into familiar Indo-European triads to much more complex tales in which the world is divided into four, five, or six parts. The first narrative I bring to attention is suggestive rather than paradigmatic of the type of cosmogonic myth we want to consider here. For although there is in this tale an account of the simultaneous creation of the members of multiple orders of things and beings, it is one that is incomplete even in its own terms. I have, here and below, left many technical Sanskrit terms untranslated in the interests of presenting an overview of the classification system explored in greater detail in subsequent chapters. I designate the following myth Cosmogony I.[5]

> The animals have Vāyu [the god of wind] as their leader, and Vāyu is breath; the animals are animated by means of breath. He [Vāyu] departed from the gods together with the animals. The gods prayed to him at the morning soma pressing, but he did not return. They prayed to him at the midday soma pressing, but he did not return. They prayed to him at the afternoon soma pressing. . . . If he had returned at the morning soma pressing, the animals would be among the Brahmins; for the *gāyatrī* [meter] is the morning soma pressing, and the *brahman* [power] is the *gāyatrī*. And if he had returned at the midday soma pressing, the animals would be among the Kshatriyas; for the midday soma pressing concerns Indra [the warrior king of the gods], and the *kṣatra* [power] is Indra. And since he returned at the afternoon soma pressing—the afternoon soma pressing concerns the Viśva Devas, and this all is the Viśva Devas—therefore the animals are everywhere here. (ŚB 4.4.1.15–16,18)

In this ritually oriented creation story, the animals are led away from the gods by their leader and animator Vāyu. The account of the animals' "return" to the other deities and their subsequent appearance "everywhere here" entails what might appear as a gratuitous excursus: a threefold classification scheme. First, the extracting of the juice in the soma sacrifice[6] is divided into the morning, midday, and afternoon pressings; and then within each of these three ritual times, a web of *bandhus* or connections is formulated between components of seemingly separate domains. The morning pressing (time) is equated to the Brahmins (society), the *gāyatrī* (meter), and the *brahman* power (metaphysics). The midday pressing (time) is connected to the Kshatriyas (society); but then, instead of following the order of the first series of associations (which would require at this point the appropriate meter), the text connects midday and Kshatriyas to Indra (deity) before returning to the expected order and supplying the *kṣatra* power (metaphysics). The linkages issuing from the afternoon pressing (time), when the animals are "returned," are limited to the Viśva Devas (deity). Then comes the tag line: "and this all is the Viśva Devas—therefore the animals are everywhere here."

The missing links can be identified, and the holes in the text filled, by comparing this story to other myths. Let us first identify the lacunae. The first category presented in Cosmogony I (morning = Brahmins = *gāyatrī* meter = *brahman* power) is the most complete, but it does not mention the deity belonging to the series as the other two do. The second set (midday = Kshatriyas = Indra = *kṣatra* power) omits the meter for this category necessary for full correspondance to the first set (which includes the *gāyatrī* meter in its string of homologies). The third and least filled out category (afternoon = Viśva Devas = animals) neglects the appropriate social class, meter, and metaphysical power of the chain but adds a component the other two have left out: an ontological class (the animals) connected to the other elements of the series.

We may begin to fill in the gaps within each set of associations, and add other components, by turning to the following text, which I will refer to as Cosmogony II:

> Prajāpati generated this [world by saying] "*bhūḥ*," the atmosphere [by saying] "*bhuvaḥ*," and the sky [by saying] "*svaḥ*." As much as these worlds are, so much is this all. . . . Prajāpati generated the *brahman* [by saying] "*bhūḥ*," the *kṣatra* [by saying] "*bhuvaḥ*," and the *viś* [by saying] "*svaḥ*." As much as the *brahman*, *kṣatra*, and *viś* are, so much is this all. . . . Prajāpati generated the Self (*ātman*) [by saying] "*bhūḥ*," the human race [by saying] "*bhuvaḥ*," and the animals [by saying] "*svaḥ*." As much as these Self, human race, and animals are, so much is this all. (ŚB 2.1.4.11-13)

The categories in Cosmogony II are generated from the creator god's ejaculation of three sacred utterances, known in Vedic ritualism as the *vyāhṛtis*. *Bhūḥ*, *bhuvaḥ*, and *svaḥ* are also the Sanskrit terms for the three cosmological worlds (earth, atmosphere, and sky), as indeed the text itself states. From these three sacred utterances—which simultaneously produce the three worlds—also are brought forth three different metaphysical powers and three different classes of beings. In sum, the paralleling chains of Cosmogony II run as follows:

1. *bhūḥ* = this world (cosmology) = the *brahman* power (metaphysics) = the Self (ontology)
2. *bhuvaḥ* = atmosphere (cosmology) = the *kṣatra* power (metaphysics) = humans (ontology)
3. *svaḥ* = sky (cosmology) = the power of the *viś* (metaphysics) = animals (ontology)

When we compare these categories of Cosmogony II to those established in Cosmogony I, we may supply some data missing from the first narrative. To the third and least complete category of Cosmogony I—afternoon (time) = Viśva Devas (deities) = animals (ontology)—we may now insert "the power of the *viś*" from Cosmogony II to complement the other metaphyical powers already supplied in the first two categories of Cosmogony I (*brahman* and *kṣatra*) and reiterated in the categories of Cosmogony II. And since in the Vedic texts "*viś*," in addition to being a kind of metaphysical power or force, is also synonymous with the Vaishya social class, we may add the Vaishyas to the third category of Cosmogony I to parallel the Brahmins and Kshatriyas of the first two orders. Finally, to the first two categories of Cosmogony I—which lack classes of beings paralleling the animals of the third category in that text—we may now add from Cosmogony II the ontological classes of the cosmic Self and the human race respectively.

The three orders of Cosmogony I, with the additions from Cosmogony II filling in some, but not all, of the lacunae, now appear thus:

1. morning (time) = Brahmins (society) = *x* (deity) = *gāyatrī* (meter) = *brahman* (metaphysics) = the Self (ontology)
2. midday (time) = Kshatriyas (society) = Indra (deity) = *x* (meter) = *kṣatra* (metaphysics) = humans (ontology)

3. afternoon (time) = Vaishyas (society) = Viśva Devas (deity) = *x* (meter) = *viś* (metaphysics) = animals (ontology)

And from the lists of Cosmogony II we may append classes of sacred utterances, scripture, and cosmological worlds to each of the three categories: (1) *bhūḥ* = this world; (2) *bhuvaḥ* = atmosphere; (3) *svaḥ* = sky.

As we learn from another text, Cosmogony III, the three sacred utterances or *vyāhṛtis* (the generative components of Cosmogony II) are also the verbal essences of the three Vedas—the Ṛg, Yajur, and Sāma Vedas respectively. This is, however, only one among several new connections the text makes:

> In the beginning, Prajāpati was the only one here. He desired, "May I be, may I reproduce." He toiled. He heated up ascetic heat. From him, from that one who had toiled and heated up, the three worlds—earth, atmosphere, and sky—were emitted. He heated up these three worlds. From those heated [worlds], three lights (*jyotis*) were born: Agni the fire, he who purifies here [Vāyu the wind], and Sūrya the sun. He heated up these three lights. From those heated [lights], three Vedas were born: from Agni, the Ṛg Veda; from Vāyu, the Yajur Veda; and from Sūrya, the Sāma Veda. He heated up those three Vedas. From those heated [Vedas], three essences (*śukras*) were born: *bhūḥ* from the Ṛg Veda, *bhuvaḥ* from the Yajur Veda, and *svaḥ* from the Sāma Veda. With the Ṛg Veda, they performed [the ritual action which] concerns the *hotṛ* priest; with the Yajur Veda, that which concerns the *adhvaryu* priest; and with the Sāma Veda, that which concerns the *udgātṛ* priest (ŚB 11.5.8.1–4).

In analyzing this cosmogony, which has many variants in the Veda,[7] one might note that one of the still unoccupied slots from the strings presented in Cosmogony I can now be filled. The deity for the first category is here declared to be Agni, while two other gods (Vāyu and Sūrya) for the other two categories are in Cosmogony III inserted in place of Indra and the Viśva Devas in Cosmogonies I and II. While the respective cosmological worlds for each of the three categories are reiterated here, we are also presented with new components: three kinds of "light," which are no different from the three deities listed; three types of scripture, which are subsequently condensed into the three sacred utterances; and three priestly offices. A close variant of Cosmogony III goes on to add the three principal sacrificial fires to the structure in the course of explicating the rules for ritual reparation of error:

Variant of Cosmogony III

> The gods said to Prajāpati, "If there should be a calamity in our sacrifice due to the Ṛg Veda, or due to the Yajur Veda, or due to the Sāma Veda, or due to unknown causes, or a total miscarriage, what is the reparation?" Prajāpati said to the gods, "If there is a calamity in your sacrifice due to the Ṛg Veda, offer in the *gārhapatya* fire saying '*bhūḥ*'; if due to the Yajur Veda, in the *āgnīdhrīya* fire [in soma sacrifices] or, in the case of *havis* sacrifices, in the *anvāhāryapacana* fire saying '*bhuvaḥ*'; if due to the Sāma Veda, in the *āhavanīya* fire saying '*svaḥ*'; (and) if due to unknown causes or a total miscarriage,

offer only in the *āhavanīya* fire saying all consecutively—'*bhūḥ*,' '*bhuvaḥ*,' '*svaḥ*.' " (AitB 5.32; cf. JB 1.358; MŚS 8.6.7)

Most of the classificatory themes stated in Cosmogony III are restated and then further expanded to envelop yet more within the fold in the next text we consider, Cosmogony IV. We observed earlier a threefold division in the realm of metaphysics. The powers of the *brahman*, *kṣatra*, and *viś* we labeled the "elemental qualities" of the *varṇa* scheme in its metaphysical application. In Cosmogony IV we encounter a set of subtypes for these elemental powers, the "essential powers." The text posits the essential powers of "splendor," "greatness," and "fame"—transformations of the elemental qualities of *brahman*, *kṣatra*, and the power of the *viś*—as the primary categories under which the principal components of the cosmological, theological, and scriptural realms are located. This cosmogony also draws homologies between them and three faculties of the human body, correlating speech with the first (Brahmin) chain, breath with the second (Kshatriya) set of homologies, and sight with the third (Vaishya) group of linkages.

Cosmogony IV

This world is splendor (*bharga*), the atmospheric world is greatness (*mahas*), the sky is fame (*yaśas*), and what other worlds there are, that is everything (*sarva*). Agni is splendor, Vāyu is greatness, Āditya is fame, and what other gods there are, that is everything. The Ṛg Veda is splendor, the Yajur Veda is greatness, the Sāma Veda is fame, and what other Vedas there are, that is everything. Speech is splendor, breath [or inhalation] is greatness, sight is fame, and what other breaths there are, that is everything. One should know this: "I have put into myself all the worlds, and into all the worlds I have put my self. I have put into myself all the gods etc., all the Vedas etc., all the breaths etc." Eternal are the worlds, the gods, the Vedas, the breaths, and eternal is the all. He who knows this crosses over from the eternal to the eternal; he conquers repeated death; he attains fullness of life. (ŚB 12.3.4.7–11)

While Cosmogonies III (and its variant) and IV expand the lists given in Cosmogony II, which is itself an amplification of Cosmogony I, the taxonomy we began with is still incomplete. The remaining missing links of our Cosmogony I (the meters for categories 2 and 3) are easily supplied by yet other cosmogonies of this type which will also, as we now can expect, add further links to each of the chains. Before we turn our attention to these other cosmogonies, we might pause to summarize a few salient points about the categorizations presented so far.

We have, in these texts, already covered a lot of classificatory ground. The *varṇa* system is here displayed as capable of categorizing elements from a variety of different domains: the realms of space and time; the gods and natural elements; the meters in which Vedic texts were composed and the Vedas into which such texts were compiled; the priests, fires, and ritual utterances of the sacrificial ritual; the metaphysical powers supposed to underlie the universe and the ontological classes of beings—not to mention the social realm which is also classified according *varṇa*. The scheme is thus presented as universal in scope; it includes but is not at all limited by the social realm.

In all four cosmogonies we have hierarchical tripartite schemes corresponding to the three "twice-born" or Āryan social classes of ancient Indian (and Indo-European) ideology (Brahmin priests, Kshatriya warriors and rulers, and Vaishya commoners). These social groupings are sometimes represented by the neuter metaphysical powers I call "elemental qualities" that underlie and are made manifest in the social classes (as well as other entities in the universe): the powers of *brahman*, *kṣatra*, and *viś*. As we shall see, other cosmogonies further expand the classification system into a fourfold typology to accommodate the Shūdra underclass and to generate a series of associations in other realms connected to the lowest of the social groups.

We have also observed thus far that parallel hierarchical orders, including the ontological, metaphysical, supernatural, temporal, spatial, and various religious and ritual orders, are intertwined with and made analogous to the social hierarchy. Under this scheme, to isolate only the ontological analogues, the Brahmins are connected to the Self, the all-encompassing ontological entity. The second-placed Kshatriyas are associated with the second-placed ontological class, the human race, of which, as rulers and warriors, the Kshatriyas are supposedly masters. The animals as a group are connected to the Vaishyas among the social classes, a perfectly consistent move in light of the fact that the Vaishyas are (or should be) herdsmen and, more generally, the element in society responsible for material prosperity and natural fecundity.

Quadripartite Schemes for Classifying the Universe

Cosmogony II suggests that the Vaishyas are "animals" in relation to the Kshatriya class (connected in that myth to the human race), the food and prey of their superiors. This theme is picked up and clarified in the following narrative, Cosmogony V, which also provides the hitherto missing elements for Cosmogony I and extends the categorical framework even further by adding new classes to a now four-part structure:

Cosmogony V

> [Prajāpati] desired, 'May I emit the sacrifice.' From his mouth he emitted the nine-versed (*trivṛt*) hymn of praise (*stoma*); along with it he emitted the *gāyatrī* among the meters, Agni among the gods, the Brahmin among men, spring among the seasons. Therefore among the hymns of praise the nine-versed is the mouth [or the first, the chief one], among the meters the *gāyatrī*, among the gods Agni, among men the Brahmin, among the seasons the spring. Therefore the Brahmin makes himself strong (*vīrya*) with his mouth, for from the mouth was he emitted. He makes himself strong with his mouth who knows this. He emitted from his chest, from his arms, the fifteen-versed (*pañcadaśa*) hymn of praise; along with it he emitted the *triṣṭubh* among the meters, Indra among the

> gods, the Kshatriya among men, the hot season among the seasons. Therefore the hymn of praise of a Kshatriya is the fifteen-versed, the meter the *triṣṭubh*, the god is Indra, the season is the summer. Therefore his strength is his arms, for he was emitted from the arms. He makes himself strong with his arms who knows this. He emitted from his middle, from his penis, the seventeen-versed (*saptadaśa*) hymn of praise; along with it he emitted the *jagatī* among the meters, the Viśva Devas among the gods, the Vaishya among men, the rainy season among the seasons. Therefore the Vaishya, although devoured [by the others] does not decrease, for he was emitted from the penis. Therefore he has abundant animals, for the Viśva Devas are his gods, the *jagatī* his meter, the rainy season his season. Therefore he is the food of the Brahmin and the Kshatriya, for he was emitted below [them]. From his feet, from his firm foundation, he emitted the twenty-one-versed (*ekaviṃśa*) hymn of praise; along with it he emitted the *anuṣṭubh* among the meters, not a single one among the gods, the Shūdra among men. Therefore the Shūdra has abundant animals but is unable to sacrifice, for he has no deity which was emitted along with him. Therefore he does not rise above simply the washing of feet, for from the feet he was emitted. Therefore the twenty-one-versed among the hymns of praise is a firm foundation, for it was emitted from the firm foundation. (PB 6.1.6–11).

We may first observe that this text does indeed plug the few remaining holes left in Cosmogony I. The meters for categories 2 and 3 left unstated in Cosmogony I are supplied. Corresponding to the *gāyatrī* for category 1, we are now informed that the *triṣṭubh* and *jagatī* are those for categories 2 and 3 respectively. The deity for category 1 is here declared to be Agni, as in Cosmogony III, and, as in Cosmogony I, Indra and the Viśva Devas are the gods for categories 2 and 3. The reconstructed structure incompletely presented in the text of Cosmogony I may now be fully charted in the following manner:

> 1. morning (time) = Brahmins (society) = Agni (deity) = *gāyatrī* (meter) = *brahman* (metaphysics) = the Self (ontology)
> 2. midday (time) = Kshatriyas (society) = Indra (deity) = *triṣṭubh* (meter) = *kṣatra* (metaphysics) = humans (ontology)
> 3. afternoon (time) = Vaishyas (society) = Viśva Devas (deity) = *jagatī* (meter) = *viś* (metaphysics) = animals (ontology)

With these additions, moreover, the tripartite connections of Cosmogonies I–IV now can be charted in their completeness, as I have done in Table 3.1.

We are also further enlightened in Cosmogony V as to the connection already established in Cosmogonies I and II between the Vaishya social class and the animals as an ontological class. The Vaishya, being "emitted from the penis" of the Cosmic Man, "has abundant animals," that is, he is rich in food and the proprietor of the means for its (re)production. But the Vaishya is also himself "the food of the Brahmin and the Kshatriya." Due to his reproductive origins and capacities, however, the Vaishya is "food" which is self-replenishing: "Therefore the Vaishya, although devoured (by the others) does not decrease, for he was emitted from the penis." The connection between the Vaishya and the animals is thus explicated—as it is reiterated and reinforced—by the connection between

TABLE 3.1. The Tripartite Scheme According to Cosmogonies I–IV

Social class	Brahmin	Kshatriya	Vaishya
Elemental quality	*brahman*	*kṣatra*	*viś*
Essential Power	splendor	greatness	fame
Ontological entity	Self	humans	animals
Deity	Agni	Indra/Vāyu	Sūrya/Āditya/Viśva Devas
Cosmological world	earth	atmosphere	sky
Natural element	fire	wind	sun
Part of day	morning	midday	afternoon
Body function	speech	breath	sight
Veda	Ṛg	Yajur	Sāma
Utterance	*bhūḥ*	*bhuvaḥ*	*svaḥ*
Meter	*gāyatrī*	*triṣṭubh*	*jagatī*
Priest	*hotṛ*	*adhvaryu*	*udgātṛ*
Sacrificial fire	*gārhapatya*	*āgnīdhrīya/ anvāhāryapacana*	*āhavanīya*

the Vaishya and food. The Vaishya is to the higher two social classes as animals are to humans and the Self: the lower is "eaten up" by the higher.

The fourth category added by this text, including within it the Shūdra social class, is also defined in part by its close association with the animals, with productivity, and with "food" in both the sense of making it and being it. The difference, however, between the Shūdra and the Vaishya, both of whom have (and are) "abundant animals," is also clarified: "The Shūdra has abundant animals but is unable to sacrifice, for he has no deity which was emitted along with him."

Furthermore, in Cosmogony IV, the Shūdra is not associated with any season and therefore may also on this score be excluded from sacrifice.[8] In this case then, as opposed to others we have encountered, the omission of links on the chain of associations is intentional and indeed the rationale for excluding one social class from participation in the all-important Vedic sacrifice. As we learn elsewhere, only Brahmins, Kshatriyas, and Vaishyas are "able to sacrifice" (*yājñiya*), and one who is consecrated for his role as a sacrificer "should not commune with everyone. [For] the consecrated one draws near to the gods; he becomes one of the gods. The gods do not commune with everyone, but only with a Brahmin, Kshatriya, or Vaishya, for only these are fit for the sacrifice."[9]

New components are also added in Cosmogony V to the series of connections already established in other texts and, in some cases, reduplicated here. The additions include what is in this text the first components of the series, those from which others in the chain of resemblances are generated—the parts of the anthropomorphically conceived divine anatomy (mouth, chest and arms, middle and penis, feet and "firm foundation" for the four categories). This cosmogonic hypothesis is also the premise of the famous Ṛg Veda hymn of the creation of the universe from the dismemberment of the Primal Man, the *puruṣa*: "When they divided the Man, into how many parts did they apportion him? What do they call his mouth, his two arms and thighs and feet? His mouth became the Brahmin; his arms were made into the Kshatriya; his thighs the Vaishya; and from his feet the Shūdras were born" (Ṛ̣V 10.90.11–12).

New also in Cosmogony V are the different *stomas* (hymns of praise) and seasons that find their place within the larger order of things. We are also told here that each of the three social *varṇas* derives a certain "strength" (or "virility," *vīrya*) from the particular part of the deity's body from which each was created. The Brahmin "makes himself strong with his mouth, for from the mouth was he emitted"; and, indeed, the ideal occupation of the Brahmin social class, according to Vedic as well as post-Vedic texts, is the priesthood (which demands much use of the mouth to recite the well-known mantras at the appropriate time and in the appropriate manner within the ritual; and to eat of the gifts and sacrificial portions designated for these "human gods"). The Kshatriya or warrior finds his strength in his arms; the Vaishya, the productive agriculturalist and pastoralist, being emitted from the divine penis is, as we have seen, said to be infinitely replenishing, "abundant" in animals, and "food" for the higher two classes.

The complexities of classification according to *varṇa* are further compounded in other texts, even while certain connections and homologies are yet again restated. In the next two myths, as in Cosmogony V, the universe is the fourfold product of the creator god's "emission" or "measuring out" from his four body parts. Many of the particular classes of things and beings linked together in each of the four categories are familiar to us by now. There are, however, still more elements infused into the structure in these narratives. Among other distinctions made in the texts to be considered, what has up until now in our survey remained the general class of "the animals" (*paśus*) is here subdivided into the particular species associated with one or another of the *varṇas*. We now turn to the text I designate Cosmogony VI:

> Prajāpati, in the beginning, was this [all]. . . . He desired, "May I become many; may I reproduce myself; may I become a multitude." He emitted from his head, from his mouth, the nine-versed hymn of praise, the *gāyatrī* meter, the *rathantara* chant (*sāman*), Agni among the gods, the Brahmin among men, the goat among the animals. Therefore the Brahmin meter is the *gāyatrī* and the divinity is related to Agni. Therefore the mouth is generation, for from the mouth he [Prajāpati] emitted him [the Brahmin]. He desired, "May I propagate myself further." He emitted from his arms, from his chest, the fifteen-versed hymn of praise, the *triṣṭubh* meter, the *bṛhat* chant, Indra among the gods, the Kshatriya among men, the horse among animals. Therefore the Kshatriya meter is the *triṣṭubh* and the divinity is related to Indra. Therefore he [Prajāpati] made from his arms virility (*vīrya*), for he emitted him [the Kshatriya] from the arms, the chest, the virility. He desired, 'May I propagate myself further.' He emitted from his belly, from his middle, the seventeen-versed hymn of praise, the *jagatī* meter, the *vāmadevya* chant, the Viśva Devas among the gods, the Vaishya among men, the cow among animals. Therefore the Vaishya meter is the *jagatī* and the divinity is related to the Viśva Devas. Therefore [the Vaishya is] procreative, for from his [Prajāpati's] belly, from his penis he emitted him. He desired, 'May I propagate myself further.' He emitted from his feet, from

> his firm foundation, the twenty-one-versed hymn of praise, the *anuṣṭubh* meter, the *yajñāyajñiya* chant, not a single one among the gods, the Shūdra among men, the sheep among animals. Therefore the Shūdra meter is the *anuṣṭubh* and the divinity is related to the Lord of the House (*veśmapati*). Therefore he [the Shūdra] seeks to make a living washing feet, for from the feet, from the firm foundation, he [Prajāpati] emitted him. With these emitted ones Prajāpati emitted the creatures. (JB 1.68–69)

The very close variant of this myth I label Cosmogony VII:

> Prajāpati desired, "May I produce offspring." He measured out from his mouth the nine-versed hymn of praise; along with it he emitted Agni among the gods, the *gāyatrī* among the meters, the *rathantara* chant, the Brahmin among men, the goat among the animals. Therefore they are foremost (or "belonging to the mouth," *mukhya*), for they were emitted from the mouth. From the chest, from the arms, he measured out the fifteen-versed hymn of praise; along with it he emitted Indra among the gods, the *triṣṭubh* meter, the *bṛhat* chant, the Kshatriya among men, the sheep among the animals. Therefore they are filled with virility, for they were emitted from virility. From the belly he measured out the seventeen-versed hymn of praise; along with it he emitted the Viśva Devas among the gods, the *jagatī* meter, the *vairūpa* chant, the Vaishya among men, the cow among the *paśus*. Therefore they are to be eaten, for they were emitted from the receptacle of food. Therefore they are more abundant than others, for they were emitted along with the most abundant among the gods. From the feet he measured out the twenty-one-versed hymn of praise; along with it he emitted the *anuṣṭubh* meter, the *vairāja* chant, the Shūdra among men, the horse among the animals. Therefore these two, the horse and the Shūdra, are dependent on those who were already created. Therefore the Shūdra is unfit for the sacrifice, for he was emitted along with no gods. Therefore they depend on the feet, for they were emitted from the feet. (TS 7.1.1.4–6)

In addition to the insertion of particular *sāmans* (chants) into each of the four categories (with some variations between the two myths), we see here the specification of four animals or *paśus*, each belonging to a string of associations with other classes of things. Cosmogony VI is, as we shall see in Chapter 8, the more standard and paradigmatic: together with the Brahmin social class and others is found the goat; the Kshatriya animal is the horse; that of the Vaishya the cow; and the sheep is assigned to the Shūdra *varṇa*. Cosmogony VII has inverted the animals belonging to the Kshatriya and the Shūdra, claiming that the horse and the Shūdra are "dependent on those already created."[10]

Despite certain divergencies in Cosmogony VII, several general points emerge when it is taken together with Cosmogony VI. First, the animals categorized among the other classes in the four chains are four of the five *paśus* in the more limited sense of "sacrificial victims," and each is associated with one or another of the four social classes. The fifth victim, the human being or *puruṣa*, is omitted, perhaps with the implicit understanding that it belongs to no particular social class but rather to the creator god himself.[11]

Second, in the course of generating their own set of connections, these two cosmogonic myths specify certain qualities or characteristics at the end of each chain. We are in this way again informed as to what the systematizers thought were the attending dominant qualities or characteristics of the four *varṇa*s generally and, more specifically, of the four social classes enumerated. Thus, in Cosmogony VI, the Brahmin category that sprang forth from the mouth of Prajāpati is characterized by "generation," the Brahmin entities being the first created and therefore not only "foremost" but also primary (and the others are secondary, tertiary, etc.). The Kshatriya is infused with "virility" owing to its origins from the arms and chest; the Vaishya, born of the belly and penis, by "procreation"; and the Shūdra, although it is not stated explicitly, is obviously characterized by service. A complementary view is provided by Cosmogony VII, where the Brahmin category is glossed as "foremost"; the members of the Kshatriya chain are "filled with virility"; those of the Vaishya *varṇa* are both "food" ("they are to be eaten, for they were emitted from the receptacle of food") and the source of its reproduction ("they are more abundant than others, for they were emitted along with the most abundant among the gods"); and the Shūdra category is characterized only by "dependence." These occupational, or even socio-ontological, traits of the four social classes in Cosmogonies VI and VII we already encountered in Cosmogony III, and they are strengthened and further delineated here. The four-part classification system exemplified by Cosmogonies V–VII is summarized in Table 3.2.

Pentadic Schemes for Classifying the Universe

The reader will, I hope, indulge me by enduring yet more cosmogonic myths that demonstrate the classificatory reach and consistencies of the *varṇa* system. In the following texts, which I call Cosmogonies VIII–XI, the taxonomical structure is extended further even as certain homologies are, once again, restated.[12] Just as the tripartite structure of Cosmogonies I–IV was expanded into a quadripartite system in Cosmogonies V–VII, so too is the fourfold taxonomy capable of elasticity, stretching out into a fivefold order of things in Cosmogonies VIII–XI.

As we shall see, the first three chains of associations retain the familiar pattern

TABLE 3.2. The Quadripartite Scheme According to Cosmogonies V–VII

Social class	Brahmin	Kshatriya	Vaishya	Shūdra
Socio-ontological quality	generation/ primacy	virility	procreation/ nutrition/ reproduction	service
Animal	goat	horse/sheep	cow	sheep/horse
Deity	Agni	Indra	Viśva Devas	no deity
Season	spring	summer	rainy	no season
Body part	mouth/head	chest/arms	belly/penis	feet
Meter	*gāyatrī*	*triṣṭubh*	*jagatī*	*anuṣṭubh*
Chant	*rathantara*	*bṛhat*	*vāmadevya*/ *vairūpa*	*yajñāyajñiya*/ *vairāja*
Hymn of praise	9-versed	15-versed	17-versed	21-versed

of the tripartite *varṇa* system in all expansions: chain number one is clearly connected to the Brahmin social class; chain two to the Kshatriyas; and chain three to the Vaishyas or commoners. When the triadic structure is enlarged into a quadripartite one, the fourth chain encompasses the Shūdra social class and correlative components from other realms. And when a quadripartite taxonomy becomes a pentadic one, the fifth chain functions as a kind of summation of the previous four set of linkages in the structure.

The text we use for Cosmogony VIII has many versions, taken as it is from a rite of the Rājasūya in which the king "ascends" and thereby "conquers" the cardinal directions.[13] The first notable item, then, is that this text adds an important component our Cosmogonies I–VII have not yet taken into account. Cosmogony VIII includes within its sets of linkages the five regions (the four cardinal directions plus the zenith).

Cosmogony VIII

> He then makes him ascend to the regions [with the following mantras from VS 10.10–14]: "Ascend to the East! May the *gāyatrī* [meter] impel you, the *rathantara* chant, the nine-versed hymn of praise, [Agni the deity,] the spring season, the *brahman* power (*draviṇa*). Ascend to the south! May the *triṣṭubh* [meter] impel you, the *bṛhat* chant, the fifteen-versed hymn of praise, [Indra the deity,] the summer season, the *kṣatra* power. Ascend to the west! May the *jagatī* [meter] impel you, the *vairūpa* chant, the seventeen-versed hymn of praise, [the Maruts the deity,] the rainy season, the power of the *viś*. Ascend to the north! May the *anuṣṭubh* [meter] impel you, the *vairāja* chant, the twenty-one-versed hymn of praise, [Mitra and Varuṇa the deity,] the autumn season, fruit [*phala*, variants read *puṣṭa* or *bala*] the power. Ascend to the zenith! May the *paṅkti* [meter] impel you, the *śakvara* and *raivata* chants, the twenty-seven- and thirty-three-versed hymns of praise, the winter and cool seasons, [Bṛhaspati the deity,] splendor [*varcas*, variants read *phala*] the power.[14]

The five chains of the text, generated from the four cardinal directions and the zenith, include meters, hymns of praise, chants, deities, and seasons for each category. Moreover, the final component of each string of associations is a metaphysical power, the first three of which act as obvious *varṇa* markers. Cosmogony VIII may be diagramed in the following fashion:

1. east = *gāyatrī* meter = nine-versed hymn of praise = *rathantara* chant = Agni = spring = the *brahman*
2. south = *triṣṭubh* meter = fifteen-versed hymn of praise = *bṛhat* chant = Indra = summer = the *kṣatra*
3. west = *jagatī* meter = seventeen-versed hymn of praise = *vairūpa* chant = Maruts = rainy season = the *viś*
4. north = *anuṣṭubh* meter = twenty-one-versed hymn of praise = *vairāja* chant = Mitra–Varuṇa = autumn = fruit (*phala*)/*bala* (physical strength)/*puṣṭa* (material prosperity)
5. zenith = *paṅkti* meter = twenty-seven- and thirty-three-versed hymn of

praise = *śakvara* and *raivata* chants = Bṛhaspati = winter and cool seasons = splendor (*varcas*)/fruit (*phala*)

It is apparent that many components—meters, hymns of praise, and chants—of the first four chains are consistent with those we have repeatedly observed in tripartite and quadripartite cosmogonies treated previously. A consistent pattern of identifications again emerges between the three highest social classes (represented here by the elemental qualities of *brahman, kṣatra* or *viś*) and their respective deities, meters, seasons, chants, and so on. Moreover, in Cosmogony VIII the fourth chain, left somewhat incomplete in quadripartite schemes examined earlier, has been filled out by the inclusion of a deity (Mitra and Varuṇa) and a season (autumn). And the major innovation here, of course, is the addition of a fifth category with its own set of components from the cardinal directions, meters, hymns of praise, chants, gods, seasons, and metaphysical powers.

The next texts we consider, Cosmogonies IX–XI, are drawn from the rites and mantras employed in the laying down of certain bricks at the Agnicayana ritual.[15] Many of the taxons found in the pentadic schemes that emerge from these texts are familiar from Cosmogony VIII, and some new ones are added. What is also noteworthy is what is not present in Cosmogonies IX–XI. For there is in none of the following three texts any explicit *varṇa* marker for the five chains (either by means of the specification of a social class or an elemental quality).

I begin with Cosmogony IX:

> This one [I put] to the east, [Prajāpati] the existent one. His breath [is born] from the existent one. From the breath [is born] spring; from spring [comes] the *gāyatrī* [meter]. From the *gāyatrī* [is born] the *gāyatra* [chant]; from the *gāyatra* [comes] the *upāṃśu* [soma cup]. From the *upāṃśu* [is born] the nine-versed [hymn of praise]; from the nine-versed [comes] the *rathantara* [chant]. From the *rathantara* [is born] the *ṛṣi* Vasiṣṭha. . . . This one [I put] to the south, [Prajāpati] the all-doer. His mind (*manas*) [is born] from the all-doer. From the mind [is born] the summer; from the summer [comes] the *triṣṭubh* [meter]. From the *triṣṭubh* [is born] the *aiḍa* [chant]; from the *aiḍa* [comes] the *antaryāma* [soma cup]. From the *antaryāma* [is born] the fifteen-versed [hymn of praise]; from the fifteen-versed [comes] the *bṛhat* [chant]. From the *bṛhat* [is born] the *ṛṣi* Bharadvāja. . . . This one [I put] to the west, [Prajāpati] the all-encompassing. His eye [is born] from the all-encompassing. From the eye [is born] the rainy season; from the rainy season [comes] the *jagatī* [meter]. From the *jagatī* [is born] the *ṛksāma* [chant]; from the *ṛksāma* [comes] the *śukra* [soma cup]. From the *śukra* [is born] the seventeen-versed [hymn of praise]; from the seventeen-versed [comes] the *vairūpa* [chant]. From the *vairūpa* [is born] the *ṛṣi* Viśvamitra. . . . This one [I put] to the north, [Prajāpati] the light (*suva*). His ear [is born] from the light. From the ear [is born] autumn; from autumn [comes] the *anuṣṭubh* [meter]. From the *anuṣṭubh* [is born] the *svāra* [chant]; from the *svāra* [comes] the *manthin* [soma cup]. From the *manthin* [is born] the twenty-one-versed [hymn of praise]; from the twenty-one-verse [comes] the *vairāja* [chant]. From the *vairāja* [is born] the *ṛṣi* Jamadagni. . . . This one [I put] up, [Prajāpati who is] thought. His speech [is born] from thought. From speech [is born] the winter; from the winter [comes] the *paṅkti* [meter]. From the *paṅkti*

> [is born] the conclusion of the chants (*nidhāna*); from the conclusion [comes] the *āgrayana* [soma cup]. From the *āgrayana* [is born] the twenty-seven-versed and thirty-three-versed [hymns of praise]. From the twenty-seven-versed and thirty-three-versed [are born] the *śakvara* and *raivata* [chants]; from the *śakvara* and *raivata* [comes] the *ṛṣi* Raivata Viśvakarman. (TS 4.3.2.1–3)

Here, as in Cosmogony VIII, the pentadic structure is generated from the four cardinal directions together with the zenith. Cosmogony IX repeats the taxons already encountered in Cosmogony VIII for the directions, seasons, meters, chants, and hymns of praise. It also adds new chants, five body functions connected with the head (breath, mind, eye/sight, ear/hearing, and thought and speech), five different cups used in the soma ritual, and five Vedic seers or *ṛṣis* to the classificatory structure. A variant of this text (ŚB 8.1.1–2), which we shall regard as supplementary to Cosmogony IX,[16] also correlates five natural elements (fire, wind, sun, the cardinal directions or regions, and the moon) with the five body functions (breath, mind, eye/sight, ear/hearing, and thought and speech) Cosmogony IX categorizes. The tripartite correspondence we observed in Cosmogony IV of fire, wind, and sun to the first three *varṇas* is thus here expanded, along with everything else in the classification system.

Cosmogony X reiterates some of the elements of Cosmogony VIII that Cosmogony IX ignores (i.e., deities and powers for each of the five categories), offers a rather different set of seers, and adds a new component, the "throws of the dice":[17]

> The eastern quarter, the spring season, Agni the divinity, the *brahman* the power (*draviṇa*), the *gāyatrī* the meter, the *rathantara* the chant, the nine-versed the hymn of praise, which is the track (*vartanī*) of the fifteen-versed [hymn of praise], Sanaga the seer (*ṛṣi*), the eighteen-month-old calf the vitality (*vayas*), of the throws of dice the *kṛta*, the east wind the wind. . . . The southern quarter, the summer season, Indra the divinity, the *kṣatra* the power, the *triṣṭubh* the meter, the *bṛhat* the chant, the fifteen-versed the hymn of praise, which is the track of the seventeen-fold [hymn of praise], Sanātana the seer, the two-year-old cow the vitality, of the throws of dice the *treta*, the south wind the wind. . . . The western quarter, the rainy season, the Viśva Devas the divinity, the *viś* the power, the *jagatī* the meter, the *vairūpa* the chant, the seventeen-versed the hymn of praise, which is the track of the twenty-one-versed [hymn of praise], Ahabhūna the seer, the three-year-old cow the vitality, of the throws of dice the *dvāpara*, the west wind the wind. . . . The northern quarter, the autumn season, Mitra and Varuṇa the divinities, prosperity (*puṣṭa*) the power, the *anuṣṭubh* the meter, the *vairāja* the chant, the twenty-one-versed the hymn of praise, which is the track of the twenty-seven-versed [hymn of praise], Purāṇa the seer, the four-year-old cow the vitality, among the throws of dice the *abhibhava* [variant: the *āskanda*], the north wind the wind. . . . The zenith quarter, the winter and the cool seasons, Bṛhaspati the divinity, fruit (*phala*) [variant: splendor (*varcas*)] the power, the *paṅkti* the meter, the *śakvara* and *raivata* the chants, the twenty-seven-versed the hymn of praise, which is the track of the thirty-three-versed [hymn of praise], Suparna the seer, the four-year-old bull the vitality, among

the throws of dice the *āskanda* [variant: the *abhibhū*], the wind from above the wind.[18]

Finally, consider the fivefold taxonomy nestled within the following text, Cosmogony XI, in which more instructions are given as to the mantras and meanings associated with certain bricks in the fire altar of the Agnicayana ritual:

> To the east he lays down [a brick]. . . . [He says the mantra that begins] "The Vasus are your gods and overlords," for the Vasus are indeed the gods and overlords of that region. "Agni is the repeller of arrows," for Agni, indeed, is here the repeller of arrows. "May the nine-versed hymn of praise support you on earth," for by the nine-versed hymn of praise it is indeed supported on earth. "May the *ājya* recitation (*uktha*) prop you for steadiness," for by the *ājya* recitation it is indeed propped up on earth for steadiness. "The *rathantara* chant for a firm foundation in the atmosphere," for by the *rathantara* hymn it is indeed firmly established in the atmosphere. . . . Then on the south side [he places a brick]. . . . [He says those mantras that begin] "The divine Rudras are your overlords." . . . "Indra is the repeller of shafts." . . . "The fifteen-versed hymn of praise may uphold you on earth". . . . "The *prauga* recitation may support you for steadiness's sake." . . . "The *bṛhat* chant for stability in the atmosphere." . . . Then to the west [he places a brick]. . . . [He says those mantras that begin] "The divine Ādityas are your overlords." . . . "Varuṇa is the repeller of shafts." . . . "The seventeen-versed hymn of praise may uphold you on earth." . . . "The *marutvatīya* recitation may support you for steadiness's sake." . . . "The *vairūpa* chant for stability in the atmosphere." . . . Then to the north [he places a brick]. . . . [He says those mantras that begin] "The divine Maruts are your overlords." . . . "Soma is the repeller of shafts." . . . "The twenty-one-versed hymn of praise may uphold you on earth." . . . "The *niṣkevalya* recitation may support you for steadiness's sake." . . . "The *vairāja* chant for stability in the atmosphere." . . . Then in the middle [he places a brick]. . . . [He says those mantras that begin] "The Viśva Devas are your overlords." . . . "Bṛhaspati is the repeller of shafts." . . . "The twenty-seven-versed and thirty-three-versed hymns of praise may uphold you on earth." . . . "The *vaiśvadeva* and *āgnimāruta* recitations may support you for steadiness's sake." . . . "The *śakvara* and *raivata* chants for stability in the atmosphere." (ŚB 8.6.1.5–9, with mantras from VS 15.10–14)

Here again, linkages are generated beginning with the cardinal directions; in this text, however, the "middle" or center takes the place of the zenith. Cosmogony XI has, comparatively, a rather straightforward taxonomical structure (directions = gods = hymns of praise = recitations = chants) but adds to the structures developed in other pentadically organized classifications by assigning particular Vedic recitations (*ukthas*). While specifying particular individual deities for each of the five categories (Agni, Indra, Varuṇa, Soma, and Bṛhaspati), the text also enumerates the groups of gods (the Vasus, Rudras, Ādityas, Maruts, and Viśva Devas) who are led by these five divine commanders.

An overview of Cosmogonies VIII–XI is found in Table 3.3. We may observe, first, that the structures created in the texts treated earlier are now filled out even

TABLE 3.3. The Pentadic Scheme According to Cosmogonies VIII–XI

Elemental quality	*brahman*	*kṣatra*	*viś*	*phala/bala/ puṣṭa*	*varcas/phala*
Deity	Agni/Vasus	Indra/Rudras	Maruts/Viśva Devas/ Varuṇa, Ādityas	Mitra, Varuṇa/ Soma/ Maruts	Bṛhaspati/ Viśva Devas
Direction	east	south	west	north	zenith/middle
Season	spring	summer	rainy	autumn	winter and cool
Bodily function	breath	mind	eye	ear	thought and speech
Meter	*gāyatrī*	*triṣṭubh*	*jagatī*	*anuṣṭubh*	*paṅkti*
Hymn of praise	9-versed	15-versed	17-versed	21-versed	27- and 33-versed
Chant	*rathantara/ gāyatra*	*bṛhat/aiḍa*	*vairūpa/ ṛksama*	*vairāja/svāra*	*śakvara/ raivata/* conclusion
Recitation	*ājya*	*prauga*	*marutvatīya*	*niṣkevalya*	*vaiśvadeva, āgnimāruta*
Soma cup	*upāṃśu*	*antaryāma*	*śukra*	*manthin*	*āgrāyana*
Seer	Vasiṣṭha/ Sanaga	Bharadvāja/ Sanātana	Viśvamitra/ Ahabhūna	Jamadagni/ Purāṇa/ Pratna	Raivata Viśvakar-man/ Supaṃa
Type of cow	18-month-old	2-year-old	3-year-old	4-year-old	4-year-old bull
Throw of dice	*kṛta*	*treta*	*dvāpara*	*abhibhava/ āskanda*	*āskanda/ abhibhū*

further with the addition of new components from previously uncharted arenas, and this in two ways: (1) chains that have already been established are here elongated (e.g., to the three and then four meters is added a fifth, the *paṅkti*; and to the list of deities and seasons is added both a fourth and a fifth); and (2) realms not previously classified (e.g., the spatial directions and Vedic recitations) are here included in the structure.

As a second comment, we might note that in some cases Cosmogonies VIII and IX provide some alternative views as to the *varṇa* affliations of certain taxons. Cosmogonies IX and X differ as to the Vedic seer assigned to each of the five chains. Cosmogony IX gives in addition to the usual chants for the five categories (*rathantara*, *bṛhat*, *vairūpa*, *vairāja*, and the pair *śakvara* and *raivata* as the fifth) five others (*gāyatra*, *aiḍa*, *ṛksāma*, *svāra*, and the conclusion of chants). More important in terms of our interpretations of these classificatory texts are alternatives and variants in the realms of theology and metaphysics. While the Brahmin and Kshatriya deities are consistently listed as Agni (together with Vasus, according to Cosmogony XI) and Indra (leading the Rudras), there is a fair amount of variation when it comes to the gods assigned to the third and fourth chains. And whereas the elemental quality or metaphysical power is straightforward for the first three categories—the expected powers of *brahman*, *kṣatra*, and *viś*—those for the fourth and fifth categories fluctuate between "fruit" (*phala*), "physical power" (*bala*), "prosperity" (*puṣṭa*), and "splendor" (*varcas*).

The texts here, it should be readily admitted, are not always absolutely consistent in their categorizations. Nevertheless, it can be said that the first three categories are here, no less than in tripartite and quadripartite structures, clearly identified with the three highest *varṇa*s. And, generally speaking, the fourth chain must also be read, as in the case of the quadripartite schemes examined in Cosmogonies VIII–XI, as generally "Shūdra" in orientation. Some of the taxons listed in the fourth category—the *anuṣṭubh* meter, the *vairāja* chant, and the twenty-one-versed hymn of praise—are the same in the pentadic structures as they are in quadripartite ones in which the Shūdra social class is also listed. Elemental qualities such as "prosperity" and "fruit" for the fourth chain, complementing those of *brahman*, *kṣatra*, and *viś* for the first three, can be understood in terms of the displacement of previously Vaishya qualities onto the Shūdras as they are added to the system. This could also be offered as the explanation for some of the interchangeability of the deities of the third and fourth chains in these structures: Varuṇa and the Maruts, for example, can function as either Vaishya or Shūdra gods.[19]

But what is the meaning of the fifth category in pentadic classifications? In many ways, the new series in these schemes is created as a kind of "transcendent fifth": here one finds the zenith or "the middle," the "wind from above," the conclusion or finale of the chants, "all the gods" (the Viśva Devas), and so on. It is in this category also that the systemizers placed certain concluding pairs that filled out the whole: thus, to the spring, summer, rainy season, and autumn are added both the winter and cool seasons. Similarly, to a list of chants (*rathantara*, *bṛhat*, *vairūpa*, and *vairāja*) for the first four categories are added *both* the *śakvara* and *raivata* chants for the summarizing and concluding fifth category.

What might also be intimated, however, is a suspicious resemblance this new transcending fifth class has to the nodes in the first and Brahmin class. In Cosmogony IX, we are informed that the fifth class contains within it thought and also the voice or speech (*vāc*), with which, as we have seen, the Brahmin is associated via "the mouth." In Cosmogonies VIII, X, and XI the deity of the fifth category is Bṛhaspati, the priest among the gods, elsewhere explicitly connected to the Brahmins (as we shall see in the Chapter 4). And the metaphysical power is said to be *varcas* or "splendor." Although in these texts the elemental quality of *brahman* and the essential power of *varcas* are found in separate categories, we saw in Chapter 2 that Brahmins have as their particular power or force the compound *brahmavarcasa*, "the splendor of the *brahman*." Category five in these texts is, in some respects at least, a kind of restatement of category one. First and last, alpha and omega, in these five-part schemes are arguably complementary proclamations of the primacy and transcendence of the Brahmin *varṇa*. The pentadic structure, in its own way, upholds the *varṇa* worldview no less than the triadic and quadripartite.

Six-Part Schemes for Classifying the Universe

We conclude our examination of Vedic cosmogonic taxonomies with the most elaborate instances of them, six-part structures in which many of the features we have discussed in our analyses of the tripartite, quadripartite, and pentadic schemes are reiterated.[20] Both of the texts surveyed here, Cosmogonies XII and XIII, reiterate the *varṇa*-encoded homologies that comprise the first three categories of the structure; in each case, the first three strings are clearly identifiable as Brahmin, Kshatriya, and Vaishya. The two texts differ, however, as to what classificatory strategy is set into motion for dealing with the second triad of the now six-part scheme.

We begin with Cosmogony XII:

> From the east arise Agni, the *gāyatrī* [meter], the nine-versed [hymn of praise], the *rathantara* [chant], the spring, inspiration (*prāṇa*), the constellations (*nakṣatras*), and the Vasus. . . . From the south arise Indra, the *triṣṭubh* [meter], the fifteen-versed [hymn of praise], the *bṛhat* [chant], the summer, the circulating breath (*vyāna*), the moon (*soma*), and the Rudras. . . . From the west arise the Maruts, the *jagatī* [meter], the seventeen-versed [hymn of praise], the *vairūpa* [chant], the rainy season, expiration (*apāna*), the planet Venus, and the Ādityas. . . . From the north arise the Viśva Devas, the *anuṣṭubh* [meter], the twenty-one-versed [hymn of praise], the *vairāja* [chant], autumn, the digestive breath (*samāna*), and Varuṇa and the Sādhyas. . . . From the zenith arise Mitra and Varuṇa. the *paṅkti* [meter], the twenty-seven- and thirty-three-versed [hymns of praise], the *śakvara* and *raivata* [chants], the winter and cool seasons, the upward breath (*udāna*), the Angirases, and the moon. . . . From the nadir arise the planet Saturn, eclipses, comets, serpents, demons, spirits, humans, birds, eight-legged mountain goats (*śarabhas*), elephants and so forth. (MaitU 7.1–6)

Cosmogony XII reasserts standard homologies in the first three categories—those linking the usual directions, gods, meters, hymns of praise, chants, and seasons in the *varṇa*-encoded chains—and adds the five breaths of Vedic physiology to the overall structure. In a way that is reminiscent of the pentadic taxonomies, here the fourth chain also serves as the "Shūdra" category (north ⇒ Viśva Devas *anuṣṭubh* meter ⇒ twenty-one-versed hymn of praise ⇒ *vairāja* chant ⇒ autumn ⇒ the digestive breath ⇒ Varuṇa and the Sādhyas); and the fifth set of analogues functions as the summarizing or "transcendent" chain (zenith ⇒ Mitra and Varuṇa ⇒ *paṅkti* meter ⇒ twenty-seven- and thirty-three-versed hymns of praise ⇒ *śakvara* and *raivata* chants ⇒ winter and the cool season ⇒ the upward breath ⇒ Angirases ⇒ moon).

The new sixth category is peculiar. In the first place, the category does not contain most of the elements of the other five categories. Having followed the pattern by listing a sixth direction (the nadir), the text does not specify a particular god, meter, hymn of praise, chant, season, or breath for this category as it had for the previous five. Second, the sixth chain here seems to function as something of the opposite of the elements of the fifth—the associations are generated from the nadir and include demons, spirits, strange astronomical phenomena, mythical animals, and so forth, in the place held by the deities in the other chains. It thus seems to be a negative inversion of the "transcendent fifth" category or a kind of "grab bag" extra category into which is relegated all that doesn't fit in the previous five categories.

In sum, Cosmogony XII demonstrates one kind of strategy the systematizers could deploy when a fundamentally tripartite scheme was unfolded to create a six-part structure. Generated out of the need to find correlates for each of the six directions (the four cardinal directions plus up and down, zenith and nadir), this text reproduces the familiar four *varṇa*s, constructs a "transcendent fifth" category, and posits a sixth category which holds its place below the scale just as the fifth is above and beyond the scale.

A rather different classificatory principle guides the six-part taxonomy of the last text we consider here, Cosmogony XIII:

> They obtain the earth by means of the first day [of the soma sacrifice], the *gāyatrī* meter, the nine-versed hymn of praise, the *rathantara* hymn, the eastern quarter, the spring of seasons, the Vasus the gods, Agni, born of the gods, the overlord. . . . They obtain the atmosphere by means of the second day, the *triṣṭubh* meter, the fifteen-versed hymn of praise, the *bṛhat* hymn, the southern quarter, the summer of the seasons, the Maruts the gods, Indra, born of the gods, the overlord. . . . They obtain the sky by means of the third day, the *jagatī* meter, the seventeen-versed hymn of praise, the *vairūpa* hymn, the western quarter, the rains of the seasons, the Ādityas the gods, Varuṇa, born of the gods, the overlord. . . . They obtain food by means of the fourth day, the *anuṣṭubh* meter, the twenty-one-versed hymn of praise, the *vairāja* hymn, the northern quarter, the autumn of seasons, the Sādhya and Ājya gods, Bṛhaspati and the moon, born of the gods, the overlords. . . . They obtain animals by means of the fifth day, the *paṅkti* meter, the twenty-seven-versed hymn of praise, the *śakvara* hymn, the zenith quarter, the winter of seasons, the Maruts the gods, Rudra, born of the gods, the overlord. . . . They obtain the waters by means of the sixth day, the *atichandas* meter, the thirty-three-versed hymn of praise, the *raivata* hymn, the zenith of the quarters, the cool season, the Viśva Devas, Prajāpati, born of the gods, the overlord. (KB 22.1, 22.5, 22.9, 23.3, 23.8)

The first three categories are, here again, easily decipherable as Brahmin, Kshatriya, and Vaishya. The second half of the taxonomy includes corresponding components for every element of the first triad (including "worlds" of "food," "animals," and "waters"), in some instances by redistributing into a sixth category what was in other schemes combined in a "transcendent fifth" (i.e., the twenty-seven- and thirty-three-versed hymns of praise, the *śakvara* and *raivata* chants, and the winter and cool seasons).

But what is the taxonomical principle at work here? In the second half of the taxonomy, we seem to have a duplication of the tripartite *varṇa* order—at least according to the semantics indicated by the deities assigned to each string. Here, it is typically Brahmin deities that are assigned to the fourth string of connections: Bṛhaspati, the priest of the gods; the Sādhyas, who are elsewhere paired with the deified *brahman* (ChU 3.10); and the moon which can also be interpreted as a

TABLE 3.4. The Six-Part Scheme According to Cosmogonies XII–XIII

Direction	east	south	west	north	zenith	nadir
Deity	Agni, Vasus	Indra, Maruts/ Rudras	Maruts, Ādityas/ Varuṇa	Viśva Devas, Varuṇa, Sādhyas/ Ājyas, moon	Mitra, Varuṇa, Angi-rases/ Maruts, Rudras	demons, etc./Viśva Devas, Prajāpati
Meter	*gāyatrī*	*triṣṭubh*	*jagatī*	*anuṣṭubh*	*paṅkti*	*atichandas*
Hymn of praise	9-versed	15-versed	17-versed	21-versed	27-versed	33-versed
Chant	*rathantara*	*bṛhat*	*vairūpa*	*vairāja*	*śakvara*	*raivata*
Season	spring	summer	rainy	autumn	winter	cool
Breath	inhalation	circulating	exhilation	digestive	upward	
Astronomical body	constella-tions	moon	Venus		moon	Saturn, eclipses, comets
Cosmological world	earth	atmosphere	sky	"food"	"animals"	"waters"

Brahmin entity.[21] The fifth and sixth chains are clearly encoded theologically as Kshatriya and Vaishya; the warrior gods Rudra and the Maruts are located in the fifth, and the creator god Prajāpati (a placeholder for the Vaishya traits of fecundity and procreation) together with the Viśva Devas (who are very often connected with the Vaishyas) are found in the sixth. It would seem that the tripartite order of things is thus simply doubled in Cosmogony XIII; the first three *varṇa*s are repositioned in the second triad of the six-part scheme.

The six-part taxonomical structure produced by Cosmogonies XII and XIII is reproduced in Table 3.4.

The Origins of Class

The centrality of the *varṇa* classificatory method in Vedic texts, its epistemological power to render the cosmos explicable, is partly demonstrated by the elasticity and adaptability of the scheme. A tripartite system expands into a quadripartite one when the social order is perceived to contain four and not three discrete classes, but also when the classificatory enterprise proceeds from a quadripartite base. When, for example, the classifiers turn their attention to the four cardinal directions, or to the linkages which fan out from the four-part division of the sacrificial animals, the scheme is constructed differently from one which has as its purpose the explanation of the three cosmological worlds or the three Vedas in terms of their analogues in other realms. A pentadic structure may be required for several kinds of reasons: to account for the five groups of deities, or the five seasons, or simply because the ritual one is contemplating lasts for five days. Similarly, a sixfold scheme is generated when the seasons are counted as six, or when to the cardinal directions are added both zenith and nadir, or, again, when the ritual which stimulates such *bandhus* is of a six day duration. Although there are different transformative methods at work in various texts, the basic *varṇa* structure undergirds all of them.

Members of different species or types of things are categorized in relation to each other while they are also categorized in relation to larger orders of things—and in the final analysis, to the order of things. The *varṇa* system is presented in the Veda as the underlying organization of the cosmos, the means of classifying at the most general level. While some the variations and inconsistencies have been duly noted in this chapter (and will be discussed at greater length in the following chapters), the continuities, consistencies, and overall coherence of the system are impressive indeed. Despite the received wisdom handed down by Indologists of the past and continually reasserted by those of the present, the connections or *bandhus* so characteristic of the Veda are not random, arbitrary, or whimsical. They are, by and large, ruled, regular, and repeated as part and parcel of the Vedic vision of the world and its categories.

In the following chapters, we devote some time and effort to unpacking what we have observed in cosmogonic shorthand in this chapter. The realms which the *varṇa* classificatory system organizes in these myths form the substance of entire chapters. Indeed, the remainder of this book might be regarded as something of an *explication de text*, with the thirteen cosmogonies presented in this chapter assuming the role of "the text."

Before leaving the cosmogonic myths of the origins of class, however, let us pause to make two general observations regarding the classificatory passages analyzed here. The first observation comes in two parts. These accounts, on the one hand, unanimously share the assumption that the hierarchical or vertically oriented structure of things is invariable. In every instance, the category which contains (explicitly or implicitly) the Brahmin social class is created and represented first. Second only to the Brahmins are the Kshatriyas and their resembling entities and phenomena. The Vaishya category is produced third and the lowly Shūdras come last. On the other hand, there is ultimately very little agreement about the sequence in which things and beings within each of the hierarchical *varṇas*—those components which are horizontally connected within each series of associations—were created. There is, in other words, no pattern as to the priority or privilege over others of one or another of the species of created things and beings in the horizontal series. Some of these cosmogonies assume that the universe was "emitted" from the body of the primordial creator god,[22] and others trace the origins of things to the ritual or one or another of the elements of the natural world. But each gives a more or less independent list of the sequence in which the links on the chain of being were created, as Table 3.5 demonstrates.

The second and very much related point I would like to call attention to at this juncture is this: in each case, it is not society which is presented as either the source of or the first component in the cosmic classification scheme. The social classes in these lists of classes are depicted neither as generative of others nor as prior to most of them. Indeed, in most of the texts covered here the social classes do not even appear in the chains of connections, although they are certainly implied. As Bruce Lincoln pointed out, "social stratification can well be—and

TABLE 3.5. Sequence of Homologies in Cosmogonies I–XIII

Cosmogony I	divisions of the day = social classes = gods = meters = metaphysical powers = types of ontological beings
Cosmogony II	sacred utterances ⇒ cosmological worlds = metaphysical powers = types of ontological beings
Cosmogony III	cosmological worlds ⇒ gods/natural elements ⇒ scriptures ⇒ sacred utterances ⇒ priestly offices (sacrificial fires)
Cosmogony IV	metaphysical powers = cosmological worlds = gods/natural elements = body functions
Cosmogony V	anatomical body parts ⇒ hymns of praise = meters = gods = social classes = seasons
Cosmogony VI	anatomical body parts (and correlative characteristics) ⇒ hymns of praise = meters = chants = gods = social classes = animal classes
Cosmogony VII	anatomical body parts (and correlative characteristics) ⇒ hymns of praise = gods = meters = chants = social classes = animal classes
Cosmogony VIII	directions = meters = hymns of praise = chants = gods = seasons = metaphysical powers
Cosmogony IX	directions ⇒ body functions ⇒ seasons ⇒ meters ⇒ chants ⇒soma cups ⇒ hymns of praise ⇒ chants ⇒ seers
Cosmogony X	directions = seasons = gods = metaphysical powers = meters = chants = hymns of praise = derivative hymns of praise = seers = types of cow = dice throw = wind
Cosmogony XI	directions = gods = hymns of praise = recitations = chants
Cosmogony XII	directions ⇒ gods = meters = hymns of praise = chants = seasons = breaths = astronomical bodies = groups of gods
Cosmogony XIII	day of ritual = cosmological worlds = meters = hymns of praise = hymns = directions = seasons = gods

often is—expressed by implication alone. . . . In ways, that which is unsaid can be far more powerful than that which is openly asserted, for by being left mute it is placed beyond question or debate."[23]

It is plain that, according to the Vedic texts and, presumably, those who wrote them, the categories of the universe are not to be reduced, at least explicitly, to either social reality or social ideology. The Vedic *varṇa* system in its fullness is not represented as generated from the Vedic social structure or an idealization of social structure. The social classes in these narratives find their source, their origin, only in the transcendent, the divine, the supernatural, or the ritual; and they are randomly located (or simply remain implicit) in such lists among entities and phenomena inhabiting the natural, supernatural, religious, and ritual spheres.

Representing the social system as intrinsic to the structure of creation itself is itself a powerful claim. Representing creation as structured by *varṇa* as the work of the deity ups the ante; the system thus "authenticates itself with the claim that the Lord instituted this order for the optimum functioning of humankind and the world. It is, therefore, eternally valid, and any discourse which attempts to step outside it or to tamper with it is a grievous sin against the Almighty and the rest of humankind."[24] And to propound such cosmogonic and theological claims anonymously obscures the social purposes that are being served by such myths of origins.

What I would like to underline at this juncture is, first, that it is most obvious these texts, like all others, were composed by *someone*, or *some group*, at a particular historical moment or series of moments. Second, the texts were *in the interests* of the someone or some group who composed them—in this case, the Brahmin priests and intelligentsia (who were also interested in the interests of their patrons, the Kshatriyas). Third, the fact that the *varṇa* system was in the particular interests of the someone or some group who composed texts like these is not accidental but rather intentional. It would be naive at best, I believe, to think that Brahmins objectively and without their own interests at heart found Brahmin deities at the top of the divine hierarchy, and Brahmin animals, trees, and plants at the forefront of the natural order. The *varṇa* system was, in sum, a totalistic ideology, by which I mean a system of ideas or categories that account for the cosmos and its parts in such a way that the interests and concerns of those who do the accounting are established, protected, and furthered.

As I suggested in the introductory chapter, the exclusive concentration on the social application of *varṇa* can prevent us from grasping its real ideological persuasiveness as a universalistic classificatory system. In this chapter, we surveyed the ways in which *varṇa* can be applied to classify the universe in many of its realms. The fact that the reach of *varṇa* is much more extensive than the social theory embedded within it should not, however, divert our attention from the powerful case that is being made for social differentiation and privilege. The *varṇa* system, a multifaceted and generalized classificatory scheme, had as its first and foremost goal to rationalize and represent an ideal form of a hierarchical social structure by projecting that form into the domains of the supernatural, the metaphysical, the natural, and the canonical. Let us begin our explication of the realms in which the *varṇa* scheme was applied with the "world of the gods."

NOTES

1. Claude Lévi-Strauss, "The Structural Study of Myth," in *Structural Anthropology*, trans. by Claire Jacobson and Brook Grundfest Schoepf (New York: Basic Books, 1963), p. 229.
2. Mircea Eliade, *Myth and Reality*, trans. by Willard R. Trask (New York: Harper & Row, 1963), p. 6.
3. Ibid.
4. Ibid., p. 15.

5. Since I refer back to the texts I label Cosmogony I, Cosmogony II, etc., throughout this work, the translated texts and their classificatory schemes are reproduced in an appendix to this book.

6. The Vedic ritual may be divided into three principal types. First, there is the domestic or *gṛhya* sacrifice which entails simple offerings into the household ritual fire. Some householders, however, established three other fires and employed several priests to offer the regular *śrauta* sacrifices, ordinarily using vegetable substances as the oblation material. These are called the *havis* type of ritual. Finally there are very elaborate sacrifices, most of them optional, involving the pressing of the soma plant and the offering of the juice.

7. See, e.g., KB 6.10–11; JB 1.357; JUB 1.1.1–4, 3.15.4–9; and ChU 4.14.1–8. In these variants, the only difference when compared to Cosmogony III is the use of the synonymous term "Āditya" instead of "Sūrya" as the name of the deity belonging to the third string of associations. Compare, however, the alternate tradition as evidenced, e.g., at TB 3.12.9.1–2: "With the verses (*ṛks*), the god [Sūrya, the sun] went to the sky in the forenoon; he stood on the Yajur Veda at midday; with the Sāma Veda he rejoiced at sunset. Sūrya goes to completion with the three Vedas. They say that from the verses all that is manifest (*mūrti*) is born; from the formulas (*yajurs*), all that is animated (*gati*) perpetually (is born); all that is luminous (*tejas*) perpetually has the form of the chants (*sāmans*); all this is emitted by the *brahman*. They say that from the verses the Vaishya class is born; they say the Yajur Veda is the womb of the Kshatriya; the Sāma Veda is the procreator of the Brahmins." One will note that in this text the Vedas and times of day associated with Brahmins and the Vaishyas are inverted in comparison to Cosmogony III and its parallels.

8. The use of the seasonal component in these linkages was often to determine (or justify) the time of initiation into Veda study and sacrificial training (*upanayana*), on the one hand, and the time of setting the sacrificial fires, on the other. Consult Brian K. Smith, "Ritual, Knowledge, and Being: Initiation and Veda Study in Ancient India," *Numen* 33, 1 (1986), pp. 69–70.

9. ŚB 3.1.1.9–10. But see also the curious text at ŚB 5.5.4.9, where it is declared that none of four *varṇa*s "vomits soma." For a study of the implications omissions such as these had for the Shūdras in later elaborations of caste theory in the traditions of Mīmāmsā and Vedānta, see Francis X. Clooney, "Finding One's Place in the Text: A Look at the Theological Treatment of Caste in Traditional India," *Journal of Religious Ethics* 17, 1 (Spring 1989): 1–29.

10. Madhava, in his commentary, accounts for the dependence of the Shūdra by pointing to his "service in relation to the other three *varṇa*s," and that of the horse because he is "a bearer": *śudrānām varṇatraya paricaryāmukhyatvena tadadhīnatvam, aśvādīnānca vahanena tadadhīnatvam*. Sāyana's gloss is similar. Cf. Ron Inden's observation: "Poor Shūdras in particular were depicted bearing loads (*bhāra*), the strength of their bodies from the tops of their heads to the soles of their feet as their only power." "Lordship and Caste in Hindu Discourse," in *Indian Religion*, ed. by R. Burghart and A. Cantlie (London: Curzon Press, 1985), p. 168. The connection of the horse and the Shūdra *varṇa* becomes much more common in post-Vedic categorizations. See, e.g., Manu 12.43, where the horse is lumped together with Shūdras, elephants, barbarians, lions, tigers, and boars as the product of "the middling states (of being) generated by darkness (*tamas*)." See also KūrmaP 1.7.53 and VishnuP 1.5 where the horse, along with certain other animals, is created from the feet of the creator god, just as the Shūdra was in the ancient account of ṚV 10.90.

11. For the identification of *puruṣa* (which can mean "man" as well as "Cosmic Man")

and Prajāpati—"That same Puruṣa became Prajāpati"—see ŚB 6.1.1.5, 6.1.1.8, 7.4.1.15, 11.1.6.2; TB 2.2.5.3; and JB 2.47. In an account of a sacrifice sponsored and performed by the gods, the list of *dakṣiṇās* or sacrificial fees given to the divine priests includes the gift of a man to Prajāpati—for, as we read elsewhere, "Man is the nearest to (*nediṣṭham*) Prajāpati [of all creatures]" (ŚB 5.1.3.8, 5.2.1.6). The human being in another text is said to be transcendent of the category of sacrificial animals because "man is all *paśus*" (ŚB 7.5.4.6).

12. For other five-part cosmogonies of this type, see also TS 1.8.13.1–2, 4.3.9.1–2, 5.3.4.1–5; KS 20.12, 21.2; MS 3.2.10; ŚB 8.4.2.1–3,20, 8.6.1.5–9.

13. For the rite and its analysis, see Jan Heesterman, *The Ancient Indian Royal Consecration: The Rājasūya Described According to the Yajus Texts and Annoted [sic]* (The Hague: Mouton, 1957), pp. 103–5.

14. ŚB 5.4.1.3–7, with variants at MS 2.6.10; TS 1.8.13; KS 15.7; and TB 1.7.7. I have inserted into the ŚB text translated here the deities for each of the five strings of associations as given in the other texts. Note, however, that in the MS and KS versions of this taxonomy the third direction is called "*prācī*," "east." Assuming that the texts do not call for emendation, the MS and KS apparently begin in the *west* and move counterclockwise through the south, east, north, and zenith. I would suggest that, given the comparative evidence, that the MS and KS "*prācī*" or "east" (followed by the *jagatī* meter, the *vairūpa* chant, and the other clearly Vaishya components) be changed to read "*pratīcī*," "west."

15. The Agnicayana, the ritual construction of a gigantic brick fire altar, is said to be a restoration of the body of the creator god Prajāpati. It is, in sum, a kind of ritualized cosmogony in reverse, returning the scattered parts of the universe back to the body from which they were originally emitted. For a comprehensive treatment of the ritual, see Frits Staal, *Agni: The Vedic Ritual of the Fire Altar*, 2 vols. (Berkeley: Asian Humanities Press, 1983).

16. The ŚB text is very nearly reduplicative of the TS passage we have labelled Cosmogony IX. There are several divergences, however. Whereas Cosmogony IX has the *aiḍa* chant in the second of the five strings of associations, and the *svāra* for the fourth, the ŚB does the opposite; and while Cosmogony IX asserts that the seers for the third and fourth chains are Viśvamitra and Jamadagni, the ŚB text reverses them.

17. The first four throws of the dice listed here become in Hinduism (and according to the commentators on the Vedic texts) names for the four *yuga*s or ages of the world (although the last and present *yuga* is usually called the *kālī* age), corresponding to the Greco-Roman notion of gold, silver, bronze, and iron ages.

18. MS 2.7.20. The variant at TS 4.3.3.1–2 is virtually identical save for the designation of Pratna rather than Purāṇa as the seer for the fourth category; *varcas* rather than *phala* for the fifth category; and the inversion of the dice throws for the fourth and fifth categories.

19. Sometimes the classificatory signals are not so clear cut, however. Cosmogonies VIII and X assign Mitra and Varuṇa to the fourth chain—royal deities representing the combined powers of the two "ruling classes," the Brahmins and Kshatriyas. And when variants of Cosmogony VIII assign the metaphysical power of physical strength or *bala* to the fourth category, a Kshatriya association would seem to be implied.

20. Others which we do not consider here may be found at AitB 4.29–5.12 and PB 10.6.1–6. A rather different organizational mode is put to work in another six-part classification scheme comprised of the mantras recited in an animal sacrifice within the Kaukili Sautrāmanī dedicated to Indra Vayodhas, a Kshatriya deity, found at TB 2.6.19.1–2. While the first three categories repeat the standardized linkages of the three *varṇa*s

and the fourth again reduplicates the third, the fifth and sixth series seem to be infused with components elsewhere contained in the second *varṇa*. For a cosmogony oriented around the first *varṇa*, see BĀU 1.4.11ff. Both are examples of one of the ways in which standard *varṇa* classificatory structures could be manipulated by individuals who, knowing the system's rules, could reorient the structure to new ends by improvisation.

21. For the connection between the moon and the Brahmin class, see JUB 3.27.11; ŚB 12.1.1.2; ŚŚS 5.1.3ff; and AitB 2.41.

22. For an analysis of the "cosmic emission" in Vedic cosmogonies, see my article "Sacrifice and Being: Prajāpati's Cosmic Emission and Its Consequences," *Numen* 32, 1 (1985): 71–87; and Chapter 3 of my *Reflections on Resemblance, Ritual, and Religion* (New York: Oxford University Press, 1989).

23. Bruce Lincoln, "The Tyranny of Taxonomy," Center for Humanistic Studies, University of Minnesota, Occasional Papers no. 1 (1985), pp. 16, 17.

24. F. Franco and Sarvar V. Sherry Chand, "Ideology as Social Practice: The Functioning of *Varṇa*," *Economic and Political Weekly* 24, 47 (Nov. 25, 1989), p. 2206.

4

Classifying the Gods

The Human Face of the Gods

The Greek philosopher Xenophanes once said, "If cattle and horses had hands, or were able to draw with their feet and produce the works which men do, horses would draw the forms of gods like horses, and cattle like cattle, and they would make the gods' bodies the same shape as their own." Many centuries later, Montesquieu more succinctly declared, "If triangles had a god, he would have three sides."

Gods are created in the image of those who imagine them. Of all the various spheres, visible and invisible, into which humans project themselves, the "world of the gods" is the least empirical and most theoretical. It is the realm in which there are fewest constraints on human creativity, and it is therefore also the arena which most obviously and directly reduplicates the needs, interests, values, and ideals of those who claim knowledge of it. Human beings certainly conceive of deities in their own likeness, in one way or another. But what is it of ourselves, exactly, that we displace into the divine sphere? Which aspects of human existence, which parts of the human psyche, which ideals of the social order, are selected to serve as qualities of the gods? Otherwise put, what is it that we have "projected" onto the divine and what, then, do the gods "represent"? What impact does such a mundane grounding for theological speculation have for the more tangible world of human life? Why might it be advantageous to theologians and those who follow them to duplicate themselves (or some part of themselves) in the divine realm?

Scholars who pursue one form or another of the reductive method in order to make sense of theology have suggested several different kinds of answers to these questions. For Sigmund Freud and his followers gods are the internalized images of parents writ large. Freud saw a "father nucleus" lying "hidden behind every divine figure,"[1] and also within every individual in the form of the conscience or superego. Melford Spiro, following in Freud's wake, argues that the dynamics of family life as perceived by the small child, when correlated to the structures of religious belief in any given culture, provide us with an explanation for both the invention of gods and goddesses and the persuasiveness with which their supposed existence is endowed:

> It is in the context of the family that the child experiences powerful beings, both benevolent and malevolent, who—by various means which are learned in the socialization process—can sometimes be induced to accede to his desires. These experiences provide the basic ingredients for his personal projective system which, if it corresponds (structurally, not substantively) to his taught beliefs, constitutes the cognitive and perceptual set for the acceptance of these beliefs. Having had personal experience with 'superhuman beings' and with the efficacy of 'ritual', the taught beliefs re-enforce, and are re-enforced by, his own projective system.[2]

Freudian-based psychological theories thus answer the question of what part of human life is projected into the divine sphere by pointing to the image of authority figures closer to home, one's parents. Why parental images are so enlarged and transcendentalized is less clear because the needs impelling the projection are nonrational. But, as Spiro points out, the effect is to provide theology with a persuasiveness it would not presumably have otherwise: social and religious beliefs in the supernatural are buttressed by, and "external" proof of, the private and psychological complexes of the individual.

Other types of reductionists, from the Euhemerists to nineteenth-century thinkers ranging from Carlyle to Feuerbach to Nietzsche, regarded the gods as either outsized versions of human heroes or the embodiments of a particular people's highest values and aspirations. From this point of view, deities are the bearers of the ideals of a culture or society as a whole, summaries of a group's notions regarding its greatest good and most esteemed goals. Deities have their source in either real humans (whose humanity is lost over time in the process of divinization) or in human ideals which, by definition, are not realizable in the purely human realm (and thus must be embodied by superhuman beings).

Closely related but nevertheless distinctive is the view perhaps best epitomized by Durkheim: gods and goddesses are "collective representations" of the group itself, anthropomorphized emblems of society. For Durkheim, "god" and "society" are merely interchangeable terms: "I see in divinity only society transfigured and conceived symbolically."[3] Durkheimians, as well as Marxists, argue that deities represent not only the social whole but also its parts and the interactions between them. Under this view, divine entities function as supernatural standard-bearers of particular social and economic classes within any given society. Gods and goddesses are created as vehicles for representing the particular qualities members of the different classes in society supposedly share; for exploring the interrelations, or conflicts, between the classes; and for positing and transposing into a divine sphere certain privileges (and liabilities) that adhere to one or another of the classes in a given social order.

The deities depicted in the Veda could be analyzed by using any one or a combination of these reductive methodologies. It is likely, for example, that certain Vedic gods could be fruitfully interpreted as ciphers for the psychological complexities entailed in ancient Indian family dynamics (although data concerning Vedic family life are sparse). Many of these deities, it seems certain, symbolically recapitulate the ideals of Vedic culture. Gods like Agni and Bṛhaspati are clearly the apotheoses of the priestly ideal, and a deity like Indra embodies the warrior ethos.

It is primarily the notion that Vedic deities represent social classes and their interactions that I explore here.[4] The gods and goddesses, like other components of the supernatural and natural worlds, are categorized according to *varṇa* in Vedic texts. They are divisible into certain categories with certain traits and characteristics—the marks of class—that link them to the social classes which, it would seem, are the foundation for them. The divine sphere thus is made into a mirror image of the social world; classifying deities into *varṇa*s meant that a particular form for ordering society was also the means by which the world of the gods was ordered. The social order and the divine order were cast as isomorphic.

And what significance might such social projection into the divine sphere have for the human beings who believed in the Vedic pantheon? The short answer is that theological claims are claims to absolute authority. The divine realm, while unseen (or perhaps *because* it is unseen), is one of the principal sources with which humans have anchored their truth claims. If the gods themselves were configured and imprinted by *varṇa*, those in human society could not dispute this social order without also tackling the order of things in the invisible world of the divine. Because the deities were categorized according the *varṇa* scheme, the authority of the divine was lent to this taxonomical method; the gods, one might say, became the guarantors of the social order because they too were subject to it.

Gods and the Social Classes

Vedic texts are often vague about the exact number of deities populating their pantheon. Several passages declare that there are 3,003 gods,[5] but go on to say that really the number is only 303, or 33, or 3, or 1½, or 1.[6] Deities are often divided into three groups: gods of the earth, the atmosphere, and the sky (e.g., ṚV 1.139.11), and these are identified as deities grouped with Agni (or fire, sometimes together with the Vasus), Vāyu (or wind, sometimes with the Rudras or the Maruts), and Āditya/Sūrya (or sun, sometimes with the Ādityas or Viśva Devas). And as we observed in Chapter 3, the three worlds and the gods located in each are also linked with the social classes: Brahmin, Kshatriya, and the peasantry respectively.

Virtually all the cosmogonies we covered in Chapter 3 (Cosmogonies I,

III–VIII, and X–XIII) list various deities in the chains of resemblances they lay out. There is much internal agreement among these texts as to which deities belong to which *varṇas*, and these assignments are confirmed in many other texts, as we shall observe in this chapter.

One such corroboration is provided in the following extract, where we learn that the gods were created in the beginning out of the elemental qualities which also underlie the four social classes, the powers called the ***brahman***, ***kṣatra***, and *viś*:

> Brahmā, in the beginning, was only one. Being one, he was indistinct. He emitted a superior form (*śreyorūpa*), the *kṣatra* power, along with the *kṣatra* gods: Indra, Varuṇa, Soma, Rudra, Parjanya, Yama, Mṛtyu, and Īśāna. Therefore there is nothing higher than the *kṣatra*. Therefore at the Rājasūya ritual the Brahmin sits below the Kshatriya. He thus bestows glory (*yaśas*) on the *kṣatra*. This same *brahman* is the womb of the *kṣatra*. Therefore, even if the king attains supremacy he still clings to the *brahman* as his own womb. Whoever injures him [the Brahmin or the *purohita*] moves against his own womb. When one harms his betters, he becomes worse. He [Brahmā] was [still too] indistinct. He emitted the *viś*, and those of the divine race known to come in groups: the Vasus, Rudras, Ādityas, Viśva Devas, and Maruts. He [Brahmā] was [still too] indistinct. He emitted the Shūdra class (*varṇa*) [in the form of] Pūṣan. Pūṣan is this [earth], for this [earth] nourishes (*puṣyati*) all, whatever is here. . . . That *brahman* [in this way became] the *kṣatra*, the *viś*, and the Shūdra. That *brahman*, by means of Agni, came to be among the gods. By means of the Brahmin [he appeared] among men. Through the Kshatriya [he appeared] as the Kshatriya, [he appeared] as a Vaishya by means of the Vaishya, and as a Shūdra by means of the Shūdra. Therefore they seek a world among the gods in Agni, and [a world] among men in the Brahmin, for Brahmā came into being [most fully] through these two forms. (BĀU 1.4.11–15)

The Kshatriya gods are here listed as Indra, Varuṇa, Soma, Rudra, Parjanya, Yama, Mṛtyu, and Īśāna;[7] the deities of the Vaishyas are all those clustered in groups—the Vasus, Rudras, Ādityas, Viśva Devas, and Maruts—while Pūṣan is the Shūdra deity. The only Brahmin god mentioned here is Agni, who is also the deity listed among the Brahmin entities in Cosmogonies I, III–VIII, and X–XIII. The text also makes a point of noting that the creator god Brahmā manifested himself most fully in the Brahmin and the Brahmin god, Agni. What's more, it is out of the *brahman* power that not only the Brahmin god and the Brahmin social class were created but also all other human classes.

In other texts, additional deities associated with the Brahmin social class are enumerated. One lists the Brahmin gods as Agni, Soma, Savitṛ, Bṛhaspati and Sarasvatī (who is equated with Vāc, the goddess of sacred speech).[8] Mitra is also often categorized as a Brahmin; he stands in for the first *varṇa* when joined with Varuṇa in the dual deity Mitra–Varuṇa in Cosmogonies VIII, X, XII, and the Vasus are also sometimes listed with Agni as Brahmin gods (see Cosmogonies XI and XIII). To the Kshatriya deities listed above should be added also the Maruts and Rudras (who accompany Indra as Kshatriya deities in Cosmogonies

XI and XIII), the wind god Vāyu, and various solar deities (Savitṛ, Āditya, and Sūrya) who are also frequently classed in this group. The gods of the lower classes include all those deities listed in groups or "bands" (*gaṇas*, i.e., the Vasus, Rudras, Ādityas, Viśva Devas, Maruts, and also the Ṛbhus), and individual deities such as Pūṣan, the god of *puṣṭi* (the essential power of material prosperity), the goddess Sarasvatī (who alternates as a Brahmin goddess), and various deities involved with creation and productivity, such as Prajāpati and Tvaṣṭṛ.

Many Vedic deities are thus apotheoses of the social classes, intimately and explicitly related to the Brahmins, Kshatriyas, and lower classes. Or they are presented as divinized representatives of the elemental qualities which are emblematic of those classes (i.e., the *brahman*, *kṣatra*, and *viś*), and are for that reason identifiable with social groups. The *varṇa* of the deities may also be recognized because many gods are linked with one or another of the essential powers that act as ciphers for the social classes (e.g., Agni = *tejas* = Brahmin; Indra = *vīrya* or *indriya* = Kshatriya; and Pūṣan = *puṣṭi* = Vaishyas and/or Shūdras).

The class orientation of each deity is fairly predictable and follows an obvious logic: sacrificial deities such as Agni and Bṛhaspati are categorized as Brahmins; deities primarily known as warriors and rulers like Indra and Varuṇa are Kshatriyas; groups of deities like the Viśva Devas are tokens of the concept of multiplicity (so definitive of the *viś*) in the divine sphere, while others like Pūṣan represent material productivity and increase and are categorized, alternatively, as either Vaishya or Shūdra.

The gods, then, like so many other entities and components of the universe, are classified according to *varṇa*. And because the gods are so obviously stand-ins for the social classes, in myth and ritual the relations (ideal or real) between the various groupings of Vedic society are symbolized, manipulated, and, most important, transposed into a transcendent sphere where they appear far less arbitrary and disputable than they otherwise might.

Brahmin Gods

The deity most often and consistently associated with the Brahmin class is Agni,[9] the god of fire (and of the earth) and therefore the god most closely connected to that special province of the priestly class, the sacrifice. Agni "is" the sacrifice (e.g., ŚB 5.2.3.6) and is "the Brahmin among the gods" (JB 1.93); therefore the Brahmin "is" or belongs to (*agneya*) Agni.[10] This god is often correlated to the Brahmin social class in the Vedic ritual. The Brahmin who sets up his sacrificial fires should offer special oblations to Agni, the divine signifier of his *varṇa*,[11] and at the New and Full Moon sacrifice, a Brahmin sacrificer takes his vow while addressing "Agni, the lord of vows."[12]

This divinity is also regularly connected to the elemental quality of the Brahmin class, the *brahman* power,[13] and one text connects Agni to both the *brahman* power and the sacrifice.[14] In a certain rite, a cake is offered to Agni as the god of the *brahman*; one who knows that Agni and *brahman* are thus connected "obtains the *brahman*, and whatever is to be won by the *brahman* all that he indeed wins" (ŚB 11.2.7.14). The connection between Agni and the *brahman* includes not only ties to the sacrifice but also to the study of the Veda (again, a predominantly Brahmin occupation) and to the mouth, the body part of the first class. According to ŚB 6.1.1.10, the *brahman* (which is also identified with the Veda) was created before anything else: "And so people say, 'The *brahman* was the first thing emitted.'. . . For even before that Cosmic Man the *brahman* was emitted; it was emitted as his mouth. Therefore they say that the one who has studied the Veda is like Agni. For the *brahman* is Agni's mouth." Agni is also known as the "mouth of the gods" and "therefore the gods eat food with Agni as their mouth. No matter which divinity one offers to, one really offers only to Agni, since it is with Agni for their mouth that the gods ate."[15]

Agni is regarded as a divinized priest,[16] the apotheosis of the Brahmin ritualist, and is the deity that carries the sacrifice to the other gods:

> "O Agni, you are great! O Brahmin, O Bhārata!" Agni is the *brahman* which is why he says, "O Brahmin!" He says, "O Bhārata!" because Agni bears (*bharati*) the oblation to the gods. Therefore people say, "Agni is the bearer (*bhārata*)." Or, he, being the breath, distributes (*vibharati*) [life among] these creatures.[17] Therefore he says, "O distributer (*bhārata*)!" (ŚB 1.4.2.2; TS 2.5.9.2ff.; cf. KB 3.2; TB 3.5.3.1)

The Brahmin connection is also clearly implied in associations between Agni and typically Brahmin essential powers such as the splendor of the *brahman* (*brahmavarcasa*)[18] and especially *tejas*: Agni is *tejas* and can endow those who supplicate him with it.[19] The god of fire is linked to other forms of "radiance" and "splendor,"[20] which also reiterate the Brahmin nature of this deity.

Agni, like other Brahmin entities, encompasses all others and is the "first" or "prior" member of his group.[21] The first brick, placed to the east (the first among the quarters) in a rite within the Agnicayana ritual is dedicated to Agni, for "Agni is the beginning of the sacrifice" and "the *brahman* is the beginning of the sacrifice" (TS 5.3.4.1). Agni is also regularly associated with the morning, the beginning of the day (discussed later in Chapter 6), for he is "the beginning of the gods, thus at the beginning he delights [all] the gods" (KB 5.5). It is for this reason that this deity can be identified with both the *brahman* and the *kṣatra*[22]—he, as a Brahmin, envelops both principles of the "ruling classes."

Perhaps second only to Agni as the Brahmin deity *par excellence* is Bṛhaspati (a.k.a. Brahmaṇaspati),[23] a god generally assumed to be the apotheosis of the Brahmin priest.[24] Bṛhaspati is very often identified with the Brahmin social class and the *brahman* power,[25] or he is designated the divine representative of the *brahman*,[26] the "lord of the *brahman*" (*brahmapati*)[27] or the overlord (*adhipati*) of the *brahman*.[28] Bṛhaspati embodies this power to the highest degree (he is *brahmiṣṭha* according to TS 2.6.8.7 and 2.6.9.3) or is the "entirety of the *brahman* power" (*sarvam brahma*, GB 2.1.3,4).

Bṛhaspati is also identified with the essential powers which are characteristic of the Brahmin class, especially *brahmavarcasa*,[29] and with typically Brahmin concerns such as the priesthood, sacrifice and sacred speech. Bṛhaspati, like Agni, is the priest (*purohita*) of the gods as well as the divine embodiment of the *brahman* power.[30] According to AitB 8.26 Bṛhaspati is the divine archetype of the human *purohita* and the Brahmin, both of whom resemble him. Another text declares that the thirty three gods have Bṛhaspati as their *purohita*, and since Bṛhaspati is the *brahman* the gods really have the *brahman* as their *purohita*.[31] While Agni is said to be the *hotṛ* priest of the gods, Bṛhaspati is often identified with the specialized priest called the *brahman*[32] who is, in turn, not surprisingly connected to the *brahman* power.[33] And if Agni and the *hotṛ* represent *tejas*, Bṛhaspati and the *brahman* priest encapsulate both the *brahman* power and *brahmavarcasa*:

> Truly *tejas* and *brahmavarcasa* pass away from him who performs the Aśvamedha. The *hotṛ* and the *brahman* priests engage in a debate (*brahmodya*), for the *hotṛ* belongs to Agni and the *brahman* priest to Bṛhaspati, Bṛhaspati being the *brahman* power. He [the priest] thus bestows on him [the sacrificer] both *tejas* and *brahmavarcasa*.[34]

Bṛhaspati, like Agni, is also directly linked to the sacrifice ("Bṛhaspati is the *brahman*, and the sacrifice also is the *brahman*," ŚB 3.1.4.15; 5.3.2.4; ĀpŚS 22.25.11) and to that essentially Brahmin characteristic, the power of speech (*vāc*).[35]

Because Bṛhaspati is so closely associated with the *brahman* power, he is specifically declared to be the god of the Brahmin social class: "Bṛhaspati is the *brahman*, and the *brahman* is the Brahmin."[36] A Brahmin "belongs to Bṛhaspati" (*bārhaspatya*, MS 2.2.3) for "Bṛhaspati is the *brahman*, the *brahman* is the father of the Brahmin; the father is the lord of the son" (KS 11.4). Bṛhaspati's identification with the Brahmins and the *brahman* power is often utilized within the Vedic ritual. An offering to Bṛhaspati is to be done in the house of a Brahmin priest in one sacrifice (TS 1.8.9.1), while a Brahmin sacrificer at the Vājapeya is instructed to perform certain rites with mantras directed to Bṛhaspati, "for Bṛhaspati is the *brahman* and a Brahmin is the *brahman*" (ŚB 5.1.5.2ff.). In the Vājapeya sacrifice, a Brahmin sacrificer carries out a certain ritual function with a mantra adjusted so that it will refer to the "highest heaven of Bṛhaspati" (ŚŚS 16.17.1–3). In other rituals, oblations to various deities are followed by one to Bṛhaspati if the sacrificer is of the Brahmin class (HŚS 13.7.18–20; ĀpŚS 18.21.9–11). After cows are sacrificed for other deities, some are offered for Bṛhaspati: "And the reason why those dedicated to Bṛhaspati come last is that Bṛhaspati is the *brahman*, and he [i.e., the sacrificer] thus establishes finally himself in the *brahman*" (ŚB 13.5.4.25, 13.6.2.16). Bṛhaspati is the *brahman* and "that which possesses the *brahman* comes to no harm" (AitB 1.13). Or again, since this god is the *brahman*, when he is pleased the ritual goes well, for "with the *brahman* he makes the sacrifice successful" (KB 9.5).

Other superhumans often connected with the Brahmins include the deification of this power of speech, the goddess Vāc, who is said to be both Bṛhaspati and the *brahman* power;[37] and the goddess Sarasvatī,[38] who is listed as one of the deities of the *brahman* (MS 4.5.8) and who is also frequently identified with speech.[39] Because Sarasvatī is speech, one who cannot speak properly is to offer a sacrifice to her,[40] and upon death the faculty of speech is said to return to her (TS 2.3.11.2; ĀpŚS 19.23.10). At JB 1.82 (cf. KS 37.2), Sarasvatī is equated to speech and speech is equated to the *brahman* power; elsewhere the Brahmin domain, the sacrifice, is added as the third element of the equation.[41] Prajāpati, the "lord of creatures" and the principal deity of many of the Vedic texts, is at times regarded as a Brahmin god, perhaps in part because of his frequent identification with Agni[42] and with, once again, speech.[43] In any event, Prajāpati is with some frequency connected to the *brahman* power,[44] the *brahman* priest,[45] and thus the Brahmin social class.

Mitra[46] is the "friend of all" (e.g., KS 7.11; MS 1.5.14), who harms no one. He is categorized as a Brahmin deity and/or identified with the *brahman* power;[47] alternatively, he is both the *brahman* and truth (*satya*).[48] The connection between Mitra and the Brahmins is also made explicit in an optional ritual for one who falls ill—the deity for a Brahmin invalid should be Mitra.[49] Mitra "is" Soma, the king of the Brahmins (ŚB 5.4.3.11), and he is also assimilated to both the sacrifice and to the Brahmin deity Bṛhaspati. When one has "veered from the path of sacrifice" by putting those who are "unworthy of sacrifice" like the Shūdras in contact with the ritual, one should offer to Mitra and Bṛhaspati, for "Mitra and Bṛhaspati are the path of the sacrifice: Mitra is the *brahman*, and the *brahman* is the sacrifice; and Bṛhaspati is the *brahman* and the *brahman* is the sacrifice. Thus he again follows the path of the sacrifice" (ŚB 5.3.2.4; cf. MS 4.8.2).

But Mitra, because of the fact that he virtually always appears with the royal god Varuṇa as a "dual deity," is also liable to be classified as a Kshatriya deity.[50] Other deities normally associated with the Kshatriyas who sometimes appear as Brahmins include the solar gods Savitṛ[51] and Āditya/Sūrya.[52] Soma is also a god with something of a dual affiliation (Brahmin and Kshatriya) when it comes to *varṇa*, a conjunction that is summed up in his epithet, the "king of the Brahmins."[53]

Kshatriya Gods

The god most frequently identified with the warriors is Indra.[54] As one scholar wrote, "The Vedic Indra was primarily a warrior-god, and consequently a champion of the Kṣattriyas."[55] In the sacrifice, the connection is made abundantly clear. A Kshatriya sacrificer should make a special offering or address a particular mantra to Indra, the deity most closely associated with his class;[56] conversely, an offering to Indra made at the Rājasūya sacrifice should take place in the house of a Kshatriya (TS 1.8.9.1), or at the consecrated king's own house, "for Indra is the *kṣatra*, and one who is consecrated is the *kṣatra*" (ŚB 5.3.1.3; cf. TB 3.8.23.2). Indra is invoked by the priest acting on behalf of the Kshatriya sacrificer in order to help him attain rule over others and victory over his rivals (AV 4.22.1), and a Kshatriya student who is setting out to study the Veda invokes Indra for the sake of "dominion" (*rāṣṭra*, JGS 1.12). Another set of texts declares that the sacrificer may be equated to Indra in a twofold way, as a Kshatriya and as a sacrificer (ŚB 5.3.5.27, 5.4.3.4,7).

In the beginning, Indra was born into the *kṣatra* power and thereby pushed out the hated enemies and made room for the gods.[57] It was Indra that the *kṣatra* power chose to enter (cf. AV 15.10.3–5) and when this god was born, the Viśva Devas proclaimed him: "The *kṣatra* has been born, the Kshatriya has been born, the overlord of all beings has been born, the eater of the *viś* has been born, the breaker of walled cities has been born, the killer of demons has been born, the protector of the *brahman* has been born, the protector of *dharma* has been born" (AitB 8.12, 8.17).

Indra is, here and elsewhere, identified with the *kṣatra*[58] or the "glory of the *kṣatra*" (KB 12.8). He is the "overlord of the *kṣatra*" (ŚB 8.4.3.10) and is asked to impart to the Kshatriya that "great *kṣatra*" that "subdues men" (TB 2.6.9.1). Indra is called upon by the Kshatriya to "enter the *viś*" and thus restore the human king to power (AV 3.3.3), to "make the [human] *viś* like-minded and wholly ours" (AV 7.94.1; cf. ŚB 4.2.4.23).

Indra, like the Kshatriya he is identified with, is a ruler and warrior. As Jan Gonda notes, "Indra, indeed, manifests himself in all that is strength and in all that is powerful in nature, in all that involves force or is attended by might."[59] He is the "leader among the gods" (JB 1.304), an overlord who rules all the gods who are his *viś*.[60] Indra is thus the "lord of the *viś*" (AV 1.21.1; cf. 8.5.22) and is invoked in a ritual for lordship (ŚB 5.3.3.11). He "stands over everything here and everything here is beneath him" (ŚB 4.5.3.2); he is the strongest among the gods (ŚB 9.2.3.3), or, as another text claims, "He is of the gods the mightiest (*ojiṣṭha*), the most powerful (*baliṣṭha*), the strongest (*sahiṣṭha*), the most real (*sattāma*), and the most effective (*pārayiṣṇutāma*)" (AitB 8.12).

Indra is thus the deity who is superior in, or born of, the Kshatriya essential powers of *ojas* (might), *bala* (physical power), and *sahas* (force, see also AitB 7.16; ṚV 10.153.2), among other similar qualities.[61] He is in particular associated with *ojas*,[62] a power that, as we saw in Chapter 2, is equated with the *kṣatra*.[63] Indra is "most endowed with *ojas*" (*ojiṣṭha*, ŚB 4.5.4.12) for the gods have concentrated all *ojas* in him (ṚV 1.80.15). This god is also the "lord of physical strength" (*balapati*, KŚS 5.13.1; cf. ŚB 11.4.3.3) or is identified with that quality,[64] and can deliver to the sacrificer *bala* together with fame (*yaśas*).[65]

Indra is filled with machismo. He possesses invincible *sahas* (ṚV 1.55.8) with which he defeated the serpent Vṛtra;[66] he is identified with "virility" (*vīrya*)[67] or manly strength (*pauṃsya*, ṚV 1.5.9); and is said to be the "strongest" or "most virile" of all the gods (ŚB 4.6.6.2-4). Indra is also equated with the power that is named after him, *indriya*:[68] at AitB 7.23, the deity is said to be the *indriya* of the Kshatriya.

Other and lesser gods that have some connection to Indra or another of the divine Kshatriya warriors and rulers are for that reason sometimes classified as Kshatriyas. In this case, the Maruts, who are Indra's henchmen, are both his subjects (and therefore regarded as deified *viś*) and extensions of his being (and thus take on Kshatriya traits).[69] This group, like their leader Indra, are said to possess *ojas*;[70] according to ṚV 5.57.6, in the arms of the Maruts reside *sahas*, *ojas*, and *bala*, courage lies in their heads, and *śrī* ("well-being, prosperity") on their bodies. The Maruts are linked with virility or physical strength (*vīrya*) at JB 1.303, and "with strength all action is done, with strength one obtains everything."

Other gods of the Kshatriya *varṇa* include various solar deities.[71] Savitṛ, the "impeller" of the gods, is called the "lord of the kingdom" (*rāṣṭrapati*, KŚS 5.13.1; cf. ŚB 11.4.3.3) and elsewhere is connected to the power of the *kṣatra* (TB 2.5.7.3). Savitṛ is sometimes associated with Bhaga, the distributer of wealth (who is also a Kshatriya deity according to TB 3.1.1.8), and is said to deliver wealth or *śriyā* to the sacrificer (TB 2.6.13.3). Other apotheoses of the sun, Āditya or Sūrya, are also identified with the *kṣatra* and are labeled the "divine *kṣatra*."[72] One who knows the sun god to be identical to the *kṣatra* becomes endowed with *indriya* (AV 15.10.7,10–11), and the solar deity is also possessed of those Kshatriya essential powers of *sahas* and *ojas* (ṚV 10.170.3). It should also be noted that the Kshatriya god par excellence, Indra, is sometimes equated with the sun.[73]

The royal divinity Soma, the "king of the gods" (e.g., KB 7.10; cf. ŚB 5.4.5.2; AitB 1.8) or the king of the plants,[74] is another Kshatriya god. Soma is very frequently said to be the *kṣatra*[75] or to embody the "glory of the *kṣatra*" (KB 12.8) and is labeled the "lord of the power of rule" (*rājapati*, KŚS 5.13.1) or is identified with the Kshatriya's ruling power (*rājya*, AitB 7.23; ŚB 11.4.3.3). Soma, like other Kshatriya deities, also "is" Indra (TS 3.1.8.2).

Another deity who embodies kingship is Varuṇa,[76] who is called "emperor" (*samrāj*, e.g., ṚV 1.17.1, 1.136.1, 8.42.1) or "lord of the imperium" (*samrāt-pati*, KŚS 5.13.1; cf. ŚB 11.4.3.3) and often "king" (*rāja*) or "king of the gods."[77] Varuṇa is the "king of the *kṣatra*" (TB 3.1.2.7); he is equated with the *kṣatra* and delivers the "glory of the *kṣatra*" to the sacrificer who invokes him.[78] This deity, like other Kshatriya gods, is often closely connected to Indra;[79] while Indra is equated to virility, Varuṇa is equal to the *kṣatra* (GB 2.6.7; cf. AitB 6.15). Elsewhere Varuṇa is connected with the *kṣatra* power and with *indriya* (TB 2.6.13.3), the *kṣatra* and *vīrya* (ŚB 9.4.2.16), *indriyam vīryam* (MS 4.3.9), and *ojas*.[80] Varuṇa is at the center of one rite that promises to deliver "superiority" and the "renown of the *kṣatra* (*prakāśa kṣatra*)" to the sacrificer (PB 15.3.30–31). Elsewhere, Varuṇa is the deity in a ritual for a Kshatriya who wishes to prosper (MS 2.1.2) or who "wishes to act wrongly towards others" by appropriating their land or property (KS 10.4).

Rudra[81] is also specified as one of the Kshatriya deities.[82] He is depicted carrying a bow and arrows, inspiring fear in the hearts of the gods (AV 11.2.12; ŚB 9.1.1.7). He is the embodiment of the *kṣatra* (e.g., ŚB 9.1.1.15,25), portrayed as a protector (ṚV 1.43.3, 6.28.7, 7.40.5, etc.) and as a giver of wealth (ṚV 2.33.12). Rudra is the "lord of the animals" (*paśupati*),[83] who is invoked for cattle (ŚB 5.3.3.11) or, more often, is asked to restrain himself from attacking one's domestic animals.[84] He is regarded as a cruel god (e.g., JB 3.26; TS 6.2.3; MS 1.10, 3.8), and it is the rapacious nature of both Rudra and the Kshatriya that seems to lie at the heart of the linkage between them. Rudra is dangerous and must be appeased; in one text he is asked not to harm the sacrificer himself, his offspring, cattle, or family (KB 6.5; cf. KB 2.4). Elsewhere, one who wishes to be an "eater of food" (an epithet almost always applied to the Kshatriya) should offer the Agnihotra when the fire is first kindled and full of smoke, for the fire is at that time identified with Rudra (ŚB 2.3.2.9).

Vāyu's place as a Kshatriya god[85] seems to stem largely from his position as the incarnation of wind which is located in what is usually classified as the Kshatriya world, the atmosphere, for Vāyu is supposedly the ruler of that world (e.g., TB 3.2.1.3). He is a warrior god (ṚV 4.48.2), invoked for protection by the weak (ṚV 1.134.5) and, as is usual for Kshatriya deities, he is closely associated with Indra.[86] At MS 2.5.1 Vāyu is said not only to be the swiftest of the gods but also the one most endowed with that Kshatriya essential power, *ojas*; elsewhere a Kshatriya sacrificer is directed to address a vow to his deity, Vāyu, at the New and Full Moon sacrifice.[87]

Among other deities who can, at least in some contexts, be classified as Kshatriyas are Yama,[88] the god of death, who is depicted as a king (TB 3.1.2.11) or as an overlord whose *viś* are the ancestors;[89] Viṣṇu, who is identified with *ojas* (see also ṚV 8.12.27) and the *kṣatra* (TS 5.3.4.2; cf. 4.3.9.1); Viśvakarman, conjoined with "youthful vigor" (*vayas*, and "*vayas* is the *kṣatra*," ŚB 8.2.3.11); and Prajāpati (with whom Viśvakarman is equated, e.g., ŚB 8.2.1.10; AitB 4.22), who is directly associated with the Kshatriyas ("He, the Kshatriya, is most obviously Prajāpati; being one, he rules over many," ŚB 5.1.5.14), with the *kṣatra* (ŚB 8.2.3.11), and with vigor (ŚB 8.2.3.11; cf. TB 3.8.7.1–2).[90]

Gods of the Peasantry

The deities who are imagined to be most akin to the commoners are very often the gods who, lacking individuality, are always referred to in the plural. As we have seen, created along with the *viś* were various groups or "troops" (*gaṇas*) of gods: the Vasus, Rudras, Ādityas, Viśva Devas, and Maruts (BĀU 1.4.11–15), and another such group is the Ṛbhus. They are, presumably like the general populace of the Vedic age, all controlled by an overlord: Agni rules the Vasus, Indra or Soma is the overlord of the Maruts or the Rudras, Varuṇa is the leader of the Ādityas, and Bṛhaspati is the chief of his *viś*, the Viśva Devas.[91]

Among the most frequently mentioned deities of the third *varṇa* are the Viśva Devas, the "all gods" or the general divine masses. Like the human commoners they represent, the Viśva Devas are the indistinguishable masses among the gods; the name can mean the "All Gods" but also "all of the gods," the divine multitude.[92] They appear in clearly demarked Vaishya categories in Cosmogonies I, V–VII, and X; they are coupled with Prajāpati (whose cosmic fertility can place him with the Vaishyas, as we shall see later) in Cosmogony XIII; and they appear as the deities of the fourth and generically "lower class" chain in Cosmogony XII.[93] In other texts too the Viśva Devas are identified as the "lords of the *viś*" (AitB 4.32) or are otherwise connected with the power of the *viś*.[94] In the ritual, the sacrificer of the Vaishya class is sometimes called upon to offer a special offering or recite a particular mantra to the Viśva Devas, the deities most closely connected to his *varṇa*.[95]

These divinities are, like the human *viś*, the "food" of others and therefore are associated with food (KB 12.8). They are often correlated with third *varṇa* traits, powers, and components such as procreation (*prajanana*, JUB 1.52.2), offspring (TS 6.6.5.2–3), and the womb (ŚB 4.2.2.16); and because of these associations, the Viśva Devas are also linked with the "lord of creatures," Prajāpati (e.g., JB 1.238ff.; Cosmogony XIII). The Viśva Devas, it is said, are the *viś* and the *viś* are equal to abundance.[96] And also like other Vaishya entities, the divine peasantry are represented by symbols of that quintessential attribute of the *viś*, multiplicity. Thus the Viśva Devas are linked with spotted animals (see Chapter 8) or clotted ghee (ŚB 3.6.3.6) or a leprous man (the victim to be offered to the Viśva Devas in the Puruṣamedha or human sacrifice according to TB 3.4.1.14)—all of which serve as ciphers for abundance, great number, or proliferation.

The Maruts, the "storm troopers" of the atmosphere, are identified with the wind, lightning, and thunderstorms and are categorized as the Vaishya deities in Cosmogonies VIII and XII. Like the Viśva Devas and Ādityas, the Maruts are proclaimed to be the *viś*.[97] The human sacrificial victim offered to the Maruts in the Puruṣamedha is a member of the Vaishya class—"For the Maruts [one should offer as a victim] a Vaishya, for the Maruts are the *viś*. He thus perfects the *viś* by means of the *viś*" (ŚB 13.6.2.10; TB 3.4.1.1). In the Rājasūya ritual, the king offers an oblation to the Maruts in the house of a Vaishya, for "the Maruts are the *viś* and the *viś* means abundance" (ŚB 5.3.1.6). And in the Vājapeya ritual, the sacrificer who is a Vaishya should adjust the mantras for certain rites so that it is addressed to the Maruts (ŚŚS 16.17.1-3).

Ritual manipulations which involve the Maruts are usually directed toward obtaining, controlling, ruling, or otherwise dominating the Vaishyas. When certain offerings are made to the Maruts it is because "the *viś* of the gods are the Maruts; by means of the *viś* of the gods he wins for him the *viś* among men" (TS 5.4.7.7; cf. TS 2.2.5.7). Through oblations and recitations to the Maruts, the sacrificer attaches the *viś* to himself and the *viś* do not desert him (PB 6.10.10, 18.1.14), or the Kshatriya surrounds himself with subjects (ŚB 14.1.3.27). Elsewhere we learn that "the Maruts are the *viś* of the gods. As the *viś* of the gods are well regulated, so he puts the human *viś* in order. He repeats the verse to the Maruts in order to regulate the *viś*" (TS 6.1.5.3; cf. AitB 1.9). Because of this equation between the Maruts and the peasantry, when the former are pleased the ruler gains power over the latter (ŚB 5.4.3.17; cf. TS 2.2.11.1, 2.3.1.3); alternatively, a sacrifice to the Maruts is to appease the commoners should they be inclined to remove a ruler from power (KS 11.1).

According to TB 2.7.2.2, the Maruts are the *viś* and also embodiments of "sustenance" (*ūrj*) and "food."[98] Elsewhere these storm gods, so intimately connected with wind and especially rain,[99] are equated to "the waters" and food (KB 12.8), to abundance (ŚB 3.9.1.17, 5.3.1.6), and to prosperity (TS 2.1.3.3). The Maruts, being sons of Rudra, are sometimes completely identified with the Rudras,[100] who are in any case fundamentally the same in characteristics and, of course, *varṇa*.[101]

The Ādityas, led by Varuṇa,[102] are classified as Vaishya deities in Cosmogony XIII. Like the Viśva Devas, the Ādityas seem sometimes to stand for the gods in general,[103] while in other instances the Ādityas are enumerated and specified[104] and are, as a group, counted among the gods of the *viś*. "The *viś*," it is said, "have the Ādityas for their deity," and by sacrificing to them the Kshatriya sacrificer "wins the *viś*" (TS 2.3.1.3–4). In the ṚV, the Ādityas are noted for bestowing such third *varṇa* boons as long life and offspring.[105]

Another group of deities with clear third *varṇa* associations[106] are the Ṛbhus. They are distributors of wealth (*śriyā*, TB 2.6.19.1-2) and material prosperity (*puṣṭi*, ṚV 4.33.2,8; 4.37.5), and are invoked to bestow cattle and horses (ṚV 4.34.10), to grant vigor, nourishment, and offspring (ṚV 1.111.2), and to utilize their reputed powers of rejuvenation.[107] They are also closely associated with that quintessential commoner trait, multiplicity: according to AitB 6.12, verses with references to "many" are "forms" (*rūpas*) of the Ṛbhus.

Of special interest is the relation between these deities and the social hybrid called the Rathakāra or "chariot-maker" (the product of the union between a Vaishya man and Shūdra woman). In some of the ritual Sūtras, this personage is allowed to set up the sacrificial fires, and as he is lighting the *gārhapatya* fire is to utter a mantra directed to the Ṛbhus.[108] The choice of the Ṛbhus to represent the "chariot-maker" or Rathakāra is interesting; the Ṛbhus are, as their name suggests ("the artificers"), craftsmen known for their dexterity and skill.[109] They are divine chariot-makers in the ṚV (1.161.3, 4.33.8, 4.36.2, 10.39.12), and so are naturally correlated to their human counterparts. Furthermore, the somewhat precarious social and religious position of the Rathakāra is nicely correlated with deities who are themselves somewhat theologically peripheral: the Ṛbhus supposedly were originally mortals who acquired immortality through their own efforts.[110]

In addition to these divine collectivities, certain individual deities also can carry Vaishya, Shūdra, or vaguely lower class connotations. The solar gods Āditya and Sūrya (who sometimes also bear first and second *varṇa* attributes) function as gods of the commoner class in Cosmogonies III (with its variants at AitB 5.32 and JB 1.358) and IV, and also indirectly through the connection to the (lower-class) cosmological world of the sky (see Chapter 5) and the Sāma Veda (see Chapter 9).[111] Prajāpati, the "lord of creatures" and principal creator god in Vedic texts, is not directly linked to the lower classes of the social realm but does have subsidiary connections to certain distinctive traits of the *viś*. Prajāpati is naturally enough characterized by his productiveness (*prajanana*),[112] and among this god's epithets are "progenitor" (*prajāyanitṛ*) or "progenitor of the earth" (*janita pṛthivyai*).[113] He is invoked to bestow offspring (ṚV 10.85.43, 10.169.4), to make livestock prolific (ṚV 10.169.4; cf. TS 3.1.5), and to produce food (AitB 6.21; ŚB 5.1.3.7, 7.1.2.4). Prajāpati is especially connected with the Vājapeya sacrifice,[114] a ritual which has as one of its main functions to ensure regeneration and food.[115]

The deity listed earlier (BĀU 1.4.13) as the Shūdra god, the agriculturalist or pastoral deity Pūṣan,[116] is elsewhere designated the "lord of the *viś*" (TB 2.5.7.4) and is connected to the Vaishyas (TB 2.7.2.1) or to both Vaishyas and Shūdras (MS 4.2.7).[117] His name is derived from the root *puṣ*, "to thrive" or "to cause to thrive,"[118] and is related to the word for "material prosperity," *puṣṭi*—a regularly employed signifier for the lower classes in general. Pūṣan is the "bringer of *puṣṭi*" (*puṣṭimbhāra*, ṚV 4.3.7), or is simply identified with this essential power of the peasantry: "Pūṣan is indeed *puṣṭi*, and *puṣṭi* belongs to the Vaishya."[119] He is said to give abundantly[120] and, as the bestower or "lord of wealth" (*bhāgapati*),[121] knows where treasure is buried (ṚV 6.48.15), enables humans to acquire wealth or property,[122] and is invoked to guard one's property (MS 4.12.6; TB 2.5.4.5ff.).

Pūṣan is also connected with *vāja* ("generative power," e.g., ṚV 10.26.7,9, 6.58.2), and thus with reproduction and childbirth (AV 1.11.1; KauśS 33.1) or with generation defined as offspring, prosperity, food, and the like (ŚB 1.2.2.3). At ŚB 5.2.5.8, a dark gray bull is the sacrificial fee for an offering to Pūṣan since this animal "belongs to Pūṣan" because of its power to bring productiveness: "There are two aspects to the dark gray [animal], the white hair and the black. The compound is [the sign of] a productive copulation and Pūṣan is productiveness."

Pūṣan is associated with food and animals (see, e.g., AV 58.10.3).[123] He is said to deliver or is simply identified with food[124] and is linked to the "eating of food" (KB 12.8). Pūṣan is charged with distributing portions to the gods (TB 1.1.2.17; ĀśvGS 1.20.4); he is the distributor of wealth (*bhāgadugha*) to the gods and is thus assimilated to the personage with the same name who is among the king's court (ŚB 5.3.1.9).[125]

Many texts regard this god as a herdsman and protector of animals.[126] Pūṣan is very often associated with livestock or animals in general (*paśus*) and is invoked to help the sacrificer obtain them.[127] He is the ruler (*adhipa*) of the animals,[128] the protector of animals (*paśupa*, ṚV 6.58.2), or the "producer of animals" (MS 4.3.7; TB 1.7.2.4), and he is invoked to retrieve lost cattle.[129] In several texts, Pūṣan is equated with livestock and *puṣṭi*, and "animals are *puṣṭi* because the sacrifice is *puṣṭi*."[130]

Another set of indicators for this deity's peasant connections is the fact that Pūṣan is closely associated with the constellation called Revatī ("the prosperous, opulent, wealthy one"). Both the god and the constellation are called lords of *puṣṭi*, protectors of livestock, and "possessors of dwellings full of generative power (*vāja*)" (TS 4.4.10.3; KS 39.13; MS 2.13.20). "Let Revatī protect our small domestic animals; let Pūṣan follow our cows and horses. Protecting food, which is various and takes many forms, let them grant to the sacrificer generative power and the sacrifice."[131] In sum, as Gonda writes, Pūṣan

> is on the whole a friendly and beneficent god, often said to bring good fortune or implored for property and other material comforts, believed to be a promoter of everything useful, not infrequently to be a representative or bringer of (re)generative power (*vāja*) and of fecundity, prosperity or a well-nourished condition (*puṣṭi*); in short—if appearances are not deceptive—especially of all well-being that depends on successful agriculture and cattle-breeding.[132]

It is no wonder that such a deity has been selected (or, rather, invented) to serve as the divine image of the social classes who are charged with much the same duties.

Another lower-class deity is Tvaṣṭṛ,[133] who sometimes appears interchangeable with Pūṣan.[134] Portrayed as a creator or builder, he "has strong connections with male and female creativity. . . . [I]t is likely that to the Vedic poets he was the principle of life and growth."[135] A victim offered to Tvaṣṭṛ is an animal with testicles, for such a one is said to produce many offspring (ŚB 3.7.2.8). Elsewhere he is connected to the thighs (TB 3.8.23.3) or androgynously depicted as a pregnant male full of milk (AV 9.4.3–6). Tvaṣṭṛ is the creator of the bride and groom (AV 6.78.3; TB 3.7.4.3) and is supposed to aid in human procreation (ṚV 1.42.10, 3.4.9, 7.2.9, 10.81.82) and childbirth (AV 6.81.3). He gives offspring and property (ĀpŚS 12.6.3) and is said to be the "maker of forms (*rūpas*)": "Truly Tvaṣṭṛ is the maker of forms for the pairs of animals."[136]

Sarasvatī, although also identified with the Brahmins through her connection to speech or *vāc*, has certain lower-class attributes as well. She is associated with not only the (Brahmin) quality of speech but also with "the eating of food" or "nourishment" (*annādya*, for "by speech is food made sweet and eaten")[137] and other forms of prosperity, material increase, and fecundity.[138] Sarasvatī is thus aptly designated the "supporter" or "nourisher" of the "*viś* (*viśobhagīna*)" (AV 6.30.1; BhŚS 4.19.7; ĀpŚS 4.13.7).

Sarasvatī, like Pūṣan, with whom she is so often conjoined,[139] is generous and is associated with wealth, plenty, and nourishment[140] or with wealth and offspring (AVP 6.19.9). She is rich in wealth (ṚV 1.3.10; 7.96.3), is beseeched to bestow abundant wealth, like Pūṣan does (ṚV 6.61.6), and is connected to Bhaga, the distributor of wealth (AV 5.7.4). She is the stereotypical "mother goddess," the very epitome of motherhood (ṚV 2.41.16). She is requested not to withhold her milk (manifest in the form of rivers) (ṚV 6.61.13); her breast feeds all beings and delivers riches of all kinds (ṚV 1.164.49; cf. AitB 4.1).

Sarasvatī is also sometimes depicted in terms of the lower-class essential power par excellence, *puṣṭi* or material prosperity. She is equated to it (ŚB 11.4.3.3,16; TB 2.5.7.4), designated the *puṣṭipati* (ŚB 11.4.3.16; KŚS 5.13.1; *puṣṭipatnī* at TB 2.5.7.4), and asked to deliver it to the sacrificer (MŚS 5.1.6.26). She is associated with the apotheosis of this quality, the deity called Puṣṭi, as well as with the goddess of wealth, Śrī, and the incarnation of "satisfaction," Tuṣṭi (BDhS 2.5.9.10). In at least one text she is specifically linked to a particular form of prosperity, livestock (AV 16.13.1).

In addition to nourishment, wealth, and prosperity, Sarasvatī is the goddess of fecundity and for this reason also might be regarded as a goddess of the peasantry. She is connected with "vitality" at ṚV 10.30.12; at ṚV 2.41.17 Sarasvatī is said to bestow both vitality and offspring; and Sarasvatī's connection with offspring is found in other texts as well (e.g., ṚV 6.6.17; AV 7.68.1, 14.2.15). At AV 6.89.8, she is invoked as the wife is prepared for sexual intercourse. She is also said to help grant progeny (ṚV 2.41.16ff.), and at ṚV 10.184.2 Sarasvatī is put in the company of other deities who assist procreation.[141]

Gods in Essence and Relations

Thus far, we have seen how certain of the gods of the Vedic pantheon are either clearly the apotheoses of the social *varṇa*s or embody certain powers, qualities, or essential traits that are also attributed to one or another of the society's groupings. Sometimes the *varṇa* of the gods is stated explicitly: Agni is the Brahmin, Indra is the Kshatriya, the Viśva Devas are the commoners, and so on. At other times the identification of the superhuman and the human is recognized because of certain adjustments in the ritual: when the sacrificer is a Brahmin, he is in some instances to offer oblations to or recite mantras that address Agni, and so forth. And in yet other texts, the *varṇa* assignment of particular gods is implicit. Tvaṣṭṛ and Sarasvatī are, we may surmise, gods of the *viś* due to the fact that they are so closely conjoined to typically lower-class kinds of concerns (fecundity, productivity, increase, fertility, etc.).

The class of various deities is made evident through the realms over which they exercise control and the traits, qualities, and occupations that characterize them. Among these attributes and responsibilities, the most certain indicators of *varṇa* are those I have labeled the elemental qualities—the neuter powers called the *brahman*, *kṣatra*, and *viś*, which are the animating forces behind the social classes and their analogues—and the "second-order" forces I have termed the essential powers which are almost inevitably indicators of the *varṇas*—*tejas* and *brahmavarcasa* (Brahmin); *ojas*, *bala*, *vīrya*, *indriya* (Kshatriya); and *puṣṭi*, *prajanana*, and *ūrj* (peasantry).

TABLE 4.1. Gods and their Powers

Brahmins	*Kshatriyas*	*Vaishyas and Shūdras*
Agni (*brahman*, *tejas*, *brahmavarcasa*, "radiance")	Indra (*kṣatra*, *ojas*, *bala*, *sahas*, *yaśas*, *vīrya*, *paumsya*, *indriya*)	Viśva Devas (*viś*, *prajanana*, multiplicity, *yaśas*)
Bṛhaspati (*brahman*, *brahmavarcasa*)	Savitṛ, Āditya, Sūrya (*kṣatra*, *rāṣṭra*, *śriyā*, *indriya*, *sahas*, *ojas*)	Ādityas (*viś*, long life, offspring)
Vāc (*brahman*, speech)	Soma (*kṣatra*, *rajyā*)	Maruts (*viś*, abundance, *ūrj*, food, prosperity)
Sarasvatī (*brahman*, speech)	Varuṇa (*kṣatra*, *samrāj*, *indriya*, *vīrya*, *ojas*)	Vasus (*viś*)
Prajāpati (*brahman*, speech)	Rudra (*kṣatra*, *paśus*)	Ṛbhus (*śriyā*, *puṣṭi*, wealth, vigor, nourishment, offspring)
Mitra (*brahman*, *satya*)	Vāyu (*kṣatra*, *ojas*)	Prajāpati (*prajanana*, offspring, food, *paśus*)
Savitṛ (*brahman*)	Yama (*kṣatra*)	Pūṣan (*viś*, *puṣṭi*, wealth, *vāja*, offspring, food, *paśus*)
Soma (*brahman*, *tejas*)	Viṣṇu (*kṣatra*, *ojas*)	Tvaṣṭṛ (*prajanana*, offspring)
	Viśvakarman (*kṣatra*, *vayas*)	Sarasvatī (nourishment, wealth, offspring, *puṣṭi*, *paśus*, vitality, procreation)
	Prajāpati (*kṣatra*, *vayas*)	Āditya, Sūrya, Savitṛ (*paśus*)

The *varṇa* classification of the gods, together with the elemental qualities they embody and the essential powers they wield, is summarized in Table 4.1. Because particular Vedic deities can thus reproduce (and transcendentalize) the essences and functions of the social classes, the interrelations between the gods become significant as statements about the real and ideal interrelations between groups of humans. The interaction of the gods that mythology relates, and the relations between the gods that ritual establishes and manipulates—these divine relations mirror, guide, or perhaps just serve as idealized hopes regarding the interactions among human beings.

What sort of relations are in this way represented? First, Brahmin deities conjoin with Kshatriya gods and form divine ruling-class pairs, often portrayed as a "dual deity" with opposing but complementary aspects,[142] thereby portraying the ideal (and close) cooperative relationship between human Brahmins and Kshatriyas. Second, Kshatriya deities are set up as overlords (and very often explicit oppressors) of divine groups conceived of as *viś*, and thus depict in the heavenly world a relationship between rulers and ruled that is presumably to apply on earth as well. Third, Brahmin gods are characterized as superior to deities representing each of the other classes, for in the divine sphere no less than in any other the Brahmin authors of the Veda made sure that their agents were granted the superiority they themselves claimed in the social realm.

Let us take a closer look at each of these three types of interrelations between gods representing the different *varṇas*.

Brahmins and Kshatriyas

Agni and Indra

The relationship of complementary opposition forged between the two highest classes is, not surprisingly, often depicted in terms of the deities that most commonly serve as the divine representatives of the Brahmins and Kshatriyas: Agni and Indra.[143] "Agni is the *brahman*, Indra the *kṣatra*. Because there is a victim dedicated to Indra and Agni, one takes into oneself the *brahman* and *kṣatra*" (TB 3.9.16.3-4; cf. KB 12.9). Agni and Indra were created in the beginning as the apotheoses of elemental qualities of the *brahman* and the *kṣatra*. They joined together to produce all other creatures:

> Now Indra and Agni were emitted as the *brahman* and the *kṣatra*—the *brahman* was Agni and the *kṣatra* was Indra. The two were separate from each other when they were first emitted. They said, "Being in this condition, we shall be incapable of producing creatures. Let us two become one form." The two became one form. (ŚB 10.4.1.5)

Conjoined and acting as the standard-bearers for the ruling class comprised of the Brahmins and Kshatriyas, Indra and Agni encompass everything: "All the gods are Indra and Agni," it is said.[144] Indra and Agni are thus both the *brahman*

(ṚV 8.16.7; cf. ŚB 4.6.6.5; JUB 1.45.1) and both are kings (ṚV 6.59.3). In true hierarchical fashion, the commoners are subsumed within the ruling-class duo: "The *brahman*, the *kṣatra*, and the *viś* are this all, and Indra and Agni are this all" (ŚB 4.2.2.14). The gods of the commoner class, the Viśva Devas, are said "to be" Indra and Agni (cf. ŚB 2.4.4.13); the divine peasantry is encompassed within the union of the deified Brahmin and Kshatriya: "It [the "imperishable" syllable *om*] is both the *brahman* and the *kṣatra*. The *brahman* is Agni, and the *kṣatra* is Indra, and the Viśva Devas are Indra and Agni. And the Viśva Devas are also the *viś*. Thus it is the *brahman*, *kṣatra*, and *viś*" (ŚB 10.4.1.9). Elsewhere, Indra and Agni, who are identified as "all the gods," are said to maintain "security (*kṣema*) in the *viś*" for the king (AV 3.3.5).

In addition to being the embodiments of the *brahman* and the *kṣatra*, Agni and Indra also "are" the essential powers of (the Brahmin) *tejas* and (the Kshatriya) "manly power" (*indriya vīrya*). By combining these complementary forces, they gained enormous strength and slew Vṛtra:

> Now comes a cake on twelve potsherds for Indra and Agni. With this they [the gods] killed [Vṛtra]. Agni is fiery luster (*tejas*) and Indra is manly power (*indriya vīrya*); with these two powers (*vīryas*) they killed him. Agni is the *brahman* and Indra is the *kṣatra*. Having taken hold of these two, having united the *brahman* and the *kṣatra*, they killed him by means of these two powers. Therefore there is a cake on twelve potsherds for Indra and Agni. (ŚB 2.5.4.8)

Indra and Agni are alternatively said to represent the essential powers of (Kshatriya) physical strength (*bala*) and (Brahmin) *tejas* and "thus [through a cake on twelve potsherds dedicated to Indra and Agni] he places the physical strength on a foundation of *tejas*" (GB 2.1.22). Or again, Indra wields might (*ojas*) or virility (*vīrya*) while Agni is associated with *tejas* (ŚB 7.4.1.40,43).

Sometimes the dual deity of Indra and Agni is regarded not as the combination of Kshatriya and Brahmin but as only a Kshatriya divinity.[145] Indra and Agni are together identified with the *kṣatra* while the Viśva Devas are equated with the *viś* (ŚB 2.4.3.6); or Indra and Agni are in combination identified with Kshatriya essential powers like *ojas* (TS 5.3.2.1) or *ojas* and *vīrya* (MS 3.2.9; KS 20.11; TS 1.1.14). Indra and Agni both act as warriors by protecting the north side of the sacrifice from demons (AitB 6.4); elsewhere we learn that Indra (working by himself) loses his *indriya vīrya* when he slays Vṛtra and gets it back with an oblation to Indra and Agni (ŚB 5.2.3.8). Indra and Agni restore *indriya vīrya* (but not the Brahmin power of *tejas*) to a sacrificer who loses it when he is establishing his fires; among all the gods it is they whose potency is never used up, who are always of unweakened strength and unimpaired freshness (*āyatayamāna*).[146] Together, Indra and Agni are the swiftest (JB 1.304), the most powerful, and the strongest of the gods, and by referring to Indra and Agni a priest can put the Kshatriya traits of might (*ojas*) and physical strength (*bala*) into the Kshatriya animal, the horse: "Therefore the horse is among the animals the mightiest and the strongest" (TB 3.8.7.1–2). Elsewhere, they are called upon to put *ojas* and *bala* into the sacrificer (TS 5.6.21). They are said to be most possessed of *ojas* among the gods (ŚB 13.1.2.5–6; PB 24.17.3; 25.11.3) and are invoked to help man who is victorious in battle restore his *ojas* and *vīrya* (MS 2.1.3).

More often, however, the two gods are clearly the representatives of both of the two highest *varṇas*. As such, they are also the signifiers of the pair that epitomizes the relations between the Brahmins and the Kshatriyas: the *purohita* and the king (HŚS 17.5; BŚS 26.32; ĀpŚS 22.13.10). The two surpass other gods, and through performing a specific rite that Indra and Agni supposedly once performed, a king and his Brahmin priest (the *purohita*) surpass all other humans.[147] They are, as the apotheosis of the Brahmin-Kshatriya ruling class synthesis, superior (*śreṣṭha*) among the gods (ŚB 8.3.1.3). Together, the Kshatriya and the Brahmin, Indra and Agni, rule over the peasantry, and invoking them in the ritual ensures both the cooperation of the two social classes and their power over others:

> The Brahmin is consecrated to Agni, the Kshatriya to Indra. This chant is consecrated to Agni and Indra. Agni is the Brahmin class, Indra the class of the Kshatriyas. Thereby he supports the Kshatriya class by means of the Brahmin class and the Brahmin class by means of the Kshatriya class. In this way he does not lose the authority over the peasantry. (JB 1.182)

Mitra and Varuṇa

Mitra and Varuṇa are often paired in Vedic texts,[148] usually as complementary opposites: "That which is of Mitra is not of Varuṇa" (ŚB 3.2.4.18). This divine synthesis of opposites, one of which is the Brahmin–Kshatriya nexus, is denoted in various ways. Mitra and Varuṇa are envisioned as inhalation and exhalation (TS 5.3.4.2), or as both sorts of breaths and also this world and "yonder world" (ŚB 12.9.2.12), or as the waxing and waning lunar half-months (PB 25.10.10), or as day and night.[149]

Keeping in mind that the Brahmin–Kshatriya combination ideally results in a "ruling-class" unity, the complementarity of Mitra and Varuṇa is sometimes represented in terms of the two aspects of kingship they seem to personify. Dumézil contends that "Mitra is the sovereign in his reasoning, clear, disciplined, calm aspect. . . . Varuṇa is the sovereign in his aggressive, somber, spirited and violent aspect."[150] The Brahmin member of the pair, Mitra, is the "friendly" ruler, whereas the Kshatriya god is "cruel": "These creatures are guarded by a friend (*mitra*) and by one who is cruel (*krūra*); Mitra is the friend, and Varuṇa is the cruel one" (KS 7.11; MS 1.5.14).

Yet another type of pairing these two gods exemplify is described by G. V. Devasthali, who writes that "it would appear that Mitra and Varuṇa represent two aspects of one and the same power that bring about the same results with the only difference that the one does it by force causing in the process some violence, break or injury, while the other does it only in a natural way, without causing any such thing."[151] Thus wood broken off by itself belongs to Mitra, while that which is hewn by the axe is Varuṇa's (ŚB 5.3.2.5); butter naturally produced belongs to Mitra, that which is churned to Varuṇa (ŚB 5.3.2.6); and plants ripening in unplowed land and coming up spontaneously (e.g., wild rice) are Mitra's, those growing in tilled ground are Varuṇa's (ŚB 5.3.3.8). Mitra thus embodies the Brahminical version of power wielded "naturally" and with ease; the Kshatriya deity Varuṇa exercises power in its more coercive form.

Finally, the nature of the complementary opposition that adheres to the Mitra–Varuṇa coupling is presented in terms of the *brahman* and *kṣatra* powers the two gods represent (e.g., AVP 6.5), and most especially in terms of the relationship between a Kshatriya ruler and his Brahmin priest or *purohita*. As Gonda writes,

> There can be no doubt whatever that the identification of the latter god [i.e., Mitra] with the brahmanical order, and of the former with the nobility is not only to be viewed in the light of Varuṇa's kingship and Mitra-and-Varuṇa's universal sovereignty, but also in that of the doctrine of the complementary relation between, and co-operation of, these two classes of society. Like these heavenly rulers who are mostly invoked together the king and his domestic priest are, for the sake of the well-being of the realm, for which both of them are responsible, an inseparable pair and each other's complement.[152]

But in the myth that establishes Mitra and Varuṇa as the deified representatives of the Brahmin *purohita* and the king, we learn some interesting facts about how that relationship was conceived (at least by the Brahmin authors of the text). Mitra, as the *brahman* and the divine *purohita*, is characterized by intelligence or inspiration (*kratu*); Varuṇa, the *kṣatra* and king, incorporates capacity for action or skillfulness (*dakṣa*) (ŚB 4.1.4.1). Here the Brahmin–Kshatriya cabal is conceived as the "brains and brawn" of rule, so to speak. The text illustrates and validates its point of view by telling the story of how this relationship between the first two *varṇa*s was established "in the beginning":

> Originally these two, the *brahman* and the *kṣatra*, were separate. Then Mitra, the *brahman*, could properly stand without Varuṇa, the *kṣatra*; but Varuṇa, the *kṣatra*, could not stand properly without Mitra, the *brahman*. Whatever action Varuṇa did uninspired by Mitra, the *brahman*, did not succeed. Varuṇa, the *kṣatra*, then summoned Mitra, the *brahman*, to him and said, "Come to me so that we may unite, and I will put you ahead (*puras*). Inspired by you, I will do deeds." Mitra consented, and the two united. . . . Such is the position of a *purohita*. Therefore a Brahmin should not wish to become the *purohita* of just any Kshatriya lest his good acts conjoin with bad, nor should a Kshatriya make any Brahmin his *purohita* lest his good acts conjoin with bad. Inspired by Mitra, the *brahman*, Varuṇa subsequently did succeed. Thus it is fitting that a Brahmin should be without a king. But if he finds a [proper] king, that makes for the success [of both]. It is, however, unfitting for a king to be without a Brahmin, for whatever act he does, unsped by Mitra, the *brahman*, does not succeed. Therefore when a Kshatriya intends to act he should seek out a Brahmin, for that act succeeds only when inspired by a Brahmin. (ŚB 4.1.4.2-6)

The text clearly establishes a hierarchical dimension to the complementary opposition entailed in the Brahmin–Kshatriya, king–*purohita*, Mitra–Varuṇa conjunction. The first member of each pair ensures the success of the second; the first is independent while the second is dependent; the first is, ultimately, superior and the second inferior. We can understand better the statement made elsewhere that Mitra and Varuṇa are embodied in the two arms of the Kshatriya (for "by his arms the Kshatriya belongs to Mitra and Varuṇa").[153] The two arms are not equally weighted. While the right one belongs to (Brahmin) Mitra and the left to (Kshatriya) Varuṇa (TB 1.7.10.1), the right arm is always considered stronger.[154]

Agni and Soma

Other combinations of Brahmin and Kshatriya gods are also described in theological terms with obvious social implications. Agni and Soma[155] serve in some texts as the ciphers for the first two social classes. Agni is identified with the Brahmin meter, the *gāyatrī*, while Soma is connected to the *triṣṭubh* meter and the *kṣatra* (KB 10.5). By combining the powers of the *brahman* and the *kṣatra*, Agni and Soma can produce beneficial effects for the ritualist: "Agni is the *brahman*, Soma is the *kṣatra*. In that on the fast day they bring forward fire (= Agni) and soma (= Soma), by means of the *brahman* and *kṣatra* they thereby strike away the evil of the sacrificer" (KB 9.5). The two also wield essential powers typical of their respective classes. Thus Agni is the Brahminical power *tejas* and Soma is *indriya*; because in a certain sacrifice there is a cake is for both, the sacrificer obtains *tejas* and *indriya*.[156]

Agni and Soma, like Mitra and Varuṇa, serve as the deities that emblemize the relationship between a Brahmin *purohita* and the Kshatriya ruler. Therefore, a Brahmin who wishes to be chosen as a king's *purohita* should offer two animals with black necks to Agni and one brown animal to Soma: "The Brahmin belongs with Agni, the Kshatriya with Soma. On either side of the animal dedicated to Soma there is one for Agni. With *tejas*, with the Brahmin, he seizes the kingdom on both sides and immediately appropriates it for himself, and he is made a *purohita*" (TS 2.1.2.9). Here again we see that the Brahmin is, through the theological and ritual correlates, the superior of the two. It is the *purohita* who "seizes the kingdom" and "appropriates it."[157]

Bṛhaspati and Indra

Bṛhaspati and Indra form another pair of divine signifiers for the union of the Brahmin and Kshatriya classes.[158] In the beginning, it is said, the *brahman* entered Bṛhaspati and the *kṣatra* entered Indra.[159] By means of offerings to Bṛhaspati which precede the consecration of a king and offerings to Indra that follow it, the sacrificer is "enclosed on both sides" by the *brahman* and the *kṣatra*.[160] Elsewhere, Bṛhaspati is the *brahman*, Indra is virility (*vīrya*), and the recitation is identified with livestock: "Therefore with virility and the *brahman* on both sides he envelops the livestock" and prevents them from wandering off (GB 2.6.7).

One myth relates that when the gods wanted to perform a sacrifice they were harassed by demons on the south side of the sacrificial grounds.

> The gods said to Indra, "You are superior (*śreṣṭha*), the most powerful (*baliṣṭha*) and the most virile (*vīryavattama*) among us. Take action against those demons." Indra said, "Let the ***brahman*** be my ally." The gods consented and made Bṛhaspati his ally, for Bṛhaspati is the ***brahman***. When by means of Bṛhaspati and Indra they struck away the evil demons in the south, they spread this sacrifice in a place free from danger and demons.

Moreover, by having the ***brahman*** priest (= Bṛhaspati and the ***brahman***) recite a particular hymn (= Indra and the *kṣatra*), the sacrifice of human beings is protected on the south from demons (ŚB 9.2.3.2–5). Once again, the point of the story seems to be that only with a Brahmin cohort can the Kshatriya, regardless of his innate strength and apparent "superiority," effectively act.

In another myth that is even more telling in regard to the social dimensions of theology and ritual, the gods, fearful of the destructive inclinations of the Kshatriya, fettered and subdued him before birth. If one (i.e., a Brahmin priest) desires that a Kshatriya be unfettered and unsubdued and become a slayer of his enemies, he should offer to Indra and Bṛhaspati, "for the Kshatriya belongs to Indra, and Bṛhaspati is the ***brahman***. By the ***brahman*** he frees him from the bond that fetters him."[161] According to other texts, because of this mythological background a sacrifice to Indra and Bṛhaspati is to be performed upon the birth of any member of the Kshatriya class (ĀpŚS 19.27.22; HŚS 22.6.28).

The myth is told somewhat differently, and the ritual performed for a somewhat different reason (for a Kshatriya who "does not rise in the world"), in the following variant:

> Aditi, desirous of offspring, cooked a rice mess and ate the remains. She fettered Indra when he was an embryo with an iron bond. He was born fettered. Bṛhaspati acted as his priest at this sacrificial rite in honor of Indra and Bṛhaspati. That bond of his [then] fell apart on its own. He [thereupon] turned around with his thunderbolt [and pervaded] these quarters of the universe. He who does not rise in the world should have this sacrificial rite in honor of Indra and Bṛhaspati performed. He is surrounded by evil; that is why he does not rise in the world. It is to Bṛhaspati that the sacrificial food is to be divided, and it is for Indra that the rite is performed. He [the priest] in this way fully liberates him. He turns around with the thunderbolt to all quarters of the universe. (MS 2.1.22)

The ritual, with oblations to Bṛhaspati (= the *brahman*) and Indra (= the *kṣatra*), may also be done for a Kshatriya who wishes to increase his power (KS 11.2) or for a man who is either desirous of being a *purohita* or desires to have a village (MŚS 5.1.9.13; cf. MŚS 5.1.7.48ff.).

Bṛhaspati and Soma

Another pair of deified Brahmins and Kshatriyas is composed of Bṛhaspati and Soma (see, e.g., AitB 2.38). The *gāyatrī* meter is connected to Bṛhaspati and Bṛhaspati is the ***brahman***, and Soma is the *kṣatra*; therefore when one recites verses in the *gāyatrī* meter to Soma one wins both the "glory of the ***brahman*** and the glory of the *kṣatra*" (KB 7.10). Elsewhere we read that Soma was once supposed to have taken away the property of his *purohita*, Bṛhaspati—a terrible mistake according to the Brahmins who relate the myth. Even after making restorations to Bṛhaspati, Soma felt guilty about acting in such a way to the apotheosis of the *brahman* power (ŚB 4.1.2.4).

Other Combinations

Among other pairings of deities representing the first two *varṇas* is the union between Mitra and Indra. At KS 12.1 and MS 2.3.1 we learn that the Brahmin belongs to Mitra and Varuṇa, and the Kshatriya to Indra and Varuṇa. "That means that in accordance with tradition there are close ties between nobility and Indra on the one hand, between *brahman*hood and Mitra on the other, but at the same time between Varuṇa and either social division."[162] Another text also regards Bṛhaspati as the Brahmin deity but then joins him with Mitra, who here functions as the Kshatriya of the pair (MS 4.3.9).[163]

These texts all corroborate the correlations between particular gods and the two highest social classes we have observed elsewhere. There are few surprises here. The Brahmin deities of the divine pairs are Agni, Bṛhaspati, and Mitra; they are coupled with the expected Kshatriya candidates—Soma, Indra, Varuṇa (and, in one text, Mitra). The relationships we observe among these deities of the first two *varṇas* are also rather predictable. On the one hand, the conjunction of the divine representatives of the ruling class, of the theological incarnations of the powers of the *brahman* and the *kṣatra*, constitutes a supposedly overwhelming power, especially over the lower classes or *viś*. On the other hand, the two terms in the relationship are ultimately not equal. While the complementary oppositions of rule are embodied in these dual deities—Brahmin–Kshatriya, *purohita*–king, spiritual authority (e.g., *tejas*)–temporal or physical power (e.g., *indriya*), organic persuasion–violent force, friendliness–cruelty, inspiration–action, and so forth—another set of terms also is obviously entailed. This would include the opposition of the independent and the dependent (the Brahmin, the *purohita*, and the god that represents them can live without a king, but not vice versa) and, finally, the opposition of the higher–lower.

Kshatriyas and the Viś

Together, the Brahmin and Kshatriya—in heaven as on earth—rule over the populace as a whole, a relationship that coalesced in the *purohita*–king duo and its divine replicates. But it is specifically the charge of the Kshatriya to implement and exercise this rule over the *viś*. While Brahmin deities also are portrayed in positions of power over gods of the peasantry,[164] it is primarily the deified signifiers of the Kshatriya and the Vaishya that encapsulate, and instruct us about, the ideal form of political rule as it was conceived in the Veda.

The relationship between the king and his subjects, between the Kshatriya and the *viś*, is nowhere more graphically portrayed than in the interactions of

Indra and the Maruts. As Alfred Hillebrandt notes, "In the entire ritual literature the Maruts are regarded as a clan, as *devānām viśaḥ*, and seen as the archetype of the Vaishyas whose fickle relations with their king have their model in those between the Maruts and Indra."[165]

The Maruts are like sons to Indra (ṚV 1.100.5) and, as the divine commoner class, attend upon their overlord (TS 4.6.5.6) and increase his strength and prowess.[166] But like *viś* on the earthly plane, the Maruts must be disciplined. Two birds can be killed with one stone: both the peasants in heaven and those on earth can be controlled, and the Kshatriya's rule strengthened, in rites that deal with Indra and the Maruts.

Because of the identification between Indra and the Kshatriya, on the one hand, and that of the Maruts and the *viś*, on the other, ritual manipulations dealing with the divine entities are supposed to have consequences for the relationship between Kshatriyas and the peasantry they rule. The Maruts "belong to" the Kshatriya god Indra (see, e.g., KB 5.5), and thus at the soma sacrifice, a certain draught of the elixer is to be offered to Indra Marutvat, the "possessor of the Maruts," for "through the *viś* the *kṣatra* becomes strong (*balavat*). Thus he now puts that strength into the *kṣatra*, and therefore he draws the cups belonging to he who possesses the Maruts." The text goes on to emphasize that cups are drawn for the Kshatriya Indra, and not for the lower-class Maruts: "For were he also to draw cups for the Maruts, he would make the *viś* rebellious towards the *kṣatra*. He thus assigns a share [to the Maruts only] after [that apportioned to] Indra, whereby he makes the *viś* subservient and obedient to the *kṣatra*" (ŚB 4.3.3.9–10).

Elsewhere, too, an offering to the Maruts follows one to Indra, for "the Maruts are the *viś*. He thus fastens the *viś* to him [the Kshatriya sacrificer]" (TS 6.6.5.2–3). Another text calls for a certain mantra dedicated to Indra Marutvat should the sacrificer be a Kshatriya, for "the Kshatriya belongs to Indra, and the *viś* to the Maruts. Thereby they make the *viś* follow the Kshatriya class. Therefore the *viś* obeys the Kshatriya class" (JB 1.95). Ritual symbols for Indra and the Maruts are, in sum, managed in such a way as to ensure that the "Kshatriyas are the controllers of the people" (ŚB 2.5.2.27).

In a certain optional sacrifice, offerings to Indra and the Maruts are recommended for one who desires possession of a village; these oblations "make his fellows subject to him." The offerings to Indra are placed on the *āhavanīya* fire, and those to the Maruts on *gārhapatya*, "for the prevention of confusion." Furthermore, "he places [the offering to the Maruts] down when the recitation is proceeding; thus he makes the *viś* obedient to him."[167] Elsewhere we learn that by offering a victim to Indra between victims offered to the Maruts and the Viśva Devas (both here equated with the *viś*) the priest "guards the *kṣatra* by the *viś*, and hence the *kṣatra* here [on earth, on the social plane] is on both sides guarded by the *viś*" (ŚB 3.9.1.18).

In other instances, it is the royal god Varuṇa that represents the Kshatriya class in the relations with the commoners as symbolized by the Maruts.[168] Thus, in one rite, a ram is dedicated to Varuṇa and a ewe to the Maruts, for "Varuṇa is the *kṣatra*, and the male represents virility (*vīrya*); thus they thereby put virility into the *kṣatra*. The female, on the other hand, is without virility, and the Maruts are the *viś*. Hence they thereby cause the *viś* to be without virility" (ŚB 2.5.2.36). In another ritual, the northern or "superior" (*uttara*) altar is connected with Varuṇa, and the southern one with the Maruts: "On the northern altar he raises the *uttara vedi*, not on the southern one. Varuṇa is the *kṣatra* and the Maruts are the *viś*. He thus makes the *kṣatra* superior (*uttar*) to the *viś*, and thus the *viś* here [on earth] serve the Kshatriya who is placed above them" (ŚB 2.5.2.6). In yet another rite in which Varuṇa and the Maruts are involved, the *adhvaryu* priest, and not the *pratiprasthātṛ* priest, calls out the offering cry ("*śrauṣat*"), for

> The *pratiprasthātṛ* is merely the imitator of what is done [by the *adhvaryu*]. For Varuṇa is the *kṣatra* and the Maruts are the *viś*. Hence he makes the *viś* the imitators, the followers of the *kṣatra*. But were the *pratiprasthātṛ* also to call for the "*śrauṣat*," he would doubtless make the *viś* equal in power to the *kṣatra*. For this reason, the *pratiprasthātṛ* does not call for the "*śrauṣat*." (ŚB 2.5.2.34)

A similar relationship exists between the Kshatriya gods Indra and Varuṇa, on the one hand, and the Viśva Devas or Ādityas on the other. The same sort of ritual patterns are formulated with the same social reverberations. Both the Kshatriya and Indra are "eaters of the peasantry" (see, e.g., AitB 8.12, 8.17); because the Viśva Devas are equated both to the *viś* and to "food," by offering a victim to Indra before that to the Viśva Devas the priest "places food before" the Kshatriya sacrificer (ŚB 3.9.1.16; cf. TS 6.6.5.2–3). In another rite, the white rice is separated from the dark:

> From the white rice he should offer a cake to the Ādityas, [for] the *viś* have the Ādityas for their deity. He thus gets power over the *viś*. "He has obtained power over the *viś*, but he has not obtained power over the realm (*rāṣṭra*)," they say. From the dark rice he should offer an oblation to Varuṇa, and he then gets power over both the *viś* and the realm. (TS 2.3.1.3–4)

Or again, having established that the dual deity Indrāgni is the *kṣatra* and the Viśva Devas are the *viś*, one text notes that Indrāgni once allowed the Viśva Devas a share in the sacrifice. An offering is thus made to them now, and thus "the *viś* is allowed to share whatever the *kṣatra* conquers" (ŚB 2.4.3.6).

Social implications are also inherent in the relations between other deities representing the Kshatriya and the peasantry. Rudra is the *kṣatra* and the Rudras are his *viś*. When ritual mantras are directed to Rudra, the Kshatriya is made to have "a share in the *viś*." Thus, "whatever belongs to the *viś*, in that the Kshatriya has a share" (ŚB 9.1.1.18). In another text, it is Pūṣan who represents "food" (and the *viś*, as we know, are food for the upper classes) and Indra who is identified with the Kshatriya, and both are represented in a he-goat victim offered at the Aśvamedha:

> [He binds a he-goat] dedicated to Indra and Pūṣan on the upper part [i.e., to the neck of the horse]. The Kshatriya belongs to Indra and Pūṣan is food. [Inasmuch as the priests bind to the horse this he-goat consecrated to Indra and Pūṣan] he

> provides him [the sacrificer] on both sides with food. And therefore the Kshatriya is an eater of food. (TB 3.8.23.2)[169]

The Authority of the Gods

In the texts analyzed in this chapter we saw how theological discourse oozes with social ramifications—and often with explicit social claims. Discussions revolving around the relations between deified Brahmins and Kshatriyas clearly are meant to be both models of and models for relations between Brahmins and Kshatriyas in less ethereal realms. The Brahmin and the Kshatriya are to cooperate and combine, but the latter is also to be subordinated to the former. And those passages dealing with divine rulers like Indra and Varuṇa and the divine *viś* (the Maruts, Viśva Devas, Ādityas, etc.) over which they rule also carry a clear message: the peasantry, divine or human, are to be controlled and exploited by the Kshatriya who rules over them, and they are to be docile, cooperative, and loyal. The divine thus recapitulates the human; or, more accurately, the idealized form of social essences and relations are projected into a divine sphere that both represents and authorizes them. The relations established between different classes of gods are designed to be both reflections of and paradigms for relations among humans.

But while the Brahmin and Kshatriya gods combine to form the heavenly ruling class that will govern the "*viś* of the gods," and while the divine Kshatriya king has special privileges with regard to his "food," his deified commoners, the texts also insist that the apotheosis of the priesthood maintains superiority over both the Kshatriya gods and the divine peasantry. Thus, although Indra or Varuṇa might elsewhere be designated the eater of the *viś*, in one text it is Agni, the Brahmin god, who is the "eater" while Soma, the Kshatriya, is "food" (ŚB 11.1.6.19). Verses in a particular ritual are addressed to both Agni and Indra, and the priest "thereby brings the *brahman* and the *kṣatra* into union." But the mantras dedicated to Agni are recited before those to Indra: "He places the *brahman* before the *kṣatra* and makes the *kṣatra* and the *viś* follow after the *brahman*" (PB 15.6.3). The Brahmin god (and also the Brahmin human, or so it is suggested) ultimately rules over "this all," the latter being emblemized in the following by the Viśva Devas:

> Then [Prajāpati once upon a time offered an oblation] for the Viśva Devas, for the Viśva Devas are all. With all Prajāpati then again strengthened himself; everything turned unto him, and he made everything subject to him. And so does this one now become strong by everything; everything turns to him, and he makes everything subject to himself. And as to why it [i.e., the offering to the Viśva Devas] follows that for Bṛhaspati, Bṛhaspati is the *brahman* and the Viśva Devas are this all. He then makes the *brahman* the head (*mukha*) of this all, and therefore the Brahmin is the head of this all. (ŚB 3.9.1.13–14)

The authority of the divine is thus lent to a social hierarchy in which the Brahmins placed themselves at the top, their Kshatriya patrons in second place, and the rest of society (the vast majority) at the bottom. The gods, not coincidentally, were categorized into the same *varṇas* as humans; they were given the same attributes and many of the same powers; and they were said to interact among themselves in the same manner that humans did—or at least were supposed to. The gods and their ways reflect the ways of humans in society; conversely, the ways of humans in society are (if we all know what's good for us) to echo those of the gods.

The *varṇa* system was in this way upheld by the very real powers of imaginary gods. It would be naive and anachronistic of us to deny or diminish the enormous persuasive force that must have accompanied the kind of theological discourse reviewed in this chapter. To contend that the divine realm was organized along the lines of *varṇa* was to appeal to a form of authority those living in traditional societies regarded as absolute. God or, in this case, the gods are not disputable, and neither is a categorical system that not only was created by the divine but was also used to classify the divinities themselves.

NOTES

1. Sigmund Freud, *The Future of an Illusion*, trans. by James Strachey (New York: W.W. Norton, 1961), pp. 33–34. See also *Totem and Taboo*, trans. by James Strachey (New York: W. W. Norton, 1950).

2. Melford E. Spiro, "Religion: Problems of Definition and Explanation," in *Anthropological Approaches to the Study of Religion*, ed. by Michael Banton, A.S.A. Monographs, Vol. 3 (London: Tavistock, 1966), p. 103.

3. Émile Durkheim, *Society and Philosophy*, trans. by D. F. Pocock (New York: The Free Press, 1974), p. 52.

4. For the gods and goddess in Vedic literature, consult A. A. Macdonell, *Vedic Mythology* (reprint Varanasi: Indological Book House, 1963); Alfred Hillebrandt, *Vedic Mythology*, 2 vols., trans. by S. Rajeswara Sarma (Delhi: Motilal Banarsidass, 1970); Jan Gonda, *Some Observations on the Relations between "Gods" and "Powers" in the Veda á propos of the Phrase śunuh sahasā* (The Hague: Mouton, 1957); and Sukumari Bhattacharji, *The Indian Theogony* (Cambridge: Cambridge University Press, 1970).

5. For the anomalous conception of the number of gods being 3,339, see ṚV 3.9.9 and 10.52.6.

6. E.g., BĀU 3.9.1ff. For the notion that the thirty three gods consist of eight Vasus, eleven Rudras, and twelve Ādityas together with two more (sky and earth, Indra and Prajāpati, or some other pair) to total thirty three, see ŚB 4.5.7.2, 11.6.3.4–5; AitB 2.18; KB 12.6; JB 1.141, 1.279–281. For thirty-three Vedic gods, see also ṚV 3.6.9, 8.35.3 (three times eleven); AV 10.7.13; etc.

7. Cf. Manu 5.96–97, 7.3–8; 9.303ff., where the king is said to be made up of the essences of the deities Indra, Vāyu, Yama, the sun, Agni, Varuṇa, the moon, and Kubera.

8. MS 4.5.8. As Jan Gonda writes in relation to this passage, "Agni and Soma are the two great ritual deities, the representatives of fire and of the power of life that circulates in the universe; Savitār is the great impeller of the gods . . . who makes the sacrifice prosper . . . ; Bṛhaspati represents and is the Brahman itself . . . and the priest of the gods. And that is why, the text continues, other people have recourse for assistance to a brahmin. A learned brahmin (*śrotriya*) has three gods, Agni, Bṛhaspati, and Sarasvatī, who are the

most important ones (*bhūyiṣṭha*) and that is why other brahmins have recourse to him." *Pūṣan and Sarasvatī* (Amsterdam: North-Holland, 1985), p. 16.

9. What few possible exceptions there are may here be noted. At TS 4.1.7.3, Agni is called the "supporter of the *kṣatra*," while at KB 19.1 Agni is variously identified with the *brahman*, the *kṣatra*, and the "supporter of the *kṣatra*." We saw earlier above how the *brahman* is said to be the "womb" of the *kṣatra*; we may have in these passages a restatement of that sentiment.

10. TS 5.6.4.5; TB 2.1.4.5, 3.7.3.2–3; ŚB 11.5.4.12; PB 15.4.8; JB 1.182.

11. E.g., MŚS 1.5.3–4. According to ŚŚS 2.3.3–7, the special offerings for a Brahmin sacrificer should be to Agni in combination with Indra (Indrāgni) or with another Brahmin deity, Soma.

12. Consult ĀpŚS 1.1, 4.1–3; 24.2.19–25; BhŚS 4.20–22.

13. For the identification of Agni and the *brahman*, ṚV 2.1.2, 4.9.4, 7.7.5; KB 9.1, 9.5, 12.8; TS 4.3.9.1; ŚB 1.3.3.19, 1.4.2.2, 1.5.1.11, 2.6.4.5, 5.3.5.32, 8.5.1.12, 10.4.1.9; AV 15.10.7,9. One text refers to this god rather enigmatically as the "calf of the *brahman*" (*brahmaṇo vatsaḥ*, JUB 2.13.1).

14. ŚB 3.2.2.7,9. Cf. AitB 7.24, where a Kshatriya in the course of being consecrated for sacrifice adopts Agni as his deity and associates himself with the *brahman* power and the Brahmin class.

15. ŚB 7.1.2.4. Agni is also the "bestower of food" (PB 17.9.2), the "eater of food" (*annādya*, JUB 1.51.6; PB 14.3.19), as well as the "lord of food" (*annapati*, KŚS 5.13.1). "Agni is the eater of food and lord of food; he becomes an eater of food, a lord of food, with his offspring he attains proper food who knows this" (AitB 1.8; cf. ŚB 11.4.3.8).

16. Epithets for Agni include *ṛtvij*, *vipra*, and *purohita*. See Macdonell, *Vedic Mythology*, pp. 96–97. Agni is specifically the *hotṛ* priest among the gods according to ṚV 8.49.1, 10.2.1, 10.7.5, 10.91.8; PB 24.13.5; ŚB 13.2.6.9; and cf. TS 4.3.13.4.

17. Agni is elsewhere identified with the "life force" (*āyus*) and by addressing Agni in a certain rite the sacrificer puts life force into himself (ŚB 6.7.3.7).

18. KB 12.8; JB 1.93; ŚB 2.3.1.31; KS 4.14,15.

19. AV 7.89.4; cf. PB 17.5.3; ŚB 5.3.5.8. For Agni and *tejas*, see also MS 2.4.6; KS 11.1; AV 9.2.19; ŚB 2.5.4.8, 5.2.3.8, 5.4.5.2, 7.4.1.39, 13.2.6.9; AitB 3.36; TB 2.1.2.9, 3.3.4.2–3. At Mbh 13.104.63, Agni (together with the cow and the *brahman*) is one of the three manifestations of *tejas*; and according to Mbh 4.2.15, Agni is the "best of all things that possess *tejas*." For Agni as the possessor of both *brahmavarcasa* and *tejas*, JB 3.165.

20. E.g., *varcas* at ŚB 4.5.4.4; *tapas*, *haras*, *arcis*, *śocis*, and *tejas* at AV 9.2.19; *bhārgas* at ṚV 10.61.14. For Agni as identified with the sun, ṚV 1.69.10, 1.70.8, 1.73.8.

21. Agni is all the gods according to MS 2.1.4; KS 13.6; ŚB 5.2.3.6; GB 2.1.16; and is both the progenitor and lord of creatures according to ŚB 3.9.1.1ff. Elsewhere, Agni is called the "womb of the gods" (*devayoni*, AitB 2.14). Thus a sacrificer who wishes to drive away the gods of his enemy sacrifices to Agni, who is all the gods (MS 1.7; KS 10.1).

22. ŚB 6.6.3.15 and 9.4.1.16 say that Agni is both the *brahman* and the *kṣatra*. See note 9 above, and cf. the statement at ṚV 7.12.3 that Agni is both the Brahmin deity Mitra and the Kshatriya god Varuṇa.

23. For Bṛhaspati's Brahmin connections, see also Cosmogonies VIII, X, XI, and XIII. The secondary literature on this deity includes Jan Gonda, *Prajāpati's Relations with Brahman, Bṛhaspati and Brahmā* (Amsterdam: North-Holland, 1989); G. M. Bailey, *The Mythology of Brahmā* (Delhi: Oxford University Press, 1983), esp. pp. 76–82;

Saraswati Bali, *Bṛhaspati in the Vedas and Purāṇas* (Delhi: Nag Publishers, 1978); Hanns-Peter Schmidt, *Bṛhaspati und Indra: Untersuchungen zur vedischen Mythologie und Kulturgeschichte* (Wiesbaden: Otto Harrassowitz, 1968); N. J. Shende, "Bṛhaspati in the Vedic and Epic Literature," *Bulletin of the Deccan College Research Institute* 8 (1946–47): 225–51; and Bhattacharji, *The Indian Theogony*, pp. 317–320.

24. Bailey, *The Mythology of Brahmā*, p. 77. For an exceptional connection between Bṛhaspati and the Kshatriya *varṇa*, see TĀ 4.5.4.

25. ṚV 2.1.3, 10.141.3; TS 1.5.4.3, 1.7.1.5, 2.2.9.1, 2.4.13.1, 5.3.4.4; VS 10.30; MS 2.1.7, 2.2.3, 3.6.4; KS 24.3, 28.5; TB 3.8.3.1; JB 1.202; AitB 1.30; KB 12.8; ŚB 3.3.1.2, 3.9.1.1ff., 5.3.3.5, 5.3.5.7–8, 5.4.5.2, 9.2.3.3, 11.4.3.13, 13.2.6.9; etc. He was born of the *ṛta* (ṚV 2.23.15) which is elsewhere identified with the *brahman*. For a more or less complete listing of the many passages in which Bṛhaspati is equated with the *brahman*, see Gonda, *Prajāpati's Relations with Brahman*, pp. 12–13.

26. E.g., TS 1.5.4.3, 1.7.1.5, 2.2.9.1; GB 2.1.3,4. According to AV 15.10.3–4, the *brahman* entered Bṛhaspati at the time of creation.

27. TB 2.5.7.4; ŚB 11.4.3.13; KŚS 5.13.1.

28. TS 3.4.5.1; ŚB 8.4.3.4; cf. ṚV 2.23.1; TB 3.11.4.2.

29. For the extremely common connection between Bṛhaspati and *brahmavarcasa*, see, e.g., KS 11.1; JUB 1.37.6, 1.51.11; TS 5.5.12.10; KB 7.10, 12.8; JB 1.362; TB 3.1.4.6, 3.8.23.3; AV 15.10.8–9. Bṛhaspati is also associated with *varcas* at AV 2.29.1; cf. AV 19.26.4.

30. ŚB 12.8.3.29; cf. TB 2.6.5.7–8. For Bṛhaspati as *purohita* of the gods, ṚV 2.24.9; TS 6.4.10; MS 1.11.5; KS 11.3, 14.5; AitB 8.26; SB 4.1.2.4, 5.3.1.2, 12.8.3.29; JB 1.125; and Shende, "Bṛhaspati in the Vedic and Epic Literature," pp. 225ff. Bṛhaspati, according to one scholar, "was originally an aspect of Agni as a divine priest presiding over devotion." Macdonell, *Vedic Mythology*, pp. 103, 104. For equivalences between Agni and Bṛhaspati, see, e.g., ṚV 2.1.3 and consult Schmidt, *Bṛhaspati und Indra*, pp. 62–72.

31. ŚB 12.8.3.29; cf. ŚB 3.1.4.15, 5.1.4.14, 5.3.5.7; AitB 1.13, 19.1, 21.1.

32. ṚV 2.1.3, 10.141.3; TB 3.7.6.3; ŚB 3.9.1.11, 9.2.3.5; TS 3.2.7.1; BhŚS 3.18.8; ĀpŚS 3.20.8. At PB 6.5.5, however, Bṛhaspati is identified with the *udgātṛ* priest.

33. E.g., ŚB 13.1.5.3, 13.2.6.9; TB 3.8.3.1, 3.12.9.3; BhŚS 3.18.7; ĀpŚS 3.20.7; AitB 5.34.

34. ŚB 13.2.6.9. Elsewhere we learn that since the *brahman* priest, who is related to Bṛhaspati, sits on the right side of the sacrificial grounds, the right side of the human body is more endowed with *brahmavarcasa* than the left (TB 3.9.5.1).

35. For Bṛhaspati's connection to speech, ŚB 5.3.3.11,31, 14.4.1.23; VS 9.39–40; TB 1.7.4.1. He is designated the "lord of speech" (*vācaspati*) at TS 1.8.10.1, 1.9.10.1; MS 2.6.6, 3.14.16, 4.9.2; KS 15.5; ŚB 5.1.4.12; TB 1.7.4.4, 2.6.19.2. In at least one text, Bṛhaspati is identified with both *vāc* and the *brahman* (ŚB 5.3.3.5).

36. AV 15.10.3ff.; ŚB 3.9.1.10–14, 5.1.1.11, 5.1.5.2,4; cf. ŚB 5.1.5.4,8,11; MS 4.4.9; AitB 1.13; PB 19.17.4–8; JUB 1.37.6.

37. JUB 2.9.6. For Vāc as the "queen" or *rāṣṭrī* (and thus potentially a Kshatriya goddess), see ṚV 8.100.10, 10.125.3; and AitB 1.19.

38. For this goddess, see Gonda, *Pūṣan and Sarasvatī* .

39. See, e.g., MS 1.11.4, 2.1.7, 3.4.4; VS 10.30; KB 12.8; ŚB 3.9.1.7, 5.2.2.13, 5.3.5.8, 5.4.5.2, 9.3.4.17; AitB 3.1.10; ĀśvŚS 3.1.14, 4.13.2; TĀ 4.5.1, 4.15.1; ŚŚS 7.10.15; KŚS 15.8.7; Mbh 9.41.31; 12.231.8; 12.306.6; and J. Gonda, *Pūṣan and Sarasvatī*, pp. 30ff. Sarasvatī is dubbed the "goddess of speech" (*vācdevi*) at BGS 3.6.2.

40. TS 2.1.2.6, 3.4.3.4; KS 13.12; cf. MS 1.10.5, 2.5.2; KS 12.12, 12.13.

41. See ŚB 3.1.4.9, 14.2.1.15; MS 1.22.10, 3.6.4; KS 2.2, 23.2.

42. E.g., ŚB 2.3.3.18, 6.2.2.4,33, 6.1.1.5, 7.1.3.7, 8.5.3.2, 10.4.1.12, 10.4.2.1. Prajāpati is also in the later literature connected with Brahmā, already at ĀśvGS 3.4.1. See Gonda, *Prajāpati's Relations with Brahman*, passim.

43. Prajāpati is the "lord of speech" according to ŚB 3.1.3.22 and 5.1.1.16.

44. E.g., MS 4.7.8, 4.8.3; ŚB 5.1.1.10, 13.6.2.8. At ŚB 7.3.1.42, Prajāpati is labeled *sarvam brahmā*.

45. GB 2.5.8; MS 1.11.7; KS 14.7.

46. The literature on this deity includes Paul Thieme, *Mitra and Aryaman* (New Haven: Connecticut Academy of Arts and Sciences, 1957); Georges Dumézil, *Mitra-Varuṇa: An Essay on Two Indo-European Representations of Sovereignty*, trans. by Derek Coltman (New York: Zone Books, 1988); and Jan Gonda, *The Vedic God Mitra* (Leiden: E. J. Brill, 1972).

47. TS 5.1.9.3; ŚB 2.3.2.12, 4.1.4.10; 5.3.2.4; ĀpŚS 25.22.11.

48. ŚB 5.3.3.8. For Mitra's connection to *satya*, see also TS 1.8.10.2, 1.3.4.5, 3.4.5.1; TB 1.7.4.1, 3.11.4.1; MS 2.6.6, 4.3.9; PGS 1.5.10; VaikhSmS 1.17.2.

49. KS 12.1; MS 2.3.1; MŚS 5.2.1.1ff.

50. For Mitra as a Kshatriya, see ṚV 8.25.8; ŚB 11.4.3.3; TB 1.7.8.4. Some texts term Mitra the "lord of the *kṣatra*" (*kṣatrapati*): "Let Mitra, the *kṣatra*, the lord of the *kṣatra*, bestow *kṣatra* upon me at this sacrifice" (KŚS 5.13.1; ŚB 5.3.5.28, 5.4.3.5, 11.4.3.11; TB 2.5.7.3,4). See also MS 4.3.9, where an offering to Mitra and Bṛhaspati is recommended for a ruler whose kingdom is tottering: "Mitra is the *kṣatra*, Bṛhaspati is the *brahman*; he takes hold of the *kṣatra* and the *brahman* when he consecrates himself." Gonda explains why Mitra can function as either a Brahmin or a Kshatriya: "The seeming contradiction Mitra = *brahman* and Mitra = *kṣatram* may probably be viewed as follows. The dual deity Mitra–Varuṇa is traditionally vested with authority, wielding also that power and influence which is called *kṣatram*. That means that either of them, if appearing individually, can represent *kṣatram*. If however they are regarded as each other's complement one of them can be associated with the complement of *kṣatram*, i.e. *brahman*, and it is interesting to see that then it is Mitra who enters into this engagement." Gonda, *The Vedic God Mitra*, p. 30. Mitra apparently stands in for the Brahmin class when joined with Varuṇa in Cosmogonies VIII, X, and XII.

51. Who is identified with the Brahmins and/or the *brahman* at MS 4.5.8; TS 5.3.4.4; JUB 3.4.5; cf. ŚānĀ 1.5. See also A. du Gubernatis, "Brahman et Savitri ou l'origine de la priere," *Actes du onzieme congrès international des orientalistes* (Paris, 1897): 9–44.

52. E.g., AitB 7.24. The sun "is" the *brahman* according to ChU 3.19.1; and MŚS 5.1.9.4 recommends a sacrifice to Sūrya for one who desires the Brahmin power of *brahmavarcasa*.

53. While others become food for the newly crowned human king, Brahmins are exempt: "Therefore the Brahmin is not to be fed upon, for he has Soma as his king" (ŚB 5.3.3.12). Soma, functioning as a Kshatriya king, is said to have oppressed his Brahmin priest, Bṛhaspati (ŚB 4.1.2.4), but elsewhere he is closely connected to the first *varṇa*. Soma is referred to as the deity of the Brahmin (KS 11.5) or is connected to the *brahman* power (ṚV 9.96.6; MS 4.5.8; JB 1.316); he is, with Agni, connected to *tejas* at TB 1.3.1.1. Other gods who are occasionally connected to the Brahmins include the divine twins, the Aśvins, who are identified with the *brahman* (ṚV 2.39.1,3) and are connected to the Brahmin essential powers of *tejas* and *brahmavarcasa* at TB 2.6.5.2; KS 38.4; cf. ŚB 12.7.2.4; JB 2.130. According to P. V. Kane, in the Mbh the Aśvins are Shūdras. *History of Dharmaśāstra*, 2d ed. (Poona: Bhandarkar Oriental Research Institute, 1975), Vol II, Pt. 1, p. 42.

54. For Indra's characteristics and mythological exploits, consult Herman Lommel,

Der arische Kriegsgott (Frankfurt: V. Klostermann, 1939); Usha Choudhuri, *Indra and Varuṇa in Indian Mythology* (Delhi: Nag Publishers, 1981); Jan Gonda, *The Indra Hymns of the Ṛgveda* (Leiden: E. J. Brill, 1989); and Bhattacharji, *The Indian Theogony*, pp. 249–83. For Indra's fairly rare association with the *brahman* power, see, e.g., ṚV 6.45.7, 8.16.7; ŚB 4.6.6.5; JUB 4.21.2.

55. Bhattacharji, *The Indian Theogony*, p. 258. In addition to texts cited below, Indra's Kshatriya affiliation is also apparent at JB 1.182; TB 2.4.7.7, 3.9.16.3, 3.8.23.2; AitB 7.23; TS 1.8.9.1; and in Cosmogonies I, V–VIII, and X–XIII.

56. See HŚS 13.7.18–20; ĀpŚS 18.21.9–11. The Kshatriya should set up his fires with mantras directed to Indra (see, e.g., VŚS 1.4.3–4; ŚŚS 2.1–4, 2.3.3–7; MŚS 1.5.3–4), and the Kshatriya sacrificer of the Vājapeya should at various points adjust the mantras so that they address Indra, for "Indra is the *kṣatra* and a Kshatriya is the *kṣatra*" (ŚB 5.1.5.2ff.; cf. ŚŚS 16.17.1–3). See also the *indrastoma* or *indrastut* sacrifice described at PB 19.16.1–7, JB 2.139,140; LŚS 9.4.29; BŚS 18.14; ĀpŚS 22.10.3; 22.13.8–9; 22.27.13–21; KŚS 22.11.15–17; ĀśvŚS 9.7.26–27; ŚŚS 14.58. The rite is to be performed for Kshatriya for the obtaining the powers of *ojas* and *vīrya*. TS 2.3.4.3 says that a Kshatriya of low rank should sacrifice to Indra to improve his standing; elsewhere we read that a Kshatriya sacrificer who is ill should offer a ritual with Indra as his deity (KS 12.1; MS 2.3.1; MŚS 5.2.1.1ff.; TS 2.3.13.1–2). For Indra's ritual connection to the Kshatriya class, see also MS 4.4.9; PB 15.4.8; ŚB 10.4.1.9.

57. ṚV 10.180.3; cf. AV 7.84.2; TS 1.6.12.4; TB 2.6.17.7.

58. See also, e.g., KB 12.8; TS 2.5.12.5, 4.3.9.1, 4.4.12.1; TB 2.6.17.7, 2.8.5.7, 3.9.16.3; ŚB 5.1.1.11, 5.3.1.3, 5.3.5.33, 5.4.3.18; AitB 4.9, 7.28; AV 15.10.3ff.

59. Jan Gonda, *Ancient-Indian ojas, Latin *augos and the Indo-European Nouns –es/–os* (Utrecht: A. Osthoek's Uitgevers Mij., 1952), p. 5.

60. AV 6.98.2; ŚB 13.4.3.14; cf. TB 3.7.9.6ff.; ĀpŚS 14.3.5.

61. For a list of Indra's attributes and epithets, see TS 4.4.8.1 and 5.4.1.1. These include all-overcoming (*viśvāsat*), self-ruling (*svarāj*), lord of strength (*śacīpati*), creator (*tvaṣṭṛ*), bountiful (*māghavan*), heavenly (*suvarga*), the slayer of Vṛtra (*vṛtraha*), supporter of the body, possessor of wealth (*gaya*), an eater of food (*annāda*), provider of "increase," the protector of the body, full of light, a drinker of Soma, a supporter of sacrifice and men, the bearer of the thunderbolt, lord, all-enveloping, unassailable, and the same as the sun. Cf. TB 2.6.19.1–2, where the following powers are bestowed on Indra by a variety of other deities, seasons, hymns of praise, and chants: *vayas*, *tejas*, *bala*, *yaśas*, *viś*, *ojas*, *śriyā*, *sahas*, *amṛta*, *kṣatra*, and *satya*. For Indra's connections to the ascetic power called *tapas*, see M. Hara, "Indra and Tapas," *Brahmavidyā* 25 (1975): 29–60.

62. Indra's connection to *ojas* is extremely common in the texts, e.g., ṚV 1.55.6, 1.57.5, 1.103.3, 1.130.4,9, 3.32.9, 3.36.4, 5.33.6, 8.6.5, 10.73.10; AV 4.24.5; ŚB 7.4.1.39; PB 9.2.7; JB 1.352; ĀśvGS 2.6. According to Gonda, "In the Ṛgveda the word *ojas* is mostly used with reference to Indra" (*Ancient-Indian ojas*, p. 9). In a text of the Atharvavedic tradition, Indra is to be invoked if one wishes to destroy the *ojas* of one's wife's lover (KauśS 36.35).

63. For the syllogism Indra = *ojas* and *ojas* = the *kṣatra*, TS 5.3.4.2–3 and cf. ṚV 1.160.5. In one rite, Indra is offered an oblation and praised as being the "possessor of might" (*ojasvin*): "for the might of the *brahman* and the *kṣatra* do I offer to you" (TS 3.3.1.1–2).

64. ŚB 11.4.3.12. According to Mbh 3.220.7, Indra was born from the *bala* of the creator god. For Indra and *bala*, see also ṚV 1.80.8, 3.53.18, 9.113.1, 10.54.2, 10.116.5, 10.133.5.

65. TB 2.6.13.3; cf. ŚB 2.3.2.11 where Indra connected to both fame and "excellence" or *śriyā*.

66. ṚV 1.80.10. According to ṚV 1.57.6, Indra is sole possessor of all *sahas* (cf. TB 2.8.5.7), and at ṚV 8.4.10, he is said to have *sahas* and also is *ojiṣṭha* (ṚV 8.4.10).

67. ŚB 5.4.5.2; TB 1.7.2.2; GB 2.6.7; AitB 6.15. Indra is connected to both *ojas* and *vīrya* at ṚV 2.22.3.

68. For Indra's connection to *indriya*, see ṚV 1.84.1; MS 2.4.6, 4.2.10; KS 11.1; TS 2.5.12.5; TB 2.5.3.3, 2.8.5.7; ŚB 5.4.3.18. For associations to both *vīrya* and *indriya*, ŚB 3.9.1.1ff.; 5.3.5.7, 12.7.1.9; TB 1.8.2.5. At AV 19.42.2, Indra asked to supply both *ojas* and *indriya*, and at TS 1.7.13.1 Indra is connected with "great power" (*mahā indriya*), strength (*sahas*), and the *kṣatra*. This god is also connected with *vayas* or "vigor" (TB 2.6.17.7), "fury" (*manyu*, AV 4.32.2), physical strength (*bala*, TS 6.6.5.2–3), and with "excellence" (*śriyā*, ŚB 2.3.2.11; JUB 1.51.8)—all typically Kshatriya essential powers.

69. Rudra's offspring or followers, designated either as the Rudras or Maruts, are sometimes also classified with the Kshatriya gods because of their close association with Rudra or Indra (see, e.g., AitB 1.7).

70. ṚV 1.19.4, 1.39.10, 3.26.6, 7.56.6,7; etc.

71. See Bhattacharji, *The Indian Theogony*, pp. 211–35. It will be remembered, however, that in Cosmogonies III and IV, the deities Sūrya and Āditya, both divinizations of the sun, appear in the third or Vaishya chain of resemblances. In these texts, however, Sūrya and Āditya function as the sun per se, in relation to the Brahmin fire (= Agni) and the Kshatriya wind (= Vāyu), and as such may be located in the "Vaishya" world of the sky.

72. ŚB 14.3.1.9; AV 15.10.7,11. At AitB 7.20, it is observed that the Brahmin and the Vaishya ask the Kshatriya for place of sacrifice. But who does the Kshatriya ask? The answer is "the divine *kṣatra* [who] is the sun; the sun is the overlord of these beings."

73. E.g., ŚB 1.6.4.18; 4.5.5.7, 4.6.7.11, 8.5.3.2; MaitU 6.33.

74. Soma often is called the king of trees and plants (e.g., KB 4.12), who are his *viś* (e.g., TS 3.1.8.2). He is also connected with food in general (ŚB 3.9.1.8–9; 12.7.3.1) or, specifically, the food of the gods (ŚB 1.6.4.5, 11.1.3.3, 11.1.4.4, 11.1.5.3, 11.2.5.3). Consult Herman Lommel, "König Soma," *Numen* 2 (1955): 196–205.

75. TS 2.1.2.9; AitB 2.38, 7.28; KB 7.10, 9.5, 10.5, 12.8, 12.11; PB 9.2.15; ŚB 3.3.2.8, 3.4.1.10, 3.9.3.3, 5.3.4.8–9, 5.3.5.8, 5.4.3.16, 12.7.3.8; TB 2.5.7.3, etc. At JB 1.90, one reads, "Men are the divine *viś*, Soma is the *kṣatra*. Thereby [by chanting a particular verse] he obtains the *viś* and the *kṣatra*."

76. For this god, consult Heinrich Luders, *Varuṇa*, 2 vols. (Göttingen: Vandenhoeck & Ruprecht, 1951–59); Choudhuri, *Indra and Varuṇa*; Georges Dumézil, *Ouranos-Varuṇa: Étude de Mythologie comparée indo-européenne* (Paris: Adrien-Maisonneuve, 1934); idem, *Mitra-Varuṇa*; and Bhattacharji, *The Indian Theogony*, pp. 23–47. For the deity's association (in conjuction with Mitra) with the Kshatriyas, see Cosmogonies VIII, X, and XII.

77. See, e.g., ṚV 2.27.10, 5.85.3, 7.34.11, 7.87.6, 10.132.4; MS 2.21; TB 2.5.7.6, 3.1.2.7; JB 3.152; PB 15.3.30. For Varuṇa as the "soul" or *ātman* of all the gods, ŚB 14.3.2.14. Varuṇa is well-known as the ruler of the cosmic-moral order (*ṛta* or *dharma*, e.g., ṚV 2.28.4, 7.88.5; ŚB 5.3.3.3ff.) and has the power to release the petitioner from his evil (ŚB 3.9.1.1ff.). As Dumézil has written, "Varuṇa is essentially a Sovereign God. . . . King par excellence, master of the King's most mystical functions, Varuṇa naturally is the King of the Universe." *Ouranos-Varuṇa*, pp. 39, 41.

78. KB 7.10; 12.8. For the relation of Varuṇa to the Kshatriyas, see also ṚV 1.136.1,3, 3.38.5, 5.62.6, 5.69.1, 7.64.2, 8.25.8; AVP 3.9.3; PB 15.3.30–31; ŚB 2.5.2.6,34,36,

4.1.4.1ff., 5.3.5.28, 5.4.3.5; ĀpŚS 24.11.13; TB 1.1.4.8, 2.5.7.3, 2.6.13.3, 3.1.2.7; GB 2.6.7; MaitU 1.6.11.

79. Indra and Varuṇa are both universal monarchs (*samrāj*, see ṚV 1.17.1; VS 8.37) and are identified at, e.g., KB 5.4. For Indra and Varuṇa, Jan Gonda, *The Dual Deities in the Religion of the Veda* (Amsterdam: North-Holland, 1974), pp. 229–70: "Indra indeed personifies the dynamic aspects of sovereignty, Varuṇa its static aspects" (p. 229). Hillebrandt refers to Varuṇa and Indra as the "two representatives of Kṣatra." Vedic Mythology, II:38.

80. ṚV 4.41.4, 7.82.2,6; ŚB 5.4.5.2,6ff.; KŚS 15.8.17. For Varuṇa's identification with *śrī*, KB 18.9.

81. For this deity, consult Ernst Arbman, *Rudra: Untersuchungen zum altindischen Glauben und Kultus* (Uppsala: Appelbergs boktryckeri aktiebolag, 1922); and Bhattacharji, *The Indian Theogony*, pp. 109–57.

82. See above, BĀU 1.4.11–15. Rudra is associated with Kshatriya components in Cosmogony XIII.

83. E.g., MS 2.6.6; KS 25.1; ŚB 5.3.3.7, 6.1.3.12; AV 11.2.24.

84. E.g., TS 3.1.9; ŚB 13.3.5.3; TB 1.1.8.4; BhŚS 9.16.15–17; ĀpŚS 9.14.11–14; HŚS 15.4.19–21; VaikhŚS 20.32; MŚS 5.1.9.26–30.

85. See Cosmogonies III and IV. For the deity, consult S. Wikander, *Vāyu: Texte und Untersuchungen zur indo-iranischen Religionsgeschichte* (Uppsala: A. B. Lundequistska Bokhandeln, 1941). For the fairly unusual connection between Vāyu and the *brahman*, AV 19.27.1; AitB 7.24; JUB 4.21.2; TU 1.1. He is the same as the Brahmin god Mitra according to ŚB 6.5.4.14.

86. E.g., ŚB 14.2.2.6. For Vāyu's connection to Indra, see also Gonda, *The Dual Deities*, pp. 209–28. Gonda remarks that Indra and Vāyu are in some texts interchangeable because "both of them were 'gods of the warrior class' " (p. 222).

87. ĀpŚS 1.1, 4.1–3, 24.2.19–25; BhŚS 4.20–22.

88. See Bhattarcharji, *The Indian Theogony*, pp. 48–108.

89. AV 5.5.13,14; TB 3.1.5.14; ŚB 7.1.1.4, 13.4.3.6. Alternatively, Yama is mentioned as the king of *dharma* (TB 3.9.16.2).

90. Prajāpati, as we have seen, may also be categorized with the Brahmins or, because of his fecundity, with the Vaishyas. Other Kshatriya deities include Paryāya, who is said to be a Kshatriya (AV 15.18.1–3); Dhātṛ, who is invoked for obtaining the power of the *kṣatra* (TS 3.3.10.1); and Vṛtra, who is identified as a Kshatriya deity (PB 18.9.6).

91. Cosmogonies VIII and XI; TS 6.2.2.1; AitB 1.24. For variants, see Cosmogonies XII and XIII; ChU 3.6–10 (Vasus and Agni, Rudras and Indra, Ādityas and Varuṇa, Maruts and Soma, Sādhyas and Brahmā); ṚV 7.10.4 and 7.35.6 (Rudra is leader of the Rudras, Varuṇa or Aditi is head of the Ādityas, and Indra is chief of the Vasus). Mitra acts in one text as the overlord of the Vasus (ŚB 6.5.1.9). Sometimes, as we have seen, the overlord's own *varṇa* is lent to the otherwise lower-class group. Thus Agni usually rules the Vasus (who as a result can categorized as Brahmins), and Indra or Soma is the overlord of the Maruts or the Rudras (thereby lending those two groups a Kshatriya status).

92. For the Viśva Devas as "all of the gods," see, e.g., ŚB 13.5.3.1; KB 4.14, 5.2; GB 2.1.20. ŚB 4.1.1.9–13 refers to them as "everything" or "everything here."

93. Cosmogony XI places these deities somewhat anomalously with the Brahmin god Bṛhaspati.

94. See, e.g., TB 2.7.2.2; ŚB 3.9.1.18; and Georges Dumézil, *L'Heritage Indo-Européen à Rome* (Paris: Gallimard, 1949), pp. 214ff.

95. E.g., HŚS 13.7.18–20; ĀpŚS 18.21.9–11; ŚŚS 2.1–4; 2.3.3–7; cf. MS 4.4.9; ŚB 2.4.3.6; 10.4.1.9. The Viśva Devas are also called upon by one who wishes to become

the Vaishya chief of his community, TS 2.3.9.1. They are sometimes assimilated to Agni (e.g., ŚB 5.2.3.6) which is why a Vaishya who is sick should sacrifice to that deity as his own (KS 12.1; MS 2.3.1; MŚS 5.2.1.1–2).

96. ŚB 5.5.1.10. These gods are also associated with *yaśas*, fame or glory, an essential power that can carry Vaishya connotations: the Viśva Devas are the "most glorious" among the gods and are called upon to put glory into the sacrificer (TB 3.8.7.2).

97. ṚV 5.56.1, 7.56.4ff., 8.12.29, 8.13.28; TS 2.2.11.1, 4.6.5.6, 6.1.5.3, 6.6.5.2–3; MS 2.1.9; TB 1.8.3.3; ŚB 2.5.1.12, 2.5.2.24,27, 3.9.1.18, 4.3.3.6,9,15, 4.5.2.16, 5.1.3.3, 5.2.1.17, 5.3.1.6, 5.4.3.8,17, 5.5.2.9, 9.3.1.3; AitB 1.9, 1.10, 2.10; KB 7.8; JB 1.95; etc.

98. TB 1.7.5.2 equates the Maruts to the *viś*, *ojas* (cf. AV 3.16), and food. For the Maruts = *viś* = food, see also ŚB 5.1.3.3.

99. E.g., ṚV 1.38.9, 1.64.5, 5.55.5, 5.59.7, 5.85.4; TS 2.4.10, 3.5.5; ŚB 7.2.2.10, 9.1.2.5.

100. E.g., ṚV 1.38.7, 1.39.4,7, 2.34.10. The Maruts and the Rudras are invoked together at ṚV 1.58.6, 1.100.5, 1.101.7, 3.32.3, 7.5.9, 7.10.4, 7.35.6; etc. At other times, however, the Rudras are clearly regarded as a group separate from the Maruts (see, e.g., ṚV 8.13.28; TĀ 1.3.3, 1.4.2; PGS 3.3.6; TS 2.1.11.3; AV 6.74.3).

101. As are the Vasus, a separate treatment of which I leave out because of the paucity of sources dealing directly with them. The Vasus are in one text enumerated as Agni, the Earth, Vāyu, the atmosphere, Āditya, the sky, the moon, and the stars (ŚB 11.6.3.6).

102. Varuṇa's Vaishya linkage here might be explicated in terms of that deity's identification with the waters and thus with the fertility they represent (the waters are connected to the penis at ŚB 10.5.4.2 and to semen at BĀU 3.9.22). See also the equation of Varuṇa and Śrī at KB 18.9, and the association with the womb at ŚB 12.9.1.17.

103. "The term Ādityas seems not infrequently to be used in a wider sense as an equivalent for the gods generally. Their nature as a class in fact resembles that of the gods in general." Macdonell, *Vedic Mythology*, p. 44.

104. ṚV 2.27.1 lists six Ādityas: Mitra, Āryaman, Bhaga, Varuṇa, Dakṣa, and Aṃśa. TB 1.1.9.1 (and Sāyana on ṚV 2.27.1) has a slightly different set: Mitra, Varuṇa, Āryaman, Aṃśa, Bhaga, Dhātṛ, Indra, Vivasvat. Most often, the Ādityas are counted as twelve (although not specified) and are sometimes identified with the twelve months of the year (e.g. BĀU 3.9.3–5).

105. Consult Macdonell, *Vedic Mythology*, p. 45.

106. Including linkages to the *jagatī* meter, the afternoon pressing of the soma, and the Ādityas (e.g., ŚB 12.3.4.1–5).

107. ṚV 1.20.4, 1.111.1, 1.161.3,7, 4.35.5, 4.36.3.

108. E.g., TB 1.1.4.8; VŚS 1.4.3–4. For a fine overview of the Rathakāra and the Vedic sacrifice, consult Christopher Minkowski, "The Rathakāra's Eligibility to Sacrifice," *Indo-Iranian Journal* 32, 3 (July 1989): 177–94.

109. See Macdonell, *Vedic Mythology*, pp. 131–34.

110. ṚV 3.60.3, 1.110.4. Cf. AitB 3.30, which claims it was *tapas* that won them their divinity and the right to drink soma, but that they were repelled from the three soma pressings by Agni and the Vasus, Indra and the Rudras, and the Viśva Devas, each of the "mainstream" *varṇa* deities, saying, "They shall not drink here, not here."

111. For linkages between the Vaishyas and the god Āditya, the sky, the Sāma Veda, the afternoon, and other correlates of the commoner *varṇa*, see ŚB 12.3.4.1ff. The solar god Savitṛ also can carry commoner traits. The deity is said to be one of the (Vaishya) Ādityas and thus is honored at the afternoon pressing of soma with verses in the *jagatī* meter (in order to obtain livestock, KB 16.2); and is connected to the western quarter (cf. ŚB 3.2.3.18; KB 7.6) and the *jagatī* meter at TS 5.5.8.2–3.

112. ŚB 5.1.3.9,13, 5.2.5.8, 5.3.1.9, 6.2.2.2, 13.2.2.6; PB 18.1.16; JB 2.129; TB 1.7.2.5, 1.7.3.6. According to ŚB 11.1.6.7, in the beginning Prajāpati, desirous of offspring, "put the power of reproduction into his own self."

113. ŚB 5.2.5.17, 6.1.2.1–11, 7.3.1.20, 8.4.2.1, 8.4.3.20; TB 2.8.1.3; JB 3.185. Cf. Manu 4.182, where the (human) father is said to be the "lord" of Prajāpati's world.

114. E.g., JB 2.193; PB 18.6.4,7, 18.7.1; GB 2.5.8; ŚB 5.1.1.8, 5.1.3.7; ĀpŚS 18.1.3; ŚŚS 15.1.14. See also Gonda, *Prajāpati's Relations with Brahman*, pp. 32–35.

115. E.g., JB 3.298; PB 15.11.12; ŚB 5.1.4.12, 5.2.2.1.

116. For this deity, see Gonda, *Pūṣan and Sarasvatī*; Samuel D. Atkins, *Pūṣan in the Ṛg Veda* (Princeton: Princeton University Press, 1941); R. N. Dandekar, "Pūṣan, the Pastoral God of the Veda," *New Indian Antiquary* 5 (1942–43): 49–66; and E. D. Perry, "Notes on the Vedic Deity Pūṣan," in *Classical Studies in Honour of Henry Drisler* (New York: Macmillan, 1894). Gonda remarks on the BĀU passage: "Since *śūdras* mostly were agricultural servants, this place may be taken to characterize Pūṣan as the god who presides over the manual labour in the fields that converts the fecundity of the earth into man's nourishment" (p. 117). It is possible that a resemblance also came to mind between the deity associated with lameness and its cure (TB 3.9.17.2) and the social class created from the feet of the creator god.

117. Gonda (*Pūṣan and Sarasvatī*, p. 89) is disingenuous when he attempts to obfuscate the connection between Pūṣan and the lower classes by redefining the term *viś*: "It has been surmised that Pūṣan was originally the countryman's deity and therefore probably a *vaiśya* god. We should rather suppose him to have been a god who was especially worshipped by the Āryan settlers in general, by the *viśaḥ*, a term which denoted a whole community, not only the 'third estate.' "

118. Macdonell, *Vedic Mythology*, p. 37: "Etymologically the word [Pūṣan] means 'prosperer' as derived from the root *puṣ*, 'to cause to thrive.' This side of his character is conspicuous both in his epithets *viśvavedas*, *anastavedas*, *purūvasu*, *puṣṭimbhara*, and in the frequent invocations to him to bestow wealth and protection." "Pūṣan is the wind," it said in a couple of texts, "for [the wind] causes everything here to prosper (*puṣyati*)" (ŚB 14.2.1.9, 14.2.2.32).

119. TB 2.7.2.1. For Pūṣan and *puṣṭi*, see also ṚV 4.3.7; AVP 2.72.2; MS 4.1.2, 4.2.10, 4.3.8, 4.7.8; KS 1.2; TB 2.5.3.3, 3.2.2.8. According to ṚV 1.89.6 and 6.56.6, this deity brings well-being (*svasti*) to his worshipers.

120. ṚV 1.42.9, 1.122.5, 1.138.1,4, 8.31.11, 6.58.4.

121. ṚV 1.90.4, 4.30.24, 5.41.4, 5.46.2, 6.54.8, 6.55.2–3, 7.34.21, 10.65.10, 10.70.9, 10.125.2; ŚB 11.4.3.3,15; KŚS 5.13.1.

122. ṚV 1.89.5–6, 1.138.2, 6.52.2, 6.54.4, 6.56.5, 6.58.4, 8.4.18.

123. Gonda, *Pūṣan and Sarasvatī*, p. 142, notes that Pūṣan "concerns himself with the fertility of the earth, with growth and the creativity of nature, the creation of new life, the acquisition of property, and occurs therefore also in passages dealing with the earth, milk, ploughing, ways and wind. . . . There seems therefore to be sufficient justification of the assertion that Pūṣan, as a god of the abodes, land, surroundings of an Āryan community, was believed to be responsible for the prosperity of men and cattle, the production of food and the promotion of agriculture and economy."

124. ṚV 1.42.9; KB 12.8, 12.14; TB 1.7.3.6, 2.1.6.1, 2.8.5.3, 3.8.23.2.

125. According to Gonda, *Pūṣan and Sarasvatī*, p. 115: "So, although it is uncertain what the functions of the *bhāgadugha* exactly were, he may be supposed to have been entrusted with the supervision of the food-supply or of the preparation of food."

126. E.g., ṚV 6.54.5ff.; TS 1.5.1.2; TB 1.7.6.6, 1.8.1.1; MS 2.2.4; TĀ 5.7.2. Macdonell refers to Pūṣan as "a god of herdsmen" (*Vedic Mythology*, p. 205). ṚV 10.17.3

calls this god the herdsman or protector (*gopa*) of the world. Sanskritists have traced the god's name to the term *paśu-san*, the "acquirer of livestock." See Dandekar, "Pūṣan," p. 60–61.

127. ṚV 6.54.5ff., 6.58.2, 10.26.3; ŚB 3.9.1.1ff., 5.2.5.7, 5.3.5.8,32,35, 5.4.5.2,9, 9.2.3.12, 13.3.8.2; MS 1.8.5, 3.10.6, 4.3.7; VS 10.30; TB 1.7.2.4, 1.7.6.6, 1.8.1.1ff.; PB 23.16.4ff.; TS 2.1.4.3; 2.2.10.3; TĀ 5.7.2,4. See also ŚB 3.9.1.12, where Pūṣan is also equated with the animals but in combination with the Brahmin god Bṛhaspati. The Brahmin class is thus put into possession of the animals that normally would be associated with the lower classes.

128. KS 10.11; MS 2.2.4; cf. KS 7.2; 7.9.

129. ṚV 6.54.10; ŚGS 3.9. Indeed, Pūṣan helps recover possessions of any kind that have been lost (see, e.g., ĀśvGS 3.7.9 and cf. ṚV 1.23.13–14).

130. ŚB 3.1.4.9; cf. MS 1.22.10; 3.6.4; KS 2.2; 23.2. For the connection between Pūṣan, *paśus*, and sacrifice, see also MS 4.4.7 and TB 1.8.1.1.

131. TB 3.1.2.9–10. According to MS 4.2.7, one may raid the herds of a Vaishya or Shūdra who is very prosperous (*bahupuṣṭa*) and take one of their cows: "For cows are granters of refreshing food, and the constellation of Pūṣan [i.e., Revatī] brings prosperity (*puṣṭi*). A fixed opinion among men who belong to the *viś* is that the constellation of Pūṣan causes to thrive. He should select [that calf from the herd] saying, 'Give me a complete span of life, give me prosperity.' He deprives him [the owner of the calf] of his property and prosperity."

132. Gonda, *Pūṣan and Sarasvatī*, pp. 94–95.

133. See K. Amner, "Tvaṣṭṛ: Ein alt-indischer Schopfergott," *Die Sprache* 1 (1949): 68–77; and Bhattacharji, *The Indian Theogony*, pp. 320–22.

134. Compare, for example, the texts at AV 1.9.1 with AVP 1.19.1.

135. Bailey, *The Mythology of Brahmā*, pp. 58, 61.

136. ŚB 13.1.8.7; TS 7.3.15.1; MS 3.12.5; TB 3.8.11.2. For the equation of Tvaṣṭṛ and "forms" (*rūpas*), see also AVP 2.72.2; KauśS 124.2; ŚB 5.4.5.2ff., 11.4.3.3; KŚS 15.8.17; cf. VS 10.30. These "forms" are explained as the "body of sons, etc." in the commentary on TB 2.5.3.3.

137. KB 12.8; cf., ŚB 3.9.1.9, 12.8.2.16; KS 5.1, 32.1; MS 3.8.11; ĀpŚS 4.10.1; MŚS 1.4.2.6.

138. One scholar attempts to explain why the goddess of speech and learning is also the goddess of fertility: "It appears that when Sarasvatī was elevated to the position of a goddess of learning, quite naturally she was regarded as a fount of all poetic creation; later on this agency of Sarasvatī generating poetic fervor in men was transferred to all kinds of creation." Shyam Kishore Lal, *Female Divinities in Hindu Mythology and Ritual* (Pune: University of Poona, 1980), p. 189.

139. I refer the interested reader to Jan Gonda's *Pūṣan and Sarasvatī*.

140. ṚV 6.61.1, 7.95.2–6, 8.21.17, 10.17.7; MS 4.14.7; AV 19.31.1,10; ŚB 11.4.3.6.

141. Before moving on, another goddess, Āditya, may also be mentioned here. The sacrificer of Vaishya class is to address his vow to Āditya in New and Full Moon sacrifice (ĀpŚS 24.2.19–25; 1.1; 4.1–3).

142. Dual deities, as Jan Gonda writes in his study of the phenomenon in Vedism, "essentially constitute biunities of conjoint principles which in their functions and activities often complement each other." *The Dual Deities*, pp. 15–16. Cf. Ananda K. Coomaraswamy, *Spiritual Authority and Temporal Power in the Indian Theory of Government* (New Haven, Conn.: American Oriental Society, 1942): "We must premise that Mitravaruṇa, and likewise Indrāgni or Indrabṛhaspati, are syzygies or progenitive pairs (*mithunāni*): Mitra, Agni and Bṛhaspati being on the one hand the divine archetypes of

the Sacerdotium or Spiritual authority (*brahma*) and Varuṇa and Indra those of the Regnum (*kṣatra*). . . . The Vedic 'dual' divinities imply, for the most part at least, a biunity (syzygy) of conjoint principles, active and passive in mutual relationship or both active in relation to things externally administered" (pp. 2, 6, n. 6).

143. For the interaction of these two deities, consult Gonda, *The Dual Deities*, pp. 271–309. As Gonda correctly observes, "The close association of Indra and Agni is also determined by the fact that they are the divine representatives of the *kṣatriya* and *brahman* classes of society" (p. 290). Cf. Jan Gonda, *Triads in the Veda* (Amsterdam: North-Holland, 1976), p. 133.

144. KB 12.6; 16.11; ŚB 3.9.2.14,16, 6.1.2.28, 6.3.3.21, 7.4.1.42, 9.5.2.10, 13.5.3.2. According to ŚB 2.5.2.8, the two deities are equivalent to inhalation and exhalation; ŚB 10.4.1.6 claims the two are immortal life; PB 15.4.8 has the two representing the universe (in the form of heaven and earth).

145. See, however, statements that seem to indicate that Indra and Agni have solely Brahmin characteristics: they are the "beginning" or "mouth" (*mukha*) of the gods (KB 4.14); Agni includes within himself Indra and Agni (*aindrāgni 'gniḥ*, ŚB 7.4.1.42); and especially ŚŚS 2.3.3ff., where Indra and Agni together represent the Brahmin class alone.

146. TB 1.1.6.4ff.; cf. TB 1.2.5.1; TS 2.1.2.3; KS 9.17; MS 2.1.1 (where the man who has won a battle is said to be depleted of *ojas* and *vīrya* and sacrifices to Indra and Agni to restore them); and ŚB 3.7.18.

147. A Brahmin who is desirous of becoming a *purohita* should also perform this sacrifice, for in the beginning Bṛhaspati received his office through the ritual. It is executed with chants of nine and fifteen verses, the former identified with the *brahman* and the latter with the *kṣatra*. See PB 19.17.1–8; JB 2.132ff.; BŚS 18.35; LŚS 9.4.30–32; ĀpŚS 22.13.10–11; KŚS 22.11.18–22.

148. For this divine duo, see Gonda, *The Dual Deities*, pp. 145–208; *The Vedic God Mitra*, pp. 18–36; and Coomaraswamy, *Spiritual Authority and Temporal Power*, passim.

149. TS 2.1.7.3,4, 6.4.8.3; TB 1.7.10.1; AitB 4.10; PB 25.10.10; BDhS 2.10.18.21. For Mitra as male and Varuṇa as female, PB 25.10.10; ŚB 2.4.4.19; and Coomaraswamy, *Spiritual Authority and Temporal Power*, passim.

150. Georges Dumézil, *Mitra-Varuṇa* (Paris: Éditions Gallimard, 1948), p. 85.

151. G. V. Devasthali, *Religion and Mythology of the Brāhmaṇas* (Poona: University of Poona, 1965), p. 160. Cf. Gonda, *The Vedic God Mitra*, p. 23: "This points to a relation of the unnatural or artificial with Varuṇa, and of the 'natural' and what is not effected by special human effort with Mitra."

152. Gonda, *The Dual Deities*, p. 156. For Mitra and Varuṇa as associated with the ordinarily Kshatriya essential power of *vīrya*, TS 1.8.14.1ff.

153. ŚB 5.4.1.16; cf. ŚB 5.3.5.28, 5.4.3.5,27; MS 4.4.6.

154. ŚB 1.2.4.6, etc. This is a Vedic instance of the apparently nearly universal favoring of the right over the left in symbolic systems. See Robert Hertz, "The Pre-eminence of the Right Hand: A Study in Religious Polarity," in *Right and Left: Essays on Dual Symbolic Classification*, ed. by Rodney Needham (Chicago: University of Chicago Press, 1973). Hertz argues that the unequal opposition between the right and left hands is biologically grounded in the "greater development in man of the left cerebral hemisphere"; thus there is an "organic asymmetry" which may account for the pre-eminence of the right over the left. He is also careful to note, however, that the preponderance of the right hand is "reinforced and fixed by influences extraneous to the organism," i.e., society and its "collective representations" (pp. 4–5).

155. See Gonda, *The Dual Deities*, pp. 363–97.

156. KS 10.2; MS 2.1.4. Cf. ŚB 5.2.5.10,12, where Agni is the "giver" while Soma

embodies the quality of "glory"; a cake offered to Agni–Soma ensures that Agni will give the sacrificer glory and success.

157. Agni and Soma can also both be regarded as Brahmin gods (Soma, as we have seen, can go either way). See, e.g., TS 2.3.3.3ff., where in a ritual for a Brahmin whose "desire is not fulfilled" one should offer to Agni and Soma, for "a Brahmin is connected with Agni, and he drinks soma." For other indications that Agni–Soma is an entity of the first *varṇa* alone, see MS 2.1.4; MŚS 5.1.5.69ff.; KS 10.2; BŚS 13.26 (a sacrifice is offered to Agni–Soma if one's wish is for *brahmavarcasa*); KS 10.2 (a sacrifice to Agni–Soma should take place in spring because that is the season of the Brahmin); TB 2.7.3.1 (the Brahmin belongs to both Agni and Soma; when the two unite, the Brahmin comes to possess virility or *vīrya* in the highest degree).

158. For these two deities in combination, consult Gonda, *The Dual Deities*, pp. 310–30. Gonda notes that "each god has his traditional relations, Indra as the god of the kṣatriya or the divine representative of nobility . . . and Bṛhaspati as the 'Lord of brahman'" (p. 323).

159. AV 15.10.3–5. See also the various adjustments made in the Vājapeya sacrifice on the basis of whether the sacrificer is a Brahmin or a Kshatriya, for Bṛhaspati is "lord of the *brahman*" and Indra the "lord of the *kṣatra*" (ŚB 5.1.5.1ff.). Elsewhere, however, we read that the *brahman* is the source for both of these deities (AV 15.10.3; ŚB 10.4.1.9).

160. ŚB 9.3.4.18. Cf. ŚB 5.3.5.7, where the same ritual setup is interpreted slightly differently: "Bṛhaspati is the *brahman*, and Indra is physical power (*indriya*) and virility (*vīrya*). With these two kinds of powers (*vīryas*) he thus encloses him on both sides."

161. TS 2.4.13.1. "If he [the priest] wants a Kshatriya to be born unbound and practicing destructive inimical powers (*vṛtrān ghnāṃs caret*)," says another text, "he should offer this Indra and Bṛhaspati oblation for him" (BŚS 13.42).

162. Gonda, *The Dual Deities*, p. 207 (n. 290).

163. A final instance has Bṛhaspati, as the *brahman*, combined with Vāc (identified with rulership, and therefore with the Kshatriyas) at AitB 1.19.

164. See, for example, the relationship between the Brahmin god Soma and the lower-class Pūṣan as displayed in KS 11.5, where a Brahmin is instructed to offer a sacrifice to Soma and Pūṣan "for a Brahmin has Soma as his deity and Pūṣan is animals." In this way the Brahmin sacrificer "makes his own deity more [i.e., higher, mightier] by means of animals." Cf. PB 23.16.4ff.: "The Brahmin is Soma, Pūṣan is cattle. They [i.e., the Brahmin priests] thereby strengthen [through a victim to Soma and Pūṣan] their own deity through animals."

165. Hillebrandt, *Vedic Mythology*, I:176.

166. ṚV 3.35.9, 6.17.11. ŚB 4.3.3.15, however, says that Indra is "bound up with evil in the shape of the *viś*, the Maruts."

167. TS 2.2.11.1; cf. MŚS 5.1.7.19–23. Similarly, at MŚS 5.1.7.1–2, an optional sacrifice is offered with oblations to Indra and the Maruts for the sacrificer who desires "well-being" (*bhūti*).

168. For Soma (= *kṣatra*) and the Maruts (= the *viś*), see ŚB 5.4.3.16–17. See also ŚB 9.3.1.13–16, where Vaiśvanara (a form of Agni) is the representative of the *kṣatra* and the Maruts are the *viś*. Oblations to the former are offered before those to the latter, and "thus, having set up the *kṣatra*, he sets up the *viś*." The oblation to Vaiśvanara is a single one, and those to the Maruts are multiple: "He thus makes the *kṣatra* to attach to a single [person], and [social] distinction to attach to a single [person]. The others are numerous; he thus bestows multiplicity on the *viś*." Again, the first oblation is offered in a "distinct" (*nirukta*) voice, "for the Kshatriya is something distinct, so to speak," while the others are offered "indistinctly," "for indistinct, so to speak, is the *viś*." The offering

to Vaiśvanara is made standing while those to the Maruts are made sitting, "for the *kṣatra* stands, so to speak" while "the *viś* sits, so to speak." Finally, the first offering is made with the ladle while standing, and the latter are made with one's hands while sitting: "He thus makes the *viś* subservient and obedient to the Kshatriya." For Vaiśvanara and the Maruts, see also TS 2.2.5.6, 5.4.7.7; ŚB 9.3.1.3; and especially TS 2.2.11.1 (Vaiśvanara = *kṣatra* = *āhavanīya* fire, Maruts = *viś* = *gārhapatya* fire).

169. The relationship between the king and his people is not always portrayed in purely exploitative terms. In the following, where the sacrificer asks Yama and the Pitṛs for a place on which to build his sacrificial fire, we learn that the people are required to approve a land grant made by the Kshatriya: "Yama is the *kṣatra* and the Pitṛs are the *viś*. And to whomever the Kshatriya, with the approval of the commoners, gives a settlement, that is well given. And in like manner does Yama, the *kṣatra*, with the consent of the Pitṛs, the *viś*, now grant to this [sacrificer] a settlement" (ŚB 7.1.1.4).

5

Classifying Space

Spatial and Social Categories

The ordering of experience within the constraints of space and time provides the framework of human intelligence. Indeed, it is impossible to imagine thought outside of the orientation provided by spatial and temporal categories. As Steven Lukes remarked, "We cannot postulate a hypothetical situation in which individuals do *not* in general think by means of space, time, class, person, cause and according to the rules of logic, since this is what thinking *is*."[1] It is for this reason that Emmanuel Kant, having posited that the capacity to perceive time was bound up with the capacity to perceive space (for time exists only by virtue of our experience of the succession of events with regard to duration in space), regarded both as instances of "categorical imperatives," categories intrinsic to the mind and given *a priori* of experience.

Émile Durkheim challenged the Kantian notion that the ability to categorize spatially and temporally was intrinsic to the human being by postulating that it is society that gives individuals such capabilities. Durkheim argued that spatial and temporal categories are epiphenomena of a prior categorization of society. The distinctions a particular culture posits in the spatial realm have their origin in social distinctions: "Thus the social organization has been the model for the spatial organization and a reproduction of it. It is thus even up to the distinction between right and left which, far from being inherent in the nature of man in general, is very probably the product of representations which are religious and collective."[2]

Durkheim's critics have often pointed out that such claims are extravagant.[3] There is no incontrovertible evidence to prove that particular forms of spatial or temporal structures are *caused* by particular social structures; Durkheim simply assumes what he ostensibly seeks to establish. Even more crucially, Durkheim seems not to have recognized the difference between a *capacity* for spatial and temporal classification and the particular *contents* of this capacity or the particular *criteria* that are brought to bear on such classifications.

Subsequent scholars have been more careful about the differences between innate and socially transmitted capabilities without giving up the notion that social forces shape spatial and temporal classification. Robert Hertz, a disciple of Durkheim, picked up the master's hints about the elementary spatial distinction between right and left. Hertz noted, however, that this opposition is biologically grounded in the "greater development in man of the left cerebral hemisphere"; thus there is an "organic asymmetry" which may account for the preeminence of the right over the left.[4] He nevertheless maintained that the preponderance of the right hand is "reinforced and fixed by influences extraneous to the organism," that is, society and its collective representations.[5] Barry Schwartz, in the course of an even more recent attempt to make a similar case for the vertically oriented categorical opposition between up and down, summarizes the middle road Hertz already had taken between innate biological classificatory models and arbitrary cultural values infused into the classes:

> On the one hand, Hertz tells us that the symbolic preeminence of the right is widespread because it is ultimately based upon a biological tendency; on the other, he insists that the meaning of this tendency is to be found in the zones of morality. There is nothing arbitrary in this. The moral world "chooses" for a representative a bipolar dimension in nature because of the dualism of morality itself [i.e., the distinction between "good" and "bad"].[6]

Whereas perception channeled by spatial and temporal classification seems to be intrinsic to the organism and therefore a universal feature of human thought, the specific *content* of the conceptual systems so structured by space and time is culturally variable and socially encoded. That is, spatial and temporal continuums are divided differently in different cultures, and the divisions created are also often differently valued.[7] In this way, space and time come to take on social meanings; the value-laden categories of the spatial and temporal orders can be read for what they tell us about the society that produced them and in which they function.

How did the authors of the Veda conceive of and categorize space? What kind of values did they impose on the spatial divisions they posited and assumed? How did the various spatial categories interrelate to one another, and how were they integrated into the larger classificatory scheme of the *varṇa*s? And how, in particular, did spatial classes relate to social classes? As we shall see in this chapter, space and its divisions became yet another screen onto which the Brahmin authors projected their social hierarchy. If the spatial realm was made to conform to the contours of the *varṇa* classification system (and thus became a counterpart of the ideal social structure), what might we conclude about the possible social, psychological, and epistemological intentions of such a move?

Correlations between particular social classes and the divisions in the space to time continuum are among the most powerful and ingrained forms of social inculcation and persuasion. Since the social class hierarchy was insinuated into (if not, as Durkheim originally contended, the cause of) the very perception of space and time, those who benefited by the social system found a very strong prop for their claim to "natural" privilege. Metaphysics and social ideology, being placed in a mutually reflective relation, here, as elsewhere, formed a duet to whose tune people found it very difficult not to march.

The Three Worlds and Their Meanings

In the classical texts of Vedic ritualism, the predominant cosmological vision assumes a tripartite universe made up of three spatial worlds or *loka*s (cognate with the Latin *locus* and the English "location"): the earth, the atmosphere, and the sky.[8] There are, however, other connotations to the Sanskrit word "*loka*." Just as in English we speak of "the world of academics," "the financial world," or "the wide world of sports" without any specific locative connotations, so too in Sanskritic metaphysical and soteriological discourse references to particular "worlds" do not always refer to a *place* but can signify a *realm of activity* or a *status*.[9]

The three spatial worlds of Vedic cosmology we focus on here, as opposed to the virtually infinite number of metaphysical or soteriological "statuses," are presented in the texts as empirically observable locations, populated by very material entities. "This world" or the earth is said to host the waters, humans, animals, plants and trees, and fire (ŚB 10.5.4.1, 11.6.2.8). The atmosphere is sometimes characterized as "wide or broad" (e.g., PB 12.5.8; KB 20.3; ŚB 4.1.1.20), "without a firm foundation" (e.g., KB 29.5), "great" (KB 26.11), and in other texts as "invisible" (e.g., PB 3.10.2, 21.7.3). The Vedic writers located the horizon, birds, rain, rays of the sun, and the wind in this middle world (ŚB 10.5.4.2, 11.6.2.6). The "yonder world" or sky contains "the heavenly waters," the gods, the stars, and the sun and moon (ŚB 10.5.4.3, 11.6.2.7).

The two meanings of "*loka*"—as cosmological locale and existential status—are sometimes conflated. In some Vedic passages, for example, there is no apparent distinction between a soteriological "world of heaven" (*svarga loka*) and a cosmological "world of the sky" (*svar*, *dyaus*). When looked at in context, however, the heaven of Vedic salvation and the sky of Vedic cosmology were usually distinct (although the difference was often enough assumed and implicit). In texts where it is the soteriology that is at the forefront, *svarga* or *svarga loka* tends to be used; in texts where the topic is more strictly cosmological, it is *svar* or *dyaus* that is most often employed.

That such a distinction was indeed made by Vedic classifiers is borne out by the following passage where in a quadripartite cosmology an explicit division between "yonder world" (here in the sense of "sky"), on the one hand, and heaven, on the other, is formulated:

> By [reciting] nine [verses] the Maitrāvaruṇa priest carries him [i.e., the sacrificer] from this world to the world of the atmosphere; by ten from the world of the atmosphere to yonder world, for the world of the atmosphere is the longest; with nine from yonder world to the world of heaven.[10]

In my analysis of cosmological texts, I assume that the meaning of "yonder world" in these contexts was equivalent to that of "sky" and distinct from that of the soteriological "world of heaven."

By representing the cosmos as comprised of three worlds, cosmological classification reflects, reinforces, and represents in spatial form the tripartite classification of other realms. Indeed, in most instances, cosmological tripartition is ensconced within chains of associations linking the three components of other and diverse arenas of things and beings—not least important among them being the social *varṇas*. The usual pattern, as we saw in Cosmogony II, is to connect, *inter alia*, Brahmins and the earth, Kshatriyas and the atmosphere, and Vaishyas and the sky.

Recall that the set of homologies drawn in Cosmogony II included the elemental qualities that identified the social implications:

1. *bhūḥ* ⇒ EARTH = the *brahman* power = the Self
2. *bhuvaḥ* ⇒ ATMOSPHERE = the *kṣatra* power = humans
3. *svaḥ* ⇒ SKY = the power of the *viś* = animals

This scheme is obviously hierarchical (as the ontological analogues—not to mention the implied social correlates—make clear) even though the spatial correlates for each of the *varṇas* are vertically inverted: the "lowest" world, earth, is associated with the "highest" of the social classes, the Brahmins; and the "highest" spatial world is connected with the "lowest" of the three *varṇas*. Our previous discussion regarding the distinction between sky and heaven here becomes relevant, for the Vaishyas are connected not to a transcendent paradise but to an observable natural realm populated with, among other things, uncountable stars—the natural analogue to the innumerable members of the social class of "the people" or "the masses." This observation is critical for a proper interpretation of the dominant cosmological pattern of Vedic taxonomies; we must realize that our usual vertically oriented sensibilities in perceiving hierarchy are apparently not, in this case at least, applicable.

Why is the earth the cosmological equivalent of the Brahmin in this scheme? Why, exactly, does the sky belong to the Vaishya? And what led classifiers to assert that the atmosphere shared the qualities of the Kshatriya class? As I show later, the earth is the "first" world, generative of the others, and is thus properly correlated with the "first" of the social classes. The atmosphere is the cosmological region of *Sturm und Drang* and therefore seems to have called up a connection with the warriors and rulers. The sky, as I already indicated, is the world in which the myriad stars and other astronomical bodies are beheld and is thus the spatial analogue of the multifarious third class, the "people" or *viś*.

Let us begin to demonstrate these correlations by recalling here the other three cosmogonies from Chapter 3 that include within them the categorization of the

TABLE 5.1. Cosmological Worlds According to Cosmogonies III, IV, and XIII

Cosmogony III (and variant)

1. EARTH ⇒ Agni/fire ⇒ Ṛg Veda ⇒ *bhūḥ* ⇒ the *hotṛ* priest (*gārhapatya* fire)
2. ATMOSPHERE ⇒ Vāyu/wind ⇒ Yajur Veda ⇒ *bhuvaḥ* ⇒ the *adhvaryu* priest (*āgnīdhrīya* or *anvāhāryapacana* fire)
3. SKY ⇒ Sūrya/sun ⇒ Sāma Veda ⇒ *svaḥ* ⇒ the *udgātṛ* priest (*āhavanīya* fire)

Cosmogony IV

1. splendor = EARTH = Agni/fire = speech
2. greatness = ATMOSPHERE = Vāyu/wind = breath
3. fame = SKY = Āditya/sun = sight

*Cosmogony XIII**

1. first day = EARTH = *gayatrī* meter = 9-versed hymn of praise = *rathantara* chant = east = spring = Vasus and Agni
2. second day = ATMOSPHERE = *triṣṭubh* meter = 15-versed hymn of praise = *bṛhat* chant = south = summer = Maruts and Indra
3. third day = SKY = *jagatī* meter = 17-versed hymn of praise = *vairūpa* chant = west = rainy season = Ādityas and Varuṇa

* Cosmogony XIII adds three more chants to the structure with "worlds" of "food," "animals," and "waters":

4. 4th day = food = *anuṣṭubh* meter = 21-versed hymn of praise = *vairāja* chant = north = autumn = Sādhyas and Ājyas and Brhaspati and the moon
5. 5th day = animals = *paṅkti* meter = 27-versed hymn of praise = *śakvara* chant = zenith = winter = Maruts and Rudra
6. 6th day = waters = *atichandas* meter = 33-versed hymn of praise = *raivata* chant = zenith = cool season = Viśva Devas and Prajāpati

three worlds. The three chains in which the cosmological worlds are located in Cosmogonies III, IV, and XIII are summarized in Table 5.1.

Many of the links connecting particular components from the natural, supernatural, ritual, and scriptural orders with one or another of the three worlds in these cosmogonies are also well attested in other texts. The linkage of earth, atmosphere, and sky to the three natural elements or principal deities of the three worlds—Agni/fire, Vāyu/wind, and Sūrya (or Āditya)/sun—is extremely widespread;[11] so is that which connects the three worlds to the Ṛg, Yajur, and Sāma Vedas;[12] and so also is that which combines in this way the three orders of cosmological worlds, gods/natural phenomena, and Vedas.[13] The sacrificial fires that are added to the set of three worlds, gods/natural phenomena, and Vedas in the variant of Cosmogony III are also found in similar linkages in other Vedic passages.[14] Finally, the correlation of the *gāyatrī* meter with the earth, the *triṣṭubh* with the atmosphere, and the *jagatī* with the sky in Cosmogony XIII recurs in other texts (where one or another deity is often also assigned to each chain)[15] and is directly and explicitly correlated with the social classes as follows: "When the meters divided these worlds, the *gāyatrī* obtain this world, the *triṣṭubh* the atmosphere, and the *jagatī* the sky. The *gāyatrī* is the Brahmin class, the *triṣṭubh* the Kshatriya class, the *jagatī* the Vaishya class" (JB 1.286).

These particular connections reinforce, or even restate, what Cosmogony II reveals about the *varṇa* attributes of the three worlds. The specific components mentioned in the previous paragraph are just those one would expect for each of the *varṇas*. The god Agni, the Ṛg Veda, the *gāyatrī* meter, the nine-versed hymn of praise—these are regularly found in association with the Brahmins. To find them correlated with the earth here is entirely in keeping with the Brahmin attribution for that world in Cosmogony II.

Even apart from the specific components which are categorized in all of these cosmogonies, at the simplest level of analysis is the significance of the order in which the strings of associations are presented. The earth, the cosmological world of the Brahmin class, it will be observed, is always the "first" (albeit vertically the "lowest"); here, it is in the sequential sense that the hierarchical order of the structure is expressed. The earth, like the Brahmins, is from this perspective logically prior, primary, and foremost; the other two worlds and the *varṇas* which characterize them are, concomitantly, presented as subsequent, secondary (and tertiary), and derivative.

The sequentially based hierarchical orientation of this cosmological taxonomy is readily visible in other texts which conform to this configuration. Some cosmological texts of this variety simultaneously categorize the worlds and certain parts of the human body. And in keeping with the interpretation of the structure as hierarchical while inverting the values placed on the "highest" and "lowest" of the cosmological worlds, we read in one passage that "the head of the man who is there in that orb [i.e., the sun] is the earth (*bhūr*). There is one head, and there is one syllable [in the word *bhūr*]. The atmosphere (*bhuvar*) is his two arms. There are two arms and two syllables. The sky (*svar*) is the foundation [or feet, *pratiṣṭhā*]. There are two feet and two syllables [for *svar* is pronounced *su-ar*]" (BĀU 5.5.3). This formulation retains the vertical hierarchy of the body posited in, for example, ṚV 10.90 and Cosmogonies V-VII (Brahmin = mouth; Kshatriya = arms; Vaishya = belly; Shūdra = feet) while turning upside down the values assigned to the spatially ascending worlds in order to maintain the implicit *varṇa* hierarchy.

The earth is the first among the worlds and, as one passage indicates, because it is first it is also the "measure" (*mā*) of the other two (ŚB 8.3.3.5). "The sky is established on the atmosphere; the atmosphere on the earth," it is said in another passage (AitB 3.6). I referred earlier to texts which homologize the three worlds to the three fires of the sacrificial cult. In one of these, where a four-part cosmological system is constructed by adding "the quarters" to the tripartite division of the worlds,[16] the association of the *gārhapatya* fire and the terrestrial world is explained as the connection between the generative components of two different realms:

> There are four [types] of fire: the one laid down, the one taken out [of the fire "laid down"], the one taken forward [from the fire "laid down"], and the one spread [over the three hearths, also taken from the fire "laid down"]. The fire which is laid down is this world, that which is taken out is the world of the atmosphere, that which is taken forward is the sky, and that which is spread is the quarters. That which is laid down is Agni (fire), that which is taken out is Vāyu (wind), that which is taken forward is Āditya (sun), and that which is spread is Candramas (moon). That which is laid down is the *gārhapatya* fire,

> that which is taken out is the *āhavanīya* fire, that which is taken forward is the fire they take eastwards from the *āhavanīya*, and that which is spread is the one they take northwards for the cooking of the sacrificial victim. (ŚB 11.8.2.1)

The *gārhapatya* fire, here and elsewhere assimilated to the earth, is the origin of all the other fires, all the other worlds.[17] Elsewhere we read that the three sacrificial ladles, the *dhruva*, *upabhṛt*, and the *juhū*, are the ritual representatives of the earth, atmosphere, and sky respectively. "It is from this world that all the worlds originate. The whole sacrifice therefore proceeds from the *dhruva*" (ŚB 1.3.2.4; cf. TB 3.3.1.1–2, 3.3.6.11).

The earth is thus both prior to and generative of the other two worlds—and, by implication, so too is the Brahmin in relation to the other two social classes. A more complex series of linkages, including within them the cosmological worlds, is displayed in the next text we consider. Here too, however, the same point is made, if a bit more obliquely: the earth, like the Brahmin class, is like a mother to the other components in its class:

> The self consists of speech, mind, and breath. These are also the three worlds: this world is speech, the atmosphere is mind; yonder world is breath. These are also the three Vedas: the Ṛg Veda is speech, the Yajur Veda is mind, the Sāma Veda is breath. These are also the gods, ancestors, and humans: the gods are speech, the ancestors are mind, human beings are breath. These are also the father, mother, and children: the father is mind, the mother is speech, children are breath. (BĀU 1.5.3–7)

The three worlds are correlated to three body functions, the three Vedas, three ontological categories (gods, ancestors, and men), and, finally, to the triumvirate of mother (equated to speech and thus the Brahmins), father, and offspring or children. The first component in each of these sets, where we must assume the Brahmins would also be placed if the social realm were being considered, contains typically Brahmin and also generative items: the earth, speech,[18] the Ṛg Veda, the gods, and the human mother. And by connecting the earth and the gods—the ontological classes of ancestors and men being assigned to the atmosphere and sky—the hierarchical superiority of the first world is underscored (as is, implicitly, the Brahmins' claim to be "gods on earth" or "human gods").[19]

This, then, would seem to be the predominant rationale for connecting the earth to the Brahmin class (or to components that are clearly encoded as "Brahmin"). By representing the Brahmin cosmological world as prior to and productive of the atmosphere and sky, the authors of the Veda were simultaneously reiterating a social message about the predominance and hierarchically encompassing nature of the Brahmin class.[20]

Second, why the connection between the atmosphere and the warrior class? To begin to explicate this assignment, let us turn our attention to still another text that aligns the three worlds with the three Vedas (earth = Ṛg Veda; atmosphere = Yajur Veda; and sky = Sāma Veda) and with the three priests associated with each Veda:

> [Prajāpati] heated up with ascetic heat these three worlds. From this world he emitted Agni, from the world of the atmosphere Vāyu, from the sky Āditya. He heated up with ascetic heat these three lights. From Agni he emitted the verses (*ṛks*), from Vāyu the formulas (*yajurs*) from Āditya the chants (*sāmans*). He heated up with ascetic heat the threefold wisdom. He stretched out the sacrifice. He recited with the Ṛg Veda, he proceeded with the Yajur Veda, and he sang with the Sāma Veda. He developed the essence of the brilliance (*tejas*) of this threefold wisdom, for the healing of these Vedas. He developed *bhūḥ* out of the verses, *bhuvaḥ* out of the formulas, and *svaḥ* out of the chants. . . . It is by the verses that the *hotṛ* priest becomes *hotṛ*, by the formulas that the *adhvaryu* priest becomes *adhvaryu*, by the chants that the *udgātṛ* priest becomes *udgātṛ*. (KB 6.10,11; cf. ŚB 11.5.8.1–4)

This text, among other things, delineates the function of each of the three Vedas and priests: the *hotṛ* uses the Ṛgvedic verses to fulfill his duties revolving around recitation (recall that speech is also located within the first or Brahmin chain); the *adhvaryu* relies on the Yajurvedic formulas to perform the ritual actions; and the *udgātṛ* depends on the Sāma Veda to supply his chants or songs. The atmosphere, connected here as elsewhere with the *adhvaryu* and the Yajur Veda, is by this associative logic the cosmic world most noted for its activity.[21] Just as the warriors are in later texts the human embodiment of the quality (or *guṇa*) called *rajas* (activity, passion), so is the atmospheric world correlated with the most physically active of the priests (the *adhvaryu* is responsible for the bulk of the actual ritual manipulations) and the Veda most concerned with the actions entailed in the performance of the sacrifice.[22]

Ruled by Vāyu, the wind, or by Indra, the fearsome bearer of the thunderbolt[23] and the leader of the storm troopers or Maruts, the atmosphere is thus the cosmic realm which, because of its natural characteristics, also suggests the tempestuous warrior on the rampage.[24] " 'You are the stormy [world], the troop of the Maruts' [he says]. The stormy [world], the troop of the Maruts, is the world of the atmosphere.[25] He thus puts into this [fire altar] the wind which is in the atmosphere" (ŚB 9.4.2.6). Elsewhere we learn that while the sky is the region of the sun, light rays, day, moon, stars, and faith and the earth is characterized by the year, space, night, quarters, intermediate quarters, and food, it is the atmosphere where one finds the rain cloud, wind, mist, lightning, thunderbolt, hailstones, and soma (ChU 5.4–6).

The atmosphere, then, seems to be the cosmological domain of the Kshatriya because of its association with activity in general (represented by connections between it and the Yajur Veda and the *adhvaryu* priest); militaristic activity in particular (it is the realm of the warrior god Indra, his thunderbolt weapon, and the demons he combats in cosmic battle); and also because of the turbulence—rain, wind, lightning, thunderstorms—which the Vedic writers observed both in the world of the atmosphere and, perhaps, in the temperament of the warrior class.

The sky, as we just observed, is said to be the region of the sun, light rays, day, moon, and stars. The innumerable stars in the sky are made to correspond to other groups or masses of things and beings in the other two worlds: to the animals or plants and trees on earth and to the birds in the atmosphere (ŚB 8.7.4.12–14; PB 5.2.3). Similarly, at PB 10.1.1 we read that each of the three worlds is itself threefold: "This world is threefold through fire, earth and plants; through wind, intermediate region and birds the atmosphere is threefold; yonder world is threefold through sun, sky and stars."[26]

The rationale for the analogy of the sky with the commoner class, the Vaishyas or *viś*, would thus seem to revolve around the concept of multiplicity. The highest spatial world, in other words, is equated with the lowest of the three social classes because of the numerous members contained in each. The countless stars, together with the other planets, sun, and moon, perhaps suggested the countless numbers that comprise the *viś*, the "people" or "the masses" of the social realm.

So far so good. But while the sky is the locale of the stars (the "*viś* of the heavens"), the chief entity of this cosmological world is the sun, divinized as Āditya, Sūrya, or Savitṛ. And this would seem to be something of an obstacle to the interpretation put forward here, namely, that the sky is the Vaishya world. For the sun is a "divine ruler" and the embodiment of the *kṣatra* power. The problem is solved, however, when we realize that, although the unitary sun is a Kshatriya, the multifarious sunbeams are the embodiment of the Viśva Devas, the *viś* of the divinities.[27] The relationship between the sun and the sunbeams within the domain that is the sky replicates that of the king and the *viś* within the kingdom. The sky may still be regarded as the cosmological realm of the Vaishya *varṇa*; it contains the multitudes of the cosmic entities (the stars and sunbeams) which are dominated by and organized around a single ruler (the sun), just as the human *viś* are dominated by and organized around a single king.

This cosmological structure inverts the expected vertical hierarchy in relation to the order of the spatial worlds—which would call for the sky as the "highest" world—but the sociological hierarchy remains intact. The sequential way in which the cosmological worlds are ordered in this paradigm reduplicates the order of the *varṇas* associated with each. Further, the characteristics of each social class find their respective analogues in the distinctive natural phenomena that define each of the three worlds. The model matches commonly assumed characteristics of the three social classes with the distinctive natural phenomena associated with the three cosmological worlds. The sociologically "foremost" class is linked to the cosmologically prior world, the earth being the measure and origin of all other worlds just as the Brahmins are supposed to serve the same function in the social realm. The Kshatriyas, second in the social hierarchy, find their spot in the second of the worlds. The warriors are matched to the realm of thunder, lightning, and other violent meteorological activity—such natural phenomena being perhaps regarded as the analogue to similar traits among the members of this social class. Finally, the Vaishyas are assigned the sky where the cosmological multitudes (the stars and sunbeams), as well as the cosmological ruler (the sun), are located.

Variations in the Cosmological Pattern

In Vedic cosmology, as in other arenas, one encounters a certain number of variations in the patterns of connections posited between things and beings. What would seem to be the dominant pattern, as we have seen, assigns the earth to the *varṇa* that includes within it the Brahmin social class, the atmosphere to the Kshatriyas, and the sky to the Vaishyas. Other, and different, configurations are also set forth in the Veda. In the interest of fairness and comprehensiveness we must pause to survey them. But we shall also see that, despite the variations, the *varṇa* system proceeds logically and in accordance with its own definitional principles.

Chief among the variants in the ways in which the three worlds are classified according to *varṇa* is that which posits the earth as the Vaishya world, the atmosphere as the world of the Kshatriyas, while the sky is associated with the Brahmins. This variant presents us with the straightforward vertically oriented hierarchical arrangement the dominant pattern examined previously inverts. Here the "lowest" world is matched with the social group at the "bottom" of the *varṇa* order (i.e., the earth = the Vaishya); the "highest" or spatially topmost world, the sky, is correlatively linked to the Brahmin, and the atmosphere is, as in the dominant model, the cosmological home of the Kshatriyas.

The social *varṇa*s are explicitly mentioned in one of the passages which illustrate the variant model. The text that follows appoints the Brahmin to the sky, the Kshatriya to the atmosphere, and the Vaishya to the earth. Other homologies link up the expected *varṇa*-encoded meters (*gāyatrī* for the Brahmins, *triṣṭubh* for the Kshatriyas, and the *jagatī* for the Vaishyas)[28] and various sacrificial sheds[29] within the sacrificial arena:

> O *gharma*, that which is your glow in the sky, in the hymns composed in the *gāyatrī* meter, in the Brahmin, in the *havirdhāna*, with this [oblation] I sacrifice to that [glow] of yours, *svāhā*! O *gharma*, that which is your glow in the atmosphere, in the hymns composed in the *triṣṭubh* meter, in the Kshatriya, in the *āgnīdhra*, with this [oblation] I sacrifice to that [glow] of yours, *svāhā*! O *gharma*, that which is your glow in the earth, in the hymns composed in the *jagatī* meter, in the Vaishya, in the *sadas*, with this [oblation] I sacrifice to that [glow] of yours, *svāhā*! (TĀ 4.11.1-2).

Closely paralleling this text is another, ŚB 14.3.1.2ff., which drops the social classes from the linkages yet implies them by repeating the associations of particular meters and sacrificial sheds with one or another of the three worlds (i.e., *gāyatrī* and *havirdhāna* = sky; *triṣṭubh* and *āgnīdhra* = atmosphere;[30] and *jagatī* and *sadas* = earth). The vertically oriented spatial hierarchy is also reinforced by the specification that each of the three offerings be made at different heights measured against the sacrificer's body, each offering representing one of the cosmological worlds. Thus an offering made while holding the ladle level with the sacrificer's mouth is for the sky, for "what is level with the mouth is, as it were, above; and above, as it were, is yonder world" (ŚB 14.3.1.3). An offering with the ladle held level with the navel is the atmosphere, "for in the middle, as it were, is what is navel high, and in the middle, as it were, is the world of the atmosphere" (ŚB 14.3.1.5). And that offered while sitting represents the earth, "for below, as it were, is he who is sitting; and below, as it were, is this world" (ŚB 14.3.1.7).[31]

In the dominant pattern, the earth (and the Brahmins) are connected with the gods, the atmosphere (and the Kshatriyas) with the ancestors, and the sky (and the Vaishyas) with men. The variant cosmological model matches the sky with the gods, the atmosphere with the ancestors, and the earth with humans (AitB 7.5; cf. ŚB 4.5.7.8). Recall also that in the dominant cosmological classification the Ṛg, Yajur, and Sāma Vedas are correlated with the earth, atmosphere, and sky, on the one hand, and the Brahmins, Kshatriyas, and Vaishyas, on the other. At TB 3.12.9.1–2, however, the correlation of Vedas and worlds may stay the same (i.e., Ṛg Veda = earth, Yajur Veda = atmosphere, and Sāma Veda = sky) but the *varṇa* attributions of the first and third chains are reversed (e.g., Ṛg Veda = earth = Vaishya; Sāma Veda = sky = Brahmin).[32]

This vertically oriented cosmological hierarchy is expressed in other modalities as well. The differential in value among three metals serves as the yardstick for the hierarchical place of each of the three worlds: iron is equated to the earth, silver to the atmosphere, and gold to the sky.[33] Another such measure of relative value is indicated at PB 17.13.18 (cf. PB 9.2.9, 20.1.3) where the three forms of sacrifice—that in which rice and barley are offered, that in which an animal is sacrificed, and that in which soma serves as the oblation material—are said to have procured for the gods the earth, atmosphere, and yonder world respectively. In an interesting twist on a passage cited earlier (BĀU 1.5.3–7), in which the earth is linked to a number of Brahmin components (speech, the Ṛg Veda, the gods) as well as to the human mother, at Manu 2.233 we read: "By loving devotion to his mother he wins this world; by loving devotion to his father, the middle world; and by obedience to his guru, the world of ultimate reality (the *brahman*)." In Manu, the last-mentioned world stands both for the "highest" cosmological world and, implicitly, for the uppermost social class.

In contrast to the sequentially based horizontal hierarchy of what we have labeled the dominant model, the variant correlates the vertical orientation of the three spatial worlds to a vertically conceived *varṇa* hierarchy. The texts which conform to this pattern make the adjustment with minimal changes in the more usual *varṇa* attributions: the Ṛg Veda remains the Veda of the earthly realm, for example, but the earth and the Ṛg Veda are both in the variant pattern encoded as Vaishya entities, and not Brahmin components as in the dominant paradigm. Or again, the *gāyatrī* meter remains that of the Brahmin *varṇa* while being assigned to the sky, and not the earth, in the variant classification.[34]

The number of elements in the structure is always stable, but the *varṇa* assignments given to the elements can change.[35] I have tried to demonstrate that no matter which world is assigned to which *varṇa* there is a rationale for doing so, and this rationale is one that always remains consistent with the essential features, qualities, and traits of the social classes. The earth, for example, is usually associated with the Brahmins because it is said to be primary and generative; but it can be correlated with the Vaishyas because it is spatially the "lowest" world, just as the commoners are the "lowest" social class. Under either of the cosmological schemes, the hierarchical place that each social class takes in the structure—whether the hierarchy is represented in a sequential or vertical modality—remains constant. The classification of the three worlds upholds the hierarchical order and does so with a consistency regarding the peculiar traits which define each of the three *varṇa*s.

Threes and Fours: The Three Worlds and the Cardinal Directions

The categorization of Āryan society into three "twice born" classes easily serves as a tripartite analogue to the cosmological conception of the three worlds. When one turns to a quadripartite spatial structure, such as that involving the four cardinal directions—the "quarters" or "regions" (*diks*)—it would seem reasonable to predict that the components of the spatial structure would be matched to a four-part social structure (the three "twice-born" Āryan classes plus the Shūdras). And in some instances, as we shall see, that is precisely what occurs. Calling up the fourth social *varṇa* was one strategy the Vedic classifiers used when moving from a tripartite scheme like that of the three worlds to a quadripartite one like that of the four cardinal directions.

Unfortunately, the situation is not always so straightforward. Some of the complexities we will observe might be regarded as reflexes of the more general reluctance to include the Shūdras in the originally tripartite *varṇa* social scheme. Thus many Vedic texts continue to assume a social triad even when faced with a quadripartite spatial division.[36] For these texts the basic problem becomes this: How can the three original social classes of many Vedic classification structures be correlated with four cardinal directions?

Correlating the three worlds and the four cardinal directions provides another, and far from unrelated, instance of this problem.[37] The three worlds together with the cardinal directions are said to be "this all," that is, the spatial totality.[38] But the coordination of the two spatial schemes is often difficult given the different ways each is divided. Attempts to harmonize the four cardinal directions and the three worlds can appear creative, or even forced.[39]

Take, for example, the following story in which we are told how five gods discovered each of the four quarters and then "improved" each one to create the three worlds:

> These five deities [Indra, Soma, Agni, Vāc, and Prajāpati] then sacrificed with that wish-fulfilling sacrifice; whatever wish they sacrificed for was fulfilled. . . . After they had sacrificed they saw the eastern (or "forwards") quarter and made it into the eastern quarter—this is that eastern quarter [as it exists today]. Therefore creatures here move along in a forward direction, for they made that the forward (or "eastern") quarter. "Let us improve it from here," they said. They made it into nourishment (*ūrj*). "Furthermore, may we see this nourishment" they said, and it became yonder sky. They then saw the southern (*dakṣiṇa*) quarter and made it the southern quarter—this is that southern quarter. This is why the *dakṣiṇa* [cows] stand to the south [of the altar] and are driven up from the south, for they made that the southern quarter. "Let us improve it from here," they said. They made it into a world. "Furthermore, may we see

> this space," they said, and it became the atmosphere, for that world is the atmosphere. Just as the foundation here in this world is obviously the earth, so the foundation there in yonder world is clearly this atmosphere. And because, being here on earth, one does not see that world, people say, "That world is invisible." They then saw the western (*pratīcī*) quarter, and made it into expectation [*āśā*, which can also mean "quarter" or "region"]. Thus, having moved forwards [or to the east] one procures [what he desires], then he goes [back] to that [western] quarter. For they made that [quarter] into expectation.[40] "Let us improve it from here," they said. They made it into excellence (*śriyā*). "Furthermore, may we see this excellence," they said, and it became this earth, for this [earth] is excellence. Thus, one who gains the most from this [earth] becomes superior (*śreṣṭha*). They then saw the northern (*udīcī*) quarter, and made it into the waters. "Let us improve it from here," they said. They made it into proper order (*dharma*), for the waters are proper order. Thus, whenever water comes to this world everything is in accordance with order. (ŚB 11.1.6.20–24)

The four directions are here represented as prior to the three worlds and generative of them—the east gives birth to the sky, the south to the atmosphere, and the west to the earth. The problem of three becoming four is solved here by adding a fourth world to complete the parallelism: the north is correlated to a world of the waters.[41] The "waters" here may function, like other fourth elements generated out of a tripartite scheme, as "something which on the one hand is added to a threefold totality and on the other hand includes the three preceding items."[42] The overlay of the three worlds—and also of the tripartite social scheme —onto the quadripartite cardinal directions often results, as we shall see, in the north becoming the direction of either the "transcendent fourth" or, alternatively, a "miscellaneous" quarter with which a variety of items are correlated.

In what I contend is the usual arrangement of the cardinal directions, east is equated with the Brahmins, south with the Kshatriyas, west with the Vaishyas. The north—the "extra" direction—is regarded as the direction of human beings as an undifferentiated mass; or, less explicitly, as that of the Vaishya or Shūdra class;[43] or as an additional direction for either of the two remaining three *varṇas*.[44] The text cited earlier, in which the three worlds are correlated to the cardinal directions, would be deciphered in the following way: 1) sky = east (= Brahmin); 2) atmosphere = south (= Kshatriya); 3) earth = west (= Vaishya); "the waters" = north (= all classes). The *varṇa* assignments of the three worlds in the text thus conform to the vertically oriented hierarchy whereby earth = Vaishyas, atmosphere = Kshatriya, and sky = Brahmin.

A somewhat different set of homologies between the worlds, the directions, and the social classes—and one which is more standard in its *varṇa* assignments and correlations between the three worlds and the spatial directions—is encountered in Cosmogony XIII. The first three chains[45] of the six-part scheme created by this cosmogony are as follows:

> 1. first day = EARTH = *gāyatrī* meter = nine-versed hymn of praise = *rathantara* chant = EAST = spring = Vasus and Agni
> 2. second day = ATMOSPHERE = *triṣṭubh* meter = fifteen-versed hymn of praise = *bṛhat* chant = SOUTH = summer = Maruts and Indra

TABLE 5.2. The *Varṇa* Of The Cardinal Directions According to Cosmogonies VIII–XIII

Cosmogony VIII

1. EAST = *gāyatrī* meter = 9-versed hymn of praise = *rathantara* chant = Agni = spring = the *brahman*
2. SOUTH = *triṣṭubh* meter = 15-versed hymn of praise = *bṛhat* chant = Indra = summer = the *kṣatra*
3. WEST = *jagatī* meter = 17-versed hymn of praise = *vairūpa* chant = Maruts = rainy season = the *viś*
4. NORTH = *anuṣṭubh* meter = 21-versed hymn of praise = *vairāja* chant = Mitra-Varuṇa = autumn = *phala, bala* or *puṣṭa*
5. ZENITH = *paṅkti* meter = 27- and 33-versed hymn of praise = *śakvara* and *raivata* chants = Bṛhaspati = winter and cool seasons = *varcas* or *phala*

Cosmogony IX

1. EAST ⇒breath ⇒ spring ⇒ *gāyatrī* meter ⇒ *gāyatra* chant ⇒ *upāṃśu* soma cup ⇒ 9-versed hymn of praise ⇒ *rathantara* chant ⇒ the seer Vasiṣṭha
2. SOUTH ⇒ mind ⇒ summer ⇒ *triṣṭubh* meter ⇒ *aiḍa* chant ⇒ *antaryāma* soma cup ⇒ 15-versed hymn of praise ⇒ *bṛhat* chant ⇒ the seer Bharadvāja
3. WEST ⇒ eye (or sight) ⇒ rainy season ⇒ *jagatī* meter ⇒ *ṛksāma* chant ⇒ *śukra* soma cup ⇒ 17-versed hymn of praise ⇒ *vairūpa* chant ⇒ the seer Viśvamitra
4. NORTH ⇒ ear (or hearing) ⇒ autumn ⇒ *anuṣṭubh* meter ⇒ *svāra* chant ⇒ *manthin* soma cup ⇒ 21-versed hymn of praise ⇒ *vairāja* chant ⇒ the seer Jamadagni
5. ZENITH ⇒ thought and speech ⇒ winter ⇒ *paṅkti* meter ⇒ conclusion of chants ⇒ *āgrāyana* soma cup ⇒ 27- and 33-versed hymns of praise ⇒ the *śakvara* and *raivata* chants ⇒ the seer Raivata Viśvakarman

Cosmogony X

1. EAST = spring = Agni = the *brahman* = *gāyatrī* meter = *rathantara* chant = 9-versed hymn of praise = track of 15-versed hymn of praise = Sanaga the seer = 18-month-old calf = *kṛta* dice throw = east wind
2. SOUTH = summer = Indra = the *kṣatra* = *triṣṭubh* meter = *bṛhat* chant = 15-verse hymn of praise = track of 17-versed hymn of praise = Sanātana the seer = 2-year-old cow = *treta* dice throw = south wind
3. WEST = rainy season = Viśva Devas = the *viś* = *jagatī* meter = *vairūpa* chant = 17-versed hymn of praise = track of 21-versed hymn of praise = Ahabhūna the seer = 3-year-old cow = *dvāpara* dice throw = west wind
4. NORTH = autumn = Mitra and Varuṇa = prosperity (*puṣṭa*) = *anuṣṭubh* meter = *vairāja* chant = 21-versed hymn of praise = track of 27-versed hymn of praise = Purāṇa [var. Pratna] the seer = 4-year-old cow = *abhibhava* [var. *askaṇḍa*] dice throw = north wind

3. third day = SKY = *jagatī* meter = seventeen-fold hymn of praise = *vairūpa* chant = WEST = rainy season = Ādityas and Varuṇa

The earth, atmosphere, and sky are here associated with east, south, and west respectively. Other elements (meters, hymns of praise, chants, deities) included within the first three chains would seem to indicate the expected *varṇa* order, Brahmin, Kshatriya, and Vaishya.

The *varṇa* assignments of the first three chains in Cosmogony XIII are confirmed when we compare them to those of Cosmogonies VIII–XII. As Table 5.2 demonstrates, all six taxonomies give much the same correlates for the east, south, and west; furthermore, Cosmogonies VIII and X specify that the meta-

5. ZENITH = winter and cool seasons = Bṛhaspati = fruit (*phala*) [var. splendor (*varcas*)] = *paṅkti* meter = *śakvara* and *raivata* chants = 27-versed hymn of praise = track of 33-versed hymn of praise = Suparṇa the seer = 4-year-old bull = *askaṇḍa* [var. *abhibhū*] dice throw = wind from above

Cosmogony XI

1. EAST = Vasus and Agni = 9-versed hymn of praise = *ājya* recitation = *rathantara* chant
2. SOUTH = Rudras and Indra = 15-versed hymn of praise = *prauga* recitation = *bṛhat* chant
3. WEST = Ādityas and Varuṇa = 17-versed hymn of praise = *mārutvatiya* recitation = *vairūpa* chant
4. NORTH = Maruts and Soma = 21-versed hymn of praise = *niṣkevalya* recitation = *vairāja* chant
5. MIDDLE = Viśva Devas and Bṛhaspati = 27-versed and 33-versed hymns of praise = *vaiśvadeva* and *āgnimaruta* recitations = *śakvara* and *raivata* chants

Cosmogony XII

1. EAST ⇒ Agni = *gāyatrī* meter = 9-versed hymn of praise = *rathantara* chant = spring = inhalation = constellations = Vasus
2. SOUTH ⇒ Indra = *triṣṭubh* meter = 15-versed hymn of praise = *bṛhat* chant = summer = the circulating breath = moon = Rudras
3. WEST ⇒ Maruts = *jagatī* meter = 17-versed hymn of praise = *vairūpa* chant = rainy season = exhalation = Venus = Ādityas
4. NORTH ⇒ Viśva Devas = *anuṣṭubh* meter = 21-versed hymn of praise = *vairāja* chant = autumn = the digestive breath = Varuṇa and the Sādhyas
5. ZENITH ⇒ Mitra and Varuṇa = *paṅkti* meter = 27- and 33-versed hymns of praise = *śakvara* and *raivata* chants = winter and the cool season = the upward breath = Angirases = moon
6. NADIR ⇒ Saturn = eclipses = comets = serpents = demons = spirits = humans, birds, eight-legged mountain goats, elephants, etc.

Cosmogony XIII

1. first day = earth = *gāyatrī* meter = 9-versed hymn of praise = *rathantara* chant = EAST = spring = Vasus and Agni
2. second day = atmosphere = *triṣṭubh* meter = 15-versed hymn of praise = *bṛhat* chant = SOUTH = summer = Maruts and Indra
3. third day = sky = *jagatī* meter = 17-versed hymn of praise = *vairūpa* chant = WEST = rainy season = Ādityas and Varuṇa
4. fourth day = food = *anuṣṭubh* meter = 21-versed hymn of praise = *vairāja* chant = NORTH = autumn = Sādhyas and Ājyas and Bṛhaspati and the moon
5. fifth day = animals = *paṅkti* meter = 27-versed hymn of praise = *śakvara* chant = ZENITH = winter = Maruts and Rudra
6. sixth day = waters = *atichandas* meter = 33-versed hymn of praise = *raivata* chant = ZENITH = cool season = Viśva Devas and Prajāpati

---

physical powers associated with the east, south, and west are the *brahman*, *kṣatra*, and *viś*. It would seem as though the *varṇa* attributes of the first three cardinal directions are fairly fixed.

The table also indicates, however, the difficulty in assigning any particular *varṇa* to the fourth direction. The north in Cosmogony XIII, for example, is connected to a fourth cosmological "world of food" (and also to the *anuṣṭubh* meter, the twenty-one-versed hymn of praise, the *vairāja* chant, autumn, and the Sādhyas, Ājyas, and Bṛhaspati). Many of these same components are repeated in Cosmogonies VIII and X, which also include the essential power of *puṣṭa*, seemingly indicating a lower-class *varṇa* assignment for this chain (and, therefore, for the north). Some of the deities assigned to this direction (the Maruts and Soma in Cosmogony XI; the Viśva Devas in Cosmogony XII) also indicate a correlation with the peasantry. But other deities linked to the north and other fourth chain components—the Brahmin-Kshatriya pair of Mitra and Varuṇa in Cosmogony X and the Brahmin deity Bṛhaspati in Cosmogony XIII—would argue for a different *varṇa* interpretation for this cardinal direction. In sum, "The problem of finding a fourth group for the North," as one scholar observes, "has been solved in different ways."[46]

Ontological and Metaphysical Correlates of the Cardinal Directions

Why are the various regions assigned to particular *varṇas*? What is the rationale behind the linking of the eastern quarter to the Brahmin class, for example? Two kinds of connections provide us with information about the supposed qualitative peculiarities of the regions; we begin our survey of the cardinal directions with these. The assimilation of different kinds of beings with one or another region, and the metaphysical powers that each quarter is thought to represent, can be used as ciphers for uncovering what the Vedic authors regarded as the distinctive features or properties of the directions. These two types of associations, ontological and metaphysical, also provide us with some of the reasons behind the *varṇa* assignments the quarters are given.

The metaphysical powers associated with the quarters are as follows. For the east, the *brahman*, "the splendor of the *brahman* power" (*brahmavarcasa*), brilliance (*tejas*), and splendor (*varcas*); the *kṣatra* and the forces of death, physical strength, and violence for the south; and qualities of procreation and generation and "the power of the *viś*" for the west. The north, the "extra" quarter when the directions are matched with the social scheme in its tripartite formulation, is variously characterized by fertility, prosperity, and success (especially in the social realm), and also by sin, disease, and weakness.

In those texts that connect the regions to one or another ontological group or class of beings, the east (or Brahmin region) is almost universally regarded as the quarter of the gods; the south (Kshatriya) belongs to the ancestors and demons; the west (Vaishya) is the quarter in which the classifiers tend to situate animals (especially snakes), the wife, and one's progeny; and the north is regarded as the quarter of offspring, men, or human beings generally. In one text, for example, the Vedic authors find various significances in what might be otherwise regarded as the haphazard bubbling of milk in different directions:

> When it swells upwards, it swells for the sacrificer; when it swells on the east side, that is for the gods; when on the south side, for the ancestors; when on the west, for the animals; and when it swells on the north, it does so for [the sacrificer's] offspring. In any case, there is no problem for the sacrificer, for it always swells upwards [in addition to swelling in a particular direction]. (ŚB 14.2.2.28)

This is indeed a kind of no-fault insurance policy for the sacrificer, for whereas others may or may not benefit from the boiling over of the milk, the sacrificer always profits from it.

The East

"The east is the region of the gods," it is declared (ŚB 1.9.3.13; cf. KB 18.10), and it is from the east that the gods are said to come to meet humans in the sacrifice: "Here they erect either a sacrificial hall or a shed, with the top beams running from west to east. The east is the quarter of the gods, and from the east westwards the gods approach men. Therefore one offers to them while facing east" (ŚB 3.1.1.6; cf. 2.6.1.11). The sacrifice as a whole is oriented eastward,[47] that is, toward the gods. As the region where the sun rises, the east is also the realm of "light," which is further equated with the day,[48] the sacrifice and the gods (ŚB 1.1.2.21).

The very fact that in Sanksrit the same word, *prāñc*, means "east," "forward," and "up" is an indicator of the importance placed on this region, and of the influence the sacrificial ideology had on ancient Indian perception. Presumably originating in the coordinates of the ritual, the assumptions here are that (1) the east always lies "in front" of the subject and (2) this quarter is the way "up." Playing on the semantic overlap of the word *prāñc*, Vedic texts often identify the eastern direction and the "world of the gods" or "heaven" (*svarga*), which is supposed to lie up from the earth (e.g., AitB 7.5; ŚB 3.5.1.9, 3.5.3.17, 3.6.3.10). The priest directs the sacrifice, conceived of as a ship, to the east, for "when he walks toward the east, he steers that [ship] eastward toward the heavenly world. By this he obtains the heavenly world" (ŚB 2.3.3.16). In one rite, a cow is released to wander freely. "If, not driven by man, she goes eastward, then he should know, 'This sacrificer has been granted [his desires]. He has won a good world [i.e., the world of heaven]' " (ŚB 4.5.8.11).

But the world of heaven and the gods, which lies to the east is permanently attained by mortals only after death. In one text, a hesitant animal victim of the sacrificial ritual is being led along to the east where, he realizes, he will "go to heaven," that is, die. His lot is made easier when the fire god Agni, the deity of this region, leads the way forward to the east: "Therefore they say, 'Every animal is connected with Agni, for it followed after Agni.' Therefore also they carry Agni [i.e., the sacrificial fire] before it [the animal victim being led to the east]" (AitB 2.6).[49]

The east is the direction of the gods, the sacrifice, and the heavenly world, all of which have apparent connections to the Brahmin *varṇa*. Should this seem speculative, the east is also explicitly said to be the quarter of the *brahman* power. The *brahman*, it is said, was "first born in the east" (TB 2.8.8.8). When constructing a burial mound, one should therefore pound a peg made of *palāśa* wood to the east, "for the *palāśa* is the *brahman* power; he thus makes him go to the heavenly world with the *brahman* power as his guide" (ŚB 13.8.4.1). Similarly, the king, upon taking a court priest (the *purohita*), is made to face east and say "homage to the *brahman*," for "when the *kṣatra* power falls under the sway of the *brahman* power, that kingdom is prosperous and filled with heroes; in it an heir is born" (AitB 8.9). In another rite, a sacrificial implement is to be pushed to the east for the attainment of "glory and the splendor of the *brahman* power" (PB 1.2.4; cf. 6.5.3). Elswhere, certain libations are made while facing in this direction if the sacrificer desires the Brahmin qualities of brilliance (*tejas*) and splendor, for "the eastern quarter is brilliance and splendor" (AitB 1.8).

The South

The association of the gods and the east is an indirect way of equating the Brahmins, who are also identified with the east, and the deities. Similarly, the Kshatriyas, who are assigned the southern quarter, share it with beings associated with death, danger, and violence—the ancestors and the demons.

The south is the realm of the deceased ancestors, those liminal figures who exist between the earthly world of living humans and the elevated place of the immortal gods.[50] The contrast between the east and the gods, on the one hand, and the south and the ancestors, on the other, is often quite pronounced: "The sacrifice to the ancestors is terminated in the south. . . . Having gone eastward they worship the sun, and the sun is the world of the gods; and the ancestors are the world of the ancestors. They thereby ascend from the world of the ancestors to the world of the gods" (KB 5.7; cf. ŚB 12.5.1.7, 13.8.2.9). The Kshatriya region and the beings who dwell there are unfavorably compared to the east (the locale of the rising sun), the gods, and (implicitly) to the Brahmins. One "ascends from the world of the ancestors" and the Kshatriyas, "to the world of the gods" and the Brahmins. The relations laid out in this text can be schematically presented—east : south :: gods : ancestors :: higher : lower :: Brahmins : Kshatriyas.

The south, the region of deceased humans, is also the quarter of death in general (see ŚānĀ 11.4; PB 9.8.1-2). Ruled by Yama (BĀU 3.9.21 and below), the king of the dead,[51] the south is often presented as the most life threatening of the quarters. If a cow that has been set free wanders southward, "he should know that the sacrificer will soon depart from this world" (ŚB 4.5.8.11). A *plakṣa* tree on the south side of one's house is said to bring death to the residents (GGS 4.7.20–22), while a room built on ground sloping to south has the potential to cause the early death of those who inhabit it.[52]

It might seem somewhat paradoxical that the quarter of the ancestors and death should also be that of offspring and "food." At AitB 1.8, one who desires food is instructed to face the south while offering certain libations: "He becomes an eater of food, a lord of food; with his offspring he gets food who knowing this turns to the south." Elsewhere (TS 5.5.3.1–6, explicating mantras from TS 4.3.9.1–2) the south is equated with both food ("he places food to the south; therefore with the right [hand, *dakṣiṇa*, also the word for 'south'] food is eaten") and offspring ("offspring is food. . . . He eats food for whom on the south these [bricks are placed], rich in food, and a son is born to him to eat food").

Such a connection between the ancestors and the propagation and sustenance of offspring may be because, as Veena Das notes, the ancestors "have a direct interest in continuation of their lines and hence the welfare of the descendants," for "the ancestor is himself, through a cycle of rebirth, the descendant"[53]—although the cycle of rebirth is anachronistic when dealing with Vedic texts before the Upanishads. But it is also said that the food one obtains through the ritual manipulation of the south is obtained at the expense of one's progeny: "[The spot for building the house should be] inclined toward the south for a person who longs for food; for offspring die there [in the south]" (MGS 2.11.2; cf. VGS 14.2; MatsyaP 256.29ff.). In the Veda, at any rate, food, offspring, and death are found clustered together in the south.

The southern region is populated with other beings also associated with death. In one text, the Maruts or divine storm troopers are said to have once come from the south in order to exterminate all living beings (ŚB 2.5.2.10). Another group of beings regularly located in the south, and also characterized as deadly, dangerous, aggressive, and evil, are the demons.[54] Stories that tell of attacks of the gods' sacrifice by the demons on the south side are (like devils themselves) legion. The gods, according to these tales, took the counteroffensive in various ways which often justify particular ritual practices. A horse (generally regarded as a Kshatriya animal) is stationed on the south side in one rite because the gods, threatened by demons from that direction, "saw that thunderbolt, yonder sun. This horse is indeed yonder sun; and by means of that thunderbolt they drove off the demons from the south" (ŚB 6.3.1.29). Two offering spoons of a particular kind of wood are placed on the south side of the sacrifice because the gods once saw a demon-killing tree, the *kārṣmarya*, in that region (ŚB 7.4.1.37). Similarly, ghee (another representation of the thunderbolt) is placed on the south by the ritualist, just as the gods did when "they warded off the danger from demons in the south by that thunderbolt, the ghee."[55]

The south is thus referred to as the "terrible" or "dreadful" quarter (TS 1.8.13.1–2), in part because of the ghouls and adversaries who supposedly dwell there.[56] As Veena Das pointed out, the south is not only the quarter of "sacred beings associated with death" (ancestors and demons), but also the realm in which "the danger emanating from these sacred beings has to be neutralized."[57] When compared to the associations made with the east, those of the south present us with a set of binary oppositions—east : south :: gods : demons :: Brahmins : Kshatriyas. But why are the Kshatriyas in this way "demons" while Brahmins are "gods"? Such linkages might be explained in two ways.

First, the south is generally conceived as the region of violence and aggression. One text claims that a room built on land sloping to south may make inhabitants quarrelsome (ĀśvGS 2.7.11), and the warrior class, at least to the Brahmin classifiers, were, it would seem, sometimes thought of as threatening folk whose berserker aspect needed to be contained. Even the gods fear the violence of the Kshatriya, and only the Brahmin class can adequately control them (see, e.g., TS 2.4.13.1). It is perhaps no coincidence that the priest who metonymically bears the name of the priestly class as a whole, the *brahman* priest, is stationed on the south side (see, e.g., ĀpŚS 1.4.8.5–6), acting as the protector (*abhigoptṛ*) of the sacrifice (ŚB 1.7.4.18; cf. 5.4.3.26, 12.6.1.38) and holding in check the martial aggression of Kshatriya-like demons and defensively protecting the sacrifice from error.[58]

As an alternative explanation, we might recall here that the Brahmins are associated with the eastern realm of the gods because it is this social class who, through their priestly duties, are charged with the care and manipulation of the deities. Similarly, the south may be the Kshatriya's quarter because the Āryan warriors, like their deified representative Indra, are best deployed in the direction of the enemy: "for it was while standing in this place that Indra drove off toward the south the danger from the demons" (ŚB 1.4.5.3).[59] The southern region is thus depicted as the site where demonic danger was defeated and protection gained thanks to the valiant efforts of the warrior god. It is perhaps significant that according to ŚB 2.3.2.6 the south is also the direction from which comes the human enemy.[60]

The south is regarded as the realm of physical strength and military power: it is dubbed the "strong" direction (MGS 2.11.2; TS 5.5.10.2), the "overpowering" region (ChU 3.15.2), or the realm of heroes (HGS 1.8.27.2), as well as the "dreadful" quarter. This region is thus aptly connected with the warrior class and other entities who are characterized by physical strength, and the qualities that are supposed to adhere to that region are transferred to various objects within the ritual. The priest stands in the south while putting power (*ojas*) and physical strength (*bala*) into a horse (and "therefore the horse is among the animals the most powerful and the strongest") (TB 3.8.7.1–2). The sacrificer is the recipient of the powers of the south in another rite where a stick is placed on the south side of the fire while the priest recites "You are the right arm of Indra" (TS 1.1.11). By this action and mantra the priest "puts strength (*indriya*) into the sacrificer" (TB 3.3.6.8).[61]

The West

The western quarter is thought to be the region of animals in general, snakes in particular, and also of the wife and offspring. The correlation of these entities and the Vaishya qualities of regeneration, fecundity, procreation, and material wealth is obvious. The west is the direction of nourishment and life, "food" and "breath," as one text puts it (PGS 3.4.16), or of "support," as it is designated elsewhere.[62] In another passage, the priest places "all life power" (*viśva āyus*) into the sacrificer by putting a stick which represents "Gandharva Viśvavasus," a demigod who "possesses all wealth," on the west side of the fire (TB 3.3.6.8).[63]

Animals were a kind of natural resource, like crops and other forms of "food,"[64] that the Vedic Indians wished to see reproduce abundantly. The Vaishyas are themselves frequently identified with animals; as pastoralists and tenders of the herds, they are equated with their beastly wards. The second-order linkage of the west and animals is thus consistent with the Vaishya association with both. Through performing certain rites involving activities done in the direction of the fertile west, the sacrificer could help his livestock multiply. A ritualist who wishes to obtain abundant domestic animals should offer oblations in the fire while facing the west (AitB 1.8).

While animals in general were located in the west, the region is the particular home of the snakes. At PB 4.9.4–6 the ritualists are instructed to face west and chant the verses known as "the queen of the snakes" (*sarparājñī*, SV 2.726–28 = ṚV 9.189.1–3), for "by means of these [verses] the Serpent Arbuda removed his dead skin. They remove their dead skin by means of these [verses]. The queen of the snakes is the earth; on the earth they obtain a firm foundation." The snake who sloughs off its skin is here, as elsewhere, most probably a symbol of regeneration and fecundity. Another text also fills the west with snakes in the course of depicting the beings associated with each of the other three quarters—east is the "faultless" quarter of the gods, the south belongs to the ancestors, and the north to men:

> For this reason one must not sleep with his head toward the west, for one would then sleep stretching [his legs, and most especially his feet] toward the gods. The southern quarter belongs to the ancestors, and the western one to the snakes. That faultless (*ahīna*) one [i.e., the east] is from where the gods ascended [into heaven]. The northern quarter belongs to men. (ŚB 3.1.1.7)

The conceptualization of the west as the quarter of natural reproduction also seems to lie behind its association with the sacrificer's wife, another fount of procreation and (re)birth. The wife takes her place within the ritual confines on the western side. A cinder which falls out of the fire toward the west before the fore-offerings are placed in the fire will bring distress to the sacrificer's wife (TB 3.7.2.6). The priest must also take care when he removes the oblation material from the *gārhapatya* fire: "If he should remove it eastward, he would cause the sacrificer to meet with grief; if southward, it would belong to the ancestors; if westward, he would cause the wife to meet with pain."[65]

The identification of the wife and the west is wholly in keeping with the more general associations of the west and the powers of fertility. This quarter is sometimes conceived, so to speak, as the region of the fertile waters which are "founded" on semen[66] or, more often, the direction of birth. For while seed is emitted into the woman "from the front" or the east, the newborn drops "down from the back" (ŚB 4.5.2.3), that is, toward the west:

> He unties the knot [that has been made in a bunch of sacrificial grass]. By that he causes procreation. That [knot] that has been twisted through upward and eastward he draws back westward. Therefore, seed is placed [into the vulva] forwards, but offspring are born backward [i.e., come out of the uterus in the opposite direction].[67]

The west is thus also the quarter identified with offspring.[68] A ritually empowered cow who wanders to the west, it is said, will bring the sacrificer a multitude of dependents as well as abundant crops (ŚB 4.5.8.11). One passage contrasts the west and east, regarding the former as the "womb of humans" while the latter is the birthplace of gods: "There are two wombs—the womb of the gods and the womb of men. The gods have their womb in the east, and men in the west" (ŚB 7.4.2.40). Here the western quarter is again presented as the region of natural fecundity, the very womb from which humans are born, while the east is realm of supernatural origins. At GGS 4.7.18, building one's house with the door facing west is prohibited, presumably because the residents would come out not facing but with their backs to the gods. Another set of binary oppositions is thus formulated, with the last member of the set perhaps implied—east : west :: divine birth : human birth :: Brahmins : Vaishyas. The west, in summary, is encoded as the region of natural wealth and the reproduction of it. Domestic animals, the wife, offspring, crops, and "food" are all located in this region where fertility and "life" are promoted and enhanced. The assignment of the Vaishya class to this quarter is thus in keeping with assumptions about the proclivities and duties of the commoner class.

The North

The north is most frequently represented as the realm of human beings in general, a categorization that lends itself to different interpretive slants on the part of the systematizers (and on the part of more distant interpreters). In some texts it appears that this direction functions as something of a catchall category, a kind of unmarked fourth in a classification system that most often operates through tripartition.

As the quarter of generalized humanity, the north is opposed to other regions and other ontological entities which reside in them. We have seen certain oppositions between the Brahmin east and the Kshatriya south or the Vaishya west: (1) east : south :: gods : ancestors :: higher : lower :: Brahmins : Kshatriyas; (2) east : south :: gods : demons :: Brahmins : Kshatriyas; (3) east : west :: divine birth : human birth :: Brahmins : Vaishyas. Regarded as "the world of the living" (KB 18.14; cf. TB 2.1.3.1), the north is sometimes contrasted to the south, the region of death and dead humans. The south lies opposite to the north, and the ancestors are thus said to be "far away from men," who serve as their ontological negative exposure (ŚB 2.4.2.21). A throne for a king who is to be consecrated is placed with two of its feet in the northern part of the sacrificial grounds and two in the south: "For the northern sacrificial grounds is this world, and the southern one the world of the ancestors. He thus consecrates him for both worlds" (ŚB 12.8.3.6). The following text, which instructs the ritualist on the site that should be chosen for construction of a tomb, also draws this sort of binary opposition between the north and south:

> Now for the choosing of the ground. He makes it on ground inclining toward the north, for the north is the region of men. He thus causes him [the deceased] to have a share in the world of men. Having given the ancestors a share in the world of men, there is offspring for him and his offspring become more distinguished. Some say, "He should make it on ground inclining toward the south, for the world of the ancestors inclines towards the south. He [in this way] thus causes him to have a share in the world of the ancestors." He should not do so, however. For the name for this kind of burial tomb is "open." [If it is constructed inclining to the south], someone else in his family quickly follows him in death. (ŚB 13.8.1.6–7)

The northern region is also set against the east in order to make an ontological division between humans and gods. For the Vedic ritualists, the human condition is often portrayed as the exact opposite of the divine, and when engaged in sacrifice, the participants must shed the practices of ordinary humanity and assume those of the gods. In contrast to the "perfection" (*samṛddha* or *sampanna*) characteristic of divine beings, the earthly and human are said to be imperfect and "unsuccessful" (*vyṛddha*).[69] "What is 'no' for the gods is 'yes' for man," says another Brāhmaṇa (AitB 3.5) in order to underline the utter difference between the two kinds of beings. Such contrasts between gods and human beings are also expressed in the opposition of east and north.[70] "Hence in human [practice] a hall or shed is constructed with the top beams running from south to north, because the north is the quarter of men. It is only for a consecrated [and therefore divinized], not for an unconsecrated person that it is [constructed] with the top beams running from west to east" (ŚB 3.1.1.7; cf. 3.6.1.23, 4.6.8.19–20).

Some texts provide a three-way comparison between the east, south, and north and the beings assigned to each—gods, ancestors, and men. The Agnihotra cow is said to be the means for conquering the three "worlds" of the ancestors, gods, and men: "He brings [the calf] to the southern side [of the cow]; by that he wins the world of the ancestors. He makes [the cow] turn toward the east; by that he wins the world of the gods. Having caused her to turn toward the north, he milks her; by that he wins the world of men" (TB 2.1.8.1).

But the godly east and the ancestoral south can also pose dangers for human beings. The king should be anointed from the direction of humans, the north, because of the metaphysical pitfalls—divinity and death—the other two quarters can pose to the leader of the living:[71]

> Some, however, anoint him on the south [or right] side of the fire altar. For it is from the right side that food is served. Thus, they anoint him from the side that represents food. One should not do this, for that [southern] quarter belongs to the ancestors. He whom they anoint in this way quickly goes to that region [i.e., dies]. And some, indeed, anoint him [on the eastern side,] near the *āhavanīya* fire. For the *āhavanīya* is the world of heaven. Thus, they anoint him in the world of heaven. One should not do this, for that [*āhavanīya* fire or world of heaven] is his divine self, and this [present self of the sacrificer] is his human one. By this action, they fasten his divine self to his mortal self if they anoint him in this way. One should anoint him only on the northern [or left] side. For that region, which is both north and east, belongs to both gods and men. One thus anoints him in his own region, his own place of safety and stability. For he who is in [that region] which is safety and stability is unharmed. (ŚB 9.3.4.11–13)

The east as the direction of the gods and the "world of heaven" is to be avoided in instances like this where the this-worldly is put to the fore. The southern region of the deceased similarly will attract the unwary ritualist to its world of extraterrestrials, the ancestors.[72] In the comparison, the north, as the quarter of living humans, or the northeast as the quarter of both gods and men, is represented as the direction of life and safety for human beings.

In this text and others, the north is grouped with the east and contrasted with the south. In such cases, both the east and north represent the regions of "life" in opposition to the south, the direction of the ancestors and death. The ground on which the sacrifice is to be performed should slope toward the east, the quarter of the gods, or the north, the region of men; but "it should rise toward the south just a little bit (*pratyucchritam iva*). That is the quarter of the ancestors. Were it to incline [more steeply] toward the south, the sacrificer would quickly go to that world [i.e., die], but this way the sacrificer lives a long time. Therefore, it should rise toward the south just a little bit."[73] We have seen that the northeast combines into one direction the ontological inhabitants of the east and north as the region of "gods and men."[74] Termed the "unconquerable" quarter,[75] the northeast is the direction toward which many rites are oriented.[76] In one such rite, animals are let loose toward the northeast, and hence "both gods and men live on animals" (ŚB 6.4.4.22); in another, a branch with points facing both northward and eastward is recommended for the "conquest of both worlds":

> If he should bring a branch [for driving the calves from the cows] with the point turned eastward, he would conquer the world of the gods. If he should bring a branch with the point turned northward, he would conquer the world of men. He brings a branch the point of which is turned toward the northeast, for the conquest of both worlds. (TB 3.2.1.3)

The north is, in sum, the region signifying all humans, the human race in general, in opposition to other categories of beings who are supposed to inhabit other regions.[77] It is opposed to the south as the living are to the dead; to the east as humans are to gods; and to the east and south as the this-worldly is to the other-worldly. The north and east together are opposed to the south as gods and men are opposed to the ancestors; furthermore, these two are contrasted to the west and south as the sacrificial versus the nonsacrificial and, ontologically, as the gods and men are opposed to all other beings.[78]

The north, one might say, is often socially neutral in relation to the other *varṇa*-encoded directions, standing as the region for human beings in general and *en masse*. Another interpretation, however, is that the semantic meaning of the north more or less reduplicates that of the west. Both directions can be envisioned as regions of "the masses" or a generalized lower class. The bifurcation of an originally undifferentiated commoner class into the Vaishyas and Shūdras may have one of its reflexes here—the north often appears to have many of the same features as the Vaishya west. Like the west, the north is said to be "the world of the living" and is associated with offspring and animals.[79] Often labeled the "firm" or "fixed" (*dhruva*) region (ŚB 4.2.4.19; cf. TS 1.1.11.1; TB 3.3.6.10; ŚB 1.3.4.4) after the pole star (which is also called *dhruva* in Sanskrit), this is where the goods of human life are secured. When a householder puts up a doorpost on the northern side of his home he is to say, "Stand here firmly, o house, rich in horses and cows, rich in delight; rich in sap, overflowing with milk, stand up for the sake of great happiness" (HGS 1.8.27.3).

The north, as the region of human beings, seems in some cases at least to be characterized by fertility and prosperity, just like the Vaishya west. It is in the north that the power of "fruit" (*phala*) or that of growth and material wealth (*puṣṭa*) is located according to Cosmogony VIII, and "the world of food" is correlated with this region in Cosmogony XIII. Like the west, the north is labeled the quarter of wealth (ChU 3.15.2) and in later Hindu texts the divinized embodiment of riches, the god Kubera, is assigned to the northern region.

The two quarters are distinguished, however, and in ways that might justify envisioning the north as the specific region of the Shūdra class.[80] Whereas I argued previously that the west is characterized by *natural* wealth (animals, offspring, crops, etc.), the north, the quarter of human beings, is sometimes portrayed as the locus of *human* wealth. By this term I mean those benefits conferred on an individual by social opinion. The released cow that wanders to the east signifies the attainment of heaven for the sacrificer, the south means death, the west means abundant dependents and crops; the bovine that heads northward indicates that the ritualist "will become more successful in this world" (ŚB 4.5.8.11). Or, again, at TB 3.8.7.1–2, the sacrificial horse is consecrated from the north with a dedication to the Viśva Devas, the divine populace or hoi polloi: "The Viśva Devas indeed are among the gods the most glorious. Thus [by reciting that formula] he puts glory (or fame, *yaśas*) into him. Therefore the horse is among the animals the most glorious." Similarly, the northern opening of the heart should be worshiped as "fame and beauty; he becomes famous and beautiful who knows this" (ChU 3.13.4).

While the north is often left vaguely depicted as the region of human beings as a whole, or as a kind of companion quarter to the west (both being characterized by the materialism associated with the lower social classes), the distinctive notion that the north is the realm of human opinion ("glory," "fame," "beauty") is perhaps suggestive of a more particular *varṇa* assignment. For while the Vaishyas have duties revolving around the increase of the natural world and the wealth it brings to humans, the Shūdras' duties are to the humans they serve.[81] Shūdras, it might be said, depend entirely on other humans for their well-being. It is not, therefore, entirely implausible that the quarter which, in some instances at least, is regarded as connected with public opinion should also be, at least implicitly, assigned to the Shūdra *varṇa*. Such a correlation between the north and the servant class might also help to explain why this quarter is sometimes said to belong to Varuṇa (e.g., ŚB 2.5.2.10 and below), who as judge and overseer of the cosmic order (*ṛta*)[82] binds creatures with their sin, and who is, with the north, connected to the cosmic (or rather chaotic) primeval waters, the moon, night, and death.[83] The ritualist is to stand to the north and declare, " 'I abandon exhaustion, languor, and sickness.' He thereby consigns to that [northern] region whatever exhaustion, languor, and sickness there is. Therefore hungry people [live] in that region" (ŚB 7.3.1.23).

If the other three regions are assigned to the other three classes, the process of elimination would seem to leave the north either to the Shūdras or to all as the generically "human" quarter. But because this region is "uninflected," so to speak, especially in relation to other directions where the class attribution is more fixed and stable, the north can function as a kind of vacuum that may be filled with any *varṇa*-encoded components. Several texts, for example, equate the north with the *brahman* power and Brahmin gods (e.g., Bṛhaspati) and claim that the north is the quarter of the Brahmin quality *varcas* or "splendor": "therefore for the Brahmins gain is produced in the north" (TS 5.3.4.4, 4.3.9.2; cf. ŚB 8.4.2.10, 8.5.1.11). In other cases, however, the north (perhaps functioning as interchangeable with its polar opposite, the south, for which see below) seems to carry Kshatriya traits. It is, as noted previously, the realm of *bala* or physical force and strength at TS 1.8.13.1–2, and at TS 5.3.4.2–3,6 (cf. TS 4.3.9.1 and ŚB 8.4.2.4) the north is the region of the *kṣatra* power, the deity Indra, the fifteen-versed hymn of praise, the power of force or *ojas*, and other Kshatriya signifiers.

We saw that the east is consistently connected with the gods, the "world of heaven," and typically Brahminical powers such as *brahmavarcasa* and *tejas*. The south is almost always regarded as the region of the ancestors and demons, the realm of death and physical (especially military) power—and is thus the appropriate region for the Kshatriya warriors. The west is populated by animals, snakes, the wife, and offspring; it signifies regeneration, fecundity, and the natural products one wishes to have reproduced, and it is aptly correlated to the agriculturalists and pastoralists. The north, according to the criteria surveyed thus far, is the wild card. It can be associated with humans in general, but is also depicted as the special direction of the Brahmins or, alternatively, of the Kshatriyas; it is also represented as the direction of the lower classes in general; further, it can appear to be the direction in which those qualities that social opinion confers are centered, as well as the region of sickness, decay, and sin—both, perhaps, in order to suggest a Shūdra affiliation.

Other Correlates for the Cardinal Directions

Having surveyed the ontological beings, metaphysical values, and social *varṇa*s assigned to the four quarters, let us now follow the chains of associations into other arenas. As we shall see, the particular *varṇa* attributions for each of the four directions—which are explicitly enunciated in some texts, and which are also reiterated in the language of ontology and metaphysics—are further reconfirmed in other idioms.

The regions are, for example, also linked to the Vedas in such a way that the *varṇa* of each can be deciphered. In our treatment of the three worlds, we observed that the Ṛg Veda was often associated with the earth and the Brahmins; the Yajur Veda was associated with the atmosphere and Kshatriyas; and the Sāma Veda, sky, and Vaishyas similarly conjoined. A comparable network of interrelations occurs with the classification of the directions at ChU 3.1–5. The Brahmin east is connected with the Ṛg Veda, as it is to the earth in other taxonomies; the south is the region of the Yajur Veda, just as the atmosphere is in other schemes; the Vaishya direction, the west, like the Vaishya world (the sky), is linked to the Sāma Veda. The fourth or "extra" direction is connected to the fourth Veda, the Atharva, and is referred to as the "very dark" region, perhaps to indicate a Shūdra affiliation.[84]

Certain chants from the Vedas, that also carry specific *varṇa* connotations, are regularly associated with one or another of the cardinal directions. Cosmogonies VIII–XIII assign the Brahmin *rathantara*, the Kshatriya *bṛhat*, and Vaishya *vairūpa* chants to the east, south, and west respectively; they also add the *vairāja* chant in a chain of associations which includes the northern quarter.[85] Also in these texts the nine-versed, fifteen-versed, seventeen-versed, and twenty-one-versed hymns of praise are assigned to the Brahmin east, the Kshatriya south, the Vaishya west, and the north, respectively.[86] At ŚB 8.4.4.4–7, the east is associated with the Brahmin hymn of praise and, as in ṚV 10.90 and elsewhere, with the head, the "top" of the body. Both the south and north are connected with the Kshatriya fifteen-versed hymn of praise and the arms, the corporeal symbol of physical strength.[87] A brick that represents the Vaishya hymn of praise, the seventeen-versed, is equated to "food" and placed within the "arms" of the Cosmic Animal, just as the Vaishyas are regarded as "food" for the warriors in other texts. Finally, the twenty-one-versed hymn of praise is identified with the feet, which are "behind" or to the west, and represented as the "foundation." The twenty-one-versed hymn of praise, which is usually connected to the northern quarter, is elsewhere specifically labeled the Shūdra hymn of praise and connected also to the feet and the "firm foundation" of the body (see, e.g., Cosmogonies V–VII), and again recalls the hymn regarding the Cosmic Man at ṚV 10.90. The west, while not usually presented as the particular realm of the servants as it is here, is nevertheless "lower class" in other formulations.[88]

The meters in which various Vedic hymns and chants are composed are also simultaneously assigned to one or another of the quarters and to one or another of the social classes. The *gāyatrī*, *triṣṭubh*, and *jagatī* are connected to the east, south, and west in Cosmogonies IX, XII, and XIII, and additionally to the Brahmin, Kshatriya, and Vaishya in Cosmogonies VIII and X. These texts also identify the *anuṣṭubh* meter and the north, the *paṅkti* meter being attributed to the zenith, and all of these linkages are repeated in other texts: "The quarters are the meters—the eastern region being the *gāyatrī*, the southern the *triṣṭubh*, the western the *jagatī*, the northern the *anuṣṭubh*, and upper region the *paṅkti*" (ŚB 8.3.1.12; cf. ŚB 8.1.1.5–8.1.2.8, 8.3.2.9, 8.3.3.1; TS 5.5.8.2–3). The *gāyatrī*, *triṣṭubh*, and *jagatī* are thus consistently linked both with the east, south, and west, on the one hand, and the Brahmins, Kshatriyas, and Vaishyas, on the other. The fourth direction is connected to the *anuṣṭubh* meter—which can be regarded either as the "Shūdra meter," as in Cosmogonies V–VII, or as an all-encompassing meter aptly connected to the quarter of human beings in general.[89]

The cardinal directions are also represented in Vedic texts as created together with the divine rulers of particular regions. While, as we have seen, "the gods" belong generically to the eastern realm (just as "men" are located in the north), individual deities are placed in each of the quarters as what are called in later Hindu literature the "guardians of the regions" (*dikpālas* or *lokapālas*).[90] Since the gods are also categorized by *varṇa*, the relationship between space and theology is another means of reiterating the relationship between the directions and the social classes.

It is Agni who leads the Vasus in the Brahmin east according to Cosmogony X and Cosmogony XIII, while Indra, Varuṇa, and Soma—deities of the south, west, and north respectively—are associated with other divine bands. There is general agreement that the Vasus are Brahmin deities and belong in the east, the Ādityas and the Viśva Devas are usually assigned to the west as Vaishya deities, while the Rudras and Maruts (Kshatriya gods) are most often located either in the south or north.[91]

When a single deity is associated with one quarter, it is almost without exception in Vedic literature Agni who is the deity of the eastern region.[92] Such is the case in Cosmogony XIII; Cosmogonies VIII and X also specifically join the *brahman* power to that god and that region. The east, Agni, the *brahman* power, and the quality of priority or precedence come together in a rite described at TS 5.3.4.1–6 (cf. ŚB 8.4.2.3, 8.1.1.4). Bricks are to be laid down on the east side of the fire altar with a mantra dedicated to Agni (TS 4.3.9.1), who is, like the east and the *brahman* power, the "beginning of the sacrifice": "He becomes foremost for whom these are placed on the east as the beginning [of the sacrifice], and his son is born to be foremost." Similarly, at TS 5.5.8.2 Agni is conjoined with the east, the Brahmin *gāyatrī* meter, and the head, "topmost" or "foremost" portion of the altar conceived of as a cosmic bird.

Agni is designated the "lord" of the eastern realm;[93] with Agni the gods conquered the east (TB 3.2.9.7–8) and drove the demons from this quarter (AitB 2.11; 6.4). Agni helps the gods discover this region, and "therefore they lead Agni [i.e., the fire] forward to the east, the sacrifice is extended eastward, and sitting eastward they offer in it, for this was the quarter he saw."[94] The land to the east fit for habitation by Āryans extends only as far as that "which has been tasted by Agni," that is, has had sacrifices performed on it.[95]

The ritual often exploits this relationship between Agni and the east.[96] A householder offers curds and honey to Agni in order to ensure the protection of his house on the eastern side (VGS 14.24); a ladle filled with clarified butter turned toward the east is commanded to "convey the oblation to Agni" (ṚV 3.6.1; TB 2.8.2.5); an oxen cart carrying fire is driven east, "for the east is Agni's region, [and] he [Agni] thus proceeds toward his own region" (ŚB 6.8.1.8). Elsewhere the ritualist is instructed to plough a furrow toward the east with the mantra, "With Agni's *tejas*," thereby linking the Brahmin quarter, a Brahmin deity, and a Brahmin essential power (ŚB 13.8.2.6). Certain bricks used to construct the great fire altar are laid down while saying, "With the eastern quarter I place you, with the *gāyatrī* meter, with Agni as the deity,"[97] thereby adding the usual Brahmin meter to the equation between Agni and the east.

The Kshatriya south[98] in Hindu texts is the region of Yama, the king of the dead and of the ancestors, and, as we saw earlier, the attribution of this realm to Yama and the deceased is found in Vedic texts as well (e.g., TS 5.5.9.3–4; ŚB 3.2.3.1–2). Elsewhere it is Soma who is declared the discoverer of the south, and "thus they say that Soma belongs to the ancestors. For through him they saw the southern region, and to him belongs the southern region."[99] The south in the older literature is also the region of the bellicose demons, and Indra is usually placed in this quarter as the warrior king defender against the enemy.[100] Indra is the sole ruler of the southern region in Cosmogony XII, and in Cosmogonies VIII and X that deity and region are also identified with the *kṣatra*. In other instances Indra rules the south together with his divine henchmen, the Rudras or Maruts, or with the ancestors. Indra is, like Agni, the "lord" of his quarter,[101] and verses to Indra recited in the meter of the Kshatriyas, the *triṣṭubh*, are equated to the thunderbolt and are said to drive off the demons in the south.[102] In another rite, the enclosing stick on the south is placed down with the mantra, "You are Indra's arm for the security of everything" (ŚB 1.3.4.3, citing VS 2.3). A variant claims that such an action "puts physical strength (*indriya*) into the sacrificer" (TB 3.3.6.8) in keeping with the Kshatriya tenor of things.[103]

The Vaishya west is, appropriately enough, associated with the "*viś* among the gods," the Viśva Devas or the Maruts,[104] and, often enough, with Varuṇa.[105] The rationale for the latter seems not to center on Varuṇa's Kshatriya-like royal qualities (which we will see sometimes result in placing that deity in the north), but rather on this deity's identification with the waters. For the waters are also equated to the penis (ŚB 10.5.4.2) and to semen (BĀU 3.9.22) and are regarded as the symbol both of fecundity and of the undifferentiated mass (and, therefore, of the Vaishyas in the social scheme). At AitB 8.13 (cf. 8.18), "Varuṇa within the waters" is invoked during the Rājasūya while the king faces west and is anointed with water strained through a branch from the *udumbara*, the tree connected rather consistently with the Vaishya class and fertility (see Chapter 7).[106] The link to the waters would seem also to explain Soma's occasional placement in the west,[107] for the waters are "Soma's world" (VS 8.26; ŚB 4.4.5.21): "He recites the offering verse for Soma. Since he recites the offering verse for Soma, therefore many rivers flow westward, for the waters are connected with Soma."[108]

Let us now move over to the more variable north. As noted previously, the north—the region of "humans" in general—can also be regarded as the quarter of "the people" or, in the terms of the *varṇa* system, as the region either of an undifferentiated commoner class or more specifically of the Shūdras. It is thus not surprising that the north is sometimes populated with divinities who carry traits associated with the lower classes. At ŚB 1.5.1.25 and 3.5.2.7 this region is said to belong to Viśvakarman, the workman of the gods, perhaps to underscore the "working-class" nature of this quarter. In several places the north is the quarter of the Viśva Devas,[109] who are also the divine representatives of the commoner class (and as the inclusive body of "all the gods" are also an appropriate choice, although for a different reason, for this the "extra" quarter).[110]

Furthermore, the north is, as we saw, the realm of debilitation and sickness, and this notion (perhaps also entailing a connection with the lower classes) is expressed theologically as well. Varuṇa is not only a regal deity, but is also known as the rather dangerous god who "binds" or "fetters" his subjects (human beings) to sin, and the north, like the south, is therefore sometimes presented as the region inhabited by superhuman beings with whom one must take care: "The northern one [oblation of curds] is offered to Varuṇa, since it was Varuṇa who seized his [Prajāpati's] creatures. He thus directly delivers them from Varuṇa's noose" (ŚB 2.5.2.10). Soma's association with the north (see below) might be similarly explicated, for Soma (or in his guise as the moon) is often connected with death, as is Varuṇa.[111] Perhaps for many of the same reasons, the north is also the realm of Rudra,[112] who must be treated with caution lest he visit sickness and death upon his "animals" or *paśus* (for he is lord of the animals)—one's livestock, one's family, or even oneself: "Twice he holds out the offering ladle to the north. Having pleased Rudra in his own quarter he lets [him] go. Therefore one should not stand to the north of the offering as it is made, for he would then be in the vicinity of this dread god" (KB 2.2).

The north, however, carries different theologically encoded correlates just as it does ontological and metaphysical ones. In addition to deities that are associated with the lower classes, the north is also where certain royal gods are assigned. In a move not unlike assigning the conglomerate of "all the gods" (the Viśva Devas) to this quarter, sometimes the Vedic classifiers placed here royal deities who also embodied the divine totality or whole. One such figure associated with the north is "king" Soma (or the moon with whom Soma is equated).[113] Varuṇa, another royal deity, is also placed in the north as the overlord of that region.[114] At TB 3.8.20.3, a portion of meat from a sacrificed horse is placed to the north of the fire altar, for "the horse belongs to Varuṇa, and that quarter is the quarter of Varuṇa." Indra is also sometimes located in the north,[115] and in at least one text, the south belongs to either of the two royal deities, Indra or Soma.[116]

The pair Mitra and Varuṇa, who can represent two different aspects of kingship, are similarly placed in the north (as in, e.g., Cosmogony X) or the zenith (e.g., Cosmogony XII). These two deities, like other royal gods, might be functioning here as ciphers for the social unity (the north being the quarter of human beings in general). Alternatively, the duo Mitra–Varuṇa may act as a theological cipher for the all-encompassing rule of the Brahmin–Kshatriya pair. As such, their occasional placement in the "extra" direction, the north, is consistent with the general transcendent quality of that region vis-à-vis the other three directions, which clearly belong to one or another of the three *varṇas*.[117]

This "transcendence" of the fourth quarter might also be why certain Brahmin deities are also assigned here. Bṛhaspati—a deity who also can be assigned to the zenith[118]—is located in the north according to Cosmogony XIII; and Savitṛ, the solar god of "instigation," is designated the deity of this region in other cosmological schemes. The explanation for the latter is not only meteorological, as in AitB 1.7 (it is "from the northwest he who blows blows most, for he blows instigated by Savitṛ"). Savitṛ is elsewhere linked with Bṛhaspati and the north, on the one hand, and the Brahmin *varṇa*, on the other:

> "You are the portion of the god Savitṛ, [the overlordship of Bṛhaspati, all the quarters saved, the four-versed stoma]." [With these words he puts a brick down] on the north. The god Savitṛ is the *brahman*, Bṛhaspati is the *brahman*, the four-versed hymn of praise is the *brahman*. Thus he places splendor in the north; therefore the northern half is more resplendent. [The verse] contains a word connected with Savitṛ, [and that is] for instigation. Therefore the gain for the Brahmins is produced in the north. (TS 5.3.4.4, with the mantra from TS 4.3.9.2; cf. ŚB 8.4.2.10)

Note here also that the fourth direction is implicated in a series of connections that include "all the quarters," indicating the "transcendence" and the all-encompassing nature that this direction and the Brahmin *varṇa* assume here.

Another Brahmin deity assimilated to the north is Vāc, the goddess of speech, a divinity with certain connections to other "transcendent" elements. Vāc is equated to the *anuṣṭubh* meter (e.g., JB 1.238ff.), which is, in turn, said to be "all the meters" (TS 5.1.3.5; JB 1.284–85; PB 6.3.14) and is associated with the north.[119] Vāc, as a Brahmin god, may therefore be connected either with the first string of associations or with a fourth chain (including the north within it) conceived as encompassing and transcending the previous three.[120] At KB 7.6, Vāc is located in the north and "therefore in the northern quarter is speech uttered with more discernment, and men go northward to learn speech." Or, again, at ŚB 3.2.3.15 we read that "through Pathyā Svasti they [the gods] recognized the northern (*uttara*) region. Therefore speech sounds more elevated (*uttara*) here among the Kuru Pañcālas. For she [Pathyā Svasti] is really Vāc, and through her they recognized the northern region, and to her belongs the northern region."

The quarters are supposedly inhabited by, or are the special provinces of, different kinds of beings: socially classified human beings, general classes of ontological beings, and, as we have now observed, various divine beings as well. The correlations between the directions and the various types of beings can themselves be correlated as in Table 5.3.

From a theological perspective, the east, south, and west regularly are associated with gods who embody qualities consistent with those of the Brahmins, Kshatriyas, and Vaishyas respectively. The deities connected to the north, unsurprisingly, seem to convey a more varied set of messages; this is in keeping with the usual pattern for this direction. The north can be the quarter of the lower classes, the royalty, or the Brahmins who apparently sometimes placed their own divine representatives in that region because of its fourth position and its association with other components (such as the *anuṣṭubh* meter) that can also signify encompassment and superiority. Despite certain variations and alternatives, and despite the complexities presented by the north or fourth direction, the Vedic classification of the spatial quarters therefore both reflects and reinforces the

TABLE 5.3. The Cardinal Directions and the Classes of Beings

East	*South*	*West*	*North*
Brahmins	Kshatriyas	Vaishyas	lower classes, Shūdras, all, royalty, Brahmins
gods	ancestors, demons	animals, snakes, wife, offspring	humans
Agni, Vasus	Indra, Maruts or Rudras (Soma, Mitra–Varuna)*	Varuṇa, Viśva Devas or Ādityas (Soma)*	Soma, Maruts or Viśva Devas (Indra, Mitra–Varuṇa, Varuṇa, Savitṛ, Vāc, Rudra)*

* Deities within parentheses are less frequently (and consistently) associated with one or another of the cardinal directions.

varṇa system as a whole and the particularities of each of the classes within that system.

Conclusion: Classifying Space

While acknowledging the various alternative formulations, the consistencies and continuities in terms of the *varṇa* system one observes in the classification of space are quite apparent and fairly impressive. Typically Brahmin connections to the gods, heaven, and the sacrifice; to the qualities and powers of the *brahman*, speech, the splendor of the *brahman*, splendor (*varcas*), and fiery luster or *tejas*; to characteristics such as generativity, primacy, and precedence; to the natural element of fire and to the god Agni; and to the Ṛg Veda, nine-versed hymn of praise, *rathantara* chant, and *gāyatrī* meter—all these connections are also made to the cosmological world of the earth (or, more rarely, to the world of the sky) and to the eastern cardinal direction. Similarly, the Kshatriya associations with death, demons, violence, war, physical strength, virility; with the gods, especially Indra, who represent such qualities; with the Yajur Veda, fiften-versed hymn of praise, *bṛhat* hymn, and *triṣṭubh* meter—these linkages are reiterated through those also made to the atmosphere and the south. Finally, the Vaishya connections to multiplicity, animals, wife and offspring, crops and nourishment, wealth and vitality; to deities who represent or promote such desiderata or who, like the Viśva Devas, are portrayed as the *viś* of the gods; and to the Sāma Veda, seventeen-versed hymn of praise, the *vairūpa* hymn, and the *jagatī* meter—these consistently Vaishya components are also those to which the sky (or, alternatively, the earth) and the west are conjoined.

The materials presented in this chapter also begin to reveal some of the complexities engendered when a fundamentally tripartite system, such as the social triad or the cosmological structure of three worlds, and a quadripartite system, such as the four cardinal directions, are co-ordered. We have also seen here some of the devices the Brahmin organizers used to achieve the feat. The fourth cardinal direction, like other "fourths" added to other triads, can be represented as the summation of the previous three, the region which encompasses and transcends the others; as such, it may be linked to royal or Brahmin entities. Alternatively, it may be regarded as the realm of "the masses" in general (usually meaning the Vaishyas and/or Shūdras). Or the fourth direction may be assigned, usually implicitly, to the Shūdra class as the social order expands into a quadripartite structure (just as a fourth "world" might be added to the tripartite cosmology) resulting in an exact parallelism with the four-part spatial order. Many of these strategies, deployed in order to categorize the fourth direction, we can also observe in other arenas where quadripartite structures are interrelated with the *varṇa* scheme.

An analysis of the connections or *bandhus* forged between the social classes, the three worlds, the cardinal directions and the entities of other realms thus furthers our understanding of the workings of the *varṇa* system—both qua system and as a set of interrelationships between three or four components. It also demonstrates something of the insidious nature of the *varṇa* scheme. A classificatory system that functions to order the social whole also is applied to spatial perception itself; the categorization of space and society is achieved within the same taxonomical economy. And if this is the case with space, so too is it with time.

NOTES

1. Steven Lukes, *Émile Durkheim: His Life and Work: A Historical and Critical Study* (Harmondsworth, Middlesex, England: Penguin Books, 1973), p. 447.

2. Émile Durkheim, *The Elementary Forms of the Religious Life*, trans. by Joseph Ward Swain (New York: Free Press, 1915), pp. 24–25.

3. For an overview of the criticism leveled at this aspect of Durkheim's sociology of knowledge, consult Lukes, *Émile Durkheim*, pp. 445ff., and Rodney Needham's introduction to Émile Durkheim and Marcel Mauss, *Primitive Classification* (Chicago: University of Chicago Press, 1963).

4. Robert Hertz, "The Pre-eminence of the Right Hand: A Study in Religious Polarity," in *Right and Left: Essays on Dual Symbolic Classification*, ed. by Rodney Needham (Chicago: University of Chicago Press, 1973), p. 4.

5. Ibid., p. 5. Hertz thus presents his study as a middle road: "Those who believe in the innate capacity to differentiate have won their victory: the intellectual and moral representations of right and left are true categories, anterior to all individual experience, since they are linked to the very structure of social thought. But the empiricists were right too, for there is no question here of immutable instincts or of absolute metaphysical data. These categories are transcendent only in relation to the individual; replaced in their original setting, namely, the collective consciousness, they appear as facts of nature, subject to change and dependent on complex conditions" (p. 22).

6. Barry Schwartz, *Vertical Classification: A Study in Structuralism and the Sociology of Knowledge* (Chicago: University of Chicago Press, 1981), pp. 31–32.

7. Although some, like the oppositions between right and left and up and down, are generally valued similarly in different cultures.

8. For an overview of Vedic cosmology, see F. B. J. Kuiper, *Ancient Indian Cosmogony* (New Delhi: Vikas Publishing House, 1983); R. F. Gombrich, "Ancient Indian Cosmology," in *Ancient Cosmologies*, ed. by C. Blacker and M. Loewe (London: George Allen & Unwin, 1975); and Jean Varenne, *Cosmogonies védique* (Paris: Société d'Édition, 1982).

9. See Brian K. Smith, *Reflections on Resemblance, Ritual, and Religion* (New York: Oxford University Press, 1989), pp. 103–4; and Jan Gonda, *Loka: The World and Heaven in the Veda*, Verhandelingen der Koninklijke Nederlandse Akademie van Wetenschappen, Afd. Letterkunde, Nieuwe Reeks, Pt. 73, No. 1 (Amsterdam: N. V. Noord-Hollandsche Uitgevers Maatschappij, 1966).

10. AitB 6.9. For heaven as the "fourth" world, beyond the sky, see also Gonda, *Loka*, p. 91; and H. W. Bodewitz, "The Waters in Vedic Cosmic Classifications," *Indologica Taurinensia* 10 (1982), p. 49 n. 27: "Heaven, regarded as the 'beyond' rather than as the sky of the day time, was also described as boundless (*ananta*)."

11. See, e.g., JUB 1.23.1–6, 1.2.1–2, 1.34.7–11, 3.4.7; TU 1.5.1–3; 1.6; MaitU 6.35; KB 6.10,11; AitB 8.27; ŚB 2.2.4.18, 6.7.4.7, 8.5.2.12, 9.3.1.3, 11.2.3.1–2, 11.5.8.1; TB

3.7.7.4–5; PB 1.2.1, 1.3.2, 20.15.2; JB 1.98. The theological specifics change, but not the *varṇa* connotations, at TS 4.4.6.1 (earth = Bṛhaspati and Agni, atmosphere = Viśvakarman and Vāyu, sky = Prajāpati and Parameṣṭhin). Cf. the variants at KB 11.2 and 18.2 (earth = Agni, atmosphere = Uṣas, sky = Aśvins). For the Vasus together with Iḍā = earth, the Rudras and Sarasvatī = atmosphere, and the Ādityas and the goddess Bhāratī = sky, see TB 3.6.13.1 (cf. TB 2.6.10.4; TS 5.1.11.3; MS 3.16.2).

12. E.g., AitĀ 1.32; KB 6.10,11; ŚB 4.6.7.1ff, 11.5.8.1–4. See also MārkP 42.4.8–11 for correlations between the three worlds, the three Vedas, and the three *guṇas*. Cf. Manu 1.23, where Agni, Vāyu, and Āditya (fire, wind, and sun) are associated with the Ṛg, Yajur, and Sāma Vedas respectively.

13. E.g., JUB 1.1.1–4; 1.8.1ff., 3.15.4ff.; JB 1.18; KB 6.10,11; ŚB 11.5.8.1–4. ŚānĀ 8.8 (cf. AitĀ 3.2.5) makes the following correlations: (1) mutes = EARTH = Agni = Ṛg Veda = the *rathantara* chant = exhalation; (2) sibilants = ATMOSPHERE = Vāyu = Yajur Veda = the *vāmadevya* chant = inhalation; (3) vowels = SKY = Āditya = the *bṛhat* chant = cross-breath. ŚB 12.3.4.1ff. links the Ṛg Veda, Yajur Veda, and Sāma Veda to the Brahmins, Kshatriyas, and Vaishyas respectively; and also to the earth, atmosphere, and sky; groups of gods (Vasus, Rudras, and Ādityas) as well as individual deities (Agni, Vāyu, and Āditya); metaphysical powers (light, might, and glory); speech, breath, and eyesight; and three times of day (morning, midday, and afternoon).

14. E.g., ChU 4.17.1–6. For other equations of the earth, atmosphere, and sky and the *gārhapatya*, *dakṣiṇa*, and *āhavanīya* fires, see below and KB 6.12; AitB 5.32 (which also adds the three Vedas to the structure of homologies); TB 2.1.5.8; ŚB 2.3.4.36, 7.1.2.7–13, 7.3.1.1ff.; MaitU 6.33; and cf. KB 2.2. At ŚB 9.2.3.14ff., the *āgnīdhra*'s fire is substituted for the *dakṣiṇa* as the analogue of the atmosphere; for the earth = *gārhapatya* and the sky = *āhavanīya* see TS 6.1.8.5 and 6.4.2.5–6.

15. E.g., KB 14.3 (with Agni, Vāyu, and the sun); KB 8.9 (with Agni, Soma, and Viṣṇu); ŚB 6.5.2.3ff. (with Vasus, Rudras, and Ādityas and adding quarters = *anuṣṭubh* meter = Viśva Devas); and ṢaḍB 2.1.9–30 (cf. JB 1.270), which gives the following strings of equations: *gāyatrī* = Agni = earth; *triṣṭubh* = Indra = atmosphere; *jagatī* = Sūrya = sky; *anuṣṭubh* = Prajāpati = "this all"; *paṅkti* = Soma = regions and seasons. Cf. TS 4.2.1.1 (earth, atmosphere, heaven, and the waters = *gāyatrī*, *triṣṭubh*, *jagatī*, and *anuṣṭubh*).

16. See also ŚB 6.5.2.22 ("as much as these worlds and the quarters are, so much is this all"), 8.5.3.5, 10.2.4.4; AitB 4.24; and cf. JUB 2.2.1–4 and MaitU 6.35.

17. For both the earth and the *gārhapatya* fire as "wombs" out of which other worlds and other fires are produced, see also ŚB 7.1.1.6–12.

18. Cf. AitĀ 2.1.7, where the earth and fire (note the connection to the Brahmin deity Agni) are first portrayed as created by speech, and then as productive entities in their own right, for "plants grow on the earth [and] fire ripens them."

19. Recall here also that in Cosmogony III the *brahman* power is equated with the cosmic Self, while the *kṣatra* = humans and the power of the *viś* = the animals.

20. The hierarchical place of the earth in this cosmological model is also due to the fact that this is the most tangible, the most real, of all the worlds: "This world is Agni's womb, for Agni is this world. Since Agni as a whole is constructed from this earth [i.e., the bricks that are used to build the altar are made from earth], it is this earth he puts down [when he lays down a brick]. He puts it down so as not to be separated from reality (*satya*); he establishes this world on reality. Therefore this world is established on reality. Therefore reality is this world, for this earth is the most certain of these worlds" (ŚB 7.4.1.8). Thus, by implication, the Brahmins are also the "most certain" or the "most real" of the social classes.

21. For an alternative explanation (based on supposed etymological connections) for the relations between the atmosphere and the Yajur Veda, see ŚB 10.3.5.1–2.

22. Similarly, when the worlds are put into correlative relationships with the breaths, the atmosphere is connected to exhalation, the expelling of breath being perhaps the equivalent of the expression of energy. See TU 1.5.1–3; ŚB 7.1.2.7ff.; and esp. AitĀ 3.2.5, where the atmosphere is also connected, *inter alia*, with exhalation in the course of classifying various realms according to a tripartite division of the Sanskrit language or "speech." For alternative assignments of the three worlds to the three breaths see KB 6.10 (earth = exhalation, atmosphere = inhalation); and ŚB 4.1.2.27; ChU 5.19.2; TU 1.7 (earth = exhalation, atmosphere = through breath, sky = inhalation).

23. See, e.g., ŚB 8.5.1.10–11 for connections between the atmosphere, the thunderbolt or *vajra*, and the *triṣṭubh* meter (all regularly linked to the Kshatriya).

24. The warriorlike qualities of this turbulent and often stormy realm perhaps also led the Vedic categorizers to conceive of the atmosphere as the locale of the demons, the warriors of the enemy camp. The connection between the Kshatriyas and the demons, mediated in texts like ŚB 1.1.2.4, 3.8.1.12, and 4.1.1.20 by their common spatial assignment in the atmosphere, and in other contexts by their sharing of the southern region, is one to which we will return in the next chapter.

25. Thus the Maruts who are regarded as "the *viś* of the gods," also can signify the Kshatriya *varṇa* because they are the "troops" of the warrior god Indra. At KB 7.8, they are said to be in the atmosphere and have the power to confound the sacrifice as the sacrificer travels to the world of heaven. Cf. the assignment of the Viśva Devas, another set of Vaishya deities, to the world of the atmosphere at, e.g., ŚB 3.8.3.32.

26. Cf. ŚB 11.8.1.2 (when Prajāpati wondered how to steady the three worlds, he did so by placing mountains and rivers on earth, birds and sun rays in the atmosphere, and clouds and stars in the sky); and ŚB 5.4.5.14: "What flowers there are of the lotus, they are a form of the sky, they are a form of the stars."

27. ŚB 12.4.4.6,7. Cf. ŚB 6.1.2.3 and also ChU 5.18.2, where the sun is called "manifold" (*viśvarūpa*).

28. For the *jagatī* = earth, *triṣṭubh* = atmosphere, and *gāyatrī* = sky, see also ŚB 1.8.2.10–13.

29. Compare the text below to TB 2.1.5.1–2, where the earth is also said to be the *sadas* shed, the atmosphere the *āgnīdhra* shed, and the sky is the *havirdhāna* shed.

30. For the identification of the *āgnīdhra* shed and the atmosphere, see also ŚB 9.2.3.15.

31. Cf. ŚB 9.1.1.11–13, where an oblation offered at the level of the knee is equated with the earth, one offered at the level of the navel is the atmosphere, and one at the level of the mouth equals the sky. Given the well-known anatomical correlates for the social classes, this text too has definite *varṇa* overtones. Cf. ŚB 5.1.5.1, 11.7.4.1 (where the varying lengths of three sacrificial stakes are similarly correlated to the worlds); and TS 2.3.6.2, where cakes which symbolize the three worlds are made in different sizes: "There are three cakes, and these worlds are three; this is in order to obtain these worlds. Each one above the other is larger, for so are these worlds; this in order to obtain prosperity."

32. See also PraśnaU 5.3–5, where the Ṛg Veda = earth, Yajur Veda = atmosphere (and "the world of the moon"), and the Sāma Veda = the highest world, the world of Brahmā. It may also be that the mantra found at AitB 8.27 is to be uttered by the Brahmin priest (the *purohita*) to the king with whom he has become connected: "I am that, you are this; you are this, I am that. I am sky, you are earth. I am the chant (*sāman*), you are the verse (*ṛk*). Let us unite. Save us from great danger." Coomaraswamy has argued on the basis of this passage and others that "it is clear that the relationship of the Sacerdotium

to the Regnum, or that of Man to Woman, or that of any Director to any Executive, can be more briefly expressed as that of Sky to Earth." Ananda K. Coomaraswamy, *Spiritual Authority and Temporal Power in the Indian Theory of Government* (New Haven, Conn.: American Oriental Society, 1942), p. 49. See also BĀU 6.4.20 (Sāma Veda = sky = man; Ṛg Veda = earth = woman) and cf. ŚB 3.2.1.3–5 where there seems to be a correlation posited between the Ṛg Veda and the sky and the Sāma Veda and the earth.

33. AitB 1.23; KB 8.8; TS 6.2.3.1; ŚB 3.4.4.3, 13.2.10.3; and cf. TB 3.9.6.5.

34. For a true alternative when it comes to the correlation of worlds and meters, see, e.g., PB 7.3.9: "These meters are [equal to] these worlds: the *gāyatrī* is this world, the *bṛhatī* is this middle world, the *triṣṭubh* is yonder highest world."

35. We have not thus far noted yet other variations in the ways the worlds are correlated to the *varṇa*s. For the earth as the "Kshatriya's world," see ŚB 11.8.4.5 and cf. ŚB 12.8.3.5 ("It is knee-high, for knee-high is this world, and it is for [the rule of] this world that the Kshatriya is consecrated"). Contrast that to the following: "The earth belongs to Agni and the Brahmin belongs to Agni; the sky belongs to Indra and the Kshatriya," it is said in one text, with the intermediate realm equated with the animals (and thus with the Vaishyas) in order to fill out the tripartite scheme (PB 15.4.8). Similarly, according to AV 15.10.4–9, *brahman* = Bṛhaspati and Agni = earth; *kṣatra* = Indra and Āditya = sky.

36. We leave aside the even more problematic case of matching the social *varṇa*s to the directions when the classificatory structures for organizing directions are pentadic (adding the zenith) or six-part (with both the zenith and nadir) in form.

37. For the problem of threes and fours in general in Indian classifications, see Troy Organ, "Three into Four in Hinduism," *Ohio Journal of Religious Studies* 1 (1973): 7–13. For the particulars of the problem in Vedic cosmology, Bodewitz, "The Waters."

38. ŚB 5.1.3.11, 6.3.1.11, 6.5.2.22, 7.5.1.27, 8.5.3.5, 10.2.4.4, 11.8.2.1, 13.6.1.3, etc. Cf. ChU 3.18.2; and F. B. J. Kuiper, *Varuṇa and Vidūṣaka: On the Origin of the Sanskrit Drama* (Amsterdam: North-Holland, 1979), p. 51, n. 163; and H. W. Bodewitz, *Jaiminīya Brāhmaṇa I, 1–65. Translation and Commentary* (Leiden: E. J. Brill, 1973), p. 87, n. 26: "The number four, often one-sidedly regarded as comprising a triad and a fourth, secret element (the *turīyam pādam*) sometimes has an encompassing function." For five-part spatial conceptions (earth, atmosphere, sky, "this all" or the waters, and the regions and seasons), see ṢaḍB 2.1.9–30 and JB 1.270, and Bodewitz's anaylsis, "The Waters," pp. 52–53.

39. At ŚB 1.2.1.10–12, for example, the west is equated to the atmosphere, and the east to the sky. But then the scheme begins to crumble: the south is identified with "all regions" and the north with "what fourth world there is or is not beyond these [three] worlds. . . . Uncertain, no doubt, is what fourth world there is or is not beyond these [three] worlds, and uncertain also are all those regions." The third "world" in this arrangement is "all the regions" while the fourth is even more indistinct. F. B. J. Kuiper has offered the opinion that the "fourth world" in this passage is "a world of disorder and formless Chaos, over which gods and men had no control." F.B.J. Kuiper, *Varuṇa and Vidūṣaka*, p. 34ff.; cf. Gonda, *Triads in the Veda*, p. 120.

40. This verse is not all that clear to me. Eggling, in a footnote to his translation of this text, comments that "what is implied, in any case, is that first some hope, or desire, is conceived in the accomplishment of which is only brought about by a forward movement, or by action; and that success in attaining the object sought for is followed by the conception of fresh desires."

41. For the north as the cardinal direction of the "world of the waters," see also ŚB 11.6.1.1–13 and JB 1.42–44.

42. Bodewitz, "The Waters," p. 47. Cf. Gonda, *Triads in the Veda*, pp. 8, 115ff.; Kuiper, *Varuṇa and Vidūṣaka*, pp. 34–35; and Bodewitz, *Jaiminīya Brāhmaṇa*, p. 87, n. 26. For the waters (or the ocean) as the fourth world, see also ṚV 9.96.19; TS 4.2.1.1; KB 18.2; ChU 4.6.3; and JB 1.270, where this "world" (in relation to the parallel at ṢaḍB 2.1.9–30) is equated to *idam sarvam*, "this whole thing."

43. Later Hindu texts do indeed correlate the north and the Shūdra class in order to match the two quadripartite schemes. See, e.g., MatsyaP 253.13–16.

44. Here, as in other chapters, we must not neglect alternative classification schemes. Particular divergences will be noted later. For now, however, we might take cognizance of two texts where the *varṇa* of the regions is stated and where the assignments differ from the ordinary paradigm. At TB 3.12.9.1–2 we read of the following correlations: (1) east = Ṛg Veda = Vaishyas; (2) south = Yajur Veda = Kshatriyas; (3) west = Atharva Veda; and (4) north = Sāma Veda = Brahmins. While the particular connections between the regions and the Vedas are not unusual, the *varṇa* assignment of the Brahmins to the north and, most especially, the Vaishyas to the east is peculiar—perhaps even unique to this text. Another apparently anomalous notion is that the Vaishyas belong to the southern quarter, for which see ŚB 8.4.2.5 and TS 5.3.4.1–2. At Manu 5.92 it is declared, "A dead Shūdra should be carried out through the southern gate of the town, but twice-born men through the western, northern, and eastern gates, as is appropriate." The commentators on this text say that the latter three directions correspond to the Vaishya, Kshatriya, and Brahmin respectively. Here we have a variant whereby the social classes of the south (ordinarily the Kshatriya) and the north (sometimes the Shūdra) are inverted in relation to the usual Vedic scheme of things.

45. The second set of three chains, which I argued in Chapter 3 reduplicate, at least in some respects, the first three, are:

> 4. fourth day = the world of food = *anuṣṭubh* meter = twenty-one-versed hymn of praise = *vairāja* chant = NORTH = autumn = Sādhyas and Ājyas and Bṛhaspati and the moon
>
> 5. fifth day = the world of animals = *paṅkti* meter = twenty-seven-versed hymn of praise = *śakvara* chant = ZENITH = winter = Maruts and Rudra
>
> 6. sixth day = the world of the waters = *atichandas* meter = thirty-three-versed hymn of praise = *raivata* chant = ZENITH = cool season = Viśva Devas and Prajāpati

46. Kuiper, *Varuṇa and Vidūṣaka*, p. 47.

47. E.g., TB 3.2.2.3. ChU 3.15.2 calls the eastern quarter by the name of the sacrificial ladle or *juhū* because, according to the commentator, one faces the east when one offers oblations. The sacrifice is "extended" eastward, symbolized by the taking of the *gārhapatya* fire forward to kindle the offering fire in the eastern direction (see, e.g., ŚB 8.1.1.4; 8.6.1.16). At ŚB 7.4.1.8 and 8.6.2.15, the fire altar is said to be built in the easterly direction.

48. For the connection between the spatial direction of the east (and the cosmological world of the earth), and the temporal component of the day, see below, pp. 195–96.

49. The text thus associates the east with the heavenly world and places the Brahmin deity Agni in that quarter, thereby strengthening the set of connections linking the first *varṇa* and the east. The animal is also in this passage placed with "his feet to the north," i.e., with the head to the east, while the priest says, "'Make its eye go to the sun; let loose its breath to the wind, its life to the atmosphere, its ear to the quarters, its body to the earth.' Truly he thus puts it in these worlds." Cf. TB 3.6.6.1.

50. See also BDhS 2.14.9–10 where the ancestors are supposed to take the form of birds and populate the atmosphere. For the south as the realm of the ancestors, see, e.g.,

TS 5.2.5.3; ŚB 2.6.1.8–9, 9.4.3.6, 11.5.3.7; and KB 2.2. For the southeast as the "door to the world of the ancestors," see ŚB 13.8.1.5.

51. See also Eggeling's note on his translation of ŚB 2.3.2.2. For an equation between Yama and the *brahman* priest (who sits on the south), see ŚBK 5.4.1.23.

52. ĀśvGS 2.7.11. For a general treatment of the spatial orientation of the Vedic house, consult Louis Renou, "La Maison védique," *Journal asiatique* 231 (1939): 481–504.

53. Veena Das, "On the Categorization of Space in Hindu Ritual," in *Text and Context: The Social Anthropology of Tradition*, ed. by Ravindra K. Jain (Philadelphia: Institute for the Study of Human Issues, 1977), pp. 15, 16. Das goes on to claim that rituals directed to the ancestors are fundamentally different from those directed to the gods. "In the latter case, the duality of the deity and the sacrifice is emphasized, hence the theme of subjugation dominates. In the former case the paradigm is the sacrifice of Puruṣa, 'of himself to himself, aided by the gods'; hence, the theme of reciprocity emerges here."

54. See also ŚB 13.8.4.1, where the great cosmic serpent and demon par excellence, Vṛtra, is said to occupy the south. At TS 5.2.5.3, however, the ancestors are located in the south and the demons in the west.

55. ŚB 3.5.3.15. For other examples of the dangers posed by the demons from the south, and of the ritual precautions that are prescribed to avert such calamities from the beings in this region, see ŚB 1.1.4.6,8, 1.3.4.13, 3.6.1.27–29, 3.7.2.2, 4.2.4.14,19, 4.6.6.1ff.; AitB 6.4.

56. The region of demons and death may also be regarded as the repository of "evil" and "impurity." In one rite within the horse sacrifice, a dog is killed by one of the officiating priests and is made to float away toward the south. "Thus he washes evil, impurity, away from him" (TB 3.8.4.2).

57. Das, "On the Categorization of Space in Hindu Ritual," p. 21.

58. For the connections between the *brahman* priest and the south, see H. W. Bodewitz, "The Fourth Priest (the *brahman*) in Vedic Ritual," in *Selected Studies on Ritual in the Indian Religions: Essays to D. J. Hoens*, ed. by Ria Kloppenborg (Leiden: E. J. Brill, 1983), pp. 43–45. Bodewitz, however, provides a different interpretation of the linkage, arguing that the south and the *brahman* priest are both connected to "the positive aspects of the supracosmic worlds, i.e. with Brahman."

59. At ŚB 4.6.6.1–4, it is again the Kshatriya deity Indra, the "strongest" of the gods, whose bellicosity protects the rest of the divine host from their antagonists to the south. See also ŚB 9.3.2.2–3.

60. In another context, the householder who is consecrating a new house is instructed to go outside and honor the southern quarter by saying " 'May that which protects and that which guards, protect me from the south' " (PGS 3.4.15).

61. Elsewhere the south is also connected with *ojas* as well as with the Kshatriya meter, the *triṣṭubh*, and the thunderbolt (ŚB 8.5.1.10). In binary oppositions between right and left, the former (south within the scheme of cardinal directions oriented toward the east) is also sometimes presented as the direction of strength; i.e., the right side of the body is said to be stronger than the left. See, e.g., TB 2.1.4.8. In other right–left dichotomies, the right is associated with virility and fertility, "for from the right side seed is infused into the womb" (ŚB 6.4.2.10; cf. ŚB 2.5.2.17; PB 8.7.10, 12.10.12). ŚB 6.3.1.30 and 7.5.1.6 state that "the male lies on the right side of the female." For right–left oppositions in general as they figure in Hindu rituals, see Veena Das, "On the Categorization of Space."

62. TS 5.3.4.3–4. At ŚB 8.4.2.9, it is *ojas* that is connected to the west.

63. See also the later Hindu text (MatsyaP 256.29ff.) that warns that an extension of a home built in the western direction only will result in the loss of wealth.

64. For the west as the quarter of "plants," see ŚB 11.6.1.1–13 and JB 1.42–44.

65. TB 2.1.3.4–5; cf. ŚB 1.3.1.20. At ŚB 1.3.1.17 and TB 3.3.3.2, however, the wife is warned not to sit exactly on the west side facing east, for this is where Aditi, the wife of the gods, sits. The human wife who usurps the place of the divine wife would cross "the wife of the gods" and "immediately go to the yonder world" (i.e., die). She thus is to take her place in the southwest. In this connection, see also ChU 3.15.2, where the western quarter is called "queen," *rājñī*.

66. BĀU 3.9.22. See also Cosmogony XIII, where the reduplicated third string of associations (generated out of the sixth day) include the waters as well as the typically Vaishya deities, the Viśva Devas and Prajāpati. On the other hand, Bodewitz has argued persuasively that the waters, the Viśva Devas, and Prajāpati, among other components in this cosmology, can be ciphers for "totality as well as indistinctness." "The Waters in Vedic Cosmic Classifications," p. 49. See below for a further discussion of the waters and their meaning for the social classification system.

67. TB 3.3.6.5; cf. PB 15.5.16. In a related metaphor, the shape of the sacrificial grounds or *vedi* widens at the bottom or west, like hips: "Toward the west he extends the two hips for the clasping of the *gārhapatya* fire [between the legs], and also for copulation" (TB 3.2.9.9).

68. Veena Das ("On the Categorization of Space," p. 21) has argued on the basis of rituals depicted in the Gṛhya Sūtras, that the "west is the direction associated with both ancestors and prosperity/fertility. . . . The westerly direction is also associated with material prosperity and the fertility of women. . . . In view of our earlier analysis of the association of ancestors with the power to bestow wealth and progeny on their descendants, it is not surprising to find that the direction in which symbols of prosperity and fertility are placed is also the direction from which ancestors enter to receive their share from their descendants. Thus the western side is associated with the benevolent aspect of ancestors and other deities of the left."

69. ŚB 1.4.1.35. In several passages we read that *satya*, here in the sense of ritual exactitude, is a quality of the gods, while *anṛta* ("error" or "disorder") is the distinguishing mark of things human (ŚB 1.1.2.17; 3.3.2.2; 3.9.4.1).

70. For the god–human opposition represented in terms of right and left, i.e., south and north, consult ŚB 3.1.3.14, 3.1.2.4–5, 5.1.4.9, 6.8.1.8, 7.2.2.6, and 9.4.2.11.

71. For the related theme of the dangers of the sacrificial journey to heaven and the ontological separation between men and gods, see also Smith, *Reflections*, pp. 104–12.

72. AitB 7.5 notes that similar kinds of dangers come to the sacrificer from the east and the west. In the course of explaining the expiation if the *gārhapatya* fire becomes extinguished, the text notes: "If he were to take out [the fire] to the east, he would fall away from his place of safety; if to the west he would perform the sacrifices like the demons; if he were to rekindle it he would produce a rival for the sacrificer; if he should make [the *āhavanīya*] also go out, breath would leave the sacrificer. Having gathered it all up together with the ashes he should put it in the place of the *gārhapatya* and from it take out the *āhavanīya* to the east. That is the reparation here."

73. ŚB 3.1.1.2; cf. ŚB 1.2.5.17. Similarly, when the tree felled for the sacrificial stake is chopped down, one should avoid having it land toward the south: "Let him cut it so as to fall toward the east, for the east is the quarter of the gods; or toward the north, for the north is the quarter of men; or toward the west. But let him take care to keep it from [falling toward] the southern quarter, for that is the quarter of the ancestors. Therefore he must take care to keep it from the southern quarter" (ŚB 3.6.4.12).

74. See also ŚB 6.6.2.3, 9.3.4.13, 13.4.2.15. But cf. TB 2.1.3.4–5 where it is the north that is associated with both gods and men. The northeast at ŚB 6.6.2.4 is also said to be the passageway to the world of heaven; but at TB 3.8.22.1, 3.9.6.4; ŚB 11.5.3.7, 13.2.8.1; and TS 5.2.5.3, it is the north that is the direction of heaven, and elsewhere heaven supposedly lies to the east.

75. AitB 1.14, 8.9; 8.10; KB 7.10. At PB 6.5.20, however, it is the east that is pronounced the "unconquerable region."

76. See, e.g., ŚB 1.3.3.7ff., 3.3.2.9, 3.5.4.20, 3.6.1.14, 3.7.1.7, 4.5.7.4, 5.2.4.15, 6.4.4.22, 6.7.2.1, 7.2.2.21, 14.1.2.2, 14.1.3.27; AitĀ 5.1.3. In other instances (e.g., ŚB 1.7.1.12, 1.8.3.18, 5.3.2.5), the action is to be performed alternatively either in the north, as the region of men, or in the east, the quarter of the gods. It is also relevant to note that according to KhGS 1.2.1; ĀpGS 2.6.10; and BGS 3.4.6,9 the sacred domestic fire is to be placed on a square mound of earth located in either the eastern or northeastern section of house.

77. Alternatives to this conclusion exist. See, e.g., the passage at JUB 2.7.1ff. where the east is the quarter of the gods, the south that of the ancestors, and the north is declared the region of the demons. On the other hand, some texts make binary oppositions between the north and south and encode the former as the region of the gods while the latter is, as usual, the quarter of the ancestors. See ŚB 2.1.3.3ff., 3.4.3.13, 12.5.1.11, 12.7.3.7, 12.8.3.6, 13.8.2.4,9. Veena Das, in "On the Categorization of Space" (p. 14), comments that "the opposition between right and left is clearly associated with 'rites to gods' and 'rites to ancestors': the right is connected with divine beings who are friendly and benevolent, the left with those supernatural beings who have to be appeased, who inspire terror and have the potential of causing great harm if they are not regularly propitiated. The pairs right/left and gods/ancestors are further associated with a number of other antithetical pairs, such as even/odd, day/night, and vegetables/meat." The right–left opposition is in Vedic texts more complex and overdetermined, however, and, when coordinated with the four cardinal directions certainly does not follow the neat scheme Das finds in her sources (p. 20): "This detailed enumeration of the contexts in which the different cardinal directions are used shows that east and north are associated with rituals in which the right dominates, and south and west with those in which the left dominates." For the right–left opposition used to distinguish gods and men, see above.

78. For the opposition between the east and north, as the auspicious regions of gods and men and therefore "sacrificial," versus the south and the west, which are deemed "unfit for sacrifice," see TB 3.2.9.8: "[In the beginning] the part of the earth that is fit for sacrifice and the part of it that is unfit for sacrifice separated. What is in the east and what is in the north is fit for sacrifice; what is in the west and what is in the south is unfit for sacrifice."

79. See GGS 4.7.16; KhGS 4.2.14–15; and ŚB 14.2.2.28, where the milk which rises on the north "does so for [the sacrificer's] offspring." Cf. ŚB 7.5.2.31; and esp. TB 3.7.2.7; ŚB 2.6.2.5ff., 5.4.2.10; KB 2.2, 5.7; where the north is identified with both animals and Rudra, also known as Paśupati or the Lord of Animals.

80. Recall that Cosmogonies V–VII explicitly declare as Shūdra the chain which includes many of the same components—the twenty-one-versed hymn of praise, the *anuṣṭubh* meter, the *vairāja* chant, etc.—which are, in other schemes, associated with the north.

81. Compare the distinction Ronald Inden makes between the Vaishyas (whose mastery is over "moveable wealth") and the Shūdras (who "was master of his body, his own labour, his own household, if he had one, but he was not the master of wealth beyond

what he required for subsistence"). "Lordship and Caste in Hindu Discourse," in *Indian Religion*, ed. by R. Burghart and A. Cantlie (London: Curzon Press, 1985), pp. 170–2.

82. For the association of the north, under the rulership of Varuṇa either alone or in partnership with Mitra, and "law and order," see TS 1.1.11.1; TB 3.3.6.8–9; VS 2.3; and ŚB 1.3.4.4, cited below.

83. Bodewitz, "The Waters," pp. 51–52: "So death, night, moon, waters, Varuṇa and *ṛta*/*satyam* belong together in the fourth position." For the north as the region of the waters, see also ŚB 11.6.1.1–13; JB 1.42–44.

84. The Upanishads are, in this formulation, connected to the zenith. Cf. ŚānĀ 3.5 and the cosmogonies in the Purāṇas (e.g., VishnuP 1.5.52–55; MārkP 48.31–34; KūrmaP 1.7.54–57; etc.) where the following homologies are entailed: (1) east = the verse (*ṛk*, i.e. the Ṛg Veda) = *gāyatrī* meter = the nine-versed hymn of praise = the *rathantara* chant = the Agniṣṭoma sacrifice; (2) south = the formula (*yajus*, i.e., the Yajur Veda) = the *triṣṭubh* meter = the fifteen-versed hymn of praise = the *bṛhat* chant = the Uktha portion of the Agnicayana sacrifice; (3) west = the chant (*sāman*, i.e., the Sāma Veda) = the *jagatī* meter = the seventeen-versed hymn of praise = the *vairūpa* chant = the Atirātra sacrifice; (4) north = the *atharvan* (i.e., the Atharva Veda) = twenty-one-versed hymn of praise = the *vairāja* chant = the Āptoryāman sacrifice. Compare, however, the unique formulation given at TB 3.12.9.1–2, where the north is connected to the Sāma Veda, the west is the region of the Atharva Veda, the east is associated with the Ṛg Veda, and the south with the Yajur Veda.

85. See also the preceding note. For an alternative formulation, consult AitĀ 5.1.2 (*gāyatra* = east, *rathantara* = south, *bṛhat* = north, *rājana* = west). Another variant is given at ŚB 8.1.1.5–1.2.4 (the *gāyatra*, *svāra*, *ṛksāma*, and *aiḍa* chants = east, south, west, north). For a somewhat different scheme, which is based on a right–left dichotomy rather than on a spatial model entailing the cardinal directions, see PB 5.1.13–15 and 5.6.7. This scheme, however, reiterates the connections between the *bṛhat* and the *triṣṭubh* meter, on the one hand, and the *rathantara* and the *gāyatrī* meter, on the other.

86. See also ŚB 8.1.1.5–1.2.4 and note 84 above. In other passages, however, the hymns of praise for the west and the north are reversed, e.g. ŚB 8.4.4.1 (nine-versed hymn of praise = east, twenty-one-versed = west, fifteen-versed = south, seventeen-versed = north). Since both are regarded as "lower-class" regions, the west and the north in this instance as elsewhere are somewhat interchangeable.

87. The north and south are sometimes represented as equally Kshatriya in *varṇa*. Compare also the text at ŚB 8.5.1.9ff., where bricks placed in the front and back (east and west) are identified with Agni, and those to the north and south with Kshatriya components: the *triṣṭubh* meter and the thunderbolt.

88. See also TS 5.3.4.1ff. (cf. TS 4.3.9.1) which has the nine-versed in the east with Agni and the *brahman* (for "the *brahman* power is the beginning of the sacrifice, and the nine-versed is the beginning of the sacrifice"); the seventeen-versed in the south (as "food"); the twenty-one-versed in the west; and the fifteen-versed (with Indra and the *kṣatra*) in the north. ŚB 8.4.1.8ff. also places the nine-versed hymn of praise in the east, but then rather independently regards the fifteen-versed (and the thunderbolt and the moon) as belonging to the west; the seventeen-versed, is placed in the north; and the twenty-one-versed is assigned to the south.

89. The zenith is represented by the *paṅkti*, the "centre in cosmic equations" according to H. W. Bodewitz, *Jaiminīya Brāhmaṇa*, p. 87 n. 26. The *anuṣṭubh* is, however, connected to the north in ŚB 13.2.2.9 in a series of equations that also identifies the horse with the *kṣatra*. The north as the region of the Kshatriyas is attested elsewhere, as we noted earlier.

The identification of particular meters and certain spatial directions is confirmed rather than disproved by cases like ŚB 1.2.5.6ff. and TB 3.2.9.7–8 (citing TS 1.1.9) where the fire or Agni is placed on the east and all the meters then shift one place clockwise (i.e., the *gāyatrī* thus takes the south, the *triṣṭubh* the west, and the *jagatī* the north). In this instance and others, the normal pattern of associations is assumed even as it is manipulated and purposefully rearranged. While some have read such passages as proof of the unsystematic nature of Vedic connections, it is perhaps more accurate to see in them the hand of creativity at work. The systematizers are here displaying a familiarity of received ideas they are simultaneously bending into new formations.

90. Many texts, beginning in the Upanishads and Sūtras and persisting through later Hindu literature, list the four lords of the cardinal directions as Indra (east), Yama (south), Varuṇa (west), and Soma or the moon (north), with Bṛhaspati or Brahman being assigned to the zenith or the "middle" region. See ŚGS 2.14.7; ĀśvGS 1.2.5–6; MGS 2.12.12–16; KGS 54.11–15; BhGS 3.14; Manu 3.87; MatsyaP 255.7–9. Compare BĀU 3.9.20–24, where the east belongs to Sūrya, the sun (and the eye and "appearance"); the south is ruled by Yama (and is the region of sacrifice, *dakṣiṇa*, and faith); Varuṇa rules the west (where water and semen are located); the north is Soma's quarter (with *dīkṣā* and truth); and the zenith is assigned to Agni (and to speech and heart). GGS 4.7.20–22 assigns Āditya/Sūrya to the east, Yama to the south, Varuṇa to the west, and Prajāpati to the north. VGS 14.2 switches the usual deities of the west and north, assigning Soma to the west and Varuṇa to the north, a move that is made by some of the older texts as well. Other Hindu sources enumerate eight deities who preside over the quarters and the intermediate regions, beginning with the east and moving clockwise: Indra, Agni, Yama, Sūrya (or Nirṛti), Varuṇa, Vāyu, Kubera, and Soma. See P. V. Kane, *History of Dharmaśāstra*, 5 vols., 2d ed. (Poona: Bhandarkar Oriental Research Institute, 1968–75), Vol. V, Pt. 2, p. 766n; Manu 5.97, 7.4. Compare the somewhat idiosyncratic enumeration at GGS 4.7.37–41 (Indra, Vāyu, Yama, the ancestors, Varuṇa, Mahārāja, Soma, Mahendra, with the nadir assigned to Vāsuki and the zenith to the *brahman*).

91. The Rudras, Ādityas, and Maruts are the deities of Indra, Varuṇa, and Soma (and the south, west, and north respectively) in Cosmogony XI. Cosmogony XII connects Indra and the Rudras, the Maruts and the Ādityas, and the Viśva Devas and Varuṇa and the Sādhyas to those three directions. The Maruts, Ādityas, and the Sādhyas and Ājyas belong with Indra, Varuṇa, and the moon (Candras and Soma being interchangeable) in Cosmogony XIII. For other texts which place the Vasus in the east, see also TB 3.1.2.7; TS 5.3.4.3; and ŚB 8.4.2.7. For texts which locate the Vasus in the east and other groups of deities in the south, west, and north, consult AitB 8.14 and 8.19 (Vasus, Rudras, Ādityas, Viśva Devas, with the Maruts and Angirases in the zenith and the Sādhyas and Āptyas in the middle); ŚB 8.6.3.3 (Vasus, Rudras, Ādityas, Maruts, with the Viśva Devas in the zenith); ŚB 3.5.2.4–7 (Indra and the Vasus in the east; the ancestors in the south; Varuṇa and the Rudras in the west; and Viśvakarma and the Ādityas in the north); and TS 5.5.9.3–4 (Vasus and Rudras in the east, the ancestors and Yama in the south; Ādityas and Viśva Devas in the west; Maruts and Dyutāna Māruta in the north; and the gods (*devas*) and Indra "below and above"). For the Maruts and the south, see ŚB 2.5.2.10. The notion that the Viśva Devas, Vaishya deities, belong in the north (as in AitB 8.14 and 8.19) is perhaps explicable insofar as the north is the direction of humanity at large, the masses, as I argued earlier. The *varṇa* scheme for these groups of gods remains constant even in cases like TB 3.2.9.7–8 (cf. ŚB 1.2.5.6ff.; 8.2.2.9), where, by assigning Agni to the east, the usual direction for each group of gods is shifted one region clockwise (the Vasus move to the south, the Rudras to the west, and the Ādityas to the north). The *varṇa* for each of the groups in this case is indicated by the meter with which each of the

groups encloses the sacrificial area on a particular side (the Vasus with the *gāyatrī*, the Rudras with the *triṣṭubh*, and the Ādityas with the *jagatī*).

92. See also AitB 2.6, cited previously, for Agni's association with the east. One exception may be found at AitB 1.7, where Pathyā, the goddess of paths, is the deity of the east (for "in that he says the offering verse for Pathyā, therefore does yonder [sun] arise in the east and set in the west, for it follows Pathyā"), Soma is located in the west, Savitṛ in the north, and Agni is placed in the southern quarter. The rationale behind such assignments, however, seems not to be connected to the *varṇa*s of the deities and directions but rather lies in other kinds of associations. The fire god Agni is the deity of the south, and "in that he says the offering verse for Agni, therefore from the south the plants come first ripe, for the plants are connected with Agni." Similarly, "he says the offering verse for Soma; in that he says the offering verse for Soma therefore westward flow many rivers, for the waters are connected with Soma. He says the offering verse for Savitṛ; in that he says the offering verse for Savitṛ, therefore on the northwest he that blows blows most, for he blows instigated by Savitṛ." See also the eccentric text at TS 5.2.5.3–4, which places Rudra in the east. One form of Agni, Agni Sviṣṭakṛt, is located in the north (ŚB 1.7.3.20), apparently because this god, who "makes well offered" (*sviṣṭakṛt*) the oblations in the sense of making them complete and final, is identified with the "last" or "final" direction.

93. TS 5.5.10.1; AV 3.27.1; MS 2.13.1; MGS 2.11.8; cf. ŚB 6.8.1.8, 9.2.3.25. In several texts, Agni is identified with the sun, and when his ritual representative is lifted toward the sky to the east "he places yonder sun upwards from here in the east, and hence yonder sun is placed upwards from here in the east" (ŚB 6.4.3.10, 7.5.1.36; cf. 8.6.1.16).

94. KB 7.6; cf. ŚB 3.2.3.16: "Through Agni they saw the eastern region. Therefore they take out Agni from behind toward the east [i.e., from the *gārhapatya* to the *āhavanīya*], and render homage to him; for through him they saw the eastern region, and to him belongs the eastern region." Similarly, in the ritual, animals are led to the east in order to search for Agni: "They [the animals searching for Agni] go eastward, for the east is Agni's region. He thus looks for him in his own region, finds him in his own region" (ŚB 6.3.2.2, cf. 6.3.2.6).

95. See, e.g., ŚB 1.4.1.14ff. and Frits Staal, *Agni: The Vedic Ritual of the Fire Altar*, 2 vols. (Berkeley: Asian Humanities Press, 1983), I:77ff.

96. In addition to the examples given below, see also ŚB 5.5.1.2–3, where the king who has "ascended the regions" ransoms himself from the east with a cake offered to Agni.

97. TS 5.5.8.2. Compare ŚB 8.5.1.9ff., where bricks placed on the eastern and western sides of the fire altar are identified with Agni, while those on the south and north are equated with Prajāpati.

98. Other deities in addition to those mentioned here are also occasionally positioned in the south. Savitṛ, the sun god and "instigator," is the deity of this quarter at ŚB 13.8.2.6, and Savitṛ in his guise as Bhaga at ŚB 1.7.4.6 is the god who sits on the south side in the gods' sacrifice. ŚB 8.1.1.7 and 8.6.1.17 place Viśvakarman, the "All-Maker," and the wind god Vāyu ("because it is in the south that he blows most") in this region. Cf., however, AitB 1.7, where Savitṛ is positioned in the northern quarter because Vāyu, instigated by Savitṛ, is said to blow most often from the northwest. At AitB 6.4, a typical myth about the attack of the demons from the south is called forth to explain why Mitra and Varuṇa are to be regarded as deities of the south.

99. ŚB 3.2.3.17. Cf. KB 7.6, where Soma is also declared to be the discoverer of the south: "Therefore they carry round in the south the soma when purchased. Standing in the south he praises; standing in the south he concludes; sitting in the south they press

it—for this was the quarter discovered by him." Soma's identification with the south in Vedic ritual texts is perhaps also one of the sources of the Upanishadic view that the world of the ancestors is to be associated with the moon (a form of Soma), darkness, sacrificial action, and rebirth (the moon being a way station in the recycling of souls); the *deva loka*, by contrast, is connected with the sun, light, mystical knowledge, and eternal liberation (BĀU 6.2.15–16; ChU 4.15.5–6, 5.10.1–3; KauṣU 1.2).

100. See above, ŚB 1.4.5.3 and 4.6.6.1–4. In later texts dealing with the *lokapālas*, the Kshatriya deity Indra is regularly assigned to the east, while Agni (the usual guardian of the east in Vedic sources and a Brahmin god) is in the later formulation moved over to the intermediate southeastern quarter. See, however, BhGS 3.14, where both Indra and Agni are located in the east. There is but one Vedic text (ŚB 3.5.2.4), to my knowledge, that concurs with the notion that the east is Indra's quarter, and even in that one Indra and the east are also associated with the group of deities known as the Vasus, who are usually regarded as Brahmin in *varṇa*. One possible explanation for the later assignment of Indra to the east is given at ŚB 4.6.6.5, where it is declared that Indra is a Brahmin.

101. TS 5.5.10.1; AV 3.27.2; MS 2.13; MGS 2.11.8.

102. ŚB 9.2.3.6. See also TS 5.5.8.2: "With the southern quarter I place you, with the *triṣṭubh* meter, with Indra as the deity."

103. Indra is also said to join forces with Bṛhaspati, the Brahmin deity often assimilated to the *brahman* priest, who is stationed on the south side of the ritual. Together, they render the south safe from demon attack. See, e.g., ŚB 9.2.3.2–3. At TB 3.8.7.1, Indra and the Brahmin Agni are associated with the south and declared to be the "the most powerful and strongest of the gods." TB 3.8.7.1, however, describes Indra and Agni in the same manner but portrays them as the deities of the east.

104. For the Vaishyas, Viśva Devas, and the west, see Cosmogony X; for the Vaishyas, Maruts, and the west, Cosmogonies VIII and XII. Cf. ŚB 5.5.1.5, where the king, who has "ascended" to the western quarter, offers an oblation to the Viśva Devas in order to "descend" from that realm; AitB 6.4, where the Viśva Devas defeat the demons who have attacked this side of the sacrifice; and TS 5.5.9.3–4, where the Viśva Devas (together with the Ādityas) protect the west.

105. E.g., Cosmogonies XI and XIII, where Varuṇa and Ādityas are located in the west; AV 3.27.3, where Varuṇa is declared the overlord of the region; and ŚB 3.5.2.5, where Varuṇa together with the Rudras protect in the west.

106. The emphasis on the fertility of the west probably also explains the linkage of that quarter to Prajāpati at GGS 4.7.20–22.

107. For Soma as the deity of the west, see TS 5.5.10; MGS 2.11.8; VGS 14.2. For the similar equation of the moon and waters, see TB 1.7.6.3 and GB 1.5.15. For Soma as the deity of the north or south, see below.

108. AitB 1.7. ŚB 9.3.1.24 also makes mention of seven rivers that flow westward. The placement of the solar god Savitṛ in the west in some texts (ŚB 3.2.3.18; KB 7.6; together with the Vaishya meter, the *jagatī*, at TS 5.5.8.2–3; and with a string of Vaishya components at ŚB 8.2.1.1–2 and 8.6.1.18), appears to have been generated primarily out of meteorological considerations. "Savitṛ is the yonder one who gives heat. Therefore men see him day by day going westward, not eastward, for this was the quarter discerned by him" (KB 7.6). Cf. TS 5.3.4.2–6, where Aditi is mentioned as a god of the west (along with Mitra and Pūṣan). Recall also that, under the most frequently encountered paradigm, the Vaishya world is the sky ruled by the sun. For the anomalous connection of the west with Vāyu, the wind god, see TB 3.8.7.1–2 and ŚB 13.8.2.6.

109. AitB 8.14; 8.19; PGS 2.9.7; and TB 3.8.7.1–2, cited previously; cf. Cosmogony XII and TS 5.5.9.3–4. At ŚB 3.6.1.28–29 the Viśva Devas are said to have originally

procured their immortality from the *āgnīdhra* fire, which is in the northern part of the sacrificial grounds. "And because the Viśva Devas gained immortality from there, therefore it belongs to the Viśva Devas."

110. Here we might also note the identification of the Viśva Devas and the *anuṣṭubh* meter (which, we will remember, is the meter of the northern region). See JB 1.238ff. and below. See also Bodewitz's comments, "The Waters," p. 47: "The fourth element often represents something which on the one hand is added to a threefold totality and on the other hand includes the three preceding items. This may refer to the Vishve Devas (the All-gods after Vasus, Rudras, and Ādityas, but at the same time 'all the gods') or to the Anuṣṭubh, which is a separate metre after Gāyatrī, Triṣṭubh and Jagatī, but does not add a number of syllables in each Pāda and is regarded as the totality of these metres." Cf., Bodewitz, *Jaiminīya Brāhmaṇa*, p. 89 n. 26: "So we may conclude that the identification of the *anuṣṭubh* with the Viśve Devas is based on their peculiar position at the end of a series in which they may act as a separate entity and at the same time as the encompassing totality. The fact that the number of the All-gods (33) almost coincides with that of the syllables may have been of secondary influence."

111. For Soma = moon and moon = death, Jan Gonda, *Change and Continuity in Indian Religion* (reprint New Delhi: Munshiram Manoharlal, 1985), p. 50. For Varuṇa and death, consult Kuiper, *Varuṇa and Vidūṣaka*, pp. 12, 62, 71–73. Soma's role as a god of death, however, can also justify positioning him in the south, as we noted earlier.

112. KB 5.7; ŚB 2.6.2.5–7 (where an oblation is to be offered to this deity north of the sacrificial grounds at the site of a crossroad); 5.4.2.10; 14.2.2.28; ĀpDhS 2.2.6. Perhaps Rudra is located in this region because of his well-known association with the mountains, i.e., particularly the Himalayas located to the north of the Āryan settlements. The mountain residence of Rudra persists as this Vedic god transmogrifies into the Hindu Śiva. For Rudra and the directions in the Veda, however, see also TS 5.2.5.3, where that god's quarter is said to be the east.

113. E.g., AV 3.27.4 and BĀU 3.9.23. Recall also that Soma together with the Maruts are the deities of the north in Cosmogony XI, and Cosmogony XIII places Candramas (the moon) in that quarter. At AitB 1.8, Soma is called the king of the north, and one who wishes to drink soma juice should turn northward while offering certain oblations.

114. See also TS 5.5.10; AV 3.27.3; MGS 2.11.8; VGS 14.2; and cf. ŚB 2.5.2.10. Varuṇa is equated with the *anuṣṭubh* meter, the meter of the north, at TB 1.7.10.4. Recall here also, as we noted previously, that the north is the region associated with the "world of the waters" in some cosmological schemes, and that the waters are ruled by Varuṇa. This deity is equated with the *kṣatra* and place in the north at ŚB 2.5.2.6: "On the northern (*uttara*) altar he raises the northern sacrificial grounds, not on the southern one. Varuṇa is the *kṣatra* and the Maruts are the *viś*. He thus makes the *kṣatra* higher (*uttara*) than the *viś*. Thus, people here serve the Kshatriya who is placed above them." The Maruts are indeed often declared the subjects or *viś* of a Kshatriya overlord (most often Indra), and they are sometimes located in the Vaishya west (see below). But they are simultaneously Kshatriya deities themselves, and therefore the text cited above might be best understood as emphasizing that *varṇa*'s claim to both the north and the south. The Maruts, it might be noted, are themselves located in the north in other texts (e.g., TS 5.5.9.3–4; and, together with Soma, in Cosmogony XI).

115. And thus there seems also to be the prospect of a Kshatriya affiliation with the north in this case. Bricks placed to the north are dedicated to Indra, the overlord of Viṣṇu, for "Indra is force (*ojas*), Viṣṇu is force, the *kṣatra* is force, the fifteen-versed hymn of praise is force. Thus, on the north he places force. Therefore he who advances to the north is victorious. . . . He becomes filled with force for whom these [are placed]

on the north, full of force, and a son who is filled with force is born to him" (TS 5.3.4.2–3,6; cf. TS 4.3.9.1; ŚB 8.4.2.4).

116. To "redeem" oneself from the southern region to which the royal sacrificer has "ascended," a cake is offered to either one of the two gods (ŚB 5.5.1.4). Alternatively, according to AitB 6.4, the north is the region of both Indra and Agni.

117. At TS 5.5.8.2–3, bricks are to be put down to the north which are dedicated to these two deities and associated with the meter of that region, the *anuṣṭubh*, which also functions as the "transcendent fourth" in relation to the *gāyatrī*, *triṣṭubh*, and *jagatī* meters. At TB 3.3.6.8–9 the divine pair are associated with the "law" and the vital breaths. An enclosing stick is placed to the north and while the priest recites (TS 1.1.11.1), "'May Mitra and Varuṇa lay you around in the north with firm law.' Mitra and Varuṇa are exhalation and inhalation. [Therefore, by saying that formula] he puts exhalation and inhalation into the sacrificer" (cf. VS 2.3; ŚB 1.3.4.4). The sacrificer who has ascended the northern quarter is "redeemed" by offering to Mitra and Varuṇa (ŚB 5.5.1.6).

118. See Cosmogonies VIII, X, and XI, and also TS 5.5.8.2–3.

119. The *anuṣṭubh* meter is equated to Vāc and all the other meters at TB 1.7.5.5 and JB 1.276. Elsewhere, the all-encompassing nature of the thirty-two-syllabled *anuṣṭubh* is explained as the summation of the *gāyatrī* (eight syllables), *triṣṭubh* (eleven), *jagatī* (twelve), plus Vāc. See JB 1.284, 2.101; and PB 10.5.9ff.

120. Bodewitz, "The Waters," p. 52 n. 40: "Vāc either occupies the first position in the usual classifications (on account of the association with Agni) or the fourth (on account of the equation with the Anuṣṭubh)."

6

Classifying Time

The Social Effects of Classifying Time

Edmund Leach wrote that "the oddest thing about time is surely that we have such a concept at all."[1] The conception of time is indeed somewhat ineffable: time is experienced, but not with our senses. "We don't see it, or touch it, or smell it, or taste it, or hear it," Leach notes. Although, as we noted at the beginning of Chapter 5, the capacity for perception oriented by space and time seems to be innate to the human being,[2] the production of an idea like that of time, "like the idea of God, is one of those categories which we find necessary because we are social animals rather than because of anything empirical in our objective experience of the world."[3]

What is the relationship between social conditions (and conditioning) and the way particular societies understand time? Durkheim argued in his *Elementary Forms of the Religious Life* that the divisions "in relation to which all things are temporally located, are taken from social life. The divisions into days, weeks, months, years, etc. correspond to the periodical recurrence of rites, feasts, and public ceremonies. A calendar expresses the rhythm of the collective activities, while at the same time its function is to assure their regularity."[4] If, as Durkheim claimed, "cosmic space was primitively constructed on the model of social space, that is, on the territory occupied by society and as society conceives it," so too is time a social product, for "time expresses the rhythm of collective life."[5]

More recently, David Pocock noted the difference between an empirically based "duration"—the simple passage of time, which is "a fact of experience"—and "time-reckoning," which presupposes social life and social categories: "If I am alone I am not the creature of my society's system of time-reckoning. My life and my activity endure and it is only through interaction with others that I am subject to time." Pocock concludes that the relation between duration and time-reckoning is a transformation of that between the individual and society: "As a temporary conclusion we can suggest that the relation of the individual person or the individual group to the larger whole is intimately related to the relation between time-reckoning and mere duration."[6]

Temporal categories ("time-reckoning"), no less than the particulars of spatial classification, are products of culture and embody social meanings. In the Veda, time is divided in such a way as to correlate with the divisions in other realms, including society itself; time, like space, is categorized according to *varṇa*. The social meaning of time is here directly manifest, for temporal classes and social classes are conjoined in Vedic taxonomies. Thus, in this context at least, the Durkheimian thesis seems to hold: the categories into which time is divided "not only come from society, but the things which they express are of a social nature. Not only is it society which has founded them, but their contents are the different aspects of the social being."[7]

But what, precisely, does this linkage between the "different aspects of the social being" and the divisions a given society imposes upon and perceives within the river of time mean? In our case, this innocuous, overly theoretical equation can be put more simply and concretely: the way the authors of the Veda classified time reflected the class divisions mandated for society by these very authors who, not coincidentally, were also the primary beneficiaries of the social order so mandated. The way that time was to be apprehended was also made to reassert class divisions in the social order—an extraordinarily subtle and powerful method of insinuating the latter into the perceptions of human beings for whom such a social order was advantageous but also those for whom it was not.

The classificatory scheme that organizes society also organizes time; the divisions of time in the Veda are isomorphic with the divisions of society. Moreover, the different units into which time is cut up are themselves placed into a relation of mutual resemblance. Periods of different duration, in other words, become analogues of one another thanks to the *varṇa* system. Because various units of time share the same class, they are regarded as transformations of one another.

In Chapter 5, we observed not only the connection between the *varṇa*s and the principal spatial correlates, but also the attempt to synchronize two different modalities of dividing space. The spatial divisions of three cosmological worlds and four cardinal directions are coordinated, albeit not without some difficulty, and both are further integrated into the larger structure of *varṇa* and its attendant components from the social, supernatural, ritual, and scriptural realms. In this chapter, we will see a similar operation of division and correlation at work as the Vedic systematizers classified time, amalgamated the different temporal units, and interwove such categorizations into the *varṇa* scheme as a whole. Also in this chapter we conclude our investigation of the classification of space and time with a look at the various ways in which spatial and temporal structures are also made to be mutually interlocking—and how both are organized within the superstructure of *varṇa*.

Time and Its Divisions

While the three worlds together with the quarters or regions comprise the spatial whole, the year functions as the temporal whole in the Veda. PB 18.9.7 states that the year contains within it both the past and the future; the "year" is thus time itself.[8] The year is represented as wheel (or the "wheel of time," as we might say) with three hubs (i.e., seasons) and twelve spokes (i.e., months), with allusions also to 360 days and 720 days and nights (ṚV 1.164.2,11,48). The year is identified both with Prajāpati, the creator god, and with *sarva* ("all that is"). The year "is" Prajāpati,[9] for Prajāpati and the year are both "this all" (ŚB 1.6.1.19, 2.6.3.1, 5.4.5.14, 6.6.4.3, 10.2.5.16, etc.). Alternatively, at ŚB 11.1.6.13 the connection is explained by the fact that Prajāpati and *saṃvatsara* ("year") both have four syllables.[10] Prajāpati is also equated with the sum of the year's parts: the 6 seasons, the 12 months, the 24 fortnights, the 360 days, or the 720 days and nights.[11] Likewise, the frequent connection between Prajāpati and the number seventeen[12] is sometimes explained by adding the number of seasons (here reckoned at five) and months: "There are twelve months in a year and five seasons. This is the seventeen-fold Prajāpati. Truly Prajāpati is all (*sarva*)."[13]

The year is broken up into intervals: half-years, three four-month periods, seasons, months, half-months, days and nights, and so on, down to infinitesimal moments.[14] The two half-years or *ayana*s are marked by the solstices: the *uttara ayana* or "northern passage" begins at the winter solstice and the *dakṣiṇa ayana* or "southern passage" of the sun's arc through the sky starts at the summer solstice. The year is also divided into three four-month periods (*cāturmāsya*s), thus constituting a twelve-month lunar year.[15] According to this calendrical model, the new year begins either with the full moon in the month of Phālguna (a.k.a. Tapasya, February–March), that is, the last day of that month, or with that of the month of Caitra (a.k.a. Madhu, March–April).[16] This full moon also inaugurates both the first *cāturmāsya*, which is sometimes called "summer" (*grīṣma*), while the second and third *cāturmāsya*s mark the beginning of the four-month "periods" known as the rainy season (*varṣa*) and winter (*hemanta*) respectively.[17]

The earliest Vedic literature knows of only three seasons or *ṛtus*.[18] Slightly later, they are expanded into six, each season encompassing two lunar months: spring (*vasanta*), summer or the hot season, the rainy season, autumn (*śarad*), winter, and the cool season (*śiśira*).[19] It is also sometimes said that there are five seasons (conflating winter and the cool season),[20] or even seven seasons (the six plus the year, or adding *pravṛṣ*, the beginning of the rains).[21] The seasons are to the year as the limbs are to the body (KB 29.8).

Each month begins with the first day after the full moon, and consists of the two fortnights of the waxing and waning moon. Each of these half-months is made up of the full moon or new moon day plus fourteen days, and each of these days is marked by two of the twenty-eight lunar mansions (*nakṣatra*s).[22] Day and night is the next principal temporal unit. There are 360 days (or 720 days and nights) each made up of 30 *muhūrta*s (the ancient Indian functional equivalent of hours), which are themselves further subdivided into even smaller units.[23]

The Vedic worldview permits these discrete but interdependent units of time to be envisioned as temporal Chinese boxes or mirroring forms of one another, just as in the spatial realm the different cosmological worlds and cardinal directions can be equated. Longer periods repeat themselves within shorter ones; units of smaller duration are homologized to the larger ones. The year, for example, is said to be recapitulated in the day, the two halves of the year in day and night, and the cycle of seasons in the tripartite division of the day (morning, midday, and afternoon or evening).

One method of establishing such connections between different temporal periods is purely numerical: six months = six seasons, twenty four days = twenty four half-months, twelve days = twelve months, six days = six seasons, and three days = three "periods"—all of which are "equivalent" to the year (ŚB 11.5.4.6–11). Smaller units of time thus can be regarded as the ritual equivalent of larger temporal units, which make up the year.[24]

Another method for interrelating temporal components divides time into oscillating binary opposites: periods which belong to the gods are opposed those belonging to the ancestors.[25] The two half-years are known generically as one day and night of the gods (see, e.g., Manu 1.65,67). The day of the gods is when the sun's arc is to the north, and this period is assigned to the gods per se; the night of the gods, when the sun's arc moves to the southern portion of the sky, belongs to the ancestors.[26] The ritual calendar is informed by this dichotomy. The sacrificer should set up his fires when the sun "moves northward," for that is when humans are "among the gods": "The gods are immortal and, although there is for him no prospect of immortality, he who sets up his fire during this time attains a long life." One who sets up his fires when the sun moves south, during the ancestors' half of the divine year, runs some risk, for "the ancestors are mortal. Therefore, one who sets up his fires during that time dies before [he has lived a long] life"(ŚB 2.1.3.3–4).

The time of the "northern passage" is thus the period of life and the gods, whereas the "southern passage" is that of death and the ancestors. This annual fluctuation between the half-year of the deities and that of the ancestors is recapitulated in other units of time, thus bringing them into a relationship of resemblance. The two half-years can in this way be homologized to the two monthly fortnights,[27] day and night,[28] and the parts of the day:

> The spring, the hot season, and the rainy season—these are the seasons which are the gods. The autumn, the winter, and the cool season—these are the ancestors.[29] The increasing half-month [i.e., the fortnight of the waxing moon] is the gods, and that which decreases [i.e., the fortnight of the waning moon] is the ancestors. The day is the gods, the night is the ancestors. And further, the forenoon is the gods, the afternoon is the ancestors. (ŚB 2.1.3.1)

The half-year of the northern passage of the sun, the first three seasons of the year, the fortnight of the waxing moon, the day, and the forenoon are all classified as belonging to the gods. Conversely, the half-year of the southern passage of the sun, the second triad of the seasons, the fortnight of the waning moon, the night, and the afternoon are times associated with the ancestors.[30] The mutual reflexivity of the components of the year, achieved by numeric equivalences or by categorizing them as belonging either to the gods or to the ancestors, constitutes half-years, seasons, fortnights, days and nights, and parts of the day as analogues of one another.

The classification of time according to *varṇa* is another, and complementary, method to attain the same end. Intratemporal coordination is made possible in part because of the reduplication of the significations, values, and concomitants with which the different discrete time periods are burdened. In other words, different temporal units (e.g., spring, day, morning) share the same *varṇa* classification; they thus are assigned the same metaphysical powers, the same ontological correlates, the same deities, and so forth. Classification of time according to *varṇa* also imposes distinctions of value onto the different components of the temporal structure. We concentrate here on the *varṇa* assignments given to the seasons of the year and the parts of the day (morning, noon, and afternoon),[31] the day being one principal resembling form of the year. As we shall see, seasons and day parts are interwoven by strings of associations that join the two temporal orders, including interconnections between these orders and the order of superclasses or *varṇa*s.

Classifying the Seasons

"The spring is the *brahman*, the hot season is the *kṣatra*, and the rainy season the *viś*," or so it is decreed. Members of particular *varṇa*s should set up the sacrificial fires in the season which is appropriate to them: "A Brahmin should therefore set up his fires in the spring, since the spring is the *brahman*; and a Kshatriya should set them up in the summer, since the hot season is the *kṣatra*; and a Vaishya should set them up in the rainy season, since the rainy season is the *viś*."[32] The three *varṇa*s are thus often assigned to the first three seasons of the year, that is, within the gods' "day" or the half of the year described as the "northern passage."

Other formulations, however, assume that the rainy season belongs to the Rathakāra or "chariot-maker," the offspring of a Vaishya male and Shūdra female, who is allowed, according to some texts, to set the sacrificial fires.[33] The Vaishya, under this scheme, drops down a season; he is sometimes instructed to set his fires in the autumn.[34] The assignment of the autumn to the Vaishya class seems to have acquired general acceptance over time; in the Gṛhya Sūtras, Brahmin boys undergo the *upanayana* (initiation into Vedic learning and sacrifice) in the spring, Kshatriyas in the hot season, and Vaishyas in the autumn.[35]

We see here that the rainy season and the autumn alternate as the seasons of the lower classes (in this case, the Vaishyas and the Rathakāras) in ways reminiscent of the similar interchangeability of the western and northern quarters. Once again we witness the indeterminacy of the lower portions of a social structure sometimes regarded as tripartite and sometimes as quadripartite, and its reverberations in other classificatory realms.

TABLE 6.1. The Seasons and Their Analogues According to Cosmogonies V, VIII–X, XII, and XIII

Cosmogony V

1. mouth ⇒ 9-versed hymn of praise = *gāyatrī* meter = Agni = Brahmin = SPRING
2. chest/arms ⇒ 15-versed hymn of praise = *triṣṭubh* meter = Indra = Kshatriya = SUMMER
3. middle/penis ⇒ 17-versed of praise = *jagatī* meter = Viśva Devas = Vaishya = RAINY SEASON
4. feet/foundation ⇒ 21-versed hymn of praise = *anuṣṭubh* meter = no god = Shūdra = NO SEASON

Cosmogony VIII

1. east = *gāyatrī* meter = 9-versed hymn of praise = *rathantara* chant = Agni = SPRING = the *brahman*
2. south = *triṣṭubh* meter = 15-versed hymn of praise = *bṛhat* chant = Indra = SUMMER = the *kṣatra*
3. west = *jagatī* meter = 17-versed hymn of praise = *vairūpa* chant = Maruts = RAINY SEASON = the *viś*
4. north = *anuṣṭubh* meter = 21-versed hymn of praise = *vairāja* chant = Mitra-Varuṇa = AUTUMN = *phala*
5. zenith = *paṅkti* meter = 27- and 33-versed hymn of praise = *śakvara* and *raivata* chants = Bṛhaspati = WINTER and COOL SEASONS = *varcas* or *phala*

Cosmogony IX

1. east ⇒ breath ⇒ SPRING ⇒ *gāyatrī* meter ⇒ *gāyatra* chant ⇒ *upāṃśu* soma cup ⇒ 9-versed hymn of praise ⇒ *rathantara* chant ⇒ the seer Vasiṣṭha
2. south ⇒ mind ⇒ SUMMER ⇒ *triṣṭubh* meter ⇒ *aiḍa* chant *antaryāma* soma cup ⇒ 15-versed hymn of praise ⇒ *bṛhat* chant ⇒ the seer Bharadvāja
3. west ⇒ eye (or sight) ⇒ RAINY SEASON ⇒ *jagatī* meter ⇒ *ṛksāma* chant ⇒ *śukra* soma cup ⇒ 17-versed hymn of praise ⇒ *vairūpa* chant ⇒ the seer Viśvamitra
4. north ⇒ ear (or hearing) ⇒ AUTUMN ⇒ *anuṣṭubh* meter ⇒ *svāra* chant ⇒ *manthin* soma cup ⇒ 21-versed hymn of praise ⇒ *vairāja* chant ⇒ the seer Jamadagni
5. zenith ⇒ thought and speech ⇒ WINTER ⇒ *paṅkti* meter ⇒ conclusion of chants ⇒ *āgrāyana* soma cup ⇒ 27- and 33-versed hymns of praise ⇒ the *śakvara* and *raivata* chants ⇒ the seer Raivata Viśvakarman

Cosmogony X

1. east = SPRING = Agni = the *brahman* = *gāyatrī* meter = *rathantara* chant = 9-versed hymn of praise = track of 15-versed hymn of praise = Sanaga the seer = 18-month-old calf = *kṛta* dice throw = east wind
2. south = SUMMER = Indra = the *kṣatra* = *triṣṭubh* meter = *bṛhat* chant = 15-verse hymn of praise = track of 17-versed hymn of praise = Sanātana the seer = 2-year-old cow = *treta* dice throw = south wind

The usual assignments of the seasons can also be articulated in terms of other *varṇa*-encoded correlates. A review of the cosmogonies that include within their chains of associations particular seasons will indicate the ways the seasons are included in strings of associations to components of other realms (see Table 6.1). We pause here to review only the theological correlates that reiterate the *varṇa* associations of the seasons.[36]

Spring and the hot season are almost invariably connected to the Brahmin deity Agni (together with the Vasus) and the Kshatriya god Indra (accompanied sometimes by the Maruts or the Rudras)[37]—no surprises here. The rainy season

3. west = RAINY SEASON = Viśva Devas = the *viś* = *jagatī* meter = *vairūpa* chant = 17-versed hymn of praise = track of 21-versed hymn of praise = Ahabhūna the seer = 3-year-old cow = *dvāpara* dice throw = west wind
4. north = AUTUMN = Mitra and Varuṇa = prosperity (*puṣṭa*) = *anuṣṭubh* meter = *vairāja* chant = 21-versed hymn of praise = track of 27-versed hymn of praise = Purāṇa [var. Pratna] the seer = 4-year-old cow = *abhibhava* [var. *askaṇḍa*] dice throw = north wind
5. zenith = WINTER and COOL SEASONS = Bṛhaspati = fruit (*phala*) [var. splendor (*varcas*)] = *paṅkti* meter = *śakvara* and *raivata* chants = 27-versed hymn of praise = track of 33-versed hymn of praise = Suparna the seer = 4-year-old bull = *askaṇḍa* [var. *abhibhū*] dice throw = wind from above

Cosmogony XII

1. east ⇒ Agni = *gāyatrī* meter = 9-versed hymn of praise = *rathantara* chant = SPRING = inhalation = constellations = Vasus
2. south ⇒ Indra = *triṣṭubh* meter = 15-versed hymn of praise = *bṛhad* chant = SUMMER = the circulating breath = moon = Rudras
3. west ⇒ Maruts = *jagatī* meter = 17-versed hymn of praise = *vairūpa* chant = RAINY SEASON = exhalation = Venus = Ādityas
4. north ⇒ Viśva Devas = *anuṣṭubh* meter = 21-versed hymn of praise = *vairāja* chant = AUTUMN = the digestive breath = Varuṇa and the Sādhyas
5. zenith ⇒ Mitra and Varuṇa = *paṅkti* meter = 27- and 33-versed hymns of praise = *śakvara* and *raivata* chants = WINTER and COOL SEASON = the upward breath = Angirases = moon
6. nadir ⇒ Saturn = eclipses = comets = serpents = demons = spirits = humans, birds, eight-legged mountain goats, elephants, etc.

Cosmogony XIII

1. first day = earth = *gāyatrī* meter = 9-versed hymn of praise = *rathantara* chant = east = SPRING = Vasus and Agni
2. second day = atmosphere = *triṣṭubh* meter = 15-versed hymn of praise = *bṛhat* chant = south = SUMMER = Maruts and Indra
3. third day = sky = *jagatī* meter = 17-versed hymn of praise = *vairūpa* chant = west = RAINY SEASON = Ādityas and Varuṇa
4. 4th day = food = *anuṣṭubh* meter = 21-versed hymn of praise = *vairāja* chant = north = AUTUMN = Sādhyas and Ājyas and Bṛhaspati and the moon
5. 5th day = animals = *paṅkti* meter = 27-versed hymn of praise = *śakvara* chant = zenith = WINTER = Maruts and Rudra
6. 6th day = waters = *atichandas* meter = 33-versed hymn of praise = *raivata* chant = zenith = COOL SEASON = Viśva Devas and Prajāpati

---

and autumn have a more diverse set of correlative deities, this in keeping with the relative interchangeability of the two seasons (and the variability of the *varṇa* attributes assigned to the autumn) mentioned previously. The divinities connected to the rainy season are always those representing the masses or the lower classes in general—usually the Viśva Devas,[38] the Maruts,[39] or the Ādityas.[40] The autumn, as the season sometimes also connected with the Vaishyas, can also be associated with some of these same deities[41] or with other gods also connected with the lower classes;[42] alternatively, it can be the season in which deities representing the kind of "transcendence" sometimes associated with the fourth are located.[43]

The pattern that emerges when one surveys the connections between deities and the seasons thus reinforces the *varṇa* associations mentioned earlier. The spring, as the Brahmin season, is ruled by Agni and his Vasus. The Kshatriya summer is Indra's, with or without his subordinates (Maruts or Rudras). The rains belong to one or another of the Vaishya groups of deities (Viśva Devas, Maruts, Ādityas), while fall is sometimes assigned to a lower-class group of deities (e.g., the Viśva Devas or Ṛbhus) as the tripartite social classification expands into a quadripartite one (stimulated in this case by the inclusion of the Rathakāra into the sacrificial cult).[44] In other cases, the autumn, like the fifth and six seasons (winter and the cool season), carries different significances which are transmitted by assigning to them Brahmin deities like Bṛhaspati or, most often, Brahmin–Kshatriya ruling class pairs like Mitra and Varuna.[45]

Why are particular seasons regularly regarded as belonging to one or another of the social classes? Past attempts to explain the underlying rationale for the correlations between the spring, summer, and rainy season, on the one hand, and the Brahmins, Kshatriyas, and Vaishyas, on the other, have included the suggestion that "we have before us different beginnings for the year in the different periods assigned to each caste and that for each member of the class concerned the installation of the fire took place at the beginning of the year."[46] There is, however, no corroborating evidence for this theory; the new year, according to sources cited above, begins in the spring, the Brahmin season, and, indeed, many texts make much of the fact that the "first" season belongs to the "foremost" social class.[47] Another notion that has been put forward to explain the match between seasons and *varṇas* provides us with what we might call a naturalistic interpretation. Under this view, the distinctive climatic features of the various seasons were correlated to the supposed proclivities of the different social classes:

> These different seasons were symbolical of the temperament and occupation of different castes. The moderation of spring symbolized the moderate life of a Brahmin; the heat of summer represented the fervour of a kṣatriya; autumn, when the commercial life of ancient India reopened after the rainy season, suggested the wealth and prosperity of a vaiśya; and the easy time of rains indicated facility for a chariot-maker.[48]

This kind of explication is intriguing and has a certain persuasiveness, although the particulars of the statement above need correction and further refinement.[49]

The spring, for example, is not merely a "moderate" period; it is also the first or foremost among the seasons and is characterized by the natural regeneration that occurs during this time. The names for the two months encompassed within this season (Madhu and Mādhava) are derived from the occurrence in the spring of plants sprouting and trees bearing their fruit: "These are the two spring [months] because in spring plants are born and trees ripen. Therefore these two are Madhu ('sweet') and Mādhava ('sweetness')" (ŚB 4.3.1.14). When the year is imaged as a bird, its face or head (*mukha*, which can also mean its "front" or "beginning") is the spring (PB 21.15.2). The spring is elsewhere called the "kindler" among the seasons; it is the time of rebirth and regeneration and, as the first of the seasons, is represented as bringing forth the rest of them: "By the second kindling stick which he now puts on he kindles the spring. The spring, when kindled, kindles the other seasons; and the seasons, when kindled, cause offspring to be produced and plants to ripen."[50]

The earth is often regarded as spatial world belonging to the Brahmin because it is supposed to be primary, primordial, and generative of other worlds—just as the Brahmin class is supposed to be in relation to the other social classes. It is thus not surprising that the temporal unit distinguished by its place at the foremost of the round of seasons and by the natural regeneration it inspires is assigned to the Brahmins, the foremost class which encompasses and "gives birth" to inferior forms of itself (i.e., the other classes).[51] Just as all other seasons are, by a particular ritual act, said to be "yoked" to the spring (ŚB 5.5.2.3), so do the Brahmins represent themselves as the foremost class in human society.

The hot season or summer—the "scorched" period of the year (ŚB 11.2.7.32) when the South Asian sun burns most ferociously (ŚB 4.3.1.15) and when the body feels warmest (KB 3.4; ŚB 1.5.3.10)—easily brought the warrior class to mind. We too speak of "hot-blooded," "hot-tempered," "fiery" temperaments, and the propounders of the ancient Indian *varṇa* scheme probably drew on much the same associations in connecting the hot season and the Kshatriyas. The rainy season and the autumn are alternatively linked to the Vaishyas, for both seasons are depicted as times of fecundity.[52] The rainy season is said to be the period when cows have most milk (ĀpŚS 8.22.3) and is the season of "life" (*jīva*, TS 3.2.5) or food: "He offers to the sacrificial food; [he thereby pleases] the rains, for through the rains sacrificial food arises."[53] Similarly, the autumn is described as the time when "the plants bear ripe fruit," insofar as rice and barley are harvested then (PB 21.15.3); or, more generally, the autumn is "when most plants ripen" (JUB 1.35.5; cf. ŚB 11.2.7.32; TĀ 1.3.3). "These plants which shrink during the summer and winter thrive because of the rains, and in autumn lie spread open" (ŚB 1.5.3.12). It is therefore the season in which the ripened plants have become edible: "These two are the autumn [months], because in autumn plants, which are nourishment (*ūrj*) and sap, ripen. Therefore these two [months] are [called] Iṣa ("possessing sap") and Ūrjas (ŚB 4.3.1.17; cf. TS 3.2.5; KB 3.4).

The winter is described as the inverse of spring (ŚB 1.5.3.13–14), that is, a period of death (cf. JUB 1.35.6; ŚB 4.3.1.18). The winter "subjects these creatures to its power. Therefore, in winter the plants wither and the leaves fall off the trees. The birds retire more and more, and fly lower and lower. The evil man's hair falls out. For the winter subjects these creatures to its power" (ŚB 1.5.4.5; cf. TĀ 1.3.3). The cool season is characterized as the time when things "freeze most intensely" (ŚB 4.3.1.19) and is the end of the year according to the Vedic calendar. Like the winter, the cool season is thus often constituted as a season of death,[54] and neither is associated with any social *varṇa* with the frequency of the other four seasons.[55]

The naturalistic explanation reduces the connections between particular seasons and the social classes to a set of homologies between climatic or calendric traits, on the one hand, and assumed social, temperamental, or even ontological traits, on the other. This kind of association is, however, but one of a multitude of *bandhus* or connections that tie the two orders of society and time together.

The connection between the social classes and the first three seasons is explicitly specified in Cosmogonies V, VIII, and X (Brahmins = spring; Kshatriyas = summer; Vaishyas = rainy season). Cosmogony V deliberately omits the season and the deity of the Shūdra string as part of the rationale for excluding the fourth *varṇa* from the sacrifice. We also observed earlier that in the ritual regulations guiding both the lighting of the sacrificial fires and the initiation into Veda study, the Shūdra is exempted. A seasonal correlate for this class is, under this logic, unnecessary.

Cosmogony X and some variants of Cosmogony VIII, however, insert *puṣṭa* (the power of material prosperity and abundance) into the slot within the fourth chain of associations occupied by the *brahman*, *kṣatra*, and *viś* in the first three chains. A lower class metaphysical power (see also the addition of the "world of food" to this chain in Cosmogony XIII) is in this way attributed to the autumn season. The homology between autumn and the power of natural and material reproduction could be called up to justify the entrance of the Rathakāra, the hybrid product of the Vaishyas and Shūdras, into the fire cult and the study of scripture. Or it might be used to argue for the assignment of the Vaishya to the autumn, rather than to the rainy season. The third and fourth seasons (like the third and fourth cardinal directions) seem to reflect the general ambiguity in the Veda about the categorization of the lower social classes. Note here again we observe the fluidity with which the systematizers alternated between the rainy season and the autumn as the season for the lower classes; such fluctuations recall similar variations in the spatial regions of the west and north.

Corroboration for these sorts of connections may be found in texts that prescribe the correct seasons in which members of the various social classes are to light the sacrificial fires:

> The spring is the *brahman*, the hot season is the *kṣatra*, and the rainy season is the *viś*. Therefore, a Brahmin should set up his fires in spring, for the spring is the *brahman*; a Kshatriya should set them up in the hot season, for the hot season is the *kṣatra*; and a Vaishya should set them up in the rainy season, for the rainy season is the *viś*. One who wants to become filled with the splendor of the *brahman* (*brahmavarcasa*) should set up his fires in spring. The spring is the *brahman*, and he will certainly become filled with *brahmavarcasa*. One who wants to become the *kṣatra*, together with excellence (*śriyā*) and fame (*yaśas*), should set up his fires in the hot seasons. The hot season is the *kṣatra*, and he will certainly become the *kṣatra*, together with excellence and fame. One who wants many offspring and livestock should set up his fires in the rainy season. The rainy season is the *viś*, and the *viś* are food. He certainly becomes one with many offspring and livestock who, knowing this, sets up his fires in the rainy season. (ŚB 2.1.3.5–8)

Here we have a text that simultaneously prescribes the season in which members of each social class should light the fires and details the powers inherent in each season. Each *varṇa* is matched with the season that holds within it the metaphysical power most appropriate to, and supposedly descriptive of, the class traits of the particular ritualist. The Brahmin should set his sacrificial fires in spring because "the spring is the *brahman*" and because such an action endows one with *brahmavarcasa*, the splendor of the *brahman* power.[56] The Kshatriya is matched to the summer, the season which "is" the *kṣatra* and which contains within it *śriyā* or "excellence" and *yaśas* or "fame."[57] The Vaishya is connected to the rainy season which is not only designated the temporal home of the *viś* but also holds within it those typically Vaishya qualities of food (for "the *viś* is food"), abundant progeny, and wealth in domestic animals. The three seasons of the half-year belonging to the gods are thus correlated with the three social *varṇa*s by means of certain inherent and differentiated powers and qualities common to the temporal and social analogues.

These inherent powers and qualities which the seasons and social classes are supposed to share are of two types. The "elemental qualities" of the *brahman*, *kṣatra*, and *viś* are the very heart and soul of what defines the three *varṇas*. But, as we observed once again in the text quoted above, the elemental qualities often entail what we have called "essential powers": the *brahman* is intimately tied to *brahmavarcasa*; the *kṣatra* is here linked to *śriyā* and *yaśas*; while the *viś* similarly has concomitant essential powers centering on nourishment ("food"), fecundity ("offspring"), and wealth ("livestock").

Often these sorts of essential powers function as surrogates for the elemental qualities, and thus provide a *varṇa* marking only slightly less explicit than the imprint of the elemental qualities themselves. TB 2.6.19.1–2 connects the spring with the quality of "fiery energy" or "brilliance" (*tejas*) along with other Brahmin signifiers such as the deities known as the Vasus, the *rathantara* chant, and the 9-versed hymn of praise; the hot season is correlated with "physical strength" (*bala*) (and also with the Rudras, the 15-versed hymn of praise, and the *bṛhat* chant); and the rainy season is associated with the *viś* and with *ojas* (as well as with the Ādityas, the 17-versed hymn of praise, and the the *vairūpa* chant). We also witnessed in Cosmogonies VIII and X how *puṣṭa*—the essential power of prosperity, abundance, and nourishment—stands within a series of associations including autumn in the place occupied by the three elemental qualities in the first three series (which include within them the spring, summer, and rainy seasons). A lower-class stamp is in this way put on the autumn season.

Another text, which assumes five seasons in the year, inflects three of the seasons with the elemental qualities and the other two with essential powers:

> Prajāpati, by means of the seasons, constructed the fire altar as the year. With the spring he built up its front half, with the hot season its right wing, with the rainy season its tail, with the autumn its left wing, and with the winter its middle. With the *brahman* he built up its front half, with the *kṣatra* its right wing, with livestock its tail, with the *viś* its left wing, and with expectation (*āśā*) its middle. (TS 5.6.10.1)

The five seasons, homologized to the body parts of the bird-shaped fire altar, are simultaneously correlated to various metaphysical powers. Spring, the hot season, and autumn are equated with the *brahman*, *kṣatra*, and *viś* respectively. The rainy season (connected to the Vaishyas in other texts) is here represented as embodying livestock or domestic animals—and, as in the case of assigning *puṣṭa* to the rains in Cosmogonies VIII and X, is thus vaguely lower class. The winter, on the other hand, is depicted as "expectation" or "hope," which carries no such *varṇa* associations. That season, the text seems to imply, is "extra" and "uninflected" in relation to the others.

A somewhat different formulation is set out at TB 1.1.2.6–8:

> A Brahmin should light the fire in spring. Spring is the Brahmin's season. He [the priest] thus places him [the Brahmin] in his own season, and he [the Brahmin] becomes filled with *brahmavarcasa*. Spring is the first (*mukham*) of the seasons. One who lights the fires in spring becomes preeminent (*mukham*). . . . A Kshatriya should light the fires in the hot season. The hot season is the Kshatriya's season. He thus places him in his own season, and he becomes filled with physical power (*indriya*). A Vaishya should light the fires in the autumn. Autumn indeed is the season of the Vaishya. He thus places him in his own season, and he becomes a possessor of livestock.

The Kshatriya and the hot season are in this passage connected with essential power called *indriya*, "physical power"; and the Vaishya is here not assigned to the rainy season, as in other texts of this sort, but rather to the autumn. Like the rainy season in other texts, however, the autumn is regarded as conducive to the obtainment of wealth in the form of domestic animals and is therefore the season of choice for the Vaishya. We thus have here another example of the seeming interchangeability of the fall and rainy season as Vaishya seasons. As in other schemes, the quality associated with both the Brahmin and the spring is declared to be *brahmavarcasa*. This text further links the Brahmin and his season by developing the notion of the spring as the "first" season of the year, and thus the analogue of the class which regards itself as "first among men": "Whoever sets the fire in spring becomes preeminent (*mukham*)."[58] The linkage of spring and the Brahmins by reason of their primordial and generative qualities—they are the components which hold within themselves all subsequent members of their category *in nuce*—may also be implied here.[59]

Texts which conjoin particular seasons with particular metaphysical powers or qualities emphasize, as expected, the Brahmin nature of the spring, the Kshatriya hue of the summer, and the Vaishya characteristics of the rainy season and/or autumn. The latter two seasons are, like the west and the north, sometimes reduplicated correlates to the *viś*, the people in general, and thus, in this case, may be assigned to either the Vaishya or the Rathakāra. The winter and cool season are "extra" seasons—just as the north is often left as the surplus spatial direction—when the fundamentally tripartite *varṇa* scheme (which sometimes expands into a quadripartite one) is overlaid upon a temporal structure of five or six categories.

The Parts of the Day

The seasons "are" the year (ŚB 8.7.1.1), and the components of the temporal whole are correlated with the elements of the social whole and their representatives in other spheres. The seasons are also assimilated to the principal divisions of another temporal unit, the solar day, which is itself said to be a resembling image of the year. "The sun is all the seasons," it is declared:[60] "When it rises, then it is spring. When the cows are herded together [for milking], it is summer. When it is midday, it is the rainy season. When it is afternoon, it is autumn. And when it sets, then it is winter" (ŚB 2.2.3.9). The progression of the five seasons of the year is here represented, in miniature, in the progression of the parts of the day. Thus the day, one of the smallest units of time in Vedic thought, can be represented as an image of the temporal whole.

The day is usually regarded as threefold:[61] morning, midday, and afternoon. These are the times when the three "pressings" or libations of soma are offered within the soma ritual. "Through these pressings they seek to obtain the sun: by the morning pressing [they obtain] the rising sun; by the midday pressing, the sun in the middle [of his daily course]; by the third pressing, the sun as it sets" (KB 18.9). These three parts of the day are identified with with larger temporal units,[62] including the spring, summer, and either the rainy season or autumn.

Observe the way the three portions of the day are identified with the spring, summer, and autumn in the following text:

> The sun up there did not shine. The gods wanted to find an expiation for him. For him they offered up these dewlapped animals—to Agni one with a black neck, to Indra one of different colors, to Bṛhaspati a white one. With these they restored his light. One who wants the splendor of the *brahman* should offer dewlapped animals—to Agni one with a black neck, to Indra one of different colors, to Bṛhaspati a white one. He thus finds help in these deities by providing each with his own share. They put the splendor of the *brahman* in him, and he becomes one who has the splendor of the *brahman*. He should offer the animal with the black neck to Agni when it is spring, and in the morning. [He should offer] the animal of different colors to Indra when it is the hot season, and at midday. [He should offer] the white animal to Bṛhaspati when it is autumn, and in the afternoon. These are the brilliances (*tejas*es) of the sun—in the spring in the morning; in the hot season at midday; in the autumn in the afternoon. (TS 2.1.2.4–5)

Morning and spring, the hot season and midday, and autumn and afternoon are presented here as analogues and pairs, and are further defined by the deities for whom the animals are slaughtered at those times. Agni and Indra, the deities of the spring and the hot season, are also the deities of morning and noon respectively, while the Brahmin god Bṛhaspati, not infrequently found connected to the fourth season, is here somewhat uncharacteristically also assigned to the afternoon.

A more frequently encountered pattern, indeed a pattern we might even call standard or paradigmatic, correlates the afternoon with the Vaishya order of things, including the Vaishya gods known as the Viśva Devas, while the morning and noon are, as above, given over to the Brahmins and Kshatriyas and their respective divine personifications. Let us here recall the filled-out chains of associations previously labeled Cosmogony I:

1. MORNING = Brahmins = Agni = *gāyatrī* = *brahman* = the Self
2. MIDDAY = Kshatriyas = Indra = *triṣṭubh* = *kṣatra* = humans
3. AFTERNOON = Vaishyas = Viśva Devas = *jagat* = *viś* = animals

The social classes connected to the three divisions of the day are explicitly set out here,[63] and they are reinforced by the appropriate elemental qualities (*brahman*, *kṣatra*, and *viś*),[64] gods (Agni, Indra, and the Viśva Devas), and ontological classes (the Self, humans, and animals), as well as the standard meters for each *varṇa* (*gāyatrī*, *triṣṭubh*, and *jagatī*).

The three parts of the day are also associated with various "essential powers" that also denote *varṇa*. The morning possesses *brahmavarcasa* (ŚB 4.1.1.7,14), midday is associated with physical power (PB 4.4.8–9), and the afternoon procures offspring, livestock, and/or prosperity for the sacrificer.[65] One text constructs a similar configuration: morning = *tejas* and *brahmavarcasa*, midday = strength, and the afternoon = food, men, livestock, and abundance.

> The [verses] at the morning service [of a soma sacrifice included within the Vājapeya ritual] contain the words "bright" (*śukra*) and "light" (*jyotis*). With these [verses] he obtains *tejas* and *brahmavarcasa*. The [verses] containing the word 'strength' (*vāja*) occur in the midday service—these in order to reach the world of heaven. The verses in the afternoon service contain the words "food" (*anna*), "troop" (*gaṇa*), and "animal" (*paśu*). With these [verses] he obtains abundance (*bhūman*). (PB 18.7.2–4)

Cosmogony I articulates the *varṇa* of the three parts of the day also in the idiom of ontology: the Brahmin morning is identified with the Self (i.e., "this all" or the cosmic whole in its ontological guise); the Kshatriya midday is equated to human beings (whom the Kshatriyas rule physically and politically); and the Vaishya afternoon is associated with domestic animals. An alternative set of homologies relays much the same message: "The morning belongs to the gods, the midday to men, and the afternoon to the ancestors" (ŚB 2.4.2.8; cf. 1.6.3.12). In both formulations, the hierarchical order of three classes of beings constitutes a hierarchical order of the three main divisions of the day.[66]

The theological encoding of morning, noon, and afternoon as the periods of the Brahmin deity Agni, the Kshatriya Indra, and the Viśva Devas (the gods of the Vaishya class) is often repeated in Vedic texts.[67] The context for such identifications between the three divisions of the day and these deities is the three pressings of the soma plant in the large-scale soma ritual. The ritualists, however, frequently identified smaller-scale sacrifices and the sacrifice of soma.[68] The following text utilizes connections between the three times of the day and the three *varṇa*-encoded deities to contend that the New Moon sacrifice recapitulates the more complex soma ritual:[69]

> And on the next day there are Agni's cake and Indra's milk offering. His [offering of] Agni's cake is, as it were, the morning libation [at the soma sacrifice], for the morning libation belongs to Agni. His [offering of] the milk offering to Indra is, as it were, the midday libation, for the midday libation belongs to Indra. And

when, at the new moon, he offers the cake dedicated to Indra–Agni on the first day, that is his third libation [at the soma sacrifice]. The third libation belongs to the Viśva Devas, and Indra and Agni are all the gods. (ŚB 2.4.4.12–13)

Among other homologies this text puts forward—including that which links Agni and the morning, Indra and the midday, and the Viśva Devas and the afternoon—note the claim that Indra and Agni, the deities of the two ruling classes, are interchangeable with the plurality known as the Viśva Devas, for the pair is declared to be "all the gods." This identification can be translated into social discourse: the Brahmins and Kshatriyas together are presented as encompassing within them "all others"—the *viś* particularly or society in general.

Agni is the deity of the morning for the same reason that he is located in the "first" world (earth) and the foremost season of the year (spring): "Agni is the beginning of the gods. Thus at the beginning [of the day] he delights the gods" (KB 5.5). As the "beginning of the gods," Agni also is said to bring all the other deities to the sacrifice at the commencement of the ritual in the morning (KB 12.7).

"Indra was not victorious at the morning pressing," or so it is written. But the warrior god conquers the next pressing, penetrating its defenses, as it were: "With these [verses] he penetrated toward the midday pressing. Because he penetrated toward, therefore these verses contain [the words] 'penetrate toward'" (AitB 6.11). Indra is equated to the center of the body and is thus also the deity of the middle of the day (ŚB 11.7.2.5), and as Alfred Hillebrandt noted, Indra's identification with the sun plays a role in the correlation between this deity and both the summer season and noon: "Thus Indra is located not only at the zenith of the day but of the year as well."[70]

The Viśva Devas are declared to be "everything here," as well as the gods of the afternoon soma pressing; furthermore, the Viśva Devas are said to be the summation of all ontological categories—gods, men, and ancestors—and also of the three Vedas (ŚB 4.4.1.9-13). The general nature of the Viśva Devas is thus called up to explicate their location in the concluding third of the day, the catchall category for everything—and everybody—not located in the Brahmin morning and the Kshatriya noon. A certain offering is made neither in the morning (which belongs to the gods) nor at noon (the time of the ancestors), for "were he to offer it at the morning pressing or at the midday pressing, he would cause strife between the gods and the ancestors. He offers it at the third pressing, because the third pressing belongs to the Viśva Devas. Thus he does not cause strife" (ŚB 4.4.2.3).

Other schemes assign groups of gods to each of the day's three divisions; but in these texts, too, the *varṇa* of each portion of the day is clear from the divine group connected with it. "The morning pressing belongs to the [Brahmin gods, the] Vasus, the midday pressing to the [Kshatriya] Rudras, the third pressing to the Ādityas [Vaishya deities]," according to one such formula (KB 16.1, 30.1). "There are three kinds of gods," according to another text, "the Vasus, the Rudras, and the Ādityas. The soma services are divided among them. The morning pressing belongs to the Vasus, the midday pressing to the Rudras, and the third pressing to the Ādityas" (ŚB 4.3.5.1; cf. ŚB 12.3.4.1; JUB 4.2.2–9; ChU 3.16.1–

5). Yet another passage agrees that the Vasus and the Rudras are the deities of the first two day parts and connects either the Ādityas or the Viśva Devas to the afternoon.[71]

Theological signifiers thus express the *varṇa* classification of the three parts of the day: the Brahmin morning is correlated with Brahmin deities such as Agni and/or the Vasus; the Kshatriya noon is connected to Indra and/or the Rudras; and the Vaishya afternoon belongs to the Viśva Devas or the Ādityas.[72]

Another set of ciphers for the *varṇa* affiliation of the parts of the day is that of the meters. Cosmogony I—and many other texts—links morning to the *gāyatrī*, noon to the *triṣṭubh*, and afternoon to the *jagatī*,[73] meters which are also routinely assigned to the Brahmins, Kshatriyas, and Vaishyas respectively.

The preeminence of both the Brahmin meter and the Brahmin portion of the day is emphasized in the following creation myth. The *gāyatrī*, it is said, once took the form of a bird:

> What she grabbed with her right foot became the morning pressing. The *gāyatrī* made that her own home. Therefore people regard it as the most perfect of all the pressings. He who knows this becomes foremost, the best, and attains preeminence. And what she grasped with her left foot became the midday pressing. But it fell apart and thus did not match the previous pressing. The gods wanted to rectify this. They put into it the *triṣṭubh* from among the meters and Indra from the deities. With that [in it] it became equal in strength (*vīrya*) to the previous pressing. He who knows this becomes successful with both pressings of equal strength and equal in relationship. What she grasped with her mouth became the third pressing. While flying she sucked out its sap, and with its sap depleted it did not equal the two previous pressings. The gods wanted to rectify this. They perceived [this pressing] in livestock. When they pour in an admixture [of milk], and proceed with the [offering of] butter and with the animal [offering], with that it became of equal strength with the previous two pressings. He who knows this becomes successful with pressings of equal strength and equal in relationship. (AitB 3.27)

The Brahmin meter, the *gāyatrī*, is here represented as not only the "first" among all meters but the creator of the others; and the morning—the Brahmin portion of the day—is the "most perfect." Brahmin components are here once again depicted as self-contained, primary, and preeminent, the womb or mother of the others.[74] And, moreover, "he who knows this becomes foremost, the best, and attains preeminence." The midday, the Kshatriya portion of the day, and the Vaishya afternoon were, it is said, originally inferior to the morning. Only when the midday was supplemented with the *triṣṭubh* meter and the warrior god Indra and the afternoon infused with livestock (the "power" of the third *varṇa*) were these two temporal units brought up to par.[75]

The almost invariable standardization of the connections between these three meters and the three day parts is revealed in part by counterinjunctions prohibiting alterations.[76] The morning pressing, for example, is not to be accompanied by verses other than the *gāyatrī* lest "he disturbs the beginning of the sacrifice from its appointed meter" (KB 25.3; cf. ŚānĀ 1.2; KB 26.8). Similarly, meters other than the *triṣṭubh*[77] are declared "unsuitable" for use in the ceremonies surrounding the midday pressing of soma (PB 4.4.8–9; cf. AitB 6.30). These well-known homologies between the day parts and the meters can also in and of themselves serve to transform, in a symbolic manner, simpler sacrifices or individual rites into resembling forms of the complex full-blown one-day soma sacrifice.[78]

These particular meters and parts of day are also connected to the appropriate deities. Agni, Indra, and the Viśva Devas are the trio usually so conjoined (e.g., Cosmogony I and ŚB 11.5.9.7). The interrelations between these gods, meters, and parts of the day are indeed so well known that in some cases a kind of shorthand code is employed. A certain recitation can be homologized to the soma sacrifice in its entirety by calling up identifications from the different paralleling orders: "He recites the *prauga* in the *gāyatrī* meter, and thus the morning pressing is obtained. [He recites it] addressed to Indra, thereby the midday pressing is obtained. [He recites it] addressed to the Viśva Devas, and thereby the third pressing is obtained" (KB 14.4). Elsewhere, the deities that participate in the triangle of triads (day parts/gods/meters, each in threes) are the groups of gods that are also identified as Brahmin, Kshatriya, and Vaishya, namely, the Vasus, Rudras, and Ādityas.[79]

In a kind of ultimate resolution of these interrelations, the three gods (Agni, Indra, and the Viśva Devas), the set of the three groups of gods (the Vasus, Rudras, and Ādityas), the three meters (*gāyatrī*, *triṣṭubh*, and *jagatī*), and the three parts of the day are all implicated in the same web of *bandhus*:

> Then they divided this sacrifice, [the soma sacrifice identified with] Viṣṇu, into three parts. The Vasus [received] the morning pressing, the Rudras the midday pressing, and the Ādityas the third pressing. Agni [received] the morning pressing, Indra the midday pressing, and the Viśva Devas the third pressing. The *gāyatrī* [received] the morning pressing, the *triṣṭubh* the midday pressing, and the *jagatī* the third pressing.[80]

We are presented here with three *varṇa*-oriented chains of homologies, one set of elements of which is the three portions of the day:

1. MORNING = Vasus = Agni = *gāyatrī* meter [Brahmin]
2. MIDDAY = Rudras = Indra = *triṣṭubh* meter [Kshatriya]
3. AFTERNOON = Ādityas = Viśva Devas = *jagatī* meter [Vaishya]

In Chapter 5 we observed how the Vedic systematizers co-ordered the two principal spatial realms—the three worlds and the four cardinal directions—with the usual pattern being earth = east, atmosphere = south, and sky = west,[81] with the north being the "extra" or "surplus" component.[82] Thus far in this chapter, we have witnessed comparable attempts to coordinate the different temporal units. The year, as the temporal whole, functions as a kind of prototype, and lesser time increments are constituted as resembling counterparts of the year. As the day and night of the gods, the two halves of the year are assimilated to the six seasons (divided into two groups of three seasons each), to the two fortnights of the lunar month, and to the solar day and night. The solar day itself is also equated to the year as a whole, while yet another identification links the half-year (the "gods' day") comprised of the first three seasons to the three times of the solar day. The five seasons are identified with the solar day conceived as pentadic in structure. And in other instances the three seasons (spring, summer, and the rains or autumn as the third) are united with the morning, midday, and afternoon.

The various temporal units are made into analogues of the whole (the year), and also of each other. And, as in the case of the classification of space, such interlocking can be done by virtue of the fact that different elements share the same *varṇa*. The spring among the seasons and the morning portion of the day (like the earth and the east) are equally regarded as Brahmin times; and the hot season and noon (like the atmosphere and the south) are categorized as Kshatriya. The afternoon, the Vaishya portion of the day, is sometimes assimilated to the rainy season. A structural parallel can thus be drawn between the first three seasons of the year (the "gods' day") and the three times of the (humans') day. Alternatively, the afternoon is conjoined with the autumn as Vaishya analogues. In any case, *varṇa* classification brings temporal units into relations of mutual resemblance, recapitulation, or even reduplication.

When interjected into different temporal structures, *varṇa* categories play an important role in constituting the affinities the components of these structures share one with another; conversely, the different temporal analogues lend cosmological weight to the rhetoric of social classification.

Correlating Space and Time

We conclude our survey of the classification of space and time in the Veda by turning to complex structures of equivalences in which spatial and temporal units are interrelated. We have seen how Vedic classifiers regarded the different units of space as themselves correlative—worlds were homologized with cardinal directions. They also viewed the different elements of time as homologous—the parts of the day and the seasons could also be connected. And, as we shall now observe, the classifiers joined both space and time together into structures composed of mutually resembling spatial and temporal taxons, structures which are often infused with, organized by, and/or generative of *varṇa* significations.[83]

One way in which spatial and temporal categories are intermixed is to represent the Cosmic One as an entity composed of twenty-one parts: twelve months, five seasons, three worlds, and the sun as the culminating twenty-first.[84] Another example of the classifiers at work integrating space and time is the portrayal of the creator god, Prajāpati or Puruṣa, as the summation of both the spatial and temporal wholes, that is, the year and the three worlds. Under the logic of resemblance, the year and the worlds can also be conceived as images of one another, for either may be regarded as the "all" (e.g., ŚB 8.2.1.17, 13.6.1.11).

The components of space and time are interdependent parts of the spatial–temporal whole, and one myth of creation puts this notion into narrative form:

> At the end of a year [floating in a golden egg on the cosmic waters] Prajāpati

> tried to speak. He uttered the syllable "*bhūḥ*" and this became this earth; he said "*bhuvaḥ*" and this became the atmosphere; he said "*svaḥ*" and this became yonder sky. Therefore a child tries to speak at the end of a year, for at the end of a year Prajāpati tried to speak. . . . These [three utterances] consist of five syllables. He made them into the five seasons, and thus there are these five seasons. (ŚB 11.1.6.3,5)

The text smoothly alternates between temporal and spatial structures, interweaving them as it goes along. The creator god lies within the cosmic egg for a year, the duration of the temporal whole, before he utters the three utterances which bring the three worlds, the spatial whole, into existence. The five syllables that constitute the three utterances (and the three spatial worlds) then re-form to create the five seasons.

More systematic identifications linking spatial and temporal orders interlace the four classificatory schemes analyzed in some depth in this and the previous chapter: the three worlds, cardinal directions, seasons, and the divisions of the day. Each of the two spatial schemes (worlds and directions) is related to each of the two temporal schemes (seasons and day parts). Let us examine these match-ups one by one.

Worlds and Parts of the Day

The cleanest correlations occur when the numerical components of the respective spatial and temporal schemes are equivalent. Connections between the three worlds and the three divisions of the day are of this sort—and both triads can easily be equated with the three principal social classes. AitB 1.23 relates how the gods used ritual means to defeat the demons and expel them from the three worlds: in the morning, they were banished from the earth, at midday from the atmosphere, and in afternoon the demons were expelled from the sky. Connections like these between morning and earth, midday and atmosphere, and afternoon and sky erase temporal and spatial boundaries in order to construct something of a Vedic space–time continuum.[85] They also correlate spatial and temporal components that, as we have seen, carry *varṇa* connotations. Thus the morning = earth homology is sensible when one knows that both are connected to the Brahmins, and so also are the other two space–time coordinates understandable as Kshatriya and Vaishya respectively.

Implicated, as they are, in a network of *bandhus*, such relatively simple equations between worlds and day parts (with social classes implied) are explicated even while being complicated by further associations the *varṇa* classificatory scheme can call upon. ChU 2.24.3–14, for example, also equates the earth and the morning, the atmosphere and midday, the afternoon and the sky, but it does so in the course of placing Brahmin deities (Agni and the Vasus) with earth and morning, Kshatriya gods (Vāyu and the Rudras) with atmosphere and midday, and Vaishya divinities (the Ādityas and Viśva Devas) with the sky and the afternoon. Theological concomitants of different sorts are interjected into several such spatial–temporal fusions, but all are markers for the same *varṇa* attributions for the three spatial-temporal pairs.[86] Thus when deities are added to the strings of associations the usual social assignation is clear: Brahmin = morning = earth; Kshatriya = midday = atmosphere; Vaishya = afternoon = sky.[87]

The same trick—correlating the three parts of the day, the three worlds, and the three social classes—can be achieved by combining the tripartite schemes of Cosmogonies I and II. Cosmogony I correlates the divisions of the day, the social classes, *varṇa*-encoded gods and meters, the elemental qualities, and three types of ontological beings:

1. MORNING = Brahmins = Agni = *gāyatrī* meter = the *brahman* power = the Self
2. MIDDAY = Kshatriyas = Indra = *triṣṭubh* meter = the *kṣatra* power = humans
3. AFTERNOON = Vaishyas = Viśva Devas = *jagatī* meter = the power of the *viś* = animals

Cosmogony II begins its series of connections with the sacred utterances that designate the three cosmological worlds (*bhūḥ*, *bhuvaḥ*, *svaḥ* = earth, atmosphere, sky), going on to link them to the same elemental qualities and ontological classes that Cosmogony I associates with the three parts of the day:

1. *bhūḥ* ⇒ EARTH = the *brahman* power = the Self
2. *bhuvaḥ* ⇒ ATMOSPHERE = the *kṣatra* power = humans
3. *svaḥ* ⇒ SKY = the power of the *viś* = animals

Combining Cosmogony I and II thus again gives us the spatiotemporal linkage between the triads of the day parts and the worlds, and does so within clearly demarked *varṇa* categorizations:

1. MORNING = Brahmins = Agni = *gāyatrī* meter = EARTH = the *brahman* power = the Self
2. MIDDAY = Kshatriyas = Indra = *triṣṭubh* meter = ATMOSPHERE = the *kṣatra* power = humans
3. AFTERNOON = Vaishyas = Viśva Devas = *jagatī* meter = SKY = the power of the *viś* = animals

Worlds and Seasons

When the three worlds are matched to another set of temporal increments—the seasons, usually enumerated as five or six—numerical congruence between the two orders is obtained only by omitting some of the seasons of the year from the syllogism, or by enumerating more than the original three spatial worlds. The first of these options is selected by the author or authors of ŚB 14.3.2.22-25, which goes to great lengths to show that offering of milk known as the *pravargya* is "everything":

> The *pravargya* is the year. The year is everything, and the *pravargya* is everything. When it is placed on the fire then it is spring; when it is burning hot then it is summer; when it is flowing over then it is the rainy season. . . . The *pravargya* is these worlds. These worlds are everything, and the *pravargya* is

> everything. When it is placed on the fire then it is this world; when it is burning hot then it is the atmosphere; and when it flows over then it is the sky. . . . The *pravargya* is those deities Agni, Vāyu, and Āditya. Those deities are everything, and the *pravargya* is everything. When it is placed on the fire then it is Agni; when it is burning hot then it is Vāyu; and when it flows over then it is Āditya. . . . The *pravargya* is the sacrificer—his self, his offspring, and his livestock. For the sacrificer is everything, and the *pravargya* is everything. When it is placed on the fire then it is his own self; when it is burning hot then it is his offspring; and when it flows over then it is his domestic animals. (ŚB 14.3.2.22–25)

The first three seasons of the year (spring, summer, and the rains)—which, we will recall, comprise the half-year known as the "gods' day" and which are also correlated with the Brahmin, Kshatriya, and Vaishya respectively—are here represented as structurally equivalent to the three worlds (earth, atmosphere, and sky). These two temporal and spatial triads are further associated with three deities (Agni, Vāyu, and Āditya) and three aspects of the sacrificer's complete being: his self, his offspring, and his domestic animals. Furthermore, the *varṇa*s of each chain are apparent on the basis of the components; thus we get the following sets: (1) Brahmin = SPRING = EARTH = Agni = the self; (2) Kshatriya = SUMMER = ATMOSPHERE = Vāyu = offspring; (3) Vaishya = RAINY SEASON = SKY = Āditya = livestock.[88] In this scheme, in order to correlate different measures of space and time the tripartite spatial cosmology (three worlds) necessitates an adjustment in the usual enumeration of the seasons—five or six contract to three (i.e., the "gods'" half of the year) in order to harmonize with the other sets.

Seasons and Directions

In other attempts at harmonizing the components of space and time, the five or six seasons of the full year are all mentioned and are correlated with the other principal spatial organizational scheme, the four cardinal directions. A problem of numerical congruence arises here too—five or six seasons must be matched with four cardinal directions. One way to solve it is to count the seasons at five and supplement the four cardinal directions with a fifth direction, the center or zenith. This is what happens in the following instance, which I cited earlier for a different purpose, where seasonal analogues for each of the "five quarters," and also metaphysical powers for all five spatial–temporal combinations, are articulated. In the beginning, "Prajāpati, by means of the seasons, constructed the fire altar as the year."

> With the spring he built up its front [eastern] half, with the hot season its right [southern] wing, with the rainy season its tail [i.e., western portion], with the autumn its left [northern] wing, and with the winter its middle. With the *brahman* he built up its front half, with the *kṣatra* its right wing, with livestock its tail, with the *viś* its left wing, and with expectation (*āśā*) its middle. (TS 5.6.10.1)

The three elemental qualities (*brahman*, *kṣatra*, and *viś*), together with the semi-metaphysical "livestock" and "expectation," provide the anchor for this pentadic spatial–temporal amalgam. Three of the seasonal and directional correlates are thus here again attached to one or another of the *varṇas*; and the connections made between *varṇas*, on the one hand, and specific seasons and cardinal directions, on the other, are consistent with the usual *varṇa* assignments given to these seasons and the cardinal directions: Brahmin = spring = east; Kshatriya = summer = south; Vaishya = west = rainy season. The fourth season (autumn) and the fourth direction (the miscellaneous north) are, as is also in keeping with texts on the seasons and directions analyzed in Chapter 5 and earlier in this chapter, imbued with a vaguely lower-class tinge by virtue of their linkage to domestic animals. The fifth triad is generated out of the need to attach a direction and metaphysical power to the fifth season, and the text does so in a suitably artificial manner (calling up the "center" direction and the very nebulous "power" of "expectation").

In another text (ŚB 8.6.1.16–20), the five seasons are also equated with the four directions plus the center. Here, additionally, appropriate deities are added to each of the five temporal–spatial pairs. Agni is the deity of both the spring and the east ("because they take him out [of the *gārhapatya* fire] toward the east, and attend upon him toward the east"); Vāyu rules the summer and south ("therefore it is in the south that he blows most"); the Āditya, the sun god, is connected (paradoxically but necessarily given the logic of the scheme) to the rainy season and the west ("for as soon as he rises all this embracing space comes into existence; and because he speaks of him as [being] behind, therefore one sees him only when he goes towards the west"); autumn and north belong to the deification of the sacrifice ("because the sacrifice is performed from the left/north side," i.e., clockwise); and winter and the center or zenith are associated with the rain god Parjanya ("because Parjanya is indeed above").

Again we observe the consistency and neatness of the first three chains of associations—the particular seasons, directions, and deities that are conjoined here are also regularly linked elsewhere, and the *varṇa* encoding of the first three strings (Brahmin, Kshatriya, and Vaishya) is readily apparent. The fourth and fifth chains in the pentadic structure are both less consistent (Parjanya, for example, one would expect to find not with the winter but with the rainy season) and less neat (one needs to add the zenith as the fifth direction to correlate with the winter season) than the first three. But this too we have come to expect; the fourth and fifth categories are often variable in meaning.

This sort of match between the directions and the seasons also occurs in several of the pentadic cosmogonies, which also correlate typically *varṇa*-encoded components (meters, hymns of praise, chants, deities, etc.) as well as elemental metaphysical powers that specify the social class entailed. As the summary of Cosmogonies VIII–X provided in Table 6.2 indicate, however, these texts count six seasons but only five directions. No matter. The cool and winter seasons are lumped together in the fifth category in order to achieve congruence. All three cosmogonies interlink the directions and the seasons: east and spring,[89] south and summer, west and the rains, north and autumn, and the zenith with the remaining two and here paired winter and cool seasons. Cosmogonies VIII and

TABLE 6.2. Summary of Space/Time Linkages in Cosmogonies VIII–X

Cosmogony VIII

1. EAST = *gāyatrī* meter = 9-versed hymn of praise = *rathantara* chant = Agni = SPRING = the *brahman*
2. SOUTH = *triṣṭubh* meter = 15-versed hymn of praise = *bṛhat* chant = Indra = SUMMER = the *kṣatra*
3. WEST = *jagatī* meter = 17-versed hymn of praise = *vairūpa* chant = Maruts = RAINY SEASON = the *viś*
4. NORTH = *anuṣṭubh* meter = 21-versed hymn of praise = *vairāja* chant = Mitra-Varuṇa = AUTUMN = *phala*
5. ZENITH = *paṅkti* meter = 27- and 33-versed hymn of praise = *śakvara* and *raivata* chants = Bṛhaspati = WINTER and COOL SEASONS = *varcas* or *phala*

Cosmogony IX

1. EAST ⇒ breath ⇒ SPRING ⇒ *gāyatrī* meter ⇒ *gayatra* chant ⇒ *upāṃśu* soma cup ⇒ 9-versed hymn of praise ⇒ *rathantara* chant ⇒ the seer Vasiṣṭha
2. SOUTH ⇒ mind ⇒ SUMMER ⇒ *triṣṭubh* meter ⇒ *aiḍa* chant ⇒ *antaryāma* soma cup ⇒ 15-versed hymn of praise ⇒ *bṛhat* chant ⇒ the seer Bharadvāja
3. WEST ⇒ eye (or sight) ⇒ RAINY SEASON ⇒ *jagatī* meter ⇒ *ṛksāma* chant ⇒ *sukra* soma cup ⇒ 17-versed hymn of praise ⇒ *vairūpa* chant ⇒ the seer Viśvamitra
4. NORTH ⇒ ear (or hearing) ⇒ AUTUMN ⇒ *anuṣṭubh* meter ⇒ *svāra* chant ⇒ *manthin* soma cup ⇒ 21-versed hymn of praise ⇒ *vairāja* chant ⇒ the seer Jamadagni
5. ZENITH ⇒ thought and speech ⇒ WINTER ⇒ *paṅkti* meter ⇒ conclusion of chants ⇒ *āgrāyana* soma cup ⇒ 27-versed and 33-versed hymns of praise ⇒ the *śakvara* and *raivata* chants ⇒ the seer Raivata Viśvakarman

Cosmogony X

1. EAST = SPRING = Agni = the *brahman* = *gāyatrī* meter = *rathantara* chant = 9-versed hymn of praise = track of 15-versed hymn of praise = Sanaga the seer = 18-month-old calf = *kṛta* dice throw = east wind
2. SOUTH = SUMMER = Indra = the *kṣatra* = *triṣṭubh* meter = *bṛhat* chant = 15-verse hymn of praise = track of 17-versed hymn of praise = Sanātana the seer = 2-year-old cow = *treta* dice throw = south wind
3. WEST = RAINY SEASON = Viśva Devas = the *viś* = *jagatī* meter = *vairūpa* chant = 17-versed hymn of praise = track of 21-versed hymn of praise = Ahabhūna the seer = 3-year-old cow = *dvāpara* dice throw = west wind
4. NORTH = AUTUMN = Mitra and Varuṇa = prosperity (*puṣṭa*) = *anuṣṭubh* meter = *vairāja* chant = 21-versed hymn of praise = track of 27-versed hymn of praise = Purāṇa [var. Pratna] the seer = 4-year-old cow = *abhibhava* [var. *askaṇḍa*] dice throw = north wind
5. ZENITH = WINTER and COOL SEASONS = Bṛhaspati = fruit (*phala*) [var. splendor (*varcas*)] = *paṅkti* meter = *śakvara* and *raivata* chants = 27-versed hymn of praise = track of 33-versed hymn of praise = Suparṇa the seer = 4-year-old bull = *askaṇḍa* [var. *abhibhū*] dice throw = wind from above

X are explicit about the *varṇa* attribution of the first three sets of homologies (correlating each with the powers of the *brahman*, *kṣatra*, and *viś* respectively) and also connect each with the deity proper to the class (the Brahmin deity Agni, the Kshatriya Indra, and the Vaishya groups, the Maruts or Viśva Devas). Both also imply a sort of generally lower class designation for the fourth set (which includes north and autumn) by connecting the essential power of *puṣṭa* (material prosperity and growth) to it. The fifth chain in these two cosmogonies is clearly a summation and transcendence of the previous four, containing two seasons, the winter and the cool season, that are linked to the zenith (as well as to the Brahmin power of *varcas* (splendor) and the Brahmin deity Bṛhaspati).[90]

Seasons, Directions, and Worlds

The seasons and the directions are made to correspond exactly in the six-part Cosmogony XIII. The two seasons collapsed into the fifth category in the pentadic taxonomies of Cosmogonies VIII–X are now separated into different categories, while the nadir is added to the zenith and the four quarters to make up six directions. Furthermore, another spatial correlate is added to the mix as the three worlds of Vedic cosmology are expanded here into six with the addition of "worlds" of food, animals, and the waters. Thus instead of omitting seasons in order to match the three worlds of Vedic cosmology as in structures mentioned previously, in this case the worlds are multiplied to match the number of seasons. Cosmogony XIII's six chains of associations are as follows (with the correlates for space and time capitalized):

1. first day = EARTH = *gāyatrī* meter = nine-versed hymn of praise = *rathantara* chant = EAST = SPRING = Vasus and Agni
2. second day = ATMOSPHERE = *triṣṭubh* meter = fifteen-versed hymn of praise = *bṛhat* chant = SOUTH = SUMMER = Maruts and Indra
3. third day = SKY = *jagatī* meter = seventeen-versed hymn of praise = *vairūpa* chant = WEST = RAINY SEASON = Ādityas and Varuṇa
4. fourth day = WORLD OF FOOD = anustubh meter = twenty-one-versed hymn of praise = *vairāja* chant = NORTH = AUTUMN = Sādhyas and Ājyas and Bṛhaspati and the moon
5. fifth day = WORLD OF ANIMALS = *paṅkti* meter = twenty-seven-versed hymn of praise = *śakvara* chant = ZENITH = WINTER = Maruts and Rudra
6. sixth day = WORLD OF WATERS = *atichandas* meter = thirty-three-versed hymn of praise = *raivata* chant = NADIR = COOL SEASON = Viśva Devas and Prajāpati

Cosmogony XIII thus provides us with a case in which both the spatial units of cosmological worlds and cardinal directions are correlated with the temporal entities of the six seasons. One could easily hypothesize the correlation of the three day parts to the first three strings of associations in this scheme; for if, as we have seen, the morning, noon, and afternoon can be matched with the earth, atmosphere, and sky (as in Cosmogonies I and II), so too could they be added here also to the triads of (1) east, south, and west, and (2) spring, summer, and the rainy season.

Directions and Parts of the Day

In Chapter 5 we observed how the three worlds can be coordinated with the cardinal directions. In this chapter we learned that temporal units can also be matched to one another: the three times of day and the first three seasons are regarded as analogues of one another. We have further witnessed how various combinations of spatial and temporal elements can occur: the three spatial worlds are integrated with the three times of the day; these worlds are also made to harmonize with the seasons; the seasons can be correlated with the cardinal directions; and the worlds, directions, and seasons can all become correlated in Cosmogony XIII.

The only permutation left to review here is the coordination of the three day parts and the (four, five, or six) directions. There are few texts, to my knowledge, which do this (and those which do often do so imperfectly). One such incomplete set of *bandhus* between the parts of the day and the directions is found at AitB 3.44:

> They should proceed with [the soma pressing] at an unhurried pace at the morning pressing, and also at the midday and third pressings. Then the sacrificer does not die suddenly. Because they proceed at an unhurried pace at the first two pressings, thus the villages of the east are densely populated. When they proceed hurriedly at the third pressing, therefore to the west there are great forests. Then the sacrificer is likely to die suddenly. Therefore they should proceed at an unhurried pace at the morning pressing, at the midday, and at the third pressing—so the sacrificer does not die suddenly.

This narrative, rather loosely, connects the morning and midday soma pressing to the "villages of the east" and the afternoon pressing to the "great forests" of the west. A second text also incompletely links the parts of the day with some of the cardinal directions:

> The demons, when they had been beaten back on the north [side of the sacrifice], ran around to the front [east] dressed in full battle array. The gods, upon realizing this, placed Agni around in the east at the time of morning pressing. With Agni in the east at the time of the morning pressing they beat back the demons and devils. . . . Therefore the morning pressing belongs to Agni. He beats back evil who knows this. The demons, beaten back on the east side, went around to the west and entered [the sacrificial grounds]. The gods, upon realizing this, placed the Viśva Devas, as their very self, around in the west at the time of the third pressing. With the Viśva Devas as their very selves, they beat back the demons and devils. Therefore the third pressing belongs to the Viśva Devas. He beats back evil who knows this. (AitB 6.4)

Here the morning belongs to Agni, who defends it from demons in the east, and the afternoon is similarly guarded by the Viśva Devas in the west. Taken together, the two texts seem to indicate that the east and the morning are analogues, as are the west and the afternoon, and that the first pair is ruled by the Brahmin god Agni and the second by the Vaishya gods. We may venture to extrapolate: the south and the midday could be interpolated into this fragmentary scheme, and they could be regarded, as a pair, as the Kshatriya component in the spatial–temporal conglomerate, just as each is regarded as Kshatriya when set within independent spatial and temporal schemes. Thus, while texts which explicitly and

TABLE 6.3. Correlations Between Different Measures of Space and Time and the Social Classes

	Brahmin	*Kshatriya*	*Vaishya*	*Other*
Worlds	earth	atmosphere	sky	"world of food"
Directions	east	south	west/north	north
Seasons	spring	summer	rainy/autumn	rainy/autumn
Partrs of the day	morning	midday	afternoon	

systematically interlink the times of the day with the directions of the compass are few and fragmentary, it is possible to reconstruct and extrapolate from texts in which the beginnings of such match-ups are found.

Conclusion

I do not wish (or need) to overstate the categorical claims here. I do not intend to present as monolithic, fixed, and complete what the Vedic systematizers often left diverse, fluid, and incomplete. Perhaps the Vedic classifiers just assumed some of what we have articulated here; perhaps we are here logically extrapolating from data the classifiers never thought to fill out. In any event, on the basis of the individual analyses of the classification of the three worlds, the cardinal directions, the seasons, and the parts of the day; on the basis of the amalgams the Vedic classifiers produced within the realms of time and space (correlating worlds and directions, on the one hand, and seasons and day parts on the other); and on the basis of the grand syntheses linking the temporal and spatial components—on these grounds, a generalized synthesis of our own is perhaps not entirely unjustified. An organizational chart of the elements of time and space together with their *varṇa* coordinates (Table 6.3), summarizes the general pattern of these *bandhus* or connections.

In the Veda, the components of space, time, and society mirrored one another. Classification in the spatial and temporal realms certainly is reflective of the classification of society and its parts; very probably, the former were generated out of the latter. Such projections from the social world into the very perception of space and time were among the more powerful of the classificatory conceits of the Brahmins. To apprehend the world as divided into discrete spatial and temporal units—directions and seasons, worlds and day parts—becomes a perpetual reaffirmation of the truth of *varṇa*, of the validity of a classificatory system that not only guides such basic perception as that of space and time but also that of social relations and hierarchy.

Categorizations of space and time arise out of fundamental cognitive needs. Furthermore, as Durkheim and others noted, spatial and temporal categories also express social needs—the need, for example, for setting aside special times and places for group activities. And one can go further. The particular modes of classifying space and time in a given society can also be an expression of class interests of those who do the classifying. The categorization of space and time can be made to be among the most subtly persuasive arguments for the social hierarchy and the different class privileges and penalties this manifestation of classification helps to legitimate and perpetuate. Precisely because the way space and time are perceived is usually unconscious, often assumed, and nearly always regarded as uncontroversial, the control of the categories through which such perception takes place is a powerful tool indeed.

In the Vedic instance, at least, there are good reasons to suppose that social categories always lie somewhere near the heart of the nexus of connections forged between spatial and temporal categories. Durkheim and Mauss proposed that all divisions of space and time had their origin in social divisions: "the first classes were social classes." While such speculation entails its own paradoxes (e.g., what provided the epistemological precedent for social classes?), and in any case lies beyond the scope of this work, it would seem indisputable that, at the very least, Vedic social categories were integrated into—and perhaps were the inspiration for—Vedic spatial and temporal categories. The classification of space and time can be understood to be just another reflex of the classification of society, an organizational effort whose success may have depended on projecting the form of the latter into other, and far less obvious, realms of social discourse.

NOTES

1. Edmund Leach, "Two Essays Concerning the Symbolic Representation of Time," in *Rethinking Anthropology* (London: Athlone Press, 1961), p. 132.

2. "Time," wrote Immanuel Kant, "is not an empirical concept that has been derived from any experience. For neither coexistence nor succession would ever come within our perception, if the representation of time were not presupposed as underlying them *a priori.*" *Critique of Pure Reason*, trans. by Norman Kemp Smith (New York: St. Martin's Press, 1965), p. 74.

3. Leach, "Two Essays," pp. 132, 125. Cf. the statement on p. 133: "Such facts show us that the regularity of time is not an intrinsic part of nature; it is a man made notion which we have projected into our environment for our own particular purposes." Similar conclusions were reached by E. E. Evans-Pritchard, *The Nuer: A Description of the Modes of Livelihood and Political Institutions of a Nilotic People* (Oxford: Clarendon Press, 1940) (see esp. p. 95: "The concept of seasons is derived from social activities rather than from the climatic changes which determine them"). Other anthropological studies of time that have problematized earlier Kantian notions of the inherent nature of temporal categories in the human mind include Henri Hubert and Marcel Mauss, "Étude sommaire de la représentation du temps dans la religion et la magie," in H. Hubert and M. Mauss, *Mélanges d'histoire des religions*, 2d ed. (Paris: Librairie Felix Alcan, 1929), pp. 189–229; Marcel Mauss, *Seasonal Variations of the Eskimo: A Study in Social Morphology*, trans. and ed. by James J. Fox (London: Routledge & Kegan Paul, 1979); A. Irving Hallowell, "Temporal Orientation in Western Civilization and in a Pre-literate Society," *American Anthropologist* 39 (1937): 647–70; and, more recently, Georges Gurvitch, *The Spectrum of Social Time*, trans. and ed. by Myrtle Korenbaum (Dordrecht: D. Reidel, 1964); and especially the essays collected in John Bender and David E. Wellbury, eds., *Chronotypes: The Construction of Time* (Palo Alto, Calif: Stanford University Press, 1991).

4. Émile Durkheim, *The Elementary Forms of the Religious Life*, trans. by Joseph Ward Swain (New York: Free Press, 1915), p. 23.

5. Quoted in Steven Lukes, *Émile Durkheim: His Life and Work: A Historical and Critical Study* (Harmondsworth, Middlesex, England: Penguin Books, 1973), p. 442. See also Hubert and Mauss, "Étude sommaire de la représentation du temps."

6. David Pocock, "The Anthropology of Time Reckoning," *Contributions to Indian Sociology* 7 (March 1964), pp. 25, 27. Pocock and others thus oppose earlier scholarship such as that of M. P. Nilsson, who in his *Primitive Time-Reckoning* (Lund: C. W. K. Gleerup, 1920) argued that "in the matter of the indications and reckoning of time we have not to do with a number of conceptions which may be supposed to be as various and numerous as we please. At the basis lies an accurately determined and limited number of phenomena, which are the same for all peoples all over the globe, and can be combined only in a certain quite small number of ways. These phenomena fall into two main groups: (1) the phenomena of the heavens—sun, moon, stars; (2) the phases of nature, the variations of the climate and plant and animal life—and these latter are of course dependent upon the sun" (pp. 2–3). Pocock points out that "it is by no means inevitable that a given society should find the movement of the heavenly bodies useful in ordering its affairs. Much of the evidence which Nilsson used shows how selective different peoples are in relation to natural phenomena in this regard" (p. 20).

7. Durkheim, *The Elementary Forms of the Religious Life*, p. 488.

8. A fairly superficial overview of this theme may be found in Siddheshwar Varma, "The Vedic Concept of Time," *Indian Linguistics* 27 (1966): 115–30.

9. E.g., ŚB 1.6.3.35, 3.2.2.4, 11.1.1.1, PB 16.4.12, JB 1.167; etc. See also Jan Gonda, *Prajāpati and the Year* (Amsterdam: North-Holland, 1984).

10. See also ŚB 12.3.2.1, cited below, where a similar equation is drawn between *saṃvatsara* and *yajamāna* ("sacrificer"). For an etymological explanation of the year as "all," ŚB 11.1.6.12: "Prajāpati reflected, 'All (*sarva*) I have obtained by stealth (*at-sāriṣam*), I who have emitted these deities.' This became *sarvatsara*, for *sarvatsara* is the same name as the year (*saṃvatsara*)."

11. For Prajāpati as the six seasons: ŚB 2.2.2.3, 5.2.1.3–4; as the twelve months: ŚB 2.2.2.4, 4.6.1.11, 5.2.1.2, 5.4.5.20; JB 1.135; as the twenty-four fortnights: ŚB 2.2.2.5, 4.6.1.12, 5.4.5.21; cf. KB 6.15; and as the 360 days and 720 days and nights, ŚB 10.4.2.2. Cf. ŚB 10.4.3.21, where the days and nights, the fortnights, the months, and the seasons are all forms of Agni (the fire altar) conceived as the year or "this all." For a complex statement of the different ways of calculating the year's numerical parts, see ŚB 8.4.1.8–28.

12. E.g., ŚB 5.2.1.5, 5.3.4.22, 5.4.5.19, PB 2.10.5, 18.6.5, 19.7.6, 20.4.2.

13. ŚB 1.3.5.10; cf. ŚB 8.4.1.11; AitB 1.1. For the numerical equation of the cosmic whole and 21, see below.

14. For the topic in general, see R. Shamashastry, *The Vedic Calendar* (reprint New Delhi: Ganga Publications, 1979). A sample of the large bibliography on time reckoning in South Asia would include M. M. Underhill, *The Hindu Religious Year* (Oxford: Oxford University Press, 1921); P. C. Sengupta, *Ancient Indian Chronology* (Calcutta: University of Calcutta, 1947); Luis Gonzalez Reimann, *Tiempo Ciclico y Eras del Mundo en la India* (Mexico City: College of Mexico, 1988); Apurba Kumar Chakravarty, *Origin and Development of Indian Calendrical Science* (Calcutta: Indian Studies Past and Present, 1975); Ruth C. Freed and Stanley A. Freed, "Calendars, Ceremonies and Festivals in a North Indian Village: Necessary Calendrical Information for Fieldwork," *Southwestern Journal of Anthropology* 20 (1964): 67–90; "Calendar in Hindu Tradition," Proceedings of a seminar held by the Institute of Traditional Cultures, Madras, *Bulletin of the Institute of*

Cultures, Madras 1 (1968): 42–144; and Judy F. Pugh, "Into the Almanac: Time, Meaning, and Action in North Indian Society," *Contributions to Indian Sociology* (n. s.) 17, 1 (1983): 27–49.

15. For the intercalary month, called Saṃsarpa, see TS 1.4.14, 6.5.3; BGS 2.10.3. For the notion of "thirteen months" (including the intercalary one), see ŚB 8.4.1.17,25 and 10.2.6.1: "The one-hundred-and-one-fold Prajāpati is the year. To him belong days and nights, half-months, months, and seasons. There are sixty days and nights of a month, and in the month the days and nights of the year are obtained. And there are twenty four half months, thirteen months, and three seasons [of four months each]; that makes a hundred parts and the year itself is the one hundred and first part."

16. BŚS 5.1. See also BŚS 5.5, 5.10, 5.18, 21.6. Assuming that the year begins on the full moon day of Phālguna, the first *cāturmāsya* includes the months of Caitra, Vaiśākha (= Mādhava, April–May), Jyaiṣṭha (= Śukra, May–June), and the first half of Āṣāḍha (= Śuci, June–July). The second *cāturmāsya* begins on the full moon day of Āṣāḍha and encompasses the second half of that month as well as the months of Śrāvaṇa (= Nabhas, July–August), Prauṣṭhapada (= Nabhasya, August–September), Āśvayuja (= Isas, September–October), and the first half of Kārtikka (= Ūrjas, October–November). The third *cāturmāsya* is inaugurated on the full moon day of Kārtikka, and lasts through Mārgaśīrṣa (= Saha, November–December), Taiṣya (= Sahasya, December–January), Magha (= Tapa, January–February) and the first half of Phālguna. If the beginning of the year is calculated at the full moon day of Caitra, the second and third four-monthly periods begin on the full moon days of Śrāvana and Mārgaśīrṣa. Consult P. V. Kane, *History of Dharmaśāstra*, 5 vols., 2d ed. (Poona: Bhandarkar Oriental Research Institute, 1974), Vol. II, Pt. 2, p. 1091.

17. For three *ṛtus*, see ṚV 10.90.6, 1.164.2,48; TB 1.3.10.3ff.; ŚB 10.2.6.1, 14.1.1.28. According to KB 11.7, there are 120 days in each season; and at ŚB 2.6.4.2ff. and elsewhere the Cāturmāsya sacrifice also assumes three *ṛtus* (for the sacrifice is performed three times a year and is divided into three parts called the *vaiśvadeva*, the *varuṇapraghāsā*, and the *śākamedhā*). As KB 29.8 makes clear these *ṛtus* are usually not, properly speaking, "seasons" but rather "periods" consisting of two seasons each. Cf. KB 14.5 ("There are six seasons. He recites each two quarter-verses [of a particular verse] separately. Therefore the season are united in pairs and called 'summer, rainy, and winter.' ") and ŚB 12.8.2.33-34 where, after declaring the three *ṛtus* as summer, the rains, and winter, ruled by Indra, Savitṛ, and Varuṇa, the text immediately observes that "there are six cups [of milk and liquor], for there are six seasons. He thereby obtains the seasons—the spring and summer by the two Āśvina [cups], the rainy season and autumn by the two Sārasvat ones, and the winter and cool season by the two Aindra ones. He thus wins and obtains the seasons for himself in accordance with their particular form and deity." ĀpŚS 8.4.13 calls the three "periods" spring, the rains, and autumn, while Śabara on JMS 11.2.13 (cited in Kane, *History of Dharmaśāstra*, Vol. II, Pt. 2, p. 1091) lists them as spring, the rains, and winter. The variability of the names used to depict these three periods would seem to indicate that they are not to be confused with the five or six seasons properly called.

18. Louis Renou, in an article entitled "Un thème litteraire en sanskrit: les saisons," found in his *Sanskrit et culture: L'apport de l'Inde à la civilisation humaine* (Paris: Payot, 1950), observes that "these six seasons break down a primary tripartite division" (p. 145, fn.). For a restatement of this claim ("the most ancient attestable Vedic year was comprised of but three seasons," p. 435, fn. 6) and a survey of the meaning of the term *ṛtu* (originally "repartition fonctionnelle" and only later coming to mean "period" or "season") see Renou, "Védique *ṛtu*," *Archiv Orientalni* 18, 1–2 (May 1950): 431–38. Consult also the

comprehensive study by V. Raghavan, *Ṛtu in Sanskrit Literature* (Delhi: Shri Lal Bahadur Shastri Kendriya Sanskrit Vidyapeeth, 1972); and, for the role of the seasons in traditional Indian medicine, Francis Zimmermann, "*Ṛtu-sātmya*: The Seasonal Cycle and the Principle of Appropriateness," trans. by McKim Marriott and John Leavitt, *Social Science and Medicine* 14B, 2 (May 1980): 99–106.

19. For early mention of the six seasons, see TS 5.1.9.1; AV 19.6. For the grouping of pairs of months into seasons, see TS 1.4.14, 4.4.11, 6.5.3; ŚB 7.4.2.29ff., 8.2.1.16ff., 8.3.2.5ff., 8.4.2.1.14ff., 8.5.2.14, 8.6.1.20, 8.7.1.1ff.; BGS 2.10.2-7; BPitṛS 2.4; BŚS 20.16.24,27, 24.12-16; BhŚS 5.1-3; ĀśvŚS 2.1; ŚŚS 2.1; VaitŚS 5; and Kauṭilya Artha Śāstra 2.20.62–68.

20 . "There are five seasons because of the union of winter and the cool season" (AitB 1.1). For five seasons, see TS 1.6.1.2, 1.6.2.3, 4.3.3.2, 7.3.8.1; ŚB 3.9.4.11, 6.2.2.3, 9.2.3.6, 11.1.6.5, 13.1.7.3; TB 3.8.10.2, 3.8.17.2; and ŚB 8.4.1.11–13 (verses 14, 21, 22, and 28, however, count six seasons while verses 15–17, 23, 25 number seven seasons).

21. See ŚB 10.2.6.2 and the previous note. The flexibility with which the Vedic ritualists operated in enumerating the seasons is demonstrable in texts like ŚB 12.3.2.1: "The year is man. Man is one thing and the year is another, but these now [because of the *bandhu*] are one and the same. In the year there are two, day and night, and in man there are these two breathings—and these now are one and the same. There are three seasons in the year, and these three breathings in man, and these are now one and the same. 'Year' (*saṃvatsara*) consists of four syllables, and so does 'sacrificer' (*yajamāna*)—and these are now one and the same. There are five seasons in the year, and these five breathings in man, and these are now one and the same. There are six seasons in the year, and these six breathings in man, and these two are now one and the same. There are seven seasons in the year, and these seven breathings in man, and these are now one and the same."

22. For an enumeration of the *nakṣatras*, often depicted as ruled by a particular deity and conducive to the acquisition of various qualities, powers, and attainments, consult TS 4.4.10.1–3; TB 1.5.1–3, 3.1.1–6; BŚS 10.46, 28.3–4; ĀpŚS 17.6.5–11; KS 39.13; MS 2.13.20; MŚS 6.2.3; BGS 1.1.20–21; BGPariS 1.2.14, 1.13.3–8; BGŚeṣaS 1.13. See also B. V. Kamesvara Aiyer, "The Lunar Zodiac in the Brāhmaṇas," *Indian Antiquary* 48 (June 1919): 95–97.

23. See ŚB 12.3.2.5: "There are 10,800 *muhūrtas* in the year; there are fifteen times as many *kṣipras* as there are *muhūrtas*; and fifteen times as many *etarhis* as there are *kṣipras*, and fifteen times as many *idānis* as there are *etarhis*; and fifteen times as many breathings as there are *idānis*," etc. Cf. Manu 1.64.

24. For a slightly different series of equations, in which the ritual *upasads* or sacrificial ceremonies are homologized with larger units of time, see ŚB 3.4.4.17–20: "He should perform three *upasads*, for since there are three seasons in the year this is made into the form of the year. He thus perfects the year. He performs each two times. This amounts to six, for since there are six seasons in the year this is made into the form of the year. He thus perfects the year. If he should perform twelve *upasads* [it is because] there are twelve months in the year, and this is made into the form of the year. He thus perfects the year. He performs each twice. This amounts to twenty-four, for since there are twenty-four half-months in the year this is made into the form of the year. He thus perfects the year." For the inverse of this phenomenon, whereby larger periods of time (e.g., days) are equated to smaller ones (e.g., parts of the day), see PB 20.16.9.

25. Cf. Leach's general statement that in "primitive societies," "time is experienced as something discontinuous, a repetition of repeated reversal, a sequence of oscillations between polar opposites: night and day, winter and summer, drought and flood, age and

youth, life and death. In such a scheme the past has no 'depth' to it, all past is equally past; it is simply the opposite of now. . . . Night and day, life and death are logically similar pairs only in the sense that they are both pairs of contraries. It is religion that identifies them, tricking us into thinking of death as the night time of life and so persuading us that nonrepetitive events are really repetitive." "Two Essays Concerning the Symbolic Representation of Time," p. 126.

26. The two halves of the year—called the "northern" and "southern passages" of the sun—thus participate in the opposition (north : south :: gods : ancestors) that I discussed in Chapter 5.

27. See, however, Manu 1.66, where the fortnight of the waning moon is said to be the ancestors' day, while that of the waxing moon is the ancestors' night: "A month is a day and a night of the ancestors, and it is divided into two lunar fortnights. The dark [fortnight] is the day for them to move about in their activity, and the bright [fortnight] is the night for their sleep."

28. E.g., ŚB 2.1.4.9: "The gods are the day. The ancestors are not free from evil, and he is not free from evil [if he churns the fire before sunrise]. The ancestors are mortal, and he who churns the fire before the sun rises dies before [he has lived a long] life. The gods are free from evil, and he is freed from evil [and becomes immortal if he churns the fire after sunrise]." Cf. ŚB 2.1.3.1. ŚB 11.1.6.7–8,11 states that the day belongs to the gods and the night to the demons. For the tripartite homology between morning, midday, and afternoon, on the one hand, and gods, men, and ancestors, on the other, see below. See also AitB 5.28, where humans and gods reciprocate in an ongoing sacrifice which alternates between day and night: humans are offered as sacrificial fees to the gods in the afternoon libation, and gods become the sacrificial fees to humans in the morning libation.

29. For the god's "day" as the first three seasons of the year and the divine "night" (equated also with the ancestors) made up of the last three seasons, see also ŚB 2.6.1.1–2.

30. For other equations between the ancestors, the fortnight of the waning moon, and the afternoon, see KB 5.6; ŚB 2.4.2.7–8; Manu 3.278. Cf. ŚB 13.8.1.3–4, where uneven years, single *nakṣatras*, the new moon (since the new moon is a single *nakṣatra*), autumn ("for the autumn is the '*svadhā*' call, and the '*svadhā*' call is the food of the ancestors"), and the hot season are declared the times of the ancestors.

31. For *varṇa* classifications of other units of time, see KB 4.8 (full moon = Brahmin, new moon = Kshatriya); and TB 3.9.14.2–3; ŚB 13.1.5.4–5 (day = Brahmin, night = Kshatriya). For the later Hindu notion that the four *yugas* or great "ages" are representative of the four *varṇas*, see the interpolated verse at Manu 1.86 in the Sanskrit edition edited by J. H. Dave (Bombay: Bhāratīya Vidyā Bhavan, 1972), p. 119: The Brahmin = the Kṛta Yuga, the Kshatriya = the Tretā Yuga, the Vaishya = the Dvāpara Yuga, and the Shūdra (of course) = the Kali Yuga. Compare this to the component of the dice throw in Cosmogony X.

32. ŚB 2.1.3.5. For an overview of the texts that prescribe the seasons in which members of the different *varṇas* were to set the fires, see R. N. Dandekar, ed. and trans., *Śrautakośa*, 2 vols. (Poona: Vaidika Saṃśodhana Maṇḍala, 1958), Vol. I, Pt. 1, pp. 1–26.

33. TB 1.1.4.8; BŚS 2.12; BhŚS 5.2.4; ĀpŚS 5.3.18–19; HŚS 3.2; VaikhŚS 1.1; cf. KŚS 1.1.9, 4.7.7, 4.9.5 (with commentary); VŚS 1.4.1.1. BŚS 20.16; BhŚS 5.1-3; ĀśvŚS 2.1; and ŚŚS 2.1 declare that the rainy season is the time when both the Rathakāra and Vaishya should set the sacrificial fires. See Christopher Minkowski, "The Rathakāra's Eligibility to Sacrifice," *Indo-Iranian Journal* 32, 3 (July 1989): 177–94.

34. E.g., TS 5.6.10.1; TB 1.1.2.7; BŚS 20.16; ĀśvŚS 2.1; BhŚS 5.2.1–5. ŚŚS 2.1–5 gives the Vaishya the option of setting his fires in either autumn or the rainy season.

35. See, e.g., ĀpGS 4.10.4; HGS 1.1.1.4; VaikhSmS 2.3; BDhS 1.2.3.10; ĀpDhS

1.1.1.19; and Brian K. Smith, "Ritual, Knowledge, and Being: Initiation and Veda Study in Ancient India," *Numen* 33, 1 (1986): 65-89. BGS 2.5.6 and BhGS 1.1 also allow for the initiation of the Rathakāra. His initiation should occur in the rainy season, just as the rainy season is the time assigned to the Rathakāra for establishing his *śrauta* fires in some texts. Shūdras, of course, are excluded from both initiation into the study of the Veda and setting up the sacrificial fires.

36. We need not be detained here with the unvarying *bandhus* between the seasons and the *varṇa*-encoded meters, hymns, and hymns of praise. For an exceptional series of correlations between the deities and the seasons, see ŚB 12.8.2.7ff., where it is stated that Indra rules the hot season, Savitṛ the rainy season, and Varuṇa the winter. Additionally, the Aśvins are said to be the deities of the spring and the hot season, Sarasvatī belongs to the rains and autumn, and winter and the cool season are related to Indra.

37. E.g., Cosmogonies V, VIII, X, XII, and XIII. For the connections between Agni and spring and Indra and the hot season, see also ŚB 13.5.4.28 and TS 2.1.2.4–5. For the Vasus and spring and the Rudras as the deities of the hot season, see also TS 7.1.18.1; TB 2.6.19.1; and TĀ 1.3.3–4.

38. As in Cosmogonies V and X.

39. For the Maruts and the rainy season, Cosmogony VIII; ŚB 9.1.2.5 (the Maruts are "rulers of rain") and 13.6.2.28 (where the Maruts alternate with Parjanya, the god of rain, as the deities of this season). ŚB 7.2.2.10 declares that "both the Viśva Devas and the Maruts rule over the rainy season."

40. See Cosmogonies XII and XIII; and also TS 7.1.18.1–2; TB 2.6.19.1–2; and TĀ 1.3.3.

41. For the Maruts as the deities of the autumn, see TĀ 1.3.3; 1.4.2; for the connection of the Viśva Devas and this season, TS 7.1.18.2. Varuṇa is the deity of the autumn in Cosmogony XII, but is represented as the god of the rainy season in Cosmogony XIII.

42. For the connections between autumn and the Ṛbhus, see TB 2.6.19.1: "The gods, the Ṛbhus, by means of the autumn season, bestowed on Indra the oblation and the vitality [which is] praised for excellence (*śriyā*) in the twenty-one-versed hymn of praise with the *vairāja* chant [which is] excellence."

43. E.g., the Brahmin–Kshatriya ruling class divine pair, Mitra and Varuṇa, as in Cosmogonies VIII and X, or the Brahmin deity Bṛhaspati in Cosmogony XIII and also at TS 2.1.2.5.

44. The text at TS 7.1.18.1–2 also confirms the *varṇa* of the first four seasons by correlating the seasons both to appropriate deities and to appropriate meters: (1) spring = Vasus = *gāyatrī*; (2) summer = Rudras = *triṣṭubh*; (3) rainy season = Ādityas = *jagatī*; (4) autumn = Viśva Devas = *anuṣṭubh*.

45. See Cosmogonies VIII, X, and XII. Cosmogony XIII's assignment of deities to the fourth, fifth, and sixth strings (which include autumn, winter, and the cool season) restates the first three *varṇas* (Brahmin, Kshatriya, and Vaishya). ŚB 13.5.4.28 associates three pairs of Brahmin–Kshatriya deities to the autumn, winter, and cool seasons: autumn is assigned to Mitra and Varuṇa; winter is the season of the Kshatriya Indra and Viṣṇu (here representing the Brahmins); and the cool season belongs to Indra and the priestly Bṛhaspati.

46. Alfred Hillebrandt, *Vedic Mythology*, 2 vols., trans. S. Rajeswara Sarma (Delhi: Motilal Banarsidass, 1970), I:61.

47. It is very much the exception to this rule that the hot season is said to mark the beginning of the year in texts like TS 5.7.2.4 and Kauṭilya Artha Śāstra 6.55.2.

48. Raj Bali Pandey, *Hindu Saṃskāras*, 2d ed. (Delhi: Motilal Banarsidass, 1969), p. 127.

49. Another kind of naturalistic argument is made at ŚB 11.2.7.32, where the seasons are connected to the different priests of the Vedic sacrifice: "The sacrificer is the year, and the seasons officiate for him. The *āgnīdhra* is the spring; therefore it is in the spring forest fires break out, for that [season and priest] is a form of Agni. The *adhvaryu* is the hot season; the hot season is heated up, as it were, and the *adhvaryu* exits [the sacrificial grounds] like something heated up [from tending the fires]. The *udgātṛ* is the rainy season; therefore, when it rains hard a sound like a chant is made. The *brahman* priest is the autumn; therefore, when the corn ripens they say, 'The creatures are filled with the *brahman*.' The *hotṛ* is the winter; therefore in the winter cattle sink into depression, having the *vaṣat*-call [made by the *hotṛ* just before offering the sacrificial oblation] uttered over them." Mention might also be made in this context of the passage at JUB 1.35.1ff. (cf. ChU 2.5.1, 2.16.1) where certain climatic and natural features of the six seasons are said to stem from the various forms of the ritual chant (*sāman*). The spring is said to be the time when animals mate, the hot season is "indistinct" (*anirukta*), the rainy season is here as elsewhere equated with the year, the autumn is when "most plants ripen," the winter is when living things die.

50. ŚB 1.3.4.7; cf. ŚB 1.5.3.8; KB 3.4. For the correlation of spring and *rasa*, the "essence" of all plants, see TS 3.2.5.

51. It is most likely in this sense that we should understand the notion that spring is "strength" and "sap" at AitB 4.26.

52. As we have seen, the spring is also a season of regeneration, but we have noted that, as the season of the Brahmin, rebirth takes on a rather different meaning in that context. For folklore linking the rainy season and fertility, see S. S. Gupta, ed., *Rain in Indian Life and Lore* (Calcutta: Indian Publications, 1963); and Pugh, "Into the Almanac," p. 45: "The monsoon rains constitute the pivot of the agricultural year. . . . In the context of agricultural production then, temporal and climatic auspiciousness is manifested as 'wetness' which ramifies into 'fertility', 'succulence' and 'plenty'." For all three seasons—spring, rainy, and autumn—as times of natural fecundity, see ŚB 7.2.4.26.

53. KB 3.4. The connection of this season with the commoners is perhaps also related to the notion that the rains are "all the seasons" or the seasons in general, for which see ŚB 2.2.3.7–8. The rainy season can thus be thought of in much the same way as the Vaishya deities, the Viśva Devas, are in theological discourse: as simultaneously a particular entity (albeit one characterized by its multiplicity), and as a general or miscellaneous category, comprised of "the masses" or undifferentiated multitudes which in the social realm are known as the *viś*. For the rainy season as the time when lots of vermin and insects come out in quest of food, see ŚB 1.5.3.11.

54. See the odd text at AitB 4.26 which depicts the cool season as the "sacrificial" time of the year during which the sacrificer of soma should be consecrated: "Therefore in these months of the cool season the animals of the village and of the wild become thin and shaggy, and thus they take on the form of consecration."

55. The climatic severity of the winter, however, can sometimes provoke an apparent linkage to the Kshatriyas: "These two are the winter [months]. Because the winter by force (*sahas*) brings these creatures into his power, therefore these two [months] are [called] Saha and Sahasya" (ŚB 4.3.1.18).

56. Cf. KS 10.2, where a Brahmin who wishes this essential power is instructed to offer a cake made of millet (because it is reddish brown, and *brahmavarcasa* is also supposed to be that color) to the Brahmin deities Agni and Soma in the spring.

57. For the triangular connection between summer, the Kshatriya, and *yaśas*, see also TB 2.6.19.1–2.

58. Other texts exploit the same concept by calling upon the imagery of the body;

the spring is the "head" of the year, its "highest" part: "Agni (the fire altar) is the year: his head is the spring, his right wing the hot season, his left wing the rainy season, his middle body (trunk) the autumn season, and his tail and feet the winter and cool seasons" (ŚB 10.4.5.2; cf. PB 21.15.2–3). For an inverse structure, however, whereby spring is correlated with the feet, summer with the middle of the leg, the rainy and autumn season with the waist, the winter with the chest, and the cool season with the head, see ŚB 13.6.1.11.

59. The connection of the spring and the Brahmin can also be witnessed in unexpected contexts. The Kshatriya patron of the horse sacrifice should begin that ritual not in the hot season (as would be expected) but in the spring. For, as a sacrificer, the Kshatriya has taken on a certain Brahminhood: "Spring is the Brahmin's season, and one who sacrifices does so having become Brahmin-like" (ŚB 13.4.1.2–3).

60. For the identification of the sun and the seasons, see also ŚB 4.1.1.3.

61. For a binary opposition between day and night, light and darkness, sky and earth, gods and demons, see ŚB 11.1.6.7–11; cf. AitB 5.30 for a somewhat different series of oppositions stimulated from that between night and day.

62. For the five days of the human sacrifice (*puruṣamedha*) as the five seasons, see ŚB 13.6.1.10–11. Periods of time even larger than the seasons are also identified with the parts of the day. For the three four-month periods (*cāturmāsyas*) obliquely connected to the three principal divisions of the day, see ŚB 11.5.2.9. JUB 4.2.1–10 and ChU 3.16.1-5 state that "man is a sacrifice" and associate the three divisions of an ideal human life span (the first twenty-four years, the second forty-four years, and the concluding forty-eight years) to the three libations of soma offered in the morning, at noon, and in the afternoon.

63. Vedic texts are almost universally in agreement as to the *varṇas* of the parts of the day. For one of the only exceptions, see TB 3.12.9.1–2, where the Vaishya (= Ṛg Veda) = morning, Kshatriya (= Yajur Veda) = midday, and Brahmin (= Sāma Veda) = afternoon.

64. See also KB 16.4: "The morning pressing is the *brahman*, the midday pressing the *kṣatra*, the third pressing is the *viś*."

65. KB 5.5, 16.2; AitB 3.10, 3.18, 6.19; ŚB 4.3.5.22.

66. AitB 7.34 presents a different scheme, connecting the morning to the ancestors, noon to "the great ones" (i.e., the gods?), and the afternoon to the sages or *ṛṣis*. ChU 2.9.2–8, in the course of an elaborate analysis of the chant (*sāman*), declares that "all beings are connected to it" and places animals in the time before sunrise, humans just after sunrise, birds in the period in the morning when the cows are gathered together for milking, the gods at midday, embryos in the early afternoon, wild animals in the late afternoon, and the ancestors in the time just after sunset.

67. In addition to Cosmogony I and the texts cited below, see, e.g., KB 14.5: "In the beginning the morning pressing [of soma] was Agni's, the midday pressing was Indra's, the third pressing belonged to the Viśva Devas." For a complex division of the day with correlations to many different deities, see JUB 4.5.1 and, with some variations, JUB 4.10.10.

68. For such homologies between larger and smaller Vedic rites, see Brian K. Smith, *Reflections on Resemblance, Ritual, and Religion* (New York: Oxford University Press, 1989), pp. 186–93.

69. See also ŚB 11.7.2.2–3, where certain rites of the animal sacrifice are correlated with the pressings of soma in the morning, midday, and afternoon so that the animal sacrifice can be equated to a "great sacrifice," i.e., a soma sacrifice.

70. Hillebrandt, *Vedic Mythology*, II:126.

71. ChU 2.24.1. Cf. ŚB 14.2.2.6, where a verse mentioning the Vasus and Rudras serves to make a particular oblation a resembling form of the morning and midday pressings of soma. KB 12.7 connects the morning to Agni, Soma (in his guise as "lord of the forest"), and the Vasus; the midday to Indra and the Rudras; and the afternoon to the Ādityas, Ṛbhus, Vibhus, Vāja, the Viśva Devas, and, somewhat incongruously, the Brahmin god Bṛhaspati.

72. See also the interesting text at KB 5.5,where theological and nontheological ciphers are deployed. Agni, it is said, as the "foremost" or "first" among the gods, is the deity of the morning; and Indra and the Maruts (depicted here as "heaters") jointly rule the scorching midday. But the Vaishya afternoon belongs here, ritually and perhaps in a pseudo-theological way, to the "householder" (*gṛhamedhīya*) and to prosperity (*puṣṭi*). The first and second divisions of the day are thus encoded theologically as Brahmin and Kshatriya—the first through the connection to the single deity Agni, the second through the association with both Indra and the Kshatriya divine band, the Maruts. The Vaishya third is not represented by a divinity or a group of gods. It is indicated by "domesticity," a kind of relatively inferior ontological condition, and by a dominant concern of the householder, material wealth, which functions as a metaphysical power of sorts. Compare this text to ŚB 2.5.3.2–4, where Agni again takes the first place in the temporal sequence, followed by the Maruts as "scorchers" in the midday slot ("for at midday indeed the scorching winds scorched Vrtra"), and the Maruts as "householders" (*gṛhamedhinas*) in the afternoon.

73. In addition to the citations adduced in the text, see also, e.g., TB 3.8.12.1–2; AitB 3.12; KB 14.3; ŚB 4.2.5.20; 4.5.3.5; 12.3.4.3-5; PB 7.4.6.

74. Cf. AitB 6.9: "He recites verses in the *gāyatrī* meter [for] the morning pressing is connected to the *gāyatrī*. He recites nine small [verses] at the morning pressing. Seed is ejaculated into that which is small. He recites ten [verses] at the midday pressing. When the seed which is ejaculated into that which is small reaches the woman's midsection it becomes that which is most broad. He recites nine small [verses] at the third pressing [for] children are born from that which is small."

75. For variants of this myth, see below, Chapter 9. All of these variants highlight the superiority of the (Brahmin) morning pressing and portray the Vaishya pressing of soma in the afternoon as defective in relation to others. See also ŚB 4.3.3.19 and KB 30.1 ("The third pressing is a pressing which has the sap sucked out").

76. Conversely, the standard associations of each meter with a particular portion of the day can be creatively manipulated in order to exploit the *varṇa*-oriented concomitants each meter entails. See, for example, AitB 3.18, where the (Vaishya) *jagatī* is used at the (Kshatriya) midday pressing to conjoin the sacrificer with livestock: "It is in *jagatī*, for livestock are connected with the *jagatī*. The midday is the self of the sacrificer; he thus confers livestock on the sacrificer." Cf. KB 16.2 (and also AitB 6.12) where the (Kshatriya) *triṣṭubh* is employed at the (Vaishya) afternoon pressing to add strength to the latter.

77. And the *bṛhatī*, which is identified with the *triṣṭubh* just as the *anuṣṭubh* is sometimes identified with the *gāyatrī* (e.g., KB 28.5; see also below, Chapter 9). For the *bṛhatī* as the meter of the midday, see also AitB 3.14 and PB 7.4.1–8 (where the *bṛhatī* is assigned to the midday even as the text declares "No matter which meter they chant at the midday service, these all amount to the *triṣṭubh*. They therefore do not depart from the *triṣṭubh* at the midday service").

78. See, e.g., ŚB 4.1.1.6ff., where the *upaṃśu graha* is made to represent the entire soma sacrifice by means of three pressings, done eight, eleven, and twelve times to correlate with the number of syllables in the three meters. Cf. AitB 6.2 where all three soma pressings are said to be accomplished at the midday pressing because certain verses

are recited in the *gāyatrī* meter (= morning pressing) and the *jagatī* meter (= the afternoon pressing).

79. See, e.g., JUB 4.2.1–10 (cf. ChU 3.16; KB 30.1): (1) morning = *gāyatrī* = Vasus; (2) midday = *triṣṭubh* = Rudras; (3) afternoon = *jagatī* = Ādityas.

80. ŚB 14.1.1.15–17. Compare the similar formulation at AitB 3.13: "Prajāpati assigned to the gods different portions of the sacrifice and the meters. He allocated the *gāyatrī* at the morning pressing to Agni and the Vasus, the *triṣṭubh* to Indra and the Rudras at the midday pressing, and the *jagatī* to the Viśva Devas and the Ādityas at the third pressing."

81. The principal alternative was sky = east, atmosphere = south, and earth = west.

82. And thus equated with "worlds" outside of the cosmological realm strictly speaking, such as the "world of waters" or the "world of food," or left without a world altogether.

83. I cannot treat here the connections between north and the first half of the year and south and the second half-year, which I touched upon earlier. Mention might be made of another amalgam of spatial and temporal categories found at TB 3.3.9.1 and 3.8.4.2, where the east seems to be regarded as the direction of the present and the west that of the future (perhaps calling upon the connection that direction has to progeny or offspring).

84. ŚB 6.2.2.3, 9.2.3.6, 13.1.7.3. Some texts refer to the components of the combined space–time unity as "worlds" and describe the cosmic whole as heaven and the *kṣatra*, among other things: "He offers twenty-one Vaiśvadeva oblations [in a rite of the horse sacrifice]. There are twenty-one worlds of the gods (*devaloka*s): the twelve months, five seasons, these three worlds, and yonder sun as the twenty-first. This is the heavenly world; this is the divine *kṣatra*, this is beauty (*śrī*), this is the summit of the ruddy one [i.e., the sun], this is called sovereignty (*svarājya*)" (TB 3.8.10.3; cf. TB 3.8.17.2).

85. For homologies between morning and earth, midday and atmosphere, and afternoon and sky, see also JB 2.431 and BĀU 3.1.10.

86. It is the Brahmin deity Agni (= earth = morning), the Kshatriya Indra (= atmosphere = midday), and the Vaishya sun god, Sūrya/Āditya (= sky = afternoon), who figure as the respective divine markers the set of equations at KB 14.1 and AitB 2.32.

87. There are exceptions. See, for example, the anomalous text at JUB 1.37.1–4, which lays out the following equations: 1) Agni = morning = earth; 2) Indra = midday = sky; 3) Viśva Devas = afternoon = atmosphere. ŚB 12.8.2.7–10 connects the Aśvins with the morning and earth, Sarasvatī with noon and atmosphere, and, curiously, the Kshatriya deity, Indra, with afternoon and sky.

88. I note in passing how in this text all the components of the Vaishya chain are symbolized in the overflowing of the *pravargya* milk as it boils on the sacrificial fire. The ritualists connect the ritual act to the overflowing bounty and fecundity of each of the elements of the Vaishya series.

89. The connection between spring and the east is made also at ŚB 2.2.3.8, where it is said that a wind blowing from the east is "a characteristic sign" of the spring.

90. See also Cosmogony XII, a six-part taxonomy which counts both a zenith and a nadir but fails to correlate the latter to a season:

1. EAST ⇒ Agni = *gāyatrī* meter = nine-versed hymn of praise = *rathantara* chant = SPRING = inhalation = constellations = Vasus

2. SOUTH ⇒ Indra = *triṣṭubh* meter = fifteen-versed hymn of praise = *bṛhat* chant = SUMMER = the circulating breath = moon = Rudras

3. WEST ⇒ Maruts = *jagatī* meter = seventeen-versed hymn of praise = *vairūpa* chant = RAINY SEASON = exhalation = Venus = Ādityas

4. NORTH ⇒ Viśva Devas = anustubh meter = twenty-one-versed hymn of praise = *vairāja* chant = AUTUMN = the digestive breath = Varuṇa and the Sādhyas

5. ZENITH ⇒ Mitra and Varuṇa = *paṅkti* meter = twenty-seven- and thirty-three-versed hymns of praise = *śakvara* and *raivata* chants = WINTER AND COOL SEASONS = the upward breath = Angirases = moon

6. NADIR ⇒ Saturn = eclipses = comets = serpents = demons = spirits = humans, birds, eight-legged mountain goats, elephants, etc.

Here also the *varṇa* of the first three chains is clearly indicated by the deities assigned to each; the fourth series of associations is here also generally lower class; and the fifth is a summation or epitomization of the preceding four.

7

Classifying Flora

Nature, the Supernatural, and Society

Conceptions of what we call "nature,"[1] no less than the ways gods are imagined or the divisions humans impose on the continuums of space and time, are cultural constructs. Nature is, of course, really "out there"; the stone Samuel Johnson kicked to disprove Bishop Berkeley's philosophy of idealism had an undeniable tangibility. But *knowledge* of the natural world is made possible and distinctively shaped by culturally given—and culturally variable—categories. What we think we know about nature is ultimately no more than an interpretation. Any culture's depiction of the natural world therefore reveals at least as much about the epistemology of that culture as it does about nature as a "thing in itself."

Furthermore, to make the claim that something—an entity or phenomenon, a particular set of practices or customs, or a full-blown classificatory scheme for categorizing the entire universe—is "natural" is to appeal to a source of considerable authority. The virtually incontestable persuasiveness of "nature" is perhaps matched only by argumentation based on the "divinely ordained" or the "word of God." Nature, like the supernatural, transcends the human beings who authoritatively pronounce on it. Truth claims that take recourse to nature thus contrive to be independent of the individuals who make them, and of the conditioning of culture, class interests, and history that shape them. As in the case of pronouncements regarding the supernatural, the appeal here is to the "objective," the indisputable, and the unquestionable—that is, the appeal is to what might be called "the sacred."[2]

As Adena Rosmarin has observed, echoing Freud's observations on religion, "'naturalness' is a compliment paid to the successful illusion rather than an insight into its working."[3] The dynamics behind this "successful illusion" entail the recasting of a cultural decision about how the world's components are to be categorized as a natural fact—the representation of nature, in other words, is itself represented as "natural." Particular cultural inventions appropriate to themselves the persuasive and prestigious power of nature when they too cease to be what they really are (opinions, interpretations, prejudices, etc.) and are reconstituted as part of the natural order of things.

The contention that something is "natural," then, draws upon the considerable authority humans invest in nature. When the classes one "discovers" in nature reprise the classes into which society is divided the latter are lent a formidible guise: the categories by which we define ourselves appear to be no other than those that order the world around us. Social classes can therefore be represented as "natural" not only because, as we saw in Chapter 3, they were created in the beginning along with other components of the natural and supernatural worlds. The organizational form of the social world may also be portrayed as part of nature by virtue of the fact that it mirrors the taxonomical structure that is supposed to define the natural world. The "prestige of origins" is complemented by what we might call the "prestige of symmetry." The classificatory contours that are projected onto both domains, society and nature, are made to appear equally "objective" and equally true, and in a manner that mutually reinforces both of them.

In this and the next chapter, we survey the Vedic texts that concern themselves with the enumeration and categorization of the inhabitants of the natural world—and with the "laws of nature" that govern the interrelations between them. After reviewing Vedic notions of the constituents of the natural world, I focus on two sectors of nature that were of special interest to the Vedic ritualists: the realm of trees and the animal kingdom. As we shall see, the *varṇa* scheme that organizes society is implicated and, ultimately, replicated in these two spheres of the natural world. The classification of trees and animals according to the *varṇa*s effectively projects social classes into nature and, conversely, makes it possible to draw upon the "evidence" of nature for the legitimacy of society organized in this fashion. Nature, like the theological, spatial, and temporal orders, can thus be marshaled, explicitly or implicitly, as "proof" of the obvious validity of the particular social order advocated in the Veda.

The Constituents of Nature

Vedic texts assume that a basic affinity exists between the principal inhabitants of the natural world. The latter are usually enumerated, in hierarchical order, as humans, animals, trees, and plants. All share a common essence or life force, although the specific nature of this essence is variously conceived. In some texts it is identified as fire[4] or light;[5] in later Vedic literature it is the *ātman*, which is further identified with the *brahman*.[6] In yet other instances it is sap (*rasa*) that is so designated, for without it there would be no juice (*payas*) in the plants, no ghee in the milk, no fat in the flesh, no hair on the skin, and no leaves on the trees (PB 24.18.3). Sap is the life force that was the mother of all things:

> [The gods] pushed upward the sap of the waters; it became the plants and the trees. They pushed upward the sap of the plants and the trees; it became fruit. They pushed upward the sap of fruit; it became food. They pushed upward the sap of food; it became seed. They pushed upward the sap of seed; it became man. (KB 2.7)

According to this text, the essence of life is squeezed out of one entity in order to vitalize another; the result is a kind of chain of being in which water, plants, trees, and humans are bound together.[7] Such an essential commonality among the types of inhabitants on earth helps to explain why trees, plants, and animals were regarded as partaking of some of the characteristics of human beings, including the traits associated with one or another of the *varṇas*.

Lists of nature's principal classes of things and beings are also articulated in terms of the various kinds of nourishment the planet provides. The earth produces food of three types—animals, humans, and trees—according to one text. Humans presumably are the food of the unearthly gods, for the text goes on to note that "the gods are above this [earth]; the gods are in heaven" (ŚB 4.1.2.8). Elsewhere (KB 20.1) a seemingly more anthropocentric view is taken; food (for humans?) is sixfold: "wild animals, domesticated animals, plants, trees, that which goes in the waters and that which swims."[8]

One frequently encounters the notion that the world is made up of nothing more than food and eaters of food.[9] As one text succinctly puts it, "The eater of food and food indeed are everything here" (ŚB 11.1.6.19), and what might appear to us as a culinary metaphor was really meant as a descriptive account of the natural world organized into a hierarchically ordered food chain. "What we in Europe, in the classical period, called 'the chain of being,'" Francis Zimmermann notes, "is presented in India as a sequence of foods."[10] Nature in the Veda was often depicted as a hierarchically ordered set of Chinese boxes, or better, Indian stomachs. The nutritional chain, comprised of an endless series of food and eaters, exactly describes the order of the species. At the top of the Vedic "natural" world were supernatural (*sic*) entities who feed on sacrificial oblations that were explicitly represented as substitutes for the human sacrificers who are next in line on the menu.[11] Humans eat animals, the next lowest life form, and animals eat plants,[12] which, in turn, "eat" rain or "the waters" from which all food is ultimately generated.[13]

Food was, of course, understood to be the source of physical survival and bodily strength; indeed, food was synonymous with life itself.[14] It was frequently identified with life sap (*rasa*, e.g., KB 2.7), nourishment (*ūrj*, ŚB 9.3.3.10; PB 8.8.19), and vigor or *vāja*.[15] Although the essence of food is said to be "invisible" (ŚB 8.5.4.4), its visible manifestation is all the inhabitants of nature. Each entity is interlinked with others in such a way that every living being is regarded as the regenerative sustenance for the one on the next rung of the ladder. Food is what eaters live on in all senses of the phrase, and "everything here lives on food" (ŚB 7.5.1.20).

Everything here also dies as food. The nutritional chain of entrées was envisioned as a closed circle of life and death, a cosmic *maṇḍala* of recirculating foodstuffs. "Those which are found on earth live by food alone, and in the end they return to it," it is said in a Upanishad (TU 2.2). And humans are, of course, not exempt from nature's cycle. We are all also destined to become food. We are fodder for Mṛtyu or "the Grim Reaper"—death personified.[16]

Another commonly encountered categorical division of the principal classes of the natural world is a binary opposition between the "stationary" and the "moving," also designated as the "rooted" and the "rootless." This pair, according to some texts (e.g., ŚB 1.8.3.15, 2.3.1.10, 5.1.3.3), sums up the totality of "all food" and is no other than the distinction between inanimate plants and trees, on the one hand, and animate humans and animals, on the other: "That which affords [the means of] subsistence is of two kinds; namely, either rooted or rootless. On both of these, which belong to the gods, men subsist. Now animals are rootless and plants are rooted."[17] Another text categorizes on the basis of the form of progeneration and enumerates three types of the "moving"—those born from an egg, those born from an embryonic sac, and those born "from moisture"—and then encompasses the "stationary" beings with the category of "those born from sprouts."[18]

In a passage which works with this division of life into the animate (here described as creatures who are "supported by breath") and the inanimate, sophisticated distinctions are drawn between (1) plants and trees versus entities with consciousness and (2) animals and humans:

> He who knows the self in a more manifest way obtains a more manifest being. There are plants and trees and whatever life there is which is supported by breath; he knows the self in a more manifest way [by examining them]. In plants and trees only life sap (*rasa*) is observable; in life which is supported by breath, there is also consciousness (*citta*). In life which is supported by breath the self becomes more manifest, for in those beings life sap is also observable, while in the others [i.e., plants and trees] there is no consciousness. In the human, the self becomes more manifest, for he is most perfected with intelligence (*prajñ-anena sampannatamo*). He articulates what he knows (*vijñatam vadati*); he observes what he knows (*vijñatam paśyati*); he knows [that there is] the future; he knows [the difference between] what is in the world and what is otherworldly. He desires the obtainment of the immortal through the mortal—thus [is his] perfection. Now among the other animals, they perceive only hunger and thirst. They do not articulate what they know; they do not observe what they know; they do not know [that there is] a future; they do not know [the difference between] what is in the world and what is otherworldly. They become only so much, according to their intelligence and capacity. (AitĀ 2.3.2)

The familiar bifurcation between animate ("those supported by breath") and inanimate nature ("plants and trees") is here analyzed and rationalized. While all of the earth's inhabitants have "life sap," inanimate nature is devoid of consciousness; and while all animals have consciousness, it is only the human being who has the power of speech,[19] who is cognizant of the world around him and able to impose his categories upon it ("he observes what he knows"), and who is endowed with the ability to imagine a future (animals live in the eternal present; they "only perceive hunger and thirst"). Furthermore, humans are distinguished from other animals in that they are capable of what we might call "religion": humans are able to separate "what is in the world" from what is "otherworldly" (i.e., they possess what we would call theology?) and have devised a set of techniques (i.e., ritual?) which utilize the worldly and "mortal" to gain access to the otherworldly and "immortal."

Another kind of subdivision within the binary opposition between animate and inanimate being distinguishes between "wild" or "jungle" and "domesticated" or "village" entities,[20] deploying a classificatory criterion that centers on a decision about which species in nature are to be domesticated and which are not. In Chapter 8 we examine in detail the way that animals (and to some extent humans) are so dichotomized. It may be observed here that this criterion also is applied to plants and "food" in general.[21] According to BŚS 24.5, "Domesticated plants are of seven kinds, those of the jungle are also of seven kinds. . . . The seven domesticated plants are: sesamum, beans, paddy, barley, *prīyaṁgu*, *aṇu*, and wheat as the seventh. Some teachers, indeed, mention *kulattha* [as the seventh]. The seven plants of the jungle are: *śyāmāka*, *nīvāra*, *jartila*, *gavīdhuka*, *gārmuta*, *vāstva*, and *veṇuyava* as the seventh."

As we will also have occasion to note in some detail in the next chapter, the opposition between wild and domesticated exactly parallels another kind of dichotomy in the world of nature, that between those things and beings which are suitable for inclusion in the all-important sacrifice and those which are not.[22] Trees and animals (and also human beings) that are excluded from the sacrifice are among those considered "wild" or belonging to the jungle; conversely, those that are regarded as "sacrificial" are also invariably classified as being of the village or domesticated.

Furthermore, as we shall see, the earth's inhabitants which are regarded as domesticated, of the village, and sacrificial are also those that become analogues to the classes of Āryan society—that is, these are the trees and animals that are among those that are classified according to *varṇa*. Let us begin our investigation of the ways the *varṇa* system operates in particular arenas in the natural world by turning attention now to the classification of a very important component of nature, the realm of trees.

Trees, the Sacrifice, and *Varṇa*

Trees, which have figured prominently in the early history of religions around the world,[23] have been featured in most all of the various strands that make up Indian religions.[24] They were certainly of importance and interest to the authors of the Veda. Plants and trees were described as having many forms (AitB 8.27) and were identified with nutrition, life sap, and food (AitĀ 1.2.4). In a metaphor not at all irrelevant here, the plants were identified with the *viś*, the commoners; they were ruled by "King Soma," the "lord of plants," who was the vegetative embodiment of the *kṣatra* power.[25] Trees, plants, water, fire, and animals describe the entities clinging to the earth's surface in one text (ŚB 1.7.2.19). More frequently, trees and plants were also supposed to embody the hair,[26] or less often the finger- and toenails (ŚB 12.1.4.1) of the earth or of the creator god Prajāpati.[27]

But it was not only as one of the primary constituents of the natural world (and of Prajāpati's cosmic body) that trees attained their significance; it was the trees that provided wood critical for the performance of the fire sacrifice.[28] They are said to be indispensable for the Vedic ritual: "Trees belong to the sacrifice (*vanaspatyo hi yajñīya*), for if there were not trees men would be unable to sacrifice" (ŚB 3.2.2.9).

And if trees are essential for the performance of sacrifice, sacrifice is necessary for the use of trees. Those who utilize trees for firewood or for the construction of wooden objects must perform a rite in order to avoid karmic retribution at the hands of trees in the next world. One who places firewood on the fire as part of the sacrifice manages to "restrain" and "conquer" the otherwise vengeful timber:

> As to those [men you saw] in the eastern quarter [of the other world] who were being dismembered by men cutting them into pieces [saying], "This one for you, this one for me," they were trees. He who places fuel from trees on [the fire] restrains the trees; by means of that [ritual act] he conquers the world of trees. (ŚB 11.6.1.8)

While all trees are to be respected, some are valued more than others. As I intimated previously, trees, like animals and humans, are subdivided into those that are fit for participation in the sacrifice and those that are not. The particular species of trees that are designated as "sacrificial" are listed in the course of ritual instructions on the types of wood to be used for various items required in the sacrifice. According to ŚB 1.3.3.19–20, the sticks used to enclose the fire are to be taken from only certain trees:

> They should be made of *palāśa*.[29] The *brahman* is the *palāśa*, and the *brahman* is fire . . . If he cannot find sticks of *palāśa*, then they may be of *vikankata*;[30] if he cannot find sticks of *vikankata*, then they may be of *kārṣmarya* (Gmelina arborea); and if he cannot find sticks of *kārṣmarya*, then they may be of the wood apple tree,[31] or of the cutch tree,[32] or of *udumbara*.[33] These are the sacrificial trees; therefore [the enclosing sticks] are of these trees.

Another list says that the four principal spoons and ladles required for the ritual are to be constructed only from the wood of the sacrificial trees, here enumerated as the cutch, *palāśa*, pipal,[34] and *vikankata*.[35]

One trait some trees share, and others lack,[36] is this sacrificial quality.[37] Largely overlapping with the category of sacrificial trees is the class of trees that are said to be infused with various metaphysical properties, and these powers are also those which characterize the members of the various social classes. In the course of a discussion setting down rules for the composition of the sacrificial stake (the *yupa*) to which the victim is tied in the animal sacrifice, we read the following:

> One who desires heaven should make the sacrificial stake out of cutch wood; by means of a sacrificial stake of cutch the gods won the world of heaven. . . . One who desires sustenance (*annādhya*, the "eating of food") or material prosperity (*puṣṭi*) should make the sacrificial stake out of the wood from a wood apple tree. The wood apple bears fruit each and every year; this is the ideal form of sustenance. It should be thick with branches right down to the root; this [is the ideal form] of material prosperity. He prospers in offspring and animals who knowing thus makes the sacrificial stake out of the wood from a wood apple tree. Now it is said with regard to the wood of the wood apple that the wood apple is light (*jyotis*). He who knows this becomes a light among his own [people]; he becomes the most excellent of his own [people]. He who desires brilliance (*tejas*) or the splendor of the *brahman* (*brahmavarcasa*) should make the sacrificial stake out of *palāśa* wood. Among the trees, the *palāśa* is brilliance and the splendor of the *brahman*, and he becomes filled with brilliance and a possessor of the splendor of the *brahman* who, knowing this, makes the sacrificial stake out of *palāśa* wood. Now it is said in regard to the *palāśa* tree that the *palāśa* is the womb (*yoni*) of all trees; therefore the word "*palāśa*" is used for trees generally, as in "the trees (*palāśas*) of so and so." The particular boon (*kāma*) that is in each and every sort of tree is obtained by him who knows this. (AitB 2.1)

Closely related is another Brāhmaṇa's discourse on this matter: "He should make [the sacrificial stake] out of *palāśa* wood if he desires the splendor of the *brahman*; out of the wood apple if he desires to be an eater of food; out of cutch if he desires heaven" (KB 10.1).

Other texts posit somewhat different views concerning the particular powers of the sacrificial trees. The wood apple tree, for example, which is said above to procure for the sacrificer sustenance, general material prosperity, and productivity ("offspring and animals"), is alternatively proclaimed to be good for the production of the splendor of the *brahman*: "These are the trees fit for use for making a sacrificial post: *palāśa*, cutch, and *rohitaka*. A sacrificer who desires the splendor of the *brahman* should make one of wood apple" (BhŚS 7.1.5–6). In still other formulations, other variations—as well as reiterations—are also to be found:

> The *palāśa*, cutch, wood apple, or *rohitaka* trees are fit for the construction of the sacrificial stake: *palāśa* if the desire is for brilliance (*tejas*) or if one desires [the ability to perform soma] sacrifices (*yajñakāma*); cutch if the desire is for heaven or virility; it should be of the wood apple if the desire is to be an eater of food or for the splendor of the *brahman*; *rohitaka* if the desire is for offspring (*prajā*) or keen eyesight (*cakṣus*). (ĀpŚS 7.1.15–16)

Or again:

TABLE 7.1. Trees and their Powers

Trees	*Powers*
palāśa	splendor of the *brahman* power (*brahmavarcasa*), brilliance (*tejas*), becoming a soma sacrificer / becoming an "eater of food"
wood apple (*bilva*)	sustenance and becoming an "eater of food," material prosperity, obtaining abundant offspring and animals, becoming a "light among one's own people" / splendor of the *brahman* power (*brahmavarcasa*)
cutch (*khadira*)	winning the world of heaven, virility
rohitaka	progeny, keen eyesight

> A sacrificer desiring abundant food or the splendor of the *brahman* should make the sacrificial post of the wood of *palāśa*; one desiring heaven, of the cutch; one desiring the splendor of the *brahman*, of the wood apple; and one desiring offspring, of the *rohitaka*. (HŚS 4.1)[38]

Despite these variations, a pattern of associations between particular trees and particular metaphysical powers emerges from a comparative reading of the passages. I summarize the data given in the texts cited above on the properties of these sacrificial trees in Table 7.1.

As we saw in other contexts, the various powers are also associated with the *varṇas*. By virtue of the fact that certain trees are linked with these powers we can infer that trees too possess *varṇa* attributes. We may surmise, for instance, that the *palāśa* is connected with some consistency to the Brahmin *varṇa*; it is supposedly infused with Brahminical powers such as the splendor of the *brahman*, *tejas*, and the ability to drink soma. The wood apple is sometimes also regarded as "Brahmin" (by virtue of its association with the splendor of the *brahman*), but more often would seem to be a Vaishya tree due to the linkages made to material prosperity, offspring, animals and so on. The cutch would seem to be a Kshatriya tree in that it is associated with virility and heaven (which is "conquered" by this tree's hard wood). The *rohitaka*, by virtue of its connection to offspring and fertility, appears to have a straightforward connection to the Vaishya *varṇa*.

In other sources there is no need for guesswork: the class designations of the trees are explicitly set forth. Particular woods are linked not only with the *varṇa*-encoded meters but also with the powers of *brahman*, *kṣatra*, and *viś* in the following text:

> The cup made of *palāśa* wood [is put down near a river] with [this mantra]: "O god Varuṇa, your bank firmly established in the *brahman*, with that *gāyatrī* meter I sacrifice to you"; that one made of banyan[39] wood with "O god Varuṇa, your bank firmly established in the *kṣatra*, with that *triṣṭubh* meter I sacrifice to you"; the cup made of pipal wood with "O god Varuṇa, your bank firmly established in the *viś*, with that *jagatī* meter I sacrifice to you." (BŚS 17.38)

The *varṇa* characteristics of particular trees, thus far deduced on the basis of more or less indirect evidence, are here explicitly stated with the introduction of the metaphysical powers which are intimately linked to the three social classes.

The connection of the *palāśa*, banyan, and pipal with the three meters also characteristically associated with the Brahmin, Kshatriya, and Vaishya reiterates the *varṇa* of the trees. The *palāśa*, as we had already posited, is a Brahmin; it is, as we have seen, elsewhere given the typical powers of its class: the splendor of the *brahman* (*brahmavarcasa*), brilliance (*tejas*), and soma. The banyan tree, we now learn, is a Kshatriya wood, and the pipal here appears as a Vaishya tree.

The *varṇa* qualities of particular trees are also articulated explicitly elsewhere,[40] and while there are some variants the consistencies are notable. One example in which the *varṇas* of trees are enunciated is provided in the texts which give the rules for performing the *upanayana* rite—the initiation of a young boy into Veda study.[41] As part of the initiate's regalia, he is given a wooden staff (*daṇḍa*) which serves to create and reinforce class differentiation and hierarchy in the boys undergoing the initiation and is constructed in particular ways according to the *varṇa* of the initiate. It is not only to be of varying lengths,[42] but also of different woods according to class—either *palāśa* or the wood apple for the Brahmin, banyan for the Kshatriya, and either the jujube tree[43] or *udumbara* for the Vaishya.[44]

In other ritual contexts, too, the same trees appear with the same class assignments. In the description of a rite within the Rājasūya or royal consecration ritual, one reads the following:

> In front of the Maitrāvaruṇa hearth are the [four] consecration vessels in which that consecration water is contained. There is a *palāśa* one. With that [water in that vessel] a Brahmin sprinkles. The *palāśa* is the *brahman*; with the *brahman* he thus sprinkles him. There is an *udumbara* one. With that one of his own [kinsmen or brothers] sprinkles. The *udumbara* is food (*anna*) and nourishment (*ūrj*). Nourishment is his own, for as far as a man's own extends, that far he does not hunger. Therefore his "own" is sustenance; therefore one of his own [kinsmen] sprinkles with an *udumbara* [vessel]. There is one made of the foot [i.e., root] of the banyan tree. With that a friendly (*mitrya*) Kshatriya sprinkles.[45] The banyan tree is firmly established by virtue of its feet, and by the friend the Kshatriya is firmly established. Therefore a friendly Kshatriya sprinkles with [the water of a vessel] made of the foot of a banyan. There is a pipal one. With that a Vaishya sprinkles. Because Indra once summoned the Maruts who were sitting on the pipal tree, therefore a Vaishya sprinkles with a pipal [vessel]. (ŚB 5.3.5.10–14)

More or less explicit homologies are drawn here between certain trees and the three social classes (*palāśa* = Brahmin; banyan = Kshatriya; pipal = Vaishya), and a fourth tree (the *udumbara*) is implicitly, and yet rather obviously, also connected to Vaishyas (who are indeed the king's own "nourishment" and "food"). Similarly, in the course of explaining the rules of an expiation, another text recommends that a Brahmin put fuel made of *palāśa* on the sacrificial fire and offer an oblation of clarified butter; a Kshatriya places fuel of banyan on the border of his kingdom and offers an oblation; and a Vaishya offers oblations having put fuel of pipal on the border of his land (ĀpŚS 9.12.4–6).

We have thus moved from indirect *varṇa* associations to direct connections

TABLE 7.2. The *Varṇa* of Trees

Trees	*palāśa*, wood apple	banyan,cutch	pipal, *udumbara*, *rohitaka*, jujube
Social Classes	Brahmin	Kshatriya	Vaishya
Powers	*brahman*	*kṣatra*	*viś*
Meters	*gāyatrī*	*triṣṭubh*	*jagatī*

between the trees and the classes. The data accumulated thus far on the *varṇa* of trees is summarized in Table 7.2.

Having surveyed the general terrain, let us now analyze the particulars of these connections between the trees, the three social classes, and other components of the natural, supernatural, and ritual worlds which are organized by the *varṇa* scheme. We start with those trees which are designated "Brahmin."

Brahmin Trees

The connection of the *palāśa* (also known as the *parṇa*) tree with the *brahman* power—and therefore with the Brahmin *varṇa*—is well established in Vedic texts. Viennot argues that "In the Brahmanic era this tree underwent a sort of apotheosis and, just as in heaven it represents the god Brahma, on earth it becomes the emblem of the sacradotal class, that of the Brahmins."[46] The *palāśa*, Viennot rightly concludes, is in Vedic texts "always the tree of the Brahmin caste."[47]

We noted earlier that the staff of the Brahmin initiate is to be made of this particular tree, and that in the royal consecration ritual a Brahmin is called upon to sprinkle the king with water from a cup made of *palāśa*, for "the *palāśa* tree is the *brahman*; it is with the *brahman* that he sprinkles him" (ŚB 5.3.5.10). In several texts, the tree is linked to both the Brahmin social class and the east, the Brahmin direction.[48] At the Cāturmāsya ritual, there is an oblation to Rudra offered at a crossroads. The central leaflet of the tripartite leaf from the *palāśa* is used as a ladle for the offering:[49] "He offers with the central leaflet of a *palāśa* leaf. The *palāśa* leaf is the *brahman*; with the *brahman*, therefore, he offers" (ŚB 2.6.2.8; cf. TB 3.7.2.2; BŚS 24.8).

Using the *palāśa* in the ritual is sometimes said to procure for the sacrificer the heavenly world through the force of the *brahman* power. In one of the funeral rites, the burial mound is surrounded by pegs, with a "*palāśa* one in front, for the *palāśa* is the *brahman*. He thus makes him go to the heavenly world with the *brahman* for his leader."[50] In other instances, the *brahman* power inherent in the *palāśa* wood is tapped in order to conquer demons and spirits. The spoon made of *palāśa* conquers demons with the power of the *brahman*, for "the *palāśa* is the *brahman*; with the *brahman* he exterminates the danger, the demons" (ŚB 5.2.4.18; cf. ŚB 13.8.2.3). Or, again, before the site chosen for the *gārhapatya* fire at the Agnicayana is ready, one must first expel the ghosts of those who have been at the place in the past:

> Wishing [to make] the *gārhapatya*, he sweeps [the site] with a branch of

> *palāśa*. When he builds the *gārhapatya*, he makes his home there. Whoever builds fire altars makes his home on this [earth]. When he sweeps [that place] he thereby sweeps away those who have made their homes [there before him]. . . . He sweeps with a branch of *palāśa*. The *palāśa* is the *brahman*; it is with the *brahman* he thus sweeps away those who have made their homes [there before him]. (ŚB 7.1.1.1,5)

Because of this intimate connection between the *palāśa* and the *brahman* power (for which see also TS 7.4.12.1), it is quite understandable that this tree should also be regularly linked to the power of *brahmavarcasa*, to the splendor of the *brahman*, or, according to one text (TB 1.7.8.7), to the power called *tviṣ*, "brilliance" or "luster."

The chain of associations joining the *palāśa* and the Brahmins is extended elsewhere to include other typically Brahmin-like items. In a passage dealing with the enclosing sticks used in the ritual, the Brahmin god Agni is added to the string: "They should be of *palāśa* wood, for the *palāśa* tree is the *brahman*, and Agni also is the *brahman*. Therefore 'the Agnis' [i.e., the enclosing sticks] should be of *palāśa* wood" (ŚB 1.3.3.19). The tree is also linked to another Brahmin deity, Soma (or the plant that carries his name). In the following quotation, which explains why the resin of the *palāśa* tree is placed in boiling water during one of the rites of the Agnicayana, a series of connections joins the *palāśa* to Agni, Soma, and the moon: "And as to why [it is done] by *palāśa* resin: the *palāśa* tree is Soma, and Soma is the moon, and that [moon] is one form of Agni. It is to obtain that form of Agni [that *palāśa* resin is used]."[51]

At AV 3.5.4 the *parṇa* (= *palāśa*) tree is called "Soma's terrible power (*ugram sahas*)," and at TB 3.8.20 it is claimed that the use of *palāśa* stakes in the Rājasūya obtains for the sacrificer "the drinking of soma," just as the use of the *palāśa* stake in the animal sacrifice also supposedly propels the sacrificer toward the soma. Indeed, in several passages the ritualists claim that the *palāśa* wood has the power to transform ordinary acts into the prestigious soma sacrifice.[52] KB 2.2, for example, claims that the placing of the kindling stick of this wood in the Agnihotra is an offering of soma: "He puts on a kindling stick of *palāśa*. The *palāśa* is soma; this is the first soma libation." A similar notion occurs at ŚB 6.6.3.7, where the *brahman* power is also included in the series of identifications: "The remaining [kindling sticks] are of *palāśa* wood. The *palāśa* is the *brahman*; with the *brahman* he thus fuels him [Agni the fire]. And again, as to why they are *palāśa* ones. The *palāśa* tree is soma, and the soma oblation is the highest oblation. It is that he now offers on this [fire], and with that he pleases him [Agni]." Or, again, at TB 3.7.4.17–18 (cf. ĀpŚS 1.13.15), adding a chip of *palāśa* wood into the milk used at the New Moon sacrifice transforms it into soma when the following mantra is recited by the priest: "Let this bark of the *palāśa*, a purifying agent which makes the milk into soma, go to its own womb."

The connection between the *parṇa*/*palāśa* tree and the soma plant and its juice is thus explained in part by the assertion that they share a common origin; they spring from the same womb (*sayonitva*, see TB 3.2.3.4). In a frequently cited myth, with many variants and different explanatory purposes, this commonality is explained. Another link is also added here to the chain of associations which includes both the *palāśa* tree and the Brahmin social class: the *gāyatrī* meter, which, like the leaf of the *palāśa* tree, is threefold (3 × 3 *padas* or verses). The myth is recalled in the following passage to explain why a branch of *palāśa* is used to drive the calves away from the cows[53] in the New and Full Moon sacrifice:

> The soma was in the third heaven from here. The *gāyatrī* seized it. A leaf (*parṇa*) of it [the soma plant] was cut off. That became the essence of the *parṇa* tree. The *parṇa* is the *brahman*. When he [the priest] drives the calves away [from the cows] with a branch of *parṇa* tree, he drives them away by means of the *brahman*. The *parṇa* tree belongs to the *gāyatrī*, and the cattle are connected with the *gāyatrī* stanza. Therefore the leaves of the *parṇa* tree are in groups of three and the *gāyatrī* has three verses. When he drives the cows [toward the pasture ground] with a branch of *parṇa* tree, he drives them by means of their own deity. (TB 3.2.1.1–2)

A slightly different variant is told elsewhere to explicate the same ritual act. In this version, the *gāyatrī* meter is represented as a bird, and the *parṇa* is said to be called so because of the linguistic overlap between the tree and the word "feather":

> He [the *adhvaryu*] drives the calves away [from the cows] with a *parṇa* branch. The reason why he drives the calves away with a *parṇa* branch is this. When the *gāyatrī* flew up to Soma, a footless archer, having taken aim at her, cut off a feather (*parṇa*)—either of the *gāyatrī* or of King Soma—while she was carrying him off. When it fell down it became the essence of the *parṇa* tree. "May that which was then infused with Soma be here with us now," [he thinks]. Therefore he drives away the calves with a *parṇa* branch. (ŚB 1.7.1.1)

Variants of the myth are also cited for justifying the use of *palāśa* in other ritual contexts, such as the driving of the cart laden with soma—again with the phrase "May that which was then infused with Soma be here now" (ŚB 3.3.4.10)—or the addition of a chip of *palāśa* into the milk offering which, as we observed, ritually transforms the milk into soma:

> From the third heaven the soma was carried by the *gāyatrī*. For the soma drink [which is here really a mixture of sweet and sour milk] I seize the inside of the bark [of a branch of the *parṇa* tree]. . . . Let the milk [be] in the houses, the milk in the cows, the milk in the calves. O milk, be firm for the oblation offered to Indra. Let the *gāyatrī*, by means of the bark of the *parṇa* tree, make the milk here into soma. (TB 3.7.4.1–2; cf. TB 3.2.1–3; ĀpŚS 1.6.8)

As we have already seen, the animal sacrifice is also made to include soma within it by means of the sacrificial stake constructed out of *palāśa*, and in justifying this practice (in the face of alternative opinions) the myth of the retrieved soma is once again cited:

> Madhuka Paingya once said, "Some perform the animal sacrifice without soma, some with soma. Soma was in the sky. The *gāyatrī*, having become a bird, carried him off. When a feather (*parṇa*) was cut off, that became the essence of the *parṇa* tree.". . . Some perform the animal sacrifice without soma, some with soma. He who makes the sacrificial stake out of wood other than *palāśa* wood performs the animal sacrifice without soma; and he who makes the sacrificial stake out of *palāśa* wood performs the animal sacrifice with soma. Therefore he should make his sacrificial stake of *palāśa* wood. (ŚB 11.7.2.8)

A rather different, and in some ways more elaborate, version of the myth is related in the course of a discussion of the proper woods for the various sacrificial ladles:

> Soma was in the third heaven from here. The *gāyatrī* carried it off. One of its leaves (*parṇa*) was cut off; that became the essence of the *parṇa* tree. His oblations become soma-like (*saumya*) whose ladle is made of *parṇa* wood; the gods are fond of his oblations. The gods were conversing about the *brahman*, and the *parṇa* overheard (*upaṣṛṇot*) it. He whose ladle is made of *parṇa* wood is one whom people have heard of (*suṣravas*); he hears no evil noise. The *parṇa* is the *brahman*, and the Maruts are the *viś*. The commoners are food, and the pipal belongs to the Maruts. He whose ladle is is made of *parṇa* wood and whose spoon is of pipal, wins food by means of the *brahman*; the *brahman* he places over the commoners. (TS 3.5.7.1–3)

The *palāśa* tree, then, is of the Brahmin *varṇa* for several reasons: it is infused with the power of the *brahman* and is thus productive of the heavenly world and the quality of *brahmavarcasa*, and it is the antithesis of the demons, who are driven away through its use. Its origin myth explains the tree's close association with soma—the "king of the Brahmins"—and the Brahmin meter, the *gāyatrī*, with which it (or rather its distinctive leaf) is also intimately related because of a numerically oriented similarity of structure.[54]

Other trees are somewhat more tentatively classifiable as Brahmin wood.[55] The wood apple, as suggested above, appears in some texts as sharing the traits of the *palāśa*, perhaps due to a similarity of appearance. For the wood apple too produces leaves of three parts,[56] and we saw earlier how in the case of the *palāśa* such tripartition calls up associations with the *gāyatrī* meter, and thus the Brahmin class. According to the BGS 2.5.18–19 the staff of the Brahmin initiate may be of either *palāśa*—which is received by the student from the teacher with the words, "You are soma. Make me a soma-drinker"—or of wood from the wood apple tree, which is taken with, "You are the splendor of the *brahman* power. You for the splendor of the *brahman*."

Other ritual texts also identify the wood apple with *brahmavarcasa* (BhŚS 7.1.1–4.4; ĀpŚS 7.1.1–5.4; HŚS 4.1) although BhŚS and ĀpŚS note that the wood procures food as well (and thus suggest a link with the commoner class). This latter observation is perhaps derived from other physical properties of the tree: "The marrow [of the creator] flowed together and burst forth from the ear. It became that tree, the wood apple. Therefore the inside of the the fruit of that [tree] is all edible, and therefore it [the tree, or wood] is yellowish, for marrow is yellowish" (ŚB 13.4.4.8). In any event, the association with food sometimes leads the ritualists to classify the wood apple among the Vaishya trees: the AitB (2.1) argues that the sacrificial stake is to be of the wood apple tree for him whose desire is for food and prosperity, for he "prospers in offspring and animals who knowing thus makes the sacrificial stake out of wood from the wood apple tree."[57] And, following the Brāhmaṇa of its tradition, the ĀsvGS (1.19.13) rules that the initiate's staff should thus be made of wood apple if he be a Vaishya.

Another tree, the *plakṣa*,[58] also has some Brahmin connotations, although here too other *varṇa* assignments are also attested. The *plakṣa* is especially noted for its infusion with the sacrificial quality (*medha*).[59] One text relates a myth of origins that explains both this association (which would thus lead to a placement of it among the Brahmin trees) and also perhaps why elsewhere (GGS 4.7.21–22) the tree is associated with Yama and death: "By means of the sacrificial animal victim (*paśu*) the gods went to the world of heaven. They reflected, 'Men will come after us.' They cut off its head and caused its sacrificial essence to flow out. It became the essence of the *plakṣa* tree" (TS 6.3.10.2).

A variant, also emphasizing the sacrificial qualities of the *plakṣa* tree, additionally provides an etymological explanation for its name:

> Having put it [the heart of the victim at the animal sacrifice] down to the south [of the fire], the priest cuts off [the various portions]. There are *plakṣa* branches as an upper layer [covering the altar]; on those he cuts off [the portions]. As to why there are *plakṣa* branches as an upper layer: When the gods, in the beginning, seized an animal [to sacrifice], Tvaṣṭṛ first spat on its head. "Surely they will not seize it now," [he thought]. For the animals belong to Tvaṣṭṛ. That [spit became] the brain in the head and the marrow in the spine; therefore it is like spit, for Tvaṣṭṛ spat on it. He should therefore not eat that, since Tvaṣṭṛ spat on it. Its sacrificial essence spilled out; a tree was born from it. The gods looked at (*prapaśyan*) it, and therefore is has the name "*prakhyā*" ("visible"), which is the same as *plakṣa*. With that same sacrificial essence he now completes it [the victim] and makes it whole. Therefore there are *plakṣa* branches as an upper layer. (ŚB 3.8.3.10–12)

Such a connection of this tree to the sacrificial essence, which in later Hinduism appears to have transformed into a connection to soma,[60] thus strengthens the possibility of an ancient association with the Brahmins.[61]

Kshatriya Trees

The *nyagrodha* or banyan tree is, as one text unambiguously puts it, "the *kṣatra* of the trees; when they bring together the banyan tree and [those ritual implements] made out of banyan wood, he [the priest] puts into him [the royal sacrificer] the *kṣatra* power that is in the trees" (AitB 8.16). Just as Indra is king of the gods, Yama the ruler of the ancestors, the king the overlord of humans, the boa constrictor the chief among snakes, the tiger the king of the beasts, the eagle the lord of the birds, and so on, so too is the banyan the king of the trees

(TS 7.3.14.1). The tree is also identified with independence of will or "self-rule" (*svadhā*) (ŚB 12.7.2.14 and below).

With its bending branches which take root in the ground, this tree is unanimously regarded as a resembling form of the Kshatriya, who not only towers over his people but is supported by them and has, so to say, spread many roots among them.[62] We have already observed the use of the banyan in the initiation ceremony (the staff of the Kshatriya boy is made of it) and in the royal consecration rite, where the king is sprinkled with water from a cup made of the root of a banyan by a friendly Kshatriya, "for by its feet [i.e., its multitudinous and enormous roots] the banyan is firmly established, and by the friend the Kshatriya is firmly established" (ŚB 5.3.5.13). It is indeed the physical peculiarities of the tree that are highlighted in the associations made between it and the ruling and warrior class:

> The banyan is the *kṣatra* power among the trees, and the Kshatriya is the *kṣatra* power [among humans]. The Kshatriya is here like a tree rooted in the kingdom, and firmly established [in it]; and the banyan is rooted in the ground by its downward growths, and firmly established [in it]. (AitB 7.31).

The origin of this tree is related in several myths, where once again the peculiarities of its structure are the salient feature and the one which leads to the connections between it and the Kshatriya *varṇa*:

> Where the gods, having offered a sacrifice, went to the heavenly world, there they turned over (*nyubjan*) the sacrificial cups. They [i.e., the overturned cups] became the banyan (*nyagrodha*) trees. Even today, in Kurukṣetra, they are called *nyubjas*. They were the first-born of the banyans; from them [all] the others were subsequently born. (AitB 7.30)

Or again:

> When the gods were performing sacrifice, they turned over those soma cups. Turned downward, they took root; therefore the banyan (*nyagrodha*) trees, when turned downward (*nyac*), take root (*roha*) [or grow downward]. (ŚB 13.2.7.3)

Among the most interesting claims made for the banyan is that the juice squeezed from its roots is a kind of Kshatriya version of the soma. This juice leads some texts to identify the tree and the "stream of self-rule" (*svadhāśravat*) which flowed from Indra's bones in the time of creation, while soma was produced from the bone marrow (ŚB 12.7.1.9). It is thus the Kshatriya's "own food" and is that class's equivalent to soma (which belongs to the Brahmins and is said to be their "king"):

> The sap (*rasa*) of [the part of] these vessels which went downward became the roots; [the essence of the part of the vessels] which went upward [became] the fruits. This Kshatriya does not abandon his own food who eats the roots and

> fruits of the banyan. Surreptitiously he obtains the soma drink; it is not consumed visibly by him. The banyan is surreptitiously King Soma. Surreptitiously does he who is a Kshatriya take on the appearance (*rūpa*) of a Brahmin by means of the Brahmin priest, by means of the consecration ritual [which transforms him into a Brahmin], and by means of the recitation of ancestors [i.e., the *pravara*, where the Kshatriya is also ritually transformed into a Brahmin for the purposes of the sacrifice]. The banyan is the *kṣatra* power among the trees, and the Kshatriya is the *kṣatra* power [among humans]. The Kshatriya is here like a tree rooted in the kingdom, and firmly established [in it]; and the banyan is rooted in the ground by its downward growths, and firmly established [in it]. Inasmuch as the Kshatriya sacrificer eats the roots and fruits of the banyan, he firmly establishes himself in the *kṣatra* among the trees [and] in the *kṣatra* which in himself [by virtue of his birth]. In the *kṣatra* which is in himself he firmly establishes the *kṣatra* which is in the trees. Like the banyan with its roots in the ground, he is firmly established in the kingdom. He who, being a Kshatriya sacrificer, eats this food has his kingdom become untroubled and formidable. (AitB 7.31)

As Ariel Glucklich observes, "The Nyagrodha, therefore, not only contains the powerful juices of royalty; its descending growth forges a downward axis-mundi, a ritual conduit for the transmission of divine powers, through royalty, to the vegetative world which the king governs as well."[63]

Other powers besides that of the *kṣatra* and rule are also inherent in the banyan tree. The staff made of this wood is taken by the Kshatriya initiate with a mantra imparting force or power (*ojas*) with which the tree is apparently infused (BGS 2.5.20). Elsewhere we read that a cup made of banyan wood is physical strength (*bala*) and is connected to the Kshatriya god Indra,[64] and one text associates this tree with "military oppression" (*śastrasampīḍa*) (GGS 4.7.21).

Other trees which occasionally, and somewhat unsystematically, are related to the Kshatriya *varṇa* include the *kārṣmarya*, which is lauded in several texts for its warriorlike ability to slay demons (TS 6.2.1.5–6; ŚB 7.4.1.37). The wood of this tree is thus used in the ritual for making the enclosing sticks which serve to keep out such cosmic riff-raff. The *kārṣmarya* is once declared to be filled with *tejas* (ŚB 7.4.1.39), and is also said to be a thunderbolt (*vajra*), the instrument of Indra, who is the Kshatriya deity par excellence.[65]

The cutch tree, as noted previously, is also associated with the Kshatriyas. Its strong, hard wood (the cutch was supposedly created from the bones of Prajāpati, ŚB 13.4.4.9) was employed in the ritual to construct the wooden sword (*sphya*) used in the sacrifice which is often identified with Indra's thunderbolt.[66] The cutch was also attributed the warriorlike powers of conquering heaven (AitB 2.1; KB 10.1; HŚS 4.1) and the attainment of virility (ĀpŚS 7.1.16). Glucklich sums up the *varṇa* characteristics of this tree by writing that the cutch "is intimately linked with the potency of the Kṣatriya, with his very essence as warrior. . . . It is the destructive warrior-like powers of the tree that produce benefits, a symbol for the powers of the sacrificing Kṣatriya, or for the royal Kṣatriya who wields that Khadira *daṇḍa* in the court of law."[67]

Another tree is also occasionally given a Kshatriya classification.[68] The pipal is said at TS 5.1.10.2 and KS 19.10 to be the overcomer of foes among the trees and is used to obtain victory for the sacrificer; at AitB 7.32 we read that this tree was born from *tejas* and thus is the overlord of trees.[69] It is also etymologically and ritually connected to the horse (*aśvattha* = *aśva*), the particular animal of the Kshatriya (TB 3.8.12.2); and the pipal is occasionally identified with Indra, who is said to be responsible for the tree's strength (ŚB 12.7.1.1–19). At ŚB 12.7.2.14, the vessel made of pipal is said to procure *apaciti* for the sacrificer—perhaps meaning "retribution" or "revenge" which is exacted by force.

Vaishya Trees

But the pipal is ordinarily classified as a Vaishya tree and is identified with that *varṇa*'s typical qualities such as fecundity and prosperity.[70] The Vaishya is to offer oblations on the border of his land using the fuel from this tree in a certain expiation rite (ĀpŚS 9.12.4–6), and the pipal is associated with the Vaishya direction, the west.[71] In the course of the royal consecration rite we read of the sprinkling of the king with water from a pipal cup: "There is a pipal one, and with that a Vaishya sprinkles. Indra once called upon the Maruts staying on the pipal tree; therefore a Vaishya sprinkles with a pipal [vessel]" (ŚB 5.3.5.14).

This latter passage apparently alludes to a myth which, as the text indicates, connects the tree to the Maruts, and therefore to the *viś* and the Vaishyas.[72] The myth in question, however, seems to be somewhat elusive. Some scholars believe the story to have originated in a misreading of a verse in the Ṛg Veda.[73] Be that as it may, there is a fairly detailed version of the myth in one text—a myth that is often referred to when making connections between the Maruts, the pipal tree, and the Vaishyas:

> Indra is the *kṣatra* power, and the Maruts are the commoners. With the commoners the Kshatriya becomes strong. . . . Indra summoned them [when they were sitting in a pipal tree], saying, "Come with me that so I can kill Vṛtra with you as my force." They said, "What's in it for us?" He drew those two Mārutvatīya draughts for them. They said, "Having put aside this one [cup] for our strength (*ojas*), we will come with you." Having thus put it aside for their strength, they joined him. But Indra tried to obtain it [thinking], "They have come with me [only] after putting aside their strength." He said, "Come with me together with your strength." "Then draw a third cup for us," they said. He drew a third cup for them [saying] "You are drawn for support; you for the strength of the Maruts." They then came with him together with their strength, and he killed and vanquished Vṛtra with them. Indra is the *kṣatra*, and the Maruts are the commoners; by means of the commoners the Kshatriya becomes strong. That strength he now puts into the *kṣatra*; therefore he draws the Mārutvatīya draughts. He should draw them only for Indra, the "possessor of Maruts," and not for the Maruts. If he were to draw [draughts] for the Maruts, he would make the commoners rebellious to the Kshatriya. He thus apportions [draughts] to the Maruts only after [that] for Indra. He thus makes the commoners subservient and obedient to the Kshatriya. (ŚB 4.3.3.6–10)

Just as Agni hides in some Brahmin trees, so do the wind gods or Maruts take refuge in the Vaishya tree, the pipal. It is for this reason that this tree is widely known as the "seat of the gods" (*devasadana*).[74]

The myth is called upon in various contexts to justify the participation of the Vaishyas in certain rites. In the Vājapeya sacrifice (one of the royal, and therefore Kshatriya, rituals), the king at one point climbs up the sacrificial post—a symbolic representation of his ascent over his people and the earth itself. Once atop his perch,

> Then they pass up bundles of salt to him. Salt is animals, and animals are food. He who offers the Vājapeya wins food, for the drink of strength (*vāja-peya*) is what is called the drink of food (*anna-peya*). Whatever food he has acquired, with that he puts himself in contact, and incorporates it into himself, now that he has gone to the goal. Therefore they pass bundles of salt up to him. They [the pieces of salt] are bound up in pipal leaves. Indra once summoned the Maruts who were sitting around in a pipal tree; therefore they are bound up in pipal leaves. Commoners pass them up to him; the Maruts are the commoners, and the commoners are food [for the king]. Therefore commoners pass them up. (ŚB 5.2.1.14–17)

The pipal leaves in this rite, signifiers for the commoner class, are employed to ensure the superiority of Kshatriya over the peasantry; they are passed up to the king, who towers over his people.

Another rite that refers to the myth of Indra calling down the Maruts from the pipal tree is that of a rice-ball offering to the Maruts (which is placed on the ground, and not in the fire) as part of a domestic sacrifice to Indra: "For the scripture says, 'The Maruts eat what is not sacrificed.' [This rice ball he offers] in pipal leaves because it is said, 'The Maruts stood in the pipal tree'" (PGS 2.15.3–4).

The association of the pipal, the Maruts, and the Vaishyas is also confirmed in passages which do not make reference to the charter myth. In an optional sacrifice dedicated to another group of the Vaishya deities, the Ādityas, which is designed to "get power over the *viś* and the realm," we read the following:

> Should he not get power over them, he should pound in seven pegs of pipal wood in the middle shaft, [saying] "I bind the Ādityas here in order that they should get power [for me] over such and such commoners." The Ādityas, their heroes bound, cause him to get power over the commoners. . . . [The pegs] are of pipal wood. The pipal is the strength (*ojas*) of the Maruts; with strength he gets power over the commoners. They are seven, and the Maruts are in seven troops. He gains power over troops of commoners. (TS 2.3.1.5)

Similarly, another optional sacrifice for a ruler who "has been or is being banished from his kingdom" cites the preceding passage:

> He should tie up the [pipal] pegs also with the sacrificial faggot and put them on the fire together with the faggot. With the faggot, verily, should he put them

> on the fire. "He thereby wins [a kingdom from which he is] not likely to be banished." So says the Brāhmaṇa. It is said in the Brāhmaṇa: "The pegs should be [made] of pipal wood. What is [known as] pipal, of the Maruts, indeed, is this vitality. Verily, by means of vitality, does one win the subjects. [The pegs] should be seven [in number]. The Maruts are, indeed, organized into seven troops. In troops, verily, does one win the subjects." So says the Brāhmaṇa.[75]

In the ritual, the *upabhṛt* ladle is supposed to be constructed out of the wood of a pipal tree (see KŚS 1.3.33–36; ĀpŚS 1.15.10; HŚS 1.4.1; BhŚS 1.16.5); in one rite it is placed under another ladle representing the Brahmins: "The *parṇa* tree is the *brahman*, the Maruts are the commoners, and the commoners are food. The pipal belongs to the Maruts; he whose ladle is made of *parṇa*, and his *upabhṛt* of pipal, by means of the *brahman* wins food and puts the Brahmins over the commoners. The *parṇa* is the *kṣatra* power, the pipal the commoners. Because the ladle is made of *parṇa* and the *upabhṛt* is of pipal, he puts the *kṣatra* over the commoners" (TS 3.5.7.2–3).

In another ritual context, however, it is the pipal which is "dominant" and placed over another wood in an act that, nevertheless, connects the pipal to the Vaishya. For it is wood of the pipal that serves as the upper of the two blocks (*araṇis*) used for generating fire, the other being made of acacia wood.[76] The pipal thus gained a reputation for fecundity and the ability to pass along that trait to those humans who are desirous of it—a reputation that extends into popular Hinduism.[77] The notion that the wood of this tree is fecund and generative is also noted in the course of a rite for the conception of a male child (KauśS 35.8), which cites AV 6.11.1: "The pipal [has] mounted the acacia; there is made the generation of a male. That is the obtainment of a son; that we bring into women." In sum, the pipal tree is characterized by the quality so often found associated with the lower classes or commoners: *puṣṭi*, "increase" or "prosperity" (TB 1.7.8.7).

The other principal Vaishya tree in Vedic texts is the *udumbara*, which perhaps even more than the pipal is thought to be filled with the very Vaishya properties of fecundity, productivity, and multiplicity.[78] The *udumbara* is the embodiment within the world of trees of the life essence and its sustenance. The tree is said to be laden with sap (*rasa*) and is virtually always identified with nourishment (*ūrj*)[79] together with "food" (*anna*) and sustenance or the "eating of food" (*annādya*).[80] Thus in the initiation rite a Vaishya receives the staff of *udumbara* by saying, "You are nourishment (*ūrj*). Put nourishment in me." (BGS 2.5.22–23). Christopher Minkowski notes that of the 107 passages in which *udumbara* appears in the Veda, 93 connect the tree to *ūrj*. Minkowski rightly claims this identity as an instance of the regularity of Vedic connections or *bandhus*:

> For everywhere, the *udumbara*'s identity is uniform; it is *ūrj* (strength/sap). . . . So widespread is the expression of the identity of *udumbara* and *ūrj*, that it is much more unusual to find a passage about *udumbara* that does not identify them than one that does. . . . It is therefore safe to say that *udumbara* is always and only associated in the Brāhmaṇa passages with *ūrj*.[81]

The reason for such an association is readily understandable from a botanical point of view. The *udumbara* is distinctive in that its fruits were not only particularly juicy but also in that it bore fruit three times a year.[82] The origin of this tree is depicted in one account which first observes that "the *udumbara* is sap and sustenance." The etiology then follows: "When the gods distributed nourishment and strength (*iṣa*),[83] the *udumbara* came into being. Therefore it ripens three times a year. In that they [the priests and the sacrificer] take hold of the *udumbara* [branch], full of sap, they take hold of nourishment and sustenance."[84]

Observable botanical features of the tree led the Vedic classifiers to generalizations: the *udumbara* was regarded as having within it the condensed essence of all the trees and served as the symbol not only for "all trees" (cf. ŚB 6.7.1.13) but for "all food" as well. The following myth of origins makes this case for the *udumbara*:

> He then puts on the fire [a stick] of *udumbara*. The gods and demons, both of them born of Prajāpati, contested with one another. Now all the trees went over to the demons, but the *udumbara* tree alone did not abandon the gods. When they conquered the demons, the gods gathered up their trees. They said, "Come on, let us put into the *udumbara* tree the nourishment and sap that is in these trees. If they then run away from us, they would desert us all used up, like a milked out cow, or like an ox [that has been tired out] by pulling." They then put into the *udumbara* tree the nourishment and sap that was in those trees; and because of that nourishment it matures [fruit] equal to all the [other] trees. Therefore that [tree] is always full of nourishment, always full of milky sap. That *udumbara* tree, [being] all the trees, is all food. He thus pleases him [Agni] with all food, and fuels him with all trees [when he puts on a stick of *udumbara*]. (ŚB 6.6.3.2ff.; cf. TS 5.7.2–3)

We shall return to the notion that the *udumbara* is "all food" as well as "all trees." For now, let us observe that the concept of the *udumbara* as metonymically representing all trees has certain ritual uses. The following text begins by asserting, as is often the case, that the *udumbara* is nourishment and sap while it also explains how, through the ritual manipulation of a mortar and pestle made of *udumbara*, trees are symbolically planted everywhere:

> They are made of *udumbara* wood. The *udumbara* is nourishment and sap; he thus puts strength, life sap into him [the sacrificer]. And also, the *udumbara* being all trees, when he puts those two up [on the altar] he puts up all trees. . . . It [the *udumbara* mortar] is four-cornered. The regions are four; he thus places trees in all the regions, and therefore there are trees in all the regions. (ŚB 7.5.1.15ff.)

The manipulation of the *udumbara* in order to tap the power of all trees also may work to the benefit of the sacrificer. Because the tree has the essence of all trees within its fruits, the eating of its fruits places this sylvan essence—the power of growth, vitality, and nourishment—in the sacrificer, regardless of his social class: "Now for the [fruits] of the *udambara*. This tree, the *udumbara*, was born of nourishment and sustenance. This is what is most delectable among the trees. He puts into this *kṣatra* the nourishment, the sustenance, and what is most delectable of the trees with the fruits of the *udumbara*" (AitB 7.32).

Just as the Vaishya class is the mass of commoners, "the people" as a kind of undifferentiated whole, so is the *udumbara* tree regarded as the forest itself. Constituting the *udumbara* as the ritual representative of all trees is tantamount to declaring it the *viś* of trees, "the masses" among the timbers. The very Vaishya quality of multiplicity, intimately related to other commoner qualities such as generation, productivity, and nourishment, is displaced onto the sap-filled, fertile, and thrice-yearly fructifying *udumbara*, and, by ritual means, is transplanted into the sacrificer.

The tree is also connected with the fertility demigods, the Gandharvas,[85] and more often with Prajāpati for similar reasons and to much the same end; the creator god who is also endowed with procreative potency and the fecund *udumbara* are regarded as resembling forms of one another (see ŚB 4.6.1.3; GGS 4.7.22). When Prajāpati was creating the world, he wiped his blood off onto the earth: "The *udumbara* was born there. Therefore it ripens [its fruits] red" (KS 6.1); or, according to the variant, "Therefore the *udumbara* belongs to Prajāpati. Therefore its fruit turns red when ripe" (MS 1.8.1). In another creation story which depicts the origins of the *udumbara* from the power of nourishment, the *udumbara* is again connected to Prajāpati, and to the middle part of the creator's body in particular:

> Prajāpati distributed the nourishment among the gods; from that the *udumbara* came into existence. The *udumbara* belongs to Prajāpati; and the *udgātṛ* priest belongs to Prajāpati. In that by his first ritual act [raising the *udumbara* pillar in the middle of the sacrificial shed is the first act for which the *udgātṛ* is required in this ritual] this priest takes hold of the pillar of *udumbara*, he chooses himself as an officiating priest by means of his own deity. . . . "You are nourishment, the giver of strength. Give me nourishment, put into me nourishment; give me food, put food into me" [he says]. The sacrificial shed is the belly of Prajāpati, the *udumbara* is nourishment. When that [pillar] of *udumbara* wood is fixed in the middle of the sacrificial shed, he puts nourishment and food from the middle into his offspring. Therefore wherever this [pillar] becomes worn out, then the offspring becomes hungry.[86]

The linkage of the *udumbara* and the "middle" part of the body, often including stomach and genitals,[87] is reiterated in texts dealing with the *udumbara* post which is placed in the center of the sacrificial shed (ŚB 3.6.1.1ff.; see also ŚB 4.6.7.8). In one such instance both the *udumbara* and barley are said to be bearers of nourishment or *ūrj*, and placing the *udumbara* post in the sacrificial shed is equated with putting nourishment in the stomach and in the sacrificer's offspring:

> He does a cruel thing when he digs [into the earth with the spade in order to make a place for the sacrificial stake made of *udumbara*]. He pours down water in order to pacify [the earth]. He pours down water mixed with barley; barley

is nourishment, and the *udumbara* is nourishment. He thus brings together nourishment with nourishment. [The post] is of *udumbara* wood of the height of the sacrificer. As much as the sacrificer is, that much nourishment does he put in him. . . . The sacrificial shed is the belly; the *udumbara* is nourishment. In the middle he fixes [the post] of *udumbara*. He puts nourishment in the middle of his offspring; therefore they consume nourishment in the middle [i.e., the stomach]. (TS 6.2.10.3,6–7; cf. TS 5.2.8.7)

The connection of the *udumbara* not only with nourishment but with the "middle," the stomach and genitals, also and again emphasizes the connection to the Vaishyas. For the "middle" is the particular anatomical part of the body belonging to the Vaishya *varṇa*—it is both the receptacle of food and the fount of the reproduction of progeny. This set of multiple but interlocking connections—between the *udumbara*, the middle part of the body, food, and semen (which originates at the navel)—is most explicitly asserted in a description of the throne constructed for carrying soma, "the king":

It is of *udumbara* wood; *udumbara* is nourishment and food. [The throne is] in order to obtain nourishment and food; therefore it is of *udumbara* wood. It reaches up to his navel, for it is there that the food is placed, and soma is food; therefore it reaches up to his navel. There also is the receptacle of the seed, and soma is seed: therefore it reaches up to his navel. (ŚB 3.3.4.27–28)

As I intimated before, and as we just observed in the prior passage, the *udumbara* tree, like the Vaishya, is closely connected to food—it is said that it was the creator's flesh, the edible portion of the body, that became the *udumbara* (ŚB 12.7.1.9). It will come as no surprise, then, that just as the *udumbara* represents all trees, so too is it associated with all food. A sacrificial spoon of *udumbara*—the wood of this tree being nourishment and strength—serves as the receptacle of "every kind of food, in order to obtain every kind of food" (TS 5.4.9.2; cf. ŚB 5.2.2.2). Furthermore, because the *paśu*s are also sometimes equated with "all food," the *udumbara* is connected to the animals, which also, once more, places the tree in the realm of the Vaishyas (this class being responsible for the tending of the herds). In a rite centering on the use of an amulet made of *udumbara*, just such an equation is made: "Both what [is] two-footed and what four-footed, what foods [there are], what saps—I seize the abundance of them, wearing the amulet of *udumbara*."[88] In other instances, the animals are declared to be nourishment, and since the *udumbara* is also nourishment, the animals and *udumbara* are connected, just as the Vaishyas and the animals in general are associated in the myths of creation we examined in Chapter 3.[89]

Elsewhere the association of the *udumbara*, food, and the animals is reiterated and extended to include curds, which are also the embodiment of the *paśu*s (cf. ŚB 5.4.3.27) and therefore of nourishment or *ūrj* (cf. ŚB 7.4.1.38; TS 5.4.7.3) and food in general: "The *udumbara* [ladle] is filled with curds. Curds are the animals, and the *udumbara* is nourishment. He thus confers nourishment upon the animals" (TS 5.2.7.3–4). In the soma sacrifice, a firestick of a forked *udum-*

bara twig (*udumbara* here being equated with nourishment and sap) is put on the fire:

> It has forked branches; forked branches are the same as the animals. With animals, that is, with food, he thus pleases [the deity]. If he cannot find one with forked branches, he should take up a glob of curds and put it on [the wood]; that [glob of curds] is a form of the animals. (ŚB 9.2.3.40)

Since curds are, additionally, the food par excellence of the Vaishyas,[90] this set of homologies reiterates the connection between the *udumbara* and the commoner class.

The *udumbara* tree is thus connected with abundance, sustenance, nourishment, and fertility; it is used in rituals to ensure that a new home will be the site of the obtainment of nourishment (ŚGS 3.2.8; ĀśvGS 2.8.11) and is used also in various ceremonies to promote childbirth.[91] "Associated uniformly throughout Vedic literature with *ūrj*," concludes Minkowski, "the *udumbara* is identified as a source of nourishing strength. It is in this capacity as source of abundance that the wood of the *udumbara* is used in many situations."[92]

Conclusion

Trees were important components in the natural world as it was understood in the Veda. Pictured as the "hair" of the earth or of the creator god, trees were regarded as close kin to humans. Together with plants, animals, water, the trees were among the inhabitants with whom humans shared the earth. From some trees, those classified as "sacrificial," came the wood so essential to the ritual; and as a further subdivision of the "sacrificial" category, certain trees were connected with the social classes. By envisioning some trees as having *varṇa* attributes (a notion that could be put into play within the ritual to create, reinforce, or represent class differences), the social world was projected into the natural world in such a way as to break down any perception of difference between the two realms. The world of trees and the social world of humans became two mutually reflecting versions of the same order of things; nature and society melded into one gigantic scheme organized by *varṇa*.

Trees were thus more than bearers of social meaning; they served to restate in another idiom the very social order itself. The forest became yet another setting in which the truth of *varṇa* could be inscribed and described. Trees could be read as ciphers for the *varṇa* system, as wooden embodiments of the classification scheme that ordered so many other nooks and crannies of the cosmos.

There was another corner of the natural world that particularly captured the interest of the Vedic taxonomers. This was the animal kingdom, to which we turn next.

NOTES

1. The circumlocution is used because it would appear that many cultures, including ancient India according to the Veda, would not regard a world of "nature" as separate from either "culture" or the "world of the gods." This fact does not, of course, invalidate the outsider's analytic and heuristic use of such categories.

2. For a definition of "the sacred" that entails "objectivity," see Mircea Eliade, *The Sacred and the Profane: The Nature of Religion* (New York: Harcourt, Brace & World, 1959); and *The Myth of the Eternal Return or, Cosmos and History*, trans. by Willard R. Trask (Princeton: Princeton University Press, 1971).

3. Adena Rosmarin, *The Power of Genre* (Minneapolis: University of Minnesota Press, 1985), p. 12.

4. See ŚB 9.2.1.8 and 10.5.4.1 for the statement that Agni is the life force of "the waters," human beings, plants, and trees. At ŚB 6.4.4.2 (citing VS 12.37) Agni is asked not to scorch heaven, earth, air, or trees (glossed as "Do not injure anything"); at 9.4.1.7 the claim is that Agni is distributed among all the plants. Cf. ŚB 1.7.2.19 where a fivefold classification of the inhabitants of the earth's surface includes fire as well as plants, trees, waters, and "these creatures."

5. See ŚB 10.2.6.4–5, where the beings of the earth are said to be infused with "the immortal sunlight" (*amṛta arci*). This vital light, however, is bestowed on creatures in different quantities, which results in varying life spans: "Now that same gift, the beneficent brilliance (*vasucitra*), Savitṛ (the sun) apportions to the different creatures, even to plants and trees. He gives more to some, and less to others. Those to whom he gives more live longest, and those to whom he gives less live less long."

6. E.g., AitĀ 3.2.3: "They see him [i.e., the *ātman*] in this earth, in heaven, in the air, in the ether, in the waters, in plants, in trees, in the moon, in the constellations, in all beings. Him they call *brahman*."

7. We shall see in Chapter 8 that similar stories are told about the way different animals were created as the sacrificial essence (*medha*) traveled among them. We also have here something of a preview of one of the formulations of transmigration in the early Upanishads, where a similar cycle of life is articulated: from the cremation fire the soul goes into space, where it becomes wind and then mist, and returns to earth as rain, where it takes the form of plants, is eaten and thus transmuted into seed, and, finally, becomes an embryo in the mother's womb (ChU 5.3–10; BĀU 6.2.9ff.).

8. These are regarded as three pairs consisting of the two types of animals, the two types of plant life, and the two types of aquatic creatures. Food is elsewhere regarded as "threefold" or "fivefold," or as vaguely "multiple" (see, e.g., ŚB 9.2.3.16 and PB 12.4.18). According to ŚB 9.1.2.23, "every kind of food" consists of animals, water, and trees.

9. For an investigation of this theme in Vedic literature, and the way Hindu conceptions of vegetarianism grew out of such notions, see Brian K. Smith, "Eaters, Food, and Social Hierarchy in Ancient India: A Dietary Guide to a Revolution of Values," *Journal of the American Academy of Religion* 58, 2 (Summer 1990): 201–29. This article forms an expanded version of the material presented in this section. See also Charles Malamoud, "Cruire le monde," *Puruṣārtha* 1 (1975): 91–135, reprinted in his *Cruire le monde: Rite et pensée dans l'Inde ancienne* (Paris: Éditions la Decouverte, 1989), pp. 35–70.

10. Francis Zimmermann, *The Jungle and the Aroma of Meats: An Ecological Theme in Hindu Medicine* (Berkeley: University of California Press, 1987), p. 1.

11. Consult Brian K. Smith and Wendy Doniger, "Sacrifice and Substitution: Ritual Mystification and Mythical Demystification," *Numen* 36, 2 (1989): 189–224.

12. Note that carnivorous animals (the "wild" or "jungle" animals in Vedic classification schemes) cannot be accounted for within this version of the food chain. Bruce Lincoln observes that "once wild animals are excluded from consideration, the groupings of fluids, plants, animals, and humans into relations of eater and eaten assume a clear and elegant form. . . . When one introduces wild animals—that is, carnivores—into this system, the system collapses, for such animals not only eat meat (the prerogative of humans) while scorning plants (the proper food of animals), they even go so far as to eat humans. Wild beasts thus not only are a physical threat, but also pose a threat to the structures of thought appropriate to cultured existence." Bruce Lincoln, *Myth, Cosmos, and Society: Indo-European Themes of Creation and Destruction* (Cambridge, Mass.: Harvard University Press, 1986), p. 200.

13. "For water is indeed food. Therefore when water comes to this world, food is produced here" (ŚB 2.1.1.3). Cf. ŚB 8.6.1.20; TB 3.2.8.1–3; PB 11.8.11–12; and KB 3.4. Alternatively, the gods in the beginning made it rain and "as many drops fell, that many plants were born" as food for animals (TB 2.1.1.1). For the cycle, see, e.g., Manu 3.76: "A burnt oblation cast properly into the fire approaches the sun; rain is created from the sun, from rain comes food, and from that, offspring."

14. "Food is life (*āyus*)," ŚB 9.2.3.16. See also PB 12.4.20 and ŚB 10.3.5.6 ("By food one is born, and by food one is propelled"). For food as *pitu* ("food" in the sense of "nourishment"), consult ŚB 1.9.2.20 and 7.2.1.15.

15. "Vigor is food. . . . For when there is food, cow, horse, and man are vigorous." PB 13.9.13, 15.11.12; JB 3.298. For food identified with *vāja*, see also ŚB 1.4.1.9, 5.1.4.3ff., 5.1.5.17,26, 7.3.1.46, 7.5.1.18, 9.3.4.1; and PB 18.6.8. For the frequent identification of the sacrifice called "Vājapeya" and "food and drink" (*annapeya*), see, e.g., ŚB 5.1.3.3, 5.2.1.13, and 5.2.2.1 ("for he who offers the Vājapeya wins food, Vājapeya being the same as *annapeya*").

16. See, e.g., ŚB 10.1.3.1, 10.4.3.10. For the relationship between this conception of the recycling of food and the later Upanishadic notion of reincarnation, see Smith, "Eaters, Food, and Social Hierarchy," pp. 181–83.

17. ŚB 2.3.1.10. Plants or the "rooted" entities are subdivided into those whose fruits appear above ground and those whose fruits appear among the roots (TB 3.8.17.4). ŚB 7.2.2.12 more generally distinguishes between "creatures and plants"; see also ŚB 13.7.1.2 for the distinction between animals and plants and a slightly more complex division between the constituents of the category of "all food." For the animals as *jagata* or "moving" (and thus connected to the *jagatī* meter), see ŚB 1.2.2.2, 1.8.2.11, 3.4.1.13, 12.8.3.13; TB 3.8.8.4; KB 8.7; and below, Chapter 9.

18. AitU 5.3. Cf. ChU 6.3.1 ("There are three sources of the beings here—those born from an egg, those born from a living being, those born from sprouts") and esp. Manu 1.39–46, where an elaborate classification based on a basic dichotomy between the "moving" and the "stationary" and the various forms of progeneration (entities born from an embryonic sac, the egg-born, those "born from moisture," and those born from sprouts). The last mentioned (the plants and trees) constitutes the "stationary" category; the first three fall under the more general rubric of "moving" life. Compare also the Āyurvedic categorization according to the Suśruta Saṃhitā (cited in Zimmermann, *The Jungle and the Aroma of Meats*, p. 199), which divides nature into four types of immobile beings—*vanaspati* (trees which do not flower); *vṛksa* (trees which give flowers and fruits); *virūḍh* (bushes and lianas); and *oṣadhi* (annual plants)—and four kinds of mobile beings—*jarāyuja* (viviparous); *aṇḍaja* (oviparous); *svedaja* (born from moisture); and *udbhijja* (grown from the ground). For similar analyses, cf. Manu 1.46–48; VishnuSm 91.4.

19. At ṚV 8.100.11 it is also declared that only the human "possesses speech."

20. See Charles Malamoud, "Village et forêt dans l'idéologie de l'Inde brahmanique," *Archives européennes de sociologie* 17, 1 (1976): 3–20; reprinted in *Cruire le monde*, pp. 93–114.

21. For the division of food and plants into wild and cultivated, see also TS 5.2.5.5, 7.3.4.1; ŚB 1.1.1.10, 11.1.7.2, 12.7.2.9, and 12.7.3.19. At ŚB 9.1.1.3 it is declared that wild sesame seeds represent "both kinds of food": "Inasmuch as they are sesamum seeds they are a domesticated [kind of food], and inasmuch as they ripen on unplowed land they are of the jungle." In many texts, honey is designated the essence of the food and plant life of the jungle (e.g., KB 4.12) or, more generally, the sap of plants and trees in general and the "highest food" (e.g., AitB 8.20; PB 13.11.17). According to ŚB 11.5.4.18, certain teachers argued that "he who is a religious student (*brahmacārin*) should not eat honey, lest he should reach the end of food. For honey is the very essence of plants." For the prohibition of honey for a student of the Veda, see also JUB 1.54.1; ĀpDhS 1.1.2.23; GautDhS 2.13; Manu 11.159. Manu 6.14 also excludes it from the diet of a *vānaprasthin* or forest dweller.

22. And, as one text notes, "the creatures that are not allowed to take part in the sacrifice are forlorn." This text goes on to give instructions for how to include, through ritual symbolism, all the creatures: "And therefore he makes those creatures here on earth that are not forlorn take part in the sacrifice. Behind the men are the animals, and behind the gods are the birds, the plants, and the trees; and thus all that here exists is made to take part in the sacrifice" (ŚB 1.5.2.4; cf. ŚB 3.6.2.26). The main purpose here is to demonstrate how, through the *bandhus* or connections, all of nature participates in the sacrifice. In the course of doing so, it also gives yet another list of the inhabitants of the world: men and animals, on the one hand, and gods, birds, plants, and trees, on the other.

23. See the older studies by James Fergusson, *Tree and Serpent Worship*, 2d ed. (1875, reprint Delhi: Oriental Publishers, 1971); and J. H. Philpot, *The Sacred Tree: The Tree in Religion and Myth* (London: Macmillan, 1897). More recent comparative studies on the topic include Mircea Eliade's *Patterns in Comparative Religion*, trans. by Rosemary Sheed (New York: World Publishing, 1958), esp. pp. 265ff. Cf. Jacques André, "Arbor felix, arbor infelix," in *Hommages à Jean Bayet*, ed. by Marcel Renard and Robert Schilling (Brussels: Collection Latomus, 1964), pp. 35–46.

24. The best work surveying trees in the history of religion in India is Odette Viennot's *Le Culte de l'arbre dans l'Inde ancienne* (Paris: Presses Universitaires de France, 1954). Other studies of the topic include M. Emeneau, *The Strangling Figs in Sanskrit Literature* (Berkeley: University of California Press, 1949); B. C. Sinha, *Tree Worship in Ancient India* (New Delhi: Books Today, 1979); Shakti M. Gupta, *Plant Myths and Traditions in India* (Leiden: E. J. Brill, 1971); S. S. Gupta, ed., *Tree Symbol Worship in India: A New Survey of a Pattern of Folk-Religion* (Calcutta: Indian Publications, 1965); M. S. Randhawa, *The Cult of Trees and Tree-Worship in Buddhist-Hindu Sculpture* (New Delhi: All India Fine Arts and Crafts Society, 1964); and E. Washburn Hopkins, "Mythological Aspects of Trees and Mountains in the Great Epics," *Journal of the American Oriental Society* (1910): 347–74.

25. E.g., TS 3.8.1.2; KB 4.12; ŚB 3.3.2.8, 3.4.1.10, 5.4.3.16, 8.4.3.17, 12.1.1.2, 12.8.3.19; AitB 3.40; TB 3.1.4.3. Other gods are also so identified: Indra is "lord of the forest" at TB 2.6.12.4 and 2.6.14.5; Agni is so labeled at KB 10.6 and trees are regarded as the "food" of Agni the fire at ŚB 9.2.3.36 and 10.3.4.4. KB 6.5 declares Rudra to be "plants and trees," and, similarly, ŚB 6.1.3.12 declares Paśupati the lord of plants (as well as of animals). Finally, at KB 12.7 and AitB 2.4. and 2.10 the honor of "lord of plants" goes to "breath."

26. See, e.g., TB 3.1.4.5; ŚB 2.2.4.3, 10.6.4.1; AitĀ 2.4.1. At ŚB 9.3.1.4 the plants

are said to be the hair of the beard of Agni. The notion that the trees and plants are the hair of the Cosmic Man or creator persists in later Hinduism, e.g., MārkP 48.3–26, KūrmaP 1.7.53; and VishnuP 1.5.45ff., where plants and trees are supposed to have been created from hair of Brahmā's body.

27. In one text, the plants and trees are regarded as part of the clothing of the earth (ŚB 6.1.1.13). Yet another imaginative variant supposes that the plants were formed when, once upon a time, the Angirases made it rain. "As many drops fell down, so many plants were born" (TB 2.1.1.2). For myths of the origin of plants and trees, see also ŚB 2.2.4.1ff. and Lincoln, *Myth, Cosmos, and Society*, esp. pp. 1–40.

28. In the ritual, the fuel used to stoke the sacrificial fires (*idhma*) is often said to be the analogue of "the trees" in general: "The sacrificial stake is yonder sun, the altar is the earth, the strew is the plants, the fuel is the trees, the sprinkling water is [all] the waters, the enclosing sticks are the quarters" (AitB 5.28; cf. TB 2.1.5.1–2; ŚB 11.1.7.2).

29. The *palāśa* is the Butea frondosa or Butea monosperma, sometimes known as the bastard teak, and appears to be the same tree that the Vedic texts also call by the name of *parṇa*. Here and in other cases where there does not appear to be a generally accepted English name for the tree I have retained the Sanskrit. According to Sinha, *Tree Worship in Ancient India*, pp. 24–25, this tree is known as the "flame of the forest" (but see below for other writers claiming this is the *plakṣa* tree) because "the flowers of this tree glitter so much in the sunlight that it appears as if the forest is in flames." According to Sinha, the flowers from the tree are offered to the gods in Hindu *pūjā* rituals and the wood from this tree is used for housebuilding.

30. Gymnosporia montana, Flacourtia sapida or Flacourtia ramontchi, apparently sometimes known as the Madagascar plum tree. Authorities agree that, whatever the species, the wood of this tree is hard and thorny.

31. The *bilva* or Aegle marmelos, also known as the *bel* or the Bengal quince. It is described by Sinha, *Tree Worship in Ancient India*, p. 26, as a deciduous tree with trifoliate leaves whose edible fruit also may be used for dye, oil, cement, etc. Gum from the trunk is also used as an adhesive. Shakti Gupta, *Plant Myths and Traditions*, p. 21, says it is "a scraggy tree with three leaves and with a crust of thick thorns."

32. The *khadira*, Acacia catechu or Mimosa catechu, known also for its very hard wood.

33. Also known as the cluster fig or the gular. It is the Ficus glomerata or, since the classification was changed in 1946 in order to subsume the tree under a larger group, the Ficus racemosa. According to Sinha, "It is a large spreading tree, without aerial roots, which is found throughout India. Its leaves are dark green and the figs are red when ripe. The wood of this tree is soft and very light. It is not durable but lasts fairly well under water." Its leaves are used as fodder for cattle, its figs are edible, and it is a good shade tree. *Tree Worship in Ancient India*, pp. 27–28. For an exhaustive survey of the citations in the Veda dealing with the *udumbara* tree, consult Christopher Minkowski, "The Udumbara and Its Ritual Significance," *Wiener Zeitschrift für die Kunde Sudasiens und Archiv für Indische Philosophie* 33 (1989): 5–23.

34. Perhaps the most renowned of India's trees, the *aśvattha* or Ficus religiosa, also called the bo or *bodhi* tree, is a large deciduous tree found throughout the subcontinent. "*Aświattha* has aerial, hanging adventitious roots which come down to earth and act as props to the trees; the slender petioles cause its leaves to tremble readily in a breeze, making a characteristic fluttering sound." Shakti Gupta, *Plant Myths and Traditions*, p. 51. Cf. Viennot, *Le culte de l'arbre*, p. 23, where the pipal tree is said to possess "lanceolate leaves, so characteristic, with their long petals which render the foliage ever quivering and melodious." See also T. K. Biswas and P. K. Debnath, "Aśvattha (*Ficus*

religiosus Linn): A Cultural and Medicinal Observation,"*Vishveshvaranand Indological Journal* 12, 1–2 (March–Sept. 1974): 39–47; S. L. Gupta, "Sacred Plants in the Hindu Religion," *India Cultures Quarterly* 22, 1 (1965): 6–19; Ananda K. Coomaraswamy, "The Inverted Tree," *Quarterly Journal of the Mythic Society* 29, 2 (Oct. 1938): 111–49; and Purna Chandra Ojha, *Aśvattha in Everyday Life as Related in the Purāṇas* (Delhi: Sundeep, 1991).

35. KŚS 1.3.33–36; ĀpŚS 1.15.10; HŚS 1.4.1; cf. BhŚS 1.16.5. Five particular species are enumerated at BŚS 2.12 as wood needed for setting up the sacrificial fires (*aśvattha*, *udumbara*, *palāśa*, acacia (*śamī*, Acacia suma, Prosopis spicigera), and *vikankata*), together with wood of a tree that has been struck by lightning. The required wood for the fuel and enclosing sticks is elsewhere said be that of *palāśa*, *khadira*, *kārṣmarya*, *bilva*, *udumbara*, *vikankata*, or *rohitaka* (Andersonia rohitaka) trees (BhŚS 1.5.2–7; BŚS 1.3; MSS 1.1.3).

36. For a list of trees prohibited from use in rituals, see KŚS 21.3.20 and GGS 1.5.14–15; for trees and plants having favorable and unfavorable characteristics, KauśS 8.15–16 and ŚB 13.8.1.16. Forbidden vegetables, fruits, foods, and herbs are also listed at ĀpDhS 1.5.17.25–27; 2.8.18.2; GautDhS 17.32–33; VāsDhS 14.33; Manu 5.5–10, 6.14; and YājSm 1.171ff.

37. The notion that certain trees contain sacrificial powers continues into later Hinduism. For a list of "sacrificial" plants and trees in Hinduism, see Shakti M. Gupta, *Plant Myths and Traditions*, p. 4 (citing the Gāruḍa Purāṇa): "The twigs of such sacrificial trees or plants, e.g. *arka* (calatropis gigantea), *palāśa*, *khadira*, *apāmārga* (Achyranthes aspera), *pippala* (Piper longum), *udumbara*, *śamī*, blades of *dūrvā* (Pao cynasuroides) and *kuśa ghās* (Eragrostis cynasuroides), soaked with curd, honey, clarified butter should be repeatedly cast in the sacrificial fire, in *homa* ceremonies celebrated for the propitiation of the planets, such as the Sun." Gupta also cites passages from Hindu texts that declare that one who gives libations of first fruits in vessels of *palāśa*, *aśvattha*, *plakṣa*, *nyagrodha*, *kāśmarī* (Gmelina arborea), *madhuka* (Jonesia asoka), *phalgu* (Ficus oppositifolia), *bilva*, or *venu* gets the benefit of all sacrifices (p. 5).

38. Cf. ŚB 12.7.2.14-15: "There is an *aśvattha* vessel: honor he thereby secures. There is an *udumbara* one: he obtains compensation (*apaciti*) [with it]. There is a *nyagrodha* one: self-rule (*svadhā*) he obtains [with it]. There are [earthen] pots: he obtains the food of the earth. There are [vessels] of *palāśa* wood near at hand. The *palāśa* is the *brahman*; it is by means of the *brahman* that he conquers the heavenly world." See also the special rules for the stake at the Aśvamedha sacrifice: "The sacrificial post for the other sacrifices is of *khadira*-, *bilva*- or *palāśa*-wood, but for the Aśvamedha it is of *nicudara*-wood" (PB 21.4.13); "For other sacrificial rituals, the sacrificial posts are made of *bilva*, *khadira*, or *palāśa*. For the Aśvamedha, [the stake is] made of *rajjudāla* (Cordia latifolia)" (TB 3.8.19.1). Cf. ŚB 13.4.4.6.

39. The *nyagrodha* or Indian fig, Ficus indica or Ficus bengalensis, is also synonymous with what the texts call the *vaṭa*. It is among the most distinctive-looking trees of India because of its ability "to support its ever growing branches and weight by the development of adventitious roots from its branches, roots which hang down and act as props over an ever widening circle." Shakti Gupta, *Plant Myths and Traditions*, p. 56. Cf. the description given by Viennot, *Le culte de l'arbre*, p. 23, where the banyan is to be distinguished "by the vigor of its aerial roots that enable it to grow horizontally to the point of covering a considerable distance."

40. In addition to the texts cited below, mention should also be made of a relatively late ritual text known as the "*yūpalakṣana*" or the "Signs of the Sacrificial Stake," where woods of different colors are said to belong to the different *varṇa*s, and thus a member

of a given social class is instructed to use a sacrificial stake with the appropriate affinities: "A white [tree] should be known to be a Brahmin, a reddish brown [tree] is mentioned to be a Kshatriya, a smoke-colored [tree] should be [regarded as] a Vaishya; and one should characterize a black [tree] as a Shūdra. In [the sacrifice of a] Brahmin, the sacrificial stake should be from a Brahmin tree; in [that of a] Kshatriya, it should be from a Kshatriya tree; in [that of a] Vaishya, it is made from a Vaishya tree; and in [that sacrifice of a] Shūdra, the sacrificial stake should be constructed from a Shūdra tree, etc. As is the soul [of a sacrifice], so is the sacrificial stake; for the soul of the sacrifice is the sacrificial stake. The soul of the sacrificer thus attains the status of the sacrificial stake." The text comes from the *Katyāyana-pariśiṣṭa*, and is translated in the *Śrautakośa*, Vol. 1, p. 1156, which, with a few adjustments, this translation follows.

41. I have analyzed this ritual and its functions (primarily to create a properly constituted human being of one or another of the three "twice-born" classes through the manipulation of *varṇa*-encoded symbols) in Brian K. Smith, "Ritual, Knowledge, and Being: Initiation and Veda Study in Ancient India," *Numen* 33, 1 (1986): 65–89. For the significance of the *daṇḍa* or staff in this ritual and others, see Ariel Glucklich, "The Royal Sceptre (*Daṇḍa*) as Legal Punishment and Sacred Symbol," *History of Religions* 28, 2 (Nov. 1988): 97–122.

42. See ĀśvGS 1.19.13; GautDhS 1.26; VāsDhS 11.55–57; Manu 2.45; BDhS 1.2.3.15. For an inversion of the normal heights recommended, however, consult ŚGS 2.1.21–23.

43. The *badarī* or *badara*—Zizyphus jujuba—also known as the jujabe or Indian plum tree. This fruit tree is particularly hardy and has given rise to many myths in later Hindu literature. See Shakti Gupta, *Plant Myths and Traditions*, pp. 108–11.The association of the jujube or *badarī* tree and the Vaishyas made in the Gṛhya Sūtras (the staff of the Vaishya initiate is optionally made of it or of the *udumbara*), and the connection one text makes between the jujube, "increase," and the Vaishya (BGS 2.5.22), apparently derives from the fruitfulness of this particular tree. Its fruits, rather than its wood, seem to be the basis for assigning a *varṇa* to the jujube tree.

44. ŚGS 2.1.18–20; BGS 2.5.17; BhGS 1.1; ĀpGS 4.11.16; HGS 1.1.1.17; VaikhSmS 2.4; JGS 1.12; ĀpDhS 1.1.1.38; VāsDhS 11.52–54. Cf. ĀśvGS 1.9.13; VGS 5.27; PGS 2.5.25–27; GGS 2.10.11; Manu 2.45; GautDhS 1.22–23.

45. Cf. TB 1.7.8.7, where the banyan is connected to the concept of "contract" (*mitranī*).

46. Viennot, *Le culte de l'arbre*, p. 35.

47. Ibid., 69.

48. MS 4.4.2; TB 1.7.8.7; ĀpŚS 18.16.3,5; KŚS 15.5.30. See also Viennot, *Le culte de l'arbre*, p. 57.

49. The central leaf of the *palāśa* is also larger than the other two. See Eggeling's note on the passage cited below. The tripartite leaf of the *palāśa* is often connected to the Hindu *trimūrti* of Viṣṇu, Śiva, and Brahmā in later Hinduism according to Sinha, *Tree Worship in Ancient India*, p. 25.

50. ŚB 13.8.4.1. See also ŚB 12.7.2.15, where *palāśa* and the *brahman* are equated, and where it is again declared that "it is by means of the *brahman* that he thus obtains the heavenly world."

51. ŚB 6.5.1.1. For the connection to soma and the moon in later Hinduism, see also Sinha, *Tree Worship in Ancient India*, pp. 24–25; and for the Hindu equation of *palāśa*, soma, the moon, and Monday (*somavāra*), Shakti M. Gupta, *Plant Myths and Traditions in India*, pp. 12–13.

52. For the phenomenon in general, see Smith, *Reflections*, pp. 187–89.

53. Some memory of this function is apparently preserved in Hinduism, for the *palāśa* is employed in Hindu ceremonies designed to make calves into good milkers. D. V. Cowen, *Flowering Trees and Shrubs in India* (Bombay: Thacker & Co., 1957), p. 4.

54. The connection of the *palāśa* and the Brahmins is perpetuated by the later belief that of the three deities of the Hindu *trimūrti*, the *palāśa* belongs to Brahmā. Sinha, *Tree Worship in Ancient India*, p. 33.

55. According to Shakti M. Gupta, *Plant Myths and Traditions in India*, p. 51, the *aśvattha* is thought by Hindus to be a Brahmin tree, largely on the strength of BhGS 10.2, where the tree is linked to the deified Brahman. Cf. Biswas and Debnath, "Aśvattha," esp. p. 41. There is little evidence for such an association in Vedic texts, however; the tree is usually regarded as belonging to the Vaishyas and, occasionally, to the Kshatriyas.

56. See Shakti M. Gupta, *Plant Myths and Traditions in India*, p. 21: "Bilva is a scraggy tree with three leaves and with a crust of thick thorns." Gupta goes on to observe that "the three leaves together, look like Trishul, or the Trident, the emblem of Śiva. . . . That is why Bilva leaves are considered effective in removing the sins of three births. The tree is sacred to Śiva and is worshipped by his followers on the 14th phase of the moon's wane between the months of Magha (Feb.) and Phālguna (March)."

57. According to K. D. Upadhyaya, the wood apple is called *śriphal*, the "fruit of prosperity," in later India. "Indian Botanical Folklore," in *Tree Symbol Worship in India: A New Survey of a Pattern of Folk-Religion*, ed. by S. S. Gupta (Calcutta: Indian Publications, 1965), p. 7.

58. Ficus infectoria or Ficus racemosa. According to Shakti Gupta, this tree is the Butea monosperma, also known as the parrot or judas tree, and also as the "flame of the forest." Gupta seems to have conflated the *plakṣa* with the *palāśa*, however, treating them as if they were the same tree; most authorities regard them as two different species.

59. TS 7.4.12.1. For a similar, although somewhat anomalous, contention that the *kārṣmarya* tree is filled with the sacrificial essence, see ŚB 3.8.2.17.

60. Shakti M. Gupta, *Plant Myths and Traditions in India*, p. 31: "The tree is associated with moon as it is believed to have sprung from the feather of a falcon imbued with Soma, the intoxicating drink of the gods and is thus immortalised. It is a common practice to use the leaves of the tree in ceremonies connected with the blessing of the calves to ensure their becoming good milkers." See also p. 31: "When a Brahmin boy renounces the worldly life and becomes a sadhu and his hair is being shorn, he is given the Plaksha leaf to eat or else he must eat off Plaksha leaves."

61. See, however, the unusual text at AitB 7.32 that links the *plakṣa* to the Kshatriya attributes of fame (*yaśas*), rule (*rājya*), and independence of rule (*svarājya*).

62. Compare the notion that the *dūrvā* grass (Cynodon dactylon) is connected to the the *kṣatra* power and the Kshatriya social class (cf. ŚB 7.4.2.12) because of its similar growth pattern: "[It] is a tenacious creeping plant, which spreads rapidly, throwing out perpetually new branches, a hard perennial grass with creeping culms rooting at nodes and forming spreading mats on the surface of the soil." Jan Gonda, *The Ritual Functions and Significance of Grasses in the Religion of the Veda* (Amsterdam: North-Holland, 1985), p. 108. Having identified the *dūrvā* and the *kṣatra*, AitB 8.8 goes on to note that "the Kshatriya is the *kṣatra* power, for the Kshatriya dwelling in the kingdom is fastened (*nitata*) here as it were, and supported (*pratiṣṭhita*) as it were. The *dūrvā* is fastened as it were to the ground (*bhūmi*) with descending growths, and is supported as it were. Thus in that there is *dūrvā* grass, truly thus he confers upon him the *kṣatra* of the plants and also a support."

63. Glucklich, "The Royal Sceptre," p. 102.

64. KŚS 19.2. Among the Hindu deities of the *trimūrti*, the banyan is connected to Śiva according to Sinha, *Tree Worship in Ancient India*, p. 33.

65. TS 5.2.7.3–4; 6.2.1.5ff.; KS 20.5. Similarly, but only once, the *vikaṅkata* tree is also said to be a thunderbolt: "If the spoon is of *vikaṅkata* wood—the *vikaṅkata* is the thunderbolt—it is with the thunderbolt that he exterminates the danger, the demons" (ŚB 5.2.4.18).

66. It is interesting to note that the *ārūndhati* plant, which was believed to have properties that healed sword wounds, is said to be the product of the union between the cutch and *aśvattha* trees. See AV 3.6.1, 4.12, 5.5.5, 8.8.3. For a myth of origins that explains why the cutch is used both for the wooden sword and for the sacrificial stake, consult ŚB 3.6.2.12. The wood's durability was also apparently a signifier for long life, as a vessel made out of cutch was employed in a ritual said to confer that quality upon the sacrificer (BŚS 13.31; ĀpŚS 19.23.10ff.).

67. Glucklich, "The Royal Sceptre," pp. 100–101.

68. Only at AitB 7.32 and ĀśvGS 1.19.13 (where the staff of a Kshatriya is required to be made of *udumbara* wood) is the *udumbara* tree so connected to the second *varṇa*. The tree's prominence in royal rituals is as a representative of the *viś* over whom the king rules. See below.

69. For other reasons for linking the pipal and the Kshatriya, see A. A. Macdonell and A. B. Keith, *Vedic Index of Names and Subjects*, 2 vols. (reprint Varanasi: Motilal Banarsidass, 1958), I:43: "It planted its roots in shoots of other trees, especially the *Khadira*, and destroyed them; hence it is called 'the destroyer' (*vaibadha*)." Cf. TS 5.4.7; AV 3.6.1ff., 8.8.3; and Viennot, *Le culte de l'arbre*, p. 63. For the notion in later literature that the pipal is a Kshatriya, consult especially Mbh 3.115, where the warrior traits of Parāsurāma are explained by his Brahmin mother's inadvertent embrace of the pipal tree.

70. For a survey of its medicinal properties, as well as its more general capabilities to generate well being, long life, prosperity, happiness, and sexual power, consult Biswas and Debnath, "Aśvattha." Sinha relays the Hindu belief in the tree's ability to make one rich, *Tree Worship in Ancient India*, p. 33; K. D. Upadhyaya, "Indian Botanical Folklore," p. 4, notes the popular belief in the tree's connection to "conjugal love and happiness"; and W. D. O'Flaherty, *Women, Androgynes, and Other Mythical Beasts* (Chicago: University of Chicago Press, 1980), p. 229, notes that the term "*pippala*" is associated with sensual pleasure and marital bliss. Rarely in Vedic texts, the tree is associated with the *brahman*, as in KU 6.1 and MaitU 6.4 (cf. ṚV 1.24.7), but this association is apparently common in later literature. See Viennot, *Le culte de l'arbre*, pp. 85–88; and Shakti Gupta, *Plant Myths and Traditions in India*, pp. 51–53: "The tree is considered to be a Brahman."

71. MS 4.4.2; TB 1.7.8.7; ĀpŚS 18.16.3,5; KŚS 15.5.30; and also in later texts like MātsyaP 255.20 and VisnuP 2.2.16. Cf. Viennot, *Le culte de l'arbre*, pp. 57, 66.

72. Alfred Hillebrandt, *Vedic Mythology*, 2 vols., trans. S. Rajeswara Sarma (Delhi: Motilal Banarsidass, 1970), II:177, traces the association to a naturalistic source: "The Maruts are Vaishyas and represent the vish. The constant fluttering of the leaves of this tree might have made it an abode for the wind gods [i.e., the Maruts] in Indian conceptions." For the connection between the Maruts and the pipal, see also ṚV 1.165.4, 5.54.12, 8.12.15.

73. See Eggeling's note on ŚB 4.3.3.6, where he writes that the association of the Maruts and the pipal "would seem to be based on a mistaken interpretation of Rig-veda I,135,8, where the bard says that 'the victorious (*jayavah*) have come nigh to the *aśvattha*,' the '*jayavah*' here evidently referring (not to the Maruts, as in I,119,3), but to the powerful draughts of Soma flowing into the *aśvattha* vessel."

74. ṚV 1.164.20–22; AV 5.4.3; cf. ṚV 5.54.12; TS 4.2.6.2, 7.2.1.3; VS 35.4; ŚB 13.8.3.1.

75. BŚS 13.21, as translated in the *Śrautakośa*, p. 553.

76. The myth of origins for the practice and for the generative properties of the pipal may be found at ŚB 11.5.1.1ff. This may also explain why this tree at GGS 4.7.21–22 is connected to fire and the sun god Āditya. For data concerning the acacia or *śamī* (Acacia suma or Prosopis spicigera), which is thought to have fire or Agni within, see Shakti Gupta, *Plant Myths and Traditions*, pp. 18–20, and M. Biardeau, "The Śāmī Tree and the Sacrificial Buffalo," *Contributions to Indian Sociology* (n.s.) 18,1 (Jan.–June, 1984): 1–23.

77. Shakti Gupta, *Plant Myths and Traditions in India*, p. 55: "The plant is a symbol of fertility and is worshipped by women for the grant of a child." For connections in Hinduism of the pipal and Viṣṇu (among the deities of the *trimūrti*), idem, pp. 51–2; Sinha, *Tree Worship in Ancient India*, p. 33; and P. Mahapatra, "Tree-Symbol Worship in Bengal," in *Tree Symbol Worship in India: A New Survey of a Pattern of Folk-Religion*, ed. by S.S. Gupta (Calcutta: Indian Publications, 1965), pp. 126–27 (where mention is also made of the tree's connection to fertility).

78. These qualities are the ones that are tapped by the frequent use of the wood in royal ceremonies. It is, however, too much to assume, as some scholars like Viennot have, that because of its "emploi si frequent dans les ceremonies royales" the tree is connected to the Kshatriya class. *Le culte de l'arbre*, p. 31. The tree is nevertheless explicitly connected to the Kshatriyas (and to the north) at MS 4.4.2; TB 1.7.8.7; ĀpŚS 18.16.3,5; and KŚS 15.5.30. For the connection of the *udumbara* and the north, see also ŚB 7.4.1.39: "And Indra took his [Prajāpati's] *ojas* away and went to the north; it became the *udumbara*."

79. For the connection of the *udumbara* to sap and nourishment, see below and also ŚB 6.7.1.13, 7.2.2.3, 7.4.1.38, 7.5.1.15, 9.2.2.3, 9.2.3.40, 14.1.2.4, 14.1.3.9. The tree is simply identified with nourishment at TS 2.1.1.6, 2.5.4.4, 5.1.10.1, 5.2.8.7, 5.4.6.1, 6.1.4.1ff., 6.6.10.1, 7.3.14.1, 7.4.12.1; KS 5.3, 5.4, 20.7, 21.9, 21.12, 25.10; MS 1.11.8, 3.1.2, 3.2.6, 3.2.7, 3.4.3, 4.4.2, 4.4.6; PB 5.5.2, 6.4.11, 16.6.4, 18.2.11; JB 1.71–72; ṢaḍB 4.3.6; ŚB 5.4.3.26; 7.5.1.21, 12.8.3.5; TĀ 5.2.4, 5.9.3, 5.10.5; and passages cited below.

80. In addition to the citations quoted below, the tree is associated with nourishment and food at TB 1.2.6.5, 1.3.8.2; JB 2.159, 2.183; AitB 5.24, 7.32, 8.8, 8.9; KB 25.13, 27.6, 27.10; ŚB 3.2.1.33, 3.3.4.27, 4.6.9.22, 5.2.1.23, 5.2.2.2, 5.3.4.2, 5.3.5.12, 9.2.2.3, 14.1.2.4; PB 18.2.11; ŚānĀ 1.7; AitĀ 1.2.3–4.

81. Minkowski, "The Udumbara and Its Ritual Significance," pp. 6,9,13.

82. See Minkowski, ibid., p. 8, for similar information conveyed from botanists.

83. Minkowski, ibid., p. 10, notes the many passages in which the synonyms *ūrj* and *iṣa* appear together.

84. AitB 5.24. Cf. TB 1.1.3.10: "Nourishment is the *udumbara*. The gods distributed vigor; from that the *udumbara* sprang up. Nourishment is the *udumbara*; he obtains nourishment who collects together what belongs to the *udumbara*."

85. See TS 3.4.8 and J. J. Meyer, *Trilogie altindischer Mächte und Feste der Vegetation*, 3 vols. (Zurich: Max Niehans, 1937), III:192, where it is noted that a staff of *udumbara* is placed in bed between newlyweds and the Gandharvas are invoked for several days after the wedding in order to aid in consummation.

86. PB 6.4.1,11–12; cf. JB 2.183. For similar statements concerning the creation of the *udumbara* from the distribution of *ūrj*, see MS 1.6.5; 3.1.9; KS 19.10; TB 1.1.3.10; ŚB 12.7.1.9.

87. The connection of the *udumbara* and diseases of the eye postulated at GGS 4.7.21 would seem to be anomalous.

88. AV 19.31.4. The entire hymn centers on the powers of the *udumbara* amulet to deliver prosperity, fat livestock, much grain, the "milk of cattle and the sap of plants," progeny, wealth and riches, etc.

89. See, e.g., TS 2.1.1.6, where in an optional animal sacrifice for one who "desires animals," the she-goat dedicated to Soma (assimilated to seed) and Pūṣan ("the producer of animals") is tied to a stake made of *udumbara*, for "the *udumbara* is vital strength, and animals are vital strength; thus by vital strength he wins for him vital strength and animals." Cf. TS 2.5.4.3–4; BŚS 17.48; 28.6; MŚS 5.2.10.7; ĀpŚS 3.16.11ff.; HŚS 2.6. See also the descriptions of the Viśvajit ritual (which entails the sacrifice of all and the subsequent recouping of wealth) where the sacrificer is clothed in the skin of a cow and dwells for a period under an *udumbara* tree in order to win vital strength and food (e.g., KB 25.15).

90. For curds identified with the Vaishyas (and clarified butter with the Brahmins, milk with the Kshatriyas, and water with the Shūdras) see ĀpŚS 22.26.1. Cf. TS 6.2.5.2-4, where the foods linked to the social classes are milk for Brahmins (for milk is associated with *tejas*), rice mash (*yavagu*) for the Kshatriya ("for rice mash is harsh, and is the form of the thunderbolt"), and curds and milk (*āmikṣā*) for the Vaishya "for obtaining material prosperity (*puṣṭi*)." For curds as "power in this world," see AitB 8.20.

91. For this topic, consult P. V. Kane, *History of Dharmaṣāstra*, 5 vols., 2d ed. (Poona: Bhandarkar Oriental Research Institute, 1968–75), Vol. 2, Pt. 1, p. 224.

92. Minkowski, "The Udumbara," p. 23.

8

Classifying Fauna

Animals and the Overdetermination of Class

For the principled nonvegetarians of Vedic India, animals were the highest form of nutrition: "Meat," it is said, "is indeed the best kind of food" (ŚB 11.7.1.3; cf. ŚB 12.8.3.12). But animals, as Claude Lévi-Strauss observed, are not only good to eat; they are also "good to think."[1] The thinking humans do with animals is most often guided by an attempt to clothe what is cultural and arbitrary in the imperial robes of what is "natural." And when humans think about animals, as when we think about gods, we are inevitably thinking about ourselves.

A survey of the ways the animal kingdom was organized in the Veda must immediately confront the fact that there are several, and at least superficially very different, methods for classifying animals. First, animals were distinguished by their various anatomical characteristics or modes of procreation—an attempt, not unlike modern Western zoology, to present classificatory decisions as "empirical." Second, animals were classified as either domesticated (*grāmya*, "of the village") or wild (*āraṇya*, "of the jungle"). Third, ritually based criteria were deployed for categorizing animals into those which were suitable for the sacrifice and those which were not. Fourth, animals were classified as either edible or inedible. And, finally, animals were subjected to the *varṇa* classificatory scheme we have seen at work in so many other domains. These apparently various methods for classifying animals were neither self-contained nor mutually exclusive; the categories of animals established by one set of taxonomic distinctions are complemented by, reinforced by, and in some cases readjusted to the others. Indeed, this categorical conflation might have been intended by those who did the classifying. The confusion of the natural and the cultural, the physiological and the ideological, the visible and invisible, and the nonhuman and human may be more than just the consequence of differing traditions and classificatory methodologies colliding and conjoining in ancient Indian texts. It might very well have been a deliberate strategy. The success of an ideology like that of *varṇa* depends in part on its ability to encompass competing systems within it. When it doesn't simply ignore them, an ideology takes account of alternative ideologies in the process of taking account of the cosmos, and it does so often enough by displaying competing visions as alternative forms of its own.[2]

Of special interest is the confusion we shall encounter between animal classes and human classes. Animal taxonomies, as many scholars have demonstrated for many cultures, have obvious social implications.[3] In this chapter, having first surveyed some of the taxonomic strategies for categorizing animals per se, we turn attention to the social ramifications of animal classificatory schemes. As we shall see, some humans were identified with certain animals in order to classify those people as altogether uncivilized and outside the realm of "proper" humanity; other kinds of humans were associated with other kinds of animals in order to reinforce the divisions of the ideal civilized society and to extend the *varṇa* scheme into the animal kingdom.

"Empirical" Criteria for Categorizing Animals

Animals, as we already saw in Chapter 3, were supposedly created in certain classes at the dawn of time by the creator god, Puruṣa (the Cosmic Man) or Prajāpati (the Lord of Creatures). Another such cosmogonic story concerning the origins of animals comes from the BĀU (1.4.1,3–4):

> In the beginning, there was only the Self (*ātman*) in the form of a person (*puruṣa*). . . . He was not sexually pleased. Therefore one who is alone is not sexually pleased. He wished for a second. He was of the same size as a man and woman copulating. He caused that body to fall apart into two. From that came to be the husband and wife. Therefore Yājñavalkya said, "Oneself is like half a piece." Therefore this space is filled with a woman. He copulated with her. From that, the human race was born. She thought to herself, 'How does he copulate with me having given birth to me from his own self? Oh, I must hide!' She became a cow, [but he became] another bull and copulated with her. From that cattle were born. She became a mare, [but he became] another stallion. She became a she-ass, [but he became] another he-ass and copulated with her. From that were born the whole-hoofed animals. She became a she-goat, [but he became] another he-goat. She became a ewe, [but he became] another ram, and copulated with her. From that were born goats and sheep. Thus he created all, whatever copulating pairs there are, right down to the ants.

In this account, the creator god is anthropomorphically represented as a primordial androgyne whose first, and highest, creation is man and woman—and, indeed, humans are ranked in all such accounts as the highest among animals.[4] Taking different forms in a cosmic game of incestuous hide and seek, the two parts of the divided creator create the species of animals "right down to the ants." As one scholar has observed in relation to this text, "The list thus encompasses all the defining species of the ancient Indian world."[5]

The text is not simply concerned to provide a general summary of the creation of animals, however. It also presents us with several specific classificatory determinations (in addition to the male–female opposition) within the animal kingdom ("whatever copulating pairs there are"). The pairs of mammals the myth enumerates—humans, cows, horses, asses, goats, and sheep—are said to produce four classes of animals: the human race, cattle, whole-hoofed animals (generated by both the pairs of horses and asses), and the class designated "goats and sheep."

This twofold division of animals into six specific male–female pairs and four general classes draws on two different types of categorical principles found also in other Vedic taxonomies. I examine these two modes of distinguishing classes within the animal kingdom one at a time: first, I shall look at texts which provide a taxonomy of animals based on selected observable physical traits; later, I analyze those systems that present divisions of animals on the bases of other and less visible criteria.

The physical or physiological characteristics elevated to principles of categorical distinction are anatomical—particularly the structures of the foot and teeth—and functional (forms of locomotion and modes of procreation).[6]

The Structure of the Foot

The text cited above derives at least one of its general classes in the animal kingdom in a rather "flat-footed" or "pedestrian" manner: the class of "whole-hoofed" animals, which originate from horses and asses.[7] Other accounts also divide mammals according to the different structures of the foot, thus utilizing different "bases" or "foundations" for the different classes. Different species are, shall we say, "put on the same footing" in this manner. In several texts, the entire animal kingdom is divisible into two classes on the strength of their footedness: "Paśupati [the lord of animals] rules over the animals (*paśus*), the four-footed (*catuśpadam*) and the two-footed (*dvipadam*)" (AV 2.34.1; cf. ṚV 3.62.14; TS 4.3.4.3; 5.2.9.4–5 etc.). As the commentator on the passage makes clear, and as other texts confirm, it is human beings who are the chief members of the "two-footed" class, all other animals comprising the four-footed category.[8]

Being "five-clawed," the human foot also serves as an anatomical paradigm for identifying animals which are not to be eaten: "One should not eat solitary animals, or unknown wild animals or birds, nor any five-clawed animals, not even those listed [in other texts] among the animals to be eaten" (Manu 5.17). The commentators specify that such inedible humanlike animals include "pseudo-men" (to whom we shall return) and apes, as well as jackals, cats, and others who are, it would seem, too much like humans to eat due to their peculiar paws. The text continues, however, by making some exceptions to the general rule, isolating certain species among the five-clawed who are not, it would seem, overly humanlike, and therefore edible: "They say that, among the five-clawed animals, the porcupine, hedgehog, iguana, rhinoceros, tortoise, and the hare are edible,

TABLE 8.1. Divisions of Animals According to Structure of the Foot

Binary Opposition		
Four-Footed		*Two-Footed*
"all animals beginning with cattle"		"all animals beginning with man"
Tripartite Division		
Whole-Hoofed	*Cloven-Hoofed*	*Five-Clawed*
horses, asses, etc.	cattle, goats and sheep, etc.	inedible: humans, apes, jackals, cats, etc. edible: porcupines, hedgehogs, iguanas, rhinoceroses, tortoises, hares, etc.

and so are the animals with incisors in the lower jaw only, except for the camel" (Manu 5.18).

The Manu passage, together with the Upanishadic text cited previously, gives us further clues as to why the classes of cattle and "goats and sheep" are distinguishable from humans and whole-hoofed animals on empirical grounds. By virtue of foot structure, cattle and "goats and sheep" both fall into the cloven-hoofed class, and are therefore distinguishable from both the whole-hoofed and five-clawed classes. The structure of the foot thus separates the class of humans from all other animals, and then horses and asses (the "whole-hoofed") may be distinguished from animals with cloven hooves—cows, goats, and sheep. The system generated from this criterion is outlined in Table 8.1.

Dental Structure

Cattle, goats, and sheep are distinct from humans, and others in that class, because they are, according to Manu, edible; and they are separated from horses and asses (and others in the whole-hoofed class) in that they are cloven-hoofed and have incisors in only the lower jaw (*anyatodant*) rather than in both jaws (*ubhayadant*). Animals with lower incisors only, which Manu decrees to be consumable, include cows, goats, "and the rest," according to the commentators. In the famous creation hymn from the ṚV (10.90), the sacrifice of the Cosmic Man creates four principal categories of animals, human beings and three others: "Horses were born from it, and those other animals that have incisors in both jaws; cows were born from it, and from it goats and sheep were born" (ṚV 10.90.10). The classificatory divisions produced on the basis of dental structure are reproduced in Table 8.2.

Cattle, goats, and sheep are categorically separable from both humans and the class of horses and asses in that they have only lower incisors, as well as by virtue of their cloven hooves. As anatomical criteria, structures of feet and teeth

TABLE 8.2. Division of Animals According to Dental Structure

Incisors Only in Lower Jaw	*Incisors in Both Jaws*
cows, goats, sheep	humans, horses, asses

thus often duplicate the separation between classes of animals; the ass, for example, is described as both whole-hoofed and having incisors in both jaws (AV 5.31.3). And as is pointed out at TS 2.2.6.3–4, were not both of these criteria simultaneously in play, humans, on the one hand, and horses and asses, on the other, would not be categorically differentiated.[9]

Modes of Procreation

We have not yet encountered "empirical" grounds for assigning cattle, on the one hand, and "goats and sheep," on the other, to different categories. Taking the Upanishadic passage we began with, together with ṚV 10.90.10, it might be argued that in both cases "goats and sheep"—the last-mentioned group in both texts—represent a kind of generic category for "everything else."

There are other grounds, however, for constituting this last-named category more specifically. Goats and sheep are said to be the beasts which are "most manifestly" like the prolific creator god, Prajāpati, in that "they bear young three times a year and produce two [offspring] three times [per year]" (ŚB 4.5.5.6,9 and 5.2.1.24; cf. TS 6.5.10.1). We may have here a category based on the fecundity (a short gestation period and the ability to produce multiple births) of the animals included.

In other formulations the general classificatory principle is the mode of procreation characteristic of different types of animals: "There are three sources of the beings here—those born from an egg, those born from a living being, those born from sprouts" (ChU 6.3.1). Or again, with the tally reckoned at four types of animals on the basis of the form of birth, we read that from the creator god are produced all the animals springing from "the various sources: those born from an egg, those born from an embryonic sac, those born from moisture, and those born from sprouts" (AitU 5.3).

The most detailed and elaborate cosmogony, which entails, among other schemes and other species, a classification of the animals according to their sources of birth, comes from Manu, where the products of the creator's labors are enumerated:

> The pseudo-men (*kinnaras*), apes, fishes, and the various kinds of birds; the domestic animals (*paśus*), wild game (*mṛgas*), and humans; the beasts of prey and the animals with incisors in both jaws; worms, bugs, and moths; and lice, flies, maggots, mosquitoes, and gnats; and stationary things of various kinds—thus this whole [universe], stationary and moving, was emitted by those great-souled ones at my command through the use of ascetic heat, each according to its own *karma*. I will tell you now what sort of *karma* is said to belong to each sort of creature here, and also their order according to birth. Domestic animals and wild game; beasts of prey and the animals with incisors in both jaws; demons (*rākṣasas*), ghouls (*piśācas*), and humans—[these are the creatures] born from an embryonic sac. [Creatures] born from an egg are birds, snakes, crocodiles, fish, turtles, and various other species (*prakaraṇas*) born on land or in water. [Creatures] born from moisture are mosquitoes and gnats, lice, flies, maggots, and other species of this sort which originate from vapor. All the stationary

> [plants] that grow from seeds or stems are born from sprouts; [and also trees] that bear many flowers and fruits and then die when the fruit ripens. [Trees] with fruit but no flowers are known as *vanaspatis*; those that bear both flowers and fruit are known as *vṛkṣas*. The various sorts [of plants that have] one root and those with many roots, the different species of grasses, and climbing vines and creepers all grow from seeds or stems. (Manu 1.39–48)

The principal division in this account is between "moving" and "stationary" life forms, and the forms of locomotion exhibited by the "moving" beings provide one implicit principle permeating the lists: animals that walk, fly, slither, hop, swim, and so on. The explicit subdivision, however, is premised on the mode of procreation: those born from an embryonic sac, the egg-born, those born from moisture, and those born from sprouts. The last mentioned (the plants and trees) constitute the "stationary" category; the first three fall under the more general rubric of "moving" life, filling out and organizing the list with which the passage begins. The classification scheme of the text is schematized in Table 8.3. Under (*a*) are listed beings enumerated in the first verses categorized on the basis of procreation, a categorization which includes, in later verses, other beings listed under (*b*).

Within the "born from embryonic sac" category, we encounter subdivisions, some of which we have met before and some new. There is a separate class for demons and ghouls, and another for humanlike animals (the pseudo-men and apes), the latter recalling the aforementioned class of "five-clawed" animals. But for present purposes, the other subdivisions are of most interest: beasts of prey and animals with incisors in both jaws; and domestic animals, wild game, and humans.

The category of "animals with incisors in both jaws," as we noted earlier, seems to refer *inter alia* to horses and asses. Their two sets of incisors distinguish them from animals like cows, goats, and sheep, which have but a single set. Here, however, the doubly dentured are opposed to "beasts of prey," and so appear to be functioning as metonyms for domesticated animals in general. Furthermore,

TABLE 8.3. Division of Beings According to Mode of Procreation

	Stationary
Born from sprouts	(*a*) plants and trees
	(*b*) plants that grow from seeds or stems; trees that have many ripenings of flowers and fruit and die when the fruit ripens; trees with fruit but no flowers; trees that bear both fruit and flowers; plants with one root; plants with many roots; grasses; climbing vines and creepers
	Moving
Born from embryonic sac	(*a*) pseudo-men and apes
	(*b*) domestic animals
Born from an egg	(*a*) fishes and various kinds of birds
	(*b*) birds
Born from moisture	(*a*) worms
	(*b*) mosquitoes

the category of "domestic animals, wild game, and humans" replicates the same distinction. *Paśus* are here domestic animals in opposition to *mṛgas* or wild animals; both are opposed to humans who form a category of animals unto themselves.

Animals of the Village and Jungle

In an explication of a creation hymn (VS 14.28–31), the ŚB provides yet another cosmogonically (and anthropomorphically) grounded structure of animal classes:

> "With seventeen they praised"—there are ten toes, four thighs and calves, and two feet, and what is below the navel is the seventeenth. With that they praised. "The village animals (*grāmya paśus*) were emitted"—the village animals were [thus] now emitted. "Bṛhaspati was the overlord"—Bṛhaspati was [thus] now overlord. . . . "With twenty-one they praised"—there are ten fingers, ten toes, and the body (*ātman*) is the twenty-first. With that they praised. "The whole-hoofed animals were emitted"—the whole-hoofed animals were [thus] now emitted. "Varuṇa was the overlord"—Varuṇa was [thus] now the overlord. "With twenty-three they praised"—there are ten fingers, ten toes, two feet, and the body is the twenty-third. With that they praised. "The small animals (*kṣudra paśus*) were emitted"—the small animals were [thus] now emitted. "Pūṣan was the overlord"—Pūṣan was [thus] now the overlord. "With twenty-five they praised"—there are ten fingers, ten toes, four limbs, and the body is the twenty-fifth. With that they praised. "The jungle animals (*āraṇya paśus*) were emitted"—the jungle animals were [thus] now emitted. "Vāyu was the overlord"—Vāyu was [thus] now the overlord. (ŚB 8.4.3.11,12–15)

We note here the creation of four distinct classes of animals: village, whole-hoofed, small, and jungle. The two classes of the whole-hoofed and the "small" animals are, it appears, just another way of designating the distinction we encountered earlier between the horses and asses, on the one hand, and the cattle, goats, and sheep, on the other. The whole-hoofed class, as we have seen, consists of those animals (primarily horses and asses) that also have incisors in both jaws. When seen in relation to the other categories, the "small" animals seem to be none other than the class of animals with cloven hooves and one set of incisors. As Macdonell and Keith point out in reference to this passage, "the two . . . classes denot[e] the tame animals. The horse and the ass are *eka-śapha* [whole-hoofed]; the *kṣudra* [small] are the sheep, the goat and the ox: this distinction being parallel to that of *ubhayadant* [animals having incisors in both jaws] and *anyatodant* [animals having incisors only in the lower jaw]."[10]

The classification of nonhuman domestic animals into whole-hoofed and small in this text thus restates other kinds of anatomical categorization (i.e., between animals with a single set of incisors and those with two, and between the whole-hoofed and the cloven-hoofed). The jungle animals are depicted as all those which are neither whole-hoofed nor small, by which is thus meant nothing more than all nondomesticated animals.

The text, it would seem, fundamentally works with a binary classificatory dichotomy between "village" or domesticated and "jungle" or wild animals found quite frequently in Vedic literature,[11] with the genus of "village" animals subsequently subdivided into the species of "whole-hoofed" and "small." The subdivisions echo those made in other texts on the basis of pedal or dental structure or the mode of procreation. The jungle animals are here left en masse in spite of, or perhaps because of, the much larger variety of species embraced by the category;[12] wild animals were in any case less available for close observation than domestic ones.

Other taxonomies make a more straightforward division between village and jungle animals. In some cases, the twofold division is analyzed into three: animals of the air (*vāyavyas*), jungle, and village (ṚV 10.90.8). More often birds become one member of the category of wild or jungle animals, with village animals forming the other general class:

> The seven village animals are the cow, horse, goat, sheep, man, ass, and camel as the seventh; some say the mule [is the seventh]. The seven jungle animals are [wild] cloven-hoofed animals, animals having feet like dogs, birds, crawling animals, elephants, monkeys, and river animals as the seventh. (BŚS 24.5)

Here anatomical criteria—as in "cloven-hoofed animals,"[13] "animals having feet like dogs,"[14] and "crawling animals"—are put into play within a culturally constituted category of seven undomesticated jungle animals posited in opposition to the complementary set of seven domesticated village animals. In another list of this kind we have a division between the animals that have been tamed and "encultured" and animals that have not, with an emphasis on the wildness of the "jungle animals":

> Among these [animals] there are fourteen kinds possessing various forms—seven dwelling in the jungle and seven dwelling in the village. The seven dwelling in the jungle are known to be lions, tigers, wild boars, buffalo, elephants, bears, and apes. The cow, goat, human, sheep, horse, mule, and the ass—these seven village animals are enumerated by the wise.[15]

While the seven animals designated as "jungle animals" in this list are mostly different from those previously enumerated, the seven "village animals" enumerated are comparable; the only dispute is whether the camel or mule should be regarded as the seventh.

Although the village animals are, as we have seen, sometimes reckoned at seven[16] or even more—it is vaguely stated that the village animals are of all forms (*viśvarūpa*), of various forms (*virūpa*), of many and yet one form (*bahudhaikarūpa*) (AV 2.34.4; cf. TB 3.9.2.4)—as will be recalled the BĀU, in speaking of the first (and paradigmatic) pairs, lists only six (the mule or camel is absent). Other, and much more common, taxonomies of village animals number only five (excluding from consideration the ass, as well as the mule or camel) and refer to them simply as "*paśus*," or "the animals": "Prajāpati is all the *paśus*—the man, the horse, the cow, the sheep and the goat."[17] The AV (11.2.9) and other texts (e.g., TS 5.2.3.6) give identical lists of the five *paśus* and also contain a corresponding fivefold taxonomy of the jungle animals.[18] In another passage, these five animals are said to have been created from one or another of the creator's body parts or functions; furthermore, the four nonhuman *paśus* are supposed to be encompassed within the man, the premier member of the category:

> Prajāpati at first was one. He desired, "May I emit food, may I be reproduced." He measured out the *paśus* from his breaths. From his mind [he measured out] the man; from his eye, the horse; from his breath, the cow, from his ear, the ram; from his voice, the goat. And since he measured them out from his breaths, they say "The *paśus* are the breaths." And since he measured out the man from his mind, they say "The man is the first, the most virile (*viryavattama*) of the *paśus*." The mind is all the breaths, for all the breaths are firmly established in the mind. And since he measured out the man from his mind, they say, "The man is all *paśus*," for they all become the man's. (ŚB 7.5.4.6)

The term *paśu*, then, can refer to the five village animals as well as to animals in general. The five domesticated species are thus metonymically "all animals," and the four nonhuman village animals are subsumed within the human who is "all *paśus*." There is a further taxonomic signification to the word *paśu*. To qualify as a *paśu* in the more limited sense of the term requires that the animal be not only domesticated but also sacrificable.

Sacrificial Animals

In certain lists—those dealing with the mammoth animal sacrifice within the Aśvamedha or horse sacrifice—the number of particular kinds of both village and jungle animals is greatly expanded.[19] In some texts dealing with this ritual, the two types of victims are said to be inclusive of all food[20] as well as all animals. They thus come to represent the cosmic totality; the village is equated with this world and the jungle with the other world:

> They sacrifice the village animals for [obtaining] this world, the jungle [animals] for [obtaining] yonder [world]. When they sacrifice the village animals, with that he obtains this world; when the jungle [animals are sacrificed], with that [he obtains] yonder [world]. He sacrifices both kinds of animals, village and jungle, for the obtainment of both worlds. He sacrifices both kinds of animals, village and forest, for the obtainment of both kinds of food. He sacrifices both kinds of animals, village and forest, for the obtainment of both kinds of animals.[21]

While the two kinds of animals are said here to be inclusive of all food, all animals, and all worlds, there is nevertheless an absolute distinction between the two classes of animals. The distinction is not merely between animals of two different habitats, nor is it merely between animals domesticated and wild. It is also the one between those that are sacrificable and those that are not: "They bind the village animals to the stakes; they keep the jungle animals in the interstices [of the stakes]—[this] for the distinguishing of the animals (*paśūnām vyāvṛttyai*). They kill the village animals; the jungle ones they release" (TB 3.8.19.2; cf. PB 21.4.13). Another text details the potential dangers of performing the animal sacrifice with the jungle animals and the advantages of sacrificing with the village animals:

> If he [the priest] were to perform the sacrifice with the jungle animals, father and son would separate, the roads would run apart, the borders of two villages would be far distant, and ravenous beasts, man-tigers, thieves, murderers, and robbers would arise in the jungles. They say regarding this, "The jungle animals are not *paśus*. If he were to perform the sacrifice with the jungle animals, they would speedily carry the sacrificer dead to the jungle, for the jungle animals are jungle dwellers." If he did not sacrifice animals, however, he would not obtain animals for this one [the sacrificer]. If he were to release them after the fire had been carried around them, he would cause the destruction of the sacrifice. When he sacrifices [the village] animals, he thus obtains animals [for the sacrificer]. When he releases them [the jungle animals] after the fire has been carried around them, [he does so] in order that the sacrifice not be destroyed. Animals are [thereby] obtained for him [the sacrificer], he does not cause the destruction of the sacrifice, and they do not carry the sacrificer dead to the jungle. He performs the sacrifice with the village animals. These animals are called "safe" (*kṣema*), [for by sacrificing them] father and son are together, the roads run together, the borders of two villages are near, and no ravenous beasts, man-tigers, thieves, murderers, and robbers arise in the jungles. (TB 3.9.1.2–4; cf. ŚB 13.2.4.1–4)

Jungle animals are thus precluded from the sacrifice and, as the text above indicates, are therefore not *paśus* in the more limited sense of the word (i.e., domestic animals). Jungle animals or "wild game" (*mṛgas*) are separable from *paśus* also by virtue of the different ways man disposes of each. As one scholar puts it, "*Pashus* are the animals that get sacrificed, whatever their origins; *mrigas* are the animals that get hunted. In both cases, the ancient Indians defined animals according to the manner in which they killed them."[22]

The village animals are therefore nothing other than the sacrificial victims of the Vedic fire ritual. "He should offer up these five *paśus*, insofar as he is able to do so," it is written, "for they were those Prajāpati was the first to offer up" (ŚB 6.2.1.39). Or, again, the origin of the *paśus* is treated from an etymological point of view in another narrative:

> Prajāpati turned his attention to the forms (*rūpas*) of Agni. He searched for that boy who had entered into the [various] forms [of Agni; see ṚV 5.2]. Agni became aware [of this and thought], "Father Prajāpati is searching for me. I will take a form unrecognizable to him." He saw those five *paśus*: man, horse, bull, ram, and he-goat. Because he saw (*paśyat*) [them], they are therefore *paśus*. He entered these five *paśus* and became these five *paśus*. (ŚB 6.2.1.1–3)

Furthermore, the order in which the five victims are listed is not random or haphazard but almost invariably fixed, and clearly hierarchical, as the following text unequivocally states:

> He offers the man first, for man is the first of the *paśus*; then [he offers] the horse, for the horse comes after the man; then the bull, for the bull comes after the horse; then the ram, for the ram comes after the bull; then the he-goat, for the he-goat comes after the ram. In this way he offers them, in hierarchical succession (*yathāpūrva*) according to their relative excellence (*yathāśreṣṭha*). (ŚB 6.2.1.18)

We have already seen how the human animal is regarded in one text as the first, "most virile," and hierarchically superior of the *paśus*, the five species of which are listed by the male member of each.[23] Not only does man come first in various enumerations of the *paśus*; he is also extolled by texts which place him closest to the creator god himself: "Man is the nearest to (*nediṣṭha*) Prajāpati [of all the animals]" (ŚB 5.1.3.8, 5.2.1.6). Because of this favored place, the man is generally proclaimed in the texts to be the highest of all possible sacrificial victims. The superiority of the human victim is underlined in a text cited earlier by claiming that he is "all *paśus*"; that is, he encompasses them all by virtue of his hierarchically superior rank (ŚB 7.5.4.6).

Whether humans were in practice sacrificed is uncertain, however;[24] and even theoretically (i.e., categorically) man does not always appear in the lists of the proper victims. We recall here Śunaḥśepha's horror when he is seized as a sacrificial victim in the famous myth: "They will slaughter me as if I were not a man" (AitB 7.16).

In a typically tautological mythical statement, the sacrificial animals were supposedly created as such in a primordial sacrifice. The five *paśus*, according to TB 2.1.2.4, were generated from the sweat of Prajāpati, which was also made into clarified butter and offered into the fire. In yet another set of stories concerning the origin, types, and relative ranking of the sacrificial victims,[25] the familiar order—from man, the highest form of *paśu*, to the he-goat, the lowest on the scale—is reiterated. The enumeration appears in the course of relating how the quality that constitutes all of these animals as worthy of sacrifice (their *medha*)[26] entered into and then left them, creating in its wake new but defective forms of each—and forms which are the wild counterparts to the domestic sacrificial prototypes.[27] So it is that we encounter a myth of origins, repeated several times in Vedic literature, for not only the sacrificial animals but also the nonsacrificial, and therefore inedible, animals:

> The gods offered man as sacrificial victim. Then the sacrificial quality (*medha*) passed out of the offered man. It entered the horse. Then the horse became fit for sacrifice and they dismissed him whose sacrificial quality had passed out of him. He [the former man, now devoid of the sacrificial quality] became a pseudo-man (*kimpuruṣa*). They offered the horse, and the sacrificial quality passed out of the offered horse. It entered the bull. . . . It [the former horse] became the wild white deer (*bos gaurus, gauramṛga*). They offered the bull. . . . The sacrificial quality entered the ram. . . . It [the former bull] became the

> gayal (*bos gavaeus*, *gavaya*). They offered the ram. . . . The sacrificial quality entered the he-goat. . . . It [the former ram] became the camel. It [the sacrificial quality] stayed the longest in the he-goat; therefore the he-goat is the *paśu* most often used [as sacrificial victim]. They offered up the he-goat, and it [the sacrificial quality] passed out of the he-goat. It entered this [earth], and therefore this [earth] became fit for sacrifice. They dismissed him whose sacrificial quality had passed out of him. He [the former goat] became the wild *śarabha*.[28] These *paśus* whose sacrificial quality had passed out of them became unfit for sacrifice. Therefore one should not eat them. (AitB 2.8; cf. MS 3.10.2)

A variant of the same myth gives an identical list of the animals created from the shells of the *paśus* once they were sacrificed and the sacrificial quality left them, and with the same tag line: the beasts unworthy of the sacrifice are not to be consumed by humans (ŚB 1.2.3.9; cf. AitB 3.33–34).

Yet another version of the myth contrasts the five sacrificial animals, who possess the *medha*, to the five nonsacrificial animals who are characterized as having *śuc* (here meaning something like "burning pain," "sorrow," or "regret"). The sacrificial quality (*medha*) is specifically equated with food (*anna*) and without it animals become unfit both for the sacrifice and for human consumption:

> The burning pain, the evil, of these [sacrificial] animals, which Prajāpati exorcised, became these [nonsacrificial] five animals. They, having had the sacrificial quality gone out of them, are without the sacrificial quality and are unfit for sacrifice. A Brahmin should not eat them. (ŚB 7.5.2.32,37)

And as still another set of parallel texts indicates, the desacralized doubles of the five sacrificial and village *paśus* are jungle animals,[29] thus reinforcing yet again the binary opposition village/sacrificial/edible vs. jungle/nonsacrificial/inedible. At TS 4.2.10.1–4 one reads of a list of five animals with five wild counterparts living in the jungle: (1) the "biped of the *paśus*" (i.e., the human being) with its counterpart, the "barbarian of the jungle" (*mayu āraṇya*); (2) the "whole-hoofed of the *paśus*" (i.e., the horse) and the *gaura* of the jungle (*gaura āraṇyaka*); (3) the bovine and the wild *gavaya*; (4) the sheep and the wild camel (*uṣṭra āraṇyaka*); and (5) the goat together with the *śarabha*.[30]

The sacrificial paradigm for constituting the category of food does not end with the animal kingdom. Other foodstuffs become so by being infused with the sacrificial essence, the *medha*. Let us pick up the myth of the movable *medha* again. When the sacrificial quality finally left the he-goat after its lengthy residency, "it entered this earth. They searched for it by digging. They found it as those two, rice and barley (*vrīhi* and *yava*). Thus even now they find those two by digging" (ŚB 1.2.3.7). The variant tells much the same story:

> They follow it [the sacrificial essence] into this [earth]; it, being followed, became rice. When they offer the rice cake in the animal sacrifice, [they do so thinking], "May our sacrifice be done with a *paśu* possessing the sacrificial quality; may our sacrifice be done with a fully constituted (*kevala*) *paśu*." His sacrifice becomes one done with a *paśu* possessing the sacrificial quality; the

> sacrifice of one who knows this becomes one done with a fully constituted *paśu*. When the rice cake [is offered], it is indeed a *paśu* which is offered up. Its stringy chaff, that is the hairs; its husk is the skin; the flour is the blood; the small grains are the flesh; whatever is the best part [of the grain] is the bone. He sacrifices with the sacrificial quality of all *paśus* who sacrifices with the rice cake. (AitB 2.8–9; cf. MS 3.10.2; ŚB 3.8.3.1)

While the primary intention of the culminating portion of this myth is to extol the merits of the vegetable offering by equating it to an animal sacrifice, it also at least implies that food is food by virtue of being "*paśu*." In another myth, in which the claim is made that killing an animal in sacrifice will not provoke revenge in the next world, the moral is similar: food consumed without a portion of it first being sacrificed will return in other worlds to consume the former eater.

> "When people in this world offer no oblation and lack true knowledge, but cook for themselves animals that cry out, those animals take the form of men in the other world and eat in return." "How does one avoid that?" "When you offer the first oblation with the voice, that is how you avoid it and are free of it." . . . "When people in this world offer no oblation and lack true knowledge, but cook for themselves rice and barley, which scream soundlessly, that rice and barley take the form of men in the other world and eat in return." "How can one avoid that?" "When you offer the last oblation with the mind, that is how you avoid it and are free of it."[31]

O'Flaherty interprets this myth by linking it to "the ancient Indian belief that it is wrong to take food without offering some, at least mentally, to the gods; in the broadest sense, all human food consists of divine leftovers."[32] More specifically, and in light of other texts we considered previously, we might say that food which has not first been categorized as a *paśu*—whether it be animal or vegetable—cannot safely and legitimately be consumed. "Proper dining" in Vedism means sacrificial dining.

Overlapping Taxons, Edibility, and a Categorical Exception

Thus far, we have observed three different, yet overlapping, criteria for animal classification. First, there is categorization on the basis of observable anatomical features such as pedal or dental structure, or modes of locomotion or procreation. Second, we have isolated another kind of taxonomy, the principal criterion of which is whether the animal is domesticated or wild, an inhabitant of the village or of the jungle. Third, we have analyzed a type of categorization which entails dividing the animals into those worthy of being sacrificial victims (the *paśus* in a more limited sense of the term) and those which lack the sacrificial quality.

Running through all these schemas, as a kind of subtext, is a fourth classificatory distinction: Is the animal suitable for consumption by humans? Animals may be excluded from the category of "food" on anatomical grounds (the "five-clawed" beasts who are too much like humans), purely cultural grounds (the wild animals), or ritualistic and religious grounds (the nonsacrificial animals). Furthermore, these criteria tautologically reinforce one another. The "five-clawed" animals (apart from man) are most often wild, wild animals are by definition nonsacrificable, and all are equally inedible.

While in many texts it is simply and generally stated that "animals (*paśus*) are food,"[33] and while others state that the village and jungle animals together constitute "all the animals" and "all food," generally the Veda specifies that the "*paśus*" who are "food" are "fivefold" (AitB 5.19), that is, they are the five village and sacrificial animals: "There are a man, a horse, a bull, a ram, and a he-goat; these are all the animals (*sarve paśavaḥ*). The animals are food; he thus puts down in front [of the altar] whatever food there is" (ŚB 6.2.1.15; cf. ŚB 7.5.2.6–7 and 10.3.4.4).

Many texts thus identify all five of the *paśus* as both food and sacrificial victims. As we have already seen, one text explicitly calls the creation of the five *paśus* the creation of food: "Prajāpati at first was one. He desired, 'May I emit food, may I be reproduced.' He measured out the *paśus* from his breaths" (ŚB 7.5.4.6). The victims are not offered up completely to the deities in the sacrifice; rather, the omentum and other bits having been consigned to the fire as food for the gods, the meat is consumed by the ritualists. Thus the victim is indeed food—for both the divine and the human eaters: "He then cuts off some goat's hair, and lets loose the animals toward the northeast; for this, the northeast, is the region of both gods and men. He thus bestows animals on that region, and hence both gods and men subsist on animals" (ŚB 6.4.4.22).

The edible animals, "food" in one sense of the word, are in these instances no other than the five "village" animals, and not, therefore, the jungle animals. The wild or "jungle" animals in ancient India, as elsewhere in the Indo-European world, do not figure into the category of food suitable for human consumption—they are categorically too distant from humans to be edible. Furthermore, often enough the human being exempts himself, although he must often do so by fudging his own categorical demands. For if the edible animals are the *paśus* in the sense of domesticated/village/sacrificial animals, one of these is man himself. "Food" is defined as those animals which share the same class as humans—that is, the edible animals also overlap with the four nonhuman domesticated village sacrificial animals. The five *paśus* are said to be "the same, all these are equal . . . in that they are called 'food'" (ŚB 6.2.1.19).

As we learn elsewhere, however, the *paśus* who are food are only the "four-footed animals" (ŚB 6.8.2.7, 7.1.1.39, 8.3.2.10) and there are not five but only "four [kinds of] four-footed animals, and animals are food" (ŚB 8.3.4.8). The human *paśu* is, of course, absent from this depiction of the "four four-footed animals" who are food; obviously man's "two-footedness" here exempts him from the category of "food" (just as his "five-clawedness" does in other texts cited above). One thus finds in the ritual literature examples of what appears to be a comprehensive list of all the principal victims, which specifies only four sacrificial animals (the horse, bull, ram, and he-goat).[34] Mythologically oriented texts corroborate ritual praxis by providing tales of how certain animals were coerced by the gods into acceptance of their sacrificial fate:

> They say, "Should the sacrificial stake stand, [or] should one toss it [into the fire]?" For one who desires animals, it should stand. The animals would not allow themselves to be taken by the gods as food. They ran away, protesting, "You shall not take us and kill us, not us." Then the gods perceived this sacrificial stake to be a thunderbolt and raised it up over them. From fear of it, they [the animals] came back, and even today they come back to it. Then the animals allowed themselves to be taken by the gods as food, and for one who knows this animals allow themselves to be taken as food.[35]

The latter portion of the passage propounds a truism of sacrificial cults worldwide: the victim is to submit voluntarily to his own execution for, ultimately, it is to his advantage anyway.[36] The first half of the text, however, seems to contradict such wish-fulfillments. For there we learn that animals, once upon a time, resisted being made into "food." The beasts become categorically correct, qua food, when they are made to cower before the sacrificial stake (pace the voluntaristic submission the second half of the passage suggests).

Man is the bipedal "overlord" of the animals and "the eater among the *paśus*" (ŚB 7.5.2.14, 10.3.4.4)—and therefore, despite the categorical imperative suggested by his inclusion in the lists of the "village" and "sacrificial" animals, not food himself.[37] Otherwise put, those who share the same class as humans are not humans themselves. Man, the paradigmatic animal of the entire category of the *paśus*, is exempt from certain of the defining properties of the class—edibility, at least, and possibly sacrificability as well. Animals, qua food, must be close to but not identical with the humans who consume them.[38] Simultaneously included within the category of "edible animals" (by reason of being "village" animals and *paśus*) and yet exempted from it (as "two-footed" and "five-clawed" beasts and as eaters of all other animals), the human classifiers make their own species anomalous and unique.

Classifying Humans with Animals

The taxonomies of (nonhuman) animals surveyed thus far coalesce into a binary opposition between village/sacrificial/edible, on the one hand, and jungle/nonsacrificial/inedible, on the other. This opposition posited among the beasts, dividing the animal kingdom into two principal categories, also has another important classificatory function. The dichotomy is reapplied to the human realm in order to categorize the peoples of the world into civilized and uncivilized. While the human being in general is regarded as a *paśu*—a domesticated, and (at least according to the strict logic of the system) edible sacrificial animal—there are some humans the authors of the Veda assimilated to the nonsacrificial, inedible wild animals of the jungle, beyond the pale of "proper" humanity altogether.

The jungle animals, as we have observed, are said to have originated as the empty shells left by the sacrificial beasts when their *medha* or sacrificial quality departed from them. The wild, nonsacrificial, inedible counterpart of the man or *puruṣa* is the *kimpuruṣa*, which I translate as the "pseudo-man." This entity is also known as the *mayu āraṇya*, the "barbarian of the jungle" (TS 4.2.10.1–4), which is explicitly equated with the *kimpuruṣa* at ŚB 7.5.2.32. Furthermore, both terms are apparently synonymous with the *kinnara* (Manu 1.39) and the *puruṣa mṛga* ("wild man," TS 5.5.15.1; MS 3.14,16; VS 24.35).

Various translations have been offered for these terms, ranging from "monkey" and "ape" to "dwarf" and "mock-man." It seems probable, however, that in Vedic texts it is the tribal peoples living outside of the Āryan settlements to which all the Sanskrit terms refer. These beastly men are the "other" of civilized Vedic society, just as the outcast wild animals are the opposites of the domesticated village animals. Because they are not "food," because they are excluded from the sacrifice, and because they dwell in the jungle, these "pseudo-men" can be regarded as ontologically inferior versions of "real" humans.

Those humans who are, on the other hand, assimilated to the category of the village/edible/sacrificial animals are subdivided into classes in part through linking them to one or another of the four nonhuman animals who are also in the category.[39] The association of certain kinds of humans with certain kinds of animals thus helps to legitimate, through recourse to "nature," a quadripartite division of society. Social *varṇa*s are justified in part by reference to the supposedly isomorphic structure in the "natural" divisions among different species of animals;[40] conversely, the animal world, like other "kingdoms," is organized in Vedic texts along the lines of *varṇa*.

Taking another angle on this issue, it might be said that in ancient Indian classification systems, the animals domesticated, eaten, and sacrificed—the horse, cow, goat, and sheep—are also those regarded as sufficiently akin to the human animal to be classed according to *varṇa*. In Cosmogony VI, it will be recalled, we encountered a creation myth in which the four nonhuman *paśus* are mentioned together, and are assigned *varṇa*s in the course of being located within a series of associations. Cosmogony VI formulated the four strings of connected phenomena in the following manner:[41]

1. head/mouth (generation) ⇒ nine-versed hymn of praise = *gāyatrī* meter = *rathantara* chant = Agni = Brahmin = goat
2 arms/chest (virility) ⇒ fifteen-versed hymn of praise = *triṣṭubh* meter = *bṛhat* chant = Indra = Kshatriya = horse
3 belly/middle/penis (procreation) ⇒ seventeen-versed hymn of praise = *jagatī* meter = *vāmadevya* chant = Viśva Devas = cow
4 feet/firm foundation (feet washing) ⇒ twenty-one-versed hymn of praise = *anuṣṭubh* meter = *yajñayajñiya* chant = no god = Shudra = sheep

The four sacrificial (and edible and domesticated) animals are here given explicit *varṇa* designations—the Brahmin animal is the goat; the horse is a Kshatriya; the cow is said to be a Vaishya; and the Shūdra animal is the sheep—and they are placed within chains of associations which link the animals to body parts, Vedic praises and hymns, meters, and deities (see Table 8.4). These associations recur with such frequency that the implied or assumed *varṇa* of a particular animal is evident even when no social class is explicitly mentioned.[42]

The four *paśus* are not always exactly matched like this with the four social classes, nor are the only animals associated with the *varṇa*s the four in the

TABLE 8.4. The *Varṇa* of Animals

Varna	Brahmin	Kshatriya	Vaishya	Shūdra
Animal	goat	horse	cow	sheep
Deity	Agni	Indra	Viśva Devas	x
Body part	head, mouth	arms, chest	belly, penis	feet
Meter	*gāyatrī*	*triṣṭubh*	*jagatī*	*anuṣṭubh*
Hymn of Praise	9-versed	15-versed	17-versed	21-versed
Chant	*rathantara*	*bṛhat*	*vāmadevya*	*yajñayajñiya*

village/sacrificial/edible category. In the following statement, for example, only three animals are mentioned; the Vaishyas and Shūdras share an animal, and one which is not one of the four nonhuman *paśu*s at all:

> They then make the animals return to the *āhavanīya* fire. The goat goes first among them, then the ass, then the horse. Now when they are led away from this [fire], the horse goes first, then the ass, then the goat. The *kṣatra* corresponds to the horse, the Vaishya and Shūdra correspond to the ass, the Brahmin corresponds to the goat. When led away from this [fire] the horse goes first, therefore the Kshatriya, going first, is followed from behind by the other three *varṇa*s. And when returning from there, the goat goes first; therefore the Brahmin, going first, is followed from behind by the other three *varṇa*s. Now since the ass does not go first, either going or returning, therefore the Brahmin and the Kshatriya never go after from behind. Therefore they walk thus to avoid inversion (*apāpavasyasāya*). And he in this way surrounds on both sides those two *varṇa*s with the Brahmin and the Kshatriya, and makes them stay in their place (*anaprakramiṇa*). (ŚB 6.4.4.12–13; cf. ŚB 6.3.1.28)

It is another of the domestic animals, the ass, which is here associated with the third and fourth social classes (a connection that is, as we shall see, repeated in other texts), while the goat and the horse are, as could be expected, assigned to the Brahmin and Kshatriya respectively. The order of precedence of the animals, and of the social classes with which they are identified, is nevertheless stated quite clearly.

The logic behind Vedic identifications between animal species and the social classes—whether that logic derives from hierarchical considerations, as above, or from other resemblances between particular animals and particular types of people—is usually straightforward enough. In this case as in others we have surveyed, the connections made are not random, even if they may be somewhat variable from text to text.

Brahmin Animals

Two of the four village/sacrificial/edible animals are at various places assigned to the Brahmin *varṇa*: the goat, and also the cow. The divergence is due to two different, perhaps competing structural configurations with the four *paśu*s as the shifting components. In the first configuration, the goat is associated with the

Brahmins due to the animal's mythological ties to the god Agni and the role this animal plays in the sacrifice. In this structure, cattle are regarded as the incarnation of wealth, multiplicity, and especially of sustenance and "the earth," and thus take the third place in the structure, that is, the Vaishya rank. A second pattern, however, requires that the cow be placed in the Brahmin *varṇa*, for reasons we will explore shortly. The goat (often coupled with the sheep) in this case is epitomized by its fecundity—and therefore is labeled the Vaishya of the sacrificial beasts. Finally, there is yet another Brahmin animal—this one consistently linked to the sacrifice and thus to the priestly order. The black antelope, although not ordinarily used as a sacrificial victim, nevertheless is intimately associated with the ritual and is in every instance regarded as bearing Brahmin traits.

The Goat

The Brahmin, as we have seen, is said to "correspond to" (*anu*) the goat, and when the goat in a certain rite is led ahead of animals representing the other classes, "therefore the Brahmin, going first, is followed from behind by the other three classes" (ŚB 6.4.4.12–13). The notions that the goat is a Brahmin and that it is hierarchically superior to others are principally explicated in terms of the relation the animal has with the deity Agni.[43] The two are even declared to have the same "self," for the goat is the animal imbued with the *brahman* power:

> He [the Brahmin priest] comes [near the fire] while holding [a lump of clay] over the he-goat; for the he-goat belongs to Agni. He thus unites him [the he-goat] with his own self, with his own divinity. And, furthermore, the he-goat is the *brahman*; he thus also unites him with the *brahman*. (ŚB 6.4.4.15)

The goat "was born from the heat of the fire" it is said (AV 4.14.1, 9.5.13). The triangular linkage between the goat, Agni or the sacrificial fire, and the Brahmin is also found in several ritual texts, where the acceptable substitutes for the offering fire are enumerated:

> If he [the priest] should not find another [fire, when the sacrificial fire goes out], he should offer the oblation on [the right ear of] a she-goat. Truly this she-goat belongs to Agni; [when the oblation is offered on a she goat] it is indeed on the fire that his oblation is offered. But [thereafter] he [the sacrificer] should not eat goats' meat. If he should eat goats' meat, he would eat the oblation that he would offer on the fire. Therefore he should not eat goats' meat. If he cannot obtain a she-goat, he should offer on the right hand of a Brahmin. He who is a Brahmin is truly Agni Vaiśvanara; [when the oblation is offered on the right hand of a Brahmin] it is indeed in fire that his oblation is offered. But thereafter he should not refuse lodging to a Brahmin, [for] he would deprive from its share the fire on which he would offer the oblation.[44]

In this list of substitutions and the explication of the consequences for employing such substitutions, fire acts as a kind of thread on which both the goat and the Brahmin are hung. The goat, no less than the Brahmin himself, duplicates the function of Agni, the fire, to mediate between the divine and the human.

Elsewhere the connection between Agni (again, here exclusively denoting the deity made manifest in the sacrificial fire) and the goat is couched in the language of origins. "Agni is born from Agni" it is declared in reference to the goat (VS 13.45; ŚB 7.5.2.21). This animal is sometimes said to be the first of Agni's creations in order to rationalize its preeminence among the animals, just as the Brahmin's preeminence among humans is legitimated by claims of that class's precedence of origins. "The she-goat as an embryo was born from Agni; she saw her procreator before [others]. Thereby those worthy of sacrifice attained pre-eminence. Thereby the gods first attained divinity."[45] Similarly, at ŚB 7.5.2.36 (cf. 7.5.2.21), the link to Agni is even more specified, while still encoded in the persuasive discourse of origins:

> "The he-goat was born from Agni's heat (*tapas*)" (VS 13.51). That which was born from Prajāpati's heat, was indeed born from Agni's heat. "He saw the procreator at first." Prajāpati is the procreator; thus, "He saw Prajāpati at first" [is what is meant]. "Thereby with that [he-goat] the gods first attained divinity."

The goat is Agni's first creation, and by means of the first goat the gods in the beginning obtained their divinity. The implication here is that by means of the sacrificial goat humans too may attain divinity and the heavenly world; the goat is thus the sacrificial victim par excellence, as we shall soon see.

But let us first follow up the statement in this text that the goat has sprung not only from Agni, the fire god, but specifically from his "heat," *tapas* or *śoka*. The notion that the goat embodies the heat which is found quintessentially in Agni the fire is fairly widespread. "Since the goat has been born from the heat (*śoka*) of Agni, it saw [its] procreator in the beginning; by it the gods in the beginning attained [their] divinity; by it those worthy of the sacrifice ascended the heights" (AV 4.14.1). The goat is elsewhere said to be *tapas* incarnate (TS 1.2.7.1; ŚB 3.3.3.8; cf. AV 18.2.8); when soma for the ritual is purchased with the goat it thereby becomes full of this heat.[46] Closely related is the belief that the goat is the beastly embodiment of *tejas*, the fiery luminosity also typically said to be inherent in the Brahmins and manifest visibly in fire. TB 2.6.4.4 and ŚB 12.7.1.2 inform us that the *tejas* in the eyes of Indra came to be instilled in the gods by means of the goat; and at the human sacrifice or Puruṣamedha the offering to a deified *tejas* is, tellingly, a goatherd (TB 3.4.9.1). Elsewhere we read that the she-goat is Agni's own form, and placing the hairs of this animal in the fire "unites him [Agni] with his own form," and thus with fiery luminosity (TS 5.1.6.2). Finally, one text in praise of the goat intersperses freely the twin qualities of heat and luminosity which supposedly characterize the animal:

> You [the goat], a fire, have come into being out of fire. . . . The goat is Agni, and they call the goat light; they say that the goat is to be given by one living to a priest (*brahman*); the goat, given in this world by one having faith, smites

far away the darknesses. . . . The goat truly was born from the heat of the fire, wise, of the wise (*vipra*), of power, he the inspired one. (AV 9.5.6,7,13)

The association of the goat with fire, and with the heat and radiance which are the fire's quintessence, acts also as the bridge to another feature of this Brahminic animal. The goat, as I intimated earlier, is the sacrificial victim par excellence; indeed, as the ritual manuals tell us, the goat is the ordinary offering at all Vedic sacrifices entailing animal sacrifice,[47] and one text (favorably) compares the sacrificial goat—the food of the gods—to the ordinary human fare, rice (ŚB 1.6.4.3). The source of the goat's heat is located not in Agni but in the sacrifice itself in the following passage: "Then [in the Pravargya ritual, he puts] goat's milk [on a skin]. For when the head of the sacrifice was cut off its luminous heat (*śuc*) went out of it; from that the goat came into being. It is with that heat that he thereby makes it [the sacrifice] successful and complete" (ŚB 14.1.2.13, cf. 25). Here the goat's link to the sacrifice is direct—which is one kind of justification for attributing Brahminhood on the animal—and here also, only obliquely but elsewhere explicitly, the animal is associated with the head (the Brahmin part of the anatomy).[48]

The goat, the preeminent sacrificial animal that embodies the sacrificial fire, the heat and light of that fire, and indeed the very sacrifice itself, and that also, as a Brahmin, encompasses the lower *varṇa*s within itself, therefore often serves as the signifier for all the animals—and especially all the sacrificial animals. The goat, in other words, metonymically represents the whole class of the *paśu*s, which is another way of presenting this animal as the sacrifice itself as well as the all-encompassing Brahmin among the beasts:

He then mixes it [the clay] with the goat's hair in order to make it firm. And as to why [it is mixed] with goat's hair: The gods collected him [Agni] from the *paśus*, and in like manner now this one collects him from the *paśus*. And [again] as to why [it is mixed] with goat's hair: It is because the form of all *paśus* is in the he-goat; and as to its being hair, form is hair. (ŚB 6.5.1.4)

Or, again, we read that the hornless he-goat, like the Brahmins in relation to other humans, envelops within its being all others of its class:

In this *paśu* is the form (*rūpa*) of all *paśu*s. The form of man [incorporated in the goat] is what is hornless and bearded, for man is hornless and bearded. The form of the horse is what is possessing a mane, for the horse possesses a mane. The form of the cow is what is eight-hoofed, for the cow has eight hooves. The form of the ram is what possesses ram-hooves, for the ram possesses ram-hooves. What is the goat, that is [the form] of the goat. Thus, when he offers this [goat], all those *paśu*s are offered by him. (ŚB 6.2.2.15; cf. TS 2.1.1.4–5; TS 5.5.1.1–2)

The Cow

The inviolability of the cow in Hinduism is well known, if not always adequately accounted for.[49] While there is no Vedic text that could serve as a real charter for the Hindu practice of not killing cows (they were regularly sacrificed according to the Veda), W. Norman Brown has suggested a "constellation of at least five elements which have produced the doctrine of the sanctity of the cow."

> These are: the importance of the cow and its products for the performance of the Vedic sacrificial ritual; the figurative uses of words for the cow in Vedic literature and the later understanding of these figurative expressions as indicating literal truth; the prohibitions against violation of the Brahman's cow; the inclusion of the cow under the general doctrine of Ahiṃsā ["nonviolence"]; and the association of the cow with the mother-goddess.[50]

Inherent in several items on Brown's list is another reason for the high esteem that Hindus accord the cow: the association, beginning in the Veda, of the animal with the Brahmin *varṇa*. Above all, there is Brown's notion that the "sanctity" of the cow is at least partly due to the "prohibitions against violation" of that possession of the Brahmins. As the priest's sacrificial fee (*dakṣiṇā*, "the rich milking one") par excellence,[51] the cow is a prized possession among the Brahmins. Several hymns (e.g., AV 5.18, 5.19, 12.4, 12.5) make it clear that, as Brown writes, "To injure the Brahman's cow is to injure the Brahman himself."[52] Brown concludes that the cow was not sacred in its own right in the Veda; rather, "It is sacred because it is a Brahman's."[53] It is, however, enough that an entity be related to the Brahmin *varṇa* to ensure its "sacrality," as we have had plenty of occasion already to witness in the course of this study.

The cow[54] is indeed found directly associated with the Brahmin class in Vedic texts. In one instance, the cow is connected to the Ṛg Veda, and both are said to be forms of the *brahman*: "They praise the calf (*vatsa*) with *ṛks*, strengthening him who is the *brahman* with the *brahman*."[55] And in the Godāna ceremony, at which a boy of sixteen has his hair cut and beard shaved, the sacrificial fee to the priest varies according to *varṇa*—for a Kshatriya it is a pair of horses and for a Vaishya it is a pair of sheep, but for the Brahmin youth the fee is a bull and cow.

In other cases, the cow is connected to typically Brahmin entities, such as the *gāyatrī* meter: "The *gāyatrī* has eight syllables. The chant is the *gāyatrī*; the *brahman* is the *gāyatrī*. Thus it [the chant] changes into the *brahman*. The cattle (*paśus*) are eight-hooved; therefore it [the chant that has turned into the *brahman* through the *gāyatrī*] belongs to the cattle" (JUB 1.1.6). Similarly, the cows are driven away from their calves during one rite of the New and Full Moon sacrifice with a branch from the *parṇa* tree which, as we have seen, has direct connections to the Brahmins: "Inasmuch as he [the priest] sets the cows in motion [toward the pasture ground] by means of a branch of *parṇa* tree, he sets them in motion by means of their own deity" (TB 3.2.1.2).

The association of the cow and the Brahmins is principally grounded, however, in the identification of both with the sacrifice.[56] The cow and her products are crucial for the performance of the ritual, and the animal is therefore often equated with the sacrifice, which is also, of course, the arena of the Brahmin priest: "Auspicious indeed is what we [gods] have produced here, who have produced the cow; for truly she is the sacrifice, and without her no sacrifice is performed" (ŚB 2.2.4.13). In the following myth of origins, the cow is not only identified with the sacrifice but also associated with the Brahmin deity Agni, whose seed has entered her and taken the form of milk:

> The gods came upon a cow which had come into being. . . . They said, "What we have produced here, the cow, is auspicious, for she is the sacrifice and without her no sacrifice is performed. She is also food, for the cow is indeed whatever food there is." This [i.e., the word *go*, "cow"] then is the name of those [cows], and of the sacrifice. He should therefore repeat it, saying, "Good, auspicious." Truly whoever knowing this repeats it, saying "Good, auspicious," has those [cows] multiply [for him] and the sacrifice will incline to him. Agni desired her: "May I copulate with her," [he thought]. He united with her and shot his seed into her; that became her milk. Therefore even though the cow is uncooked, that [milk] which she brings forth is cooked, for it is Agni's seed. Therefore whether it be in a black or in a red [cow], it is ever white and looks like fire, because it is Agni's seed. Therefore it is warm when first milked, because it is Agni's seed.[57]

In addition to the connections made in this text to the sacrifice and the Brahmin deity Agni, we also note here that the cow is also said to be "whatever food there is." Elsewhere too the chain comprised of the cow, sacrifice, and food is encountered. At the horse sacrifice, the priest "seizes the cow [as a victim]. The cow is the sacrifice, and it is the sacrifice he thus obtains. And the cow is food, and it is food he thus obtains" (TB 3.9.8.3; cf. ŚB 2.2.4.13). This notion that the cow "is indeed food" is one reason why this animal is sometimes regarded as a Vaishya, and not a Brahmin, as we shall soon see.[58]

The Black Antelope

In addition to the goat and the cow, a third animal which is very often related to the Brahmin *varṇa* is the black antelope (*kṛṣṇa*). In the initiation rite, the upper garment given to the boy is to be a skin from the black antelope if the initiate is a Brahmin,[59] and the practice is consistent with linkages established also in the ritual of consecration for the soma sacrifice: "Being consecrated, he [the sacrificer, regardless of class[60]] attains Brahminhood in that he puts on the black antelope's skin," says one text (AitB 7.23); similarly, in another it is declared, "In that he puts on a black antelope's skin, and the black antelope's skin is the *brahman*. He thus unites the sacrifice with the *brahman*" (KB 4.11). Elsewhere the black antelope skin is called the very form (*rūpa*) of the *brahman* power (TS 6.1.3.1; TB 2.7.1.4, 2.7.3.3) or is connected to the splendor of the *brahman* power (*brahmavarcasa*) (PB 17.11.8; ŚB 9.3.4.14; cf. ĀpDhS 1.1.3.9 and BhGS 1.1). The skin of this animal is said to represent the meters which carry the sacrificer to heaven (ŚB 6.7.1.6, 9.3.4.10, 12.8.3.3), or it denotes the Veda (TS 1.2.2, 6.1.3.1ff.), the knowledge of which helps to define the class of Brahmins. And as the following text indicates, the black antelope is also intimately associated with the sacrifice (identified also with the triple Veda), the workplace of the Brahmin priest:

> He now takes the black antelope skin, for the universality (*sarvatva*) of the sacrifice. The sacrifice went away from the gods, and having become a black antelope roamed about. The gods found it, stripped off its skin, and took it [the skin] away with them. Its white and black hairs are forms of the verses (*ṛks*) and the chants (*sāmans*). The white is the chant and the black the verse; or conversely, the black is the chant and the white the verse. The brown and the yellow ones are forms of the formulas (*yajurs*). This same threefold knowledge is the sacrifice. The manifold art (*etaśilpa*) and that class (*varṇa*) of this [knowledge] is this black antelope skin. For the universality of the sacrifice [he thus takes the skin].[61]

Kshatriya Animals

The Horse

The horse (*aśva*) is preeminently the animal of the Kshatriya *varṇa*.[62] In addition to the texts already cited, a more or less direct correlation between the horse and the warrior class is frequently made in the course of asserting the horse's physical and quasi-political superiority over the other animals. The horse, identified with the *kṣatra*,[63] rules over its "subjects" in the animal kingdom like a king and is physically dominant like a warrior. The horse is not only "the most fortunate (*bhagitama*) of animals" (ŚB 6.3.3.13) or the animal that possesses the greatest quantity of *ojas* (ŚB 13.1.2.6); it also "surpasses" (*ati*) the others, "and therefore the horse attains preeminence (*śraiṣṭhya*) over [all] the animals" (ŚB 13.1.6.1; TB 3.8.9.1). Thus the horse may metonymically serve as "all animals" (TB 3.9.11.4) insofar as he, like the human ruler, is their chief.

The horse is very frequently associated with the god Prajāpati; this animal "belongs to Prajāpati" (*prājāpatya*),[64] and the sacrifice of the horse, the Aśvamedha, is declared to be Prajāpati's own ritual (ŚB 13.2.2.1,13; TB 3.8.14.1). "By means of the sacrificial horse," claims one text, the sacrificer "obtains union (*sayujya*) and commonality of world (*salokata*) with Prajāpati" (TB 3.9.20.2). In one of the many ritual contexts in which this connection is put into play, the New and Full Moon sacrifice calls for the priest to cut the grass needed for the ritual with a horse's rib. The explanation for the practice centers on the "commonality of origin" (*sayonitvāya*) of the horse and Prajāpati, the "lord of creatures":

> He who knows the plants inside and out (*parvaśa*) does not injure them. Prajāpati indeed knows the plants inside and out; he does not injure them. He [the priest] approaches the sacrificial grass with a horse's rib [in hand]. The horse belongs to Prajāpati. [When the priest approaches the sacrificial grass with a horse's rib in hand], it is so there is a commonality of origin [between the grass, the horse, and Prajāpati]. (TB 3.2.2.1)

The horse and Prajāpati are also intimately linked in several different creation mythologies. In one such cycle, Prajāpati takes the form of the steed in order to create the universe (PB 11.3.4–5, 20.4.5). In another, the creator god in the guise of a horse is seized by the deities as a victim in a primordial sacrifice: "Since Prajāpati, having been seized, became a horse, therefore of [all] the victims that are offered to Prajāpati the horse is the one that most resembles (*anurūpatama*) him" (TB 3.9.22.1–2). A third set of myths draws on an etymological explanation for the origin of the horse, here said to arise from the swollen eye of Prajāpati:[65] "The eye of Prajāpati swelled (*aśvayat*). It fell out and became the horse (*aśva*); hence the horse has its name. By means of the Aśvamedha, the gods restored it to its place. He who performs the Aśvamedha makes Prajāpati complete."[66]

The connection with the prolific Prajāpati does seems not to be derived primarily from the reproductive capacities of the horse (a connection more apt to be made when dealing with Vaishya entities).[67] Rather, it is in the sense of surpassing hierarchical rank and lordship that the very frequent connection between the horse and the deity who goes beyond all others, Prajāpati, is explicable. By means of a mantra dedicating the horse to Prajāpati, the beast is made preeminent among animals just as Prajāpati is the chief among the deities (ŚB 13.1.8.2). In another ritual, thirty-three cows are to be given as the sacrificial gift to the priests: "These make thirty-three sacrificial gifts [of cows]. There are thirty-three deities; he [thus] reaches to the deities. The horse is the thirty-fourth sacrificial gift. Prajāpati is the thirty-fourth of the deities; he [thus] reaches Prajāpati" (PB 17.11.3; cf. KB 1.1; PB 18.1.20–23).

The horse in relation to the other animals, then, is as a king to his subjects, just as Prajāpati is the ruler over the other deities who are his "people," his *viś*. The horse is thus set apart from the other animals offered at the horse sacrifice; and although other authorities recommend that the same mantras be used for both the horse and the other animals, the ŚB cautions against such a practice:

> Let him not do so. The horse is the *kṣatra*, and the other animals are the *viś*. And those who do this make the *viś* equal to and contrary toward the *kṣatra*. Those who do this deprive the sacrificer of his longevity. Therefore the horse alone belongs to Prajāpati, and the others belong to the various other gods. He makes the *viś* dependent on and obedient to the *kṣatra* alone; and he also supplies the sacrificer with long life. (ŚB 13.2.2.15)

It is also in this same sense of surpassing rule that the triangular connection between Prajāpati, the horse, and virility (*vīrya*) is explicable. For just as Prajāpati is the most virile, potent, and (meta)physically strong (*vīryavattama*) among the gods, so is the horse the most powerful animal.[68]

The physical power of the horse, this animal's *kṣatra*, led the ritualists to connect it to other Kshatriya deities and metaphysical powers. In one text, which depicts the ritual consecration of the sacrificial horse, some of these associations are summarized. Beginning with what is now for us a familiar statement of the horse's association with Prajāpati, and thus with the "eating of food" and virility, the text goes on to link this animal to other Kshatriya divinities and qualities:

> From the east, standing with his face turned westward, he [the priest] sprinkles [the horse], saying, "I sprinkle you, agreeable to Prajāpati." Prajāpati indeed is, among the gods, the eater of food and the most virile. Thus he [the priest] puts into him [the horse] food and virility; therefore the horse is, among the animals, the eater of food and the most virile. From the south [he sprinkles the horse], saying, "[I sprinkle] you, [agreeable] to Indra and Agni." Indra and Agni are the most powerful (*ojiṣṭha*) and the physically strongest (*baliṣṭha*) of the gods. Thus he puts power and physical strength into him [the horse]; therefore the horse is the most powerful and the strongest of the animals. From the west [he sprinkles the horse] saying, "[I sprinkle] you [agreeable] to Vāyu." Vāyu (or the wind) is the quickest (*aśu*), the fastest racer (*sārasāritama*), of the gods. Thus he puts speed (*java*) into him; therefore the horse is the quickest, the fastest racer, of the animals. From the north [he sprinkles] saying "[I sprinkle] you [agreeable] to the Viśva Devas." The Viśva Devas are indeed among the gods the most famous (*yaśasvitama*). Thus he puts fame into him; therefore the horse is the most famous of the animals.[69]

In addition to the already explored connection to Prajāpati, this text posits bonds between the horse and (1) Indra and Agni, and the powers of *ojas* and *bala*; (2) Vāyu and swiftness (*java*); and (3) the Viśva Devas and fame, *yaśas*. Let us follow some of the threads with which the horse is thus ensnared.

The connection to the warrior god Indra and the typically Kshatriya powers of power (*ojas*) and physical strength (*bala*) is fairly typical. It is with offerings of horses that the gods put virility and physical strength (*bala*) into Indra (TB 2.6.13.3); and the horse is directly connected both with Indra ("the horse is Indra," KB 15.4) and with the *kṣatra*: "With a horse chariot Indra ran the race; therefore it, loudly neighing and snorting, is a form of the *kṣatra*, for it is connected to Indra" (AitB 4.9). The notion that the horse and the Viśva Devas have an intimate relationship, on the other hand, is not often encountered (the Viśva Devas being preeminently Vaishya deities).[70] Another text does, however, explicate the connection to *yaśas* ("fame"), although here with a more typical reference to Indra: "From his (Indra's) ear his fame flowed out and became the one-hoofed animals, the horse, mule, and ass" (ŚB 12.7.1.5).

The link of the horse with Vāyu, the wind god, is also not widely attested but was apparently called to mind by the often noted speediness of the horse, which was regarded as, one might say, "swift as the wind"; indeed one text indulges in what for us would be just such a metaphor (ŚB 7.5.2.18). In the Puruṣamedha, a groom (*aśvapā*) is to be offered to a deified "swiftness" (*java*) (TB 3.4.9.1), and in the Aśvamedha a mantra is recited over the horse to instill in the animal a quality it is also said to possess from the dawn of time: "He says, 'May the steed [be] quick (*aśu*).' He thereby bestows swiftness on the horse. For it is because of that [formula] that formerly [in the beginning] the horse was born quick" (TB 3.8.13.1; ŚB 13.1.9.1; cf. TB 3.9.5.3). The horse's speed is equated with its virility in another text (ŚB 13.4.2.2), thus reattaching this particular equine characteristic to Kshatriya machismo. In a myth of origins, the speed of the horse is explained at the same time as is the brute's vicious backward kick:

> They [the demons] went after them [the gods, who had gone to heaven] and joined up with them. [The gods], having become horses, knocked [the demons] away with their hooves. Since [the gods], having become horses, knocked [the demons] away with their hooves, that [power of the hooves] is the essence of the horse—he who knows this attains whatever he wants. Therefore a horse is the swiftest of animals; therefore a horse strikes backwards with his foot—he who knows this strikes evil away. (AitB 5.1)

Agni, another god mentioned in the summary above as related to the horse, is not readily identifiable as a Kshatriya deity, being more usually closely associated with the Brahmins. And, indeed, in the text cited previously which connects the fire god to the horse (as well as to *ojas* and physical strength), it is really a "dual deity" that is so joined—Indrāgni, the deified coalescence of the Brahmin–Kshatriya ruling class. There are, however, other passages in the Veda where a direct connection is indeed made ("The horse is Agni," ŚB 6.3.3.22); and there are also more indirect associations between Agni and the horse to be found in Vedic literature (see, e.g., ŚB 6.6.3.4; AitB 3.49). The logic of the linkage with Agni and the horse, however, seems to be guided primarily by a kind of second-order identification.

In the first place, there is the idea that both the horse and Agni are bearers or conveyers, the fire being the transporter of oblations to the gods and the horse being the vehicle both of man and also of Agni himself.[71] Second, this connection is explicated by the assertion that there is an equivalence between Agni and Prajāpati, and therefore a roundabout link to the horse: "He [the priest] now perfumes it [the fire] with horse dung [to protect it from injury]. For the horse belongs to Prajāpati, and Prajāpati is Agni, and one does not injure one's own self" (ŚB 6.5.3.9). Third, in one narrative of origins, the horse's relationship to Agni is explained somewhat differently. Prajāpati, taking the form of the horse, discovers fire, although not without cost:

> Agni ran away from the gods and entered the water. The gods said to Prajāpati, "Go look for him; he will show himself to you, his own father." He [Prajāpati] became a white horse, and looked for him [Agni]. He found him, who had slid out of the water, on a lotus leaf. He gazed upon him, and he [Agni] burned him. Therefore the white horse has a burnt [red] mouth, as it were, and is prone to poor vision. He [Agni] thought he had hit and hurt him, and said to him, "I grant you a boon." He [Prajāpati] said, "Whoever, in that form [of a white horse], looks for you shall find you." Thus, he who, in that form [of a white horse] looks for him finds him. (ŚB 7.3.2.14–15)

The text goes on to note that the fire-discovering horse "should be white, for that [kind of horse] is a form of him who burns yonder [i.e., the sun]" (ŚB 7.3.2.16). This leads us to the final, and most important, reason why the horse and Agni should be equated in Vedic classifications. For Agni is not only the deity incarnate in the earthly, sacrificial fire (which would ordinarily call up the Brahmin category) but is also manifest in the atmosphere (in the form of lightning) and in the sky (in the guise of the sun)—and both the thunderbolt (*vajra*)[72] and sun are widely assumed to be linked both with the horse and with Kshatriya power. For it is with the thunderbolt, which is no different from the sun, which is, in turn, said to be the horse, that the gods defeated the demons:

> Then they led a white horse to the front [of the fire]. The gods were fearful, [thinking,] "Let the demons and danger not attack us here [in front]." They saw that thunderbolt, yonder sun; and that horse is yonder sun. Having beaten off the demons and danger in front with that thunderbolt, they obtained well being in [a place] free from fear and danger. (ŚB 7.3.2.10)

Similarly, in another text, the horse/thunderbolt/sun is called a "protector," just as the Kshatriya is called upon to defend and protect the social order. And whom does the horse protect but Agni, who has hid himself from the other deities?

> Then he makes it [the horse] step on [a lump of clay]. When it [the horse] discovered him [Agni], it pointed him out to the gods, as if [to say], "He is right here!" And, again, as to why he makes it step on [the lump of clay]. The gods were fearful, [thinking,] "Let the demons and danger not attack us here." They placed that thunderbolt, yonder sun, as a protector above. The horse is the sun; therefore this [priest] now places that thunderbolt as a protector above.[73]

With the notion that the horse, in a form of Agni, protects the god of fire, the animal's connection to the deity is thus tied up with the ropes of the homological worldview. The point, however, is that both the declaration that the horse (especially the white horse) is the sun[74] and that which assimilates this animal to the thunderbolt[75] reemphasize the association with the Kshatriya. For the sun, like the horse, and like the king, is said to be "unrivaled," without a competitor to sovereignty: "And as to its [the horse] being yoked without its partner on the right side [in a certain rite], it is in order to obtain him who burns [above, i.e., the sun], for that [horse] is indeed he [who burns above], and there is really no match for him" (ŚB 13.4.2.2). The thunderbolt, which is also believed to be Indra's weapon of choice, when incorporated into the horse makes that animal a leader (ŚB 4.3.4.27) and more powerful than others (TS 5.1.2.6). Possessing the thunderbolt is yet another of the signs of the horse's virility (ŚB 7.5.2.24, 13.5.1.7); by means of the horse (called *vajrin*, "he who posseses the thunderbolt") the sacrificer "stamps out the evil enemy" (TB 3.8.4.2). Finally, lest there be any doubt about the *varṇa* to which this thunderbolt, and therefore the horse that manifests it, belongs, we read in the ŚB (13.4.4.1) that "the horse is the *kṣatra*, and the Kshatriya is the *kṣatra*. The *kṣatra* is delivered by means of thunderbolt. Thus he receives the *kṣatra* by means of the thunderbolt."

There is one more string of associations tying the horse to Kshatriya deities and powers. For the horse is said to belong not only to Prajāpati, Indra, Agni, and Vāyu; the animal is also the particular animal of Varuṇa, the royal deity of the sea.[76] One text goes so far as to oppose the usual association of the horse with Prajāpati in favor of this relationship: "The horse belongs to Varuṇa. When he makes him a victim for Prajāpati he deprives him of his deity. He [the priest] says, 'Homage to the king! Homage to Varuṇa!' The horse belongs to Varuṇa;

thus he provides him with his own deity."[77] And in an interesting variant of the myth of the horse's origins from the swollen eye of Prajāpati, we read the following: "Varuṇa once gave king Soma a black eye. It swelled up (*aśvayat*); from that the horse came into being. And because it came into being from a swelling, therefore it is called *aśva*" (ŚB 4.2.1.11).

The linkage of the horse with the northern direction[78] is also explicable in part due to the connection to Varuṇa. At the Aśvamedha, the portions of the flesh cut from the horse are carved off north of the sacrificial altar: "The horse belongs to Varuṇa. And that quarter [the north] is the quarter of Varuṇa. It is in the horse's own quarter that he cuts the portions [of the horse's flesh]" (TB 3.8.20.3–4). So too the often noted idea that the horse is "born of the waters"[79] is explained in part by the association with Varuṇa, the Indian Neptune:

> He then sprinkles the horses with water, either when they are being led down to be watered, or when they are brought up after being watered. In the beginning the horse came into being from the water. Coming into being from the water, it came into being incomplete. Therefore it does not stand on all four feet, but rather stands lifting up one foot or another. What was at that time left behind of it [the horse] in the water, with that he now restores it and makes it whole. Therefore he sprinkles the horses with water, either when they are being led down to be watered, or when they are brought up after being watered. (ŚB 5.1.4.5)

The Bull

The other domestic animal associated with the Kshatriya *varṇa* is the bull (*ṛṣabha, vṛṣan*), for both are regarded as rulers over their respective kingdoms. One Vedic ritual is called "The Bull," and the priest "should perform it for a Kshatriya. The bull is the overlord of the animals and the Kshatriya [is the overlord] of men. He who is [a bull] becomes the overlord" (PB 19.12.4; cf. 6.10.9). The chant called the "bull chant" (*ārṣabha*, SV 1.161 = ṚV 8.45.22–24) is said to be "the same as the *kṣatra* power; by it he becomes the *kṣatra*" (PB 9.2.15). Similarly, the king who performs the Rājasūya becomes supreme, like a bull:

> He [the king] rubs it [consecration water] over himself with [the mantra from VS 10.19], 'Forward from the top of the mountain, from the top of the bull.' Just as the mountain stands out here [on earth], just as the bull stands out among the animals, so does he who sacrifices with the Rājasūya stand out over everything; everything is below him.[80]

Another rite performed at the royal consecration ritual and its effect on the king who undergoes it entails an offering to Indra at the sacrificer's home, "for Indra is the *kṣatra*, and he who is consecrated is the *kṣatra*; therefore it is for Indra. The sacrificial fee for this is a bull, for the bull belongs to Indra" (ŚB 5.3.1.3). The bull is indeed regularly associated with Indra, the Kshatriya deity par excellence.[81] The creator sacrificed a bull to Indra in the first sacrifice (ŚB 6.2.1.5), and Indra, in another myth, after creating the world is restored by means of his animal alter-ego (ŚB 12.7.1.13). In one ritual which is assimilated to Indra's conquest of the great demon Vṛtra (cf. ŚB 2.6.4.1), the deity is summoned by means of a bull:

> Now he [the priest] should instruct him [the sacrificer] to make a bull call out. "If it bellows," say some, "then that [sound] is the call to offer (the *vaṣat*). He should offer when [he hears] that call." Then he indeed calls Indra in his own form; he comes to [this rite,] the slaying of Vṛtra. The bull is indeed a form of Indra; thus he calls Indra in his own form to the slaying of Vṛtra. If it bellows, Indra has come to his sacrifice; he [may then think,] "Indra is my sacrifice." (ŚB 2.5.3.18)

The sacrificial fee to the priests at this ritual is a bull, for the sacrifice belongs to Indra (KB 5.5).

The bull is also associated with other Kshatriya signifiers. The second day of one ritual contains the recitation of verses to the bull in the meter of the Kshatriyas, the *triṣṭubh*: "This second day is combined with the bull; it belongs to Indra and to the *triṣṭubh* meter" (PB 11.8.4). More often, both the animal and Indra are connected with powers characteristic of the warrior, such as physical strength (*bala* or *indriya*)—for it was "from his [Indra's] mouth that strength flowed out; it became that animal, the bull."[82] The connection between the bull and the Kshatriya is also duc to the virility of the animal. In Vedic texts, "No symbol of virility comparcs to the bull," as W. Norman Brown noted.[83] "We sacrifice to the strong bull. . . . Let him give us an abundance of virility (*suvīrya*)" (TB 3.7.5.13; cf. 2.8.8.12; PB 18.9.14).

Other Kshatriya Animals

Other Kshatriya animals include the spotted deer (*ruru*), the skin of which is prescribed for a Kshatriya initiate,[84] and the lion and tiger among the wild animals. The latter two beasts are connected with Indra: "From the insides of his [Indra's] bowels flowed out ardor; that became the tiger, the king of the jungle animals. From his blood his might flowed out; that became the lion, the lord of the jungle animals" (ŚB 12.7.1.8). Thus in the Puruṣamedha a lion and tiger are to be offered to Indra (TS 5.5.21.1). At the royal consecration ritual, the throne for the king is covered with tiger skin, for "the tiger is the *kṣatra* of the jungle animals, and the Kshatriya is the *kṣatra*. He thus makes the *kṣatra* prosper with the *kṣatra*."[85] Hairs from the tiger are added to the liquor in the Sautrāmaṇī ritual (which is limited to Kshatriya sacrificers) in order to obtain ardor and the "kingship of the jungle animals," while those of the lion procure might and the "lordship of the jungle animals" (ŚB 12.7.2.8). Elsewhere it is said that by taking on the traits of the lion, the warrior "devours all the commoners," and by assuming the aspect of a tiger he beats down his foes (AV 4.22.7; cf. KauśS 13.4).

Vaishya Animals

The particular species classified, in one place or another, as belonging to the Vaishyas include sheep, goats, and cattle. The species associated with the Vaishya *varṇa* are so because of their fecundity or their numbers. Alternatively, any animal can call up a Vaishya connection if it possesses the right markings: a dappled hide is rather consistently regarded as the indicator of the *viś*. It is, in sum, often the very numbers in the herd, the prolific reproductive capacities of certain species, or particular markings which are regarded as signs of multiplicity, that provoke the association with the commoner class.

The Goat

In discussing of the Brahmin animals, I noted that while the goat may, under certain circumstances, be classified among the entities of the first *varṇa*, it also may be conceived as a Vaishya animal under an alternative vision concerning the connections between animals and social classes. When the cow takes the role of the Brahmin among the sacrificial animals, the goat is relegated to the Vaishya class, and both the cow and the goat are classified as Vaishya when the black antelope has been designated as the Brahmin. Thus, for example, the Vaishya initiate wears the skin of either the cow or the goat in the initiation ritual as it is presented in the Sūtras.

The connection between the goat and the Vaishya seems to follow from the link between this prolific animal and the creator god, the cosmically fertile Prajāpati. The goat is said to be the animal form (*rūpa*) of this deity (ŚānĀ 1.1) and to belong to "Prajāpati's *varṇa*" (TS 1.2.7.1; MŚS 2.1.4.11; BhŚS 10.17.4; ĀpŚS 10.25.12, etc.). The explication of this union makes clear that it is the goat's fecundity and ability to produce "abundance" for the sacrificer that links the animal to the creator god:

> He then makes him [the sacrificer] recite over the she-goat, which stands facing the west: "You are the body of ascetic heat." That she-goat came into existence from the ascetic heat of Prajāpati; therefore he says, "You are the body of ascetic heat." [He then says,] "[You are] of the same class as Prajāpati." She gives birth three times in the year; therefore she is of Prajāpati's class. "You are purchased with the most excellent animal." She gives birth three times in a year; therefore she is the most excellent of animals. "May I become prosperous with a thousandfold prosperity!" With that he asks for a wish. A thousand is the same as the earth; he [thus really] says, "May I obtain [the prosperity of] the earth." (ŚB 3.3.3.8; cf. ŚB 5.2.1.24; TS 6.5.10.1)

Elsewhere we read that Prajāpati created the hornless goat in order to create all animals, all offspring; and with the hornless goat, the sacrificer also wins offspring and animals:

> Prajāpati was alone here. He desired, "May I emit offspring and animals." He extracted the omentum from his body and placed it in the fire. The hornless goat

then came into existence. He offered it to its own deity; then he emitted offspring and animals. He who desires offspring and animals should offer to Prajāpati a hornless goat. He pleases Prajāpati with his own share; [and then] he [Prajāpati] produces offspring and animals for him. (TS 2.1.1.4–5; cf. TS 5.5.1.2)

Furthermore, the goat is connected to food insofar as it "eats all kinds of plants" (ŚB 6.5.4.16). So it is that a sacrificer wishing for material increase and prosperity (*puṣṭi*) should be consecrated for the soma sacrifice on a skin of the he-goat (ŚB 9.3.4.14), and, elsewhere, the she-goat is declared the "form of material prosperity": "He steps on the skin of the goat. He thus firmly establishes material prosperity in [his] offspring" (TB 1.3.7.7). The goat's connection with the deity Vāc is similarly explained: "The he-goat is Vāc, and from Vāc Viśvakarman produced living beings" (ŚB 7.5.2.21). A barren she-goat is also offered to the Vaishya deities, the Viśva Devas and the Ādityas, to obtain animals and progeny.[86]

Goats and Sheep

Goats and sheep are animals that herd together,[87] and it would seem to be partly their aggregation and numbers[88] which lead to a connection between them and the Vaishya qualities of earthly abundance (*bhūman*) and material increase (*puṣṭi*): "[At the horse sacrifice] he [the priest] seizes goats and sheep in great abundance [as victims]. Abundance is material increase; it is material increase he [the sacrificer] thus obtains" (TB 3.9.8.3). There are other grounds too for connecting the goats and sheep to the Vaishyas. The two species are said elsewhere to be the beasts which are "most manifestly" like the prolific creator god, Prajāpati, in that "they bear young three times a year and produce two [offspring] three times [per year]."[89]

Just as the Vaishyas are opposed to the upper classes of the Brahmins and Kshatriyas, so too do we often find sheep and goats opposed to cattle and horses.[90] It might be argued that in the famous creation hymn from the Ṛg Veda (10.90), the sacrifice of the Cosmic Man creates four principal categories of animals, human beings and three others with the "goats and sheep" forming a category unto themselves, perhaps of "all others": "Horses were born from it, and those other animals that have two rows of teeth [meaning humans, perhaps?]; cows were born from it; and from it goats and sheep were born" (ṚV 10.90.10).

Cattle

It would indeed seem that there was a tradition of regarding goats and sheep in a general way as "all animals," the great unwashed mass of beasts, for in several texts we find objections to such a view. Rather, the disputants argue, the cattle are the true *Lumpenproletariat* of the beasts, and are therefore sacred to the Vaishya deities par excellence, the Viśva Devas:

About this they say, "These goats, sheep, and the jungle animals, are not all

> animals. Rather, those cattle are really all animals." On the last day he seizes the cattle [as victims], for they are all animals. They are for the Viśva Devas, and the horse belongs to the Viśva Devas; [they are sacrificed] for universality (*sarvatva*). They are of many types; therefore there are many types of animals. They are of various types; therefore the animals are of various types. (ŚB 13.3.2.3; cf. TB 3.9.9.2)

Elsewhere also the cattle are declared the masses among the beasts—"The Āditya cup is drawn with the largest number of verses; therefore cattle are the most numerous among the animals" (TS 6.5.10.1; cf. ŚB 4.5.5.8)—and are related to the deities which form the *viś* of the gods, the Ādityas (AitB 4.17; ŚB 4.3.5.22) and Maruts (KB 23.3; TB 2.6.18.4). The cow is also the animal connected with Prajāpati (sometimes a Vaishya deity) and the Vaishya meter, the *jagatī* (MS 2.13.14; cf. TS 4.3.7.1).

In Cosmogonies VI and VII, cattle are created from the middle of the Cosmic Man together with the most numerous of the deities and the most populous of the social classes, the Vaishya: "Therefore they are to be eaten, for they were created from the receptacle of food. Therefore they are more numerous than others, for they were created after the most numerous of the gods" (TS 7.1.1.5). The cow is elsewhere equated with "all food," and thus is appropriately the animal of the Vaishya agriculturalist and herdsman.[91] As Brown notes, "No symbol of fecundity or maternity or source of nourishment compared in the Veda to the cow,"[92] and the frequent reference to the cow as a "mother," the identification of the animal with the earth (who is also a mother), and the connection of the cow with one or another of the fertility goddesses bears this out.

Dappled Animals

In some texts, it is the speckled or dappled cow (*pṛṣni*) that is, directly or indirectly, the animal of the *viś* and of Vaishya divinities, the multiplicity of markings being the sign of the Vaishya nature of the beast.[93] In the course of the Rājasūya sacrifice, the king visits the houses of his "jewels" or retainers, including that of the Vaishya village headman (*grāmaṇī*):

> He goes to the house of the village headman. He prepares a cake on seven potsherds for the Maruts. The Maruts are the *viś*, and the village headman is a Vaishya; therefore it is for the Maruts. . . . The sacrificial fee for this [rite] is a spotted cow, for there is an abundance of forms in the spotted cow. The Maruts are the *viś*, and the *viś* are abundance. Therefore the sacrificial fee is a spotted cow. (ŚB 5.3.1.6)

Similarly, in another rite where yet another group of Vaishya deities, the Viśva Devas, are offered an oblation, the sacrificial fee is also a spotted cow, with the same rationale given.[94] Elsewhere a dappled pregnant cow is offered for the Maruts because "the Maruts are the commoners; he thereby makes him [the king] the embryo of the commoners."[95] Still another connection between the spotted cow, Vaishya deities, and the commoners also entails the notion that the *viś* are "food" (and thus are "eaten" by the king) and that the cow of many colors is the earth which generates food:

> Then he seizes a spotted sterile cow (*vāśa*) for the victorious Maruts. For the spotted sterile cow is this [earth]. Whatever food here, rooted and rootless, is established on her. Now he who offers the Vājapeya sacrifice with that spotted sterile cow wins food; for the Vājapeya is so named because it means food and drink (*annapeya*). And the Maruts are the commoners, and the commoners are food.[96]

Lower-Class Animals

Some animals are regarded as alternatively or simultaneously belonging to both the Vaishya and Shūdra *varṇas*; the lower two classes were not, as we have seen elsewhere, always regarded as distinct. The sheep, to take one example, is associated not only with the Vaishyas—for reasons already explicated—but also with the servant classes. This sort of connection is often made via Tvaṣṭṛ, whose animal is the sheep, or more particularly the ram (e.g., ŚB 6.2.1.5, 7.5.2.19ff.; PB 1.8.8), and who can be either a Vaishya or a Shūdra deity. The vaguely lower-class status of the sheep is also indicated at TS 2.2.6.3, where it is written that "he who accepts a sheep [as a sacrificial gift] accepts the nature of the sheep. Having accepted a sheep he should offer to Agni Vaiśvanara. Agni Vaiśvanara is the year; he accepts [the sheep] made suitable by the year, and does not accept the nature of the sheep."

The ass, too, as we saw earlier, is explicitly said to be related to both of the two lower orders (ŚB 6.4.4.12); indeed, it is the double nature of the ass that is featured in Vedic texts.[97] One myth of origins explains why the ass comes to represent two *varṇas* at once:

> Agni ran away from the gods. The gods said, "Agni is the *paśu*. Let us look for him by means of the animals: he will show himself to his own [animal] form." They looked for him by means of the animals, and he showed himself to his own [animal] form. Therefore even now the animal shows itself to its own form, cow to cow, horse to horse, and man to man. They said, "If we look for him with all of them, they will become depleted and not useful for subsistence; and if [we do] not [look for him] with all [the animals], we will get him [Agni] incomplete." They saw one animal [as a substitute] for two animals—the ass [as a substitute for] the cow and the sheep; and because they saw that one beast [would do] for two beasts, therefore that one [the he-ass], while being one has a double seed. (ŚB 6.3.1.22–23)

The text thus justifies the use of the ass as the representative of the Vaishyas and Shūdras by asserting that it is the substitute for both the cow and the sheep, the ordinary Vaishya and Shūdra animals. Furthermore, the myth concludes, this is the reason why the ass, "while being one has a double seed," can impregnate both the mare and the she-mule.[98] Being double seeded, the ass is doubly symbolic: he is of two *varṇa*s at once. He is also the signifier for illicit sexuality. One who breaks a vow of celibacy offers an ass to the goddess of disorder, Nirṛti.[99]

And as other texts make clear, the ass is among the lowest of the animals and therefore is doubly symbolic of only the lowest of the social classes. In one rite, fire is placed on the back of an ass, which is explained in the following fashion:

> Therefore he yokes it for strength. He gathers with the ass; therefore the ass is the best burden-gatherer of animals. He gathers with the ass; therefore the ass, even when grazing is bad, becomes fat beyond other animals. Therefore by it he gathers food and light. He gathers with the ass; therefore the ass, being double seeded, is born least of animals, for Agni burns his place of birth. (TS 5.1.5.5)

The ass, the "least of animals," is the also the "burden-gatherer"[100] and grows fat on very little—a rather telling description of an animal elsewhere equated with the Shūdra class: "When he [student] is going to mount a he-ass, he addresses it: 'You are a Shūdra, a Shūdra by birth. You belong to Agni, with double seed. Make me arrive safely.'"[101] It is no wonder that, as one text notes, the ass when compared to the (Kshatriya) horse is filled with sorrow.[102]

The "Natural" Status of Society

It is usually assumed that the purpose of classificatory schemes is to create epistemological clarity out of what otherwise would be confusion or ignorance; classification does indeed impose order on chaos. But categorical schemes can also be multiplied, overlapped, and superimposed one on top of another in such a way as to produce their own kind of confusion. What results is a sort of classificatory overkill which obfuscates the methods and helps to mask the true purpose and end of the classificatory enterprise.

Ancient Indian animal classification schemes seem to have been designed to conflate "empirical" criteria (pedal structure, dental structure, and the form of procreation) with criteria less obvious and indisputable (whether the animal was domesticated or wild, sacrificable or not, edible or inedible). The redundancy of results—for no matter which set of criteria were used, the same animals were relegated to the same two classes—tended to obscure the relative contestability of the different decisions. Determining the structure of an animal's foot is not the same kind of observation as whether or not the animal is edible or sacrificable—but it is made to appear to be.

A second result of classificatory overkill was that cultural institutions and customs were made to bolster and legitimize one another. Culinary habits and customs regarding domestication of animals were reinforced by the rules of religious ritual: animals that could not be sacrificed to the gods were not to be eaten or tamed by humans. Conversely, the religious ritual was represented as integral to the economy of ordinary life, dealing as it did with the essences of food and wealth.

Even more significant is the fact that in texts dealing with animal classification the institution of the sacrificial ritual is revealed to be the *fons et origo* of all such categorical distinctions. This is not surprising given that in the Veda the entire cosmos is said to have been created out of the sacrifice. It is, we will recall, whether or not the animal possesses the *medha* or sacrificial essence that determines if it is edible or inedible, village or jungle; thus the sacrificial order of things is supposedly prior even to the natural order of things.

Animal classification becomes another occasion for reiterating what is something of a leitmotiv in the Veda—the enormous creative power of the sacrificial ritual, in this case, the power to create categorical differentiation between species of animals. And given that the Brahmin priests are those charged with manipulating the ritual, this too is not surprising in texts that were written by (and largely for) Brahmins. The priests did indeed stand to benefit from a classificatory system that was supposedly grounded in the sacrifice they controlled. But this was only one way in which animal categories effectively served the interest of those who created them.

Animal classification schemes were used in various ways to justify the "naturalness" of the Āryans' own ideal social order, at least as that order was conceived by the Brahmin authors of the Veda. The *varṇa* system was represented in Vedic texts as restating the class divisions within the category of domesticated/edible/sacrificial animals and thus could be harmonized with—or even fully disappear into—the natural order. The social and the natural become thoroughly confused, just as do the "empirical" and the "cultural" or "religious."

In another instance of classificatory overkill and taxonomic mystification, then, animal categories were used in various and yet complementary ways to create and/or buttress social distinctions. Redeploying the fundamental binary opposition among animals to humans, the Āryans could see themselves as part of the valuable and useful side of things (that which belonged to the village, which was edible, and which was suitable for the sacrifice) while relegating their non-Āryan neighbors to the status of "pseudo-men," the wild, inedible, nonsacrificial other, the empty shells of real human beings. And they could envision their particular social order—divided and hierarchically ranked according to *varṇa*—as part of the same "natural" order of things that divided and hierarchically ranked animal species. Such a variety of arguments for the "natural" status of the social order were not necessarily explicitly stated, nor were they necessarily consistent with one another. They were, however, stunningly overwhelming in their redundancy and reapplicability.

NOTES

1. Claude Lévi-Strauss, *Totemism*, trans. by Rodney Needham (Boston: Beacon Press, 1963), p. 89.

2. This is one form of the "encompassment of the opposite" in hierarchical systems which is explored in Louis Dumont's work on the caste system, for which see especially his *Homo Hierarchicus: The Caste System and Its Implications*, trans. by Mark Sainsbury, Louis Dumont, and Basia Gulati (Chicago: University of Chicago Press, 1980). Dumont's

insight on the ways an ideology envelops principles foreign to those guiding the ideology is limited, however, to the notion that power is encompassed by purity (and the Kshatriya by the Brahmin). The notion of hierarchical encompassment in the history of Indian religion and ideas could be applied far more generally than Dumont himself cares to do.

3. The immense anthropological literature on classification of animals includes recent works by Roy G. Willis, *Man and Beast* (London: Granada Publishing, 1974); Tim Ingold, *The Appropriation of Nature* (Manchester: Manchester University Press, 1986); the essays included in Roy G. Willis, ed., *Signifying Animals: Human Meaning in the Natural World* (London: Unwin Hyman, 1990); and in Tim Ingold, ed., *What Is an Animal?* (London: Unwin Hyman, 1988). For an introductory overview of animals in Vedism, see Alfred Hillebrandt, "Tiere und Götter im vedischen Ritual," *Schlesische Gesellschaft für Vaterländische Cultur* 83 (1905): 1–12; and Jan Gonda's "Mensch und Tier im alten India," in his *Selected Studies*, Vol. 4 (Leiden: E. J. Brill, 1975), pp. 484–95. See also the closely related materials presented in Hanns-Peter Schmidt's "Ancient Iranian Animal Classification," *Studien zur Indologie und Iranistik* 5/6 (1980): 209–44. For animals in other Indian traditions, consult Padmanabh S. Jaini, "Indian Perspectives on the Spirituality of Animals," in *Buddhist Philosophy and Culture: Essays in Honour of N. A. Jayawickrema*, ed. by David J. Kalupahana and W. G. Weeraratne, (Colombo: Jayawickrema Felicitation Volume Committee, 1987); and James McDermott, "Animals and Humans in Early Buddhism," *Indo-Iranian Journal* 32, 4 (Oct. 1989): 269–80.

4. For man as the "overlord" (*adhipati*) of the animals, see KS 20.10 and TS 5.3.1.5; cf. ŚB 4.5.5.7 and the commentary of Govinda on Manu 1.39, where humans are clearly distinguished from other kinds of animals: "*manuṣyānāṃ paśutvepi prādhānyāt pṛthakgrahaṇam*." For man as "first" among the animals, see ŚB 6.2.1.18, 7.5.2.6,17; and below. See also ŚB 1.5.2.4 (cf. 3.6.2.26) where it is said that the animals are "behind" humans, just as birds, plants, and trees are "behind" the gods. The most articulate and sophisticated statement of the superiority of the human over both fauna and flora may be found at AitĀ 2.3.2, cited and analyzed in Chapter 7.

5. W. D. O'Flaherty, "The Case of the Stallion's Wife: Indra and Vṛṣanaśva in the Ṛg Veda and the Brāhmaṇas," *Journal of the American Oriental Society* 105, 3 (1985), p. 497.

6. I do not take into account here another "empirically" grounded dichotomy of animals represented in two texts: "The expounders of the Veda say, 'What sacrifice is performed from which comes, on the one hand, the animals who take up [food] by the hand (*hastadāna*) and, on the other hand, the animals who take up [food] by the mouth?' When one takes up [the soma] with one's hand silently, from that the monkey (*makata*), the man (*puruṣa*), and the elephant (*hastin*) [are created]—these are [the animals] who take up [food] by the hand. The mouth is [that draught of soma] related to Vāyu. When they take up the several [soma] draughts related to Vāyu, from that [are born] the several kinds of animals who take up [food] by the mouth" (MS 4.5.7; cf. TS 6.4.5.7).

7. Cf. ŚB 12.7.1.5: "From his [Indra's] ear fame (*yaśas*) flowed, and became the whole-hoofed animals—the horse, mule, and ass."

8. Sāyana glosses "four-footed" with *gavādīnam*, animals "beginning with the cow," and *manuṣyādīnam*, animals "beginning with man," for the "two-footed." Cf. TS 4.2.10.1–2; VS 17.47–48; ŚB 7.5.2.32, 13.3.6.3–4; AitB 3.31.

9. The text notes that the recipient of a gift of an animal with incisors in both jaws, "whether horse or man," has in fact accepted "a measure of his very self." At BŚS 13.9 we read:"Having received as sacrificial fee an animal with incisors in both jaws, [namely] a horse or a man, one should offer a cake on twelve potsherds to Vaiśvanara Agni." Cf. TS 5.1.2.6, where it is claimed that the horse, by virtue of its two rows of teeth, is more

powerful than animals with just one, and by virtue of its hair it is more powerful than other animals with two rows of teeth (i.e., humans?).

10. A. A. Macdonell and A. B. Keith, *Vedic Index of Names and Subjects*, 2 vols. (reprint Varanasi: Motilal Banarsidass, 1958), I:510. Cf. Schmidt, "Ancient Iranian Animal Classification," p. 233.

11. For stock phrases like "both kinds of *paśus*, those of the village and those of the jungle," see, MS 3.2.3, 3.9.7; AV 2.34.4, 3.31.3; ŚB 12.7.3.18; etc. The dichotomy is also sometimes indicated by the opposition of wild game (*mṛga*) and domesticated animals (*paśu*), e.g., AV 11.2.24, or, in at least one passage (AV 7.5.11), of "moving" (*jagat*) animals and animals with feet like dogs. For an overview of the distinction made between the "village" and the "jungle" in Vedic texts, see Charles Malamoud, "Village et forêt dans l'idéologie de l'Inde brahmanique," in *Cruire le monde: Rite et pensée dans l'Inde ancienne* (Paris: Éditions la Découverte, 1989), pp. 93–114.

12. This seems to be a widespread feature of animal classification systems. See S.J. Tambiah's observation that "as a class, forest animals have a greater variety of members than the domesticated category." "Animals Are Good to Think and Good to Prohibit," *Ethnology* 8 (1969), p. 440. But note that AV 2.34.4 (cf. TB 3.9.2.4) declares that the village animals are "of all forms (*viśvarūpa*), of various forms (*virūpa*), of many and yet one form (*bahudhaikarūpa*)." For general references to *mṛga* (wild beast), see ṚV 1.173.2, 1.191.4, 8.1.20, 8.5.36, 10.146.6; AV 4.3.6, 10.1.26, 12.1.48, 19.38.2; PB 6.7.10, 24.11.2; AitB 3.31.2, 8.23.3. For "terrible (*bhīma*) *mṛga*," ṚV 1.154.2, 1.190.3, 2.33.1, 2.34.1, 10.180.2. And for *mṛga* in the sense of a gazelle-type animal, ṚV 1.38.5, 1.105.7, 6.75.11, 9.32.4; AV 5.21.4; TS 6.1.3.7; TB 3.2.5.6; ŚB 11.8.4.3.

13. The text obviously refers only to *wild* animals with cloven hooves; as we saw previously, the term "cloven-hoofed animals" ordinary refers to one type of village animal (cows, sheep, and goats).

14. This term sometimes is used to designate wild animals as a class, and especially those feared by man. See, e.g., ŚB 4.2.4.16, AV 7.5.11, 8.5.11, 19.39.4; and Sāyana on AV 3.31.3.

15. Mbh 6.5.12–14. See also the difficult AV passages (translated here by Whitney) listing the wild jungle animals: "To you [o Rudra] the jungle animals, the wild beasts in the wood (*mṛgāh vane*) are assigned; the geese (*haṃsas*), the eagles (*suparṇas*), the hawks (*śakunas*), the winged animals (*vayases*). O Paśupati, the spirit within the waters is yours; the divine waters flow for your increase. The crocodiles (*śiṃśumāras*), the alligators (*ajagaras*), the *purīkayas*, *jaṣas*, and the *matsyas* (all types of fish); the *rajasas* (insects?) at which you throw" (AV 11.2.24–25). "The jungle animals of yours, the wild beasts lying in the woods—the lion, the tiger—who go around eating men; the *ula* (owl? jackal?), the wolf (*vṛka*), the demoness of calamity (*ducchunā*), the ravenous beasts (*ṛkṣīkas*), the demon whom one must beware; O earth, drive them away from us here. . . . She to whom the two-legged birds flock—the geese (*haṃsas*), eagles (*suparṇas*), hawks (*śakunas*), the smaller birds (*vayases*) . . . " (AV 12.1.49,51). For an interpretation of these passages, see below.

16. For seven village animals, see also AV 3.10.6 (with Sāyana's commentary); PB 22.4.4 (and commentary); and ŚB 9.3.1.18–25, where it is declared that there are seven (unspecified) village animals along with other sets of seven (rivers flowing eastward, *ṛṣis*, breaths, meters, rivers flowing westward, and the number of deities within each of the troops of the Maruts).

17. ŚB 10.2.1.1; see also, e.g., TS 5.2.3.6. The contraction of a sevenfold class of domestic animals into a category with only five components raises the question as to why the ass, mule, and camel—which appear in other lists of domesticated village animals—

dropped from enumerations of this kind. While the three would indeed appear to be "village animals," they are not, it would seem, "*paśus*" in the more limited sense of the word as it is deployed in the fivefold schemes. The ass and the mule are possibly dropped from lists of this kind because they are regarded as subsumed under "horse"—the first because it can reproduce with a horse, and the second because it is the hybrid product of the ass and horse and therefore is said to be "of double seed." See TS 5.1.5.5, 7.1.2–3; ŚB 6.3.1.23, 12.7.2.21; PB 6.1.4–5; and JB 1.67. The rationale for dropping the camel from lists of "village animals" is much more difficult to determine. It will be recalled that at Manu 5.18 the camel is specifically excepted from the general class of edible animals. Since village animals (excepting humans) are regarded as edible, the camel may have appeared as a problematic species in that category. The meaning of the term translated here as "camel" (*uṣṭra* or *uṣṭī*) is, in any event, questionable. According to Macdonell and Keith, *Vedic Index of Names and Subjects*, Western Sanskritists have guessed that the word in some passages (ṚV 1.138.2, 8.5.37, 8.6.48; AV 20.127.2; VS 8.50; ŚB 1.2.3.9; AitB 2.8) refers to a humped bull or buffalo.

18. See also AV 11.2.24–25, 12.1.49,51; and Heinrich Zimmer, *Altindisches Leben: Die Cultur der vedischen Arier nach den samhita dargestellt* (Berlin: Weidmannsche Buchhandlung, 1879), pp. 77–78. Zimmer argues that the five classes of jungle animals are: (1) those of jungle described as "the dread beasts which are in the wood" (*mṛgā bhīmā vane hitā*); (2) winged creatures (represented by the *haṃsa*, *suparṇa*, and *śakuna*); (3) amphibia (the alligator or *śiṃśumāra* and the *ajagara* or crocodile); (4) fish (*purīkaya*, *jaṣa*, *matsya*); and (5) insects and worms (*rajasas*). Macdonell and Keith believe "this division is more ingenious than probable." *Vedic Index*, I:511. For an even more explicit fivefold classification of the jungle animals, however, see TS 4.2.10.1–4, and below.

19. See the lists of 111 and 180 animal victims at the Aśvamedha, divided into village and jungle; for the first list, TS 5.5.11–24; KS 5.7; MS 3.14.11ff.; VS 24.30ff.; and TB 3.9.1–4; for the second list, TS 5.6.11–20; KS 5.9; MS 3.13.3ff.; VS 24.2ff.; and TB 3.8.19–3.9.1.

20. KB 20.1 also speaks of "sixfold food" and includes both wild and domesticated animals (as well as plants, trees, "that which goes in the water," and "that which swims"). As we shall see, however, the great majority of texts exclude the beasts of the jungle from the category of edible animals.

21. TB 3.9.3.1. Cf. TB 3.9.2.1–2: "Prajāpati desired, 'May I obtain both worlds.' He saw (*apaśyat*) both these *paśus*, the village and the jungle. He sacrificed them; with this [sacrifice] he obtained both worlds. With the village animals he obtained this world; with the jungle animals the yonder [world was obtained]. When he sacrifices the village animals, with that he obtains this world; when the jungle [animals are sacrificed], with that [he obtains] the yonder [world]."

22. Wendy Doniger, *Other People's Myths*, (New York: Macmillan, 1988), p. 83.

23. See also ŚB 11.7.1.3: "He who sacrifices with the animal sacrifice redeems himself—a male for a male. For the *paśu* is a male, and the sacrificer is a male."

24. The Vedic categorical system is ambiguous on the question of human sacrificial victims. For, on the one hand, insofar as sacrificial victims are edible, the explicit rules against eating human flesh would seem to preclude human sacrifice. On the other hand, insofar as humans are among the five sacrificial *paśus*, they were eminently sacrificable. For arguments for the probability of human sacrifice in ancient India, consult G. R. Sharma, *The Excavations at Kauśambi (1957–1959)* (Allahabad: Institute of Archeology, Allahabad University, 1960), pp. 87ff.; Dieter Schlinghoff, "Menschenopfer in Kauśambi," *Indo-Iranian Journal* 11 (1969): 176–98; Asko Parpola, "The Pre-Vedic Indian

Background of the Śrauta Rituals," in *Agni: The Vedic Ritual of the Fire Altar*, ed. by Frits Staal (Berkeley: Asian Humanities Press, 1983), II:41–75, esp. pp. 49–53; James L. Sauvé, "The Divine Victim: Aspects of Human Sacrifice in Viking Scandinavia and Vedic India," in *Myth and Law among the Indo-Europeans*, ed. by Jaan Puhvel (Los Angeles: University of California Press, 1970), pp. 173–91; and Willibald Kirfel, "Der Aśvamedha und der Puruṣamedha," in *Festschrift für Walther Schubring* (Hamburg: Walter de Gruyter, 1951), pp. 39–50. The argument that human sacrifice was "only a priest's fantasy of the sacrifice to end all sacrifices" has been put forward most recently by Bruce Lincoln, in *Myth, Cosmos, and Society: Indo-European Themes of Creation and Destruction* (Cambridge, Mass.: Harvard University Press, 1986), p. 183.

25. Mention also might be made here of the passage at ŚB 6.2.1.39: "He should offer up these five *paśus*, insofar as he is able to do so. For these were the ones that Prajāpati was the first to offer up, and [it was these that] Śyāparṇa Sāyakāyana was the last [to offer up], and between these two these [were the victims] people offered up."

26. Compare Tambiah's observation about the Thai conception of *khwan*: "The close association of buffalo with human beings is also manifest in the fact that to the buffalo alone of all animals is attributed *khwan* (spiritual essence), a pre-eminently human possession." "Animals Are Good to Think," p. 437.

27. Tambiah notes the same phenomenon in Thailand, where certain wild animals are constituted as the "counterparts of domesticated animals." In that context, however, the "forest counterparts" to the village animals are classified as edible. "Animals Are Good to Think," pp. 433, 440.

28. Macdonell and Keith, *Vedic Index*, write that in Vedic texts the *śarabha* "is spoken of as akin to the goat; it was probably a kind of deer." See also AV 9.5.9 and VS 13.51. In later Hinduism, the animal is depicted as having eight legs and living in the Himalayan mountains. See also Francis Zimmermann, *The Jungle and the Aroma of Meats: An Ecological Theme in Hindu Medicine* (Berkeley: University of California Press, 1987), pp. 82–83.

29. In this regard, one might also point to the tale told at AitB 3.33–34 about the incestuous mating of Prajāpati/Rudra, in the form of a deer, with his own daughter. The creator god spills his seed, which is surrounded by Agni the fire, and which thus becomes a kind of sacrificial oblation. A list of animals created from the scorched earth and ashes of the completed "sacrifice" follows: "The charred [earth] became the black *paśus*, the reddened ground became the ruddy [animals]. The ash spread out in different forms: the *gaura*, the *gavaya*, the *ṛṣya* antelope, the camel, the ass, and those [other] tawny animals." Here, as in those texts which account for the origins of the inedible jungle animals from the spent husks of the sacrificed village animals, it is the presence or absence of the sacrificial quality which bifurcates the animals into two general categories. Certain animals are created within the sacrifice, and the others are created when the sacrifice has been completed, "out of its ashes."

30. Cf. MS 2.7.17 and KS 16.17, which differ only by positing the *meṣam āraṇyakam* or wild ram as the jungle equivalent of the domesticated sheep.

31. JB 1.43, translated in W.D. O'Flaherty, *Tales of Sex and Violence: Folklore, Sacrifice, and Danger in the Jaiminīya Brāhmaṇa*, (Chicago: University of Chicago Press, 1984), pp. 33–34. Cf. KB 11.2 and ŚB 12.9.1.1: "Whatever food a man consumes in this world, that [food] in return consumes him in yonder world."

32. O'Flaherty, *Tales of Sex and Violence*, p. 36.

33. E.g., ŚB 3.2.1.12, 5.2.1.16, 8.3.1.13, 8.3.3.2ff., 8.5.2.1, 8.6.2.1,13, 9.2.3.40, and esp. 7.5.2.42. For particular hymns of praise identified with "food and animals," see PB 15.9.13, 16.15.8, 22.3.4–5, 22.10.2, 25.2.3, and cf. 19.9.4. For a particular sacrifice

intended for one who "desires animals or food," see KB 4.5. For sacrificial food as "food and animals," KB 3.7, 13.6.

34. See, e.g., the optional sacrifice called the *sarvapṛṣṭheṣṭi* described at BŚS 13.29–30, ĀpŚS 19.22.7–23.2, and HŚS 22.3.17,18, which requires a *dakṣiṇā* of a horse, bull, ram, and he-goat. See also BŚS 28.6, where it is stated that cows and horses are substitutes for one another, as are goats and sheep (with no mention of the human).

35. AitB 2.3; cf. ŚB 3.7.3.1–5. See also AitB 2.6 and the text at ŚB 4.6.9.1–2, where the animals, identified with food, fearfully run away from the gods who intended to sacrifice them (in order to attain excellence, *śriyā*, and fame, *yaśas*, and to become eaters of food). The animals are lured back by the *gārhapatya* fire, which is a house (*gṛha*) and a "firm foundation" (*pratiṣṭhā*). "They thereby contained them in the house, and thus that food, gained by them, did not go away from them."

36. Consult Brian K. Smith and Wendy Doniger, "Sacrifice and Substitution: Ritual Mystification and Mythical Demystification" *Numen* 36, 2 (1989): 189–224.

37. Another way to exclude the human from the edible animals is found in another text where we learn that "food" is precisely all animals who are not in "the same class as men": "Of these [animals], those who have two rows of teeth, and who are categorized in the [same] class [as that] of man (*puruṣasyānu vidhāṃ vihitās*) are eaters of food; the other animals are food" (AitĀ 2.3.1). This translation follows the interpretation of the text first put forward by Heinrich Zimmer, *Altindisches Leben*, pp. 74–76. For other options, see A. B. Keith's *Aitareya Āraṇyaka* ("Of animals, those who have teeth above and below and are formed like men . . ."); and Hanns-Peter Schmidt, "Ancient Iranian Animal Classification," p. 234: "Of the (animals) those who have incisors in both jaws and are disposed according to the disposition of man. . . . " Compare the passage with that at Manu 5.18, where animals with one row of teeth are declared edible (with some exceptions).

38. Similarly, the animal victim in the sacrifice must resemble the (human) sacrificer —and is indeed often said "to be" the sacrificer in the ritual—but cannot really be fully equated, for then the act of sacrifice would be indistinguishable from suicide. On this point in general, with examples from the Vedic and Hindu contexts, see Smith and Doniger, "Sacrifice and Substitution."

39. Recall also that one of the social classes, the Vaishyas, are identified with animals in general, and therefore are regarded as "food" for the higher two classes. Linkages to the western or northern quarter (see above, Chapter 5), the rainy season (said to be "rich in offspring and animals" as well as food, see above, Chapter 6), the *jagatī* meter (also identified with food and animals, see below, Chapter 9) and the *vairūpa* meter (ditto, for both food and animals are multiform, *virūpa*, see Chapter 9), and other signifiers corroborate the notion that the Vaishyas "are" animals (and that they are to be "tended" as well as "eaten" by the higher *varṇas*).

40. Cf. Claude Lévi-Strauss's hypothesis regarding "totemism": "It is this direct perception of the class, through the individuals, which characterizes the relation between man and the animal or plant, and it is this also which helps us to understand 'this singular thing that is totemism.'" *Totemism*, p. 93.

41. Cosmogony VII differs in the order in which the links on the chain are produced by the creator god and, more importantly here, in reversing the assignments of the horse and the sheep:

1. mouth (primacy) ⇒ nine-versed hymn of praise = Agni = *gāyatrī* meter = *rathantara* chant = Brahmin = goat
2. chest/arms (virility) ⇒ fifteen-versed hymn of praise = Indra = *triṣṭubh* meter = *bṛhat* chant = Kshatriya = sheep

3. belly (food and abundance) ⇒ seventeen-versed hymn of praise = Viśva Devas = *jagatī* meter = *vairūpa* chant = Vaishya = cow

4. feet (dependency) ⇒ twenty-one-versed hymn of praise = no god = *anuṣṭubh* meter = *vairāja* chant = Shūdra = horse

For this inversion of the horse and sheep, see above, Chapter 3, n. 10.

42. In other cases, too, the *varṇa* of particular animals is clear even without specific attributions. See, e.g., the text at ŚB 6.1.2.4–5. Agni has fled from Prajāpati and has hidden in the sacrificial animals: "He [Prajāpati] saw those five animals. Because he saw (*apaśyat*) them, therefore they are animals (*paśus*). Because he saw him [Agni] in them, therefore they are animals. He thought, 'They are Agni; I will make them into my own self. Just as Agni, when kindled, gleams, so does their eye gleam; as Agni's smoke rises, so does vapor rise from them; as Agni burns up what is put in him, so do they devour; and as Agni's ashes drop down, so do their turds. They are indeed Agni; I will make them into my own self.' He wanted to anoint them for different deities: the man for Viśvakarman; the horse for Varuṇa; the bull for Indra; the ram for Tvaṣṭṛ; the he goat for Agni."

The correlations between the animals and gods at the end of this passage mostly differ from those made in Cosmogony VI cited earlier (the goat and Agni, the horse and Indra, the cow and the Viśva Devas, and the sheep and "not a single one among the gods"). Nevertheless, the implicit *varṇa* of each is apparent—for the *varṇas* of the deities are fairly obvious—and the assignments do not contradict the classification of Cosmogony VI. The he-goat, the animal of Agni in both instances, is the Brahmin animal; the horse's royal and warriorlike qualities are highlighted by the association with either Indra or Varuṇa, both of whom are Kshatriya deities; the male bull, in one of the two texts connected with Indra, has been separated from the (female) cows (and the Vaishyas) and given a Kshatriya classification; and the ram, by virtue of the its deity, Tvaṣṭṛ, is perhaps implicitly categorized as a Shūdra animal, just as the sheep generally were regarded as the Shūdra beasts in the scheme of Cosmogony VI.

43. In addition to the texts cited below, the goat is also said to be Agni's animal at TS 2.2.2.4–5, 5.4.3.2, 5.5.22.1, 5.5.24.1; ŚB 6.3.2.9, 6.4.4.4, 13.2.7.2; TB 3.7.3.1; MŚS 5.2.10.15. See also PB 1.8.4,6 where the he-goat is attached to Agni and the she-goat to Agni and Soma. The goat is the particular animal associated with the priest who bears Agni's name, the *āgnīdhra* (ŚB 1.2.4.13, 2.1.4.3), and this priest is also directly connected with the Brahmin *varṇa* (ŚB 4.3.4.19), and is linked to one of the priests who bears the *brahman* power, the *subrahmaṇya* (PB 18.9.19). For the connection of the she-goat to another Brahmin deity, Bṛhaspati, see MS 2.13.14 and TS 4.3.7.1.

44. TB 3.7.3.1–3. The Sūtras which repeat this series of substitutions for fire include BŚS 24.8; BhŚS 9.4.5ff.; cf. ĀpŚS 9.3.3ff.; HŚS 15.1.51ff.; VaikhŚS 20.7; KŚS 25.4.1ff. At MŚS 11.1.2.1 the priest indicates his acceptance of a goat given as a *dakṣiṇā* by touching the animal's ear.

45. TS 4.2.10.4. See also the etymological origin myth told at ŚB 6.1.1.11 and 6.3.1.28 where the goat is said to have been produced from the juice adhering to the shell of the cosmic egg and is therefore known as aja (= *a-ja*, "unborn"). A variant is found at ŚB 6.2.2.6: "He then seizes [as a sacrificial victim] for Vāyu Niyutvat that white hornless [he-goat]. Prajāpati, having emitted the creatures, looked around. Because of his great bliss, he shed his seed. It became that white, hornless, bearded he-goat (*aja*, 'unborn one'). Seed is life sap; as far as life sap reaches, so far extends the self. And when he seizes that one he reaches to the very end of Agni. It is white because seed is white. It is hornless because seed is hornless."

46. See TS 6.1.10.1 and ŚB 3.3.3.8. For other relations between the goat, soma, and

the *gāyatrī* meter (which reiterates the Brahmin connection), see TS 6.1.6.3. See also ŚB 3.3.3.9: "With that [mantra] he gives the she-goat, with that he takes the king [soma]. For she [the she-goat, *ajā*] is the name for her who is conquering (*ajaitaya*). She finally conquers him [king Soma]. It is thus a mysterious sense in which they call her the she-goat."

47. Consult, e.g., BŚS 24.9. ŚB 5.5.4.1, in recommending the use of the goat as an option if animals which are harder to come by are unobtainable, notes that goats are "easier to cook."

48. For the goat's creation from the head, see Cosmogonies VI and VII, and also ŚB 6.5.4.16. For a similar connection to the mouth and speech, a connection equally laden with Brahmin connotations, see ŚB 7.5.2.21 and esp. ŚB 7.5.2.36: "The he-goat is speech, and with speech the gods at first obtained their divinity. 'With that the wise ones went to the heights.' The heights are the heavenly world; [it therefore is the same as saying] 'With that the wise ones went to the heavenly world.'"

49. As Bruce Lincoln notes in his *Priests, Warriors, and Cattle: A Study in the Ecology of Religions* (Berkeley: University of California Press, 1981), both the Kshatriyas and the Brahmins "had legitimate claims to the possession of cattle, warriors because they procured the animals in raids and priests because the animals are important for sacrifice" (p. 153), and the "sacrality" of the cow may be derived from economic or ritualistic sources or, more likely, both. Lincoln's analysis of what might be regarded as something of a charter myth for the association of Brahmins and cattle (at the expense of Kshatriya claims to the cow) found at Rāmāyana 1.50ff. is also relevant to our discussion here (see pp. 143–54).

50. W. Norman Brown, "The Sanctity of the Cow in Hinduism," in *India and Indology: Selected Articles by W. Norman Brown*, ed. by Rosane Rocher (Delhi: Motilal Banarsidass, 1978), p. 95.

51. In BŚS (28.13), it is said that the standard *dakṣinā* for a sacrifice is comprised of a cow, some gold, and a garment.

52. Brown, "The Sanctity of the Cow," p. 97.

53. Ibid., p. 98.

54. For a specified list of animals generally known as cattle or the bovines (*gavya*) see ĀpŚS 19.16.16: "A bull with protruding horns, bull with horns turned backwards, an ox (*ukṣan*), a barren cow, a pregnant cow, a milch-cow, a calf, a bull, bull to be yoked to a cart, ox which has been let loose again, and a gayal—these are the bovines."

55. TB 2.8.8.9. Cf. Mbh 13.104.63, where the cow, together with Agni or fire and the *brahman* power, are said to be the three manifestations of *tejas*.

56. Cf. Lincoln's remark that "cattle are ultimately destined for the priest, to be used for the ritual return of their products to the gods." *Priests, Warriors, and Cattle*, p. 154. In this connection, it might also be noted that the apotheosis of sacred speech, Vāc (who is also equated to the sacrifice), is often connected with cows (e.g., KS 29.1; PB 21.3.1; ŚB 4.5.8.3,11, 14.2.1.15).

57. ŚB 2.2.4.12–15. See also TB 2.1.6.2–3 where the cow is said to have originated from the breath of Agni, the body of Vāyu, and the eyesight of Āditya the sun: "Truly the Agnihotra sacrifice is a cow. He who knows that the Agnihotra is a cow endows Agni with his inhalation and exhalation."

58. The association of Sarasvatī and the milch cow (*dhenu*) (MS 3.11.2,3; KS 38.8; TB 2.6.12.1,4) also is ambiguous, given that Sarasvatī can function as a Brahmin god (given her identification with speech) or as a Vaishya deity (because of her fertility attributes).

59. ĀśvGS 1.19.10; ŚGS 2.1.2–5; BGS 2.5.16; HGS 1.1.4.7; BhGS 1.1; VaikhSmS

2.4; PGS 2.5.17–19; GGS 2.10.9; JGS 1.12; ĀpDhS 1.1.3.3–6; BDhS 1.2.3.14; VāsDhS 11.61–63; GautDhS 1.16.

60. Kshatriya and Vaishya sacrificers become Brahmins when consecrated for sacrifice since they are "born out of the *brahman*, out of the sacrifice," according to ŚB 3.2.1.40; cf. ŚB 13.4.1.3; AitB 7.23. It is in this sense that the antelope skin upon which the king sits during the royal consecration is called the "womb" and "navel" of the *kṣatra* (see, e.g., TB 2.6.5.1), for the *kṣatra* is often said to be born out of the *brahman*.

61. ŚB 1.1.4.1–3; cf. the variant at TS 5.2.6.4–5. Other texts linking the black antelope to the sacrifice include AitB 1.13 (which further associates both with speech and heaven), ŚB 3.2.1.8,28, 6.4.1.6,9, 12.8.3.9,21, 14.1.2.2. In the later *dharma* literature, the territory which was deemed fit for habitation by the Āryans was defined, on the one hand, by where the black antelope naturally roams and, on the other hand, where it is suitable to sacrifice. See, e.g., Manu 2.22–23.

62. The connection made between the horse and the *brahman* at VS 23.14 and ŚB 13.2.7.10 is exceptional.

63. As in ŚB 13.2.2.17, where the slaughtering knife used for cutting up the horse is to be made of gold: "But indeed the horse is also the *kṣatra*, and this gold is a form of the *kṣatra*. He thus combines the *kṣatra* with the *kṣatra*." Cf. ŚB 13.2.2.15, cited below.

64. E.g., PB 18.9.11; ŚB 6.5.3.9, 13.1.1.1, 13.2.6.8; TB 3.8.8.4, 3.9.16.1–2.

65. See also ŚB 7.5.2.6 and 7.5.4.6, cited above.

66. PB 21.4.2; cf. JB 2.268; TS 5.3.12.1; ŚB 13.4.2.3–4. See also the variant at ŚB 13.3.1.1–2, which goes on to specify that it was Prajāpati's left eye from which the horse originated, thus justifying the practice of cutting the meat portion from the left side of the horse in the Aśvamedha. A somewhat different etymologically centered myth is recounted at TB 3.9.21.1–2: "The Ādityas and the Angirases were battling for the heavenly world. [After the Ādityas, by means of their sacrifice, had obtained the heavenly world] the Angirases brought to the Ādityas the sun which had become a white horse as a sacrificial gift. They [the Ādityas] said [to the Angirases], 'The one you have brought us as a sacrificial gift has [because of this] become excellent (*vārya*).' Therefore people call the horse very excellent (*suvārya*). Therefore, at the sacrifice, a boon (*vāra*) is given [as a sacrificial gift]. Inasmuch as Prajāpati, having been seized [for the sacrifice] became the horse, that is the origin of the name 'horse.' Inasmuch as he swelled (*śvayat*) and was sore (*aru*), that is the origin of the name *arvan* ('courser'). Inasmuch as he immediately conquered booty (*vāja*), that is the origin of the name *vājin* ('heroic steed')." For yet another etymological myth on the origins of the horse, see ŚB 6.1.1.11; 6.3.1.28: "And the tear (*aśru*) which had formed itself became the tear; 'tear' is what they mysteriously call the horse (*aśva*), for the gods love the mysterious."

67. Passages which link the horse with the procreative power of the creator god are to be found, however. See, e.g., PB 11.3.4–5: "There is the horse chant. Prajāpati, having become a horse, emitted the creatures; he was reproduced [and] became multiple. He who has chanted the horse chant is reproduced and becomes multiplied"; and PB 20.4.5: "Prajāpati emitted the creatures. These [creatures] did not procreate. He saw this chant, and changing himself into a horse, he sniffed at them [and] they procreated. This chant is procreation." See also TB 3.9.8.2 (the horse is Prajāpati and equated with *śrī*, bountiful good fortune) and TB 3.8.8.4, where the horse is connected both with Prajāpati and the *jagatī*, the Vaishya meter. Perhaps even more to the point is the frequently observed fact that the mare is doubly procreative, being able to mate with both the stallion and the mule (PB 6.1.4; JB 1.67; TS 7.1.1–3; ŚB 6.3.1.23, 12.7.2.21; cf. PB 12.4.15).

68. ŚB 13.1.2.5. The virility of the horse also had ritual applications: "He [the priest] then makes the horse walk [on the place of the *āhavanīya* fire]. When he has made it

walk on it, he leads it out toward the east, makes it turn round again and lets it loose to the west. The horse is virility; therefore he makes it turn round again so that this virility does not turn away from him [the sacrificer]. He places that [fire] into the horse's footprint. The horse is virility; into virility he places it" (ŚB 2.1.4.23–24).

69. The horse is also the most honored (*apacitatama*), thanks to the Devas, and the most energetic (*tviṣīmat*) and fullest with fiery energy (*harasvitama*), due to the Sarva Devas. TB 3.8.7.1–3; cf. ŚB 13.1.2.5–8.

70. See, however, ŚB 13.3.2.3 and TB 3.9.2.4.

71. E.g., ŚB 1.4.3.6, 6.4.4.3,7. See also ŚB 10.6.4.1, which declares the horse to be the universe: "As the mare (*hayā*) it carried the gods; as the steed (*vājin*) the Gandharvas; as the racer (*arvan*) the demons; and as the horse (*aśva*) [it carried] men." ŚB 14.1.3.25 states that the earth is called "the mare of man," and "having become a mare, she [the earth] carried Manu; he, Prajāpati, is her lord." Cf. AitB 4.27; and esp. 3.47: "The meters, having carried the oblation to the gods, are tired and stand at the back part of the sacrifice—just as if a horse or a mule stands having carried [its load]." For both the horse and Agni the fire as "leaders," consult PB 8.8.4.

72. The thunderbolt is equated with the *kṣatra* power at ŚB 13.4.4.1 and 13.7.1.10; it is called "harsh" (*krūra*) like the Kshatriya at TS 6.2.5.2. See also the interesting text at ŚB 5.4.4.15, describing a rite at the Rājasūya: "Then a Brahmin, either the *adhvaryu* priest or he who is his [the king's] *purohita*, hands him a wooden sword [saying], 'You are Indra's *vajra*. With that serve me.' The *vajra* is the wooden sword. That Brahmin, by means of the *vajra*, makes the king to be weaker than himself (*ātmano 'baliyamsam-kurute*), for the king who is weaker than the Brahmin becomes stronger (*balīyas*) than his enemies. Thus he makes him stronger than his enemies."

73. ŚB 6.3.3.9–10. For similar statements see ŚB 2.1.4.15ff.; 6.3.1.28, and 7.3.2.18–19.

74. For this equation see also AitB 3.11, 6.35; KB 30.6; PB 16.12.4; TB 2.8.6.1; ŚB 3.5.1.13ff.

75. For the horse as thunderbolt, see also ŚB 6.3.3.12 and 13.1.2.9.

76. See above, ŚB 6.1.2.5, and also PB 1.8.2; ŚB 4.3.4.31, 5.3.1.5.

77. TB 3.9.16.1. The text later goes on, however, to state that "the horse belongs to Prajāpati."

78. The north is ordinarily the direction of the lower classes or the Shūdra, and indeed as we witness in Cosmogony VII, the horse (together with the *anuṣṭubh* meter) is sometimes associated with that *varṇa*. Elsewhere, too, the horse is connected with the *anuṣṭubh* and northern quarter (e.g., ŚB 7.5.2.15) but, as we learn from ŚB 13.2.2.17ff., such associations may also be conceived in Kshatriya terms: having established that the horse is the *kṣatra*, and all other animals are commoners, the text then notes that "the horse belongs to the *anuṣṭubh*, and that [northern] quarter belongs to the *anuṣṭubh*. He thus places that [horse] in its own quarter." Cf. PB 21.4.6 and ŚB 13.3.3.1 for the declaration that the horse is the highest animal and the *anuṣṭubh* the highest meter. For the north as the way to heaven, and the claim that it is the horse (and not man) who knows the way to the heavenly world, see TB 3.8.22.1, 3.9.6.4; ŚB 13.2.3.1, 13.2.8.1.

79. ŚB 6.1.1.11, 5.1.4.5, 7.5.2.18, 10.6.4.1, 13.2.2.19, 13.3.1.3; TB 3.8.4.3, 3.8.19.2, 3.8.20.4; etc.

80. ŚB 5.4.2.5. Cf. ŚB 13.1.2.2, where the Aśvamedha is designated "the bull of sacrifices" to indicate its superiority. PB 18.6.14, however, labels a certain chant "the bull of the *brahman*; he makes him [the sacrificer] reach the status of the bull."

81. In addition to the texts cited, see, e.g., TS 1.8.9.1; ŚB 1.4.1.33, 5.5.4.1, 12.9.1.4;

ŚānĀ 1.1; MŚS 5.2.10.15,35–37. The bull is once said to provide a "fine shelter" (*sūpasthā*) for Indra (TB 2.6.15.2).

82. ŚB 12.7.1.4. For other connections between Indra, the bull, and *bala* or *indriya*, see, e.g., ŚB 12.7.2.3; TB 2.6.4.5, 2.6.11.3, 2.6.18.4.

83. Brown, "The Sanctity of the Cow," p. 95.

84. ĀśvGS 1.19.10; ŚGS 2.1.2–5; BGS 2.5.16; HGS 1.1.4.7; BhGS 1.1; VaikhSmS 2.4; PGS 2.5.17–19; GGS 2.10.9; JGS 1.12; ĀpDhS 1.1.3.3–6; BDhS 1.2.3.14; VāsDhS 11.61–63; GautDhS 1.16. A variant opinion on the proper skin for a Kshatriya initiate recommends that of the tiger (KGS 41.13), and a commentary on a different text (Rāghavānanda on Manu 2.41) equates the spotted deer and the tiger.

85. AitB 8.6. Cf. AV 4.8.4, where the consecrated Kshatriya is called a tiger; and ŚB 5.5.4.10, where the tiger is regarded as the foremost member of the class of wild animals.

86. MŚS 5.2.10.12. For connections between the goat, the Viśva Devas, and Pūṣan, the protector of animals and a lower-class deity, see TS 4.6.8.1 and cf. 5.5.12.1. In the ṚV, the goat is often identified with Pūṣan (1.138.4, 6.55.3,4, 6.58.2, 9.67.10, 10.26.7; cf. TB 1.3.4.5), and at ṚV 1.162.2–3 Pūṣan's vehicle is drawn by goat. Jan Gonda, writes that "we cannot exclude the possibility that the god's relations with the cultivation of land and prosperity have contributed much to his association with this animal which is a powerful representative of vigour and generative force, the *vāja* which is so often implored." *Pūṣan and Sarasvatī* (Amsterdam: North-Holland, 1985), p. 89.

87. PB 24.11.5; cf. ŚB 4.5.5.4: "And because of those two [cups] which are together he offers the *upāṃśu* first, therefore, of goats and sheep when they are together, the goats go first and the sheep behind them."

88. See also AV 8.7.25: "Of how many the goats and sheep, let so many plants, being brought, extend protection to you."

89. ŚB 4.5.5.6,9, 5.2.1.24. Cf. TS 6.5.10.1 for the ewe giving birth to "two or three." For other references to a single category containing goats and sheep, see PB 24.11.5 (goats and sheep "go together"); and KB 11.2 ("the *uṣṇih* meter is sheep and goats"). For the ewe's connection to the Vaishya-like fertility goddess Sarasvatī, see TS 5.5.22.1; ŚB 5.5.4.1, 12.7.2.7; and especially ŚB 13.2.2.4, where the female ewe is subservient to the male horse, just as the Vaishya is to be subservient to the Kshatriya: "An ewe, for Sarasvatī [he sacrifices at the Aśvamedha] beneath the [horse's] jaws; he thereby makes women obedient. Therefore women are predisposed to be obedient to the man." For an association between Sarasvatī and the ram, consult ŚB 12.7.1.3.

90. E.g., AV 7.62.5, 10.6.23, 11.2.21, 12.2.15. Cf. KB 11.2 where the *bṛhatī* meter is equated with cows and horse, and the *uṣṇih* with sheep and goats.

91. E.g., ŚB 2.2.4.13, 3.1.2.21, 4.3.4.25. Cf. the contention at ĀpŚS 8.22.3 that it is during the rainy season, the Vaishya time of year, when the cow gives most milk; and the ritual called the "Vaiśyastoma," described as KŚS 22.9.6–12, which is to be performed "by a Vaishya or one who desires cattle" and features the cow and dairy products throughout.

92. Brown, "The Sanctity of the Cow," p. 95.

93. It would seem that the Vaishya nature of the cow is in some cases less important than the multicolored markings. See, for example, TS 2.1.3.2–3, where the dappled animal is a bull, and thus connected with the Kshatriya deity Indra: "He who desires a village should offer [a bull] with dappled thighs to Indra with the Maruts. . . . In that it is a bull it is Indra's; in that it is dappled, it belongs to the Maruts, for prosperity. It has dappled thighs behind; he thus makes the *viś* dependent on him."

94. ŚB 5.5.1.10. For other associations between the Viśva Devas and dappled animals,

see ŚB 4.5.1.11; MS 4.8.6; ĀpŚS 13.23.12; KŚS 10.9.12, 15.9.19 (the Viśva Devas and Maruts are interchangeable here); MŚS 5.2.1.10–18 (a milk-giving spotted cow is given as *dakṣiṇā* in a sacrifice dedicated to Viśva Devas and Indra).

95. ŚB 5.5.2.9. For other connections between dappled animals and the Maruts, consult also MS 2.1.7; TS 1.8.9.1, 2.1.3.2, 2.2.11.4, 2.5.6.12; TB 1.7.3.4,8. In the ṚV, the deified dappled cow, Pṛṣni, is declared to be the mother of the Maruts (ṚV 5.52.16, 8.83.1, 1.85.3, 8.20.8) and, according to A. A. Macdonell, "The coursers which draw their [the Maruts'] cars . . . are spotted, as appears from the epithet *pṛṣadaśva*, 'having spotted steed,' which is several times and exclusively connected with the Maruts." *The Vedic Mythology* (reprint Delhi: Motilal Banarsidass, 1974), p. 79,

96. ŚB 5.1.3.3. Cf. ŚB 1.8.3.15, where the earth is also identified with the spotted cow because of "rooted and rootless" food. See also ŚB 8.7.3.21, where speckled cows are equated with food and juxtaposed to the Vaishya class.

97. For connections between the ass and twins, TS 7.1.1.2–3; for the ass and the Aśvins, the divine twins, see ṚV 1.116.2, 10.85.8–9,15–16; and esp. AitB 4.9: "With an ass chariot the Aśvins won [the race], the Aśvins attained [victory]. In that the Asvins won [the race], in that the Aśvins attained [victory by means of the ass], therefore his swiftness departed, milked out—he is the least swift of all beasts of burden here. They did not take away the virility of his seed; therefore this potent one possesses a double seed."

98. For the ass's double (male) seed and the mare's double (female) seed, see TS 5.1.5.5, 7.1.1.2–3; JB 1.67; PB 6.1.4–5, 24.11.5; AV 5.31.3, 8.6.10, 10.1.4; BĀU 1.4.8; AitB 3.34, 4.9; ŚB 4.5.1.9, 6.2.1.23, 12.7.1.5.

99. BhŚS 9.17.1–5; ĀpŚS 9.15.1–5; HŚS 15.4.22–25; VaikhŚS 20.32. Cf. KŚS 1.1.13–17; PGS 3.12; BDhS 2.1.30–35; ĀpDhS 1.26.8–9; GautDhS 23.17.

100. For the ass as bearer of others, consult also ŚB 6.4.4.3 where mantras are recited over the animal in order to make it broad, easy to sit on, and the "bearer of Agni's excrement (*agneh purīṣavāhana*)".

101. PGS 3.15.6. For the ass, together with dogs, crows, and, significantly Shūdras and untouchables, as polluting of the sacrifice, see BŚS 27.8 and 28.10.

102. ŚB 6.4.4.7. For an etymological myth of origins which claims that the ass (*rāsabha*) was created from that which cried (*rās*), see ŚB 6.1.1.11, 6.3.1.28.

9

Classifying Revelation

The Authority of the Veda and the Authority of Varṇa

The particular social ideology of the Brahmin authors of the Veda was, as we saw in past chapters, legitimated and propounded in several different but interrelated ways. The appeal to the "prestige of origins" was one modality of argumentation: the social classes were supposedly brought into being at the beginning of time by the creator god and therefore are part of the original nature of the cosmos. A second method for legitimating the Vedic vision of the ideal society was to appeal to the authority of the divine and the metaphysical order of things. If the realm of the gods was organized in accordance with the *varṇa* system, and if the very structure of space and time could be show to be patterned in this way, then why should the social world be any different? Third, we have witnessed how the Vedic social ideology could be made to appear as just another part of "nature," with all the authority such an implication entails.

In this chapter we explore yet another source of legitimating power and authoritative persuasiveness for the ancient Indian social system. By the very fact that the framework for the caste system is laid out in the Veda, it can claim a certain canonical status. The social scheme, in other words, derives at least part of its compelling nature and historical endurance from the fact that it appears in the Veda itself. The canonical status of the Veda and its teachings, including teachings on the ideal social order, was claimed even at the time of authorship. Unlike some other comparable "canons" or "holy books" in the world's religions, the Veda represented itself—and was not only represented later—as absolutely authoritative, as the summation of all truth, as the unquestionable wisdom of the ages.[1]

The Veda is thus self-consciously canonical, and what is declared in the Veda is meant to have a force it would not have outside of such "sacred speech." Moreover, in the Veda both the Veda itself and the *varṇa* scheme are traced back to the dawn of time. Canon and a particular form of social classification are part of creation itself according to Vedic cosmogonies, and thus in addition to their canonical status both Veda and *varṇa* are portrayed as aboriginal.

The Veda and the Vedic social classes are not only canonical and primordial; they are also represented—again in the Veda itself—as structurally reduplicative of the generalized tripartite cosmic pattern we have seen operative in so many realms. Because both Veda and *varṇa* are predominantly regarded as divisible into three components, canon and class are made to appear isomorphic and significance can be attached to this resemblance.

Constituting a canon (a finite set of "texts" which are regarded as foundational and absolutely authoritative),[2] constructing a mechanism for its transmission, and establishing the means for its infinite interpretability (so that the canon will perpetually be "relevant")[3] generate the conditions of possibility for what we call a religious tradition.[4] The Veda is the canon of Hinduism.[5] Like other such works, the Veda was deemed canonical retroactively by those later religious traditions which created themselves through this very act of canon formation. But the Veda, as I have indicated, also represented itself (and was not only represented later) as the summation of all truth, the unassailable wisdom of the ages. The canonical status of the Veda was first established, self-referentially and tautologically, in Vedic texts; the absolute truth and authority of the Hindu canon was posited from its Vedic inception and reasserted in its later reception.

The three Vedas, or "triple wisdom,"[6] are declared equal to *satya*, or "truth" (ŚB 9.5.1.18), or to *vāc*, "speech" or "the word," also in the sense of "truth." *Vāc* is the "mother of the Vedas" (TB 2.8.8.5) and is divided into three forms which are no other than the three Vedas.[7] Alternatively, the Vedas are equated with the *brahman*, the universal principle which is the ground and end of all knowledge.[8] The Vedas, it is said in the Veda, are "endless" like great mountains while human knowledge of them is likened to mere handfuls of dirt (TB 3.10.11.3–5).

The Veda frequently wrote itself into its own accounts of the creation of the world; the canon is not only absolutely authoritative but is also primeval. In some texts, it is even claimed that the universe in its totality was originally encapsulated in the three Vedas and was generated out of them.[9] The structure of the cosmos as a whole is thus patterned on the structure of the Veda.[10] Conversely, the very tripartite form of the Veda is proof of the eternal verity of its contents since it produces and reproduces the form of the world.

The canonical Veda is also the sanctifying source of the ancient Indian social system; the superiority of the Brahmin class was ensured by the Brahmin authors of the canonical Veda. The social system presented in the Veda is structurally reduplicative of the tripartite form of the canon, which is in turn itself a mirror image of the structure of the cosmos.[11] Society becomes merely one expression of a universe created in the image of the Veda. Caste and Brahmin privilege thus derive at least part of their subsequent endurance and persuasiveness in India from the fact that they have canonical authorization; unlike many other Hindu beliefs and practices that claim Vedic legitimacy, caste and the superiority of the Brahmins actually are ordained in the Veda.

The prestige of the Brahmin class within the social hierarchy was underwritten by the Brahmin authors of the canonical Veda. The *varṇa* scheme, like the Vedas themselves, is traced back in the Vedic texts to the dawn of time: canon and social classification are both part of creation itself according to Vedic cosmogonies. Canon and class are not only primordial; both are also represented in the Veda as structurally reduplicative of a generalized cosmic pattern and are therefore both supposedly part of the "natural order of things." Finally, because both Veda and *varṇa* are predominantly regarded as divisible into three components, canon and class are isomorphic. Thus, in addition to the legitimation the social structure receives by being part of the *content* of the Veda, the *formal authority* of the structure of the canon (which is also the structure of the universe as a whole) is lent to a vision of society also comprised of three principal parts. Because of the *bandhus* or connections that govern Vedic philosophy, the two tripartite structures of Vedas and *varṇas* are regarded as transformations of one another, reduplicative manifestations of the fundamental triadic form.

Although direct equations between the Vedas and *varṇas* were usually not drawn,[12] the absence of explicit connections equating the three Vedas and the three social classes does not mean that such homologies were not implied or even presupposed. It is even possible that direct connections between the Vedas and *varṇas* were not articulated for a reason. As Bruce Lincoln pointed out in another context, "social stratification can well be—and often is—expressed by implication alone. . . . In ways, that which is unsaid can be far more powerful than that which is openly asserted, for by being left mute it is placed beyond question or debate."[13]

The Vedas and the *varṇas* share mutual linkages to components of other realms—metaphysical, spatial, temporal, ontological, theological, ritual, anatomical, zoological—which are their analogues. Canonical and sociological classes can thus be interrelated by tracking the connections they have in common, and one can assume that these homologies were so well known to the Brahmin theologians that they, just as we, could easily extrapolate from them to conjoin scripture and society.

In this chapter I delineate two ways in which Vedas and social classes are implicitly represented in Vedic texts as homological transformations of one another.

First, the three Vedas are often metonymically represented by their essential kernels, the three *vyāhṛtis* or utterances: "The *vyāhṛtis* are [the utterances] *bhūḥ*, *bhuvaḥ*, and *svaḥ*," one text explains, "and they are the three Vedas. *Bhūḥ* is the Ṛg Veda, *bhuvaḥ* is the Yajur Veda, and *svaḥ* the Sāma Veda" (AitĀ 1.3.2; cf. TU 1.5.3). Furthermore, the three *vyāhṛtis* are also names for the three worlds of Vedic cosmology, earth (*bhūḥ*), atmosphere (*bhuvaḥ*), and sky (*svaḥ*), and, as we already know, the worlds are regularly associated with the three social classes: earth = Brahmins, atmosphere = Kshatriyas, and sky = Vaishyas. If the Vedas = the three worlds, and the social classes = the three worlds, then the Vedas = the social classes.

The second mode of indirectly equating Vedas and society centers around the various meters (*chandas*es) in which the Veda was composed. Particular meters are, *inter alia*, explicitly connected to particular social classes, the "elemental powers" that are the essences of each *varṇa* (i.e., the *brahman*, *kṣatra*, and *viś*), and certain distinctive metaphysical qualities (e.g., *tejas*, "brilliance" or "fiery luster" for the Brahmin meter, "physical power" or *indriya* for the meter of the Kshatriya class, and a certain animal nature characteristic of Vaishyas). Furthermore, the meters are connected to components of various realms that are also direct analogues of the Vedas, for example, the three worlds. We are therefore again led to logical, although unstated, equations of the social classes and the Vedas: if the meters = the *varṇa*s = the worlds = the Vedas, then the *varṇa*s = the Vedas.[14]

The Creation of the Vedas and the Universe

Recall the following passage, one that has many repetitions and variants in Vedic texts, which was earlier labeled Cosmogony III:

> In the beginning, Prajāpati was the only one here. He desired, "May I be, may I reproduce." He toiled. He heated up ascetic heat. From him, from that one who had toiled and heated up, the three worlds—earth, atmosphere, and sky—were emitted. He heated up these three worlds. From those heated [worlds], three lights (*jyotis*) were born: Agni the fire, he who purifies here [Vāyu the wind], and the sun. He heated up these three lights. From those heated [lights], three Vedas were born: from Agni, the Ṛg Veda; from Vāyu, the Yajur Veda; and from Sūrya, the Sāma Veda. He heated up those three Vedas. From those heated [Vedas], three essences (sukras) were born: *bhūḥ* from the Ṛg Veda, *bhuvaḥ* from the Yajur Veda, and *svaḥ* from the Sāma Veda. With the Ṛg Veda, they performed [the ritual action which] concerns the *hotṛ* priest; with the Yajur Veda, that which concerns the *adhvaryu* priest; and with the Sāma Veda, that which concerns the *udgātṛ* priest.[15]

Five different orders of things and beings, each order divided into three parts, are here (and elsewhere) depicted as coeval: the three cosmological worlds of earth, atmosphere, and sky (the spatial order); three natural elements or "lights" (fire, wind, and sun) which are identical to three deities (Agni, Vāyu, and Sūrya/Aditya);[16] the three Vedas; the three verbal essences of the Vedas (*bhūḥ*, *bhuvaḥ*, and *svaḥ*); and the three principal priests of the Vedic sacrifice. The Vedas and their verbal essences are thus situated within a primordial nexus of connections to other cosmological, natural, superhuman, and ritual realms.[17] The three chains of associations which co-order the cosmological worlds, natural elements/gods, scriptures, and sacred utterances are, in sum:

1. earth = fire/Agni = Ṛg Veda = *bhūḥ* = *hotṛ* priest
2. atmosphere = wind/Vāyu = Yajur Veda = *bhuvaḥ* = *adhvaryu* priest
3. sky = sun/Sūrya = Sāma Veda = *svaḥ* = *udgātṛ* priest

As noted in Chapter 3, a set of texts that form a close variant of Cosmogony III goes on to add the three principal sacrificial fires to the three associative chains:

> The gods said to Prajāpati, "If there should be a calamity in our sacrifice due to the Ṛg Veda, or due to the Yajur Veda, or due to the Sāma Veda, or due to unknown causes, or a total miscarriage, what is the reparation?" Prajāpati said to the gods, "If there is a calamity in your sacrifice due to the Ṛg Veda, offer in the *gārhapatya* fire saying '*bhūḥ*'; if due to the Yajur Veda, in the *āgnīdhrīya* fire [in soma sacrifices] or, in the case of *havis* sacrifices, in the *anvāhāryapacana* fire saying '*bhuvaḥ*'; if due to the Sāma Veda, in the *āhavanīya* fire saying '*svaḥ*'; [and] if due to unknown causes or a total miscarriage, offer only in the *āhavanīya* fire saying all consecutively—'*bhūḥ*,' '*bhuvaḥ*,' '*svaḥ*.'" (AitB 5.32; cf. 5.34; KB 6.12; ChU 4.17.1–8)

By combining the components of these two texts with those established above, the scheme now looks like this:

1. earth = Agni/fire = Ṛg Veda = *bhūḥ* = the *hotṛ* priest = *gārhapatya* fire
2. atmosphere = Vāyu/wind = Yajur Veda = *bhuvaḥ* = the *adhvaryu* priest = *āgnīdhrīya* or *anvāhāryapacana* fire
3. sky = Sūrya/sun = Sāma Veda = *svaḥ* = the *udgātṛ* priest = *āhavanīya* fire

Still other triads from other arenas fill out these three sets of homologies even further. Let us reconsider the text we labeled Cosmogony IV, where three metaphysical qualities—"light," "might," and "fame" –are depicted as the primary generative categories. Components from the cosmological, theological, scriptural, and bodily realms[18] are then asserted as analogues:

> This world is light (*bharga*), the atmospheric world is might (*mahas*), the sky is fame (*yaśas*), and what other worlds there are, that is everything (*sarva*). Agni is light, Vāyu is might, Āditya is fame, and what other gods there are, that is everything. The Ṛg Veda is light, the Yajur Veda is might, the Sāma Veda is fame, and what other Vedas there are, that is everything. Speech is light, breath is might, sight is fame, and what other breaths there are, that is everything. One should know this: "I have put into myself all the worlds, and into all the worlds I have put my self. I have put into myself all the gods etc., all the Vedas etc., all the breaths etc." Eternal are the worlds, the gods, the Vedas, the breaths, and eternal is the all. He who knows this crosses over from the eternal to the eternal; he conquers repeated death; he attains fullness of life.

In this text, light, might, and fame generate the three worlds (earth, atmosphere, and sky), the three naturalistic deities (Agni the fire, Vāyu the wind, and Āditya the sun), the three Vedas (Ṛg, Yajur, and Sāma), and three physical functions (speech, breath, and sight).[19] The passage may be compared to the following text from AitĀ 3.2.5 (cf. ŚānĀ 8.8), where the categorical system proceeds from an analysis of speech (that is, recited Sanskrit) into consonants, sibilants, and vowels:

> And now for this secret teaching (*upaniṣad*) concerning all speech. . . . The consonants are the earth, the sibilants the atmosphere, and the vowels the sky. The consonants are Agni [or fire], the sibilants Vāyu [or air], the vowels Āditya [or the sun]. The consonants are the Ṛg Veda, the sibilants the Yajur Veda, the vowels the Sāma Veda. The consonants are the eye, the sibilants the ear, the vowels the mind. The consonants are the inhalation, the sibilants the exhalation, the vowels the circulatory breath.

The constituent parts of the Sanskrit language in which the Veda was composed are here equated to that tripartite Veda, among other cosmic components. Note here the addition of three breaths to the triads which include, as in other passages already encountered, the three worlds, the three gods/natural forces, and the three Vedas. Corresponding to the Ṛg, Yajur, and Sāma Vedas, however, are in this instance different bodily organs: the eye, the ear, and the mind, respectively, as opposed to speech, breath, and sight as one of the texts cited previously argues.

The tripartite Veda is thus depicted in many Vedic texts as created in the beginning as part of the cosmos in which we live. The three worlds, three natural elements, three deities (or types of deities), the ritual components of three fires and three principal priests, three qualities (light, might, and fame), three bodily parts or functions, three aspects or speech, three kinds of breaths—all are homologized to the three Vedas and their verbal essences. We arrive at a composite tripartite structure, here reconfigured in order to present the three Vedas first:

1. Ṛg Veda = earth = fire/Agni = *bhūḥ* = *gārhapatya* fire = *hotṛ* priest = light = speech or eye = consonants = inhalation
2. Yajur Veda = atmosphere = wind/Vāyu = *bhuvaḥ* = *āgnīdhrīya* or *dakṣiṇa* fire = *adhvaryu* priest = might = breath or ear = sibilants = exhalation
3. Sāma Veda = sky = sun/Sūrya/Āditya = *svaḥ* = *āhavanīya* fire = *udgātṛ* priest = fame = sight or mind = vowels = circulatory breath

It will be noted that nowhere in the texts cited thus far are there specific social attributions given to the Vedas or their analogues; the social classes, in other words, are not mentioned in any of these cosmogonies. From other associations found elsewhere in the Veda, many of which we have surveyed in previous chapters, we may now assume what the authors of these texts undoubtedly did. Though unstated in the texts above, each chain of resemblances includes a social component too.

Light, might, and fame, for example, may be regarded as ideal qualities of the three social classes (Brahmin priest, Kshatriya warrior, and Vaishya commoner respectively) or as transformations of the three elemental metaphysical powers which are the essences of the three Āryan social classes: *brahman*, *kṣatra*, and *viś*. The three worlds, we know, are also regularly associated with the three groups comprising society—the earth belongs to the Brahmin *varṇa*, the atmosphere to the Kshatriyas, and the sky to the Vaishyas. The deities included in the three chains are also *varṇa*-encoded: Agni and the Vasus are Brahmin deities; Vāyu, Indra, and the Rudras are Kshatriya divinities; and Āditya, Sūrya, Varuṇa, and the Ādityas are Vaishya gods.

Evidence of a similar kind comes from the ChU (3.1–5). That text associates the Ṛg Veda with the east, the south is linked to the Yajur Veda, and the west is connected to the Sāma Veda.[20] As we saw in Chapter 5, the cardinal directions are regularly given *varṇa* attributions with the east being the Brahmin direction, the south the Kshatriya quarter, and the west (or north) belonging to the Vaishyas. The directions thus also serve as mediators linking Vedas and social classes: Ṛg Veda = east = Brahmins; Yajur Veda = south = Kshatriyas; and Sāma Veda = west (or north) = Vaishyas.

The Ṛg Veda, we may surmise, is the Brahmin Veda, for typically Brahmin components such as the earth, Agni, speech, and the east are regularly associated with it. We can infer on the same grounds that the Yajur Veda is that of the Kshatriyas, and the Sāma Veda belongs with the Vaishyas. These assumptions regarding the social correlates for each of the three Vedas are corroborated when we isolate one triadic set of the structure, the three *vyāhṛtis* or syllabic essences of the Vedas which are also, as we have observed, the three worlds of Vedic cosmology.

In Cosmogony II, these metonymical representatives of the Vedas are directly correlated with the three *varṇas* (portrayed in the form of neuter elemental powers) and also with cosmological and ontological triads:

> Prajāpati generated this [world by saying], "*bhūḥ*," the atmosphere [by saying] "*bhuvaḥ*," and the sky [by saying] "*svaḥ*." As much as these worlds are, so much is this all . . . Prajāpati generated the *brahman* [by saying] "*bhūḥ*," the *kṣatra* [by saying] "*bhuvaḥ*," and the *viś* [by saying] "*svaḥ*." As much as the *brahman*, *kṣatra*, and *viś* are, so much is this all . . . Prajāpati generated the Self (*ātman*) [by saying] "*bhūḥ*," the human race [by saying] "*bhuvaḥ*," and the animals [by saying] "*svaḥ*." As much as these Self, human race, and animals are, so much is this all.

This text confirms what we assumed earlier—that connections can be drawn between the Vedas (since the three *vyāhṛtis* are equated with the three Vedas) and the three *varṇas* (which are here also correlated to the *vyāhṛtis*). Because the *vyāhṛtis* are also the names for the worlds which, as we have seen, are said to have *varṇa* attributes, the text formulates the equation between the Vedas and the *varṇas* through the mediation of the three worlds: Vedas = worlds = social classes. Here too we have the establishment of a hierarchical ranking for each of the three strings of associations. And so, too, we may conclude, are the three Vedas similarly hierarchically ranked in the eyes of the Vedic classifiers. Ṛg, Yajur, and Sāma correspond to the Brahmin (and the Self), Kshatriya (and humans), and Vaishya (and animals), and in that order.[21]

The Meters, the Vedas, and the Social Classes

The Veda is also analyzable into the meters (*chandases*) in which the Vedic verses (*ṛks*), formulas (*yajurs*), and chants (*sāmans*) are composed. The meters are even given the same primordial standing as the three Vedas themselves: "From that sacrifice in which everything was offered," one reads in the famous creation hymn, "the verses [i.e., the Ṛg Veda] and chants [the Sāma Veda] were born, the meters were born from it, and from it the formulas [the Yajur Veda] were born."[22] Or again, by means of speech the creator "emitted all this, whatever there is: verses, chants, meters, sacrifices, humans, and animals" (ŚB 10.6.5.5).

Just as the worlds act as the mediating components for connections between the Vedas and the social classes, so do they form the basis for another set of homologies, this time conjoining also Vedic meters and social classes: "When the meters divided these worlds, the *gāyatrī* obtain this world, the *triṣṭubh* the atmosphere, and the *jagatī* the sky. The *gāyatrī* is the Brahmin class, the *triṣṭubh* the Kshatriya class, and the *jagatī* is the Vaishya class."[23] Such linkages—mediated or unmediated—between certain meters and the social classes are regularly forged in Vedic texts, most notably in those places where the ritual mantras are modified according to the class of the sacrificer.[24] Each of the meters is supposed to embody a power or quality that is particularly characteristic of the inborn and ritually actualized traits of one or another of the three *varṇas*. In one rite (described at AitB 1.28) which entails taking the sacrificial fire forward from one fireplace to another, a *gāyatrī* verse (a triplet consisting of eight syllables in each verse) is recited if the sacrificer is a Brahmin, for "the Brahmin is connected with the *gāyatrī*. The *gāyatrī* is fiery luster (*tejas*) and the splendor of the *brahman* (*brahmavarcasa*), and with those he makes him prosper." If the sacrificer is a Kshatriya, a different verse in the *triṣṭubh* meter (a quartet of verses each containing eleven syllables) is used, for "the Kshatriya is connected with the *triṣṭubh*. The *triṣṭubh* is force (*ojas*), power (*indriya*), and virility (*vīrya*); truly thus with force, power, and virility he makes him prosper." Alternatively, in the case of a Vaishya sacrificer the verse is composed in the *jagatī* meter (a quartet with each verse comprised of twelve syllables), for "the Vaishya is connected with the *jagatī* and animals are connected with the *jagatī*. Truly thus with animals he makes him prosper."

In the initiation or *upanayana* described in the Gṛhya Sūtras,[25] the *sāvitrī* verse (ṚV 3.62.10: "We contemplate the excellent glory of the divine Savitṛ; may he inspire our intellect!") was imparted to the boy to inaugurate his period of Veda study. The verse is to be composed in different meters for members of the different classes. Brahmins were to learn the verse in the *gāyatrī* meter, Kshatriyas in the *triṣṭubh*, and Vaishyas in the *jagatī*.[26] The adjustment was not only in order to match the boy's *varṇa* to the meter that bore the proper power. The syllabic composition of the meters (eight syllables for each line in the *gāyatrī* meter, eleven in the *triṣṭubh*, and twelve in the *jagatī*) was also reduplicative of the respective ages for initiation of boys from different classes (eight for the Brahmin, eleven for the Kshatriya, and twelve for the Vaishya).[27]

There are many other examples of the ritual uses of the meters "according to *varṇa*" (*yathāvarṇa*). Upon setting up the sacrificial fires the mantras recited are sometimes so tailored: "With [a mantra in] the *gāyatrī* meter when it is a Brahmin, with the *triṣṭubh* meter when it is a Kshatriya, with the *jagatī* meter when it is a Vaishya."[28] In all instances, the meters were thought to embody and instill certain properties that were characteristic of the ontology of members of the different social classes. *Varṇa*-encoded properties were ritually injected into the appropriate person through the metrical medium.

"The *gāyatrī* is the Brahmin class,"[29] and the Brahmin meter was supposed to hold within it typically Brahmin traits. The text cited earlier which connects this meter to the powers of fiery luster (*tejas*) and the splendor of the *brahman* (*brahmavarcasa*) is by no means alone in making such a claim.[30] Other texts regard the *gāyatrī* as the representative of speech or the mouth;[31] of light (*bharga* or *jyoti*);[32] of the sacrifice (ŚB 4.2.4.20); of perfection (ŚānĀ 2.15); or as the bearer of the elemental metaphysical power invigorating the Brahmin class, the *brahman*.[33]

The *gāyatrī*, like other Brahmin entities, is regarded as the primary and foremost member of its realm: no other meter surpasses it (JB 1.290). When the priest puts a kindling stick on the fire with a *gāyatrī* verse, "He thereby kindles the *gāyatrī*; the *gāyatrī*, when kindled, kindles the other meters; and the meters, when kindled, carry the sacrifice to the gods" (ŚB 1.3.4.6). At PB 8.4.2–4, the *triṣṭubh* and *jagatī* are said to have been created from the primordial *gāyatrī*. The Brahmin meter, like other Brahmin components of the universe, is prior to and generative of others. When verses in the Brahmin meter are recited before those in the *triṣṭubh*, "truly he makes the *kṣatra* dependent on the *brahman*. Therefore the Brahmin is foremost. He becomes foremost who knows thus" (TS 2.6.2.5).

The Kshatriya meter, the *triṣṭubh*, is the meter of force (*ojas*), power (*indriya*), and virility (*vīrya*), as we observed previously. Verses in this meter are to be used by one who desires strength, for "the *triṣṭubh* is force, power, and virility."[34] Or, again, "the Kshatriya is connected with the *triṣṭubh*" for both are characterized by this triumvirate of qualities.[35] The *triṣṭubh* "is the Kshatriya class and the Kshatriya class is glory (*yaśas*). He who thus considers this *triṣṭubh* to be glory becomes the best in whatever country he may be, and even kings approach him as inferiors" (JB 1.272). Elsewhere similar Kshatriya attributes such as physical strength (*bala*) as well as the elemental *kṣatra* power itself are said to be inherent in that meter.[36] The eleven-syllabled verses of the *triṣṭubh* are also homologized to Indra's great weapon, the thunderbolt or *vajra*, and thus replicate the coercive force of that cosmic armament within the ritual.[37]

The *jagatī* is frequently associated with the Vaishyas[38] and with animals that are, in turn, connected to the commoner class.[39] An etymological basis for the correlation is also sometimes encountered: "He offers [oblations] with *jagatī* verses, for animals are mobile (*jagata*). By means of the *jagatī* he thus obtains animals for him."[40] And in at least one text (ŚB 8.3.3.4), the Vaishya meter is connected to both animals and food. Elsewhere, this meter is identified with "procreation" (*prajanana*), as well as with animals and offspring (JB 1.93); or with "abundance" and procreation: "He who thus considers this *jagatī* to be abundance and procreation, he becomes rich in offspring and cattle and to whatever community of kinsmen he belongs, there he becomes the chief" (JB 1.272). The meter of the third *varṇa* is also said to be weaker than the other two, just as Vaishyas are supposedly weaker (although numerically larger) than the Brahmin and Kshatriya elites: "The *gāyatrī* and the *triṣṭubh* are the strongest among the meters. In that these are on either side and the *jagatī* is in the middle [in this chant], thereby, he encompasses the animals with the strongest of the meters" (PB 20.16.8). Furthermore, it is by means of this meter that a king can "enter" the people or *viś* (PB 19.17.6).

Varṇa encodings for the three meters are reconfirmed when one turns to other realms. Witness the tripartite classification scheme of the reconstructed Cosmogony I, where chains of associations explicitly link the three meters with the social classes and their elemental metaphysical qualities, with three theological and ontological classes, and also with the three parts of the day which are in this text generative of all other associations:

1. morning = Brahmins = Agni = *gāyatrī* meter = the *brahman* = the Self
2. midday = Kshatriyas = Indra = *triṣṭubh* meter = the *kṣatra* = humans
3. afternoon = Vaishyas = Viśva Devas = *jagatī* meter = the *viś* = animals

We shall return to the theological correlates for each of the three meters. First, however, let us note that the linkage made here in Cosmogony I of the Brahmin morning, the Kshatriya midday, and the Vaishya evening with the *gāyatrī*, *triṣṭubh*, and *jagatī* respectively is extremely common, as we also observed in Chapter 6.[41] By means of certain manipulations, "The morning pressing [of soma] becomes *gāyatrī*-like, the midday pressing *triṣṭubh*-like, and the third pressing *jagatī*-like. He who knows this obtains glory as if he were a Kshatriya and wealth and prosperity as if he were a Vaishya, even though he is a Brahmin" (JB 1.243). Or again, in a text that also supplies an interesting list of class-specific "luxuries" or accoutrements for the Kshatriyas and the Vaishyas, we read the following:

> The morning service is connected with the *gāyatrī*, the midday service with the *triṣṭubh*, and the third service with the *jagatī*. When during the morning service which is connected with the *gāyatrī* one sings a *gāyatrī* verse—the *gāyatrī* is the Brahmin class, and the morning service is the Brahmin class—one thereby places the Brahmin class in its own proper place. When one sings a *triṣṭubh* verse—the *triṣṭubh* is the Kshatriya class and these are luxuries used in the Kshatriya class, namely, elephants and golden ornaments for the neck, a chariot with a she-mule, a chariot with a horse, a golden ornament for the breast and a golden cup—one thereby offers these to the Brahmins and decorates them with them. When one sings a *jagatī* verse—the *jagatī* is the Vaishya class and these are the luxuries current among the Vaishyas, namely, cows and horses, elephants and gold, goats and sheep, rice and barley, sesame and beans, clarified butter, milk, wealth and comfort—one thereby offers these to the Brahmins and decorates them with them. (JB 1.263)

These three meters, which are sometimes said to be the very "forms" (*rūpas*) of the three day parts,[42] are here and elsewhere routinely assigned to the Brahmins, Kshatriyas, and Vaishyas (see also JB 1.265, 266). The connections to the three day parts are, therefore, yet another transformation of the *varṇa* of the meters. Furthermore, one text goes on to draw complex homologies between all of the above (meters, day parts, and social classes) and another set of *varṇa*-encoded components, the three worlds (JB 1.284).

Creation stories for the three meters explain why each belongs to one or another of the social classes and the day parts correlative to each of those classes. One myth tells how the *gāyatrī* flew to heaven and procured the soma:

> What she [the *gāyatrī* in the form of a bird] grabbed with her right foot became the morning pressing [of the soma plant at the soma sacrifice]. The *gāyatrī* made that her own home, and therefore they regard it as the most perfect of all the pressings. He who knows this becomes foremost, the best; he attains preeminence. And what she grasped with her left foot became the midday pressing. That crumbled off and thus did not match the former pressing. The gods wanted to fix this, so in it they put the *triṣṭubh* from the meters and Indra from the deities. With that [in it] it became equal in strength to the first pressing. He who knows this becomes successful with both pressings of equal strength and equal in relationship. That which she grabbed with her mouth became the third pressing. While flying she sucked out its sap. With its sap sucked out it did not equal the two previous pressings. The gods wanted to fix this. They saw it in domestic animals. When they pour in an admixture [of milk], and proceed with the [offering of] butter and the animal [offering], with that it became of equal strength with the previous two pressings. He who knows this becomes successful with pressings of equal strength and equal in relationship. (AitB 3.27)

Hierarchy and inequality—with the Brahmin *gāyatrī* and the morning pressing presented as "perfect," and the other two pressings as defective in various ways—are transformed into pressings of "equal strength" and "similar quality" through *varṇa* supplementation: the *triṣṭubh* meter and the warrior god Indra beef up the midday, while different symbols for animals bring the third pressing up to par. The Brahmin components of morning and the *gāyatrī* meter are thus depicted as self-contained, primary, and preeminent, the "womb" of the others.[43]

A variant also assumes original inequality but tells the story somewhat differently.

> [Originally] the *gāyatrī* was composed of eight syllables, the *triṣṭubh* of three, the *jagatī* of one. The eight-syllabled *gāyatrī* carried the morning pressing upward. The three-syllabled *triṣṭubh* was unable to carry the midday pressing upward. The *gāyatrī* said to her, "I will come [to the midday pressing]. Let there be something here for me too." "Okay," replied the *triṣṭubh*. "Add these eight syllables to me." "Alright," [the *gāyatrī* said]. She added herself to her. Thus at the midday [pressing] the last two [verses] of the introductory verse dedicated to Indra Marutvat and the response belong to the *gāyatrī*. She [the *triṣṭubh*] became eleven-syllabled and carried up the midday pressing. The *jagatī* had one syllable and was unable to carry the third pressing upward. The *gāyatrī* said to her, "I will come [to the evening pressing]. Let there be something here for me too." "Okay," replied the *jagatī*. "Add these eleven syllables to me." "Alright," [the *gāyatrī* said]. She added herself to her. Thus at the third [pressing] the last two [verses] of the introductory verse dedicated to the Viśva Devas and the response belong to the *gāyatrī*. She (the *jagatī*) became twelve-syllabled and carried up the third pressing. This is how the *gāyatrī* became eight-syllabled, the *triṣṭubh* eleven-syllabled, and the *jagatī* twelve-syllabled. He who knows

> this becomes successful with pressings of equal strength and equal in relationship. (AitB 3.28)

The Brahmin *gāyatrī* meter of eight syllables is once again represented as perfect and self-sufficient, capable of "supporting" on its own the morning pressing to which it is assigned. The Kshatriya and Vaishya representatives are, as in the other version, originally smaller and thus unable to carry out their functions. But in this account they are not supplemented by other props; rather, they are infused with the *gāyatrī*'s eight syllables in order to attain their proper syllabic strength, and thus all the meters are made "of equal strength and of equal quality." The myth, in sum, belies its own overt message of equality among the meters, the day parts, and (implicitly) the *varṇa*s by arguing that such equality was achieved by the incorporation of the *gāyatrī* (i.e., Brahmin) component into those representing the Kshatriyas and Vaishyas.

Yet another version of the story (ŚB 4.3.2.7–11; cf. JB 1.287–88) starts with the opposite premise: the meters were originally equal. The conclusion, however, is identical to those reached in variants that begin differently. Equal at first, the *varṇa*-encoded meters are soon rendered unequal, only to be made again equal—but as slightly transformed versions of the all-encompassing Brahmin meter. Here, as elsewhere, the *gāyatrī* is, mythically, the meter not only of the morning soma pressing but of them all, for "all the soma pressings are connected to the *gāyatrī*."

The meters, no less than the social classes they signify, are clearly structured in a hierarchical fashion. The Brahmin meter, like the Brahmin class, is the "first" of the meters—hierarchically and chronologically—and also the meter of the fewest syllables, just as the elite Brahmin social class is numerically small: "The *gāyatrī*, while being the smallest meter, is the meter yoked first on account of its strength (*vīrya*)" (ŚB 1.8.2.10). The "larger" Kshatriya and Vaishya meters, on the other hand, are displayed as subsequent to and the inferior offspring of the *gāyatrī*. Less, indeed, is more.

The *gāyatrī*, like the social class it represents, is also said to encompass all the other meters. This notion is ritually put into play according to ŚB 4.1.1.7–12, where the well-known code of morning = *gāyatrī*, midday = *triṣṭubh*, and evening = *jagatī* is tapped in order to efficiently and efficaciously collapse the soma sacrifice into a single rite. All three of the day's ritual pressings of soma are symbolically condensed into the morning pressing through manipulating the number of pressings of the soma plant:[44]

> They complete the entire sacrifice at the morning pressing only. . . . He presses [the soma] eight times. The *gāyatrī* consists of eight syllables and the morning pressing is connected to the *gāyatrī*. Thus this [pressing of the soma eight times] is made to be the morning pressing. . . . He then presses [the soma at the morning pressing] eleven times. The *triṣṭubh* consists of eleven syllables and the midday pressing is connected to the *triṣṭubh*. Thus this [pressing of the soma eleven times at the morning pressing] is made to be the midday pressing. . . . He then presses [the soma] twelve times. The *jagatī* consists of twelve syllables and the

evening pressing is connected to the *jagatī*. Thus this [pressing of the soma twelve times] is made to be the evening pressing.

The linkage of the *gāyatrī*, *triṣṭubh*, and *jagatī* meters and three *varṇa*-encoded deities is well attested. Often the three gods thus connected to the meters are Agni, the divine priest;[45] Indra, the deified exemplar of the warrior;[46] and the Viśva Devas, the "masses" among the gods.[47] Alternatively, the three groups called the Vasus, Rudras, and Ādityas are those linked with the three meters.[48] This series of correlates between meters and divinities can include within it the Brahmin morning, the Kshatriya midday, and the Vaishya evening: "Prajāpati assigned to the gods the sacrifice and the meters in portions. He allotted the *gāyatrī* at the morning pressing to Agni and the Vasus, the *triṣṭubh* to Indra and the Rudras at the midday [pressing], the *jagatī* to the Viśva Devas and the Ādityas at the third pressing."[49]

Numerological explanations are put forward to explain the particular bonds between meters and deities. The connection between the three meters (containing verses with eight, eleven, and twelve syllables respectively) and the Vasus, Rudras, and Ādityas is explicated in one passage which declares that there are thirty-three gods who drink soma: "eight Vasus, eleven Rudras, twelve Ādityas, Prajāpati and the *vaṣat* call" (AitB 2.18). Or again:

> The *gāyatrī* has eight syllables. There are eight Vasus. The morning pressing is connected with the *gāyatrī* and belongs to the Vasus. To every syllable corresponds a deity. The *triṣṭubh* has eleven syllables. There are eleven Rudras. The midday pressing is connected with the *triṣṭubh* and belongs to the Rudras. To every syllable corresponds a deity. The *jagatī* has twelve syllables. There are twelve Ādityas. The third pressing is connected with the *jagatī* and belongs to the Ādityas. To every syllable corresponds a deity. (JB 1.141; cf. 1.281)

Furthermore, in some texts the deities that are elsewhere connected to the meters and the three parts of the day are conjoined with the meters and the three worlds:[50] meters (*gāyatrī*, *triṣṭubh*, and *jagatī*), gods (Agni and/or the Vasus;[51] Indra and/or the Rudras or Maruts; and one or more of the Vaishya deities), space (earth, atmosphere, and sky), and time (morning, noon, and evening) are thus brought together in triadic equations.

In the realm of anatomy, the *gāyatrī* is, unsurprisingly, assimilated to the head (and "the head means excellence," comments ŚB 4.2.4.20) or the mouth, the usual Brahmin body parts; the *triṣṭubh*, like the Kshatriya, was created from the chest or arms of the Cosmic Man;[52] and the Vaishya meter, the *jagatī*, is connected to the hips (e.g., ŚB 8.6.2.6–8; 10.3.2.1–6), belly, or penis.[53] Indeed, in several texts (Cosmogonies V, VI, VII) the meters and the social classes are produced from these distinctive body parts of the creator, as are deities (Agni, Indra, and the Viśva Devas), seasons (spring, summer, and rains), and animals (goat, horse, and cow). In yet other cosmogonies (e.g. Cosmogonies VIII and IX; cf. TS 5.5.8.2–3), the expected cardinal directions are added to the chains of connections (east, south, and west for the Brahmin and *gāyatrī*, Kshatriya and *triṣṭubh*, and Vaishya and *jagatī* respectively).

Such cosmogonies regularly associate certain Vedic chants (*sāmans*) and hymns of praise (*stomas* or *stotras*) with the three meters—and with the three social classes. Particular chants from the Sāma Veda and hymns of praise taken from all the Vedas, like particular meters, are thus regarded as the *varṇa*-encoded elements comprising the Veda as a whole. In cosmogonies already cited in this chapter and others from Chapter 3 we consistently observe that the Brahmin chain of associations is also where the classifiers place the ***rathantara*** chant and all nine-versed hymns of praise; the ***bṛhat*** chant and fifteen-versed hymns of praise belong with the Kshatriya; and the ***vairūpa*** chant together with the seventeen-versed hymns of praise are assigned to the Vaishyas.[54]

The connections posited between the hymns of praise, chants, and the *varṇas* in these cosmogonic texts are as standardized in a wide variety of other sources as those made between the *varṇas* and the meters. First, the nine-versed hymn of praise is regularly equated with the Brahmin class (JB 1.232); Brahmin powers such as *tejas* and the splendor of the ***brahman*** (PB 20.10.1, 25.6.3; JB 1.66; TS 6.3.3.6); the Brahmin deity Agni (JB 1.240; ŚB 6.3.1.25; TB 1.5.10.4; KB 28.5); or with three Brahmin components—Agni, speech, and the ***brahman*** power (ŚB 8.4.2.3). Like the social class it represents, the nine-versed hymn of praise surpasses all others (JB 1.290). Second, the fifteen-versed hymn of praise "is" the Kshatriya class (JB 1.232); it is connected with strength, might, and virility,[55] and with the thunderbolt or *vajra* (JB 1.195; PB 2.4.2; 16.2.5). This hymn of praise is connected to Indra (JB 1.110) and also directly to the *kṣatra* (ŚB 8.4.2.4). And third, the Vaishya seventeen-versed hymn of praise is equated with the *viś* (ŚB 8.4.2.5), Prajāpati and offspring (TS 6.3.3.6), food,[56] and with the three benefits of offspring, livestock, and procreation (JB 1.66).

The *rathantara* or Brahmin chant[57] is, in texts other than the cosmogonic ones just mentioned, identified with the ***brahman*** power (PB 11.4.6) or ***tejas*** (TB 2.6.19.1); with the cosmological world of the Brahmin class, the earth (JB 1.88, 1.327, 1.328; PB 6.8.18; ṢaḍB 2.1.35); with the Brahmin deity Agni (JB 1.332, 1.335); with one of the Brahmin animals (the cow, JB 1.333); and with the Brahmin attribute of speech or *vāc* (JB 1.128, 1.230, PB 7.6.3). The *bṛhat* chant is said to be the "end of the chants" just as "the Kshatriya is the end of men" (PB 19.12.8). It is connected to Indra (cf. AitB 4.31) and the *kṣatra* power (TS 4.4.12.1–2); to physical strength (*bala*) and "fame" (*yasas*) (TB 2.6.19.1); to the Kshatriya animal, the horse (JB 1.333); and to the Kshatriya entities of the south, the summer, the ***triṣṭubh***, the fifteen-versed hymn of praise, and the *kṣatra* (ŚB 5.4.1.4). The *bṛhat* is, in sum, the Kshatriya's chant and is intimately connected with his life (AitB 7.23); thus a Kshatriya's sacrifice is perfect (*samṛddha*) when it has a *bṛhat* chant in it (AitB 8.3). "The *bṛhat* is the ***kṣatra***. This [chant] is also the offspring of a member of the Kshatriyas. In the offspring of him who knows thus an excellent ruler, and excellent man, of good appearance and good looking, is born" (JB 1.187). By utilizing this chant in a ritual, even a sacrificer from the first class "attains everything which belongs to the Kshatriya class" and "obtains the glory of a Kshatriya although he is a Brahmin."[58]

The *rathantara* and the *bṛhat* chants are homologized not only to the Brahmin and the Kshatriya respectively, but also to speech and mind, the Ṛg and Sāma

Vedas (cf. JB 1.333), and this world and yonder world;[59] morning (= *bṛhat*) and afternoon (= *rathantara*) can also added to this list of pairs (JB 1.298). When employed together in the ritual, the two chants can serve either to establish hierarchical relations between the two highest social classes[60]—in one rite, the *rathantara* is to be chanted first, because "the *brahman* is prior to the *kṣatra*" (AitB 8.1; cf. PB 7.6.5)—or to help the two coalesce into a ruling class: taken together, the *rathantara* and *bṛhat* chants are said to be equal to "supremacy" (PB 19.13.5; 22.18.6) or "honor" (PB 19.8.3). By employing both of them at once within the ritual, "on the *brahman* is the *kṣatra* established, and on the *kṣatra* the *brahman*" (AitB 8.2).

As for the Vaishya chants, the *vairūpa* is associated, typically, with food and animals (PB 12.4.18; 14.9.8); with the power of the *viś* (but also the ordinarily Kshatriya power of *ojas*, TB 2.6.19.2); or with the prolific goat (JB 1.333). Another chant often associated either with the Vaishyas or with the lower classes in general, the *vāmadevya*, is also equated with animals in general (JB 1.133; 1.138) or with the lower class sheep (JB 1.333); with procreation or *prajanana* (ŚB 5.1.3.12); or with the deity most closely associated with procreation, Prajāpati (JB 1.229, 1.327; PB 4.8.15, 11.4.7; ŚB 13.3.3.4).

Many of the cosmogonies mentioned above actually lay out quadripartite or pentadic structures into which meters we have not discussed are associated with components of the fourth and fifth chains. Cosmogony V, which traces creation to the head, arms, and middle of the body of the creator god, goes on to state:

> From his feet, from his firm foundation, he emitted the twenty-one-versed hymn of praise; along with it he emitted the *anuṣṭubh* [four verses, each with eight syllables] among the meters, not a single one among the gods, the Shūdra among men. Therefore the Shūdra has abundant animals but is unable to sacrifice, for he has no deity which was emitted along with him. Therefore he does not rise above simply the washing of feet, for from the feet he was emitted. Therefore the twenty-one-versed among the hymns of praise is a firm foundation, for it was emitted from the firm foundation.

Cosmogonies VI and VII also lay out a fourth chain of entities created from the feet of the primordial god which includes on it the twenty-one-versed hymn of praise, the *anuṣṭubh* meter, the *yajñayajñiya* chant, and the Shūdra social class.

According to AitB 3.47,48, the *gāyatrī*, *triṣṭubh*, *jagatī*, and *anuṣṭubh* are called "all the meters," for "on [them] the others [depend], for these are performed most prominently at the sacrifice. By means of these meters the sacrificer who knows this sacrifices with all the meters."[61] The *anuṣṭubh* meter in the texts cited above thus completes the structure by adding a fourth to the previous three—in these cases, at the bottom. And other texts confirm the identification, for example, of the *anuṣṭubh* and the "lowest": it is connected to the "foundation" (JB 1.229; or the "feet" (ṢaḍB 2.3) or "this earth" (PB 8.7.2; ŚB 1.3.2.16), or, again as previously in Cosmologies VI and VII, to the Shūdras or servant class (JB 1.263, 1.265–66).

It is, however, in another sense of completion that elsewhere we read of that which is "subsequent to" the three soma pressings of the day as participating in the nature of the *anuṣṭubh* (ŚB 11.5.9.7); or that this meter is "above and beyond" (*atirikta*) the other three (ŚB 4.5.3.5); or that the *anuṣṭubh* is correlated with speech (while the other three meters are connected to breath, sight, and hearing), and "speech is the *brahman*";[62] or that this meter "is" heaven in comparison to the other three meters, which are equated to earth, atmosphere, and the quarters (JB 1.104).

We witness here, once again, the ambiguity the authors of Vedic texts displayed when it comes to the fourth element added to a triadic structure. Rather than the lowest meter, the *anuṣṭubh* is sometimes extolled as the highest, the "transcendent fourth" of the meters. One manifestation of this is the connection of the meter and deities that emblemize totality—the Viśva Devas ("All the Gods," e.g., JB 1.239.) or Prajāpati[63]—or the claim that the *anuṣṭubh* "is all meters" (e.g., JB 1.285). Another way in which the superiority of the meter is expressed is with the connections to royal signifiers. In texts dealing with the Aśvamedha or horse sacrifice, we read that "the *anuṣṭubh* is the highest meter, and the horse is the highest of animals."[64] "Highest" here and elsewhere seems to mean "kingly" or "royal"; the horse is both the *kṣatra* and "belongs to the *anuṣṭubh*."[65] With the *anuṣṭubh* meter, it is said, one attains "preeminence" (AitB 3.13).

Taking on yet another role, the *anuṣṭubh* sometimes acts as one of the ciphers for the combination of Brahmin spiritual authority and Kshatriya temporal power. In the pentadic Cosmogony VIII, the fourth chain encompasses the *anuṣṭubh* meter and the dual deity Mitra-Varuṇa, representing the Brahmin–Kshatriya ruling class. This text also specifies the northern direction for the *anuṣṭubh* meter (and for the twenty-one-versed hymn of praise and the *vairāja* chant), and like other pentadic cosmogonies, also adds the zenith to the string of associations that include within them the meters. The fifth category, in which is placed another meter (the *paṅkti*, five verses of eight syllables each), is something of an apotheosis of the first, Brahmin chain. The chain as a whole is marked by the quintessential Brahmin deity, Bṛhaspati, and as we learn elsewhere, the *paṅkti* is indeed sometimes connected to the *brahman* power (ŚānĀ 11.7) and the sacrifice (AitB 1.5).

Finally we turn to the six-part structure created in Cosmogony XIII,[66] where yet another meter (the *atichandas*) is brought into service as the homologue to entities of a sixth string of associations. The structure of the text is as follows:

1. first day = earth = *gāyatrī* meter = nine–versed hymn of praise = *rathantara* chant = east = spring = Vasus and Agni
2. second day = atmosphere = *triṣṭubh* meter = fifteen-versed hymn of praise = *bṛhat* chant = south = summer = Maruts and Indra
3. third day = sky = *jagatī* meter = seventeen-versed hymn of praise = *vairūpa* chant = west = rainy season = Ādityas and Varuṇa
4. fourth day = food = *anuṣṭubh* meter = twenty-one-versed hymn of praise = *vairāja* chant = north = autumn = Sādhyas and Ājyas and Bṛhaspati and the moon

5. fifth day = animals = *paṅkti* meter = twenty-seven-versed hymn of praise = *śakvara* chant = zenith = winter = Maruts and Rudra

6. sixth day = waters = *atichandas* meter = thirty-three-versed hymn of praise = *raivata* chant = zenith = cool season = Viśva Devas and Prajāpati

The six days of the ritual, six cosmological worlds, six hymns of praise, hymns, directions, seasons, and gods are each assigned a meter. In this structure, as suggested in Chapter 3, the *varṇa* connotations of the first three chains seem to be reproduced in the second three. Thus, in terms of the meters, here the *anuṣṭubh* reduplicates the function of the Brahmin *gāyatrī*; and indeed, many other texts provide corroboration for this thesis. Verses for Agni are recited at the morning pressing in the *anuṣṭubh* meter, for "the *anuṣṭubh* is the *gāyatrī*, and the meter of Agni is the *gāyatrī*" (KB 10.5, 14.2, 28.5). The virtual interchangeability of the two meters is also expressed in the following: "He recites a *gāyatrī*; the *gāyatrī* is the mouth. He recites an *anuṣṭubh*; the *anuṣṭubh* is speech. Thus he places speech in the mouth, and by the mouth he utters speech" (KB 11.2; cf. ŚB 7.1.2.21; 7.2.4.19).

According to this hypothesis, the *paṅkti* meter should thus be a Kshatriya component, and the *atichandas* (seven verses of eight syllables each) would be Vaishya in orientation. Unfortunately, things are not quite so simple. The *paṅkti* seems here to have been assimilated to the fifth chain simply because it is, as the text says, "five-footed"; a numerical equivalence rather than one based on *varṇa* seems to have guided the classifiers.[67] And the placing of the *atichandas* in the sixth and final string of connections is probably because of its reputation for being the equivalent of "all meters" (ŚB 4.6.9.13, 5.4.3.22). Its connection with the belly, food, and animals,[68] however, might also have led the ritualists to equate it with other Vaishya entities such as Prajāpati (see also ŚānĀ 11.7) and the Viśva Devas in this cosmogony.

Despite these and other variants and exceptions, the Vedas and the social classes are, as we have seen, related indirectly through the mediation of the meters, just as we have seen they can be through the mediation of the *vyāhṛtis*. The *gāyatrī*, *triṣṭubh*, and *jagatī* meters are explicitly equated not only to the three social classes but also to the metaphysical qualities that are so often definitive of each *varṇa* (e.g., fiery luster, force and power, and animality), the parts of the day, deities, worlds, parts of the body, seasons, animals, and directions—all of which are all well-known signs for the social classes.

Meters, then, like the *vyāhṛti* syllables which function as the condensed representatives of the three Vedas, act as switches to link up components from the realms of society and scripture. As a comparison of Table 9.1 (which maps the analogues of the three Vedas) and Table 9.2 (surveying the analogues of the three meters) demonstrates, the shared connections are so numerous that we may conclude (ourselves employing the homologic typical of the Veda) that each of the meters is an analogue of one of the three Vedas (*gāyatrī* = Ṛg Veda, *triṣṭubh* = Yajur Veda, and *jagatī* = Sāma Veda).[69] Since the meters are given *varṇa* attributions and are implicitly connected to the Vedas, the Vedas are thus in this way too analogues of the social classes.

TABLE 9.1. The Three Vedas and Their Analogues

	Ṛg Veda	Yajur Veda	Sāma Veda
Social Class	Brahmin	Kshatriya	Vaishya
Elemental Power	*brahman*	*kṣatra*	*viś*
Quality	light	might	fame
Cosmological World	earth	atmosphere	sky
Season	spring	summer	rainy
Part of Day	morning	midday	evening
Cardinal Direction	east	south	west
Natural Element	fire	wind	sun
Deity	Agni, Vasus	Vāyu, Indra, Rudras	Sūrya/Āditya, Varuṇa, Ādityas
Ontological Entity	self	humans	animals
Body Part	eye	ear	mind
Physical Function	speech	breath	sight
Breath	inhalation	exhalation	circulatory
Sacrificial Fire	*gārhapatya*	*āgnīdhrīya/dakṣiṇa*	*āhavanīya*
Priest	*hotṛ*	*adhvaryu*	*udgātṛ*
Linguistic Component	consonants	sibilants	vowels

Canonical Authority and Social Structure

One of the questions that remains unaddressed, however, is why particular Vedas were correlated to particular *varṇas*. Why, in other words, were these particular *bandhus* between canon and class formulated? For this I do not claim to have definitive answers but feel compelled to offer some speculations.

The Ṛg Veda is often accorded a status above that of the other two Vedas. Like the Brahmins in the social realm, the morning or spring in temporal cat-

TABLE 9.2. The Three Meters and Their Analogues

	Gāyatrī	*Triṣṭubh*	*Jagatī*
Social Class	Brahmin	Kshatriya	Vaishya
Elemental Power	*brahman*	*kṣatra*	*viś*
Quality	fiery luster, splendor of the *brahman*, generation	force,power, virility, physical strength	animal and food, procreation
Cosmological World	earth	atmosphere	sky
Season	spring	summer	rainy
Part of Day	morning	midday	evening
Deity	Agni, Vasus	Indra, Rudras,	Viśva Devas/Āditya, Ādityas
Animal	goat	horse	cow
Body Part	head, mouth	chest, arms	belly, penis
Physical Function	speech		
Hymn of Praise	9-versed	15-versed	17-versed
Chant	*rathantara*	*bṛhat*	*vāmadevya*

egorizations, and the eastern direction in spatial structures, the Ṛg Veda is the "first" or "primary" member of its class.[70] Moreover, as the Veda of the *hotṛ* priest, who is the "reciter" of verses in the sacrifice, it is also connected to speech. Since the Veda as a whole, as we have also noted, is sometimes said to be the summation of all speech, the Ṛg Veda might have been regarded as the metonymical placeholder for the Veda qua creative, sacred speech—for the "essence of speech is the verse (*ṛk*)" (ChU 1.1.2). As the metonym for all the Vedas, the Ṛg Veda stands in the same relation to the other parts of the canon as the Brahmin (the fullest representative of the human being) does vis-à-vis the lesser social classes.

The Yajur Veda, the Veda of the *adhvaryu* priest or the officiant who is charged with much of the actual ritual maneuvers, is appropriately classified with the Kshatriyas, the social class noted for physical activity. Other associations—with might, force, power, and virility; with the turbulent realm of the atmosphere; and with Vāyu the wind and the microcosmic anatomical equivalent, breath[71]—are in keeping with the "active" nature of both the Kshatriya *varṇa* and the Yajur Veda.[72]

Finally, the connection between the Sāma Veda and the Vaishyas[73] would seem to follow from the fact that both are characterized by multiplicity. The Sāma Veda is used by the *udgātṛ* priest in the Soma sacrifices where he is employed accompanied by a group of supporting chanters or singers. Just as the sky is the analogue of the *viś* in cosmology (owing to the countless heavenly orbs), and just as the dappled or spotted animal belongs to the Vaishya because of its multiple markings, so too, it would seem, do the Sāma Veda and the multitude of priests connected with it indicate a connection to the commoner class. Furthermore, the third place given to the Sāma Veda in these structures[74] may also be attributed to the fact that the Sāma Veda is dependent (like the commoners are supposed to be): all its chants are reworkings of the hymns of the Ṛg Veda.

The Brahmins are thus, in this context as in so many others, represented as primary and generative; the Kshatriyas are activity incarnate; and the Vaishyas are the embodiment of reproduction. But more important than the specifics of the equations forged between the Vedas and the social classes is the fact that such homologies are made at all, albeit in a roundabout way.

By means of such equations, the several and considerable canonical powers of the Veda can be, through the logic of analogy, applied also to the class structure of society. The Veda is said to be eternal and unsullied by human authorship (it is *apauruṣeya*, "not derived from humans"); thus the Veda—and, by implication, the *varṇa* system too—is reputedly not subject to the personal idiosyncrasies and class interests brought to ordinary books written by ordinary authors.[75] The Veda, and also the *varṇas*, is primordial and eternal, and therefore not subject to the contingencies and quirks of historical time. And the Veda—and, by implication, the *varṇas* too—is regarded as infallible and unquestionable (see Manu 2.10) and not subject to contestation. All these "canonical powers," all these claims to absolute authority, are brought to bear simultaneously on the Vedas and on the hierarchical social order of the *varṇas* because of the connections that serve to equate the two.

For later Hinduism, the caste system (or at least caste *in nuce*) can thus be presented as canonical: the authority of caste derives from the authority of Veda, but more than that caste is made to appear as a social transformation or reduplication of canon. The legitimacy, or even indisputability, of the distinctive social scheme of historical and contemporary India rides piggyback on the unquestionable truth of the Veda, and both are part of the eternal cosmic order of things. Any challenge to either the sociological or the scriptural structure can be debunked as obviously "unnatural" and false.

We here begin to understand how the most common two definitional criteria for that entity we call "Hinduism" (see Chapter 1) interrelate. Among those who have attempted to define Hinduism, one will recall, two features of the religion often are mentioned: (1) the claim that the Veda is absolutely authoritative and "sacred," and (2) the importance of the caste system for structuring "Hindu" doctrines, practices, and, of course, society. Definitions centering around the first feature focus on the canonical status of the Veda within Hinduism; those revolving around the second construe the religion in terms of its distinctive social theory. But what correlation there might be between these two criteria for "Hinduism" is rarely, if ever, spelled out.

The materials surveyed in this chapter could very well provide the key (and one that goes back to the time of the Veda itself) for such a correlation. The social system presented in the Veda is structurally reduplicative of the tripartite form of the canon, which is itself but one manifestation among many of a universal triadic pattern. Society and scripture are two rather privileged expressions of what Barbara Holdrege calls the "cosmic blueprint";[76] both partake of aboriginality, and both are represented as hard-wired into reality. Vedas and *varṇa*, canon and class, are regarded as transformations of one another and thus can later function as mirroring definitional criteria for "Hinduism."

NOTES

1. For a comprehensive comparison of the function of the Veda in Hinduism and the Torah in Judaism, together with important ruminations regarding the relationship of canon and tradition in the history of religions in general, see Barbara A. Holdrege, *Veda and Torah: Transcending the Textuality of Scripture* (Albany, N.Y.: SUNY Press, 1993).

2. For the etymological history of the term "canon" (originally "rule" or "measure," and later "list"), see William A. Graham, *Beyond the Written Word: Oral Aspects of Scripture in the History of Religion* (Cambridge: Cambridge University Press, 1987), pp. 52–53. Graham prefers the word "scripture" to denote a religiously authoritative text: "A book is only 'scripture' insofar as a group of persons perceive it to be sacred or holy, powerful and portentous, possessed of an exalted authority, and in some fashion transcendent of, and hence distinct from, all other speech and writing" (p. 5). "Canon," as I use the term here, avoids the literary connotations of "scripture": nonliterate groups can and do have the oral equivalent of a written canon (a set of myths, stories of origins, legends, histories, etc.), not to mention the case of the Veda, which was preserved only orally until recently.

3. "Where there is a canon, it is possible to predict the *necessary* occurrence of a hermeneute, of an interpreter whose task it is continually to extend the domain of the closed canon over everything that is known or everything that exists without altering the canon in the process. . . . [A] canon cannot exist without a tradition and an interpreter." Jonathan Z. Smith, "Sacred Persistence: Toward a Redescription of Canon," in *Imagining Religion: From Babylon to Jonestown* (Chicago: University of Chicago Press, 1982), pp. 48, 49.

4. "Canon" or "scripture" thus does not exist apart from the perception of it as such by a community and a tradition. One cannot but agree with William Graham when he writes that "neither form nor content can serve to distinguish or identify scripture as a general phenomenon or category. . . . [F]rom the historian's perspective, the sacrality or holiness of a book is not an a priori attribute of a text but one that is realized historically in the life of communities who respond to it as something sacred or holy. A text becomes 'scripture' in active, subjective relationship to persons, and as part of a cumulative communal tradition. No text, written or oral or both, is sacred or authoritive in isolation from a community." *Beyond the Written Word*, p. 5. On the other hand, religious traditions and communities come into existence only when they assign to themselves a point of origins (to which they endlessly return) and absolute authority—that is, a canon.

5. See Brian K. Smith, *Reflections on Resemblance, Ritual, and Religion* (New York: Oxford University Press, 1989), pp. 3–29; and "Exorcising the Transcendent: Strategies for Defining Hinduism and Religion," *History of Religions* 27, 1 (Aug. 1987): 32–55. For a recent treatment of the theme as it pertains to Tamil literature, consult John B. Carman and Vasudha Narayanan, *The Tamil Veda: Pillan's Interpretation of the Tiruvaymoli* (Chicago: University of Chicago Press, 1989), esp. pp. 3–12. See also the essays collected in Laurie Patton, ed., *Authority, Anxiety and Canon: Essays in Vedic Interpretation* (Albany, N.Y.: SUNY Press, 1993); David Carpenter, "Language, Ritual and Society: Reflections on the Authority of the Veda in India," *Journal of the American Academy of Religion* 60, 1 (Spring 1992): 57–78; and Barbara Holdrege's comparative study, *Veda and Torah*.

6. To the three principal Vedas— the Ṛg, Yajur, and Sāma—is sometimes added a fourth Veda, the Atharva. The latter attained its status relatively late in the scheme of things and became one example of adding an inferior fourth to a prior triad. The other principal instance of this phenomenon is, coincidentally enough, the addition of the Shūdra or servant class to the basement of the previously tripartite *varṇa* structure.

7. For the three Vedas as the three forms of *vāc*, ŚB 6.5.3.4; 10.5.5.1,5; and PB 10.4.6,9 (with Sāyana's commentary); and for a later transformation in which Sarasvatī similarly functions as the maternal source of the Vedas, Mbh 12.326.52. The three (or four in the case of the Atharvavedic GB, e.g., 1.5.28) Vedas are also equated with the sacrifice, another all-encompassing entity in Vedic thought. See, e.g., JB 1.358; ŚB 1.1.4.3, 3.1.1.12, 4.6.7.13, and esp. 5.5.5.10 ("The whole sacrifice is equivalent to that threefold Veda"). This chain of connections also entails the linkage of speech (*vāc*) and sacrifice, for which consult G. U. Thite, *Sacrifice in the Brāhmaṇa-Texts* (Poona: University of Poona, 1975), pp. 288–290.

8. E.g., ŚB 10.1.1.8; 10.2.4.6; JUB 4.25.2. For connections between *vāc* and the *brahman*, ŚB 2.1.4.10; AitĀ 1.1.1; BĀU 4.1.2.

9. E.g., ŚB 10.4.2.21–22, where it is said that in the beginning Prajāpati "surveyed all beings and perceived all beings in the triple wisdom. For in that [Veda] is the essence (*ātman*) of all meters, of all hymns of praise, of all breaths, and of all the gods. This indeed exists for it is immortal, and what is immortal exists; and this [contains also] that which is mortal. Prajāpati reflected to himself, 'Truly all beings are in the triple wisdom.'"

Cf. the later text in Manu where the Veda is said to contain within it all beings, all time (past, present, and future), the three worlds, and, importantly, also the social *varṇas* (Manu 12.97–99).

10. This is a notion that continues into recent history. The nineteenth-century Hindu apologist Haracandra Tarkapancanana could declare, "If there is to be faith in a book, let it be in the Veda, since it has prevailed on earth from the time of creation onward." Cited and translated in Richard Fox Young, *Resistant Hinduism: Sanskrit Sources on Anti-Christian Apologetics in Early Nineteenth-Century India* (Vienna: Publications of the De Nobili Research Library, 1981), p. 99. Swami Dayānanda Sarasvatī, the founder of the nineteenth-century neo-Hindu organization called the Ārya Samāj, similarly argued that the Vedas were superior to Christian scriptures because they lie outside of or before history and do not refer to historical persons or events or to geographical locales. See J. T. F. Jordens, *Dayānanda Sarasvatī: His Life and Ideas* (Delhi: Oxford University Press, 1978), pp. 271–72.

11. The authority of the Veda can thus be established in two tautological ways: first, because it was the creative source of the cosmos that is patterned after it; and second, the very tripartite *form* of the Veda can be constituted as proof of the eternal verity of its contents since it produces and reproduces the form of world.

12. The only exception to this rule I have encountered is provided by TB 3.12.9.2: "They say that the Vaishya class is born from the verses (*ṛks*, i.e., the Ṛg Veda). They say the Yajur Veda is the womb of the Kshatriya. The Sāma Veda is the procreator of the Brahmins." The Vedas associated here with Brahmins and the Vaishyas are inverted in comparison to the usual homologies, as we shall see. The fact that the passage does indeed directly connect the *varṇas* and the Vedas, however, is significant in itself. It demonstrates that such *bandhus* were not only theoretically possible but actually articulated.

13. Bruce Lincoln, "The Tyranny of Taxonomy," Center for Humanistic Studies, University of Minnesota, Occasional Papers No. 1 (1985), pp. 16, 17.

14. And, as we shall see, the meters can also be metonymically equated to the Vedas, although again usually only with the worlds as the connective intermediaries.

15. Other variants include ŚB 4.6.7.1–2; JB 1.357; AitB 5.34; KB 6.12; JUB 1.1.1–4; 1.23.1–6; 3.15.4–9; and PraśnaU 5.3–5.

16. Manu 1.23 also connects Agni (fire), Vāyu (wind), and Āditya (the sun) with the Ṛg Veda, Yajur Veda, and Sāma Veda respectively. ChU 3.6–10, alternatively, associates the Ṛg Veda with Agni and the Vasus, the Yajur Veda with Indra and the Rudras, and the Sāma Veda with Varuṇa and the Ādityas (and goes on to connect Soma and the Maruts with the Atharva Veda, and Brahmā and the Sādhyas with the Upanishads). Under either formulation, however, the *varṇa* of the deities linked with the Vedas remains constant: Brahmin (Agni, with or without his divine retinue, the Vasus) for the Ṛg Veda, Kshatriya (Vāyu or Indra and the Rudras) for the Yajur Veda, and Vaishya (Āditya or Varuṇa and the Ādityas) for the Sāma Veda.

17. Cf. JUB 1.1.1–4 where the following homologies are posited: Ṛg Veda = *bhūḥ* = earth = Agni; Yajur Veda = *bhuvaḥ* = atmosphere = Vāyu; Sāma Veda = *svaḥ* = Āditya.

18. KauśU 1.7 anomalously connects the Yajur Veda and the belly, the Sāma Veda and the head, and the Ṛg Veda and "form," while JUB 4.24.12 regards the various parts of the right eye as analogues of the various Vedas.

19. Cf. JUB 1.25.8–10 where Ṛg Veda = speech, Yajur Veda = mind, and Sāma Veda = breath.

20. The text goes on to connect the Atharva Veda (and the *itihāsa* and *purāṇa* literature) to the north, and the Upanishads are associated with the zenith. Cf. ŚānĀ 3.5;

VishnuP 1.5.52–55; MārkP 48.31–34; KūrmaP 1.7.54–57; and TĀ 2.3, which declares the Yajur Veda the head (= east) of the fire altar regarded as a person; Ṛg Veda the right side (= south); Sāma Veda the left side (= north); and Atharva Veda, the lower part, the foundation (= west).

21. One wonders whether a hierarchy of the Vedas is also being posited in a post-Vedic text that works with slightly different ontological correlates (gods, men, and ancestors respectively): "One should never recite the recitations (*ṛks*) or formulas (*yajurs*) when there is the sound of chants (*sāmans*)," says Manu, for "the Ṛg Veda is known to be sacred to the gods, the Yajur Veda to men, and the Sāma Veda to the ancestors. Therefore the sound of the latter is impure (*aśuci*)" (Manu 4.123–4). Elsewhere, however, are encountered passages where the Sāma Veda, and not the Ṛg Veda, is exalted as the "highest Veda." See, e.g., ŚB 12.8.3.23, where "the *sāman*" is said to be "the essence of all the Vedas"; or ŚB 11.5.6.4ff., where the Ṛg Veda = milk, Yajur Veda = ghee, Atharva Veda = fat, and the Sāma Veda = soma. Alternatively, a Kshatriya connection for the Sāma Veda is suggested or stated at ŚB 13.4.3.14, 14.3.1.10; AitB 3.23; TS 1.6.10.3–4; JB 1.88 (where the Sāma Veda = the *kṣatra* or the Kshatriya class and the Ṛg Veda = the *viś*); and especially ŚB 12.8.3.23: "He then sings a *sāman*. The *sāman* is the *kṣatra* power. With *kṣatra* he thus sprinkles him [i.e., consecrates a king]. And the *sāman* is imperial rule. With imperial rule he thus brings him to imperial rule." Recall also the apparently anomalous connection between the Yajur Veda and the Brahmins (and also the Sāma Veda = Kshatriyas, Ṛg Veda = Vaishyas) at TB 3.12.9.2.

22. ṚV 10.90.8. The hymn from which this citation is taken, the famous "Puruṣa Sūkta," also provides the best known example of the Vedic claim that the Vedas and *varṇas* were created together at the beginning of time. Following the verse already cited we read: "His mouth became the Brahmin, his arms were made into the Kshatriya, his thighs the commoners, and from his feet the Shūdras were born" (ṚV 10.90.12).

23. JB 1.286. The text goes on to draw the following interesting moral of the story: "Since now the *gāyatrī* had given her whole self, therefore the Brahmin goes with his whole self to the Kshatriya. And because the *jagatī* did not give its whole self, the Vaishya class shrinks from the Kshatriyas." Cf. JB 1.339. For another set of associations between earth and the *gāyatrī*, the atmosphere and the *triṣṭubh*, and the quarters and the *jagatī*, see JB 1.104.

24. The phenomenon is in general called *mantra ūha*, the details of which are described in S. C. Chakrabarti's The *Paribhāṣās in the Śrautasūtras* (Calcutta: Sanskrit Pustak Bhandar, 1980), pp. 132–36; 154–65.

25. For the following, see also Brian K. Smith, "Ritual, Knowledge, and Being: Initiation and Veda Study in Ancient India," *Numen* 33, 1 (1986): 65–89.

26. ŚGS 2.5.4–7; MGS 1.22.13; PGS 2.3.7–9; BDhS 1.2.3.11. According to other texts (VGS 5.26; KGS 41.20; cf. MGS 1.2.3), wholly different Vedic verses, each in the appropriate meter, were to be imparted to initiates of different classes. See also Radha Kumud Mookerji, *Ancient Indian Education (Brahmanical and Buddhist)* (London: Macmillan, 1947), p. 182; and P. V. Kane, *History of Dharmaśāstra*, 5 Vols., 2nd ed. (Poona: Bhandarkar Oriental Research Institute, 1974), Vol. II, Pt. 1, pp. 300–304.

27. The difference between these ages and the last ages possible for performing the *upanayana* for members each class (also eight, eleven, and twelve respectively) numerologically strengthened the bond between the *varṇas* and the meters.

28. VādhŚS 1.1.3.16; cf. 1.1.3.43. For other correlations of the three meters and the three social classes when the *adhvaryu* priest puts firesticks into the fire within the ritual of setting up the sacred fires for a new *āhitāgni*, consult the texts brought together in R. N. Dandekar, ed., *Śrautakośa (English Section)*, 2 vols. (Poona: Vaidika Saṃśodhana

Manṇḍala, 1958), Vol. I, Pt. 1, pp. 16, 20, and 24. For similar mantra adjustments in the Agnicayana ritual, e.g. TS 5.1.4.5; 5.2.2.4; and for those in the funeral rites for members of each social class, consult the Bhāradvāja Pitṛmedha Sūtra, translated in Dandekar, *Śrautakośa*, Vol. I, Pt. 1, pp. 1102–3. See also the text at JB 1.287: "Thus food is surrounded on both sides, by the Brahmins [through the employ of the *gāyatrī* meter] and the Kshatriyas [through the employ of the *triṣṭubh*]. The food surrounded on both sides by the Brahmins and the Kshatriyas is at the service of him who knows this."

29. JB 1.229; cf. PB 11.11.9; AitB 4.11; KB 3.5; ŚB 1.3.5.5; JUB 1.1.8.

30. See also KB 17.2, 17.9; AitB 1.5, 1.28; TS 5.1.4.5, 6.3.3.6; AitĀ 1.1.3; ŚB 4.1.1.14; PB 5.1.9, 6.9.25, 8.10.1ff., 12.1.2, 15.1.8, 15.10.6, 19.7.6; JB 1.229, 1.131; TB 2.7.3.3, 3.9.4.6; GB 2.5.3; 2.5.5.

31. TS 5.4.10.4, 7.2.8.1; KB 11.2; PB 14.5.28; 19.11.4; JUB 4.8.1.

32. KB 17.6; JB 1.93; PB 6.9.25, 12.1.2, 15.10.6; GB 2.5.15.

33. For the equation of the *gāyatrī* and the *brahman*, AitB 3.5, 3.34, 7.23; KB 3.5, 7.10; AitĀ 1.1.3; ŚB 1.3.5.4–5, 4.1.1.14, 8.5.3.7; JUB 1.1.8, 1.6.6, 1.33.11, 1.34.2; JB 1.264.

34. AitB 1.5. Cf. JB 1.68, 1.93, 1.229, 1.132.

35. AitB 8.2. Cf. AitB 1.28, 8.3, 8.4; PB 14.1.5, 14.5.19, 14.7.10; TS 6.3.3.6.

36. TS 5.4.1.5; AitB 3.5, 4.3, 6.21, 7.23; AitĀ 1.1.3; KB 3.5, 7.10, 8.7, 10.5, 11.2, 16.1, 16.2, 17.2, 17.9, 18.6, 30.11; TB 3.3.9.8; PB 18.10.7; JUB 4.8.1; ŚB 1.3.5.5, 3.4.1.10.

37. ŚB 7.5.2.24, 10.2.3.2, and 13.6.2.4,6 ("The *triṣṭubh* consists of eleven syllables, and the *triṣṭubh* is the thunderbolt and vigor"). Cf. ŚB 7.5.2.24, 8.5.1.10–11, 9.2.3.6; AitB 2.2, 2.16.

38. TB 1.1.9.7; TĀ 4.11.1–2; AitB 1.28. For an exception to the association of the *jagatī* and the Vaishyas or their signifiers, see KB 11.2, where the meter is connected to the ordinarily Kshatriya attributes of physical strength and virility (*bala* and *vīrya*).

39. AitĀ 1.1.3; KB 16.2, 17.2, 17.9, 18.6; ŚB 8.3.3.3, 13.1.3.8, 13.2.6.6, 13.6.2.5; TS 2.5.10.1, 6.1.6.2, 3.2.9.4; AitB 1.5, 3.18, 3.25, 3.48, 4.3; PB 18.11.9–10; JB 1.69, 1.104, 1.229, 1.132, 1.339.

40. ŚB 12.8.3.13; cf. ŚB 1.2.2.2, 1.8.2.11, 3.4.1.13, 13.6.2.5; TB 3.8.8.4; and KB 8.7.

41. Other texts that draw homologies between these three meters and the three day parts include ŚB 4.1.1.15–18, 4.2.5.20, 4.5.3.5, 14.1.1.17; AitB 3.12, 6.12; KB 14.3; TB 3.8.12.1–2; PB 7.4.6; JB 1.74, 1.103, 1.242, 1.280, 1.342.

42. E.g., TB 3.8.12.1–2; AitB 3.12; KB 14.3; ŚB 4.2.5.20, 4.5.3.5; PB 7.4.6.

43. See also AitB 6.9: "They are [verses in the] *gāyatrī* meter which he recites. The morning pressing is connected to the *gāyatrī*. Nine small [verses in the *gāyatrī* meter] he recites at the morning pressing; in what is small is seed poured. He recites ten at the midday pressing; seed poured in the small having attained the middle part of the woman becomes most firm. Nine small [verses] he recites at the third pressing; from what is small are offspring born."

44. For some different symbolic uses to which the syllabic content of the meters are put, see AitB 6.2; ŚB 1.7.3.22–25; TB 3.2.7.4–5; KB 10.1; JUB 4.2.1–10; and ChU 3.16. In other passages, however (e.g., KB 25.3, 26.8; AitB 6.21, 6.30; PB 4.4.8; ŚānĀ 1.2; ŚB 1.8.2.13), the ritualists warn against recitations in meters inappropriate to the time of the pressing.

45. E.g., at ŚB 1.3.5.4 and 2.1.4.14 (cf. KB 10.5), the *gāyatrī* is called "Agni's meter." At MS 2.13.14, KS 39.4, and TS 4.3.7.1, however, the *gāyatrī* is connected to the other principal Brahmin deity, Bṛhaspati; and at ŚB 13.6.2.8 the meter is associated with both Prajāpati and the *brahman*.

46. For the connection between the *triṣṭubh* and Indra, see also ṚV 10.130.5; ŚB 12.7.2.18; TS 3.2.9.3; TB 1.7.9.2.

47. See Cosmogonies I, V, VI, VII, X; ŚB 11.5.9.7; KB 14.3, 14.4, 30.1; AitB 8.6; JB 1.299. For other correlations between these meters and individual gods, see ŚB 10.3.2.1–6 (*gāyatrī* = Agni, *triṣṭubh* = Indra, and *jagatī* = Āditya); TS 4.3.2.1ff., 5.5.8.2ff.; and Cosmogonies VIII and XII (*gāyatrī* = Agni, *triṣṭubh* = Indra, and *jagatī* = the Maruts); AitB 3.47 (*gāyatrī* = Anumati, *triṣṭubh* = Rākā, *jagatī* = Sinīvālī); KB 7.10 (*gāyatrī* = *brahman* = Bṛhaspati; *triṣṭubh* = *kṣatra* = Varuṇa); KB 10.5 (*gāyatrī* = Agni, *triṣṭubh* = Soma = *kṣatra*); and MS 2.13.14, KS 39.4, and TS 4.3.7.1 (*gāyatrī* = Bṛhaspati; *jagatī* = Prajāpati).

48. See, e.g., ŚB 6.5.2.3–5, 12.3.4.1–6, 13.2.6.4ff.; JB 1.73, 1.78, 1.81, 1.239, 1.280, 1.281, 1.283–84; JUB 1.18.4–6, 4.2.1–9; ChU 3.16.1–5.

49. AitB 3.13; cf. ŚB 14.1.1.15ff.; JB 1.239; and Cosmogony XIII, where the deities of the three chains are Agni and the Vasus, Indra and the Maruts, and Varuṇa and the Ādityas respectively.

50. E.g., KB 8.9 (Agni = *gāyatrī* = earth; Soma = *triṣṭubh* = atmosphere; Visnu = *jagatī* = sky); KB 14.3 (with the respective deities being Agni, Vāyu, Āditya); ṢaḍB 2.1.9ff., JB 1.102, 1.270 (the gods here being Agni, Indra, Sūrya); and Cosmogony XIII (Agni and the Vasus; Indra and the Maruts; and Varuṇa and the Ādityas). For an inversion of the usual pattern, see ŚB 14.3.1.4–8 (*gāyatrī* = sky, *triṣṭubh* = atmosphere, *jagatī* = earth). And for an idiosyncratic formulation, AitB 3.48 (sky = Anumati = *gāyatrī*; Uṣas = Rākā = *triṣṭubh*; cow = Sinīvālī = *jagatī*; earth = Kuhū = *anuṣṭubh*).

51. For the linkage between the *gāyatrī* and the Brahmin deity Bṛhaspati, MS 2.13.14 and TS 4.3.7.1.

52. But also see ŚānĀ 2.4: "Then he recites [the verse called] 'the collarbone.' It is in the *triṣṭubh* meter. Therefore the collarbone is the strongest."

53. For the fairly common correlation between the *gāyatrī* and breath, the *triṣṭubh* and sight, and the *jagatī* and hearing, consult JB 1.99, 1.101–103, 1.253, 1.260, 1.268–70. For the identifications of the three meters and three breaths—inhalation, exhalation, and circulation—see JB 1.156.

54. See Cosmogonies V (listing the appropriate hymns of praise but no chants), VI (with the Vaishya chant as the *vāmadevya*), VII, VIII, IX, X, XI, XII, XIII; and cf. TB 2.6.19.1–2, where the following strings of connections are forged:

1. Vasus ⇒ spring ⇒ nine-versed hymn of praise ⇒ *rathantara* chant ⇒ *tejas*
2. Rudras ⇒ summer ⇒ physical strength (*bala*) ⇒ fifteen-versed hymn of praise ⇒ *bṛhat* chant ⇒ fame (*yaśas*)
3. Ādityas ⇒ rainy season ⇒ seventeen-versed hymn of praise ⇒ *vairūpa* chant ⇒ the *viś* and ojas
4. Ṛbhus ⇒ autumn ⇒ *śriyā* ⇒ twenty-one-versed hymn of praise ⇒ *vairāja* chant ⇒ *śriyā*
5. Maruts ⇒ winter ⇒ force (*sahas*) ⇒ twenty-seven-versed hymn of praise⇒ *śakvara* chant ⇒ physical strength (*bala*).
6. The gods (*devas*) ⇒ cool season ⇒ thirty-three-versed hymn of praise ⇒ immortality (*amṛta*) and the *kṣatra* ⇒ *revati* chant ⇒ *satya*

See also the later Hindu cosmogonic texts at VishnuP 1.5.52–55; MārkP 48.31–34; KūrmaP 1.7.54–57.

55. E.g., KB 1.66; PB 11.6.11, 11.11.13–14, 19.4.11, 19.16.4,7, 19.18.3, 20.10.1, 25.6.3; JB 1.253.

56. E.g., ŚB 8.4.4.7; PB 17.9.1–3, 19.18.3, 20.10.1, 25.6.3. At PB 19.11.4–5, the Brahmin *gāyatrī* meter is "the mouth," and the Vaishya seventeen-versed hymn of praise

is "food": "He thereby puts food in his [own] mouth. He who knows this eats food, becomes an eater of food."

57. This chant is closely associated with generation (which can be a Brahmin trait but also might call up associations with the *viś*). For connections between the *rathantara* and Prajāpati and the quality of procreation, see JB 1.231 and PB 7.7.16. For the *rathantara* and the emission of seed, JB 1.305; for this chant and "prosperity," JB 1.328, 1.330; and for *rathantara* and the house and land, JB 1.330.

58. JB 1.137. For this concept, see H. W. Bodewitz, *Jaiminī Brāhmaṇa 1, 1–65. Translation and Commentary* (Leiden: E. J. Brill, 1973), p. 77, n. 17.

59. JB 1.128, 1.291, 1.293, 1.343, 1.359. It is this homology that guides the identification of the *rathantara* and luster or glory and heaven, on the one hand, and of the *bṛhat* and "firm support" on the other (JB 1.229; cf. PB 9.1.28). For the *rathantara* = this world; *vāmadevya* = atmosphere; *bṛhat* = sky, see JB 1.146, 1.219, 1.298. For an even more complex equation (*rathantara* = earth = exhalation; *vāmadevya* = atmosphere = circulating breath; *bṛhat* = sky = inhalation), see JB 1.129.

60. For an interesting myth whereby originally the Kshatriya chant, the *bṛhat*, won a race thereby making the *rathantara* feel inferior and provoking the latter to ask the former for concessions that will render the two chants equal, see JB 1.298.

61. Cf. JB 1.300: "There are four meters that conduct the sacrifice: the *gāyatrī*, the *triṣṭubh*, the *jagatī*, and the *anuṣṭubh*." Elsewhere, however, "all the meters" are the *gāyatrī*, *triṣṭubh*, and *jagatī* (AitB 1.9). At BŚS 24.5 they are listed as seven, "each one consisting of four more syllables than the preceding one": *gāyatrī*, *uṣṇih*, *anuṣṭubh*, *bṛhatī*, *paṅkti*, *triṣṭubh*, and *jagatī*.

62. JB 1.102. For the connection of the *anuṣṭubh* meter and speech, consult also JB 1.99, 1.161, 1.188, 1.253, 1.260, 1.267–270, 1.306, 1.352. At JB 1.239, the *anuṣṭubh* = speech and mind. Cf. JB 1.272, where the meter is identified with "fame" or "renown" (*yaśas*) as well as speech: "He who thus considers this *anuṣṭubh* to be fame, for him this speech, the *anuṣṭubh*, fame continuously roams higher and higher above [that of] the others and he becomes an authority." For a correlation of *gāyatrī* = breath = wind; *triṣṭubh* = sight = sun; *jagatī* = hearing = quarters; and *anuṣṭubh* = speech = Prajāpati, see JB 1.317.

63. E.g., JB 1.211, 1.239, 1.290, 1.299, 1.317.

64. ŚB 13.3.3.1; cf. PB 21.4.6: "The horse is the last [i.e., the culmination, the highest, most perfect] of the animals, the *anuṣṭubh* [is the last] of the meters, Viṣṇu of the gods, the four-versed of the hymns of praise, the three-day rite of the sacrifices."

65. And to the northern direction, ŚB 13.2.2.17–19. See also TB 1.7.10.4, where the meter is connected to the royal deity Varuṇa; AitB 8.6 for an association of this meter with Soma; and for the connection between the *anuṣṭubh* and the Kshatriyas, PB 18.8.14, 19.12.8; TB 1.8.8.2–3.

66. Compare also the six-part Cosmogony XII, which fails, however, to give a meter for the sixth category.

67. Other associations the ritualists posited demonstrate no consistent *varṇa* classification for the meter. The *paṅkti* is equated variously with food (AitĀ 1.1.3), a "firm foundation" (KB 11, 17), the *brahman* (ŚānĀ 11.7), man (ŚB 8.2.4.3), animals (KB 23), Mitra and Varuṇa (AitB 8.6; ŚB 4.2.5.22), Bṛhaspati (TS 5.5.8.3), and Soma (ṢaḍB 2.1.30; JB 1.270).

68. See, e.g., ŚB 8.6.2.13: "An *atichandas* is the belly. For the meters are livestock, and livestock are food, and food is [what fills] the belly, because it is the belly that eats the food. Therefore when the belly gets the food, it becomes eaten and used up. And

inasmuch as this [brick] eats (*atti*) the meters (*chandas*), the cattle, it is called *attichandas*, for *attichandas* is really what is secretly called *atichandas*. For the gods love the occult."

69. The thesis is borne out in a later Hindu text, the KūrmaP (1.7.54–57): "From his eastern mouth he [Brahmā Prajāpati] measured out the *gāyatrī* meter and the verse [i.e., the Ṛg Veda], and also the nine-versed hymn of praise, the *rathantara* chant, and the Agniṣṭoma among the sacrifices. Then, from his southern mouth were emitted the formulas [i.e., the Yajur Veda], the *triṣṭubh* meter, the fifteen-versed hymn of praise, the *bṛhat* chant, and the Uktha sacrifice. From his western mouth he then emitted the chants [i.e., the Sāma Veda], the *jagatī* meter, the seventeen-versed hymn of praise, the *vairūpa* chant, and the Atirātra sacrifice. And from his northern mouth he emitted the twenty-one-versed hymn of praise, the Atharva [Veda], the Aptoryāman sacrifice, the *anuṣṭubh* meter, and the *vairāja* chant." Cf. VishnuP 1.5.52–55; and MārkP 48.31–34.

70. This is specifically articulated in later Hindu texts (e.g., MārkP 42.4.8–11, 102.1–7,19–21; VishnuP 2.11.12–13), where the Ṛg Veda is identified with the creator god of the *trimūrti*, Brahmā. It is in those texts, however, also identified with the *guṇa* of "activity" (*rajas*), which is elsewhere said to be the principle behind the Kshatriya *varṇa*.

71. For this point, see also ŚB 10.3.5.1–5, where the formula or *yajur* is etymologically equated with the wind and the breath.

72. Mention might be made here also of the homologies made between the Yajur Veda and "food," "the eating of food," and becoming "first" or "a leader" among one's people. See ŚB 10.2.5.6ff. For a connection between "eating food" and the Ṛg Veda, however, see TS 4.4.8.1.

73. For exceptions, see ŚB 12.8.3.23 (where "the *sāman*" is equated with the *kṣatra* and rule) and also ŚB 14.3.1.10 (where "the *sāman*" is said to repel the demons and prevent injury, thus seeming also to indicate a Kshatriya linkage for the Sāma Veda).

74. Elsewhere, however, one encounters passages where the Sāma Veda is exalted. See, e.g., ŚB 12.8.3.23, where "the *sāman*" is said to be "the essence of all the Vedas"; cf. ŚB 13.4.3.14 and esp. AitB 3.23, where the Sāma Veda is presented as the masculine superior to the feminine Ṛg Veda.

75. This point holds for other traditions that claim their canon was written by divinely inspired humans, and also for "secular" traditions whose classics are regarded as the work of "genius." In all cases, the end result is to exempt the text from the limitations entailed by ordinary authorship. For a different explication of the "authorless" Veda and its corollaries in contemporary Western literary theory, see Francis X. Clooney, "Why the Veda Has No Author: Language as Ritual in Early Mīmāṃsā and Post-Modern Theology," *Journal of the American Academy of Religion* 55, 4 (Winter 1987): 659–84. For a meditation on the similarities and differences between religious "scripture" and secular "classics," consult Graham, *Beyond the Written Word*, p. 3.

76. Holdrege, *Veda and Torah*, passim.

10

Conclusion

The *varṇa* system examined in this book supplied its propagators with a contrivance for classifying—and thereby knowing and controlling—the universe in its entirety. The Vedic epistemological project of discovering the "connections" or "homologies" (*bandhus*) that conjoined components from different realms was made possible by the resemblances thought to adhere to members of the same class, of the same *varṇa*. These linkages between elements of different species, realms, or "worlds" that share the same class—the Brahmin, Agni, the earth, the eastern direction, the morning, spring, the he-goat, the Ṛg Veda, and the *gāyatrī* meter, for example—I dub "horizontal connections." Such class-oriented resemblances are located within a cosmos that was, in each of its parts, hierarchically ordered. *Varṇa*s also functioned to rank elements of particular realms in the same way that society's classes were: members of the "Brahmin" class were placed first, those of Kshatriya *varṇa* are second, and the elements associated with the commoner class come third. The *varṇa* system thus entailed as well what I call "vertical connections," with the "Brahmin" component within each categorical sphere being the "all-encompassing" prototype while others were somewhat less complete versions of or counterparts to this prototype.

This classificatory system assumed that certain traits, qualities, functions, characteristics, or powers were inherent in, and definitive of, each of the *varṇa*s. These definitive classificatory taxons were often straightforward and expressed in terms of what I label the "elemental qualities": the he-goat "is" the *brahman*, Indra "is" the *kṣatra*, and the rainy season "is" the *viś*—and therefore each of these components is the correlate for, respectively, the Brahmin, Kshatriya, and Vaishya class which are the social manifestations of these same elemental qualities. The "essential powers" that are attributed to various things and beings are secondary indicators of their *varṇa*. Thus the god Bṛhaspati is the deified bearer of *brahmavarcasa* (the "splendor of the *brahman*"), *brahmavarcasa* is an essential power clearly related to the elemental quality of the *brahman*, and the Brahmin "is" the *brahman*. Therefore, even when the equation is not explicitly stated (as it often is), through this method of following out the homologies one can conclude that Bṛhaspati and the Brahmin are co-members (albeit in different spheres) of the same class.

Other forms of resemblance also lead to placing different elements in the same *varṇa* or class. The star-filled sky, dappled animals, or leprous men call to mind "multiplicity," and therefore are connected to the commoner class. The morning and the season of spring, the east, the Ṛg Veda, Agni, the *palāśa* tree, and the earth are all the "first" members of their particular realms or the "womb" of all others, and are therefore classified with the Brahmin, who is "first among men." The sometimes stormy world of the atmosphere, the warrior god Indra, the Yajur Veda, and the horse are "Kshatriya" entities because of the active, physical, and militaristic imagery they called forth. Yet other and different sorts of resemblances and homologies also provoke or reinforce *varṇa* classification. The syllabic composition of the each of the principal meters (eight syllables for each line in the *gāyatrī* meter, eleven in the *triṣṭubh*, and twelve in the *jagatī*) were numerical homologues of the respective ages for initiation of boys from different classes (eight for the Brahmin, eleven for the Kshatriya, and twelve for the Vaishya)—and for this reason (among others) are the meters of the three *varṇas*.

Connections from elements of a given sphere to one or another of the *varṇas* were not always directly forged but can nevertheless be inferred by means of intermediaries. As we observed in Chapter 9, the three Vedas are indirectly correlated to the three *varṇas*: first, because of the mediation of the three worlds (if the Vedas = the three worlds, and the social classes = the three worlds, then the Vedas = the social classes); and second, because of the mediation of the three *meters* and the three worlds (if the meters = the *varṇas* = the worlds = the Vedas, then the *varṇas* = the Vedas).

The system is enormously complicated and not always easily understood. No single trait adheres to every member of a given *varṇa*, although a constellation of such taxons can be identified.[1] More than one member of a given realm can be assigned to the same *varṇa*—thus the cow, the goat and the black antelope are all "Brahmin" animals; and the pipal and *udumbara* are both Vaishya trees. Third, as we have also seen, the same entity can be classified into different *varṇas* for different reasons: the cow is a Brahmin animal because of its connections to the sacrifice, but it is a Vaishya animal insofar as it is associated with productivity and "food"; and the sky is usually the realm of the commoners because it is, so to say, "overpopulated," but in other cases it can be the Brahmin region because it is "highest."

I have tried to be careful to note all such alternatives, variations, and discrepancies in the course of this work. I have also tried, when possible, to provide explanations for why they occur and to show how differing *varṇa* assignments nevertheless follow a consistent *varṇa* classificatory ideology. And, most important, I have, I hope, somewhat overwhelmed the reader with the much larger number of recurring consistencies that appear, in stunning redundancy, in Vedic homological thinking guided by *varṇa*.

The universe can be classified into *varṇa*s because all of the components of the universe can be understood as bearing one or another of a limited number of what Wittgenstein called "family resemblances." There are a certain number of definitional criteria for these classes which are fixed and invariable, even while that which is placed within those classes is indeed subject to some variability. Things and beings that had special importance for the sacrificial sphere, that were created first or otherwise took precedence, that could be seen as "mild" or "temperate"—these all could be understood as "Brahmin." Entities that were characterized by strength and physical power, rulership over subjects, activity, components of the cosmos that were notably "hot"—these were Kshatriya entities. And those that were multiple and "indistinct," that were intimately related to fecundity, productivity, and regeneration, or that could be shown to be dependent on others and relatively weak—these were the Vaishya components of the cosmos.

The epistemological dimension of the *varṇa* system made it possible to reduce the vast array of things and beings in the universe to a small number of classes into which all things, for one reason or another, could be fitted. But such knowledge was not just theoretical; it was not "knowledge for its own sake," if indeed such a thing even exists. Given the overweening importance of ritual action, of *karman*, to Vedic religion and philosophy, the classificatory fruit produced by the *varṇa* system was generated in order to be put into action. Knowledge is power, and for the Vedic ritualists, knowledge that informs and interprets the workings and meanings of the sacrifice is the most powerful.

The resemblances that guided classification according to *varṇa* made ritual activity possible. Ritual depends for its supposed efficacy on "symbols," that is, on the substitution of a controllable thing for another that is not so easily manipulated. Classification of the type we have covered here assumes that any member of the class can substitute for any other[2] and makes it possible for the ritualists to effect changes on one entity through operations performed on a substance which shares its same class. Priests who wielded such knowledge could, by means of the substitutes the *varṇa* system provided, control the natural, supernatural, and social worlds from within the confines of their ritual world.

Both classification (as the basis for and the equivalent of "knowledge") and the ritual efficacy classification makes possible (insofar as it allows for substitution and interchangeability) have, in the Veda, a social foundation and a social function. As we have seen throughout this book, the *varṇa* system, with all its epistemological power, had a particular social theory at its base; and ritual manipulations of entities with *varṇa* codings had obvious social implications and were often directed to specific social ends. The king is made to rule over his subjects when the ladle that represents the former is placed over the spoon that symbolizes the latter. Brahmins exempt themselves from the king's rule by withholding hymns of praise that are nine-versed (and therefore sharing the same *varṇa* as the priests) from the royal consecration rite. The commoners are made to be plentiful when a multitude of sacrificial hearths, which are identified with the *viś*, are constructed in the sacrifice. And so on . . . throughout the Veda. Because of *varṇa* classifications, the ritual world of the Vedic priests could function as the workshop for social control.

With roots in an Indo-European "ideology" of tripartition, the *varṇa*s were first and foremost geared to establishing and upholding a hierarchical social order. Subsequently, the distinctively Indic system of social theory and practice known as the "caste system" would find its rationale (as well as its historical origins) in the Vedic classificatory system we have studied here. Already in the Veda (as we saw in Chapter 2 and, indeed, throughout this work) and subsequently also in later texts dealing with *dharma* or "duty," society was (at least ideally and theoretically) said to be comprised of three and then four hierarchically ordered *varṇa*s or classes. This relatively simple system (simple, that is, in structure) is the predecessor of and the theoretical basis for the much more complicated social framework of historical and contemporary India, in which thousands of castes or *jāti*s are counted.[3]

What, exactly, is the relationship between the ancient theory of society comprised of three or four classes, on the one hand, and the multitude of castes that anthropologists tend to regard as the more empirical social units of historical and contemporary India on the other? On what grounds can it be contended, as I have, that *varṇa* provides the roots and rationale for such a complex social formation as that of the later Indian caste system?

Different answers to the query regarding the relationship between class (*varṇa*) and caste (*jāti*) have been put forth. In the scholarly literature, the terms "*varṇa*" and "*jāti*" have sometimes been regarded as virtually interchangeable.[4] Dumont more cautiously argues that the *varṇa* and caste systems are "homologous," and that the *varṇa* system is indeed the caste system in embryo, "both of which are structural, and both of which culminate in the Brahmans."[5] At the other end of the spectrum we find those who regard the *varṇa*s as purely theoretical constructs which refer "at best only to the broad categories of the society and not to its real and effective units."[6]

Still others view the *varṇa*s as the "base categories" which "are subject to combination by means of the application of certain operations or rules . . . thereby generating a number of new ranked categories which we can identify as *jāti* (castes) or their analogues";[7] the *varṇa* system thus provides a unifying and pan-Indian superstructure for the complex, unruly, and locally divergent multiplicity of castes. As M. N. Srinivas sums up the last position in his 1952 classic, *Religion and Society among the Coorgs*, "*Varṇa* systematizes the chaos of *jāti*s and enables the sub-castes of one region to be comprehended by people in another area by reference to a common scale."[8] Srinivas, like many others, thus regards the relationship between the *varṇa*s and the *jāti*s as one reflex of Robert Redfield's notion of the interplay between the "great" or "Sanskritic" tradition and the "little" tradition of village India. Richard G. Fox sees this as a "quasi-political" function by which the *varṇa*s help to unite an otherwise fragmented polity, acting as "ideological models which provide culturally stereotyped standards to be absorbed by local caste groups. The acceptance of these models promotes a minimal behavioral consistency over regions, and a minimal cultural (attributional) homogeneity."[9] R. S. Khare in like manner envisions the *varṇas* as "genres in the Indian ideology":

> To emphasize these genres is to investigate the place of the archetype in Indian social classification, where symbolic elements and their relations are expected to guide the actual social relations. . . . In being remote rather than immediate, and guiding rather than definitely classifying, *varṇa* acts as a true symbolic *archetype* should. It makes a member of a *jāti* always apperceive of himself (or herself) as a Brahman or a Kshatriya or a Vaishya or a Shūdra.[10]

Having briefly reviewed the anthropological literature on the subject, let me say this: the social classes or *varṇas* are, I think it is safe to say, theoretical entities (although they do have very real social functions). But then again, so too are the *jātis* that some anthropologists think have some kind of harder reality than the *varṇas*. Both class and caste in India are conceptual ways of concretizing more or less fluid social groupings;[11] both are ways of categorizing and classifying. While social classes and castes do "exist" and are "real" in an epistemological way, they are not empirical facts. They are what Durkheim called "collective representations." Both class and caste are ideas, or better, "ideologics" as defined by Franco and Chand: "Therefore, we also understand 'ideology' as a social practice, comprising two different yet dialectically united elements: discourse (language, ideas, propositions, theories, symbols, etc.) and activity (specific actions, gestures, behaviour patterns, and institutions as specimens of reified activity)."[12]

Be that as it may, it is also quite clear that post-Vedic Indian texts and present-day Indian informants regard the ancient *varṇa* scheme as the historical source and continuing basis of caste. Whether or not anthropologists think of the social classes as "real" in relation to the *jātis* or castes is, ultimately, beside the point—just as is the "irrelevance" of the Veda for the actual doctrines and practices of Hinduism—in the face of the fact that those living within the system identify themselves as belonging to one or another of the four *varṇas*.

The *varṇa* system (in its social expression) comes to be a generalized, pan-Indic way of representing Hindu society; the *jāti* system is a more specific and localized method of doing the same thing. Class has an ancient, Brahminical, and orthodox pedigree; caste, although known also from ancient texts, perhaps came into prominence (qua "system") only with the rise of the modern state and its bureaucratic requirements.[13] Just as it might be said that Vedism forms the archaic and prestigious predecessor to Hinduism, the *varṇas* provide the Vedic form for the Hindu *jātis*.

If caste and class are both ideas, they may very well be ideas of somewhat different sorts. The ancient Sanskritic texts do their best to explain how it is that a society supposedly comprised of three or four classes actually seems to contain hundreds and thousands of subgroups—the castes or *jātis*. Simple, the texts say; the castes are the product of intermixtures of the classes (*varṇasaṃkara*).[14] By offering such an explanation, however, the theorists are in fact obliged to admit that there are two different, even opposed, social principles at work in India: an ideal separation of the complementary but exclusivistic classes and the actual interrelation between those classes that results in castes. J. C. Heesterman pinpoints the dilemma:

> So far, we have spoken of caste as a single, coherent system. But it is striking that, where we have only a single word, caste, India has at least two terms: the well-known set of four *varṇa*s and the numerous *jāti*s. The question then is how the *jāti*s are related to the *varṇa*s. The answer is obvious: through mixed unions. But here is the catch. Such unions represent the abomination of *varṇa-saṃkara*, the confusion of the *varṇa* order, which is based on strict separation of the *varṇa*s. The interesting point is that the *jāti*s came about through exchange in its weightiest form, namely, marriage. The *jāti*s stand for asymmetrical exchange relationships, and that is exactly what is rejected by the *varṇa* theory. . . . The *varṇa* order and the *jāti* order are each other's opposites. Hierarchical interdependence upheld by "worshipful" and disinterested exchange may mask the pivotal problem, but it will not solve it. . . . Of course, no society can rest on the single principle of separation alone. And so *varṇa*, like *dharma*, has to encompass its own opposite, namely *varṇasaṃkara*, the confusion of the *varṇa*s, resulting in the proliferation of the innumerable *jāti*s. The seemingly monolithic caste order, then, is torn apart by two diametrically opposed principles, strict separation as required by the *varṇa* theory and conflictual interlinking in the actual *jāti* order.[15]

The paradox does not end there either. For the caste or *jāti* system itself adheres to the principle of separation characteristic of the *varṇa* scheme: it is a strictly endogamous social system. While the origin of castes is explained as a corruption of *varṇa* integrity, members of the castes thus created out of interclass unions are prohibited from marrying outside their own group. The caste system thus attempts to retrieve the apartheid ideology of the ancient Indian class scheme that caste has contravened in its origins. By doing so, the *jāti*s also come to reclaim the ideological premise of *varṇa*: the social classes (like other classes of the universe) should be separate and interdependent.

The caste system, like the *varṇa* system upon which it rests and which it recapitulates, is justified and explicated in terms of religious ideas. Louis Dumont and his followers have insisted on the opposition of the fundamentally religious conceptions of "purity" (supposedly manifest in the Brahmin) and "impurity" (represented by the Untouchable) as the religious core of the caste system. Those who oppose or rework Dumont have either attempted to fine-tune the purity–impurity opposition or suggest other abstractions for the religious bases of caste hierarchy.[16]

Few scholars of caste or contemporary Hinduism seem to fully recognize and appreciate what this book is dedicated to proving: that there are multiple sources of religious authority underwriting the *varṇa* scheme which, in turn, provide legitimation for the caste system. The authority on which caste depends, insofar as it is dependent on *varṇa*, has many tentacles. The failure to recognize these multitudinous and interlocking sources of religious power the caste ideology draws upon is in part due to Indology's failure to represent the *varṇa* system in the Veda in all its grandeur and partly, perhaps, because of a limited sense of what "religion" is and does in any culture.

In the first place, as noted at the end of Chapter 9, the ideology of social hierarchy is authoritative in historical and contemporary India because it is authorized by the ancient and canonical Veda. The Veda functions as the guarantor for truth in Hindu India; all sorts of ideas, practices, and institutions are validated and repositioned as themselves authoritative by the claim that they are, somehow, "Vedic." Traditionally, Hindu texts achieve their prestige by representing themselves as the "fifth Veda," and Hindu ideas and practices—ranging from nonviolence or *ahiṃsā* to pilgrimage, from devotionalism or *bhakti* to the ritual of *pūjā*—seek legitimation by claiming that they all are, in one way or another, "Vedic" and therefore both "ancient" and "right."[17]

Such reliance on the authority of the ancient Veda for legitimating the new and what would otherwise appear to be the non-Vedic continues even in recent times. In the nineteenth century, for example, the Veda was called upon as part of the Indian response to the perception that India was materially, technologically, and scientifically backward in comparison with the West. Swami Dayānanda Sarasvatī, the founder of the Ārya Sāmaj, argued that since the Vedas embody the totality of all truth, the truths of modern science must already be in the Vedas. Dayānanda thus claimed to have found knowledge of high-tech telecommunications, capabilities for the construction of aircraft, and advanced theories of gravitational attraction already documented in Indian texts nearly three thousand years old.[18]

If the technological accoutrements of modern life can be found prefigured in the all-embracing and absolutely authoritative Veda, how much easier to attach Vedic legitimation to the caste hierarchy? For the basic structure of caste ideology really is ordained in the Vedic texts, and the well-known creation myth at ṚV 10.90 often cited by Hindus to provide such Vedic pedigree for the social system is not, by a long shot, the only such text within the canon to authorize this particular form of social hierarchy. Caste is indeed Vedic in its origins, and merely by being Vedic can appropriate for itself the authority such a designation carries in historical and contemporary India. The *varṇa* or ancient class system may therefore be regarded as having the same religious power for the more recent *jāti* or caste system that Vedism as a whole has over Hinduism: Vedic *varṇa*s provide canonical sanction for Hindu *jātis*.[19]

The caste system relies on the *varṇa* system and its Vedic authority. But another closely related source for the enduring and persuasive authority of the caste hierarchy in India is its supposed primordial status. Because the caste system finds itself presaged in the Veda, the former borrows the prestige of antiquity (as well as absolute authority) associated with the latter. But in addition, within the Veda itself the social classes are portrayed as aboriginal, as we saw in Chapter 3.

Cosmogony legitimizes the present insofar as it conforms to what things were like "in the beginning." Creation stories ensure that departures from a status quo appear as deviations from a god-given norm, as degenerations vis-à-vis a pristine time of original perfection. To pronounce on how things were at the dawn of time is to describe how things really are—or, at least, how they really should be. Religions have always depended on myths of origins to validate the dictates of particular human beings living in particular historical eras. Both Vedic and Hindu religions bestowed such cosmogonic legitimations on the social system they advocated and instituted in India.

Class distinctions (and the social hierarchy) were supposedly created by the Vedic creator god; *varṇa*s are the organizational pattern into which the universe was originally shaped. These classes are part of the uncorrupted nature of the cosmos and continue to participate pantheistically in the nature of the divine creator. It is cosmogony, and not secondary abstractions like "purity," to which the indigenous tradition has often appealed to legitimate social hierarchy, as R. S. Khare also notes:

> The indigenous perspective on *varṇa* and *jāti* implies such crucial cultural assumptions as (1) the reality of *varṇa* and *jāti* is connected to the reality of the Supreme Being; (2) its conception is as a cosmic rather than a social or political order . . .; and (3) connections produced in sacred texts, whether direct or metaphorical, offer the true, eternally verifiable basis between a *jāti* member, a *jāti*, a *varṇa*, and the Purusha. . . . If *varṇa* is a cultural taxon for *jāti*s, it has, in turn, to be connected to its archetype, the Cosmic Man (Purusha).[20]

Social classification is said to be so ordered by the divine will as that will is represented in the ancient and authoritative Veda and purportedly implemented at the time of creation. But society is not created and organized in isolation; Vedic myths of the origins of society's classes are also stories of the origins of all things and beings in God's universe. The social classes were created at the same mythical moment as the classes within the supernatural and natural worlds. Knowledge of the true organizational patterns of the worlds of the gods, of space and time, and of the flora and fauna on earth can conversely revert back to what we are supposed to know about the social classes themselves. Here we confront another dimension of the power of cosmogony—the conflation of one sphere with all others. Cosmogony, by its very nature, presents the origins of one type of thing as concurrent, and often as in the Vedic case, in conformity with all other things that came into being.

Among other things and beings created concomitantly with the social classes are classes of gods; the structure of divine society reduplicates that of human society. Here, then, is another source of the authority of caste in India. For not only is society patterned in a certain way created by a divine hand, but the divine realm itself is categorized along class lines—as on earth, so in heaven. Theology recapitulates sociology; a particular conception of the social order is buttressed by the supernatural order wherein deities were given class attributes and participated in class-governed interrelations. The *varṇa* system, and the caste hierarchy it gave rise to, was divinely legitimated, and in two ways: it was created by God, and gods were created (and organized) in its image.

If the class structure of Indian society could be read in the heavens, it also pervaded the world all around. The very structures of space and time testified to the validity of this mode of social organization; perception itself, channeled as it is by spatiotemporal categories infused with *varṇa* significations, was recruited to prove the authenticity of this form of social classification. Vedic categorizations of space (dividing the universe into three worlds and spatial coordinates here on earth into four cardinal directions) and Vedic categorizations of time (dividing the parts of the day and the seasons of the year) were endowed with social meanings. Spatiotemporal reality, in turn, became yet another witness to the truth of what was, after all, an arbitrarily designated form of social classification.

The Vedic divisions in space and time largely continue in later Indic cosmology, with or without the explicit memory of the *varṇa* attributes the Veda bequeathed them. But the notion that a class hierarchy of this sort was "natural" certainly perseveres, and the insinuation of class into spatiotemporal categories cannot be ignored when it comes to the question of the authoritative planks on which caste stands.

Nor can the fact that flora and fauna were so represented. "Nature" is a social construct, but it is one that human beings (not excluding ourselves) continually draw upon to lend an aura of "objectivity" to constructs of other sorts. "Nature," no less than the "supernatural," transcends the particularities and subjectivities of those who pronounce upon it. Constituting plants and animals as carriers of *varṇa* repositioned social class as natural truth.

All of this, as we have seen, was encoded in texts that themselves were classified in accordance with the *varṇa* system. Veda and *varṇa* are, in the Veda itself, conceived of as isomorphic: the triadic form of the former is redolent with the triadic structure of the latter. And since the revelation that is encapsulated in the Veda is supposedly the *fons et origo* of the universe as a whole, we are once again back to cosmogony and its validating authority. The legitimizing power of the Veda for Indian social theory can thus be established in two ways: the Veda was the source of a cosmos that is patterned in the same way as society, and second, the very tripartite *form* of the Veda is proof of the eternal verity both of its contents and of the social order since both reproduce the form of world.

Caste relies on *varṇa* as its ancient and Vedic prototype, and *varṇa* draws its legitimating power from some of the most powerful strategies human beings have invented for transcending their own inherently limited claims to truth. Subjectivity, cultural and historical relativity, the skewed perspectives of particular points of view—all these are obliterated by representing the truth-claim as ancient or "original," as God-given and divinely ordained, as part of the "way things are" in "nature," as "objective" and intrinsic to "reality," and as "revealed" in texts with eternal validity. Each one of these, I would contend, is a fundamentally "religious" claim, for each entails an appeal to something transcendent of the human beings who make them. All of these various kinds of appeals to transcendence were brought to bear on the *varṇa* system, and all of them (explicitly or implicitly) provide the religious props for a caste hierarchy that survives into present-day India.

Authoritative discourse depends on erasing the human origins of that discourse. Use of the impersonal or passive ("it is known," "it is a fact that," etc.) is one way to achieve the illusion of objectivity necessary for authority. Another method, frequently used in religion, is to claim simply to be repeating what the gods say or impassively transmitting the revelations from the transcendent realm. The true sources of such truth, human beings, make themselves invisible. The authority they wish to stand on is not their own (for that would be obviously human, subjective, contingent, limited, and eminently disputable); the authority which the religious wishes to appropriate comes from, as Rudolph Otto once put it, the realm of the *ganz andere*, the "wholly other."

We have seen how the Brahmin authors of the Vedic texts in which *varṇa* is first encoded consistently attempted to conceal their own authorship, if not their own interests. The Veda itself is "authorless" (*apauruṣeya*), the social order in which Brahmins are placed at the top is simply part of creation, part of nature, part of the "way things are." We have often observed in the course of this work how the *varṇa* classificatory scheme could be deployed to make assertions with obvious social relevance without ever directly speaking about social class at all. Anonymity lends considerable authority to a discourse by obscuring its source.

One of the inevitable tasks of the analyst of religion, however, is to pull the curtain back and reveal that the wizard of Oz is but a humbug from Kansas. Or, to phrase it more delicately, we are obliged to reveal what others have taken such pains to hide: the particularistic, subjective, intrinsically interested, and always human origins of all claims to "absolute truth," "objective reality," "transcendent authority," "nature," and the like. Questions and answers that are never posed or given by the religious need not be left mute by scholars of religion. Among the most important is "Says who?"[21] To leave unsaid who said what was said is scholastically irresponsible and inappropriately pious. "Says who?" may alternatively be phrased as "To whose advantage?" or "In whose interests?" And religious discourse no less than other varieties always is to the advantage and serves the interests of some more than others (or of some and not others).

Knowledge is never disinterested. Classifications, such as those made possible by the *varṇa* system, reflect the interests of those who are classifying. And those who do the classifying for a particular culture and time do so because they can, because they have seized (or have been given) the ability to imperiously decree what is what. But the student of religion, to put a fine point on it, must not be content to repeat the claims of the religious elite he or she studies. Despite the pretensions to universality and generalized truth, the spokespersons for any tradition (including our own) obviously represent the interests and viewpoint of but one segment of a much larger and diverse group, a more complicated time, and a more culturally varied place. The scholar must, of course, attempt to grasp the details of the perspective under scrutiny, not only because it is an obvious *sine qua non* of the enterprise but also because such particular perspectives have often enough *succeeded* in their quest for ideological hegemony.

This I have tried to do here with the *varṇa* system. But to conclude without emphasizing, once again, whose hand lay behind such intricate labor, who benefited (and at whose expense) from such elaborate systematical classification, leaves too much unseen and unsaid. These texts, as I underscored in the introductory chapter, were written by the Brahmin class. They do not and cannot give us an unalloyed snapshot of life as it was lived, thought as it was conceived, in

Vedic India. The Veda is the Brahmin's account of the world; it was written in part to establish and promote Brahmin interests; and while it certainly represents the ideals and hopes of the Brahmin community, it very probably distorts the historical, political, and social realities of Vedic India "as it was" in order to do so.

A secularized and humanistic study of religion has a necessary obligation to its secularism and humanism. This obligation is to avoid a conclusion that does nothing more than reposition, restate, and relegitimate the very claims of our object of study (particular individuals and classes) to natural and supernatural superiority and privilege.[22] This is precisely what happens, whether intended or not and whether stated or not, when any form of the nonreductive approach to "symbol systems" such as that entailed in the *varṇa* structure is adopted. Furthermore, the study of religion, in a way unique to it, has an opportunity to point out the transformations religiously based discourse has undergone as it moves away from a transcendent God only to find new masks for its human origins. The claims behind modern and "scientific" knowledge are often not much different from those discussed in this work. We often enough continue to hear, from the mouths of humans like ourselves, pronouncements made in the passive voice about "nature" or "natural law," or about the "objectively" observable organizational patterns of the universe.

Assuming that there were human origins, particular class interests, and historical and cultural conditionality at work in religious (and all other) discourse seems to me a necessary methodological starting point, as well as (in this case) part of a concluding summary. But such a stance will also pit the scholar of religion against the religious he or she studies. While some in the profession fervently wish to avoid such a stark drawing of the lines between themselves and the religious they study, I cannot see how such a conclusion can be avoided.

Consider the following: the Indian social system was *not*, from one point of view, created by a primordial superhuman Cosmic Man; it was *not* merely the "natural" way of organizing human beings, replicating in the social sphere what was "objectively discovered" in other realms; and it was *not* ordained from the beginning of time as part of the "way things just are." Such, however, are the claims made for the *varṇa* system in the sacred texts known as the Veda, and such are the claims many in contemporary India continue to make in order to defend the caste system. Nor are these sorts of transcendentalizing, ahistorical, and impersonal truth claims unique to Vedic religion. They are, in fact, rather commonplace contentions in religious discourse, which, as I pointed out earlier, depend on erasing the mundane, human signatures from their own decrees. The study of religion, insofar as it assumes that religion is a human product, conditioned (like all other human products) by the space and time in which the humans concerned lived, busily rewrites what the religious have tried so hard to elide.

Claude Lévi-Strauss unhesitatingly stated, "No common analysis of religion can be given by a believer and a non-believer, and from this point of view, the type of approach known as 'religious phenomenology' should be dismissed."[23] Liberal-minded students of comparative religion have long been concerned with being properly empathetic toward and tolerant of the claims of religion in general and those of other peoples' religions especially. There was a time—and for some of us it is surely not yet passed—when such an emphasis served as a necessary corrective to crude ethnocentrism and jingoistic sectarianism and denominationalism. However, perhaps the time has now come also to begin to reflect more deeply about the ways in which being religious and being a scholar within that larger tradition called the humanities or the human sciences are often, and perhaps inevitably, fundamentally opposed enterprises.

NOTES

1. Thus the system is in some respects guided by "polythetic" taxonomical principles, which "means that no single feature is either essential to group membership or is sufficient to make an organism a member of the group." Rodney Needham, "Polythetic Classification: Convergence and Consequences," *Man* (n.s.) 10, 3 (Sept. 1975), p. 355, citing Peter H. A. Sneath, "The Construction of Taxonomic Groups," in *Microbial Classification*, ed. by G. C. Ainsworth and P. H. A. Sneath (Cambridge: Cambridge University Press, 1962). For an application of the polythetic concept to the caste system, consult Gabriella Eichinger Ferro-Luzzi, "The Polythetic-Prototype Concept of Caste," *Anthropos: International Review of Ethnology and Linguistics* 81, 4-6 (1986): 637–42.

2. "Of every class, so far as it is correctly formed, the great principle of substitution is true, and whatever we know of one object in a class we also know of the other objects, so far as identity has been detected between them." W. Stanley Jevons, *The Principles of Science: A Treatise on Logic and Scientific Methods*, 2 vols. (London: Macmillan, 1874), II:345; cited in Needham, "Polythetic Classification," p. 350. Such a view is, it should be noted, outmoded in contemporary Western thought about classification.

3. For a history of the term "caste" and an analysis of its comparative utility outside the Indian situation, see Julian Pitt-Rivers, "On the Word 'Caste,'" in *The Translation of Culture: Essays Presented to E. E. Evans-Pritchard*, ed. by T. O. Beidelman (London, Tavistock, 1970), pp. 231–56.

4. E.g., Max Weber in *The Religion of India: The Sociology of Hinduism and Buddhism*, trans. and ed. by Hans H. Gerth and Don Martindale (New York: Free Press, 1958). It might be pointed out here that in the ancient Sanskrit lawbooks themselves the terms *varṇa* and *jāti* are also sometimes used interchangeably. See Manu 3.15, 9.86, 10.27,31,41, etc.

5. Louis Dumont, *Homo Hierarchicus: The Caste System and its Implications*, trans. by Mark Sainsbury, Louis Dumont, and Basia Gulati (Chicago: University of Chicago Press, 1980), p. 73. Dumont goes on to argue that the "caste system is influenced by the theory of *varṇas*" in two ways: by the separation of status and power, which results in the Brahmins given a higher rank than the Kshatriyas; and by the elevation of the ruling class (who are "impure" in that they are generally carnivorous and occupationally involved in violence) over even vegetarian Vaishyas, for the *varṇa* theory, "whilst it subordinates king to priest, power to status, establishes a solidarity between them which opposes them conjointly to the other social functions" (p. 75). For critiques of Dumont's theory, see M. N. Srinivas, "Some Reflections on the Nature of Caste Hierarchy," *Contributions to Indian Sociology* (n.s.) 18, 2 (1984): 151–67; McKim Marriott, "Interpreting Indian Society: A Monistic Alternative to Dumont's Dualism," *Journal of Asian Studies* 36, 1 (1976): 189–95; idem, review of *Homo Hierarchicus*, *American Anthropologist* 71 (1969): 1166-

75; the articles in T. N. Madan et al., "On the Nature of Caste in India: A Review Symposium on Louis Dumont's *Homo Hierarchicus*," *Contributions to Indian Sociology* (n.s.) 5 (1971): 1–81.; Nicholas B. Dirks, "The Original Caste: Power, History and Hierarchy in South Asia," *Contributions to Indian Sociology* (n.s.) 23, 1 (1989): 59—77; and Arjun Appadhurai, "Is Homo Hierarchicus?" *American Ethnologist* 13, 4 (Nov. 1986): 745–61.

6. M. N. Srinivas, "*Varṇa* and Caste," in *Caste in Modern India and Other Essays* (Bombay: Asia Publishing House, 1962), p. 65. The author concludes that "the *varṇa*-model has produced a wrong and distorted image of caste. It is necessary for the sociologist to free himself from the hold of the *varṇa*-model if he wishes to understand the caste system" (p. 66). See also Émile Senart's much earlier insistence on the radical difference between *varṇa* and caste, in *Caste in India: The Facts and the System*, trans. by Sir E. Denison Ross (London: Methuen, 1930), pp. 114–19; and the fairly recent articulation of the position that *varṇa* is "of little real use to the analyst of the present system" by Morton Klass, *Caste: The Emergence of the South Asia Social System* (Philadelphia: Institute for the Study of Human Issues, 1980), p. 90. Heesterman's variant of this position (to which we return later) holds that the relationship of ideal and theoretical *varṇa*s and real castes is one form of what he calls "the inner conflict of tradition." "The seemingly monolithic caste order, then, is torn apart by two diametrically opposed principles, strict separation as required by the *varṇa* theory and conflictual interlinking in the actual *jāti* order." J. C. Heesterman, *The Inner Conflict of Tradition: Essays in Indian Ritual, Kingship, and Society* (Chicago: University of Chicago Press, 1985), pp. 200–201; cf. pp. 8, 103, 190, 199.

7. S. J. Tambiah, "From Varṇa to Caste through Mixed Unions," in *The Character of Kinship*, ed. by Jack Goody (Cambridge: Cambridge University Press, 1973), p. 194, rephrasing the indigenous theory of the origins of castes from the intermixture (*saṃkara*) of the four *varṇa*s, for which see below.

8. M. N. Srinivas, *Religion and Society among the Coorgs of South India* (Oxford: Oxford University Press, 1952), p. 25.

9. Richard G. Fox, "*Varṇa* Schemes and Ideological Integration in Indian Society," *Comparative Studies in Society and History* (Ann Arbor) 11 (1969), p. 43.

10. R. S. Khare, "The One and the Many: Varṇa and Jāti as a Symbolic Classification," in *American Studies in the Anthropology of India*, ed. by Sylvia Vatuk (New Delhi: Manohar, 1978), pp. 40–41, 49.

11. For an attempt to more adequately represent this fluidity and the "transactional" dimension of the caste system, consult the work of McKim Marriott, esp. his review of *Homo Hierarchicus*; "Interactional and Attributional Theories of Caste Ranking," *Man in India* 39, 2 (1959): 92–107; "Interpreting Indian Society"; "Caste Ranking and Food Transactions: A Matrix Anaylsis," in *Structure and Change in Indian Society*, ed. by M. Singer and B. Cohn (Chicago: Aldine, 1968), pp. 133–71; "Hindu Transactions: Diversity without Dualism," in *Transactions and Meaning*, ed. by B. Kapferer (Philadelphia: Institute for the Study of Human Issues, 1976), pp. 109–42; "Toward an Ethnosociology of South Asian Caste Systems," in *The New Wind: Changing Identities in South Asia*, ed. by Kenneth David (The Hague: Mouton, 1977), pp. 423–38; and with Ronald B. Inden, "Caste Systems," *Encyclopaedia Britannica, macropaedia* (1974), Vol. 3, pp. 982–91.

12. F. Franco and Sarvar V. Sherry Chand, "Ideology as Social Practice: The Functioning of *Varṇa*," *Economic and Political Weekly* 24, 47 (Nov. 25, 1989), p. 2601.

13. See the interesting speculations of J. C. Heesterman, *The Inner Conflict of*

Tradition, p. 8: "The universal order propounded by the modern state implied a novel, analytic view of society. Rejecting the pervasivenss of conflict, it could only conceive of society as made up of separate, self contained units. Hence the notion of the self-sufficient 'village republic.' Hence also the exclusivist census definition of caste as a world unto itself, which disregards the interrelations of castes as well as other, noncaste groupings, such as guilds or brotherhoods. This definition translates the scriptural notion of *varṇa*, but distorts the living realities of *jāti*. Identifying the conflict-free ideal of *varṇa* separation with the conflictive interdependence of *jāti*, the modern state sought to establish its universal order."

14. Studies of the *varṇasaṃkara* theory include H. Brinkhaus, Die Altindischen *Mischkastensysteme* (Wiesbaden: Steiner, 1978); V. N. Jha, "Varṇasaṃkara in the Dharmasūtras: Theory and Practice," *Journal of the Economic and Social History of the Orient* (Leiden) 13, 3 (1970): 273–88; and Tambiah, "From Varṇa to Caste."

15. Heesterman, *The Inner Conflict of Tradition*, pp. 190, 200–201.

16. See, e.g., Veena Das's reapplication of Durkheim's sacred–profane dichotomy to complicate the purity–impurity opposition (*Structure and Cognition: Aspects of Hindu Caste and Ritual* [Delhi: Oxford University Press, 1977; 2d ed., 1982]). For auspiciousness–inauspiciousness as the dominant categories, consult Frederique Apffel Marglin, *Wives of the God-King: The Rituals of the Devadāsīs of Puri* (Delhi: Oxford University Press, 1985). For other critiques and revisions, see John B. Carman and Frederique A. Marglin, eds., *Purity and Auspiciousness in Indian Society* (Leiden: E. J. Brill, 1985); Dirks, "The Original Caste"; and Appadhurai, "Is Homo Hierarchicus?"

17. Consult Brian K. Smith, *Reflections on Resemblance, Ritual, and Religion* (New York: Oxford University Press, 1989), esp. Chapters 1 and 8.

18. Swami Dayānanda Sarasvatī, *Ṛgveda-bhāṣyam*, 3 vols., ed. by Yudhisthira Mimamsaka (Karanala, Harayana: Ramala Kapure Trasta, 1973), I:160ff., 234ff., 255ff. See also J. T. F. Jordens, *Dayānanda Sarasvatī: His Life and Ideas* (Delhi: Oxford University Press, 1978), pp. 82, 272.

19. This is an observation also recently implied by Francis X. Clooney, who argues that the religious significance of the caste system is borrowed from that of the *varṇa* system. "As distinguished from *varṇas*," Clooney writes, "*jātis* do not have directly religious significance; they are the 'secular' correlates of the theological categories and religiously meaningful due to the correlation." "Finding One's Place in the Text: A Look at the Theological Treatment of Caste in Traditional India," *Journal of Religious Ethics* 17, 1 (Spring 1989), p. 7.

20. Khare, "The One and the Many," p. 50. For an interesting survey of the very different reinterpretations two modern Indian thinkers have put forward of such cosmogonic legitimations of the class/caste system, see J. T. F. Jordens, "Two Giants Look at the Cosmic Man: Ambedkar and Dayānanda Interpret the *Puruṣa-Sūkta*," *Journal of the Oriental Institute* (Baroda) 33,1 (Sept.-Dec. 1983): 1–10.

21. Other questions that the religious leave unasked and unanswered often also include "When?" and "Where?" Religious truth, like some contemporary claims to "scientific fact," is not represented by the religious as historically or culturally contingent; it is supposedly universal and absolute.

22. I have also argued this point from somewhat different angles in different contexts. See my review article of the work of Jan Heesterman, "Ideals and Realities in Indian Religion," *Religious Studies Review* 14, 1 (Jan. 1988): 1–10; and "Exorcising the Transcendent: Strategies for Defining Hinduism and Religion," *History of Religion* 27, 1 (Aug. 1987), esp. pp. 52–53; and *Reflections*, esp. pp. 19–20, 27–28, 44, and 222–24.

23. Claude Lévi-Strauss, "The Bear and the Barber," in *Reader in Comparative Religion: An Anthropological Approach*, 3d ed., ed. by William A. Lessa and Evon Z. Vogt (New York: Harper Row, 1972), p. 188. Cf. the same author's concluding remarks in *Totemism*, trans. by Rodney Needham (Boston: Beacon Press, 1963), pp. 103–4.

Appendix

Cosmogony I

(ŚB 4.4.1.15–16,18)

The animals have Vāyu [the god of wind] as their leader, and Vāyu is breath; the animals are animated by means of breath. He [Vāyu] departed from the gods together with the animals. The gods prayed to him at the morning soma pressing, but he did not return. They prayed to him at the midday soma pressing, but he did not return. They prayed to him at the afternoon soma pressing. . . . If he had returned at the morning soma pressing, the animals would be among the Brahmins; for the *gāyatrī* [meter] is the morning soma pressing, and the ***brahman*** [power] is the *gāyatrī*. And if he had returned at the midday soma pressing, the animals would be among the Kshatriyas; for the midday soma pressing concerns Indra [the warrior king of the gods], and the ***kṣatra*** [power] is Indra. And since he returned at the afternoon soma pressing—the afternoon soma pressing concerns the Viśva Devas, and this all is the Viśva Devas—therefore the animals are everywhere here.

Scheme of Cosmogony I

1. morning = Brahmins = *gāyatrī* = ***brahman***
2. midday = Kshatriyas = Indra = ***kṣatra***
3. afternoon = Viśva Devas = animals

Completed Scheme of Cosmogony I

1. morning = Brahmins = Agni = ***gāyatrī*** = ***brahman*** = the Self
2. midday = Kshatriyas = Indra = ***triṣṭubh*** = ***kṣatra*** = humans

3. afternoon = Vaishyas = Viśva Devas = *jagatī* = *viś* = animals

divisions of the day = social classes = gods = meters = metaphysical powers
⇒ types of ontological beings

Cosmogony II

(ŚB 2.1.4.11–13)

Prajāpati generated this [world by saying], "*bhūḥ*," the atmosphere [by saying] "*bhuvaḥ*," and the sky [by saying] "*svaḥ*." As much as these worlds are, so much is this all. . . Prajāpati generated the *brahman* [by saying] "*bhūḥ*," the *kṣatra* [by saying] "*bhuvaḥ*", and the *viś* [by saying] "*svaḥ*". As much as the *brahman*, *kṣatra*, and *viś* are, so much is this all. . . Prajāpati generated the Self (*ātman*) [by saying] "*bhūḥ*," the human race [by saying] "*bhuvaḥ*", and the animals [by saying] "*svaḥ*". As much as these Self, human race, and animals are, so much is this all.

Scheme of Cosmogony II

1. *bhūḥ* ⇒ this world = the *brahman* power = the Self
2. *bhuvaḥ* ⇒ atmosphere = the *kṣatra* power = humans
3. *svaḥ* ⇒ sky = the power of the *viś* = animals

sacred utterances ⇒ cosmological worlds = metaphysical powers = types of ontological beings

Cosmogony III

(ŚB 11.5.8.1–4)

In the beginning, Prajāpati was the only one here. He desired, "May I be, may I reproduce." He toiled. He heated up ascetic heat. From him, from that one who had toiled and heated up, the three worlds—earth, atmosphere, and sky—were emitted. He heated up these three worlds. From those heated [worlds], three lights (*jyotis*) were born: Agni the fire, he who purifies here [Vāyu the wind], and Sūrya the sun. He heated up these three lights. From those heated [lights], three Vedas were born: from Agni, the Ṛg Veda; from Vāyu, the Yajur Veda; and from Sūrya, the Sāma Veda. He heated up those three Vedas. From those heated [Vedas], three essences (*śukras*) were born: *bhūḥ* from the Ṛg Veda, *bhuvaḥ* from the Yajur Veda, and *svaḥ* from the Sāma Veda. With the Ṛg Veda, they performed [the ritual action which] concerns the *hotṛ* priest; with the Yajur Veda, that which concerns the *adhvaryu* priest; and with the Sāma Veda, that which concerns the *udgātṛ* priest.

Variant of Cosmogony III (AitB 5.32; cf. JB 1.358; MŚS 8.6.7)

The gods said to Prajāpati, "If there should be a calamity in our sacrifice due to the Ṛg Veda, or due to the Yajur Veda, or due to the Sāma Veda, or due to unknown causes, or a total miscarriage, what is the reparation?" Prajāpati said to the gods, "If there is a calamity in your sacrifice due to the Ṛg Veda, offer in the *gārhapatya* fire saying '*bhūḥ*'; if due to the Yajur Veda, in the *āgnīdhrīya* fire [in soma sacrifices] or, in the case of *havis* sacrifices, in the *anvāhāryapacana* fire saying '*bhuvaḥ*'; if due to the Sāma Veda, in the *āhavanīya* fire saying '*svaḥ*'; [and] if due to unknown causes or a total miscarriage, offer only in the *āhavanīya* fire saying all consecutively—'*bhūḥ*,' '*bhuvaḥ*,' '*svaḥ*.'"

Scheme of Cosmogony III and Variant

1. earth ⇒ Agni/fire ⇒ Ṛg Veda ⇒ *bhūḥ* ⇒ the *hotṛ* priest (*gārhapatya* fire)

2. atmosphere ⇒ Vāyu/wind ⇒ Yajur Veda ⇒ *bhuvaḥ* ⇒ the *adhvaryu* priest (*āgnīdhrīya* or *anvāhāryapacana* fire)

3. sky ⇒ Sūrya/sun ⇒ Sāma Veda ⇒ *svaḥ* ⇒ the *udgātṛ* priest (*āhavanīya* fire)

cosmological worlds ⇒ gods/natural ⇒ elements ⇒ scriptures ⇒ sacred utterances ⇒ priestly offices (sacrificial fires)

Cosmogony IV

(ŚB 12.3.4.7–11)

This world is splendor (*bharga*), the atmospheric world is greatness (*mahas*), the sky is fame (*yaśas*), and what other worlds there are, that is everything (*sarva*). Agni is splendor, Vāyu is greatness, Āditya is fame, and what other gods there are, that is everything. The Ṛg Veda is splendor, the Yajur Veda is greatness, the Sāma Veda is fame, and what other Vedas there are, that is everything. Speech is splendor, breath [or inhalation] is greatness, sight is fame, and what other breaths there are, that is everything. One should know this: "I have put into myself all the worlds, and into all the worlds I have put my self. I have put into myself all the gods etc., all the Vedas etc., all the breaths etc." Eternal are the worlds, the gods, the Vedas, the breaths, and eternal is the all. He who knows this crosses over from the eternal to the eternal; he conquers repeated death; he attains fullness of life.

Scheme of Cosmogony IV

1. splendor = earth = Agni/fire = speech
2. greatness = atmosphere = Vāyu/wind = breath
3. fame = sky = Āditya/sun = sight

metaphysical powers = cosmological worlds = gods/natural forces = body functions

Cosmogony V

(PB 6.1.6–11)

[Prajāpati] desired, "May I emit the sacrifice." From his mouth he emitted the nine-versed (*trivṛt*) hymn of praise (*stoma*); along with it he emitted the *gāyatrī* among the meters, Agni among the gods, the Brahmin among men, spring among the seasons. Therefore among the hymns of praise the nine-versed is the mouth [or the first, the chief one], among the meters the *gāyatrī*, among the gods Agni, among men the Brahmin, among the seasons the spring. Therefore the Brahmin makes himself strong (*vīrya*) with his mouth, for from the mouth was he emitted. He makes himself strong with his mouth who knows this. He emitted from his chest, from his arms, the fifteen-versed (*pañcadaśa*) hymn of praise; along with it he emitted the *triṣṭubh* among the meters, Indra among the gods, the Kshatriya among men, the hot season among the seasons. Therefore the hymn of praise of a Kshatriya is the fifteen-versed, the meter the *triṣṭubh*, the god is Indra, the season is the summer. Therefore his strength is his arms, for he was emitted from the arms. He makes himself strong with his arms who knows this. He emitted from his middle, from his penis, the seventeen-versed (*saptadaśa*) hymn of praise; along with it he emitted the *jagatī* among the meters, the Viśva Devas among the gods, the Vaishya among men, the rainy season among the seasons. Therefore the Vaishya, although devoured [by the others] does not decrease, for he was emitted from the penis. Therefore he has abundant animals, for the Viśva Devas are his gods, the *jagatī* his meter, the rainy season his season. Therefore he is the food of the Brahmin and the Kshatriya, for he was emitted below [them]. From his feet, from his firm foundation, he emitted the twenty-one-versed (*ekaviṃśa*) hymn of praise; along with it he emitted the *anuṣṭubh* among the meters, not a single one among the gods, the Shūdra among men. Therefore the Shūdra has abundant animals but is unable to sacrifice, for he has no deity which was emitted along with him. Therefore he does not rise above simply the washing of feet, for from the feet he was emitted. Therefore the twenty-one-versed among the hymns of praise is a firm foundation, for it was emitted from the firm foundation.

Scheme of Cosmogony V

1. mouth ⇒ nine-versed hymn of praise = *gāyatrī* meter = Agni = Brahmin = spring
2. chest/arms ⇒ fifteen-versed hymn of praise = *triṣṭubh* meter = Indra = Kshatriya = summer
3. middle/penis ⇒ seventeen-versed of praise = *jagatī* meter = Viśva Devas = Vaishya = rainy season
4. feet/foundation ⇒ twenty-one-versed hymn of praise = *anuṣṭubh* meter = no god = Shūdra = no season

anatomical body parts ⇒ hymns of praise = meters = gods = social classes = seasons

Cosmogony VI

(JB 1.68–69)

Prajāpati, in the beginning, was this [all]. . . . He desired, "May I become many; may I reproduce myself; may I become a multitude." He emitted from his head, from his mouth, the nine-versed hymn of praise, the *gāyatrī* meter, the *rathantara* chant (*sāman*), Agni among the gods, the Brahmin among men, the goat among the animals. Therefore the Brahmin meter is the *gāyatrī* and the divinity is related to Agni. Therefore the mouth is generation, for from the mouth he [Prajāpati] emitted him [the Brahmin]. He desired, "May I propagate myself further." He emitted from his arms, from his chest, the fifteen-versed hymn of praise, the *triṣṭubh* meter, the *bṛhat* chant, Indra among the gods, the Kshatriya among men, the horse among animals. Therefore the Kshatriya meter is the *triṣṭubh* and the divinity is related to Indra. Therefore he [Prajāpati] made from his arms virility (*vīrya*), for he emitted him [the Kshatriya] from the arms, the chest, the virility. He desired, "May I propagate myself further." He emitted from his belly, from his middle, the seventeenfold hymn of praise, the *jagatī* meter the *vāmadevya* chant, the Viśva Devas among the gods, the Vaishya among men, the cow among animals. Therefore the Vaishya meter is the *jagatī* and the divinity is related to the Viśva Devas. Therefore [the Vaishya is] procreative, for from his [Prajāpati's] belly, from his penis he emitted him. He desired, "May I propagate myself further." He emitted from his feet, from his firm foundation, the twenty-one-versed hymn of praise, the *anuṣṭubh* meter, the *yajñayajñiya* chant, not a single one among the gods, the Shūdra among men, the sheep among animals. Therefore the Shūdra meter is the *anuṣṭubh* and the divinity is related to the Lord of the House (*veśmapati*). Therefore he [the Shūdra] seeks to make a living washing feet, for from the feet, from the firm foundation, he [Prajāpati] emitted him. With these emitted ones Prajāpati emitted the creatures.

Scheme of Cosmogony VI

1. head/mouth (generation) ⇒ nine-versed hymn of praise = *gāyatrī* meter = *rathantara* chant = Agni = Brahmin = goat
2. arms/chest (virility) ⇒ fifteen-versed hymn of praise = *triṣṭubh* meter = *bṛhat* chant = Indra = Kshatriya = horse

3. belly/middle/penis (procreation) ⇒ seventeen-versed hymn of praise = *jagatī* meter = *vāmadevya* chant = Viśva Devas = cow
4. feet/firm foundation (feet washing) ⇒ twenty-one-versed hymn of praise = *anuṣṭubh* meter = *yajñayajñiya* chant = no god = Shūdra = sheep

anatomical body parts (and correlative characteristics) ⇒ hymns of praise = meters = chants = gods = social classes = animals

Cosmogony VII

(TS 7.1.1.4–6)

Prajāpati desired, "May I produce offspring." He measured out from his mouth the nine-versed hymn of praise; along with it he emitted Agni among the gods, the *gāyatrī* among the meters, the *rathantara* chant, the Brahmin among men, the goat among the animals. Therefore they are foremost (or "belonging to the mouth," *mukhya*), for they were emitted from the mouth. From the chest, from the arms, he measured out the fifteen-versed hymn of praise; along with it he emitted Indra among the gods, the *triṣṭubh* meter, the *bṛhat* chant, the Kshatriya among men, the sheep among the animals. Therefore they are filled with virility, for they were emitted from virility. From the belly he measured out the seventeen-versed hymn of praise; along with it he emitted the Viśva Devas among the gods, the *jagatī* meter, the *vairūpa* chant, the Vaishya among men, the cow among the animals. Therefore they are to be eaten, for they were emitted from the receptacle of food. Therefore they are more abundant than others, for they were emitted along with the most abundant among the gods. From the feet he measured out the twenty-one-versed hymn of praise; along with it he emitted the *anuṣṭubh* meter, the *vairāja* chant, the Shūdra among men, the horse among the animals. Therefore these two, the horse and the Shūdra, are dependent on those who were already created. Therefore the Shūdra is unfit for the sacrifice, for he was emitted along with no gods. Therefore they depend on the feet, for they were emitted from the feet.

Scheme of Cosmogony VII

1. mouth (primacy) ⇒ nine-versed hymn of praise = Agni = *gāyatrī* meter = *rathantara* chant = Brahmin = goat
2. chest/arms (virility) ⇒ fifteen-versed hymn of praise = Indra = *triṣṭubh* meter = *bṛhat* chant = Kshatriya = sheep
3. belly (food and abundance) ⇒ seventeen-versed hymn of praise = Viśva Devas = *jagatī* meter = *vairūpa* chant = Vaishya = cow
4. feet (dependency) ⇒ twenty-one-versed hymn of praise = no god = *anuṣṭubh* meter = *vairāja* chant = Shūdra = horse

anatomical body parts (and corresponding characteristics) ⇒ hymns of praise = gods = meters = chants = social classes = animals

Cosmogony VIII

(ŚB 5.4.1.3–7/VS 10.10–14; with variants at MS 2.6.10; TS 1.8.13; KS 15.7; TB 1.7.7)

He then makes him ascend to the regions [with the following mantras from VS 10.10–14]: "Ascend to the East! May the *gāyatrī* [meter] impel you, the *rathantara* chant, the nine-versed hymn of praise, [Agni the deity,] the spring season, the *brahman* power (*draviṇa*). Ascend to the south! May the *triṣṭubh* [meter] impel you, the *bṛhat* chant, the fifteen-versed hymn of praise, [Indra the deity,] the summer season, the *kṣatra* power. Ascend to the west! May the *jagatī* [meter] impel you, the *vairūpa* chant, the seventeen-versed hymn of praise, [the Maruts the deity,] the rainy season, the power of the *viś*. Ascend to the north! May the *anuṣṭubh* [meter] impel you, the *vairāja* chant, the twenty-one-versed hymn of praise, [Mitra and Varuṇa the deity,] the autumn season, fruit [*phala*, variants read *puṣṭa* or *bala*] the power. Ascend to the zenith! May the *paṅkti* (meter) impel you, the *śakvara* and *raivata* chants, the twenty-seven- and thirty-three-versed hymns of praise, the winter and cool seasons, [Bṛhaspati the deity,] splendor [*varcas*, variants read *phala*] the power.

Scheme of Cosmogony VIII

1. east = *gāyatrī* meter = nine-versed hymn of praise = *rathantara* chant = Agni = spring = the *brahman*
2. south = *triṣṭubh* meter = fifteen-versed hymn of praise = *bṛhat* chant = Indra = summer = the *kṣatra*
3. west = *jagatī* meter = seventeen-versed hymn of praise = *vairūpa* chant = Maruts = rainy season = the *viś*
4. north = *anuṣṭubh* meter = twenty-one-versed hymn of praise = *vairāja* chant = Mitra-Varuṇa = autumn = *phala*, *bala*, or *puṣṭa*
5. zenith = *paṅkti* meter = twenty-seven- and thirty-three-versed hymn of praise = *śakvara* and *raivata* chants = Bṛhaspati = winter and cool seasons = *varcas* or *phala*

directions = meters = hymns of praise = chants = gods = seasons = metaphysical powers

Cosmogony IX

(TS 4.3.2.1–3; cf. ŚB 8.1.1–2)

This one [I put] to the east, [Prajāpati] the existent one. His breath [is born] from the existent one. From the breath [is born] spring; from spring [comes] the *gāyatrī* [meter]. From the *gāyatrī* [is born] the *gāyatra* [chant]; from the *gāyatra* [comes] the *upāṃśu* [soma cup]. From the *upāṃśu* [is born] the nine-versed [hymn of praise]; from the nine-versed [comes] the *rathantara* [chant]. From the *rathantara* [is born] the *ṛṣi* Vasiṣṭha. . . This one [I put] to the south, [Prajāpati] the all-doer. His mind (*manas*) [is born] from the all-doer. From the mind [is born] the summer; from the summer [comes] the *triṣṭubh* [meter]. From the *triṣṭubh* [is born] the *aiḍa* [chant]; from the *aiḍa* [comes] the *antaryāma* [soma cup]. From the *antaryāma* [is born] the fifteen-versed [hymn of praise]; from the fifteen-versed [comes] the *bṛhat* [chant]. From the *bṛhat* [is born] the *ṛṣi* Bharadvāja. . . . This one [I put] to the west, [Prajāpati] the all-encompassing. His eye (or sight) [is born] from the all-encompassing. From the eye (or sight) [is born] the rainy season; from the rainy season [comes] the *jagatī* [meter]. From the *jagatī* [is born] the *ṛksāma* [chant]; from the *ṛksāma* [comes] the *śukra* [soma cup]. From the *śukra* [is born] the seventeen-versed [hymn of praise]; from the seventeen-versed [comes] the *vairūpa* [chant]. From the *vairūpa* [is born] the *ṛṣi* Viśvamitra. . . . This one [I put] to the north, [Prajāpati] the light (*suva*). His ear (or hearing) [is born] from the light. From the ear (or hearing) [is born] autumn; from autumn [comes] the *anuṣṭubh* [meter]. From the *anuṣṭubh* [is born] the *svāra* [chant]; from the *svāra* [comes] the *manthin* [soma cup]. From the *manthin* [is born] the twenty-one-versed [hymn of praise]; from the twenty-one-verse [comes] the *vairāja* [chant]. From the *vairāja* [is born] the *ṛṣi* Jamadagni. . . . This one [I put] up, [Prajāpati who is] thought. His speech [is born] from thought. From speech [is born] the winter; from the winter [comes] the *paṅkti* [meter]. From the *paṅkti* [is born] the conclusion of the chants (*nidhāna*); from the conclusion [comes] the *āgrayaṇa* [soma cup]. From the *āgrayaṇa* [is born] the twenty-seven-versed and thirty-three-versed [hymns of praise]. From the twenty-seven-versed and thirty-three-versed [are born] the *śakvara* and *raivata* [chants]; from the *śakvara* and *raivata* [comes] the *ṛṣi* Raivata Viśvakarman.

Scheme of Cosmogony IX

1. east ⇒ breath ⇒ spring ⇒ *gāyatrī* meter ⇒ *gāyatra* chant ⇒ *upāṃśu* soma cup ⇒ nine-versed hymn of praise ⇒ *rathantara* chant ⇒ the seer Vasiṣṭha
2. south ⇒ mind ⇒ summer ⇒ *triṣṭubh* meter ⇒ *aiḍa* chant ⇒ *antaryāma* soma cup ⇒ fifteen-versed hymn of praise ⇒ *bṛhat* chant ⇒ the seer Bharadvāja
3. west ⇒ eye (or sight) ⇒ rainy season ⇒ *jagatī* meter ⇒ *ṛksāma* chant ⇒ *śukra* soma cup ⇒ seventeen-versed hymn of praise ⇒ *vairūpa* chant ⇒ the seer Viśvamitra
4. north ⇒ ear (or hearing) ⇒ autumn ⇒ *anuṣṭubh* meter ⇒ *svāra* chant ⇒ *manthin* soma cup ⇒ twenty-one-versed hymn of praise ⇒ *vairāja* chant ⇒ the seer Jamadagni
5. zenith ⇒ thought and speech ⇒ winter ⇒ *paṅkti* meter ⇒ conclusion of chants ⇒ *āgrayaṇa* soma cup ⇒ twenty-seven-versed and thirty-three-versed hymns of praise ⇒ the *śakvara* and *raivata* chants ⇒ the seer Raivata Viśvakarman

directions ⇒ body functions ⇒ seasons ⇒ meters ⇒ chants ⇒ soma cups ⇒ hymns of praise ⇒ chants ⇒ seers

Cosmogony X

(MS 2.7.20; with variant at TS 4.3.3.1–2)

The eastern quarter, the spring season, Agni the divinity, the *brahman* the power (*draviṇa*), the *gāyatrī* the meter, the *rathantara* the chant, the nine-versed the hymn of praise, which is the track (*vartanī*) of the fifteen-versed [hymn of praise], Sanaga the seer (*ṛṣi*), the eighteen-month-old calf the vitality (*vāyas*), of the throws of dice the *kṛta*, the east wind the wind. . . . The southern quarter, the summer season, Indra the divinity, the *kṣatra* the power, the *triṣṭubh* the meter, the *bṛhat* the chant, the fifteen-versed the hymn of praise, which is the track of the seventeen-fold [hymn of praise], Sanātana the seer, the two-year-old cow the vitality, of the throws of dice the *treta*, the south wind the wind. . . . The western quarter, the rainy season, the Viśva Devas the divinity, the *viś* the power, the *jagatī* the meter, the *vairūpa* the chant, the seventeen-versed the hymn of praise, which is the track of the twenty-one-versed [hymn of praise], Ahabhūna the seer, the three-year-old cow the vitality, of the throws of dice the *dvāpara*, the west wind the wind. . . . The northern quarter, the autumn season, Mitra and Varuṇa the divinities, prosperity (*puṣṭa*) the power, the *anuṣṭubh* the meter, the *vairāja* the chant, the twenty-one-versed the hymn of praise, which is the track of the twenty-seven-versed [hymn of praise], Purāṇa the seer, the four-year-old cow the vitality, among the throws of dice the *abhibhava* [variant: the *āskanda*], the north wind the wind. . . . The zenith quarter, the winter and the cool seasons, Bṛhaspati the divinity, fruit (*phala*) [variant: splendor (*varcas*)] the power, the *paṅkti* the meter, the *śakvara* and *raivata* the chants, the twenty-seven-versed the hymn of praise, which is the track of the thirty-three-versed [hymn of praise], Suparṇa the seer, the four-year-old bull the vitality, among the throws of dice the *āskanda* [variant: the *abhibhū*], the wind from above the wind.

Scheme of Cosmogony X

1. east = spring = Agni = the *brahman* = *gāyatrī* meter = *rathantara* chant = nine-versed hymn of praise = track of fifteen-versed hymn of praise = Sanaga the seer = eighteen-month-old calf = *kṛta* dice throw = east wind
2. south = summer = Indra = the *kṣatra* = *triṣṭubh* meter = *bṛhat* chant = fifteen-verse hymn of praise = track of seventeen-versed hymn of praise = Sanātana the seer = two-year-old cow = *treta* dice throw = south wind

3. west = rainy season = Viśva Devas = the *viś* = *jagatī* meter = *vairūpa* chant = seventeen-versed hymn of praise = track of twenty-one-versed hymn of praise = Ahabhūna the seer = three-year-old cow = *dvāpara* dice throw = west wind

4. north = autumn = Mitra and Varuṇa = prosperity (*puṣṭa*) = *anuṣṭubh* meter = *vairāja* chant = twenty-one-versed hymn of praise = track of twenty-seven-versed hymn of praise = Purāṇa [var. Pratna] the seer = four-year-old cow = *abhibhava* [var. *āskanda*] dice throw = north wind

5. zenith = winter and cool seasons = Bṛhaspati = fruit (*phala*) [var. splendor (*varcas*)] = *paṅkti* meter = *śakvara* and *raivata* chants = twenty-seven-versed hymn of praise = track of thirty-three-versed hymn of praise = Suparna the seer = four-year-old bull = *āskanda* [var. *abhibhū*] dice throw = wind from above

directions = seasons = gods = metaphysical powers = meters = chants = hymns of praise = derivative hymns of praise = seers = type of cow = dice throw = wind

Cosmogony XI

(ŚB 8.6.1.5–9/VS 15.10–14)

To the east he lays down [a brick]. . . . [He says the mantra that begins] "The Vasus are your gods and overlords," for the Vasus are indeed the gods and overlords of that region. "Agni is the repeller of arrows," for Agni, indeed, is here the repeller of arrows. "May the nine-versed hymn of praise support you on earth," for by the nine-versed hymn of praise it is indeed supported on earth. "May the *ājya* recitation (*uktha*) prop you for steadiness," for by the *ājya* recitation it is indeed propped up on earth for steadiness. "The *rathantara* chant for a firm foundation in the atmosphere," for by the *rathantara* hymn it is indeed firmly established in the atmosphere. . . . . Then on the south side [he places a brick]. . . . [He says those mantras that begin] "The divine Rudras are your overlords." . . . "Indra is the repeller of shafts." . . . "The fifteen-versed hymn of praise may uphold you on earth." . . . "The *prauga* recitation may support you for steadiness's sake." . . . "The *bṛhat* chant for stability in the atmosphere." . . . Then to the west [he places a brick]. . . . [He says those mantras that begin] "The divine Ādityas are your overlords." . . . "Varuṇa is the repeller of shafts." . . . "The seventeen-versed hymn of praise may uphold you on earth." . . . . "The *marutvatīya* recitation may support you for steadiness's sake." . . . "The *vairūpa* chant for stability in the atmosphere." . . . Then to the north [he places a brick]. . . . [He says those mantras that begin] "The divine Maruts are your overlords." . . . "Soma is the repeller of shafts." . . . "The twenty-one-versed hymn of praise may uphold you on earth." . . . "The *niṣkevalya* recitation may support you for steadiness's sake." . . . "The *vairāja* chant for stability in the atmosphere." . . . Then in the middle [he places a brick]. . . . [He says those mantras that begin] "The Viśva Devas are your overlords." . . . "Bṛhaspati is the repeller of shafts." . . . "The twenty-seven-versed and thirty-three-versed hymns of praise may uphold you on earth." . . . "The *vaiśvadeva* and *āgnimāruta* recitations may support you for steadiness' sake." . . . "The *śakvara* and *raivata* chants for stability in the atmosphere."

Scheme of Cosmogony XI

1. east = Vasus and Agni = nine-versed hymn of praise = *ājya* recitation = *rathantara* chant

2. south = Rudras and Indra = fifteen-versed hymn of praise = *prauga* recitation = *bṛhat* chant

3. west = Ādityas and Varuṇa = seventeen-versed hymn of praise = *marutvatīya* recitation = *vairūpa* chant

4. north = Maruts and Soma = twenty-one-versed hymn of praise = *niṣkevalya* recitation = *vairāja* chant

5. middle = Viśva Devas and Bṛhaspati = twenty-seven-versed and thirty-three-versed hymns of praise = *vaiśvadeva* and *āgnimāruta* recitations = *śakvara* and *raivata* chants

directions = gods = hymns of praise = recitations = chants

Cosmogony XII

(MaitU 7.1–6)

From the east arise Agni, the *gāyatrī* [meter], the nine-versed [hymn of praise], the *rathantara* [chant], the spring, inspiration (*prāṇa*), the constellations (*nakṣatras*), and the Vasus. . . . From the south arise Indra, the *triṣṭubh* [meter], the fifteen-versed [hymn of praise], the *bṛhat* [chant], the summer, the circulating breath (*vyāna*), the moon (*soma*), and the Rudras. . . . From the west arise the Maruts, the *jagatī* [meter], the seventeen-versed [hymn of praise], the *vairūpa* [chant], the rainy season, expiration (*apāna*), the planet Venus, and the Ādityas. . . . From the north arise the Viśva Devas, the *anuṣṭubh* [meter], the twenty-one-versed [hymn of praise], the *vairāja* [chant], autumn, the digestive breath (*samāna*), and Varuṇa and the Sādhyas. . . . From the zenith arise Mitra and Varuṇa, the *paṅkti* [meter], the twenty-seven- and thirty-three-versed [hymns of praise], the *śakvara* and *raivata* [chants], the winter and cool seasons, the upward breath (*udāna*), the Angirases, and the moon. . . . From the nadir arise the planet Saturn, eclipses (*rāhus*), comets (*ketus*), serpents, demons (*rakṣases*), spirits (*yakṣases*), humans, birds, eight-legged mountain goats (*śarabhas*), elephants and so forth.

Scheme of Cosmogony XII

1. east ⇒ Agni = *gāyatrī* meter = nine-versed hymn of praise = *rathantara* chant = spring = inhalation = constellations = Vasus
2. south ⇒ Indra = *triṣṭubh* meter = fifteen-versed hymn of praise = *bṛhat* chant = summer = the circulating breath = moon = Rudras
3. west ⇒ Maruts = *jagatī* meter = seventeen-versed hymn of praise = *vairūpa* chant = rainy season = exhalation = Venus = Ādityas
4. north ⇒ Viśva Devas = *anuṣṭubh* meter = twenty-one-versed hymn of praise = *vairāja* chant = autumn = the digestive breath = Varuṇa and the Sādhyas
5. zenith ⇒ Mitra and Varuṇa = *paṅkti* meter = 27- and thirty-three-versed hymns of praise = *śakvara* and *raivata* chants = winter and the cool season = the upward breath = Angirases = moon
6. nadir ⇒ Saturn = eclipses = comets = serpents = demons = spirits = humans, birds, eight-legged mountain goats, elephants, etc.

directions ⇒ gods = meters = hymns of praise = chants = seasons = breaths = astronomical bodies = groups of gods

Cosmogony XIII

(KB 22.1, 22.5, 22.9, 23.3, 23.8)

They obtain the earth by means of the first day [of the soma sacrifice], the *gāyatrī* meter, the nine-versed hymn of praise, the *rathantara* chant, the eastern quarter, the spring of seasons, the Vasus the gods, Agni, born of the gods, the overlord. . . . They obtain the atmosphere by means of the second day, the *triṣṭubh* meter, the fifteen-versed hymn of praise, the *bṛhat* chant, the southern quarter, the summer of the seasons, the Maruts the gods, Indra, born of the gods, the overlord. . . . They obtain the sky by means of the third day, the *jagatī* meter, the seventeen-versed hymn of praise, the *vairūpa* chant, the western quarter, the rains of the seasons, the Ādityas the gods, Varuṇa, born of the gods, the overlord. . . . They obtain food by means of the fourth day, the *anuṣṭubh* meter, the twenty-one-versed hymn of praise, the *vairāja* chant, the northern quarter, the autumn of seasons, the Sādhya and Ājya gods, Bṛhaspati and the moon, born of the gods, the overlords. . . . They obtain animals by means of the fifth day, the *paṅkti* meter, the twenty-seven-versed hymn of praise, the *śakvara* chant, the zenith quarter, the winter of seasons, the Maruts the gods, Rudra, born of the gods, the overlord. . . . They obtain the waters by means of the sixth day, the *atichandas* meter, the thirty-three-versed hymn of praise, the *raivata* chant, the zenith of the quarters, the cool season, the Viśva Devas, Prajāpati, born of the gods, the overlord.

Scheme of Cosmogony XIII

1. first day = earth = *gāyatrī* meter = nine-versed hymn of praise = *rathantara* chant = east = spring = Vasus and Agni
2. second day = atmosphere = *triṣṭubh* meter = fifteen-versed hymn of praise = *bṛhat* chant = south = summer = Maruts and Indra
3. third day = sky = *jagatī* meter = seventeen-versed hymn of praise = *vairūpa* chant = west = rainy season = Ādityas and Varuṇa
4. fourth day = food = *anuṣṭubh* meter = twenty-one-versed hymn of praise = *vairāja* chant = north = autumn = Sādhyas and Ājyas and Bṛhaspati and the moon

5. fifth day = animals = *paṅkti* meter = twenty-seven-versed hymn of praise = *śakvara* chant = zenith = winter = Maruts and Rudra

6. sixth day = waters = *atichandas* meter = thirty-three-versed hymn of praise = *raivata* chant = zenith = cool season = Viśva Devas and Prajāpati

day of ritual = cosmological worlds = meters = hymns of praise = chants = directions = seasons = gods

Bibliography

Sanskrit Texts and Translations

Aitareya Āraṇyaka. Ed. and trans. by A. B. Keith. Oxford: Clarendon Press, 1909; reprint Oxford: Oxford University Press, 1969.

Aitareya Brāhmaṇa. 2 vols. Ānandāśrama-saṃskṛta-granthāvaliḥ, granthānkha 32. Poona: Ānandāśrama, 1931.

———. Trans. by A. B. Keith. In *Ṛgveda Brāhmaṇas*. Harvard Oriental Series, Vol. 25. Cambridge, Mass.: Harvard University Press, 1920; reprint Delhi: Motilal Banarsidass, 1971.

Aitareya Upaniṣad. Ed. by V. P. Limaye and R. D. Vadekar. In *Eighteen Principal Upaniṣads*. Poona: Vaidika Saṃśodhana Maṇḍala, 1958.

———. Trans. by Robert Hume. In *The Thirteen Principal Upanishads*, 2d ed. Oxford: Oxford University Press, 1931.

Āpastamba Dharma Sūtra. Ed. by U. C. Pandeya. Kashi Sanskrit Series, no. 93. Varanasi: Chowkhamba Sanskrit Series Office, 1969.

———. Trans. by Georg Bühler. In *The Sacred Books of the Āryas*. Sacred Books of the East, Vol. 2. Oxford: Clarendon Press, 1879; reprint Delhi: Motilal Banarsidass, 1965.

Āpastamba Gṛhya Sūtra. Ed. by U. C. Pandey. Kashi Sanskrit Series, no. 59. Varanasi: Chowkhamba Sanskrit Series Office, 1971.

———. Trans. by Hermann Oldenberg. In *The Gṛhya Sūtras*. Sacred Books of the East, Vol. 30. Oxford: Oxford University Press, 1886; reprint Delhi: Motilal Banarsidass, 1964.

Āpastamba Śrauta Sūtra. 3 vols. Ed. by R. Garbe. Calcutta: Royal Asiatic Society of Bengal, 1882–1902.

———. 3 vols. Trans. into German by W. Caland. Calcutta: Vandenhoeck and Ruprecht, 1921; reprint Wiesbaden: Dr. Martin Sandig, 1969.

Āśvalāyana Gṛhya Sūtra. Ed. and trans. by N. N. Sharma. Delhi: Eastern Book Linkers, 1976.

———. Trans. by Hermann Oldenberg. In *The Gṛhya Sūtras*. Sacred Books of the East, Vol. 29. Oxford: Oxford University Press, 1886; reprint Delhi: Motilal Banarsidass, 1964.

Āśvalāyana Śrauta Sūtra. Ed. by R. Vidyaratna. Calcutta: Asiatic Society of Bengal, 1874.

———. Incomplete trans. by H. G. Ranade. Poona: R. H. Ranade, 1981.

Atharva Veda Saṃhitā (Paippalāda recension). Ed. by Raghu Vira. New Delhi: Meharchand Lachhmandas, 1976.

Atharva Veda Saṃhitā (Śaunaka recension). 4 vols. Ed. by V. Bandhu. Hoshiarpur: Vishveshvaranand Vedic Research Institute, 1960–62.

———. 2 vols. Trans. by W. D. Whitney. Harvard Oriental Series, Vols. 7 and 8. Cambridge, Mass.: Harvard University Press, 1905; reprint Delhi: Motilal Banarsidass, 1962.

Baudhāyana Dharma Sūtra. Ed. by U. C. Pandeya. Kashi Sanskrit Series, no. 104. Varanasi: Chowkhamba Sanskrit Series Office, 1972.

———. Trans. by Georg Bühler. In *The Sacred Books of the Āryas*. Sacred Books of the East, Vol. 14. Oxford: Clarendon Press, 1879; reprint Delhi: Motilal Banarsidass, 1965.

Baudhāyana Gṛhya, Paribhāṣā, Śeṣa, and Pitṛmedha Sūtras. Ed. by R. Shama Sastri. Mysore: Government Branch Press, 1920; reprint New Delhi: Meharchand Lachhmandas, 1982.

Baudhāyana Śrauta Sūtra. 3 vols. Ed. by W. Caland. Calcutta: Asiatic Society of Bengal, 1904–24; reprint New Delhi: Munshiram Manoharlal, 1982.

Bhagavad Gītā. Ed. and trans. by J. A. B. van Buitenen. Chicago: University of Chicago Press, 1981.

Bhāradvāja Gṛhya Sūtra. Ed. by H. J. W. Salomons. Leyden: E. J. Brill, 1913; reprint Delhi: Meharchand Lachhmandas, 1981.

Bhāradvāja Śrauta Sūtra. Ed. and trans. by C. G. Kashikar. Poona: Vaidika Saṃśodhana Maṇḍala, 1964.

Bṛhadāraṇyaka Upaniṣad. Ed. by V. P. Limaye and R. D. Vadekar. In *Eighteen Principal Upaniṣads*. Poona: Vaidika Saṃśodhana Maṇḍala, 1958.

———. Trans. by Robert Hume. In *The Thirteen Principal Upanishads*, 2d ed. Oxford: Oxford University Press, 1931.

Bṛhat Saṃhitā. Ed. and trans. by M. Ramakrishna Bhat. Delhi: Motilal Banarsidass, 1981–82.

Chandogya Upaniṣad. Ed. by V. P. Limaye and R. D. Vadekar. In *Eighteen Principal Upaniṣads*. Poona: Vaidika Saṃśodhana Maṇḍala, 1958.

———. Trans. by Robert Hume. In *The Thirteen Principal Upanishads*, 2d ed. Oxford: Oxford University Press, 1931.

Gautama Dharma Sūtra. Ed. by Manmatha Nath Dutt. In *The Dharma Śāstra Texts*. Calcutta: M. N. Dutt, 1908.

———. Trans. by Georg Bühler. In *The Sacred Books of the Āryas*. Sacred Books of the East, Vol. 14. Oxford: Clarendon Press, 1879; reprint Delhi: Motilal Banarsidass, 1965.

Gobhila Gṛhya Sūtra. Ed. by Chintamani Bhattacharya. Calcutta: Metropolitan Printing and Publishing House, 1936.

———. Trans. by Hermann Oldenberg. In *The Gṛhya Sūtras*. Sacred Books of the East, Vol. 30. Oxford: Oxford University Press, 1886; reprint Delhi: Motilal Banarsidass, 1964.

Gopatha Brāhmaṇa. Ed. by R. Mitra and H. Vidyabhusana. Calcutta: Bibliotheca Indica, 1872; reprint Delhi: Indological Book House, 1972.

Hiraṇyakeśin Śrauta and Gṛhya Sūtras. 10 vols. Ed. by K. Agase and S. Marulakara. Poona: Ānandāśrama, 1907–32.

Jaiminīya Brāhmaṇa. Ed. by R. Vira and L. Chandra. Nagpur: Sarasvati Vihara Series, 1954.

———. Incomplete trans. by H. W. Bodewitz. In *Jaiminīya Brāhmaṇa I: 1–65*. Leiden: E. J. Brill, 1973.

———. Incomplete trans. by H. W. Bodewitz. In *The Jyotiṣṭoma Ritual: Jaiminīya Brāhmaṇa* I,66–364. Leiden: E. J. Brill, 1990.

Jaiminīya Gṛhya Sūtra. Ed. and trans. by W. Caland. Punjab Sanskrit Series, no. 2. Lahore: Moti Lal Banarsi Dass, 1922; reprint Delhi: Motilal Banarsidass, 1984.

Jaimini Mīmāṃsā Sūtras. 2 vols. Ed. and trans. by Mohan Lal Sandal. Reprint Delhi: Motilal Banarsidass, 1980.

Jaiminīya Śrauta Sūtra. Ed. by Premnidhi Shastri. In *Jaiminīya-Śrauta-Sūtra-Vṛtti of Bhavatrāta*. Śata-Piṭaka Series, Vol. 40. New Delhi: International Academy of Indian Culture, 1966.

Jaiminīya Upaniṣad Brāhmaṇa. Ed. and trans. by Hanns Oertel. *Journal of the American Oriental Society* 16 (1896): 79–260.

Kātha Upaniṣad. Ed. by V. P. Limaye and R. D. Vadekar. In *Eighteen Principal Upaniṣads*. Poona: Vaidika Saṃśodhana Maṇḍala, 1958.

———. Trans. by Robert Hume. In *The Thirteen Principal Upanishads*, 2d ed. Oxford: Oxford University Press, 1931.

Kāṭhaka Gṛhya Sūtra. Ed. by W. Caland. Lahore: Research Depts., D. A. V. College, 1925.

Kāṭhaka Saṃhitā. Ed. by V. Santavalekar. Bombay: Bhāratamudraṇālayam, 1943.

Kātyāyana Śrauta Sūtra. Ed. by Albrecht Weber. Chowkhamba Sanskrit Series, no. 104. Reprint Varanasi: Chowkhamba Sanskrit Series Office, 1972.

———. Trans. by H. G. Ranade. Pune: Dr. H. G. Ranade and R. H. Ranade, n.d.

Kauśika Sūtra. Ed. by Maurice Bloomfield. Reprint Delhi: Motilal Banarsidass, 1972.

Kauṣītaki Brāhmaṇa. Ed. by H. Bhattacharya. Calcutta Sanskrit College Research Series, no. 73. Calcutta: Sanskrit College, 1970.

———. Trans. by A. B. Keith. In *Ṛgveda Brāhmaṇas*. Harvard Oriental Series, Vol. 25. Cambridge, Mass.: Harvard University Press, 1920; reprint Delhi: Motilal Banarsidass, 1971.

Kauṣītaki Upaniṣad. Ed. by V. P. Limaye and R. D. Vadekar. In *Eighteen Principal Upaniṣads*. Poona: Vaidika Saṃśodhana Maṇḍala, 1958.

———. Trans. by Robert Hume. In *The Thirteen Principal Upanishads*, 2d ed. Oxford: Oxford University Press, 1931.

Kauṭiliya Artha Śāstra. 2d ed. 3 vols. Ed. and trans. by R. P. Kangle. Reprint Delhi: Motilal Banarsidass, 1986.

Khādira Gṛhya Sūtra. Ed. by A. M. Sastri and L. Srinivasacharya. Mysore: Government Branch Press, 1913.

———. Trans. by Hermann Oldenberg. In *The Gṛhya Sūtras*. Sacred Books of the East, Vol. 29. Oxford: Oxford University Press, 1886; reprint Delhi: Motilal Banarsidass, 1964.

Kūrma Purāṇa. Ed. by Sri Anand Swarup Gupta; trans. by Sri Ahibhusham Bhattacharya et al. Varanasi: All-India Kashi Trust, 1972.

Lātyāyana Śrauta Sūtra. Ed. by Anandachandra Vedantavagisa. Calcutta: Asiatic Society of Bengal, 1972.

Mahābhārata. Ed. by Vishnu S. Sukthankar. 19 vols. Poona: Bhandarkar Oriental Research Institute, 1933–60.

Maitrāyaṇī Saṃhitā. Ed. by Sripada Damodara Satavalekara. Delhi: Prakashaka Svadhyaya Mandala, n.d.

Maitrāyaṇī Upaniṣad. Ed. by V. P. Limaye and R. D. Vadekar. In *Eighteen Principal Upaniṣads*. Poona: Vaidika Saṃśodhana Maṇḍala, 1958.

———. Trans. by Robert Hume. In *The Thirteen Principal Upanishads*, 2d ed. Oxford: Oxford University Press, 1931.

Mānava Gṛhya Sūtra. Ed. by R. H. Shastri. Reprint Delhi: Meharchand Lacchmandas, 1982.

———. Trans. by M. J. Dresden. Groningen: J. B. Wolters Uitgevers, 1941.

Mānava Śrauta Sūtra. Ed. and trans. by J. M. van Geldner. Śata-Piṭaka Series, Vol. 27. New Delhi: International Academy of Indian Culture, 1963.

Manu Smṛti. 5 vols. Ed. by J. H. Dave. Bhāratīya Vidyā Series. Bombay: Bhāratīya Vidyā Bhavan, 1972–82.

———. Trans. by Wendy Doniger with Brian K. Smith. London: Penguin Books, 1991.

Mārkaṇḍeya Purāṇa. Trans. by F. Eden Pargiter. Reprint Delhi: Indological Book House, 1969.

Matsya Purāṇa. Ed. by Rama Sarma Acarya. Bareli: Saṃskṛti Saṃsthāna, 1970.

Pañcaviṃśa Brāhmaṇa. 2 vols. Ed. by P. A. Cinnaswami Sastri and P. Pattachirama Sastri. Kashi Sanskrit Series, no. 105. Benares: Sanskrit Series Office, 1935.

———. Trans. by W. Caland. Bibliotheca Indica, no. 255. Calcutta: Asiatic Society of Bengal, 1931.

Pāraskāra Gṛhya Sūtra. Ed. by M. G. Bakre. Bombay: Gujrati Printing Press, 1917; reprint Delhi: Meharchand Lachhmandas, 1982.

———. Trans. by Hermann Oldenberg. In *The Gṛhya Sūtras*. Sacred Books of the East, Vol. 29. Oxford: Oxford University Press, 1886; reprint Delhi: Motilal Banarsidass, 1964.

Praśna Upaniṣad. Ed. by V. P. Limaye and R. D. Vadekar. In *Eighteen Principal Upaniṣads*. Poona: Vaidika Saṃśodhana Maṇḍala, 1958.

———. Trans. by Robert Hume. In *The Thirteen Principal Upanishads*, 2d ed. Oxford: Oxford University Press, 1931.

Ṛg Veda Saṃhitā. 4 vols. Ed. by F. Max Müller. Chowkhamba Sanskrit Series, Vol. 99. Reprint Varanasi: Chowkhamba Sanskrit Series Office, 1966.

———. 4 vols. Trans. into German by Karl Friedrich Geldner. Harvard Oriental Office, Vols. 33–36. Cambridge, Mass.: Harvard University Press, 1951–57.

———. Partial trans. by Wendy Doniger O'Flaherty. New York: Penguin Books, 1981.

Ṣaḍviṃśa Brāhmaṇa. Ed. by B. R. Sharma. Kendriya Sanskrit Vidyapeetha Series, no. 9. Tirupati: Kendriya Sanskrit Vidyapeetha, 1967.

Śāṅkhāyana Āraṇyaka. Ed. by Bhim Dev. Hoshiarpur: Vishveshvaranand Vedic Research Institute, 1980.

———. Trans. by A. B. Keith. Reprint New Delhi: Oriental Books Reprint Corp., 1975.

Śāṅkhāyana Gṛhya Sūtra. Ed. and trans. by S. R. Sehgal. Delhi: Munshiram Manoharlal, 1960.

———. Trans. by Hermann Oldenberg. In *The Gṛhya Sūtras*. Sacred Books of the East, Vol. 29. Oxford: Oxford University Press, 1886; reprint Delhi: Motilal Banarsidass, 1964.

Śāṅkhāyana Śrauta Sūtra. 2 vols. Ed. by A. Hillebrandt. Reprint New Delhi: Meharchand Lachhmandas, 1981.

———. Trans. by W. Caland. Nagpur: International Academy of Indian Literature, 1953; reprint Delhi: Motilal Banarsidass, 1980.

Śatapatha Brāhmaṇa (Kāṇva recension). Ed. by W. Caland; rev. by Raghu Vira. Delhi: Motilal Banarsidass, 1983.

Śatapatha Brāhmaṇa (Mādhyaṇdina recension). 5 vols. Bombay: Laxmi Venkateshwar Steam Press, 1940.

———. 5 vols. Trans. by Julius Eggeling. Sacred Books of the East, Vols. 12, 26, 41, 43, 44. Oxford: Clarendon Press, 1882–1900; reprint Delhi: Motilal Banarsidass, 1963.

Śrautakośa. 2 vols. Ed. by R. N. Dandekar. Poona: Vaidika Saṃśodhana Maṇḍala, 1958–82.

Taittirīya Āraṇyaka. 2 vols. Ānandāśrama-saṃskṛta-granthāvaliḥ, granthānkha 36. Poona: Ānandāśrama, 1981.

Taittirīya Brāhmaṇa. 3 vols. Ānandāśrama-saṃskṛta-granthāvaliḥ, granthānkha 37. Poona: Ānandāśrama, 1979.

———. Partial trans. by P.-E. Dumont. In *Proceedings of the American Philosophical Society* 92, 95, 98, 101, 107, 108, 109, 113.

Taittirīya Saṃhitā. 8 vols. Ānandāśrama-saṃskṛta-granthāvaliḥ, granthānkha 42. Poona: Ānandāśrama, 1978.

———. 2 vols. Trans. by A. B. Keith. Harvard Oriental Series, Vols. 18 and 19. Cambridge, Mass.: Harvard University Press, 1914; reprint Delhi: Motilal Banarsidass, 1967.

Taittirīya Upaniṣad. Ed. by V. P. Limaye and R. D. Vadekar. In *Eighteen Principal Upaniṣads*. Poona: Vaidika Saṃśodhana Maṇḍala, 1958.

———. Trans. by Robert Hume. In *The Thirteen Principal Upanishads*, 2d ed. Oxford: Oxford University Press, 1931.

Vādhūla Śrauta Sūtra. Partial ed. and trans. by M. Sparreboom and J. C. Heesterman. In *The Ritual Setting Up of the Sacrificial Fires According to the Vādhūla School (Vādhūlaśrautasūtra 1.1–1.4)*. Vienna: Verlag der Österreichischen Akademie der Wissenschaften, 1989.

Vaikhānasa Smārta Sūtra. Ed. by W. Caland. Bibliotheca Indica, no. 242. Calcutta: Asiatic Society of Bengal, 1927.

———. Trans. by W. Caland. Bibliotheca Indica, no. 251. Calcutta: Asiatic Society of Bengal, 1929.

Vaikhānasa Śrauta Sūtra. Ed. by W. Caland. Bibliotheca Indica, no. 265. Calcutta: Royal Asiatic Society of Bengal, 1941.

Vaitāna Śrauta Sūtra. Ed. by Vishva Bandhu. Hoshiarpur: Vishveshvaranand Institute, 1967.

Vājasaneya Saṃhitā. 3d ed. Ed. and trans. by Devi Chand. New Delhi: Munshiram Manoharlal, 1980.

Vārāha Gṛhya Sūtra. Ed. and trans. into French by Pierre Rolland. Aix-en-Provence: Publications universitaires de lettres et sciences humaines, 1971.

Vārāha Śrauta Sūtra. Ed. by W. Caland and R. Vira. Reprint Delhi: Meharchand Lachhmandas, 1971.

Vāsiṣṭha Dharma Sūtra. Ed. by Manmatha Nath Dutt. In *The Dharma Śāstra Texts*. Calcutta: M. N. Dutt, 1908.

———. Trans. by Georg Bühler. In *The Sacred Books of the Āryas*. Sacred Books of the East, Vol. 14. Oxford: Clarendon Press, 1879; reprint Delhi: Motilal Banarsidass, 1965.

Viṣṇu Purāṇa. 2 vols. Ed. and trans. by H. H. Wilson; enlarged and arranged by Nag Sharan Singh. Delhi: Nag Publishers, 1980.

Viṣṇu Smṛti. 2 vols. Ed. by Pandit V. Krishnamacharya. Adyar Library Series, Vol. 93. Adyar: The Adyar Library and Research Centre, 1964.

Yājñavalkya Smṛti. 2d ed. Ed. by Mahamahopadhyaya T. Ganapati Sastri. New Delhi: Munshiram Manoharalal, 1982.

Secondary Sources (Indological)

Agarwal, V. S. "Roots of Indian Plants as Source for Medicine." *Indian Museum Bulletin* (Calcutta) 4, 2 (1969): 81–101.

Aiyer, B. V. Kamesvara. "The Lunar Zodiac in the Brāhmaṇas." *Indian Antiquary* 48 (June 1919): 95–7.

Ambedkar, B. R. *Who Were the Shūdras? How They Came to Be the Fourth Varṇa in the Indo-Aryan Society*. Bombay: Thackers, 1946; reprint Bombay: Thackers, 1970.

Amner, K. "Tvaṣṭṛ: Ein alt-indischer Schopfergott." *Die Sprache* 1 (1949): 68–77.

Appadhurai, Arjun. "Is Homo Hierarchicus?" *American Ethnologist* 13, 4 (Nov. 1986): 745–61.

Apte, V. M. *Social and Religious Life in the Gṛhyasūtras*. Ahmedabad: V. M. Apte, 1939.

———. "Were Castes Formulated in the Age of the Rig Veda?" *Bulletin of the Deccan College Research Institute* 2 (1940): 34–46.

Arbman, Ernst. *Rudra: Untersuchungen zum altindischen Glauben und Kultus*. Uppsala: Appelbergs boktryckeri aktiebolag, 1922.

Atkins, Samuel D. *Pūṣan in the Ṛg Veda*. Princeton: Princeton University Press, 1941.

Bailey, G. M. *The Mythology of Brahmā*. Delhi: Oxford University Press, 1983.

———. "Trifunctional Elements in the Mythology of the Hindu *trimūrti*." *Numen* 25 (1979): 152–63.

Bali, Saraswati. *Bṛhaspati in the Vedas and Purāṇas*. Delhi: Nag Publishers, 1978.

Banerjea, A. C. *Studies in the Brāhmaṇas*. New Delhi: Motilal Banarsidass, 1963.

Banerjee, Santi. "Prajāpati in the Brāhmaṇas." *Vishveshvaranand Indological Journal* 19, 1–2 (June–Dec. 1981): 14–19.

Basu, J. *India in the Age of the Brāhmaṇas*. Calcutta: Sanskrit Pustak Bhandar, 1969.

Beaudry, Thomas. "Social Paradigm: For the Synthesis of Material Difference and Spiritual Oneness." *Clarion Call* 2, 3 (Summer 1989): 32–35, 59–63.

Benveniste, Émile. "La doctrine médicale des indo-européens." *Revue de l'histoire des religions* 130 (1945): 5–7.

———. *Le Vocabulaire des institutions Indo-Européens, Vol. 1: Économie, parenté, société*. Paris: Éditions de minuit, 1969.

———. "Les classes sociales dans la tradition avestique." *Journal asiatique* 221 (1932): 117–34.

———. "Traditions indo-iraniennes sur les classes sociales." *Journal asiatique* 230 (1938): 529–49.

Bhargava, P. L. *India in the Vedic Age: A History of Āryan Expansion in India*. 2d ed. Aminabad: Upper India Publishing House, 1971.

Bhattacharji, Sukumari. "Rise of Prajāpati in the Brāhmaṇas." *Annals of the Bhandarkar Oriental Research Institute* 64 (1983): 205–13.

———. *The Indian Theogony*. Cambridge: Cambridge University Press, 1970.

Bhattacharya, D. "Cosmogony and Rituo-Philosophical Integrity in the Atharvaveda." *Vishveshvaranand Indological Journal* 15 (March 1977): 1–12.

Bhattacharya, Jogendra Nath. *Hindu Castes and Sects*. Calcutta: 1896; reprint Calcutta: Editions Indian, 1968.

Bhide, V. V. *The Cāturmāsya Sacrifices*. Pune: University of Poona, 1979.

Biardeau, M. "Études de mythologie hindou: Cosmogonies purāniques: 1,2,3." *Bulletin de l'École Francaise de l'Extreme Orient* 54 (1968): 19–45; 55 (1969): 59–105; 56 (1971): 19–81.

———. "The *śamī* Tree and the Sacrificial Buffalo." *Contributions to Indian Sociology* (n.s.) 18,1 (Jan.–June, 1984): 1–23.

———. and Charles Malamoud. *Le Sacrifice dans l'Inde ancienne*. Bibliothèque de l'École des Hautes Études, Sciences religieuses, Vol. 79. Paris: Presses Universitaires de France, 1976.

Biswas, T. K., and P. K. Debnath. "Ashoka (*Saraca indica Linn*)—A Cultural and Scientific Evaluation." *Indian Journal of the History of Science* 7, 2 (1972): 99–114.

———. "Aśvattha (*Ficus religiosus Linn*): A Cultural and Medicinal Observation." *Vishveshvaranand Indological Journal* 12, 1–2 (March–Sept. 1974): 39–47.

Bloomfield, Maurice. *The Atharva-Veda and the Gopatha Brāhmaṇa*. Strassburg: Karl J. Trübner, 1899; reprint New Delhi: Asian Publication Services, 1978.

———. *The Religion of the Veda*. New York: G. P. Putnam's Sons, 1908.

Bodewitz, H. W. *Jaiminīya Brāhmaṇa I, 1–65. Translation and Commentary*. Leiden: E. J. Brill, 1973.

———. *The Daily Evening and Morning Offering (Agnihotra) According to the Brāhmaṇas*. Leiden: E. J. Brill, 1976.

———. "The Fourth Priest (the *brahman*) in Vedic Ritual." In *Selected Studies on Ritual in the Indian Religions: Essays to D. J. Hoens*, pp. 33–68. Ed. by Ria Kloppenborg. Leiden: E. J. Brill, 1983.

———. *The Jyotiṣṭoma* Ritual: *Jaiminīya Brāhmaṇa* I, 66–364. Leiden: E. J. Brill, 1990.

———. "The Waters in Vedic Cosmic Classification." *Indologica Taurinensia* 10 (1982): 43–54.

Bonnerjea, B. "Possible Origin of the Caste System in India." *Indian Antiquary* 60 (1931): 49–52.

Bose, D. M., and S. N. Sen, eds. *A Concise History of Science in India*. New Delhi: Indian National Science Academy, 1971.

Bose, N. K. "Caste in India." *Man in India* 31, 3–4 (1951): 107–23.

Bouglé, C. *Essays on the Caste System*. Trans. with an introduction by D. F. Pocock. Cambridge: Cambridge University Press, 1971.

Brinkhaus, H. *Die Altindischen Mischkastensysteme*. Wiesbaden: Steiner, 1978.

Briquel, Dominique. "Sur l'équipment royal indo-européen." *Revue de l'histoire des religions* 200 (1983): 67–74.

Brown, W. Norman. *Man in the Universe: Some Cultural Continuities in Indian Thought*. Berkeley: University of California Press, 1970.

———. "The Creation Myth of the Ṛg Veda." *Journal of the American Oriental Society* 62 (1942): 85–98. Reprinted in *India and Indology: Selected Articles by W. Norman Brown*, pp. 20–33. Ed. by Rosane Rocher. Delhi: Motilal Banarsidass, 1978.

———. "Theories of Creation in the Ṛg Veda." *Journal of the American Oriental Society* 85 (1965): 23–34.

———. "The Sanctity of the Cow in Hinduism." *Journal of Madras University*, Section A, 28, 2 (Jan. 1957): 29–49. Reprinted in *India and Indology: Selected Articles by W. Norman Brown*, pp. 90–101. Ed. by Rosane Rocher. Delhi: Motilal Banarsidass, 1978.

———. "The Sources and Nature of Puruṣa in the Puruṣa Sūkta." *Journal of the American Oriental Society* 51 (1931): 108–18. Reprinted in *India and Indology: Selected*

Articles by W. Norman Brown, pp. 5–10. Ed. by Rosane Rocher. Delhi: Motilal Banarsidass, 1978.

Burghart, R. "Hierarchical Models of the Hindu Social System." *Man* (n.s.) 13 (1978): 519–36.

Burrow, T. "Sanskrit *rajas*." *Bulletin of the School of Oriental and African Studies* 12 (1947–48): 645–51.

Caland, Wilhelm, and V. Henry. *L'Agniṣṭoma: Description complète de la forme normale du sacrifice de Soma dans le cult védique*. 2 vols. Paris: Ernest Leroux, 1906.

"Calendar in Hindu Tradition." Proceedings of a seminar held by the Institute of Traditional Cultures, Madras. *Bulletin of the Institute of Cultures, Madras* 1 (1968): 42–144

Carman, John B., and Frederique A. Marglin, eds. *Purity and Auspiciousness in Indian Society*. Leiden: E. J. Brill, 1985.

———, and Vasudha Narayanan. *The Tamil Veda: Pillan's Interpretation of the Tiruvaymoli*. Chicago: University of Chicago Press, 1989.

Carpenter, David. "Language, Ritual and Society: Reflections on the Authority of the Veda in India." *Journal of the American Academy of Religion* 60, 1 (Spring 1992): 57–78.

Chakladar, H. C. "On the History of the Indian Caste System." *Indian Antiquary* 49 (1920): 205–14, 224–31.

Chakrabarti, S. C. *The Paribhāṣās in the Śrautasūtras*. Calcutta: Sanskrit Pustak Bhandar, 1980.

Chakrabarti, S. K. "On the Transition of the Vedic Sacrificial Lore." *Indo-Iranian Journal* 21 (1979): 181–88.

Chakravarty, Apurba Kumar. *Origin and Development of Indian Calendrical Science*. Calcutta: Indian Studies Past and Present, 1975.

Chatterjee, H. N. *Studies in Some Aspects of Hindu Saṃskāras in Ancient India*. Calcutta: Sanskrit Pustak Bhandar, 1965.

———. "Vedic Exemplarism." *Harvard Journal of Asiatic Studies* 1 (1936): 44–64.

Choudhuri, Usha. *Indra and Varuṇa in Indian Mythology*. Delhi: Nag Publishers, 1981.

Clooney, Francis X. "Finding One's Place in the Text: A Look at the Theological Treatment of Caste in Traditional India." *Journal of Religious Ethics* 17, 1 (Spring 1989): 1–29.

———. *Thinking Ritually: Rediscovering the Pūrva Mīmāṃsā of Jaimini*. Vienna: Institut für Indologie, 1990.

———. "Why the Veda Has No Author: Language as Ritual in Early Mīmāṃsā and Post-Modern Theology." *Journal of the American Academy of Religion* 55, 4 (Winter 1987): 659–84.

Conger, G. P. "Cosmic Persons and Human Universes in Indian Philosophy." *Journal of the Asiatic Society of Bengal* (n.s.) 29 (1933): 255–70.

Coomaraswamy, Ananda K. *Spiritual Authority and Temporal Power in the Indian Theory of Government*. New Haven, Conn.: American Oriental Society, 1942.

———. "The Inverted Tree." *Quarterly Journal of the Mythic Society* 29, 2 (Oct. 1938): 111–49.

Cowen, D. V. *Flowering Trees and Shrubs in India*. Bombay: Thacker & Co., 1957.

Crooke, W. "The Veneration of the Cow in India." *Folklore* 23 (1912): 275–306.

Dandekar, R. N. "Pūṣan, the Pastoral God of the Veda." *New Indian Antiquary* 5 (1942–43): 49–66.

Daniélou, A. *Les Quatre sens de la view et la structure sociale de l'Inde traditionelle*. Paris: Libraire academique Perrin, 1963.

Das, Veena. "A Sociological Approach to the Caste Purāṇas." *Sociological Bulletin* (New Delhi) 17 (1968): 141–64.

———. "On the Categorization of Space in Hindu Ritual." In *Text and Context: The Social Anthropology of Tradition*, pp. 9–27. Ed. by Ravindra K. Jain. Philadelphia: Institute for the Study of Human Issues, 1977.

———. *Structure and Cognition: Aspects of Hindu Caste and Ritual*. Delhi: Oxford University Press, 1977; 2d ed., 1982.

———. "The Uses of Liminality: Society and Cosmos in Hinduism." *Contributions to Indian Sociology* (n.s.) 10 (1976): 245–63.

———, and J. P. S. Uberoi. "The Elementary Structure of Caste." *Contributions to Indian Sociology* 5 (1971): 33–43.

Dastur, J. F. *Useful Plants of India and Pakistan*. Bombay: Taraporevala, 1962.

Davis, M. "A Philosophy of Hindu Rank from Rural West Bengal." *Journal of Asian Studies* 36 (1976): 5–24.

Deussen, Paul. *Philosophy of the Upanishads*. Trans. by A. S. Geden. New York: Dover Publications, 1966.

Devasthali, G. V. *Religion and Mythology of the Brāhmaṇas*. Poona: University of Poona, 1965.

Dikshit, Shankar Balakrishn. "The Method of Calculating the Week-days of Hindu Tithis and the Corresponding English Dates." *Indian Antiquary* 16, 195 (April 1887): 113–22.

Dirks, Nicholas B. "The Original Caste: Power, History and Hierarchy in South Asia." *Contributions to Indian Sociology* (n.s.) 23, 1 (1989): 59–77.

Doniger, Wendy. *Other People's Myths*. New York: Macmillan, 1988.

———, with Brian K. Smith, trans. *The Laws of Manu*. London: Penguin Books, 1991.

Drekmeir, C. *Kingship and Community in Early India*. Stanford, Calif: Stanford University Press, 1962.

Drury, Naama. *The Sacrificial Ritual in the Śatapatha Brāhmaṇa*. Delhi: Motilal Banarsidass, 1981.

du Gubernatis, A. "Brahman et Savitri ou l'origine de la prière." *Actes du onzieme congrès international des orientalistes* (Paris), 1897: 9–44.

Dubuisson, Daniel. "L'équipement de l'inauguration royale dans l'Inde védique et en Irelande." *Revue de l'histoire des religions* 193 (1978): 153–64.

———. "Le roi indo-européen et la synthèse des trois fonctions." *Annales: Économiés, Sociétés, Civilisations* 33 (1978): 21–34.

———. "Structure sociales et structure idéologique: l'apport de Georges Dumézil." In *Georges Dumézil*, pp. 147–58. Ed. by J. Bonnet. Paris: Centre Georges Pompidou, 1981.

———. "The Apologues of Saint Columba and Solon, or the 'Third Function' Denigrated." *Journal of Indo-European Studies* 6 (1978): 231–42.

Dumézil, Georges. *Destiny of a King*. Trans. by Alf Hiltebeitel. Chicago: University of Chicago Press, 1973.

———. *Destiny of a Warrior*. Trans. by Alf Hiltebeitel. Chicago: University of Chicago Press, 1970.

———. *L'Heritage Indo-Européen à Rome*. Paris: Gallimard, 1949.

———. *L'Idéologie tripartie des Indo-Européens*. Brusels: Collection Latomus, 1958.

———. "La Préhistoire indo-iranienne des castes." *Journal asiatique* 216 (1930): 109–30.

———. *Les Dieux des Indo-Européens*. Paris: Presses Universitaires de France, 1952.

———. *Les Dieux souverains des indo-européens*. Paris: Gallimard, 1977.

———. "Métiers et classes fonctionnelles chez divers peuples Indo-Européens." *Annales: Économiés, Sociétés, Civilisations* 13, 4 (Oct.–Dec. 1958): 716–24.

———. "Mitra-Varuṇa, Indra, les Nasaty comme patrons des trois fonctions cosmiques et sociales." *Studia Linguistica* 2 (1948): 121–29.

———. *Mitra-Varuṇa: An Essay on Two Indo-European Representations of Sovereignty.* Trans. by Derek Coltman. New York: Zone Books, 1988.

———. *Mythe et épopée.* 3 vols. Paris: Gallimard, 1968–73.

———. *Naissance d'Archanges.* Vol. 3 of *Jupiter, Mars, Quirinus,* 4 vols. Paris: Gallimard, 1941–45.

———. *Ouranos-Varuṇa*: Étude de Mythologie comparée indo-européenne. Paris: Adrien-Maisonneuve, 1934.

———. "Triades de calamités et triades de délits à valeur trifonctionnelle chez divers peuples indo-européens." *Latomus* 14 (1955): 173–85.

Dumont, Louis. "A. M. Hocart on Caste: Religion and Power." *Contributions to Indian Sociology* 2 (1958): 45–63.

———. *Homo Hierarchicus: The Caste System and Its Implications.* Complete Revised English Edition. Trans. by Mark Sainsbury, Louis Dumont, and Basia Gulati. Chicago: University of Chicago Press, 1980.

———. *La Civilisation indienne et nous.* Paris: Armand Colin, 1975.

———. *Religion/Politics and History in India: Collected Papers in Indian Sociology.* The Hague: Mouton, 1970.

———, and D. Pocock. "Pure and Impure." *Contributions to Indian Sociology* 3 (1959): 9–39.

Dumont, P.-E. *L'Agnihotra: Description de l'agnihotra dans le rituel védique d'après les Śrautasūtras.* Baltimore: Johns Hopkins Press, 1939.

———. *L'Aśvamedha: Description du sacrifice solennel du cheval dans le culte védique d'après les textes du Yajurveda blanc.* Paris: P. Geuthner, 1927.

Dutt, U. C., George King, et al. *The Materia Medica of the Hindus.* Rev. ed. Calcutta: Madan Gopal Dass, 1922.

Edgerton, Franklin. "Dominant Ideas in the Formation of Indian Culture." *Journal of the American Oriental Society* 62 (1942): 151–56.

———. "Philosophical Materials of the Atharvaveda." In *Studies in Honor of Maurice Bloomfield,* pp. 119–35. New Haven, Conn.: Yale University Press, 1920.

Eliot, Charles. *Hinduism and Buddhism: An Historical Sketch.* 3 vols. New York: Barnes and Noble, 1954.

Emeneau, M. *The Strangling Figs in Sanskrit Literature.* Berkeley: University of California Press, 1949.

Ferro-Luzzi, Gabriella Eichinger. "The Polythetic-Prototype Concept of Caste." *Anthropos: International Review of Ethnology and Linguistics* 81, 4–6 (1986): 637–42.

Filliozat, Jean. "La Force organique et la force cosmique dans la philosophie médicale de l'Inde et dans le Véda." *Revue philosophique* 116 (1933): 410–29.

———. *The Classical Doctrine of Indian Medicine: Its Origins and Greek Parallels.* Trans. by Dev Raj Chanana. Delhi: Munshiram Manoharlal, 1964.

Fitzgerald, James. "India's Fifth Veda: The Mahābhārata's Presentation of Itself." *Journal of South Asian Literature* 20 (1980): 125–40.

Fleming, John. "A Catalogue of Indian Medicinal Plants and Drugs, with Their Names in the Hindustani and Sanscrit Languages." *Asiatic Researches* 11 (1812): 153–96.

Fox, R. G. "*Varṇa* Schemes and Ideological Integration in Indian Society." *Comparative Studies in Society and History* (Ann Arbor) 11 (1969): 27–45.

Franco, F., and Sarvar V. Sherry Chand. "Ideology as Social Practice: The Functioning of *Varṇa*." *Economic and Political Weekly* 24, 47 (Nov. 25, 1989): 2601–12.

Freed, Ruth C., and Stanley A. Freed. "Calendars, Ceremonies and Festivals in a North Indian Village: Necessary Calendrical Information for Fieldwork." *Southwestern Journal of Anthropology* 20 (1964): 67–90.

Frenkian, Aram. "Puruṣa—Gayomard—Anthropos." *Revue des études indo-européens* 3 (1943): 118–31.

Fugier, Huguette. "Quarante ans de récherchés sur l'idéologie indo-européens: La methode de M. Georges Dumézil." *Revue d'histoire et de philosophie religieuses* 45 (1965): 358–74.

Fuller, C. "Gods, Priests and Purity: On the Relation Between Hinduism and the Caste System." *Man* (n.s.) 14, 3 (1979): 459–76.

Gajendragadkar, S. N. "Caste System in the Mahābhārata." *Journal of the University of Bombay* (n.s.) 30 (1961): 23–38.

Ghosh, N. N. "The Origin and Development of the Caste System in India." *Indian Culture* 12 (1945): 177–91.

Ghoshal, U. N. "The Status of Brāhmaṇas in the Dharmasūtras." *Indian Historical Quarterly* 23, 2 (1947): 83–92.

———. "The Status of Śūdras in the Dharmasūtras." *Indian Culture* 14, 4 (April–June 1948): 21–27.

Glucklich, Ariel. "Karma and Pollution in Hindu Dharma: Distinguishing Law from Nature." *Contributions to Indian Sociology* (n.s.) 18, 1 (1984): 25–43.

———. "The Royal Sceptre (*Daṇḍa*) as Legal Punishment and Sacred Symbol." *History of Religions* 28, 2 (Nov. 1988): 97–122.

Gombrich, R. F. "Ancient Indian Cosmology." In *Ancient Cosmologies*, pp. 110–142. Ed. by C. Blacker and M. Loewe. London: George Allen & Unwin, 1975.

Gonda, Jan. *Ancient Indian Kingship from the Religious Point of View*. Leiden: E. J. Brill, 1966.

———. *Ancient Indian ojas, Latin *augos and the Indo-European Nouns –es/–os*. Utrecht: A. Oosthoek's Uitgevers Mij., 1952.

———. *Bandhu* in the Brāhmaṇas." *Adyar Library Bulletin* 29 (1965): 1–29.

———. *Change and Continuity in Indian Religion*. Disputations Rheno-Trajectinae, Vol. 9. The Hague: Mouton, 1965.

———. "Dumézil's Tripartite Ideology: Some Critical Observations." *Journal of Asian Studies* 34, 1 (Nov. 1974): 139–49.

———. "Etymologies in the Ancient Indian Brāhmaṇas." *Lingua* 5 (1955): 61–85.

———. "In the Beginning." *Annals of the Bhandarkar Oriental Research Institute* 63 (1982): 43–62.

———. *Loka: The World and Heaven in the Veda*. Verhandelingen der Koninklijke Nederlandse Akademie van Wetenschappen, Afd. Letterkunde, Nieuwe Reeks, Pt. 73, No. 1. Amsterdam: N. V. Noord-Hollandsche Uitgevers Maatschappij, 1966.

———. "Mensch und Tier im alten Indian." In Jan Gonda, *Selected Studies*, Vol. 4, pp. 484–95. Leiden: E. J. Brill, 1975.

———. *Notes on Brahman*. Utrecht: J. L. Beyers, 1950.

———. *Prajāpati and the Year*. Amsterdam: North-Holland, 1984.

———. *Prajāpati's Relations with Brahman, Bṛhaspati and Brahmā*. Amsterdam: North-Holland, 1989.

———. *Prajāpati's Rise to Higher Rank*. Leiden: E. J. Brill, 1986.

———. "Purohita." In *Studia Indologica: Festschrift für Willibald Kirfel*, pp. 107–24. Ed. by O. Spies. Bonn: Universität Bonns, 1955.

———. *Pūṣan and Sarasvatī*. Amsterdam: North-Holland, 1985.
———. "Reflections on *sarva-* in Vedic Texts." *Indian Linguistics* 16 (Nov. 1955): 53–71.
———. "Some Observations on Dumézil's View of Indo-European Mythology." *Mnemosyne* 4 (1960): 1–14.
———. *Some Observations on the Relations between "Gods" and "Powers" in the Veda à propos of the Phrase śunuh sahasā*. The Hague: Mouton, 1957.
———. *The Dual Deities in the Religion of the Veda*. Amsterdam: North-Holland, 1974.
———. *The Indra Hymns of the Ṛgveda*. Leiden: E. J. Brill, 1989.
———. *The Meaning of the Sanskrit Term Āyatana*. Adyar: Adyar Library and Research Centre, 1969.
———. *The Ritual Functions and Significance of Grasses in the Religion of the Veda*. Amsterdam: North-Holland, 1985.
———. *The Vedic God Mitra*. Leiden: E. J. Brill, 1972.
———. *Triads in the Veda*. Amsterdam: North-Holland, 1976.
———. "Upanayana." *Indologica Taurinensia* 7 (1979): 253–59.
———. "Vedic Gods and the Sacrifice." *Numen* 30, 1 (July 1983): 1–34.
Gopal, Ram. *India of the Vedic Kalpasūtras*. Delhi: National Publishing House, 1959.
Greenwold, S. "Caste: A Moral Structure and a Social System of Control." In *Culture and Morality*, pp. 126–52. Ed. by A. C. Mayer. Delhi: Oxford University Press, 1981.
Grottanelli, Cristiano. "Temi Duméziliani fuori dal mondo indoeuropeo." *Opus* 2 (1983): 365–89.
Gupta, S. L. "Sacred Plants in Hindu Religion." *Indian Cultures Quarterly* (Jabalpur) 21, 3 (1964): 2–10; 22, 1 (1965): 6–19.
Gupta, Shakti M. *Plant Myths and Traditions in India*. Leiden: E. J. Brill, 1971.
Gupta, S. S., ed. *Rain in Indian Life and Lore*. Calcutta: Indian Publications, 1963.
———. ed. *Tree Symbol Worship in India: A New Survey of a Pattern of Folk-Religion*. Calcutta: Indian Publications, 1965.
Hale, Wash Edward. *Asura- in Early Vedic Religion*. Delhi: Motilal Banarsidass, 1986.
Hara, M. "Indra and Tapas." *Brahmavidyā* 25 (1975): 29–60.
Harper, E. B. "Ritual Pollution as an Integrator of Caste and Religion." *Journal of Asian Studies* 23, 1 (1964): 151–97.
Hayden, R. "Excommunication as Everyday Event and Ultimate Sanction: The Nature of Suspension from an Indian Caste." *Journal of Asian Studies* 42, 2 (1983): 291–307.
Heesterman, J. C. "Brahmin, Ritual, and Renouncer." *The Inner Conflict of Tradition: Essays in Indian Ritual, Kingship, and Society*, pp. 26–44. Ed. by Jan Heesterman. Chicago: University of Chicago Press, 1985.
———. *The Ancient Indian Royal Consecration: The Rājasūya Described According to the Yajus Texts and Annoted [sic]*. Disputations Rheno-Trajectinae, Vol. 2. The Hague: Mouton, 1957.
———. *The Inner Conflict of Tradition: Essays in Indian Ritual, Kingship, and Society*. Chicago: University of Chicago Press, 1985.
———. "Veda and Dharma." In *The Concept of Duty in South Asia*, pp. 80–95. Ed. by Wendy Doniger O'Flaherty and J. D. M. Derrett. Columbia, Mo.: South Asia Books, 1978.
———. "Veda and Society: Some Remarks apropos of the Film 'Altar of Fire.'" In *Proceedings of the Nordic South Asia Conference, Held in Helsinki, June 10–12, 1980*, pp. 51–64. Ed. by Asko Parpola. Helsinki: Studia Orientalia, 1981.

Hillebrandt, Alfred. "Tiere und Götter im vedischen Ritual." *Schlesische Gesellschaft für Vaterländische Cultur* 83 (1905): 1–12.

———. *Vedic Mythology*. 2 vols. Trans. by S. Rajeswara Sarma. Delhi: Motilal Banarsidass, 1970.

Hiltebeitel, Alf. "Die glühende Axt: Symbolik, Struktur, und Dynamik in Chandogya Upanishad 6." In *Sehnsucht nach dem Ursprung: Zu Mircea Eliade*, pp. 394–405. Ed. by Hans-Peter Duerr. Stuttgart: Syndikat, 1983.

———. "Dumézil and Indian Studies." *Journal of Asian Studies* 34, 1 (Nov. 1974): 129–37.

———. *The Ritual of Battle: Krishna in the Mahābhārata*. Ithaca, N.Y.: Cornell University Press, 1976.

Hoang-sy-Quy, Hoang-son. "Le mythe indien de l'homme cosmique dans son contexte culturel et dans son évolution." *Revue de l'histoire des religions* 175 (1969): 133–54.

Holdrege, Barbara A. *Veda and Torah: Transcending the Textuality of Scripture*. Albany, N.Y.: SUNY Press, 1993.

Hooker, J. D. *The Flora of British India*. London: Reeve & Co., 1872.

Hopkins, E. Washburn. "Holy Numbers of the Rig-Veda." In *Oriental Studies: A Selection of the Papers Read before the Oriental Club of Philadelphia*, pp. 141–59. Boston: Ginn and Co., 1894.

———. "Mythological Aspects of Trees and Mountains in the Great Epics." *Journal of the American Oriental Society* (1910): 347–74.

———. *The Mutual Relations of the Four Castes according to the Mānavadharmaśāstra*. Reprint Delhi: Ajanta Books, 1976.

———. *The Social and Military Position of the Ruling Caste in Ancient India*. Reprint Varanasi: Bharat-Bharati, 1972.

Inden, Ronald. *Imagining India*. Oxford: Basil Blackwell, 1990.

———. "Lordship and Caste in Hindu Discourse." In *Indian Religion*, pp. 159–79. Ed. by R. Burghart and A. Cantlie. London: Curzon Press, 1985.

Institute of Traditional Cultures, Madras. "Calendar in Hindu Tradition." Proceedings of a seminar on this topic held by the Institute of Traditional Cultures. *Bulletin of the Institute of Traditional Cultures, Madras* 1 (1968): 42–144.

Iyengar, B. R. Keshava. *The Ṛgvedic Purushasūkta*. Bangalore: Vedanta Book Agencies, 1977.

Jackson, A. M. T. "Note on the History of the Caste System." *Journal of the Asiatic Society of Bengal* (n.s.) 3, 7 (July 1907): 509–15.

Jaini, Padmanabh S. "Indian Perspectives on the Spirituality of Animals." In *Buddhist Philosophy and Culture: Essays in Honour of N. A. Jayawickrema*, pp. 169–78. Ed. by David J. Kalupahana and W. G. Weeraratne. Colombo: N. A. Jayawickrema Felicitation Volume Committee, 1987.

Jha, V. N. "Stages in the History of Untouchables." *Indian Historical Review* 2 (July 1975): 14–31.

———. "Varṇasaṃkara in the Dharmasūtras: Theory and Practice." *Journal of the Economic and Social History of the Orient* (Leiden) 13, 3 (1970): 273–88.

Jordens, J. T. F. *Dayānanda Sarasvatī: His Life and Ideas*. Delhi: Oxford University Press, 1978.

———. "Two Giants Look at the Cosmic Man: Ambedkar and Dayānanda Interpret the *Puruṣa-Sūkta*," *Journal of the Oriental Institute* (Baroda) 33, 1 (Sept.–Dec. 1983): 1–10.

Joshi, J. R. "Prajāpati in Vedic Mythology and Ritual." *Annals of the Bhandarkar Oriental Research Institute* 53 (1972): 101–25.

Kamble, B. R. *Caste and Philosophy in Pre-Buddhist India*. Aurangabad: Parimal, 1979.

Kane, P. V. *History of Dharmaśāstra*: Ancient and Mediaeval, Religious and Civil Law. 5 vols. 2d ed. Poona: Bhandarkar Oriental Research Institute, 1968–75.

Karambelkar, K. W. "Brahman and Purohita in Atharvanic Texts." *Indian Historical Quarterly* 26 (1950): 293–300.

Kaushik, Meena. "The Symbolic Representation of Death." *Contributions to Indian Sociology* (n.s.) 10 (1976): 265–92.

Keith, Arthur Berriedale. *The Religion and Philosophy of the Veda and Upaniṣads*. 2 vols. Harvard Oriental Series, Vols. 31 and 32. Cambridge, Mass.: Harvard University Press, 1925; reprint Delhi: Motilal Banarsidass, 1976.

Khare, R. S. "Encompassing and Encompassed: A Deductive Theory of Caste System." *Journal of Asian Studies* 31, 4 (1971): 859–68.

———. "Ritual Purity and Pollution in Relation to Domestic Sanitation." *Eastern Anthropologist* 15, 2 (1962): 125–39.

———. "The One and the Many: Varṇa and Jāti as a Symbolic Classification." In *American Studies in the Anthropology of India*, pp. 35–64. Ed. by Sylvia Vatuk. New Delhi: Manohar, 1978.

Kirfel, Willibald. "Der Aśvamedha und der Puruṣamedha." In *Festschrift für Walther Schubring*, pp. 39–50. Hamburg: Walter de Gruyter, 1951.

Kirtikar, K. R., and B. D. Basu. *Indian Medicinal Plants*. 4 vols. 2d ed. Ed., rev., and en. by E. Blatter et al. Delhi: Bishen Singh Mahendra Pal Singh, 1975.

Klass, Morton. *Caste: The Emergence of the South Asia Social System*. Philadelphia: Institute for the Study of Human Issues, 1980.

Kosambi, D. D. "Early Brahmins and Brahminism." *Journal of the Bombay Branch of the Royal Asiatic Society* (n.s.) 23 (1947): 39–46.

———. "Early Stages of the Caste System in Northern India." *Journal of the Bombay Branch of the Royal Asiatic Society* (n.s.) 22 (1946): 33–48.

Kuiper, F. B. J. *Ancient Indian Cosmogony*. New Delhi: Vikas Publishing House, 1983.

———. "Some Observations on Dumézil's Theory." *Numen* 8 (1961): 34–45.

———. *Varuṇa and Vidūṣaka: On the Origin of the Sanskrit Drama*. Amsterdam: North-Holland, 1979.

Lal, Shyam Kishore. *Female Divinities in Hindu Mythology and Ritual*. Pune: University of Poona, 1980.

Lévi, Sylvain. *La Doctrine du sacrifice dans les Brāhmaṇas*. Bibliothèque de l'École des Hautes Études, Sciences religieuses, Vol. 11. Paris: Ernest Leroux, 1898.

Lincoln, Bruce. *Death, War, and Sacrifice: Studies in Ideology and Practice*. Chicago: University of Chicago Press, 1991.

———. *Myth, Cosmos, and Society: Indo-European Themes of Creation and Destruction*. Cambridge, Mass.: Harvard University Press, 1986.

———. *Priests, Warriors, and Cattle: A Study in the Ecology of Religions*. Berkeley: University of California Press, 1981.

———. "The Indo-European Myth of Creation." *History of Religions* 15 (1975): 121–45.

———. "The Tyranny of Taxonomy." *Occasional Papers of the University of Minnesota Center for Humanistic Studies* 1 (1985).

Lingat, Robert. *Classical Law of India*. Trans. by J. Duncan M. Derrett. Berkeley: University of California Press, 1973.

———. "Time and the Dharma." *Contributions to Indian Sociology* 6 (1962): 7–16.

Littleton, F. Scott. *The New Comparative Mythology: An Anthropological Assessment of the Theories of Georges Dumézil*. Berkeley: University of California Press, 1973.

Locchi, Giorgio. "Le myth cosmogonique indoeuropéen: Réconstruction et réalité." *Nouvelle école* 19 (1972): 87–95.

Lommel, Herman. "Bhrigu im Jenseits." *Padeuma* 4 (1950): 93–109.

———. *Der arische Kriegsgott*. Frankfurt: V. Klostermann, 1939.

———. "König Soma." *Numen* 2 (1955): 196–205.

Luders, Heinrich. *Varuṇa*. 2 vols. Göttingen: Vandenhoeck and Ruprecht, 1951–59.

Macdonald, A. W. "À propos de Prajāpati." *Journal asiatique* 240 (1953): 323–28.

———. "On Prajāpati." In *Essays on the Ethnology of Nepal and South Asia*, pp. 1–13. Kathmandu: Ratna Pustak Bhandar, 1975.

Macdonald, K. S. *The Brāhmaṇas of the Vedas*. Reprint Delhi: Bharatiya Book Corporation, 1979.

Macdonell, A. A. *The Vedic Mythology*. Grundriss der Indo-Arische Philologie und Alterthumskunde, Vol. 3, No. 1A. Strassburg: K. J. Trübner, 1894; reprint Delhi: Motilal Banarsidass, 1974.

———, and A. B. Keith. *Vedic Index of Names and Subjects*. 2 vols. Reprint Varanasi: Motilal Banarsidass, 1958.

Madan, T. N., et al., "On the Nature of Caste in India: A Review Symposium on Louis Dumont's *Homo Hierarchicus*." *Contributions to Indian Sociology* (n.s.) 5 (1971): 1–81.

Madan, T. N., ed. *Way of Life: King, Householder, Renouncer. Essays in Honour of Louis Dumont*. New Delhi: Vikas, 1982.

Mahapatra, P. "Tree-Symbol Worship in Bengal." In *Tree Symbol Worship in India: A New Survey of a Pattern of Folk-Religion*, pp. 125–39. Ed. by S. S. Gupta. Calcutta: Indian Publications, 1965.

Majumdar, Girijaprasanna. "Vedic Plants." In *B. C. Law Volume, Pt. 1*, pp. 644–68. Ed. by D. R. Bhandarkar et al. Calcutta: Indian Research Institute, 1945.

Malamoud, Charles. "Cruire le monde." *Puruṣārtha* 1 (1975): 91–135. Reprinted in Charles Malamoud, *Cruire le monde: Rite et pensée dans l'Inde ancienne*, pp. 35–70. Paris: Éditions la Découverte, 1989.

———. *Le Svādhyāya: Recitation personelle du Veda*. Paris: Institut de Civilisation Indienne, 1977.

———. "Village et forêt dans l'idéologie de l'Inde brahmanique." *Archives européennes de sociologie* 17, 1 (1976): 3–20. Reprinted in Charles Malamoud, *Cruire le monde: Rite et pensée dans l'Inde ancienne*, pp. 93–114. Paris: Éditions la Découverte, 1989.

Manessy, J. *Les substantifs en –as– dans la Ṛk-Saṃhitā*. Dakar: n.p., 1961.

Marglin, Frederique Apffel. *Wives of the God-King: The Rituals of the Devadāsīs of Puri*. Delhi: Oxford University Press, 1985.

Marriott, McKim. "Caste Ranking and Food Transactions: A Matrix Anaylsis." In *Structure and Change in Indian Society*, pp. 133–71. Ed. by M. Singer and B. Cohn. Chicago: Aldine, 1968.

———. "Constructing an Indian Ethnosociology." *Contributions to Indian Sociology* (n.s.) 23, 1 (1989): 1–39.

———. "Hindu Transactions: Diversity without Dualism." In *Transactions and Meaning*, pp. 109–42. Ed. by B. Kapferer. Philadelphia: Institute for the Study of Human Issues, 1976.

———. "Interactional and Attributional Theories of Caste Ranking." *Man in India* 39, 2 (1959): 92–107.

———. "Interpreting Indian Society: A Monistic Alternative to Dumont's Dualism." *Journal of Asian Studies* 36, 1 (1976): 189–95.

———. Review of Louis Dumont's *Homo Hierarchicus*. *American Anthropologist* 71 (1969): 1166–75.

———. "Toward an Ethnosociology of South Asian Caste Systems." In *The New Wind: Changing Identities in South Asia*, pp. 423–38. Ed. by Kenneth David. The Hague: Mouton, 1977.

———. ed. *India Through Hindu Categories*. Newbury Park, Calif.: Sage Publications, 1990.

———, and Ronald B. Inden. "Caste Systems." *Encyclopaedia Britannica, macropaedia* (1974), Vol. 3, pp. 982–91.

Mayrhofer-Passler, E. "Haustieropfer bei dem Indoiraniern und den andern indo-germanischen Volkern." *Archiv Orientalni* 21 (1953): 182–205.

McDermott, James. "Animals and Humans in Early Buddhism." *Indo-Iranian Journal* 32, 4 (Oct. 1989): 269–80.

Mees, G. H. *Dharma and Society: A Comparative Study of the Theory and Ideal of Varṇa ("Natural Class") and the Phenomenon of Caste and Class*. London, 1935; reprint Delhi: Seema, 1980.

Meyer, J. J. *Trilogie altindischer Mächte und Feste der Vegetation*. 3 vols. Zurich: Max Niehans, 1937.

Minkowski, Christopher. "The Rathakāra's Eligibility to Sacrifice." *Indo-Iranian Journal* 32, 3 (July 1989): 177–94.

———. "The Udumbara and Its Ritual Significance." *Wiener Zeitschrift füur die Kunde Sudasiens und Archiv für Indische Philosophie* 33 (1989): 5–23.

Molé, Marijan. *Culte, mythe, et cosmologie dans l'Iran ancien*. Paris: Presses universitaires de France, 1963.

Mookerji, Radha Kumud. *Ancient Indian Education (Brahmanical and Buddhist)*. London: Macmillan, 1947.

Muir, J. "Relation of Priests to the Other Classes of Indian Society in the Vedic Age." *Journal of the Royal Asiatic Society* (n.s.) 2 (1866): 257–302.

Müller, R. F. G. "Die Medizin im Ṛg Veda." *Asia Major* 6 (1930): 377–85.

Mus, Paul. *Barabadur: Esquisse d'une histoire du Bouddhism fondée sur la critique archéologique des textes*. Paris and Hanoi: Paul Geuthner, 1935.

———. "Du Nouveau sur Ṛg Veda 10.90?" In *Indological Studies in Honor of W. Norman Brown*, pp. 165–85. Ed. by Ernest Bender. American Oriental Series, Vol. 47. New Haven, Conn.: American Oriental Society, 1962.

———. "Ou finit Puruṣa?" *Mélanges d'Indianisme à la mémoire de Louis Renou*, pp. 539–63. Paris: E. de Boccard, 1968.

Mylius, Klaus. "Die Ideenwelt des Śatapatha Brāhmaṇa." *Wissenschaftliche Zeitschrift der Karl Marx Universität* (Leipzig) 16 (1967): 47–55.

———. "Die Identifikationen der Metren in der Literatur des Ṛgveda." *Wissenschaftliche Zeitschrift der Karl Marx Universität* (Leipzig) 17 (1968): 267–73.

———. "Die Identifikationen im *Kauṣītaki-Brāhmaṇa*." *Altorientalische Forschungen* 5 (1977): 237–44.

———. "Die Rolle des vedischen Rituals in sozialen Konflikten." *Zeitschrift des Zentralen Rates für Asien-, Afrika- un Lateinamerika Wissenschaften in der DDR* 1 (1974): 123–34.

———. "Die vedischen Identifikationen am Beispiel des *Kauṣītaki-Brāhmaṇa*." *Klio* 58 (1976): 145–66.

O'Flaherty, W. D. *Tales of Sex and Violence: Folklore, Sacrifice, and Danger in the Jaiminīya Brāhmaṇa*. Chicago: University of Chicago Press, 1984.

———. "The Case of the Stallion's Wife: Indra and Vṛṣanaśva in the Ṛg Veda and the Brāhmaṇas." *Journal of the American Oriental Society* 105, 3 (1985): 485–98.

———. *Women, Androgynes, and Other Mythical Beasts*. Chicago: University of Chicago Press, 1980.

———, and J. D. M. Derrett, eds. *The Concept of Duty in South Asia*. Columbia, Mo.: South Asia Books, 1978.

Oguibenine, Boris. "*Bandhu* et *dakṣiṇā*. Deux termes védique illustrant le rapport entre le signifiant et le signifié." *Journal asiatique* 276 (1983): 263–75.

———. *Structure d'un mythe védique: Le Mythe cosmogonique dans le Ṛg Veda*. The Hague: Mouton, 1973.

Ojha, Purna Chandra. *Aśvattha in Everyday Life as Related in the Purāṇas*. Delhi: Sundeep, 1991.

Oldenberg, Hermann. *Vorwissenschaftliche Wissenschaft: Die Weltanschauung der Brāhmaṇa-texte*. Göttingen: Vandenhoeck and Ruprecht, 1919.

———. "Zur Geschichte des Indien Kastenwesens." *Zeitschrift der Deutschen Morgenländischen Gesellschaft* 51 (1897): 267–90.

Orenstein, H. "Toward a Grammar of Defilement in Hindu Sacred Law." In *Structure and Change in Indian Society*, pp. 115–31. Ed. by M. Singer and B. S. Cohn. Chicago: Aldine, 1968.

Organ, Troy. "Three into Four in Hinduism." *Ohio Journal of Religious Studies* 1 (1973): 7–13.

Pandey, Raj Bali. *Hindu Saṃskāras*. 2d ed. Delhi: Motilal Banarsidass, 1969.

Parpola, Asko. "On the Symbol Concept of the Vedic Ritualists." In *Religious Symbols and Their Functions*, pp. 139–53. Ed. by H. Biezais. Stockholm: Almquist and Wiksell, 1979.

———. "The Pre-Vedic Indian Background of the Śrauta Rituals." In *Agni: The Vedic Ritual of the Fire Altar*, II:411–75. 2 vols. Ed. by Frits Staal. Berkeley: Asian Humanities Press, 1983.

Patton, Laurie, ed. *Authority, Anxiety and Canon: Essays in Vedic Interpretation*. Albany, N.Y.: SUNY Press, 1993.

Patyal, H. C. "Significance of *varaṇa* in the Veda." *Oriens* 21–22 (1968–69): 300–306.

Perry, E. D. "Notes on the Vedic Deity Pūṣan." In *Classical Studies in Honour of Henry Drisler*. New York: Macmillan, 1894.

Pillai, D. B., and L. D. Swamikanny. *Indian Chronology (Solar, Lunar and Planetary): A Practical Guide to the Interpretation and Verification of Tithis, Nakshatras, Horoscopes and Other Indian Time-Records, B.C. 1 to A.D. 2000*. New Delhi: Asian Educational Services, 1982.

Pitt-Rivers, Julian. "On the Word 'Caste.'" In *The Translation of Culture: Essays Presented to E. E. Evans-Pritchard*, pp. 231–56. Ed. by T. O. Beidelman. London: Tavistock, 1970.

Pohlman, E. W. "Evidence of Disparity between the Hindu Practice of Caste and the Ideal Type." *American Sociological Review* 16 (1951): 37–59.

Prasad, N. *The Myth of the Caste System*. Patna: Samjña Prakashan, 1957.

Pryzluski, Jean. "Le Loi de symétrie dans la Chandogya Upanishad." *Bulletin of the School of Oriental Studies* 5 (1928–30): 491–94.

Pugh, Judy F. "Into the Almanac: Time, Meaning, and Action in North Indian Society." *Contributions to Indian Sociology* (n.s.) 17, 1 (1983): 27–49.

Puhvel, Jaan. "Mythological Reflections of Indo-European Medicine." In *Indo-European and Indo-Europeans*, pp. 369–82. Ed. by George Cardona et al. Philadelphia: University of Pennsylvania Press, 1970.

———. "Victimal Hierarchies in Indo-European Animal Sacrifice." *American Journal of Philology* 99 (1978): 354–62.

Raghavan, V. *Ṛtu in Sanskrit Literature*. Delhi: Shri Lal Bahadur Shastri Kendriya Sanskrit Vidyapeeth, 1972.

Raheja, Gloria Goodwin. *The Poison in the Gift: Ritual, Prestation, and the Dominant Caste in a North Indian Village*. Chicago: University of Chicago Press, 1988.

Randhawa, M. S. *The Cult of Trees and Tree-Worship in Buddhist-Hindu Sculpture*. New Delhi: All India Fine Arts and Crafts Society, 1964.

Reimann, Luis Gonzalez. *Tiempo Ciclico y Eras del Mundo en la India*. Mexico City: College of Mexico, 1988.

Renou, Louis. "La Maison védique." *Journal asiatique* 231 (1939): 481–504.

———. *Les Écoles védiques et la formation de Veda*. Cahiers de la Societé Asiatique, Vol. 9. Paris: Imprimerie nationale, 1947.

———. "Un thème litteraire en sanskrit: les saisons." In *Sanskrit et culture: L'apport de l'Inde à la civilisation humaine*, pp. 43–54. Paris: Payot, 1950.

———. "Védique *ṛtu*." *Archiv Orientalni* 18, 1–2 (May 1950): 431–38.

———, and Lillian Silburn. "Nirukta and Anirukta in Vedic." In *Sarūpa-Bhāratī or the Homage of Indology: The Dr. Lakshman Sarup Memorial Volume*, pp. 68–79. Ed. by J. N. Agrawal and B. D. Shastri. Hoshiarpur: Vishveshvaranand Institute Publications, 1954.

Rice, S. "The Origin of Caste." *Asiatic Review* 25 (1929): 147–57.

Ritschl, Eva. "Brahmanische Bauern: Zur Theorie und Praxis der brahmanische Standeordnung im alten Indien." *Altorientalische Forschungen* 7 (1980): 177–87.

Rocher, Ludo. "Caste and Occupation in Classical India: The Normative Texts." *Contributions to Indian Sociology* (n.s.) 9, 1 (1975): 139–51.

———, and Rosane Rocher. "La Sacralité du pouvoir dans l'Inde ancienne d'aprés les textes de dharma." *Annales du Centre d'études des Religions* (Brussels) (1962): 123–37.

Rolland, Pierre. "Le Cérémonial d'exclusion de la caste dans l'Inde ancienne." In *K. A. Nilakanta Sastri Felicitation Volume*, pp. 487–97. Madras: K. A. Nilakanta Sastra Felicitation Committee, 1971.

Roth, R. "Brahma und die Brahmanen." *Zeitschrift der Deutschen Morgenländischen Gesellschaft* 1 (1847): 66–86.

Ruben, W. *Über die frühesten Stufen der Entwicklung der altindischen Śūdras*. Berlin: Academie-Verlag, 1965.

Sarasvatī, Swami Dayānanda. *Ṛgveda-bhāṣyam*. 3 vols. Ed. by Yudhisthira Mimamsaka. Karanala, Harayana: Ramala Kapure Trasta, 1973.

Sauvé, James L. "The Divine Victim: Aspects of Human Sacrifice in Viking Scandinavia and Vedic India." In *Myth and Law among the Indo-Europeans*, pp. 173–91. Ed. by Jaan Puhvel. Los Angeles: University of California Press, 1970.

Schayer, Stanislov. "Die Struktur der magischen Weltanschauung nach dem Atharva-Veda und den Brāhmaṇa-Texten." *Zeitschrift für Buddhismus* 6 (1925): 259–99.

Schlerath, Bernfried. *Die Indogermanen: Das Problem der Expansion eines Volkes im Lichte seiner sozialen Struktur*. Innsbruck: Innsbruck Beiträge zur Sprachwissenschaft, 1973.

Schlinghoff, Dieter. "Menschenopfer in Kauśambi." *Indo-Iranian Journal* 11 (1969): 176–198.

Schmidt, Hanns-Peter. "Ancient Iranian Animal Classification." *Studien zur Indologie und Iranistik* 5/6 (1980): 209–44.

———. *Bṛhaspati und Indra: Untersuchungen zur vedischen Mythologie und Kulturgeschichte*. Wiesbaden: Otto Harrassowitz, 1968.

———. "The Origin of ahiṃsā." In *Mélanges d'indianisme à la mémoire de Louis Renou*, pp. 625–55. Ed. by Jean Filliozat. Paris: E. de Boccard, 1968.

Schwab, J. *Das altindische Thieropfer*. Erlangen: Andreas Deichert, 1886.

Senart, Émile. *Caste in India: The Facts and the System*. Trans. by Sir E. Denison Ross. London: Methuen, 1930.

———. "*Rajas* et le théorie indienne des trois *guṇas*." *Journal asiatique* 6 (1915): 151–64.

Segupta, P. C. *Ancient Indian Chronology*. Calcutta: University of Calcutta, 1947.

Sergent, Bernard. "Penser—et mal penser—les indo-européens." *Annales: Économiés, Sociétés, Civilisations* 37 (1982): 669–81.

Sewell, Robert. *Indian Chronography*. London: George Allen and Co., 1912.

Shamashastry, R. *The Vedic Calendar*. Reprint New Delhi: Ganga Publications, 1979.

Sharma, A. "Analysis of Three Epithets Applied to the Śūdras in AitB 7.29.4." *Journal of Economic and Social History of the Orient* (Leiden) 18, 3 (1975): 300–317.

Sharma, G. R. *The Excavations at Kauśambi (1957–1959)*. Allahabad: Institute of Archeology, Allahabad University, 1960.

Sharma, K. N. *Brahmins through the Ages: Their Social, Religious, Cultural, Political and Economic Life*. Delhi: Ajanta Books, 1977.

———. *Culture and Civilization as Revealed in the Śrautasūtras*. Delhi: Nag Publishers, 1977.

———. "On the Word 'varṇa.'" *Contributions to Indian Sociology* (n.s.) 9, 2 (1975): 293–97.

Sharma, R. S. "Caste and Marriage in Ancient India, ca. 630 BC to 500 AD." *Journal of the Bihar Research Society* (Patna) 40 (1954): 39–54.

———. "Class Formation and Its Material Basis in the Upper Gangetic Basin (ca. 1000–500 BC)." *Indian Historical Review* (July 1975): 1–13.

———. "Politico-Legal Aspects of the Caste System, ca. 600 BC–500 AD." *Journal of the Bihar Research Society* (Patna) 39 (1953): 306–30.

———. *Śūdras in Ancient India*. 2d ed. Delhi: Motilal Banarsidass, 1980.

Shende, N. J. "Bṛhaspati in the Vedic and Epic Literature." *Bulletin of the Deccan College Research Institute* 8 (1946–47): 225–51.

———. *Religion and Philosophy of the Atharva Veda*. Poona: Bhandarkar Oriental Research Institute, 1952.

———. "The *hotṛ* and Other Priests in the Brāhmaṇas of the Ṛgveda." *Journal of the University of Bombay* (n.s.) 32, 2 (1963): 48–88.

Shivaganesha Murthy, R. S. *A Study of the Important Brāhmaṇas*. Mysore: Prasaranga, University of Mysore, 1974.

Silburn, Lilian. *Instant et cause: Le Discontinu dans la pensée philosophique de l'Inde*. Paris: Libraire philosophique J. Vrin, 1955.

Sinha, B. C. *Tree Worship in Ancient India*. New Delhi: Books Today, 1979.

Smith, Brian K. "Canonical Authority and Social Classification: Veda and *Varṇa* in Ancient Indian Texts." *History of Religions* 32, 2 (Nov. 1992): 103–25.

———. "Classifying the Universe: Ancient Indian Cosmogonies and the Varṇa System." *Contributions to Indian Sociology* (n.s.) 23, 2 (1989): 241–60.

———. "Classifying Animals and Humans in Ancient India." *Man* (n.s.) 26 (Sept. 1991): 323–341.

———. "Eaters, Food, and Social Hierarchy in Ancient India: A Dietary Guide to a

Revolution of Values." *Journal of the American Academy of Religion* 58, 2 (Summer 1990): 201–29.

———. "Exorcising the Transcendent: Strategies for Defining Hinduism and Religion." *History of Religions* 27, 1 (Aug. 1987): 32–55.

———. "Ideals and Realities in Indian Religion." *Religious Studies Review* 14, 1 (Jan. 1988): 1–10.

———. *Reflections on Resemblance, Ritual, and Religion*. New York: Oxford University Press, 1989.

———. "Ritual, Knowledge, and Being: Initiation and Veda Study in Ancient India." *Numen* 33, 1 (1986): 65–89.

———. "Sacrifice and Being: Prajāpati's Cosmic Emission and Its Consequences." *Numen* 32, 1 (1985): 71–87.

———. "The Veda and the Authority of Class." In *Authority, Anxiety and Canon: Essays in Vedic Interpretation*. Ed. by Laurie Patton. Albany, N.Y.: SUNY Press, 1993.

———, and Wendy Doniger. "Sacrifice and Substitution: Ritual Mystification and Mythical Demystification." *Numen* 36, 2 (1989): 189–224.

Smith, Frederick Marcus. *The Vedic Sacrifice in Transition: A Translation and Study of the Trikāṇḍamaṇḍana* of *Bhāskara Miśra*. Bhandarkar Oriental Series, no. 22. Poona: Bhandarkar Oriental Research Institute, 1987.

Smith, Pierre, and Dan Sperber. "Mythologiques de Georges Dumézil." *Annales: Économiés, Sociétés, Civilisations* 26 (May–Aug. 1971): 559–86.

Sparreboom, M., and J. C. Heesterman. *The Ritual Setting Up of the Sacrificial Fires according to the Vādhula School* (*Vādhulaśrautasūtra* 1.1–1.4). Vienna: Verlag der Österreichischen Akademie der Wissenschaften, 1989.

Srinivas, M. N. *Religion and Society among the Coorgs of South India*. Oxford: Oxford University Press, 1952.

———. "Some Reflections on the Nature of Caste Hierarchy." *Contributions to Indian Sociology* (n.s.) 18,2 (1984): 151–67.

———. "Varṇa and Caste." In M. N. Srinivas, *Caste in Modern India and Other Essays*. Bombay: Asia Publishing House, 1962.

Staal, Frits. *Agni: The Vedic Ritual of the Fire Altar*. 2 vols. Berkeley: Asian Humanities Press, 1983.

Tambiah, S. J. "From Varṇa to Caste through Mixed Unions." In *The Character of Kinship*, pp. 191–230. Ed. by Jack Goody. Cambridge: Cambridge University Press, 1973.

Thapar, Romila. *The Past and Prejudice*. Delhi: National Book Trust, 1975.

Thieme, Paul. *Mitra and Aryaman*. New Haven: Connecticut Academy of Arts and Sciences, 1957.

Thite, G. U. *Sacrifice in the Brāhmaṇa-Texts*. Poona: University of Poona, 1975.

Tull, Herman. *The Vedic Origins of Karma: Cosmos as Man in Ancient Indian Myth and Ritual*. Albany, N.Y.: SUNY Press, 1989.

Underhill, M. M. *The Hindu Religious Year*. Oxford: Oxford University Press, 1921.

Upadhyay, Govind Prasad. *Brāhmaṇas in Ancient India*. New Delhi: Munshiram Manoharlal, 1979.

Upadhyaya, K. D. "Indian Botanical Folklore." In *Tree Symbol Worship in India: A New Survey of a Pattern of Folk-Religion*, pp. 1–18. Ed. by S. S. Gupta. Calcutta: Indian Publications, 1965.

Varenne, Jean. *Cosmogonies védique*. Paris: Société d'Édition, 1982.

Varma, Siddheshwar. "The Vedic Concept of Time." *Indian Linguistics* 27 (1966): 115–30.

Verpoorten, Jean-Marie. "Unité et distinction dans les spéculations rituelles védique." *Archiv für Begriffsgeschichte* 21 (1977): 59–85.

Viennot, Odette. *Le Culte de l'arbre dans l'Inde ancienne.* Paris: Presses Universitaires de France, 1954.

Vogel, J. P. *Het Sanskrit woord tejas (= gloed, vuur) in de beteekenis van magische kracht.* Amsterdam: Mededelingen der Koninktijke Nederlandse Akademie van Wetenschappen, 1930.

Vyas, R. T. "The Concept of Prajāpati in Vedic Literature." *Bhāratīya Vidyā* 38 (1978): 95–101.

Wayman, Alex. "The Body as a Microcosm in India, Greek Cosmology, and Sixteenth-Century Europe." *History of Religions* 22 (1982): 172–90.

Weber, Max. *The Religion of India: The Sociology of Hinduism and Buddhism.* Trans. and ed. by Hans H. Gerth and Don Martindale. New York: Free Press, 1958.

Weber, Albrecht. "Über Maschenopfer bei den Indern der vedischen Zeit." *Zeitschrift der Deutschen Morgenländischen Gesellschaft* 18 (1864): 262–287.

Wikander, S. *Vāyu: Texte und Untersuchungen zur indo-iranischen Religionsgeschichte.* Uppsala: A. B. Lundequistska Bokhandein, 1941.

Witzel, Michael. "On the Localisation of Vedic Texts and Schools." In *India and the Ancient World*, pp. 173–213. Ed. by G. Pollet. Louvain: Departement Orientalistiek, 1987.

Young, Richard Fox. *Resistant Hinduism: Sanskrit Sources on Anti-Christian Apologetics in Early Nineteenth-Century India.* Vienna: Publications of the De Nobili Research Library, 1981.

Zaehner, R. C. *Hinduism.* New York: Oxford University Press, 1966.

Zimmer, Heinrich. *Altindisches Leben: Die Cultur der vedischen Arier nach den samhita dargestellt.* Berlin: Weidmannsche Buchhandlung, 1879.

Zimmermann, Francis. "*Rtu-sātmya*: The Seasonal Cycle and the Principle of Appropriateness." Trans. by McKim Marriott and John Leavitt. *Social Science and Medicine* 14B, 2 (May 1980): 99–106.

———. *The Jungle and the Aroma of Meats: An Ecological Theme in Hindu Medicine.* Berkeley: University of California Press, 1987.

Zysk, Kenneth. *Religious Healing in the Veda.* Philadelphia: American Philosophical Society, 1986.

Secondary Sources (General)

Anderson, Walter Truett. *Reality Isn't What It Used to Be: Theatrical Politics, Ready-to-Wear Religion, Global Myths, Primitive Chic, and Other Wonders of the Post-modern World.* San Francisco: Harper & Row, 1990.

André, Jacques. "Arbor felix, arbor infelix." In *Hommages à Jean Bayet*, pp. 35–46. Ed. by Marcel Renard and Robert Schilling. Brussels: Collection Latomus, 1964.

Baird, Robert. *Category Formation and the History of Religions.* The Hague: Mouton, 1971.

Barkan, Leonard. *Nature's Work of Art: The Human Body as Image of the World.* New Haven, Conn.: Yale University Press, 1975.

Bender, John, and David E. Wellbury, eds. *Chronotypes: The Construction of Time.* Palo Alto, Calif.: Stanford University Press, 1991.

Bendix, Reinhard, and Bennett Berger. "Images of Society and Problems of Category Formation in Sociology." In *Looking for America*, pp. 258–87. Ed. by B. Berger. Englewood Cliffs, N.J.: Prentice-Hall, 1971.

Berger, Peter. *The Sacred Canopy: Elements of a Sociological Theory of Religion*. New York: Doubleday, 1967.

Bulmer, Ralph. "The Uncleanness of the Birds of Leviticus and Deuteronomy." *Man* (n.s.) 24, 2 (June 1989): 304–20.

———. "Why Is the Cassowary Not a Bird? A Problem of Zoological Taxonomy among the Karam of the New Guinea Highlands." *Man* (n.s.) 2 (1967): 5–25.

Capdeville, Gérard. "Substitution de victimes dans les sacrifices d'animaux à Rome." *Mélanges d'archéologie et d'histoire de l'école fancaise de Rome* 83 (1971): 283–323.

Cavanaugh, M. "Pagan and Christian: Sociological Euhemerism versus American Sociology of Religion." *Sociological Analysis* 43, 2 (1982): 109–30.

Crosby, Donald A. *Interpretive Theories of Religion*. The Hague: Mouton, 1981.

De Gré, Gerard L. *Society and Ideology*. New York: Columbia University Press, 1943.

Derrida, Jacques. "Structure, Sign, and Play in the Discourse of the Human Sciences." In *Writing and Difference*, pp. 278–93. Translated with an introduction and additional notes by Alan Bass. Chicago: University of Chicago Press, 1978.

Detienne, Marcel, and Jean-Pierre Vernant, eds. *La cuisine du sacrifice en pays grec*. Paris: Gallimard, 1979.

Douglas, Mary. "Animals in Lele Religious Thought." *Africa* 27,1 (1957): 46–58.

———. *Purity and Danger: An Analysis of Concepts of Pollution and Taboo*. London: Routledge & Kegan Paul, 1966.

———. "The Abominations of Leviticus." In *Purity and Danger: An Analysis of Concepts of Pollution and Taboo*, pp. 41–57. London: Routledge & Kegan Paul, 1966.

Durkheim, Émile. *Society and Philosophy*. Trans. by D. F. Pocock. New York: The Free Press, 1974.

———. *The Elementary Forms of the Religious Life*. Trans. by Joseph Ward Swain. New York: Free Press, 1915.

———, and Marcel Mauss. *Primitive Classification*. Trans. by Rodney Needham. Chicago: University of Chicago Press, 1963.

Eliade, Mircea. *Myth and Reality*. Trans. by Willard R. Trask. New York: Harper & Row, 1963.

———. *Patterns in Comparative Religion*. Trans. by Rosemary Sheed. New York: World Publishing, 1958.

———. *The Myth of the Eternal Return or, Cosmos and History*. Trans. by Willard R. Trask. Princeton: Princeton University Press, 1971.

———. *The Sacred and the Profane: The Nature of Religion*. New York: Harcourt, Brace & World, 1959.

Ellen, Roy F., and David Reason. *Classifications in Their Social Contexts*. London: Academic Press, 1979.

Evans-Pritchard, E. E. *The Nuer: A Description of the Modes of Livelihood and Political Institutions of a Nilotic People*. Oxford: Clarendon Press, 1940.

Fallers, Lloyd A. *Inequality*. Chicago: University of Chicago Press, 1973.

Fenton, John Y. "Reductionism in the Study of Religions." *Soundings* 53 (Spring 1970): 61–76.

Fergusson, James. *Tree and Serpent Worship*. 2d ed. Reprint Delhi: Oriental Publishers, 1971.

Foa, Uriel, and Edna B. Foa. *Societal Structures of the Mind*. Springfield, Ill.: Charles C Thomas, 1974.

Fortes, M. "Totem and Taboo." *Proceedings of the Royal Anthropological Institute of Great Britain and Ireland for 1966*, pp. 5–22. London, 1967.

Freud, Sigmund. *The Future of an Illusion*. Trans. by James Strachey. New York: W. W. Norton, 1961.

———. *Totem and Taboo*. Trans. by James Strachey. New York: W. W. Norton, 1950.

Garret, W. R. "Troublesome Transcendence: The Supernatural in the Scientific Study of Religion." *Sociological Analysis* 35 (1974): 167–79.

Godelier, Maurice. *L'Idéel et le matériel*. Paris: Fayard, 1984.

Godlove, Terry. "In What Sense Are Religions Conceptual Frameworks?" *Journal of the American Academy of Religion* 52 (1984): 289–306.

Gombrich, E. H. *Art and Illusion: A Study in the Psychology of Pictorial Representation*. 2d ed., rev. Princeton: Princeton University Press, 1960.

Gomes da Silva, José Carlos. "Mythe et idéologie." *L'Homme* 16 (1976): 49–75.

Gordon, R. L., ed. *Myth, Religion and Society*. Cambridge: Cambridge University Press, 1981.

Graham, William A. *Beyond the Written Word: Oral Aspects of Scripture in the History of Religion*. Cambridge: Cambridge University Press, 1987.

Gurvitch, Georges. *The Spectrum of Social Time*. Trans. and ed. by Myrtle Korenbaum. Dordrecht: D. Reidel, 1964.

Hallowell, A. Irving. "Temporal Orientation in Western Civilization and in a Pre-literate Society." *American Anthropologist* 39 (1937): 647–70.

Halverson, John. "Animal Categories and Terms of Abuse." *Man* (n.s.) 11, 4 (Dec. 1976): 505–16.

Hamilton, David. "A Theory of the Social Origin of the Factors of Production." *American Journal of Economic Sociology* 15 (1955): 73–83.

Hamilton, Peter. *Knowledge and Social Structure*. London: Routledge & Kegan Paul, 1974.

Hamnett, Ian. "Sociology of Religion and Sociology of Error." *Religion* 3 (1973): 1–12.

Harnad, Stevan, ed. *Categorical Perception: The Groundwork of Cognition*. Cambridge: Cambridge University Press, 1987.

Hertz, Robert. *Death and the Right Hand*. Trans. by R. and C. Needham. London: Cohen and West, 1960.

———. "The Pre-eminence of the Right Hand: A Study in Religious Polarity." In *Right and Left: Essays on Dual Symbolic Classification*, pp. 3–31. Ed. by Rodney Needham. Chicago: University of Chicago Press, 1973.

Hocart, A. M. *Caste: A Comparative Study*. Reprint London: Methuen, 1950.

———. *Kings and Councillors*. Reprint Chicago: University of Chicago Press, 1970.

Hodges, Daniel L. "Breaking a Scientific Taboo: Putting Assumptions about the Supernatural into Scientific Theories of Religion." *Journal of the Scientific Study of Religion* 13 (1974): 393–408.

Hubert, Henri, and Marcel Mauss. "Étude sommaire de la représentation du temps dans la religion et la magie." *École pratique des hautes études, section des sciences religieuses* (1905): 1–39; reprinted in H. Hubert and M. Mauss, *Mélanges d'histoire des religions*, pp. 189–229. 2d ed. Paris: Librairie Felix Alcan, 1929.

———. *Sacrifice: Its Nature and Function*. Trans. by W. D. Halls. Chicago: University of Chicago Press, 1964.

Ingold, Tim. *The Appropriation of Nature*. Manchester: Manchester University Press, 1986.

———, ed. *What Is an Animal?*. London: Unwin Hyman, 1988.

Jarvi, I. C. *Concepts and Society*. London: Routledge & Kegan Paul, 1972.

Jevons, W. Stanley. *The Principles of Science: A Treatise on Logic and Scientific Methods*. 2 vols. London: Macmillan, 1874.

Kant, Immanuel. *Critique of Pure Reason*. Trans. by Norman Kemp Smith. New York: St. Martin's Press, 1965.

Kelsen, Hans. *Society and Nature*. Chicago: University of Chicago Press, 1943.

Kuper, Hilda. "Costume and Cosmology: The Animal Symbolism of the Ncwala." *Man* (n.s.) 8 (1973): 613–30.

Lakoff, George. *Women, Fire, and Dangerous Things: What Categories Reveal about the Mind*. Chicago: University of Chicago Press, 1987.

Landtman, Gunnar. *The Origin of the Inequality of the Social Classes*. Chicago: University of Chicago Press, 1938.

Leach, Edmund. "Anthropological Aspects of Language: Animal Categories and Verbal Abuse." In *New Directions in the Study of Language*, pp. 23–63. Ed. by Eric H. Lenneberg. Cambridge, Mass.: MIT Press, 1964.

———. "Two Essays Concerning the Symbolic Representation of Time." In *Rethinking Anthropology*, pp. 124–36. London: Athlone Press, 1961.

Lenski, Gerhard. *Power and Privilege*. New York: McGraw-Hill, 1966.

Levering, Miriam, ed. *Rethinking Scripture: Essays from a Comparative Perspective*. Albany, N.Y.: SUNY Press, 1989.

Lévi-Strauss, Claude. "The Bear and the Barber." *Journal of the Royal Anthropological Institute* 93 (1963): 1–11; reprinted in *Reader in Comparative Religion: An Anthropological Approach*. Ed. by William A. Lessa and Evon Z. Vogt. 3d ed. New York: Harper & Row, 1972.

———. "The Structural Study of Myth." In *Structural Anthropology*. Trans. by Claire Jacobson and Brook Grundfest Schoepf. New York: Basic Books, 1963.

———. *Totemism*. Trans. by Rodney Needham. Boston: Beacon Press, 1963.

Lincoln, Bruce. "Notes Toward a Theory of Religion and Revolution." In *Religion, Rebellion, Revolution*, pp. 266–92. Ed. by Bruce Lincoln. London: Macmillan, 1985.

Londow, John. *Comitatus, Individual, and Honor*. Berkeley: University of California Press, 1976.

Lovin, Robin, and Frank E. Reynolds, eds. *Cosmogony and Ethical Order: New Studies in Comparative Ethics*. Chicago: University of Chicago Press, 1985.

Lukes, Steven. *Émile Durkheim: His Life and Work: A Historical and Critical Study*. Harmondsworth, Middlesex, England: Penguin Books, 1973.

———. "The Theoretical Polemics of Anti-ideology." *American Journal of Sociology* 84 (1978): 186–90.

MacIntyre, Alisdair. "Is Understanding Religion Compatible with Believing?" In *Faith and the Philosophers*, pp. 115–33. Ed. by J. Hick. London: Macmillan, 1964.

Mandelbaum, Maurice. "Societal Facts." *British Journal of Sociology* 6 (December 1955): 305–17.

Mannheim, Karl. *Ideology and Utopia*. New York: Harcourt, Brace and World, 1936.

Mauss, Marcel. *Seasonal Variations of the Eskimo: A Study in Social Morphology*. Trans. and ed. by James J. Fox. London: Routledge & Kegan Paul, 1979.

Mayr, Ernst. *Principles of Systematic Zoology*. New York: McGraw-Hill, 1969.

Merton, Robert K. *Social Theory and Social Structure*. Glencoe, Ill.: Free Press, 1957.

Morris, Rudolph. "The Concept of the Spiritual and the Dilemma of Sociology." *Sociological Analysis* 25 (1964): 167–73.

Murray, S. O. "Fuzzy Sets and Abominations." *Man* (n.s.) 18 (1983): 396–99.

Needham, Rodney. "Polythetic Classification: Convergence and Consequences." *Man* (n.s.) 10, 3 (Sept. 1975): 349–69.

———. *Symbolic Classification*. Santa Monica, Calif.: Goodyear Publishing Co., 1979.

———, ed. *Right and Left: Essays on Dual Symbolic Classification*. Chicago: University of Chicago Press, 1973.

Nielsen, Kai. *Contemporary Critiques of Religion*. New York: Herder and Herder, 1971.

Nilsson, M. P. *Primitive Time-Reckoning*. Lund: C. W. K. Gleerup, 1920.

O'Neil, W. M. *Time and the Calendars*. Sydney: Sydney University Press, 1975.

Ornstein, E. *On the Experience of Time*. Baltimore: Penguin, 1969.

Ossowski, Stanislaw. *Class Structure in the Social Consciousness*. New York: Free Press, 1963.

Parsons, Talcott. *The Structure of Social Action*. 2d ed. New York: Free Press, 1968.

Peel, J. D. Y. "Understanding Alien Belief-Systems." *British Journal of Sociology* 20 (March 1969): 69–84.

Penner, Hans. "Structure and Religion." *History of Religions* 25 (1986): 236–54.

———, and Edward Yonan. "Is a Science of Religion Possible?" *Journal of Religion* 52 (1952): 107–33.

Phillips, D. Z. *Faith and Philosophical Enquiry*. London: Routledge & Kegan Paul, 1970.

———. *Religion without Explanation*. Oxford: Oxford University Press, 1976.

Philpot, J. H. *The Sacred Tree: The Tree in Religion and Myth*. London: Macmillan, 1897.

Pocock, David. "The Anthropology of Time Reckoning." *Contributions to Indian Sociology* 7 (March 1964): 18–29.

Rickett, Mac Linscott. "In Defence of Eliade." *Religion* 3 (Spring 1973): 13–34.

Rosch, E., and B. B. Lloyd, eds. *Cognition and Categorization*. Hillsdale, N.J.: Lawrence Erlbaum Associates, 1978.

Rosmarin, Adena. *The Power of Genre*. Minneapolis: University of Minnesota Press, 1985.

Said, Edward. *Orientalism*. New York: Pantheon Books, 1978.

Saliba, John A. *"Homo Religiosus" in Mircea Eliade*. Leiden: E. J. Brill, 1976.

Salzman, P. C. "Does Complementary Opposition Exist?" *American Anthropologist* 80 (1978): 53–70.

Schaub, E. "A Sociological Theory of Knowledge." *Philosophical Review* 29 (1920): 319–39.

Schwartz, Barry. *Vertical Classification: A Study in Structuralism and the Sociology of Knowledge*. Chicago: University of Chicago Press, 1981.

Segal, Robert. "In Defense of Reductionism." *Journal of the American Academy of Religion* 51 (1983): 97–124.

———. "The Social Sciences and the Truth of Religious Belief." *Journal of the American Academy of Religion* 48 (1980): 403–13.

Seger, Imogen. *Durkheim and His Critics on the Sociology of Religion*. New York: Bureau of Applied Social Research, Columbia University, 1957.

Shepherd, William C. "On the Concept of 'Being Wrong' Religiously." *Journal of the American Academy of Religion* 42 (March 1974): 66–81.

Simpson, George G. *Principles of Animal Taxonomy*. New York: Columbia University Press, 1961.

Smart, Ninian. *The Science of Religions and the Sociology of Knowledge: Some Methodological Questions*. Princeton: Princeton University Press, 1973.

Smith, Jonathan Z. "Sacred Persistence: Toward a Redescription of Canon." In *Imagining Religion: From Babylon to Jonestown*. Chicago: University of Chicago Press, 1982.

Sneath, Peter H. A. "The Construction of Taxonomic Groups." In *Microbial Classifica-*

tion. Ed. by G. C. Ainsworth and P. H. A. Sneath. Cambridge: Cambridge University Press, 1962.

Spiro, Melford E. "Religion: Problems of Definition and Explanation." In *Anthropological Approaches to the Study of Religion*, pp. 85–126. Ed. by Michael Banton. A.S.A. Monographs, Vol. 3. London: Tavistock, 1966.

Tambiah, S. J. "Animals Are Good to Think and Good to Prohibit." *Ethnology* 8 (1969): 423–59.

Turner, Bryan S. *Religion and Social Theory: A Materialistic Perspective*. Atlantic Highlands, N. J.: Humanities Press, 1983.

Turner, Victor. "Color Classification in Ndembu Ritual." In *The Forest of Symbols: Aspects of Ndembu Ritual*, pp. 59–92. Ithaca, N.Y.: Cornell University Press, 1967.

Urton, G., ed. *Animal Myths and Metaphors in South America*. Salt Lake City: University of Utah Press, 1985.

Vernant, Jean-Pierre. "Sacrificial and Alimentary Codes in Hesiod's Myth of Prometheus." In *Myth, Religion, and Society*. Ed. by R. L. Gordon. Cambridge: Cambridge University Press, 1981.

Widengren, Geo. "Macrocosmos—Microcosmos: Speculation in the Rasa'il Ikhwan al-Safa and Some Hurufi Texts." *Archivio di Filosofia* (1980): 297–312.

Wiebe, Donald. "Beyond the Sceptic and the Devotee: Reductionism in the Scientific Study of Religion." *Journal of the American Academy of Religion* 52, 1 (March 1984): 157–64.

———. *Religion and Truth: Towards an Alternative Paradigm for the Study of Religion*. The Hague: Mouton, 1981.

Wijewardene, G. "Address, Abuse and Animal Categories in Northern Thailand." *Man* (n.s.) 3 (1968): 76–93.

Willis, Roy G. *Man and Beast*. London: Granada Publishing, 1974.

———. ed. *Signifying Animals: Human Meaning in the Natural World*. London: Unwin Hyman, 1990.

Wood, Ellen Meiksins, and Neal Wood. *Class Ideology and Ancient Political Theory: Socrates, Plato, and Aristotle in Social Context*. New York: Oxford University Press, 1978.

Worsley, P. M. "Émile Durkheim's Theory of Knowledge." *Sociological Review* (n.s.) 4, 1 (1956): 47–62.

Wrong, Dennis H. "The Oversocialized Conception of Man in Modern Sociology." *American Sociological Review* 26 (April 1961): 183–93.

Index and Glossary

Abundance. *See also Bhūman*
and Ādityas, 43
and afternoon, 184
and dappled animals, 272
and goat, 270–71
and goats and sheep, 271
and *jagatī*, 295
and Maruts, 97
and *puṣṭi*, 271
and *viś* or Vaishya, 31, 43–44, 272
and Viśva Devas, 97
Acacia (type of tree)
and pipal, 226
Activity. *See also Karma*; *Rajas*
and atmosphere, 128, 132, 315
and horse, 315
and Indra, 315
and Kshatriya, 305
and Yajur Veda, 315
Adhidevatā (relating to the macrocosmos), vii
Adhiyajña (relating to the sacrifice), vii
Adhvaryu (type of priest), 39, 110
and atmosphere, 132
and hot season, 203
and Yajur Veda, 63, 132, 290, 305
Adhyātman (relating to the microcosmos or self), vii
Aditi (name of goddess), 107, 163
Āditya or Sūrya (name of solar deity). *See also* Sun
and Ādityas, 88
and Brahmin, 93
and *indriya*, 95
and *kṣatra*, 95, 133
and Kshatriya, 90, 95
and *ojas*, 95
and rainy season, 191–12
and *sahas*, 95
and Sāma Veda, 63, 98, 132, 290
and sky, 63, 98, 129–30, 132–33, 191
and Vaishya, 98, 185, 292
and Viśva Devas, 88
and west, 192
and *yaśas*, 64, 291
Ādityas (group of deities)
and abundance, 43
and Āditya or Sūrya, 88
and afternoon, 185–87, 189
as all the gods, 119
and cow, 272
and goat, 271
and *jagatī*, 299
and long life, 98
number of, 119, 299
and offspring, 98
and rainy season, 177–78, 181
and sky, 78, 189
and Varuṇa, 96–97
and *viś* or the Vaishya, 89–90, 96–98, 110, 152, 272, 292
and Viśva Devas, 299
and west, 74, 77, 152
Afternoon
and Ādityas, 185–87, 189
and ancestors, 184
and animals, 184, 186
and autumn, 183, 188
and *bhūman*, 184
and Bṛhaspati, 183
and food, 184
and *jagatī*, 184, 296–99
and offspring, 184